Borland C++ Builder™:
The Complete Reference

ONE WEEK LOAN

About the Authors

Herbert Schildt is the world's leading
programming author. He is an authority on the
C, C++, Java, and C# programming languages,
and a master Windows programmer. His
programming books have sold over three
million copies worldwide and have been
translated into all major foreign languages.
He is the author of numerous best-sellers,
including *C++: The Complete Reference*,
C: The Complete Reference, *Java 2: The Complete
Reference*, *Java 2: A Beginner's Guide*, *C#: A
Beginner's Guide*, *Windows 2000 Programming
from the Ground Up*, and many more. Schildt
holds a master's degree in computer science
from the University of Illinois.

Greg Guntle has been programming and
working with PC's for the last 20 years. He also
provides technical editing skills for computer
books and has done that for the past 15 years.

Borland® C++ Builder™:
The Complete Reference

Herbert Schildt
Greg Guntle

Osborne/**McGraw-Hill**

New York   Chicago   San Francisco
Lisbon   London   Madrid   Mexico City
Milan   New Delhi   San Juan
Seoul   Singapore   Sydney   Toronto

Osborne/**McGraw-Hill**
2600 Tenth Street
Berkeley, California 94710
U.S.A.

To arrange bulk purchase discounts for sales promotions, premiums, or fund-raisers, please contact Osborne/**McGraw-Hill** at the above address. For information on translations or book distributors outside the U.S.A., please see the International Contact Information page immediately following the index of this book.

Borland C++® Builder™: The Complete Reference

1234567890 CUS CUS 01987654321

ISBN 0-07-212778-3

Publisher
Brandon A. Nordin

Vice President & Associate Publisher
Scott Rogers

Editorial Director
Wendy Rinaldi

Project Editor
Carolyn Welch

Acquisitions Coordinator
Tim Madrid

Copy Editor
Robert Campbell

Indexer
Sheryl Schildt

Project Manager
Dave Nash

Computer Designers
Elizabeth Jang, Tara A. Davis,
Lauren McCarthy

Illustrators
Michael Mueller, Lyssa Sieben-Wald

Series Design
Peter F. Hancik

This book was composed with Corel VENTURA™ Publisher.

Contents

Part I

The Foundation of C++: The C Subset

v

Part II

The C++ Builder Function Library

Part III

C++

Part IV

The C++ Builder Integrated Development Environment

Preface

by Herbert Schildt

This book is about Borland's C++ Builder. Borland has been making state-of-the-art compilers since the 1980s. C++ Builder is their most powerful and full-featured compiler yet. It is known for its compilation speed and for the efficiency of the code it produces. C++ Builder is really two compilers in one. First, it is a C compiler. (C is the language upon which C++ is built.) Second, it is a C++ compiler. C++ Builder can produce programs for Windows 95/98/NT/2000 and the DOS environment provided by Windows. By any measure, it is one of the finest programming development environments available. The purpose of this book is to help you get the most out of it.

About This Book

I have been writing about the Borland line of compilers for many years now. No doubt, many readers will be familiar with one or more of my earlier Borland C++ books. This book is the latest edition in my series of Borland C++ "Complete References." The previous edition was called *Borland C++: The Complete Reference*. This book is unique, though, because it is the first to cover the new "Builder" environment.

In addition to the new "Builder" environment, another event of significant importance has occurred which makes this book profoundly different than its earlier editions: The ANSI/ISO standard for C++ was adopted. This standard contains many new features, functions, and classes, which greatly expand the power of the C++ language. As you would expect, C++ Builder fully supports this standard. Thus, this book has been completely updated to cover all of the new features defined by ANSI/ISO Standard C++. For example, there is now extensive coverage of the STL, the new I/O classes, and the **string** class. Coverage of templates has also been expanded. Frankly, the changes caused by the standardization of C++ are very significant in several chapters.

What's Inside

This book describes the entire C++ Builder programming environment. As such, it discusses both the C and the C++ languages and their libraries in significant detail. It also shows how to use the integrated development environment (IDE) and the various application development tools supplied by C++ Builder. Numerous example programs are included to help illustrate the elements of C++ and the Builder environment.

    This book is designed for programmers at all skill levels. If you are just learning to program, this guide makes an excellent companion to any tutorial, providing answers to your specific questions. If you are an experienced C/C++ programmer, this book serves as a handy desk reference.

How This Book Is Organized

As you can surmise given the size of this book, C++ Builder is a large topic. To help bring order to such a vast amount of information, this book is organized into these four parts:

Part I   The Foundation of C++: The C Subset

Part II   The C++ Builder Function Library

Part III   The C++-Specific Features

Part IV   The C++ Builder Integrated Development Environment

This organization allows the C programmer to quickly find material related to C while at the same time letting the C++ programmer find the material appropriate to C++. Further, if you are currently a C programmer who is moving to C++, this organization lets you avoid "wading through" reams of information you already know. You can simply concentrate on the C++ sections of the book.

Conventions Used in This Book

Throughout, keywords, operators, function names, and variable names are shown in bold when referenced in text. General forms are shown in italics. Also, when referencing a function name in text, the name is followed by parentheses. In this way, you can easily distinguish a variable name from a function name.

Source Code on the Web

The source code for all of the programs in this book is available at Osborne's Web site **www.osborne.com**, free of charge.

Special Thanks

I wish to thank Greg Guntle for his help in the preparation of this book. Because of my very busy writing schedule and the extensive changes that were required, it was not possible for me to single-handedly prepare this edition within the time frame required by my publisher. To solve this problem, I turned to Greg Guntle. Greg is an expert programmer who has helped me in the past as a technical reviewer for several of my books. He went through each chapter with a fine-tooth comb, updating and fixing where needed. He also wrote the initial drafts for Chapters 28, 29, and 30. He did a fine job and much of the credit for this book goes to Greg. Again, I say a wholehearted "Thanks!"

Acknowledgments

I want to thank my beautiful wife Carla for her love and support. Without those, I would not have been able to do this book. I love you, Hon! I also need to thank my children, Phil, Colin, and Olivia, for being so understanding when Dad did not have time to share with them. Thanks to the fine staff at Osborne/McGraw-Hill, especially Wendy Rinaldi and Tim Madrid. Most of all I want to thank Herb Schildt for giving me this wonderful opportunity to work with him on this project. His leadership, guidance, and technical prowess helped me tremendously. He is the best!

Greg Guntle

For Further Study

Borland C++ Builder: The Complete Reference is part of the "Herb Schildt" series of programming books. Here are some others that you will find of interest.

To learn about C++, you will find these books especially helpful.

C++: The Complete Reference

Teach Yourself C++

C++ From the Ground Up

STL Programming From the Ground Up

The C/C++ Programming Annotated Archives

The C/C++ Programmer's Reference

If you want to learn more about the C language, then the following titles will be of interest.

C: The Complete Reference

Teach Yourself C

To learn about Java programming, we recommend the following:

Java 2: The Complete Reference

Java 2: A Beginner's Guide

Java 2: Programmer's Reference

To learn about Windows programming we suggest the following Schildt books:

Windows 98 Programming From the Ground Up

Windows 2000 Programming From the Ground Up

MFC Programming From the Ground Up

The Windows Programming Annotated Archives

To learn about C# try this book from Herb.

C#: A Beginner's Guide

When you need solid answers fast, turn to Herbert Schildt, the recognized authority on programming.

The Complete Reference

Borland C++ Builder

Part I

The Foundation of C++: The C Subset

This book divides its description of the C++ language into two parts. Part One discusses the C-like features of C++. This is commonly referred to as the *C subset* of C++. Part Three describes those features specific to C++. Together, they describe the entire C++ language.

As you may know, C++ was built upon the foundation of C. In fact, C++ includes the entire C language, and (with minor exceptions) all C programs are also C++ programs. When C++ was invented, the C language was used as the starting point. To C were added several new features and extensions designed to support object-oriented programming. However, the C-like aspects of C++ were never abandoned, and the 1989 ANSI/ISO C standard was a *base document* for Standard C++. Thus, an understanding of C++ implies an understanding of C.

Because C is a subset of C++, any C++ compiler is, by definition, also a C compiler. C++ Builder is no exception. C++ Builder allows you to compile both C programs and C++ programs. When used as a C compiler, C++ Builder fully supports the C language. When used as a C++ compiler, it fully supports C++.

In a book such as this *Complete Reference,* dividing the C++ language into two pieces—the C foundation and the C++-specific features—achieves three major benefits:

1. The dividing line between C and C++ is clearly delineated.

2. Readers already familiar with C can easily find the C++-specific information.

3. It provides a convenient place in which to discuss those features of C++ that relate mostly to the C subset—for example, the C I/O system.

Understanding the dividing line between C and C++ is important because both are widely used languages and it is very likely that you will be called upon to write or maintain both C and C++ code. When working on C code, you need to know where C ends and C++ begins. Many C++ programmers will, from time to time, be required to write code that is limited to the "C subset." This will be especially true for embedded systems programming and the maintenance of existing applications. Knowing the difference between C and C++ is simply part of being a top-notch professional C++ programmer.

A clear understanding of C is also valuable when converting C code into C++. To do this in a professional manner, a solid knowledge of C is required. For example, without a thorough understanding of the C I/O system, it is not possible to efficiently convert an I/O-intensive C program into C++.

Many readers already know C. Covering the C-like features of C++ in their own section makes it easier for the experienced C programmer to quickly and easily find information about C++ without having to "wade through" reams of information that he or she already knows. Of course, throughout Part One, any minor differences between C and C++ are noted. Also, separating the C foundation from the more advanced, object-oriented features of C++ makes it possible to tightly focus on those advanced features because all of the basics have already been discussed.

Although C++ contains the entire C language, not all of the features provided by the C language are commonly used when writing "C++-style" programs. For example, the C I/O system is still available to the C++ programmer even though C++ defines its own, object-oriented version. The preprocessor is another example. The preprocessor is very important to C, but less so to C++. Discussing several of the "C-only" features in Part One prevents them from cluttering up the remainder of the book.

Remember: The C subset described in Part One constitutes the core of C++ and the foundation upon which C++'s object-oriented features are built. All the features described here are part of C++ and available for your use.

One last point: Because the programs in Part One are C programs, you must compile them as C programs. To do this, just make sure that their filenames use the .C (not the .CPP) extension. Whenever C++ Builder compiles a file that has the .C extension, it automatically compiles it as a C, rather than a C++, program. For information on how to compile programs, see Part Four.

Chapter 1

An Overview of C

This chapter presents an overview of the origins, uses, and philosophy of the C programming language.

The Origins of the C Language

Dennis Ritchie invented and first implemented the C programming language on a DEC PDP-11 that used the UNIX operating system. The language is the result of a development process that started with an older language called BCPL. Martin Richards developed BCPL, which influenced Ken Thompson's invention of a language called B, which led to the development of C in the 1970s.

For many years, the de facto standard for C was the version supplied with the UNIX operating system. It was first described in *The C Programming Language* by Brian Kernighan and Dennis Ritchie (Englewood Cliffs, N.J.: Prentice-Hall, 1978). In the summer of 1983, a committee was established to create an ANSI (American National Standards Institute) standard that would define the C language. The standardization process took six years (much longer than anyone reasonably expected).

The ANSI C standard was finally adopted in December 1989, with the first copies becoming available in early 1990. The standard was also adopted by ISO (International Standards Organization), and the resulting standard was typically referred to as ANSI/ISO Standard C, or simply ANSI/ISO C. In 1995, Amendment 1 to the C standard was adopted, which, among other things, added several new library functions. The 1989 standard for C, along with Amendment 1, became a base document for Standard C++, defining the *C subset* of C++. The version of C defined by the 1989 standard is commonly referred to as C89. This is the version of C that C++ Builder supports.

It must be noted that recently a new standard for C, called C99, has been created. For the most part, it leaves the features of C89 intact and adds a few new ones. However, C++ Builder does not support the new features added by C99. This is not surprising because at the time of this writing, no commonly available compiler supports C99, and C89 still describes what programmers think of as C. Furthermore, as just explained, it is the C89 version of C that forms the C subset of C++. Because the version of C supported by C++ and C++ Builder is C89, it is the version of C described in this book. (The interested reader can find a full description of the C99 standard in *C: The Complete Reference, 4th Ed.* by Herbert Schildt, Berkeley: Osborne/McGraw-Hill, 2000.)

A Middle-Level Language

C is often called a *middle-level computer language*. This does not mean that C is less powerful, harder to use, or less developed than a high-level language such as Pascal; nor does it imply that C is similar to, or presents the problems associated with, assembly language. The definition of C as a middle-level language means that it combines elements of high-level languages with the functionalism of assembly language. Table 1-1 shows how C fits into the spectrum of languages.

As a middle-level language, C allows the manipulation of bits, bytes, and addresses—the basic elements with which the computer functions. Despite this fact, C code is surprisingly portable. *Portability* means that it is possible to adapt software written for one type of computer to another. For example, if a program written for one type of CPU can be moved easily to another, that program is portable.

All high-level programming languages support the concept of data types. A *data type* defines a set of values that a variable can store along with a set of operations that can be performed on that variable. Common data types are integer, character, and real. Although C has several basic built-in data types, it is not a strongly typed language like Pascal or Ada. In fact, C will allow almost all type conversions. For example, character and integer types may be freely intermixed in most expressions. Traditionally C performs no run-time error checking such as array-boundary checking or argument-type compatibility checking. These checks are the responsibility of the programmer.

A special feature of C is that it allows the direct manipulation of bits, bytes, words, and pointers. This makes it well suited for system-level programming, where these operations are common. Another important aspect of C is that it has only 32 keywords (5 more were added by C99, but these are not supported by C++), which are the commands that make up the C language. This is far fewer than most other languages.

Highest level	Ada
	Modula-2
	Pascal
	COBOL
	FORTRAN
	BASIC
Middle level	C#
	Java
	C++
	C
	FORTH
	Macro-assembly language
Lowest level	Assembly language

Table 1-1.   *C's Place in the World of Languages*

A Structured Language

In your previous programming experience, you may have heard the term "block structured" applied to a computer language. Although the term *block-structured language* does not strictly apply to C, C is commonly referred to simply as a *structured* language. Technically, a block-structured language permits procedures or functions to be declared inside other procedures or functions. Since C does not allow the creation of functions within functions, it cannot formally be called block structured.

The distinguishing feature of a structured language is *compartmentalization* of code and data. Compartmentalization is the language's ability to section off and hide from the rest of the program all information and instructions necessary to perform a specific task. One way of achieving compartmentalization is to use subroutines that employ local (temporary) variables. By using local variables, the programmer can write subroutines so that the events that occur within them cause no side effects in other parts of the program. This capability makes it very easy for C programs to share sections of code. If you develop compartmentalized functions, you only need to know what a function does, not how it does it. Remember that excessive use of global variables (variables known throughout the entire program) may allow bugs to creep into a program by allowing unwanted side effects. (Anyone who has programmed in traditional BASIC is well aware of this problem!)

 The concept of compartmentalization is greatly expanded by C++. Specifically, in C++, one part of your program can tightly control which other parts of your program are allowed access.

A structured language allows a variety of programming possibilities. It directly supports several loop constructs, such as **while, do-while,** and **for.** In a structured language, the use of **goto** is either prohibited or discouraged and is not the common form of program control that it is in old-style BASIC or traditional FORTRAN. A structured language allows you to indent statements and does not require a strict field concept.

Here are some examples of structured and nonstructured languages:

Structured	Nonstructured
Pascal	FORTRAN
Ada	BASIC
C++	COBOL
C	
C#	
Modula-2	
Java	

Structured languages are newer; nonstructured languages are older. Today, few programmers would seriously consider a nonstructured language for new software development.

Note *New versions of many older languages have attempted to add structured elements. BASIC is an example. However, the shortcomings of these languages can never be fully mitigated because they were not designed with structured features from the start.*

The main structural component of C is the function—C's stand-alone subroutine. In C, functions are the building blocks in which all program activity occurs. They allow the separate tasks in a program to be defined and coded separately, thus allowing your programs to be modular. After a function has been created, you can rely on it to work properly in various situations, without creating side effects in other parts of the program. The fact that you can create stand-alone functions is extremely critical in larger projects where one programmer's code must not accidentally affect another's.

Another way to structure and compartmentalize code in C is to use code blocks. A *code block* is a logically connected group of program statements that is treated as a unit. In C a code block is created by placing a sequence of statements between opening and closing curly braces. In this example,

```
if(x < 10) {
  printf("too low, try again");
  reset_counter(-1);
}
```

the two statements after the **if** and between the curly braces are both executed if **x** is less than 10. These two statements together with the braces are a code block. They are a logical unit: one of the statements cannot execute without the other. Code blocks not only allow many algorithms to be implemented with clarity, elegance, and efficiency, but also help the programmer conceptualize the true nature of the routine.

A Programmer's Language

One might respond to the statement, "C is a programmer's language," with the question, "Aren't all programming languages for programmers?" The answer is an unqualified "No!" Consider the classic examples of nonprogrammers' languages, COBOL and BASIC. COBOL was designed to enable nonprogrammers to read and, presumably, understand a program. BASIC was created essentially to allow nonprogrammers to program a computer to solve relatively simple problems.

In contrast, C was created, influenced, and field-tested by real working programmers. The end result is that C gives the programmer what the programmer wants: few restrictions, few complaints, block structures, stand-alone functions, and a compact set of keywords. It is truly amazing that by using C, a programmer can achieve nearly the efficiency of assembly code, combined with the structure of ALGOL or Modula-2. It is no wonder that C became one of the most popular programming languages.

The fact that C can often be used in place of assembly language contributed greatly to its success. Assembly language uses a symbolic representation of the actual binary code that the computer executes. Each assembly language operation maps into a single task for the computer to perform. Although assembly language gives programmers the potential for accomplishing tasks with maximum flexibility and efficiency, it is notoriously difficult to use when developing and debugging a program. Furthermore, since assembly language is unstructured, the final program tends to be spaghetti code—a tangled mess of jumps, calls, and indexes. This lack of structure makes assembly language programs difficult to read, enhance, and maintain. Perhaps more important, assembly language routines are not portable between machines with different CPUs.

Initially, C was used for systems programming. A *systems program* is part of a large class of programs that forms a portion of the operating system of the computer or its support utilities. For example, the following are usually called systems programs:

Operating systems

Interpreters

Editors

Compilers

File utilities

Performance enhancers

Real-time executives

As C grew in popularity, many programmers began to use it to program all tasks because of its portability and efficiency—and because they liked it! At the time of its creation, C was a much longed-for, dramatic improvement in programming languages. Of course, C++ has carried on this tradition.

With the advent of C++, some thought that C as a distinct language would die out. Such has not been the case. First, not all programs require the application of the object-oriented programming features provided by C++. For example, applications such as embedded systems are still typically programmed in C. Second, a substantial amount of C code is still in use, and those programs will continue to be enhanced and maintained. While C's greatest legacy is as the foundation for C++, it will continue to be a vibrant, widely used language for many years to come.

Compilers Versus Interpreters

It is important to understand that a computer language defines the nature of a program and not the way that the program will be executed. There are two general methods by which a program can be executed: it can be *compiled* or it can be *interpreted*. While programs written in any computer language can be compiled or interpreted, some languages are designed more for one form of execution than the other. For example, Java was designed to be interpreted and C was designed to be compiled. However, in the case of C, it is important to understand that it was specifically optimized as a compiled language. Although C interpreters have been written and are available in some environments (especially as debugging aids or experimental platforms), C was developed with compilation in mind. Since C++ Builder is a compiler, you will be compiling and not interpreting programs. Since the difference between a compiler and an interpreter may not be clear to all readers, the following brief description will clarify matters.

In its simplest form, an interpreter reads the source code of your program one line at a time, performing the specific instructions contained in that line. This is the way that earlier versions of BASIC worked. In languages such as Java, a program's source code is first converted into an intermediary form that is then interpreted. In either case, a run-time interpreter is still required to be present to execute the program.

A compiler reads the entire program and converts it into *object code*, which is a translation of the program's source code into a form that the computer can execute directly. Object code is also referred to as *binary code* or *machine code*. Once the program is compiled, a line of source code is no longer meaningful in the execution of your program.

In general, an interpreted program runs slower than a compiled program. Remember, a compiler converts a program's source code into object code that a computer can execute directly. Therefore, compilation is a one-time cost, while interpretation incurs an overhead each time a program is run.

The Form of a C Program

Table 1-2 lists the 32 keywords that, combined with the formal C syntax, form the C programming language as defined by the C89 standard. These are the keywords that form the C subset of C++ and the ones that are supported by C++ Builder. Also shown are 12 extended keywords added by Borland that may also be included in a C program. Of course, using the extended keywords renders your program nonportable. (Additional Borland extended keywords are defined for use with C++. See Part Three.)

All C keywords are lowercase. In C uppercase and lowercase are different: **else** is a keyword; ELSE is not. A keyword may not be used for any other purpose in a C program—that is, it cannot serve as a variable or function name.

All C programs consist of one or more functions. The only function that absolutely must be present is called **main( )**, and it is the first function called when program execution begins. In well-written C code, **main( )** outlines what the program does. The outline is composed of function calls. Although **main( )** is not a keyword, treat it as if it were. Don't try to use **main** as the name of a variable, for example.

The general form of a C program is illustrated in Figure 1-1, where **f1( )** through **fN( )** represent user-defined functions.

The Library and Linking

Technically speaking, it is possible to create a useful, functional C program that consists solely of the statements actually created by the programmer. However, this is rarely done because C does not contain any keywords that perform such things as I/O

```
Global declarations

int main(parameter list)
{
  statement sequence
}

return-type f1(parameter list)
{
  statement sequence
}

return-type f2(parameter list)
{
  statement sequence
}
  .
  .
  .
return-type fN(parameter list)
{
  statement sequence
}
```

Figure 1-1.   *The general form of a C program*

The keywords defined by C subset of C++

auto	double	int	struct
break	else	long	switch
case	enum	register	typedef
char	extern	return	union
const	float	short	unsigned
continue	for	signed	void
default	goto	sizeof	volatile
do	if	static	while

These additional keywords added by Borland are allowed in a C program:

asm	_cs	_ds	_es
_ss	cdecl	far	huge
interrupt	near	pascal	_export

Table 1-2.   *A List of the C Keywords Supported by C++ Builder*

operations, high-level mathematical computations, or string handling. As a result, most programs include calls to various functions contained in C's *standard library*.

The C language defines a standard library that provides functions that perform most commonly needed tasks. (This library is also supported by C++.) When you call a function that is not part of the program you wrote, the compiler "remembers" its name. Later the *linker* combines the code you wrote with the object code already found in the standard library. This process is called *linking*.

The functions that are kept in the library are in *relocatable* format. This means that the memory addresses for the various machine-code instructions have not been absolutely defined; only offset information has been kept. When your program links with the functions in the standard library, these memory offsets are used to create the actual addresses used. There are several technical manuals and books that explain this process in more detail. However, you do not need any further explanation of the actual relocation process to program in C or use C++ Builder.

Separate Compilation

Most short C programs are completely contained within one source file. However, as a program gets longer, so does its compile time, and long compile times make for short tempers! Because of this, C allows a program to be broken into pieces and contained in many files, and for each file to be compiled separately. Once all files have been compiled, they are linked together, along with any library routines, to form the complete object code. The advantage of separate compilation is that a change in the code of one file does not necessitate the recompilation of the entire program. On all but the simplest projects, the time saving is substantial.

A C Program's Memory Map

A compiled C program creates and uses four logically distinct regions of memory that serve specific functions. The first region is the memory that actually holds the code of your program. The next region is the memory where global variables are stored. The remaining two regions are the stack and the heap. The *stack* is used for a great many things while your program executes. It holds the return address of function calls, arguments to functions, and local variables. It is also used to save the current state of the CPU. The *heap* is a region of free memory, which your program can use via C's dynamic allocation functions, for things like linked lists and trees. The diagram in Figure 1-2 shows conceptually how your C programs appear in memory.

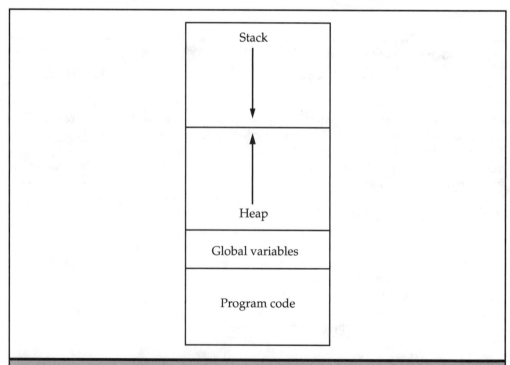

Figure 1-2.   *A conceptual memory map of a C program*

A Review of Terms

The terms that follow will be used frequently throughout the remainder of this book. You should be completely familiar with their meaning.

Source code	The text of a program that a user can read; commonly thought of as the program. The source code is input into the C compiler.
Object code	Translation of the source code of a program into machine code, which the computer can read and execute directly. Object code is the input to the linker.
Linker	A program that links separately compiled functions together into one program. It combines the functions in the standard C library with the code that you wrote. The output of the linker is an executable program.
Library	The file containing the standard functions that can be used by your program. These functions include all I/O operations as well as other useful routines.
Compile time	The events that occur while your program is being compiled. A common occurrence during compile time is a syntax error.
Run time	The events that occur while your program is executing.

Borland
C++
Builder

Chapter 2

Variables, Constants, Operators, and Expressions

V ariables and constants are manipulated by operators to form expressions. These are the atomic elements of the C and C++ language. This chapter will examine each element closely.

Identifier Names

The names that are used to reference variables, functions, labels, and various other user-defined objects are called *identifiers.* Identifiers can vary from one to several characters in length. C defines two kinds of identifiers: *external* and *internal.* An external identifier will be involved in an external link process. These identifiers, called *external names,* include function names and global variable names that are shared between source files. If an identifier is not used in an external link process, then it is internal. This type, called an *internal name,* includes the names of local variables, for example. The C language guarantees that at least the first 6 characters are significant for an external identifier, as are the first 31 characters for an internal identifier. C++ Builder recognizes the first 250 characters as being significant. (In C++, all characters are significant.)

In an identifier, the first character must be a letter or an underscore with subsequent characters being either letters, numbers, or the underscore. Here are some examples of correct and incorrect identifier names:

Correct	Incorrect
Count	1count
test23	hi!there
high_balance	high..balance

In C/C++, upper- and lowercase are treated differently. Hence, **count**, **Count**, and **COUNT** are three separate identifiers. An identifier cannot be the same as a keyword, and it should not have the same name as any function that you wrote or that is in the standard library.

Data Types

There are five atomic data types in the C subset of C++: character, integer, floating-point, double floating-point, and valueless. Values of type **char** are used to hold ASCII characters or any 8-bit quantity. Variables of type **int** are used to hold integer quantities. Variables of type **float** and **double** hold real numbers. (Real numbers have both an integer and a fractional component.) The **void** type has three uses. The first is to declare explicitly a function as returning no value; the second is to declare explicitly a function as having no parameters; the third is to create generic pointers. Each of these uses is discussed in subsequent chapters.

Note   *ANSI/ISO C99 added three more data types to the five basic types just listed: _Bool, _Complex, and _Imaginary, but these are not part of the C subset of C++.*

C supports several *aggregate* types, including structures, unions, bit fields, enumerations, and user-defined types. These complex types are discussed in Chapter 7.

Type Modifiers

Except type **void**, the basic data types may have various *modifiers* preceding them. A type modifier is used to alter the meaning of the base type to fit the needs of various situations more precisely. The list of modifiers is shown here:

signed

unsigned

long

short

The modifiers **signed, unsigned, long,** and **short** can be applied to integer base types. The character base type can be modified by **unsigned** and **signed**. You can also apply **long** to **double**. Table 2-1 shows all valid data types, along with their bit widths and ranges as implemented by C++ Builder.

The use of **signed** on integers is redundant (but allowed) because the default integer declaration assumes a signed number.

The difference between signed and unsigned integers lies in the way the high-order bit of the integer is interpreted. If a signed integer is specified, then the compiler will generate code that assumes the high-order bit of an integer is to be used as a *sign flag*. If the sign bit is 0, then the number is positive; if it is 1, then the number is negative. Here is an overly simplified example:

127 in binary is 0 0 0 0 0 0 0 0 0 1 1 1 1 1 1 1
–127 in binary is 1 0 0 0 0 0 0 0 0 1 1 1 1 1 1 1

↑

sign bit

The reader is cautioned that virtually all computers (including those that run C++ Builder) use *two's complement* arithmetic, which will cause the representation of –127 to appear different than the simplified example just shown. However, the use of the sign bit is the same. To form the negative of a number in two's complement form, reverse all bits and add one to the number. For example, –127 in two's complement appears like this:

1 1 1 1 1 1 1 1 1 0 0 0 0 0 0 1

Type	Bit Width	Range
char	8	–128 to 127
unsigned char	8	0 to 255
signed char	8	–128 to 127
int	32	–2,147,483,648 to 2,147,483,647
unsigned int	32	0 to 4,294,967,295
signed int	32	–2,147,483,648 to 2,147,483,647
short int	16	–32,768 to 32,767
unsigned short int	16	0 to 65,535
signed short int	16	–32,768 to 32,767
long int	32	–2,147,483,648 to 2,147,483,647
unsigned long int	32	0 to 4,294,967,295
signed long int	32	–2,147,483,648 to 2,147,483,647
float	32	1.18E–38 to 3.40E+38
double	64	2.23E–308 to 1.79E+308
long double	80	3.37E–4932 to 1.18E+4932

Table 2-1.   *The C Data Types as Implemented by C++ Builder*

Signed integers are important for a great many algorithms, but they have only half the absolute magnitude of their unsigned relatives. For example, here is 32,767:

0 1 1 1 1 1 1 1   1 1 1 1 1 1 1 1

If the high-order bit were set to 1, the number would then be interpreted as –1. However, if you had declared this to be **unsigned**, then when the high-order bit is set to 1, the number becomes 65,535.

Access Modifiers

C/C++ has two type modifiers that are used to control the ways in which variables may be accessed or modified. These modifiers are called **const** and **volatile**.

Variables of type **const** may not be changed during execution by your program. For example,

```
const int a;
```

will create an integer variable called **a** that cannot be modified by your program. It can, however, be used in other types of expressions. A **const** variable will receive its value either from an explicit initialization or by some hardware-dependent means. For example, this gives **count** the value of 100:

```
const int count = 100;
```

Aside from initialization, no **const** variable can be modified by your program.

The modifier **volatile** is used to tell the compiler that a variable's value can be changed in ways not explicitly specified by the program. For example, a global variable's address can be passed to the clock routine of the operating system and used to hold the time of the system. In this situation, the contents of the variable are altered without any explicit assignment statements in the program. This is important because C automatically optimizes certain expressions by making the assumption that the content of a variable is unchanging inside that expression. Also, some optimizations may change the order of evaluation of an expression during the compilation process. The **volatile** modifier prevents these changes from occurring.

It is possible to use **const** and **volatile** together. For example, if **0x30** is assumed to be the address of a port that is changed by external conditions only, then the following declaration is precisely what you would want to prevent any possibility of accidental side effects:

```
const volatile unsigned char *port = (const volatile char *) 0x30;
```

Declaration of Variables

As you probably know, a *variable* is a named location in memory that is used to hold a value that can be modified by the program. All variables must be declared before they are used. The general form of a declaration is shown here:

type variable_list;

Here, *type* must be a valid C data type and *variable_list* may consist of one or more identifier names with comma separators. Some declarations are shown here:

```
int i, j, l;

short int si;

unsigned int ui;

double balance, profit, loss;
```

Remember, the name of a variable has nothing to do with its type.

There are three basic places where variables can be declared: inside functions, in the definition of function parameters, or outside all functions. These variables are called local variables, formal parameters, and global variables, respectively.

Local Variables

Variables that are declared inside a function are called *local variables*. In some literature, these variables may be referred to as *automatic variables* in keeping with the use of the (optional) keyword **auto** that can be used to declare them. Since the term *local variable* is more commonly used, this guide will continue to use it. Local variables can be referenced only by statements that are inside the block in which the variables are declared. Stated another way, local variables are not known outside their own code block. You should remember that a block of code is begun when an opening curly brace is encountered and terminated when a closing curly brace is found.

One of the most important things to understand about local variables is that they exist only while the block of code in which they are declared is executing. That is, a local variable is created upon entry into its block and destroyed upon exit.

The most common code block in which local variables are declared is the function. For example, consider these two functions:

```
void func1(void)
{
   int x;

   x = 10;
}

void func2(void)
{
   int x;

   x = -199;
}
```

The integer variable **x** was declared twice, once in **func1( )** and once in **func2( )**. The **x** in **func1( )** has no bearing on, or relationship to, the **x** in **func2( )** because each **x** is only known to the code within the same block as the variable's declaration.

The C language contains the keyword **auto**, which can be used to declare local variables. However, since all nonglobal variables are assumed to be **auto** by default, it is virtually never used and the examples in this book will not use it. (It has been said that **auto** was included in C to provide for source-level compatibility with its predecessor, B. Further, **auto** is supported in C++ to provide compatibility with C.)

It is common practice to declare all variables needed within a function at the start of that function's code block. This is done mostly to make it easy for anyone reading the code to know what variables are used. However, it is not necessary to do this because local variables can be declared within any code block. To understand how this works, consider the following function:

```
void f(void)
{
  int t;

  scanf("%d", &t);

  if(t==1) {
    char s[80];  /* s exists only inside this block */
    printf("enter name:");
    gets(s);
    process(s);
  }
  /* s is not known here */
}
```

Here, the local variable **s** is created upon entry into the **if** code block and destroyed upon exit. Since **s** is known only within the **if** block, it may not be referenced elsewhere—not even in other parts of the function that contains it.

There is one small restriction that you must observe when declaring local variables when using C if you want the widest portability: they must be declared at the start of a block, prior to any "action" statements. This restriction does not apply to C++.

One reason you might want to declare a variable within its own block, instead of at the top of a function, is to prevent its accidental misuse elsewhere in the function. In essence, declaring variables inside the blocks of code that actually use them allows you to compartmentalize your code and data into more easily managed units.

Because local variables are destroyed upon exit from the function in which they are declared, they cannot retain their values between function calls. (As you will see shortly, however, it is possible to direct the compiler to retain their values through the use of the **static** modifier.)

Unless otherwise specified, local variables are stored on the stack. The fact that the stack is a dynamic and changing region of memory explains why local variables cannot, in general, hold their values between function calls.

Formal Parameters

If a function is to use arguments, then it must declare variables that will accept the values of the arguments. These variables are called the *formal parameters* of the function. They behave like any other local variables inside the function. As shown in the following program fragment, their declaration occurs inside the parentheses that follow the function name.

```
/* return 1 if c is part of string s; 0 otherwise */
int is_in(char *s, char c)
{
  while(*s)
    if(*s==c) return 1;
    else s++;

  return 0;
}
```

The function **is_in( )** has two parameters: **s** and **c**. You must tell C what type of variable these are by declaring them as just shown. Once this has been done, they may be used inside the function as normal local variables. Keep in mind that, as local variables, they are also dynamic and are destroyed upon exit from the function.

You must make sure that the formal parameters you declare are the same type as the arguments you will use to call the function. If there is a type mismatch, unexpected results can occur. Unlike many other languages, C is very robust and generally will do something, even if it is not what you want. There are few run-time errors and no bounds checking. As the programmer, you have to make sure that errors do not occur.

As with local variables, you may make assignments to a function's formal parameters or use them in any allowable expression. Even though these variables perform the special task of receiving the value of the arguments passed to the function, they can be used like any other local variable.

Global Variables

Unlike local variables, *global variables* are known throughout the entire program and may be used by any piece of code. Also, they will hold their values during the entire execution of the program. Global variables are created by declaring them outside of any function. They may be accessed by any expression regardless of what function that expression is in.

In the following program, you can see that the variable **count** has been declared outside of all functions. Although its declaration occurs before the **main( )** function, you could have placed it anywhere prior to its first use, as long as it was not in a function. However, it is usually best to declare global variables at the top of the program.

```c
#include <stdio.h>

void func1(void), func2(void);

int count;   /* count is global  */

int main(void)
{
  count = 100;
  func1();

  return 0;
}

void func1(void)
{
  func2();
  printf("count is %d", count); /* will print 100 */
}

void func2(void)
{
  int count;

  for(count=1; count<10; count++)
    putchar(' ');
}
```

Looking closely at this program fragment, it should be clear that although neither **main( )** nor **func1( )** has declared the variable **count**, both may use it. However, **func2( )** has declared a local variable called **count**. When **func2( )** references **count**, it will be referencing only its local variable, not the global one. If a global variable and a local variable have the same name, all references to that variable name inside the function where the local variable is declared refer to the local variable and have no effect on the global variable. This is a convenient benefit. However, forgetting this can cause your program to act very strangely, even though it "looks" correct.

Storage for global variables is in a fixed region of memory set aside for this purpose by the compiler. Global variables are very helpful when the same data is used in many functions in your program. You should avoid using unnecessary global variables, however, for three reasons:

1. They take up memory the entire time your program is executing, not just when they are needed.

2. Using a global variable where a local variable will do makes a function less general because it relies on something that must be defined outside itself.

3. Using a large number of global variables can lead to program errors because of unknown, and unwanted, side effects.

One of the principal points of a structured language is the compartmentalization of code and data. In C, compartmentalization is achieved through the use of local variables and functions. For example, here are two ways to write **mul( )**—a simple function that computes the product of two integers:

Two Ways to Write mul( )

General	Specific
	int x, y;
int mul(int x, int y)	int mul(void)
{	{
return(x*y);	return(x*y);
}	}

Both functions will return the product of the variables **x** and **y**. However, the generalized, or *parameterized*, version can be used to return the product of *any* two numbers, whereas the specific version can be used to find only the product of the global variables **x** and **y**.

Storage Class Specifiers

Four storage class specifiers are supported by C. They are

extern

static

register

auto

These specifiers tell the compiler how to store the subsequent variable. The general form of a variable declaration that uses one is shown here:

storage_specifier type var_name;

Notice that the storage specifier precedes the rest of the variable declaration. Each specifier will be examined in turn.

 *C++ adds another storage-class specifier called **mutable**, which is described in Part Three.*

extern

Because C allows separately compiled modules of a large program to be linked together to speed up compilation and aid in the management of large projects, there must be some way of telling all the files about the global variables required by the program. The solution is to declare all of your globals in one file and use **extern** declarations in the other, as shown in Table 2-2.

In File Two, the global variable list was copied from File One and the **extern** specifier was added to the declarations. The **extern** specifier tells the compiler that the following variable types and names have been declared elsewhere. In other words, **extern** lets the compiler know what the types and names are for these global variables without actually creating storage for them again. When the two modules are linked, all references to the external variables are resolved.

In real world, multifile programs, **extern** declarations are normally contained in a header file that is simply included with each source code file. This is both easier and less error prone than manually duplicating **extern** declarations in each file.

When a declaration creates storage for a variable, it is called a *definition*. In general, **extern** statements are declarations, but not definitions. (If an **extern** declaration includes an initializer, it becomes a definition.) They simply tell the compiler that a definition exists elsewhere in the program.

Here is another example that uses **extern**. Notice that the global variables **first** and **last** are declared *after* **main( )**.

```
#include <stdio.h>

int main(void)
{
  extern int first, last;  /* use global vars */
  printf("%d %d", first, last);

  return 0;
}

/* global definition of first and last */
int first = 10, last = 20;
```

File One	File Two
int x, y;	extern int x, y;
char ch;	extern char ch;
int main(void)	void func22(void)
{	{
/* ... */	x = y / 10;
}	}
void func1(void)	void func23(void)
{	{
x = 123;	y = 10;
}	}

Table 2-2.   *Using Global Variables in Separately Compiled Files*

This program outputs **10 20** because the global variables **first** and **last** used by the **printf( )** statement are initialized to these values. Because the **extern** declaration tells the compiler that **first** and **last** are declared elsewhere (in this case, later in the same file), the program can be compiled without error even though **first** and **last** are used prior to their definition.

It is important to understand that the **extern** variable declarations as shown in the preceding program are necessary only because **first** and **last** had not yet been declared prior to their use in **main( )**. Had their declarations occurred prior to **main( )**, then there would have been no need for the **extern** statement. Remember, if the compiler finds a variable that has not been declared within the current block, the compiler checks if it matches any of the variables declared within enclosing blocks. If it does not, the compiler then checks the global variables. If a match is found, the compiler assumes that that is the variable being referenced. The **extern** specifier is needed when you want to use a variable that is declared later in the file.

static Variables

Variables declared as **static** variables are permanent variables within their own function or file. They differ from global variables in that they are not known outside their function or file but they maintain their values between calls. This feature makes them very useful when you write generalized functions and function libraries, which may be used by other programmers. Because the effect of **static** on local variables is different from its effect on global ones, they will be examined separately.

static Local Variables

When **static** is applied to a local variable, it causes the compiler to create permanent storage for it in much the same way that it does for a global variable. The key difference between a **static** local variable and a global variable is that the **static** local variable remains known only to the block in which it is declared. In simple terms, a **static** local variable is a local variable that retains its value between function calls.

It is very important to the creation of stand-alone functions that **static** local variables are available because there are several types of routines that must preserve a value between calls. If **static** variables were not allowed, then globals would have to be used—opening the door to possible side effects. A simple example of how a **static** local variable can be used is illustrated by the **count( )** function in this short program:

```c
#include <stdio.h>
#include <conio.h>

int count(int i);

int main(void)
{
  do {
    count(0);
  } while(!kbhit());
  printf("count called %d times", count(1));

  return 0;
}

int count(int i)
{
  static int c=0;

  if(i) return c;
  else c++;

  return 0;
}
```

Sometimes it is useful to know how many times a function has been executed during a program run. While it is certainly possible to use a global variable for this purpose, a better way is to have the function in question keep track of this information itself, as is done by the **count( )** function. In this example, if **count( )** is called with a value of 0 then the counter variable **c** is incremented. (Presumably in a real application, the function would also perform some other useful processing.) If **count( )** is called with any other value, it returns the number of times it has been called. Counting the number of times a function is called can be useful during the development of a program so that those functions called most frequently can receive the most attention.

Another good example of a function that would require a **static** local variable is a number series generator that produces a new number based on the last one. It is possible for you to declare a global variable for this value. However, each time the function is used in a program, you would have to remember to declare that global variable and make sure that it did not conflict with any other global variables already declared—a major drawback. Also, using a global variable would make this function difficult to place in a function library. The better solution is to declare the variable that holds the generated number to be **static**, as in this program fragment:

```
int series(void)
{
   static int series_num;

   series_num = series_num+23;
   return series_num;
}
```

In this example, the variable **series_num** stays in existence between function calls, instead of coming and going the way a normal local variable would. This means that each call to **series( )** can produce a new member of the series based on the last number without declaring that variable globally.

You may have noticed something that is unusual about the function **series( )** as it stands in the example. The static variable **series_num** is never explicitly initialized. This means that the first time the function is called, **series_num** will have the value zero, by default. While this is acceptable for some applications, most series generators will need a flexible starting point. To do this requires that **series_num** be initialized prior to the first call to **series( )**, which can be done easily only if **series_num** is a global variable. However, avoiding having to make **series_num** global was the entire point of making it **static** to begin with. This leads to the second use of **static**.

static Global Variables

When the specifier **static** is applied to a global variable, it instructs the compiler to create a global variable that is known only to the *file* in which the **static** global variable is declared. This means that even though the variable is global, other routines in other files have no knowledge of it and are unable to alter its contents directly; thus it is not subject to side effects. For the few situations where a local **static** cannot do the job, you can create a small file that contains only the functions that need the **static** global variable, separately compile that file, and use it without fear of side effects.

To see how a **static** global variable can be used, the series generator example from the previous section is recoded so that a starting "seed" value can be used to initialize the series through a call to a second function called **series_start( )**. The entire file containing **series( )**, **series_start( )**, and **series_num** follows:

```
/* This must all be in one file - preferably by itself */

static int series_num;

int series(void);
void series_start(int seed);

int series(void)
{
  series_num = series_num + 23;
  return series_num;
}

/* initialize series_num */
void series_start(int seed)
{
  series_num = seed;
}
```

Calling **series_start( )** with some known integer value initializes the series generator. After that, calls to **series( )** will generate the next element in the series.

To review: The names of **static** local variables are known only to the function or block of code in which they are declared; the names of **static** global variables are known only to the file in which they reside. This means that if you place the **series( )** and **series_start( )** functions in a separate file, you can use the functions, but you cannot reference the variable **series_num**. It is hidden from the rest of the code in your program. In fact, you may even declare and use another variable called **series_num** in your program (in another file, of course) and not confuse anything. In essence, the **static** modifier permits variables that are known only to the functions that need them, without unwanted side effects.

By using **static** variables, you can hide portions of your program from other portions. This can be a tremendous advantage when trying to manage a very large and complex program. The **static** storage specifier lets you create generalized functions that can go into libraries for later use.

register Variables

C has one last storage specifier that originally applied only to variables of type **int,** **char,** or pointer types. However, when C was standardized, its scope was broadened. The **register** specifier requests the compiler to store a variable declared with this modifier in a manner that allows the fastest access time possible. For integers, characters, and pointers, this typically means in a register of the CPU rather than in memory, where normal variables are stored. For other types of variables, the compiler may use any other means to decrease their access time. In fact, it can also simply ignore the request altogether.

In C++ Builder, the **register** specifier can be applied to local variables and to the formal parameters of a function. You cannot apply **register** to global variables. Also, because a **register** variable may be stored in a register of the CPU, you cannot obtain the address of a **register** variable. (This restriction applies only to C, not to C++.)

In general, operations on **register** variables occur much faster than on variables stored in main memory. In fact, when the value of a variable is actually held in the CPU, no memory access is required to determine or modify its value. This makes **register** variables ideal for loop control. Here is an example of how to declare a **register** variable of type **int** and use it to control a loop. This function computes the result of M^e for integers.

```
int int_pwr(register int m, register int e)
{
   register int temp;

   temp = 1;

   for(; e; e--) temp *= m;

   return temp;
}
```

In this example, **m, e,** and **temp** are declared to be **register** variables because they are all used within the loop. In general practice, **register** variables are used where they will do the most good, that is, in places where many references will be made to the same variable. This is important because not all variables can be optimized for access time.

It is important to understand that the **register** specifier is just a request to the compiler, which the compiler is free to ignore. In general, you can count on at least two **register** variables of type **char** or **int** actually being held in a CPU register for any one function. Additional **register** variables will be optimized to the best ability of the compiler.

Assignment Statements

The general form of the *assignment statement* is

> *variable_name = expression;*

where an expression may be as simple as a single constant or as complex as a combination of variables, operators, and constants. Like BASIC and FORTRAN, C/C++ uses a single equal sign to indicate assignment (unlike Pascal or Modula-2, which use the := construct). The target, or left part, of the assignment must be a variable, not a function or a constant.

Multiple Assignments

You can assign many variables the same value by using multiple assignments in a single statement. For example, this program fragment assigns **x**, **y**, and **z** the value 0:

```
x = y = z = 0;
```

In professional programs, variables are frequently assigned common values using this method.

Type Conversion in Assignments

Type conversion refers to the situation in which variables of one type are mixed with variables of another type. When this occurs in an assignment statement, the *type conversion rule* is very easy: The value of the right (expression) side of the assignment is converted to the type of the left side (target variable), as illustrated by this example:

```
int x;
char ch;
float  f;
void func(void)
{
  ch = x;      /* line 1 */
  x = f;       /* line 2 */
  f = ch;      /* line 3 */
  f = x;       /* line 4 */
}
```

In line 1, the left, high-order bits of the integer variable **x** are lopped off, leaving **ch** with the lower 8 bits. If **x** were between 255 and 0, **ch** and **x** would have identical values. Otherwise, the value of **ch** would reflect only the lower order bits of **x**. In line 2, **x** receives the nonfractional part of **f**. In line 3, **f** receives the 8-bit integer value stored in **ch**, converted into floating-point format. In line 4, **f** receives the value of integer **x** converted into floating-point format.

When converting from integers to characters, long integers to integers, and integers to short integers, the basic rule is that the appropriate number of high-order bits will be removed. For C++ Builder, 24 bits will be lost when converting from an integer to a character, and 16 bits will be lost when converting from an integer or long integer to a short integer.

Table 2-3 summarizes several common assignment type conversions as they relate to the way that C++ Builder implements the built-in data types. You must remember two important points that can affect the portability of the code you write:

1. The conversion of an **int** to a **float**, or a type **float** to **double** and so on, will not add any precision or accuracy. These kinds of conversions will only change the form in which the value is represented.

2. Some C compilers (and processors) will always treat a **char** variable as positive, no matter what value it has when converting it to an integer or a floating-point value. Other compilers may treat **char** variable values greater than 127 as negative numbers when converting (as does C++ Builder). Generally speaking, you should use **char** variables for characters, and use **int**, **short int**, or **signed char** when needed to avoid a possible portability problem in this area.

To use Table 2-3 to make a conversion not directly shown, simply convert one type at a time until you finish. For example, to convert from a **double** to an **int**, first convert from a **double** to a **float** and then from a **float** to an **int**.

Target Type	Expression Type	Possible Info Loss
signed char	unsigned char	If value > 127, the targets will be negative
char	short int	High-order 8 bits
char	int	High-order 24 bits
char	long int	High-order 24 bits
short int	int	High-order 16 bits
int	long int	None
int	float	Fractional part and possibly more
float	double	Precision, result rounded
double	long double	Precision, result rounded

Table 2-3. *The Outcome of Common Type Conversions for C++ Builder*

If you have used a computer language like Pascal, which prohibits this automatic type conversion, you may think that C is very loose and sloppy. However, keep in mind that C was designed to make the life of the programmer easier by enabling work to be done in C rather than assembler. To do this, C has to allow such type conversions.

Variable Initializations

You can give variables a value at the time they are declared by placing an equal sign and a constant after the variable name. This is called an *initialization*; its general form is:

type variable_name = constant;

Some examples are

```
char ch = 'a';

int first = 0;

float balance = 123.23;
```

Global variables are initialized only at the start of the program. Local variables are initialized each time the block in which they are declared is entered. However, **static** local variables are only initialized once, at program startup and not each time the block is entered. All global variables and **static** local variables are initialized to zero if no other initializer is specified. Local variables that are not initialized will have indeterminate values.

Constants

Constants refer to fixed values that may not be altered by the program. They can be of any data type, as shown in Table 2-4. Constants are also called *literals*.

By default, floating-point constants are of type **double**. An integer constant is fit into the smallest integer type that will hold it. Often, these defaults are adequate. However, you can specify precisely the type of numeric constant you want by using a suffix. For floating-point types, if you follow the number with an F, the number is treated as a **float**. If you follow it with an L, the number becomes a **long double**. For integer types, the U suffix stands for **unsigned** and the L for **long**. The type suffixes are not case dependent, and you can use lowercase, if you like. For example, both F and f specify a **float** constant.

C supports one other type of constant in addition to those of the predefined data types. This is a *string*. All string constants are enclosed between double quotes, such as **"this is a test"**. You must not confuse strings with characters. A single character constant is enclosed by single quotes, such as **'a'**. Because strings are simply arrays of characters, they will be discussed in Chapter 5.

Data Type	Constant Examples
char	'a' '9'
int	1 123 21000 –234
long int	35000L –34L
short int	10 –12 90
unsigned int	10000U 987U 40000U
float	123.23F 4.34e–3F
double	123.23 12312.333 –0.9876324
long double	1001.2L

Table 2-4.   *Constant Examples for Data Types*

Backslash Character Constants

Enclosing all character constants in single quotes works for most printing characters, but a few, such as the carriage return, are impossible to enter from the keyboard. For this reason, C supplies the special backslash character constants, shown in Table 2-5. These are also referred to as *escape sequences*.

You use a backslash code exactly the same way you would any other character. For example,

```
ch = '\t';
printf("%c this is a test\n", ch);
```

first assigns a tab to **ch** and then prints a tab, "this is a test", and then a new line.

Code	Meaning
\b	Backspace
\f	Form feed
\n	Newline

Table 2-5.   *Backslash Codes*

Code	Meaning
\r	Carriage return
\t	Horizontal tab
\"	Double quote
\'	Single quote
\0	Null
\\	Backslash
\v	Vertical tab
\a	Alert
\?	Question mark
\N	Octal constant (where N is an octal value)
\xN	Hexadecimal constant (where N is a hexadecimal value.

Table 2-5.   *Backslash Codes* (continued)

Operators

C is very rich in built-in operators. An *operator* is a symbol that tells the compiler to perform specific mathematical or logical manipulations. There are four general classes of operators in C: *arithmetic, relational, logical,* and *bitwise.* In addition, there are some special operators for particular tasks.

Arithmetic Operators

Table 2-6 lists C's *arithmetic operators.* The operators +, −, *, and / all work the same way in C as they do in most other computer languages. They can be applied to almost any built-in data type allowed by C. When / is applied to an integer or character, any remainder is truncated; for example, **10 / 3** equals 3 in integer division.

The modulus division operator (%) also works in C the way it does in other languages. Remember that the modulus division operation yields the remainder of

Operator	Action
–	Subtraction, also unary minus
+	Addition
*	Multiplication
/	Division
%	Modulus
– –	Decrement
++	Increment

Table 2-6. *Arithmetic Operators*

an integer division. However, as such, % cannot be used on type **float** or **double**. The following code fragment illustrates its use:

```
int x, y;

x = 10;
y = 3;

printf("%d", x/y);    /* will display 3 */
printf("%d", x%y);    /* will display 1, the remainder of
                         the integer division */

x = 1;
y = 2;

printf("%d %d", x/y, x%y); /*  will display 0 1 */
```

The reason the last line prints a 0 and 1 is because **1 / 2** in integer division is 0 with a remainder of 1. **1 % 2** yields the remainder 1.

The unary minus, in effect, multiplies its single operand by –1. That is, any number preceded by a minus sign switches its sign.

Increment and Decrement

C allows two very useful operators not generally found in other computer languages. These are the increment and decrement operators, **++** and **– –**. The operation **++** adds 1 to its operand, and **– –** subtracts 1. Therefore, the following are equivalent operations:

```
x = x + 1;
```

is the same as

```
++x;
```

Also,

```
x = x - 1;
```

is the same as

```
--x;
```

Both the increment and decrement operators may either precede or follow the operand. For example,

```
x = x + 1;
```

can be written

```
++x;
```

or

```
x++;
```

However, there is a difference when they are used in an expression. When an increment or decrement operator precedes its operand, C performs the increment or decrement operation prior to obtaining the operand's value. If the operator follows its operand, C obtains the operand's value before incrementing or decrementing it. Consider the following:

```
x = 10;
y = ++x;
```

In this case, **y** is set to 11. However, if the code had been written as

```
x = 10;
y = x++;
```

y would have been set to 10. In both cases, **x** is set to 11; the difference is when it happens. There are significant advantages in being able to control when the increment or decrement operation takes place.

The precedence of the arithmetic operators is as follows:

highest	++ --
	– (unary minus)
	* / %
lowest	+ –

Operators on the same precedence level are evaluated by the compiler from left to right. Of course, parentheses may be used to alter the order of evaluation. Parentheses are treated by C in the same way they are by virtually all other computer languages: They give an operation, or set of operations, a higher precedence level.

Relational and Logical Operators

In the term *relational operator* the word *relational* refers to the relationships values can have with one another. In the term *logical operator* the word *logical* refers to the ways these relationships can be connected together using the rules of formal logic. Because the relational and logical operators often work together, they will be discussed together here.

The key to the concepts of relational and logical operators is the idea of *true* and *false*. In C, *true* is any value other than 0. *False* is 0. Expressions that use relational or logical operators will return 0 for false and 1 for true.

Table 2-7 shows the relational and logical operators. The truth table for the logical operators is shown here using 1s and 0s:

p	q	p && q	p II q	!p
0	0	0	0	1
0	1	0	1	1
1	1	1	1	0
1	0	0	1	0

Both the relational and logical operators are lower in precedence than the arithmetic operators. This means that an expression like **10 > 1 + 12** is evaluated as if it were written **10 > (1 + 12)**. The result is, of course, false.

Several operations can be combined in one expression, as shown here:

    10>5 && !(10<9) I I 3<=4

which will evaluate true.

Relational Operators

Operator	Action
>	Greater than
>=	Greater than or equal
<	Less than
<=	Less than or equal
==	Equal
!=	Not equal

Logical Operators

Operator	Action
&&	AND
I I	OR
!	NOT

Table 2-7.   *Relational and Logical Operators*

The following shows the relative precedence of the relational and logical operators:

highest   !

                        > >= < <=

                        == !=

                        &&

lowest ||

As with arithmetic expressions, it is possible to use parentheses to alter the natural order of evaluation in a relational or logical expression. For example,

!1 && 0

will be false because the **!** is evaluated first, then the **&&** is evaluated. However, when the same expression is parenthesized as shown here, the result is true:

!(1 && 0)

Remember, all relational and logical expressions produce a result of either 0 or 1. Therefore the following program fragment is not only correct but also prints the number 1 on the display:

```
int x;

x = 100;
printf("%d", x > 10);
```

Bitwise Operators

Unlike many other languages, C supports a complete complement of *bitwise operators*. Since C was designed to take the place of assembly language for most programming tasks, it needed the capability to support many operations that can be done in assembler. *Bitwise operations* are the testing, setting, or shifting of the actual bits in a byte or word, which correspond to the standard **char** and **int** data types and variants. Bitwise operators cannot be used on type **float**, **double**, **long double**, **void**, or other more complex types. Table 2-8 lists these operators.

The bitwise AND, OR, and NOT (one's complement) are governed by the same truth table as were their logical equivalents except that they work on a bit-by-bit level. The exclusive OR ^ has the truth table shown here:

p	q	p^q
0	0	0
0	1	1
1	0	1
1	1	0

Operator	Action
&	AND
|	OR
^	Exclusive OR (XOR)
~	One's complement
>>	Shift right
<<	Shift left

Table 2-8.   *The Bitwise Operators*

As the table indicates, the outcome of an XOR is true only if exactly one of the operands is true; it is false otherwise.

Bitwise operations most often find application in device drivers, such as modem programs, disk file routines, and printer routines, because the bitwise operations can be used to mask off certain bits, such as parity. (The parity bit is used to confirm that the rest of the bits in the byte are unchanged. It is usually the high-order bit in each byte.)

The bitwise AND is most commonly used to turn bits off. That is, any bit that is 0 in either operand causes the corresponding bit in the outcome to be set to 0. For example, the following function reads a character from the modem port using the function **read_modem( )** and resets the parity bit to 0:

```
char get_char_from_modem(void)
{
  char ch;

  ch = read_modem(); /* get a character from the
                        modem port */
  return(ch & 127);
}
```

Parity is indicated by the eighth bit, which is set to 0 by ANDing it with a byte that has bits 1 through 7 set to 1 and bit 8 set to 0. The expression **ch & 127** means to AND together the bits in **ch** with the bits that make up the number 127. The net result is that the eighth bit of **ch** will be set to 0. In the following example, assume that **ch** had received the character '**A**' and had the parity bit set:

```
    parity bit
       |
       ↓
    1 1 0 0 0 0 0 1        ch containing an 'A' with parity bit set
    0 1 1 1 1 1 1 1        127 in binary
&   ----------------       do bitwise AND
    0 1 0 0 0 0 0 1        'A' without parity
```

The bitwise OR, as the reverse of AND, can be used to turn bits on. Any bit that is set to 1 in either operand causes the corresponding bit in the outcome to be set to 1. For example, **128 | 3** is

```
    1 0 0 0 0 0 0 0        128 in binary
    0 0 0 0 0 0 1 1        3 in binary
|   --------------         bitwise OR
    1 0 0 0 0 0 1 1        result
```

An exclusive OR, usually abbreviated XOR, will turn a bit on only if the bits being compared are different. For example, **127 ^ 120** is

```
    0 1 1 1 1 1 1 1        127 in binary
    0 1 1 1 1 0 0 0        120 in binary
^   ----------------       bitwise XOR
    0 0 0 0 0 1 1 1        result
```

In general, bitwise ANDs, ORs, and XORs apply their operations directly to each bit in the variable individually. For this reason, among others, bitwise operators are not usually used in conditional statements the way the relational and logical operators are. For example if **x = 7**, then **x && 8** evaluates to true (1), whereas **x & 8** evaluates to false (0).

Relational and logical operators always produce a result that is either 0 or 1, whereas the similar bitwise operations may produce any arbitrary value in accordance with the specific operation. In other words, bitwise operations may create values other than 0 or 1, while the logical operators will always evaluate to 0 or 1.

The shift operators, >> and <<, move all bits in a variable to the right or left as specified. The general form of the shift right statement is

variable >> number of bit positions

and the shift left statement is

variable << number of bit positions

As bits are shifted off one end, bits are brought in the other end. Remember, a shift is *not* a rotate. That is, the bits shifted off one end *do not* come back around to the other. The bits shifted off are lost, and 0s are brought in. However, a right shift of a negative number shifts in ones. (This maintains the sign bit.)

Bit shift operations can be very useful when decoding external device input, like D/A converters, and reading status information. The bitwise shift operators can also be used to perform very fast multiplication and division of integers. A shift left will effectively multiply a number by 2, and a shift right will divide it by 2, as shown in Table 2-9.

The one's complement operator, ~, will reverse the state of each bit in the specified variable. That is, all 1s are set to 0, and all 0s are set to 1.

The bitwise operators are used often in cipher routines. If you wished to make a disk file appear unreadable, you could perform some bitwise manipulations on it. One of the simplest methods would be to complement each byte by using the one's complement to reverse each bit in the byte as shown here:

Original byte	00101100	
After 1st complement	11010011	— same
After 2nd complement	00101100	

Notice that a sequence of two complements in a row always produces the original number. Hence, the first complement would represent the coded version of that byte. The second complement would decode it to its original value.

You could use the **encode( )** function shown here to encode a character:

```
/* A simple cipher function. */
char encode(char ch)
{
  return(~ch); /* complement it */
}
```

	x as Each Statement Executes	Value of x
char x;		
x = 7;	0 0 0 0 0 1 1 1	7
x = x << 1;	0 0 0 0 1 1 1 0	14
x = x << 3;	0 1 1 1 0 0 0 0	112
x = x << 2;	1 1 0 0 0 0 0 0	192
x = x >> 1;	0 1 1 0 0 0 0 0	96
x=x >> 2;	0 0 0 1 1 0 0 0	24

Each left shift multiplies by 2. You should notice that information has been lost after x << 2 because a bit was shifted off the end.

Each right shift divides by 2. Notice that subsequent division will not bring back any lost bits.

Table 2-9.   *Multiplication and Division with Shift Operators*

The ? Operator

C has a very powerful and convenient operator that can be used to replace certain statements of the if-then-else form. The ternary operator ? takes the general form

Exp1 ? Exp2 : Exp3

where *Exp1, Exp2,* and *Exp3* are expressions. Notice the use and placement of the colon.

The ? operator works like this. *Exp1* is evaluated. If it is true, then *Exp2* is evaluated and becomes the value of the expression. If *Exp1* is false, then *Exp3* is evaluated and its value becomes the value of the expression. For example:

```
x = 10;
y = x>9 ? 100 : 200;
```

Here, **y** will be assigned the value **100**. If **x** had been less than or equal to 9, **y** would have received the value **200**. The same code written using the **if/else** statement would be:

```
x = 10;
if(x>9) y = 100;
else y = 200;
```

The **?** operator will be discussed more fully in Chapter 3 in relationship to C's other conditional statements.

The & and * Pointer Operators

A *pointer* is the memory address of a variable. A *pointer variable* is a variable that is specifically declared to hold a pointer to a value of its specified type. Knowing a variable's address can be of great help in certain types of routines. Pointers have three main uses in C:

1. They can provide a very fast means of referencing array elements.

2. They allow C functions to modify their calling parameters.

3. They support dynamic data structures, such as linked lists.

These topics and uses will be dealt with in Chapter 6, which is devoted exclusively to pointers. However, the two operators that are used to manipulate pointers will be presented here.

The first pointer operator is **&**. It is a unary operator that returns the memory address of its operand. Remember that a unary operator only requires one operand. For example,

```
m = &count;
```

places into **m** the memory address of the variable **count**. This address is the computer's internal location of the variable. It has nothing to do with the *value* of **count**. The operation of the **&** can be remembered as returning the "the address of." Therefore, the preceding assignment statement could be read as "m receives the address of count."

To better understand the preceding assignment, assume the variable **count** resides at memory location 2000. Also assume that **count** has a value of 100. After this assignment, **m** will have the value 2000.

The second operator, *, is the complement of the &. It is a unary operator that returns the *value of the object located at the address that follows.* For example, if **m** contains the memory address of the variable **count**, then

```
q = *m;
```

places the value of **count** into **q**. Following the preceding example, **q** will have the value 100 because 100 is stored at location 2000, which is the memory address that was stored in **m**. The operation of the * can be remembered as "at address." In this case, the statement could be read as "q receives the value at address m."

Unfortunately, the multiplication sign and the "at address" sign are the same, and the bitwise AND and the "address of" sign are the same. These operators have no relationship to each other. Both **&** and * have a higher precedence than the binary arithmetic operators.

Variables that will hold memory addresses, or pointers as they are called in C, must be declared by putting a * in front of the variable name to indicate to the compiler that it will hold a pointer to that type of variable. For example, to declare a **char** pointer variable called **pch**, you would write

```
char *pch;
```

Here, **pch** is not a character, but rather a pointer to a character—there is a big difference. The type of data that a pointer will be pointing to, in this case **char**, is called the *base type* of the pointer. However, the pointer variable itself is a variable that will be used to hold the address to an object of the base type. Hence, a character pointer (or any pointer, for that matter) will be of sufficient size to hold an address as defined by the architecture of the computer on which it is running. The key point to remember is that a pointer should only be used to point to data that is of that pointer's base type.

You can mix both pointer and nonpointer directives in the same declaration statement. For example,

```
int x, *y, count;
```

declares **x** and **count** to be integer types, and **y** to be a pointer to an integer type.

Here, the * and **&** operators are used to put the value 10 into a variable called **target**:

```
#include <stdio.h>

/* Assignment with * and &. */
int main(void)
```

```
{
  int target, source;
  int *m;

  source = 10;
  m = &source;
  target = *m;

  printf("%d", target);

  return 0;
}
```

The sizeof Compile-Time Operator

The **sizeof** operator is a unary compile-time operator that returns the length, in bytes, of the variable or parenthesized type-specifier it precedes. For example, assuming that integers are four bytes and **double**s are eight bytes, this fragment will display 8 4.

```
double f;

printf("%f ", sizeof f);
printf("%d", sizeof(int));
```

Remember that to compute the size of a type, you must enclose the type name in parentheses (like a cast, which is explained later in this chapter). This is not necessary for variable names.

The principal use of **sizeof** is to help generate portable code when that code depends upon the size of the built-in data types. For example, imagine a database program that needs to store six integer values per record. If you want to port the database program to a variety of computers, you must not assume the size of an integer, but determine its actual length using **sizeof**. This being the case, you could use the following routine to write a record to a disk file:

```
/* Write 6 integers to a disk file */
void put_rec(FILE *fp, int rec[6])
{
  int size, num;

  size = sizeof(int) * 6;
  num = fwrite(rec, size, 1, fp);
  if(num!=1) printf("Write Error");
}
```

The key point of this example is that, coded as shown, **put_rec( )** will compile and run correctly on any computer—including those that use 16- and 32-bit integers. One final point: **sizeof** is evaluated at compile time, and the value it produces is treated as a constant within your program.

The Comma Operator

The comma operator strings together several expressions. The left side of the comma operator is always evaluated as **void**. This means that the expression on the right side will become the value of the total comma-separated expression. For example,

```
x = (y=3, y+1);
```

first assigns **y** the value 3 and then assigns **x** the value of 4. The parentheses are necessary because the comma operator has a lower precedence than the assignment operator.

Essentially, the comma causes a sequence of operations to be performed. When you use it on the right side of an assignment statement, the value assigned is the value of the last expression of the comma-separated list. For example:

```
y = 10;
x = (y=y-5, 25/y);
```

After execution, **x** will have the value 5 because **y**'s original value of 10 is reduced by 5, and then that value is divided into 25, yielding 5 as the result.

The comma operator has somewhat the same meaning as the word "and" in English, as used in the phrase "do this and this and this."

The Dot (.) and Arrow (–>) Operators

The **.** (dot) and **–>** (arrow) operators access individual elements of structures and unions. *Structures* and *unions* are compound data types that can be referenced under a single name. Structures and unions are thoroughly covered in Chapter 7, but a short discussion of the operators used with them is given here.

The dot operator is used when working with a structure or union directly. The arrow operator is used with a pointer to a structure or union. For example, given the fragment,

```
struct employee {
  char name[80];
  int age;
  float wage;
```

```
} emp;

struct employee *p = &emp; /* address of emp into p */
```

you would write the following code to assign the value 123.23 to the **wage** member of
structure variable **emp:**

```
emp.wage = 123.23;
```

However, the same assignment using a pointer to structure **emp** would be

```
p->wage = 123.23;
```

The [ ] and ( ) Operators

Parentheses are operators that increase the precedence of the operations inside them.
Square brackets perform array indexing (arrays are discussed fully in Chapter 5).
Given an array, the expression within square brackets provides an index into that
array. For example,

```
#include <stdio.h>

char s[80];

int main(void)
{
    s[3] = 'X';
    printf("%c", s[3]);

    return 0;
}
```

first assigns the value 'X' to the fourth element (remember, all arrays begin at 0) of
array **s,** and then prints that element.

Precedence Summary

Table 2-10 lists the precedence of all operators defined by C. Note that all operators,
except the unary operators and **?,** associate from left to right. The unary operators
(*, &, –) and **?** associate from right to left.

Highest	() [] -> .
	! ~ ++ -- + - (type) * & sizeof
	* / %
	+ -
	<< >>
	< <= > >=
	== !=
	&
	^
	|
	&&
	||
	?:
	= *= /= %= += -= &= ^= |= <<= >>=
Lowest	,

Table 2-10. *Precedence of C Operators*

Expressions

Operators, constants, functions, and variables are the constituents of expressions. An *expression* is any valid combination of these elements. Because most expressions tend to follow the general rules of algebra, they are often taken for granted. However, a few aspects of expressions relate specifically to C.

Type Conversion in Expressions

When constants and variables of different types are mixed in an expression, they are all converted to the same type. The compiler converts all operands "up" to the type of the largest operand, which is called *type promotion*. First, all **char** and **short int** values are automatically elevated to **int**. This process is called *integral promotion*. Once this step has been completed, all other conversions are done operation by operation, as described in the following type conversion algorithm:

IF an operand is a **long double**

THEN the second is converted to **long double**

ELSE IF an operand is a **double**

THEN the second is converted to **double**

ELSE IF an operand is a **float**

THEN the second is converted to **float**

ELSE IF an operand is an **unsigned long**

THEN the second is converted to **unsigned long**

ELSE IF an operand is **long**

THEN the second is converted to **long**

ELSE IF an operand is **unsigned int**

THEN the second is converted to **unsigned int**

There is one additional special case: If one operand is **long** and the other is **unsigned int**, and if the value of the **unsigned int** cannot be represented by a **long**, both operands are converted to **unsigned long**.

Once these conversion rules have been applied, each pair of operands is of the same type, and the result of each operation is the same as the type of both operands.

For example, consider the type conversions that occur in Figure 2-1. First, the character **ch** is converted to an integer. Then the outcome of **ch/i** is converted to a **double** because **f * d** is **double**. The outcome of **f + i** is **float**, because **f** is a **float**. The final result is **double**.

Casts

You can force an expression to be of a specific type by using a *cast*. The general form of a cast is:

(*type*) *expression*

where *type* is valid data type. For example, to cause the expression **x / 2** to evaluate to type **float**, write:

```
(float) x/2
```

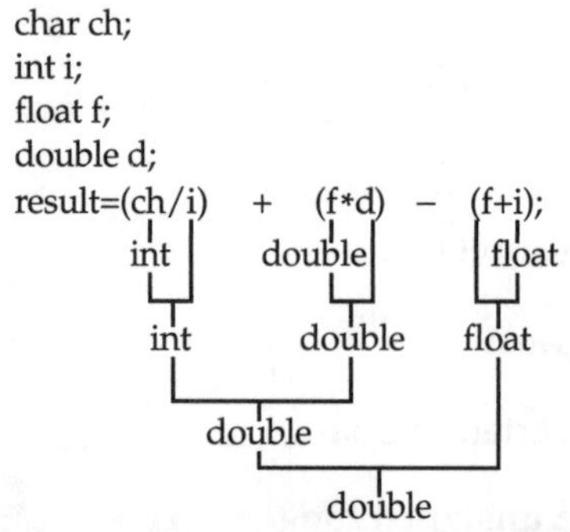

```
char ch;
int i;
float f;
double d;
result=(ch/i)  +  (f*d)  -  (f+i);
         int      double    float
          int     double   float
              double
                 double
```

Figure 2-1.   *An example of type conversion*

Casts are technically operators. As an operator, a cast is unary and has the same precedence as any other unary operator.

Casts can be very useful. For example, suppose you want to use an integer for loop control, yet to perform computation on it requires a fractional part, as in the following program:

```
#include <stdio.h>

/* Print i and i/2 with fractions. */
int main(void)
{
  int i;

  for(i=1; i<=100; ++i )
    printf("%d / 2 is: %f\n", i, (float) i/2);

  return 0;
}
```

Without the cast (**float**), only an integer division would have been performed; but the cast ensures that the fractional part of the answer is displayed.

Note   *C++ adds four additional casting operators, which are described in Part Three.*

Spacing and Parentheses

To aid readability, an expression may have tabs and spaces added in it at your discretion. For example, the following two expressions are the same.

```
x=10/y~(127/x);

x = 10 / y ~(127/x);
```

Redundant or additional parentheses do not cause errors or slow down the execution of an expression. You should use parentheses to clarify the exact order of evaluation, both for yourself and for others. For example, which of the following two expressions is easier to read?

```
x=y/3-34*temp&127;

x = (y/3) - (34*temp) & 127;
```

C Shorthand

C has a special shorthand that simplifies the coding of a certain type of assignment statement. For example

```
x = x + 10;
```

can be written, in C shorthand, as

```
x += 10;
```

The operator pair **+=** tells the compiler to assign the value of **x** plus 10 to **x**. This type of assignment is formally called a *compound assignment*.

This shorthand works for all binary operators (those that require two operands). The general form of the shorthand

var = var operator expression;

is the same as

var operator = expression;

Here is another example,

```
x = x - 100;
```

is the same as

```
x -= 100;
```

You will see compound assignments used widely in professionally written C/C++ programs.

The
Complete
Reference

Borland
C++
Builder

Chapter 3

Program Control Statements

T his chapter discusses C/C++'s rich and varied program control statements. C and C++ categorize statements into these groups:

- Selection
- Iteration
- Jump
- Label
- Expression
- Block

The selection statements are the **if** and **switch**. The term *conditional statement* is often used in place of selection statement. The iteration statements are **while**, **for**, and **do/while**. These are also commonly called *loop* statements. The jump statements are **break**, **continue**, **goto**, and **return**. The label statements include the **case** and **default** statements (discussed along with the **switch** statement) and the label statement itself (discussed with **goto**). Expression statements are statements composed of a valid expression. Block statements are simply blocks of code. (A block begins with a { and ends with a }.) Block statements are also referred to as *compound statements*.

Since many statements rely upon the outcome of some conditional test, let's begin by reviewing the concepts of true and false.

True and False

Many C/C++ statements rely on a conditional expression that determines what course of action is to be taken. The conditional expression evaluates to either a true or false value. Unlike many other computer languages that specify special values for true and false, a true value in C/C++ is any nonzero value, including negative numbers. A false value is zero. This approach to true and false allows a wide range of routines to be coded very efficiently.

 *C++ also defines the values **true** and **false**, which stand for the two Boolean values, but they are not supported by the C subset. See Part Three for details.*

Selection Statements

C/C++ supports two types of selection statements: **if** and **switch**. In addition, the **?** operator is an alternative to **if** in certain circumstances.

if

The general form of the **if** statement is

if*(expression) statement;*
else *statement;*

where *statement* may consist of a single statement, a block of statements, or nothing (in the case of empty statements). The **else** clause is optional.

The general form of the **if** using a block of statements is

if*(expression)* {
  statement sequence
}
else {
  statement sequence
}

If *expression* evaluates to true (anything other than 0), the statement or block that forms the target of the **if** is executed; otherwise, the statement or block that is the target of the **else** is executed. Remember, only the code associated with the **if** or the code that is associated with the **else** executes, never both.

For example, consider the following program, which plays a very simple version of the "guess the magic number" game. It prints the message "** Right **" when the player guesses the magic number.

```
#include <stdio.h>

/* Magic number program. */
int main(void)
{
  int magic = 123;  /* magic number */
  int guess;

  printf("Enter your guess: ");
  scanf("%d", &guess);

  if(guess == magic) printf("** Right **");

  return 0;
}
```

This program uses the equality operator to determine whether the player's guess matches the magic number. If it does, the message is printed on the screen.

Taking the magic number program further, the next version illustrates the use of the **else** statement to print a message in response to the wrong number.

```c
#include <stdio.h>

/* Magic number program - improvement 1. */
int main(void)
{
  int magic = 123;  /* magic number */
  int guess;

  printf("Enter your guess: ");
  scanf("%d",&guess);

  if(guess == magic) printf("** Right **");
  else printf(".. Wrong ..");

  return 0;
}
```

Nested ifs

One of the most confusing aspects of **if** statements is nested **ifs**. A *nested if* is an **if** that is the target of another **if** or **else**. The reason that nested **ifs** are so troublesome is that it can be difficult to know what **else** associates with what **if**. For example:

```c
if(x)
  if(y) printf("1");
  else printf("2");
```

To which **if** does the **else** refer? Fortunately, there is a very simple rule for resolving this type of situation. The **else** is associated with the closest preceding **if** (at the same scope level) that does not already have an **else** statement associated with it. In this case, the **else** is associated with the **if(y)** statement. To make the **else** associate with the **if(x)**, you must use braces to override its normal association, as shown here:

```c
if(x) {
  if(y) printf("1");
}
else printf("2");
```

The **else** is now associated with the **if(x)** because it is no longer part of the **if(y)** block. Because of the scope rules, the **else** now has no knowledge of the **if(y)** statement because they are no longer in the same block of code.

You can use a nested **if** to further improve the magic number program by providing the player with feedback about how close each guess is.

```c
#include <stdio.h>

/* Magic number program - improvement 2. */
int main(void)
{
  int magic = 123;   /* magic number */
  int guess;

  printf("Enter your guess: ");
  scanf("%d", &guess);

  if(guess == magic) {
    printf("** Right ** ");
    printf("%d is the magic number", magic);
  }
  else {
    printf(".. Wrong .. ");
    if(guess > magic) printf("Too high");
    else printf("Too low");
  }

  return 0;
}
```

The if-else-if Ladder

A common programming construct is the *if-else-if ladder,* sometimes called the *if-else-if staircase* because of its appearance. Its general form is

if *(expression)*
   statement;
else if *(expression)*
   statement;
else if *(expression)*
   statement;

.
.
.

else
statement;

The conditions are evaluated from the top downward. As soon as a true condition is found, the statement associated with it is executed and the rest of the ladder is bypassed. If none of the conditions are true, the final **else** is executed. The final **else** often acts as a default condition; that is, if all other conditional tests fail, the last **else** statement is performed. If the final **else** is not present, then no action takes place if all other conditions are false.

Using an if-else-if ladder, the magic number program becomes

```
#include <stdio.h>

/* Magic number program - improvement 3. */
int main(void)
{
  int magic = 123;  /* magic number */
  int guess;

  printf("Enter your guess: ");
  scanf("%d", &guess);

  if(guess == magic) {
    printf("** Right ** ");
    printf("%d is the magic number", magic);
  }
  else if(guess > magic)
    printf(".. Wrong .. Too High");
  else printf(".. Wrong .. Too low");

  return 0;
}
```

The ? Alternative

You can use the ? operator to replace **if-else** statements of the general form:

if(*condition*) *expression;*
else *expression;*

The key restriction is that the target of both the **if** and the **else** must be a single expression—not another statement.

The **?** is called a *ternary operator* because it requires three operands. It takes the general form

Exp1 ? Exp2 : Exp3

where *Exp1*, *Exp2*, and *Exp3* are expressions. Notice the use and placement of the colon.

The value of a **?** expression is determined as follows. *Exp1* is evaluated. If it is true, *Exp2* is evaluated and becomes the value of the entire **?** expression. If *Exp1* is false, then *Exp3* is evaluated and its value becomes the value of the expression. For example, consider

```
x = 10;
y = x>9 ? 100 : 200;
```

In this example, **y** is assigned the value 100. If **x** had been less than or equal to 9, **y** would have received the value 200. The same code written using the **if-else** statement would be

```
x = 10;
if(x>9) y = 100;
else y = 200;
```

The use of the **?** operator to replace **if-else** statements is not restricted to assignments only. Remember, all functions (except those declared as **void**) return a value. Thus, you can use one or more function calls in a **?** expression. When the function's name is encountered, the function is executed so that its return value can be determined. Therefore, you can execute one or more function calls using the **?** operator by placing the calls in the expressions that form the **?**'s operands. Here is an example:

```
#include <stdio.h>

int f1(int n), f2(void);

int main(void)
{
  int t;

  printf("Enter a number: ");
  scanf("%d", &t);
  /* print proper message */
```

```
    t ? f1(t) + f2() : printf("zero entered.");

    return 0;
}

int f1(int n)
{
  printf("%d ",n);
  return 0;
}

int f2(void)
{
  printf("entered ");
  return 0;
}
```

The program first prompts the user for a value. Entering 0 causes the **printf( )** function to be called, which displays the message **zero entered**. If you enter any other number, both **f1( )** and **f2( )** execute. Note that the value of the **?** expression is discarded in this example. You don't need to assign it to anything. Even though neither **f1( )** nor **f2( )** returns a meaningful value, they cannot be defined as returning **void** because doing so prevents their use in an expression. Therefore, the functions simply return zero.

Using the **?** operator, you can rewrite the magic number program again as shown here:

```
#include <stdio.h>

/* Magic number program - improvement 4. */
int main(void)
{
  int magic = 123;   /* magic number */
  int guess;

  printf("Enter your guess: ");
  scanf("%d", &guess);
  if(guess == magic) {
    printf("** Right ** ");
    printf("%d is the magic number", magic);
  }
  else
    guess > magic ? printf("High") : printf("Low");
```

```
    return 0;
}
```

Here, the **?** operator displays the proper message given the outcome of the test **guess > magic**.

switch

Although the if-else-if ladder can perform multiway tests, it is hardly elegant. The code can be difficult and confusing to follow. For these reasons, C/C++ has a built-in multiple-branch selection statement, called **switch**, which successively tests the value of an expression against a list of integer or character constants. When a match is found, the statements associated with that constant are executed. The general form of the **switch** statement is

```
switch(expression) {
    case constant1:
        statement sequence
        break;
    case constant2:
        statement sequence
        break;
    case constant3:
        statement sequence
        break;
        .
        .
        .
    default:
        statement sequence
}
```

The **default** statement is executed if no matches are found. The **default** is optional, and if it is not present, no action takes place if all matches fail. When a match is found, the statement sequence associated with that **case** is executed until the **break** statement or the end of the **switch** statement is reached.

There are three important things to know about the **switch** statement:

1. The **switch** differs from the **if** in that **switch** can only test for equality, whereas **if** can evaluate any type of relational or logical expression.

2. No two **case** constants in the same **switch** can have identical values. Of course, a **switch** statement enclosed by an outer **switch** may have **case** constants of the same value.

3. If character constants are used in the **switch** statement, they are automatically converted to integer (as specified by the type conversion rules).

The **switch** statement is often used to process keyboard commands, such as menu selection. As shown here, the function **menu( )** displays a menu for a spelling-checker program and calls the proper procedures:

```
void menu(void)
{
  char ch;

  printf("1. Check Spelling\n");
  printf("2. Correct Spelling Errors\n");
  printf("3. Display Spelling Errors\n");
  printf("Strike Any Other Key to Skip\n");
  printf("      Enter your choice: ");

  ch = getche(); /* read the selection from the keyboard */

  switch(ch) {
    case '1':
      check_spelling();
      break;
    case '2':
      correct_errors();
      break;
    case '3':
      display_errors();
      break;
    default :
      printf("No option selected");
  }
}
```

Technically, the **break** statements inside the **switch** statement are optional. They terminate the statement sequence associated with each constant. If the **break** statement is omitted, execution continues on into the next **case**'s statements until either a **break** or the end of the **switch** is reached. You can think of the **cases** as labels. Execution starts at the label that matches and continues until a **break** statement is found, or the **switch** ends. For example, the following function uses the "drop through" nature of the **cases** to simplify the code for a device-driver input handler:

```
void inp_handler(void)
{
  int ch, flag;
```

```
ch = read_device(); /* read some sort of device */
flag = -1;

switch(ch) {
  case 1:  /* these cases have common statement */
  case 2:  /* sequences */
  case 3:
    flag = 0;
    break;
  case 4:
    flag = 1;
  case 5:
    error(flag);
    break;
  default:
    process(ch);
  }
}
```

This example illustrates two aspects of **switch**. First, you can have **case** statements that have no statement sequence associated with them. When this occurs, execution simply drops through to the next **case**. In this example, the first three **cases** all execute the same statements, which are

```
flag = 0;
break;
```

Second, execution of one statement sequence continues into the next **case** if no **break** statement is present. If **ch** matches 4, **flag** is set to 1 and, because there is no **break** statement at the end of the **case**, execution continues and the call to **error(flag)** is executed. In this case, **flag** has the value 1. If **ch** had matched 5, **error(flag)** would have been called with a **flag** value of –1 (rather than 1). The fact that **cases** can run together when no **break** is present prevents the unnecessary duplication of statements, resulting in more efficient code.

Nested switch Statements

You can have a **switch** as part of the statement sequence of an outer **switch**. Even if the **case** constants of the inner and outer **switch** contain common values, no conflicts arise. For example, the following code fragment is perfectly acceptable:

```
switch(x) {
  case 1:
```

```
switch(y) {
  case 0: printf("Divide by zero error.");
          break;
  case 1: process(x,y);
          break;
}
  break;
case 2:
  .
  .
  .
```

Iteration Statements (Loops)

Iteration statements (also called loops) allow a set of instructions to be repeatedly executed until a certain condition is reached. This condition may be predetermined (as in the **for** loop), or open-ended (as in the **while** and **do-while** loops).

The for Loop

The general design of the **for** loop is reflected in some form or another in all procedural programming languages. However, in C/C++, it provides unexpected flexibility and power.

The general form of the **for** statement is

for(*initialization*; *condition*; *increment*) *statement*;

The **for** loop allows many variants, but there are three main parts:

1. The *initialization* is usually an assignment statement that sets the loop control variable.

2. The *condition* is a relational expression that determines when the loop exits.

3. The *increment* defines how the loop control variable changes each time the loop is repeated.

These three major sections must be separated by semicolons. The **for** loop continues to execute as long as the condition is true. Once the condition becomes false, program execution resumes on the statement following the **for**.

In the following program, a **for** loop is used to display the numbers 1 through 100 on the screen:

```
#include <stdio.h>
```

```
int main(void)
{
  int x;

  for(x=1; x <= 100; x++) printf("%d ", x);

  return 0;
}
```

In the loop, **x** is initially set to 1 and then compared to 100. Since **x** is less than 100, **printf( )** is called and the loop iterates. This causes **x** to be increased by 1 and again tested to see if it is still less than or equal to 100. This process repeats until **x** is greater than 100, at which point the loop terminates. In this example, **x** is the *loop control variable*, which is changed and checked each time the loop repeats.

Here is an example of a **for** loop that iterates a block of statements:

```
for(x=100; x != 65; x -= 5) {
  z = x*x;
  printf("The square of %d, %d", x, z);
}
```

Both the squaring of **x** and the call to **printf( )** are executed until **x** equals 65. Note that the loop is negative running: **x** was initialized to 100, and 5 is subtracted from it each time the loop repeats.

An important point about **for** loops is that the conditional test is always performed at the top of the loop. This means that the code inside the loop may not be executed at all if the condition is false to begin with. For example:

```
x = 10;
for(y=10; y != x; ++y) printf("%d", y);
printf("%d", y); /* this is the only printf()
                    statement that will execute */
```

This loop never executes because **x** and **y** are equal when the loop is entered. Because this causes the conditional expression to evaluate to false, neither the body of the loop nor the increment portion of the loop executes. Thus, **y** still has the value 10, and the only output produced by the fragment is the number 10 printed once on the screen.

for Loop Variations

The previous discussion described the most common form of the **for** loop. However, several variations of the **for** are allowed that increase its power, flexibility, and applicability to certain programming situations.

One of the most common variations uses the comma operator to allow two or more variables to control the loop. (Remember, the comma operator strings together a number of expressions in a "do this and this" fashion. See Chapter 2.) For example, the variables **x** and **y** control the following loop, and both are initialized inside the **for** statement.

```
for(x=0, y=0; x+y < 10; ++x) {
  scanf("%d", &y);
    .
    .
    .
}
```

Commas separate the two initialization statements. Each time the loop repeats, **x** is incremented and **y**'s value is set by keyboard input. Both **x** and **y** must be at the correct value for the loop to terminate. Even though **y**'s value is set by keyboard input, **y** must be initialized to 0 so that its value is defined before the first evaluation of the conditional expression. (If **y**'s value is not set, it could, by chance, contain the value 10, making the conditional test false and preventing the loop from executing.)

Another example of using multiple loop-control variables is found in the **reverse( )** function shown here. **reverse( )** copies the contents of the first string into the second string, in reverse order. For example, if "hello" is stored at **s**, then after the call **r** will point to "olleh."

```
/* Copy s into r backwards. */
void reverse(char *s, char *r)
{
  int i, j;

  for(i=strlen(s)-1, j=0; i > =0; j++, i--) r[i] = s[j];
  r[j] = '\0'; /* append null terminator */
}
```

The conditional expression does not have to involve testing the loop control variable against some target value. In fact, the condition may be any relational or logical statement. This means that you can test for several possible terminating conditions. For example, you could use the following function to log a user onto a remote system. The user has three tries to enter the password. The loop terminates when the three tries are used up, or when the user enters the correct password.

```
void sign_on(void)
{
  char str[20];
  int x;
```

```
  for(x=0; x<3 && strcmp(str,"password"); ++x) {
    printf("enter password please:");
    gets(str);
  }
  if(x==3) hang_up();
}
```

This loop uses **strcmp( )**, the standard library function that compares two strings and returns 0 if they match.

Remember, each of the three sections of the **for** loop may consist of any valid expression. The expressions need not actually have anything to do with what the sections are generally used for. With this in mind, consider the following example:

```
#include <stdio.h>

int readnum(void), prompt(void);
int sqrnum(int num);

int main(void)
{
  int t;

  for(prompt(); t=readnum(); prompt()) sqrnum(t);
  return 0;
}

int prompt(void)
{
  printf("Enter a number: ");
  return 0;
}

int readnum(void)
{
  int t;

  scanf("%d", &t);
  return t;
}

int sqrnum(int num)
```

```
{
  printf("%d\n", num*num);
  return 0;
}
```

Look closely at the **for** loop in **main( )**. Notice that each part of the **for** is composed of function calls that prompt the user and read a number entered from the keyboard. If the number entered is 0, the loop terminates because the conditional expression will be false. Otherwise, the number is squared. Thus, this **for** loop uses the initialization and increment portions in a nontraditional but completely valid manner.

Another interesting trait of the **for** loop is that pieces of the loop definition need not be there. In fact, there need not be an expression present for any of the sections— the expressions are optional. For example, this loop will run until the user enters **123**:

```
for(x=0; x != 123; ) scanf("%d", &x);
```

Notice that the increment portion of the **for** definition is blank. This means that each time the loop repeats, **x** is tested to see if it equals 123, but no further action takes place. If you type 123 at the keyboard, however, the loop condition becomes false and the loop terminates.

The initialization of the loop control variable can occur outside the **for** statement. This most frequently happens when the initial condition of the loop control variable must be computed by some complicated means, as in this example:

```
gets(s);  /* read a string into s */
if(*s) x = strlen(s); /* get the string's length */
else x = 10;

for( ; x < 10; ) {
  printf("%d", x);
  ++x;
}
```

The initialization section has been left blank, and **x** is initialized before the loop is entered.

The Infinite Loop

One of the most interesting uses of the **for** loop is to create an infinite loop. Since none of the three expressions that form the **for** loop are required, you can make an endless loop by leaving the conditional expression empty, as here:

```
for(;;) printf("This loop will run forever.\n");
```

When the conditional expression is absent, it is assumed to be true. You may have an initialization and increment expression, but C programmers more commonly use the **for(;;)** construct to signify an infinite loop.

Actually, the **for(;;)** construct does not guarantee an infinite loop, because a **break** statement, encountered anywhere inside the body of a loop, causes immediate termination. (**break** is discussed later in this chapter.) Program control then resumes at the code following the loop, as shown here:

```
ch = '\0';

for( ; ; ) {
  ch = getchar();  /* get a character */
  if(ch == 'A') break;  /* exit the loop */
}

printf("you typed an A");
```

This loop will run until the user types an **A** at the keyboard.

for Loops with No Bodies

A statement may be empty. This means that the body of the **for** loop (or any other loop) may also be empty. You can use this fact to simplify the coding of certain algorithms and to create time delay loops.

Removing spaces from an input stream is a common programming task. For example, a database program may allow a query such as "show all balances less than 400." The database needs to have each word fed to it separately, without leading spaces. That is, the database input processor recognizes "show" but not " show" as a command. The following loop shows one way to accomplish this. It advances past leading spaces in the string pointed to by **str**:

```
for( ; *str == ' '; str++) ;
```

As you can see, this loop has no body—and no need for one either.

Time delay loops are sometimes useful. The following code shows how to create one by using **for**:

```
for(t=0; t < SOME_VALUE; t++) ;
```

The while Loop

The second iteration statement in C/C++ is the **while** loop. Its general form is

while(*condition*) *statement* ;

where *statement* is either an empty statement, a single statement, or a block of statements. The *condition* may be any expression, and true is any nonzero value. The loop iterates while the condition is true. When the condition becomes false, program control passes to the line of code immediately following the loop.

The following example shows a keyboard input routine that loops until **A** is pressed:

```
char wait_for_char(void)
{
  char ch;

  ch = '\0';  /* initialize ch */
  while(ch != 'A')  ch = getchar();
  return ch;
}
```

First, **ch** is initialized to null. The **while** loop then checks to see if **ch** is not equal to **A**. Because **ch** was initialized to null, the test is true and the loop begins. Each time you press a key, the condition is tested again. Once you enter an **A**, the condition becomes false because **ch** equals **A**, and the loop terminates.

Like **for** loops, **while** loops check the test condition at the top of the loop, which means that the body of the loop will not execute at all if the condition is false to begin with. This feature may eliminate the need to perform a separate conditional test before the loop. The **pad( )** function provides a good illustration of this. It adds spaces to the end of a string to fill the string to a predefined length. If the string is already at the desired length, no spaces are added.

```
/* Add spaces to the end of a string. */
void pad(char *s, int length)
{
  int l;
  l = strlen(s);  /* find out how long it is */

  while(l < length) {
    s[l] = ' ';    /* insert a space */
```

```
    l++;
  }

  s[l] = '\0';  /* strings need to be
                   terminated in a null */
}
```

The two arguments of **pad( )** are **s**, a pointer to the string to lengthen, and **length**, the number of characters that **s** should have. If the length of string **s** is already equal to or greater than **length**, the code inside the **while** loop does not execute. If **s** is shorter than **length**, **pad( )** adds the required number of spaces. The **strlen( )** function, part of the standard library, returns the length of the string.

In cases in which any one of several separate conditions can terminate a **while** loop, often a single loop-control variable forms the conditional expression. In this example

```
void func1(void)
{
  int working;

  working = 1;    /* i.e., true */

  while(working) {
    working = process1();
    if(working)
      working = process2();
    if(working)
      working = process3();
  }
}
```

any of the three routines may return false and cause the loop to exit.

There need not be any statements in the body of the **while** loop. For example,

```
while((ch=getchar()) != 'A') ;
```

will simply loop until the user types **A**. If you feel uncomfortable putting the assignment inside the **while** conditional expression, remember that the equal sign is just an operator that evaluates to the value of the right-hand operand.

do-while

Unlike **for** and **while** loops, which test the loop condition at the top of the loop, the **do-while** loop checks its condition at the bottom of the loop. This means that a **do-while** loop always executes at least once. The general form of the **do-while** loop is

do {
    statement sequence
} while(*condition*);

Although the curly braces are not necessary when only one statement is present, they are usually used to improve readability and avoid confusion (to you, not the compiler) with the **while**.

This **do-while** loop will read numbers from the keyboard until it finds a number less than or equal to 100:

```
do {
   scanf("%d", &num);
} while(num > 100);
```

Perhaps the most common use of the **do-while** is in a menu selection function. When the user enters a valid response, it is returned as the value of the function. Invalid responses cause a reprompt. The following code shows an improved version of the spelling-checker menu shown earlier in this chapter:

```
void menu(void)
{
   char ch;

   printf("1. Check Spelling\n");
   printf("2. Correct Spelling Errors\n");
   printf("3. Display Spelling Errors\n");
   printf("      Enter your choice: ");

   do {
     ch = getche(); /* read the selection from the keyboard */
     switch(ch) {
       case '1':
         check_spelling();
         break;
       case '2':
         correct_errors();
```

```
        break;
      case '3':
        display_errors();
        break;
    }
  } while(ch!='1' && ch!='2' && ch!='3');
}
```

In the case of a menu function, you always want it to execute at least once. After the options have been displayed, the program will loop until a valid option is selected.

Jump Statements

C/C++ has four statements that perform an unconditional branch: **break**, **return**, **goto**, and **continue**. Of these, you can use **return** and **goto** anywhere inside a function. You can use the **break** and **continue** statements in conjunction with any of the loop statements. As discussed earlier in this chapter, you can also use **break** with **switch**. The **return** statement is discussed in Chapter 4, when functions are described. The other **jump** statements are discussed here.

break

The **break** statement has two uses. You can use it to terminate a **case** in the **switch** statement (covered in the section on the **switch**, earlier in this chapter). You can also use it to force immediate termination of a loop, bypassing the normal loop conditional test. This use is examined here.

When the **break** statement is encountered inside a loop, the loop is immediately terminated, and program control resumes at the next statement following the loop. For example,

```
#include <stdio.h>

int main(void)
{
  int t;

  for(t=0; t<100; t++) {
    printf("%d ", t);
    if(t == 10) break;
  }
  return 0;
}
```

prints the numbers 0 through 10 on the screen. Then the loop terminates because **break** causes immediate exit from the loop, overriding the conditional test **t < 100**.

Programmers often use the **break** statement in loops in which a special condition can cause immediate termination. For example, here a keypress can stop the execution of the **look_up( )** routine:

```
int look_up(char *name)
{
  char tname[40];
  int loc;

  loc = -1;
  do {
    loc = read_next_name(tname);
    if(kbhit()) break;
  } while(!strcmp(tname, name));
  return loc;
}
```

You might use a function like this to find a name in a database file. If the search is taking a very long time and you are tired of waiting, you could strike a key and return from the function early. The **kbhit( )** function returns 0 if no key has been hit, and non-0 otherwise.

A **break** causes an exit from only the innermost loop. For example,

```
for(t=0; t<100; ++t) {
  count = 1;
  for(;;) {
    printf("%d ", count);
    count++;
    if(count == 10) break;
  }
}
```

prints the numbers 1 through 9 on the screen 100 times. Each time the program encounters **break**, control is passed back to the outer **for** loop.

A **break** used in a **switch** statement will affect only that **switch**. It does not affect any loop the **switch** happens to be in.

THE FOUNDATION OF C++

exit( )

Although **exit( )** is not a program control statement, a short digression that discusses it is in order at this time. Just as you can break out of a loop, you can break out of a program by using the standard library function **exit( )**. This function causes immediate termination of the entire program, forcing a return to the operating system. In effect, the **exit( )** function acts as if it were breaking out of the entire program. The general form of the **exit( )** function is

```
void exit(int status);
```

It uses the **<stdlib.h>** header. The value of *status* is returned to the calling process, which is usually the operating system. Zero is commonly used as a return code to indicate normal program termination. Other values indicate some sort of error. You can also use the predefined macros **EXIT_SUCCESS** and **EXIT_FAILURE** as values for *status.*

Programmers frequently use **exit( )** when a mandatory condition for program execution is not satisfied. For example, imagine a virtual-reality computer game that requires a special graphics adapter. The **main( )** function of this game might look like this,

```
#include <stdlib.h>

int main(void)
{
  if(!special_adapter()) exit(1);
  play();
  return 0;
}
```

where **special_adapter( )** is some function that returns true if the needed special adapter is present. If the adapter is not in the system, **special_adapter( )** returns false and the program terminates.

As another example, this version of **menu( )** uses **exit( )** to quit the program and return to the operating system:

```
void menu(void)
{
  char ch;
```

```
  printf("1. Check Spelling\n");
  printf("2. Correct Spelling Errors\n");
  printf("3. Display Spelling Errors\n");
  printf("4. Quit\n");
  printf("      Enter your choice: ");

  do {
    ch = getche(); /* read the selection from the keyboard */

    switch(ch) {
      case '1':
        check_spelling();
        break;
      case '2':
        correct_errors();
        break;
      case '3':
        display_errors();
        break;
      case '4':
        exit(0);   /* return to OS */
    }
  } while(ch!='1' && ch!='2' && ch!='3');
}
```

continue

The **continue** statement works somewhat like the **break** statement. Instead of forcing termination, however, **continue** forces the next iteration of the loop to take place, skipping any code in between. For example, the following routine displays only positive numbers:

```
do {
  scanf("%d", &x);
  if(x < 0) continue;
  printf("%d ", x);
} while(x != 100);
```

In **while** and **do-while** loops, a **continue** statement forces control to go directly to the conditional test and then continue the looping process. In the case of the **for**, first the increment part of the loop is performed, then the conditional test is executed, and finally the loop continues. The previous example can be changed to allow only 100 numbers to be printed, as shown here:

```
for(t=0; t<100; ++t) {
  scanf("%d", &x);
  if(x < 0) continue;
  printf("%d ", x);
}
```

The following example shows how you can use **continue** to expedite the exit from a loop by forcing the conditional test to be performed sooner:

```
void code(void)
{
  char done, ch;

  done = 0;
  while(!done) {
    ch = getchar();
    if(ch=='.') {
      done = 1;
      continue;
    }
    putchar(ch+1);  /* shift the alphabet one position */
  }
}
```

This function codes a message by shifting all characters you type one letter higher. For example, 'a' would become 'b'. The function will terminate when you type a period. After a period has been input, no further output will occur, because the conditional test, brought into effect by **continue**, will find **done** to be true and will cause the loop to exit.

Labels and goto

Since C/C++ has a rich set of control structures and allows additional control using **break** and **continue**, there is little need for **goto**. Most programmers' chief concern about the **goto** is its tendency to render programs unreadable. Although the **goto** statement fell out of favor some years ago, it occasionally has its uses. This book will not judge its validity as a form of program control. While there are no programming situations that require **goto**, it is a convenience, which, if used wisely, can be a benefit in a narrow set of programming situations, such as jumping out of a set of deeply nested loops. The **goto** is not used in this book outside of this section.

The **goto** statement requires a label for operation. (A *label* is a valid identifier followed by a colon.) Furthermore, the label must be in the same function as the **goto** that uses it—you cannot jump between functions. For example, a loop from 1 to 100 could be written using a **goto** and a label as shown here:

```
x = 1;

loop1:
  x++;
  if(x <= 100) goto loop1;
```

One good use for the **goto** is to exit from several layers of nesting. For example:

```
for(...) {
  for(...) {
    while(...) {
      if(...) goto stop;
      .

      .

      .

    }
  }
}
stop:
  printf("error in program\n");
```

Eliminating the **goto** would force a number of additional tests to be performed. A simple **break** statement would not work here because it would only exit from the innermost loop.

Expression Statements

Chapter 2 covers expressions thoroughly. However, a few special points are mentioned here. Remember, an expression statement is simply a valid expression followed by a semicolon, as in

```
func();   /* a function call */
a = b+c;  /* an assignment statement */
b+f();    /* a valid, but strange statement */
;         /* an empty statement */
```

The first expression statement executes a function call. The second is an assignment. The third expression, though strange, is still evaluated by the compiler because the function **f( )** may perform some necessary task. The final example shows that a statement can be empty (sometimes called a *null statement*).

Block Statements

Block statements are groups of related statements that are treated as a unit. The statements that make up a block are logically bound together. Block statements are also called *compound statements*. A block begins with a { and terminates by its matching }. Block statements are most commonly used to create a multistatement target for some other statement, such as **if**.

Borland
C++
Builder

Chapter 4

Functions

Functions are the building blocks of C and C++ and the place where all program activity occurs. This chapter examines their features, including function arguments, return values, prototypes, and recursion.

The General Form of a Function

The general form of a function is

```
ret-type function_name(parameter list)
{
  body of the function
}
```

The *ret-type* specifies the type of data that the function returns. A function can return any type of data except an array. The *parameter list* is a comma-separated list of variable names and their associated types. The parameters receive the values of the arguments when the function is called. A function can be without parameters, in which case the parameter list is empty. An empty parameter list can be explicitly specified by placing the keyword **void** inside the parentheses.

The return Statement

The **return** statement has two important uses. First, it causes an immediate exit from the function. That is, it causes program execution to return to the calling code. Second, it can be used to return a value. The following section examines how the **return** statement is applied.

Returning from a Function

A function terminates execution and returns to the caller in one of two ways. The first is when the last statement in the function has executed and, conceptually, the function's ending curly brace (}) is encountered. (Of course, the curly brace isn't actually present in the object code, but you can think of it in this way.) For example, this function takes an address to a string as a parameter and displays the string backward:

```
void pr_reverse(char *s)
{
  register int t;

  for(t=strlen(s)-1; t >= 0; t--) printf("%c", s[t]);
}
```

Once the string has been displayed, there is nothing left for **pr_reverse()** to do, so it returns to the place from which it was called.

Actually, not many functions use this default method of terminating their execution. Most functions rely on the **return** statement to stop execution either because a value must be returned or to make a function's code simpler and more efficient. A function may contain several **return** statements. For example, the **find_substr()** function, shown next, returns either the starting position of a substring within a string or –1 if no match is found. It uses two **return** statements to simplify the coding:

```
int find_substr(char *s1, char *s2)
{
  register int t;
  char *p, *p2;

  for(t=0; s1[t]; t++) {
    p = &s1[t];
    p2 = s2;
    while(*p2 && *p2==*p) {
      p++;
      p2++;
    }
    if(!*p2) return t; /* substring was found */
  }
  return -1; /* substring not found */
}
```

Returning Values

All functions, except those of type **void**, return a value. This value is specified by the **return** statement. In C89, if a non-**void** function executes a **return** statement that does not include a value, then a garbage value is returned. In C++ (and C99), a non-**void** function *must* use a **return** statement that returns a value. As long as a function is not declared as **void**, you can use it as an operand in an expression. Therefore, each of the following expressions is valid:

```
x = power(y);
if(max(x, y) > 100) printf("greater");
for(ch=getchar(); isdigit(ch); ) ... ;
```

As a general rule, a function call cannot be on the left side of an assignment. A statement such as

```
swap(x, y) = 100;    /* incorrect statement */
```

is wrong. C++ Builder will flag it as an error and will not compile a program that contains it.

If a function is declared as **void**, it cannot be used in any expression. For example, assume that **f( )** is declared as **void**. The following statements will not compile:

```
t = f();   /* no value to assign to t */

f()+f();   /* no value to add */
```

When you write programs, your functions will be of three types. The first type is simply computational. These functions are specifically designed to perform operations on their arguments and return a value based on that operation. A computational function is a "pure" function. Examples are the standard library functions **sqrt( )** and **sin( )**, which compute the square root and sine of their arguments.

The second type of function manipulates information and returns a value that simply indicates the success or failure of that manipulation. An example is the library function **fwrite( )**, which writes information to a disk file. If the write operation is successful, **fwrite( )** returns the number of items successfully written. If an error occurs, **fwrite( )** returns a number that is not equal to the number of items it was requested to write.

The last type of function has no explicit return value. In essence, the function is strictly procedural and produces no value. An example is **srand( )**, which initializes the random number generator function **rand( )**. Sometimes, functions that really don't produce an interesting result often return something anyway. For example, **printf( )** returns the number of characters written. Yet, it is unusual to find a program that actually checks this. In other words, although all functions, except those of type **void**, return values, you don't have to use the return value for anything. A common question concerning function return values is, "Don't I have to assign this value to some variable since a value is being returned?" The answer is no. If there is no assignment specified, the return value is simply discarded. Consider the following program, which uses **mul( )**:

```
#include <stdio.h>

int mul(int a, int b);
```

```
int main(void)
{
  int x, y, z;

  x = 10;    y = 20;
  z = mul(x, y);              /* 1 */
  printf("%d", mul(x, y));    /* 2 */
  mul(x, y);                  /* 3 */

  return 0;
}

int mul(int a, int b)
{
  return a*b;
}
```

In line 1, the return value of **mul( )** is assigned to **z**. In line 2, the return value is not actually assigned, but it is used by the **printf( )** function. Finally, in line 3, the return value is lost because it is neither assigned to another variable nor used as part of an expression.

What Does main() Return?

The **main( )** function returns an integer to the calling process, which is generally the operating system. Returning a value from **main( )** is the equivalent of calling **exit( )** with the same value. A return value of 0 indicates that the program terminated normally. All other values indicate that some error occurred with the exiting program.

Understanding the Scope of a Function

The scope rules of a language are the rules that govern whether a piece of code knows about or has access to another piece of code or data.

Each function is a discrete block of code. Thus, a function defines a block scope. This means that a function's code is private to that function and cannot be accessed by any statement in any other function except through a call to that function. (For instance, you cannot use **goto** to jump into the middle of another function.) The code that makes up the body of a function is hidden from the rest of the program, and unless it uses global variables, it can neither affect nor be affected by other parts of the program. Stated another way, the code and data defined within one function cannot interact with the code and data defined in another function because the two functions have different scopes.

Variables that are defined within a function are local variables. A local variable comes into existence when the function is entered and is destroyed upon exit. Thus, a local variable cannot hold its value between function calls. The only exception to this rule is when the variable is declared with the **static** storage class specifier. This causes the compiler to treat it like a global variable for storage purposes, but limits its scope to the function. (See Chapter 2 for additional information on global and local variables.)

All functions have file scope. Thus, you cannot define a function within a function. This is why C and C++ are not technically block-structured languages.

Function Arguments

If a function is to accept arguments, it must declare the parameters that will receive the values of the arguments. As shown in the following function, the parameter declarations occur after the function name:

```
/* return 1 if c is part of string s; 0 otherwise */
int is_in(char *s, char c)
{
  while(*s)
    if(*s==c) return 1;
    else s++;

  return 0;
}
```

The function **is_in( )** has two parameters: **s** and **c**. This function returns 1 if the character **c** is part of the string pointed to by **s**; otherwise, it returns 0.

As with local variables, you can make assignments to a function's formal parameters or use them in any allowable expression. Even though parameters perform the special task of receiving the value of the arguments passed to the function, they behave like any other local variable.

Call by Value, Call by Reference

In a computer language, there are two ways that arguments can be passed to a subroutine. The first is *call by value*. This method copies the *value* of an argument into the formal parameter of the subroutine. In this case, changes made to the parameter have no effect on the argument. *Call by reference* is the second way of passing arguments to a subroutine. In this method, the *address* of an argument is copied into the parameter. Inside the subroutine, the address is used to access the actual argument used in the call. This means that changes made to the parameter affect the argument.

By default, C/C++ uses call by value to pass arguments. In general, this means that code within a function cannot alter the arguments used to call the function. Consider the following program:

```
#include <stdio.h>

int sqr(int x);

int main(void)
{
  int t=10;

  printf("%d %d", sqr(t), t);
  return 0;
}

int sqr(int x)
{
  x = x*x;
  return x;
}
```

In this example, the value of the argument to **sqr( )**, 10, is copied into the parameter **x**. When the assignment **x = x * x** takes place, only the local variable **x** is modified. The variable **t**, used to call **sqr( )**, still has the value 10. Therefore, the output is **100 10**.

Remember that it is a copy of the value of the argument that is passed into a function. What occurs inside the function has no effect on the variable used in the call.

Creating a Call by Reference

Even though C/C++ uses call by value for passing parameters, you can create a call by reference by passing a pointer to an argument instead of passing the argument itself. Since the address of the argument is passed to the function, code within the function can change the value of the argument outside the function.

Pointers are passed to functions just like any other argument. Of course, you need to declare the parameters as pointer types. For example, the function **swap( )**, which exchanges the values of the two integer variables pointed to by its arguments, shows how:

```
void swap(int *x, int *y)
{
  int temp;
```

```
    temp = *x;   /* save the value at address x */
    *x = *y;     /* put y into x */
    *y = temp;   /* put x into y */
}
```

The **swap( )** function is able to exchange the values of the two variables pointed to by **x** and **y** because their addresses (not their values) are passed. Within the function, the contents of the variables are accessed using standard pointer operations, and their values are swapped.

Remember that **swap( )** (or any other function that uses pointer parameters) must be called with the *addresses of the arguments*. The following program shows the correct way to call **swap( )**:

```
#include <stdio.h>

void swap(int *x, int *y);

int main(void)
{
  int x, y;

  x = 10;
  y = 20;
  printf("x and y before swapping: %d %d\n", x, y);
  swap(&x, &y);
  printf("x and y after swapping: %d %d\n", x, y);

  return 0;
}
```

The output from the program is shown here.

```
x and y before swapping: 10 20
x and y after swapping: 20 10
```

In this example, the variable **x** is assigned the value 10, and **y** is assigned the value 20. Then **swap( )** is called with the addresses of **x** and **y**. (The unary operator **&** is used to produce the addresses of the variables.) Therefore, the addresses of **x** and **y**, not their values, are passed into the function **swap( )**.

THE FOUNDATION
OF C++

*C++ allows you to fully automate a call by reference through the use of reference
parameters. Reference parameters are not supported by C.*

Calling Functions with Arrays

Arrays are covered in detail in Chapter 5. However, this section discusses passing arrays
as arguments to functions because it is an exception to the normal call-by-value
parameter passing convention.

When an array is used as a function argument, its address is passed to a function.
This is, when you call a function with an array name, a pointer to the first element in
the array is passed to the function. (Remember that an array name without any index is
a pointer to the first element in the array.) The parameter declaration must be of a
compatible pointer type. There are three ways to declare a parameter that is to
receive an array pointer. First, it can be declared as an array, as shown here:

```
#include <stdio.h>

void display(int num[10]);

int main(void)   /* print some numbers */
{
  int t[10], i;

  for(i=0; i<10; ++i) t[i]=i;
  display(t);
  return 0;
}

void display(int num[10])
{
  int i;

  for(i=0; i<10; i++) printf("%d ", num[i]);
}
```

Even though the parameter **num** is declared to be an integer array of 10 elements,
the compiler automatically converts it to an integer pointer because no parameter can
actually receive an entire array. Only a pointer to an array is passed, so a pointer
parameter must be there to receive it.

A second way to declare an array parameter is an unsized array, as shown here:

```
void display(int num[])
{
```

```
   int i;

   for(i=0; i<10; i++) printf("%d ", num[i]);
}
```

Here, **num** is an integer array of unknown size. Since C/C++ provides no array boundary checks, the actual size of the array is irrelevant to the parameter (but not to the program). This method of declaration also defines **num** as an integer pointer.

The final way that **num** can be declared—and the most common form in professionally written programs—is as a pointer, as shown here:

```
void display(int *num)
{
  int i;

  for(i=0; i<10; i++) printf("%d ", num[i]);
}
```

Declaring **num** as a pointer works because any pointer can be indexed using [ ] as if it were an array. (Actually, arrays and pointers are very closely linked.)

All three methods of declaring an array parameter yield the same result: a pointer.

On the other hand, an array *element* used as an argument is treated like any other variable. For example, the program just examined could have been written without passing the entire array, as shown here:

```
#include <stdio.h>

void display(int num);

int main(void) /* print some numbers */
{
  int t[10], i;

  for(i=0; i<10; ++i) t[i] = i;
  for(i=0; i<10; i++) display(t[i]);

  return 0;
}
```

```
void display(int num)
{
  printf("%d ", num);
}
```

The parameter to **display( )** is of type **int**. It is not relevant that **display( )** is called by using an array element, because only that one value of the array is passed.

It is important to understand that when an array is used as a function argument, its address is passed to a function. This is an exception to the call-by-value parameter passing convention. In this case, the code inside the function is operating on, and potentially altering, the actual contents of the array used to call the function. For example, consider the function **print_upper( )**, which prints its string argument in uppercase:

```
#include <stdio.h>
#include <ctype.h>

void print_upper(char *str);

int main(void)  /* print string as uppercase */
{
  char s[80];

  printf("Enter a string: ");
  gets(s);
  print_upper(s);
  printf("\ns is now uppercase: %s", s);

  return 0;
}

void print_upper(char *str)
{
  register int t;

  for(t=0; str[t]; ++t) {
    str[t] = toupper(str[t]);
    putchar(str[t]);
  }
}
```

After the call to **print_upper( )**, the contents of array **s** in **main( )** are changed to uppercase. If this is not what you want, you could write the program like this:

```
#include <stdio.h>
#include <ctype.h>

void print_upper(char *str);

int main(void)   /* print string as uppercase */
{
  char s[80];

  printf("Enter a string: ");
  gets(s);
  print_upper(s);
  printf("\ns is unchanged: %s", s);

  return 0;
}

void print_upper(char *str)
{
  register int t;

  for(t=0; str[t]; ++t)
    putchar(toupper(str[t]));
}
```

In this case, the contents of array **s** remain unchanged because its values are not altered inside **print_upper( )**.

The standard library function **gets( )** is a classic example of passing arrays into functions. Although the **gets( )** in C++ Builder's library is more sophisticated, the following example will give you an idea of how it works. To avoid confusion with the standard function, this one is called **xgets( )**:

```
/* A simple version of the gets() library function. */

char *xgets(char *s)
{
  char ch, *p;
  int t;
```

```
    p = s;

    for(t=0; t<80; ++t) {
      ch = getchar();
      switch(ch) {
        case '\n':
          s[t] = '\0'; /* terminate the string */
          return p;
        case '\b':
          if(t>0) t--;
          break;
        default:
          s[t] = ch;

      }
    }
    s[79] = '\0';
    return p;
}
```

The **xgets( )** function must be called with a **char** * pointer. This, of course, can
be the name of a character array, which by definition is a **char** * pointer. Upon entry,
xgets( ) establishes a **for** loop from 0 to 79. This prevents larger strings from being
entered at the keyboard. If more than 80 characters are entered, the function returns.
(The real **gets( )** function does not have this restriction.) Because C/C++ has no built-in
bounds checking, you should make sure that any array used to call **xgets( )** can accept
at least 80 characters. As you type characters on the keyboard, they are placed in the
string. If you type a backspace, the counter **t** is reduced by 1, effectively removing the
previous character from the array. When you press ENTER, a null is placed at the end
of the string, signaling its termination. Because the array used to call **xgets( )** is
modified, upon return it contains the characters that you type.

argc and argv—Arguments to main( )

Sometimes it is useful to pass information into a program when you run it. Generally,
you pass information into the **main( )** function via command line arguments. A *command
line argument* is the information that follows the program's name on the command line
of the operating system. For example, when you compile programs using C++ Builder's
command line compiler, you type something like

    bcc32 *program_name*

where *program_name* is a command line argument that specifies the name of the program you want to compile.

C++ Builder supports three arguments to **main( )**. The first two are the traditional arguments: **argc** and **argv**. These are also the only arguments to **main( )** defined by standard C/C++. They allow you to pass command line arguments to your program.

The **argc** parameter holds the number of arguments on the command line and is an integer. It is always at least 1 because the name of the program qualifies as the first argument. The **argv** parameter is a pointer to an array of character pointers. Each element in this array points to a command line argument. All command line arguments are strings—any numbers will have to be converted by the program into the proper binary format, manually. Here is a simple example that uses a command line argument. It prints **Hello** and your name on the screen, if you specify your name as a command line argument:

```
#include <stdio.h>

int main(int argc, char *argv[])
{
  if(argc!=2) {
    printf("You forgot to type your name\n");
    return 1;
  }
  printf("Hello %s", argv[1]);

  return 0;
}
```

If you called this program **name** and your name were Jon, you would type **name Jon**. The output from the program would be **Hello Jon**. For example, if you were logged into drive A, you would see

```
A>name Jon
Hello Jon
A>
```

after running **name**.

For C++ Builder, each command line argument must be separated by a space or a tab. Commas, semicolons, and the like are not considered separators. For example,

```
run Spot run
```

is made up of three strings, while

```
Herb,Rick,Fred
```

is a single string because commas are not generally legal separators.

If you want to pass a string that contains spaces or tabs as a single argument, you must enclose that string within double quotes. For example, this is a single argument:

```
"this is a test"
```

You must declare **argv** properly. The most common method is

```
char *argv[];
```

The empty brackets indicate that the array is of undetermined length. You can now access the individual arguments by indexing **argv**. For example, **argv[0]** points to the first string, which is always the program's name; **argv[1]** points to the next string, and so on.

Another short example using command line arguments is the program called **countdown**, shown here. It counts down from a starting value (which is specified on the command line) and beeps when it reaches 0. Notice that the first argument containing the starting number is converted into an integer using the standard function **atoi( )**. If the string **display** is the second command line argument, the countdown will also be displayed on the screen.

```c
/* Countdown program. */

#include <stdio.h>
#include <stdlib.h>
#include <string.h>

int main(int argc, char *argv[])
{
  int disp, count;

  if(argc<2) {
    printf("You must enter the length of the count\n");
    printf("on the command line. Try again.\n");
    exit(1);
  }

  if(argc==3 && !strcmp(argv[2],"display")) disp = 1;
  else disp = 0;
```

```
    for(count=atoi(argv[1]); count; --count)
      if(disp) printf("%d\n", count);

    putchar('\a');   /* this will ring the bell */
    printf("Done");
    return 0;
}
```

Notice that if no command line arguments have been specified, an instructional
message is printed. A program with command line arguments often issues instructions
if the user attempts to run the program without entering the proper information.

To access an individual character in one of the command line arguments, add a
second index to **argv**. For example, the next program displays all the arguments with
which it was called, one character at a time:

```
#include <stdio.h>

int main(int argc, char *argv[])
{
  int t, i;

  for(t=0; t<argc; ++t) {
    i = 0;
    while(argv[t][i]) {
      printf("%c", argv[t][i]);
      ++i;
    }
    printf(" ");
  }

  return 0;
}
```

Remember, for **argv**, the first index accesses the string and the second index accesses
the individual characters of the string.

You generally use **argc** and **argv** to get initial commands, which are needed at
start-up, into your program. The command line arguments often specify a filename, an
option, or an alternate behavior, for example. Using command line arguments gives
your program a professional appearance and facilitates its use in batch files.

If you link the file WILDARGS.OBJ (provided with C++ Builder) with your
program, command line arguments like *.EXE automatically expand into any matching
filenames. (C++ Builder automatically processes the wildcard filename characters and
increases the value of **argc** appropriately.) For example, if you link the following

program with WILDARGS.OBJ, it shows you how many files match the filename
specified on the command line:

```
/* Link this program with WILDARGS.OBJ. */

#include <stdio.h>

int main(int argc, char *argv[])
{
  register int i;

  printf("%d files match specified name\n", argc-1);

  printf("They are: ");

  for(i=1; i<argc; i++)
    printf("%s ", argv[i]);

  return 0;
}
```

If you call this program **WA**, then executing it in the following manner tells you the
number of files that have the .EXE extension, and lists their names:

```
C>WA *.EXE
```

C++ Builder also allows a third command line argument, **env**. The **env** argument
lets your program access the environmental information associated with the operating
system. The **env** parameter must follow **argc** and **argv** and is declared like this:

```
char *env[]
```

As you can see, **env** is declared like **argv**. Like **argv**, it is a pointer to an array of
strings. Each string is an environmental string defined by the operating system. The
env parameter does not have a corresponding **argc**-like parameter that tells your
program how many environmental strings there are. Instead, the last environmental
string is null. The following program displays all the environmental strings currently
defined by the operating system:

```
/* This program prints all the environmental
   strings.
*/
```

```
#include <stdio.h>

int main(int argc, char *argv[], char *env[])
{
  int t;

  for(t=0; env[t]; t++)
    printf("%s\n", env[t]);

  return 0;
}
```

Even though **argc** and **argv** are not used in this program, they must be present in the parameter list. C/C++ does not actually know the names of the parameters. Instead, their usage is determined by the order in which the parameters are declared. In fact, you can call the parameters anything you like. Since **argc**, **argv**, and **env** are traditional names, it is best to use them so that anyone reading your program will instantly know that they are arguments to **main( )**.

It is common for a program to need to find the value of one specific environmental string. For example, knowing the value of the PATH string allows your program to utilize the search paths. The following program shows how to find the string that defines the default search paths. It uses the standard library function **strstr( )**, which has this prototype:

char *strstr(const char *str1, const char *str2);

The **strstr( )** function searches the string pointed to by *str1* for the first occurrence of the string pointed to by *str2*. If it is found, a pointer to the first occurrence is returned. If no match exists, then **strstr( )** returns null.

```
/* This program searches the environmental
   strings for the one that contains the
   current PATH.
*/
#include <stdio.h>
#include <string.h>

int main(int argc, char *argv[], char *env[])
{
  int t;

  for(t=0; env[t]; t++) {
```

THE FOUNDATION
OF C++

```
    if(strstr(env[t], "PATH"))
      printf("%s\n", env[t]);
  }

  return 0;
}
```

Function Prototypes

In well-written C code, and in all C++ code, functions must be declared before they are used. This is normally accomplished using a *function prototype*. Function prototypes were not part of the original C language, but they were added when C was standardized. While prototypes are not technically required by C, their use is strongly encouraged. Prototypes have always been *required* by C++. In this book, all examples include full function prototypes. Prototypes enable both C and C++ to provide stronger type checking. When you use prototypes, the compiler can find and report any illegal type conversions between the type of arguments used to call a function and the type definition of its parameters. The compiler will also catch differences between the number of arguments used to call a function and the number of parameters in the function.

The general form of a function prototype is

type func_name(type parm_name1, type parm_name2,. . ., type parm_nameN);

The use of parameter names is optional. However, they enable the compiler to identify any type mismatches by name when an error occurs, so it is a good idea to include them.

The following program illustrates the value of function prototypes. It produces an error message because it contains an attempt to call **sqr_it( )** with an integer argument instead of the integer pointer required:

```
/* This program uses a function prototype to
   enforce strong type checking. */

void sqr_it(int *i); /* prototype */

int main(void)
{
  int x;

  x = 10;
  sqr_it(x);  /* type mismatch */
```

```
    return 0;
}

void sqr_it(int *i)
{
  *i = *i * *i;
}
```

A function's definition can also serve as its prototype if the definition occurs prior to the function's first use in the program. For example, this is a valid program:

```
#include <stdio.h>

/* This definition will also serve
   as a prototype within this program. */
void f(int a, int b)
{
  printf("%d ", a % b);
}

int main(void)
{
  f(10,3);

  return 0;
}
```

In this example, since **f( )** is defined prior to its use in **main( )**, no separate prototype is required. While it is possible for a function's definition to serve as its prototype in small programs, it is seldom possible in large ones—especially when several files are used. The programs in this book include a separate prototype for each function because that is the way C/C++ code is normally written in practice.

The only function that does not require a prototype is **main( )**, since it is the first function called when your program begins.

Because of the need for compatibility with the original version of C, there is a small but important difference between how C and C++ handle the prototyping of a function that has no parameters. In C++, an empty parameter list is simply indicated in the prototype by the absence of any parameters. For example,

```
int f(); /* C++ prototype for a function with no parameters */
```

However, in C this prototype means something different. For historical reasons, an empty parameter list simply says that *no parameter information* is given. As far as the compiler is concerned, the function could have several parameters or no parameters. In C, when a function has no parameters, its prototype uses **void** inside the parameter list. For example, here is **f( )**'s prototype as it would appear in a C program:

```
int f(void);
```

This tells the compiler that the function has no parameters, and any call to that function that has parameters is an error. In C++, the use of **void** inside an empty parameter list is still allowed, but redundant.

 In C++, f( ) and f(void) are equivalent.

Function prototypes help you trap bugs before they occur. In addition, they help verify that your program is working correctly by not allowing functions to be called with mismatched arguments.

One last point: Since early versions of C did not support the full prototype syntax, prototypes are technically optional in C. This is necessary to support pre-prototype C code. If you are porting older C code to C++ you may need to add full function prototypes before it will compile. Remember: Although prototypes are optional in C, they are required by C++. This means that every function in a C++ program must be fully prototyped.

Standard Library Function Prototypes

Any standard library functions used by your program should be prototyped. To accomplish this, you must include the appropriate *header* for each library function. All standard headers are provided by C++ Builder. In C, library headers use the **.h** extension and are (usually) contained in files. A header contains two main elements: any definitions used by the library functions and the prototypes for the library functions. For example, **<stdio.h>** is included in almost all programs in this part of the book because it contains the prototype for **printf( )**. If you include the appropriate header for each library function used in a program, it is possible for the compiler to catch any accidental errors you may make when using it. (Also, when you write a C++ program, all functions must be prototyped.) All of the programs in this book include the appropriate headers. The headers for the functions provided by C++ Builder are discussed in Part Two, when the C++ Builder's function library is described.

Old-Style Versus Modern Parameter Declarations

Early versions of C used a different parameter declaration method than do modern versions of C. This old-style approach is sometimes called the *classic* form. The declaration approach used in this book is called the *modern* form. Although C++ Builder supports both forms for use in C code, new code should use only the modern form. Also, C++ supports only the modern form. However, since the old-style approach can still be found in older C programs, it is described here for the sake of completeness.

The old-style function parameter declaration consists of two parts: a parameter list, which goes inside the parentheses that follow the function name, and the actual parameter declarations, which go between the closing parenthesis and the function's opening curly brace. The general form of the old-style parameter definition is shown here:

```
type function_name(parm1, parm2,. . .parmN )
type parm1;
type parm2;
    .
    .
    .
type parmN;
{
function code
}
```

For example, this modern declaration:

```
char *f(char *str1, int count, int index)
{
  /* ... */
}
```

will look like this when declared in the old style:

```
char *f(str1, count, index)
char *str1;
int count, index;
{
  /* ... */
}
```

Notice that in the old style, more than one parameter can be listed after the type name.

Even though the old-style declaration form is outdated, C++ Builder can still correctly compile C programs that use this approach. Therefore, you need not worry if you want to compile a C program that uses the old approach. Remember, however, that C++ programs *must use* the modern form.

The "Implicit int" Rule

The original version of C included a feature that is sometimes described as the "implicit int" rule (also called the "default to **int**" rule). This rule states that in the absence of an explicit type specifier, the type **int** is assumed. This rule was included in the C89 standard but has been eliminated by C99. It is also not supported by C++. Since the implicit **int** rule is obsolete and not supported by C++, this book does not use it. However, since it is still employed by many older C programs, it is still supported by C++ Builder for C programs and a brief discussion is warranted.

The most common use of the implicit **int** rule was in the return type of functions. Years ago, many (probably, most) C programmers took advantage of the rule when creating functions that returned an **int** result. Thus, years ago a function such as

```
int f(void) {
  /* ... */
  return 0;
}
```

would often have been written like this:

```
f(void) { /* return type int by default */
  /* ... */
  return 0;
}
```

In the first instance, the return type of **int** is explicitly specified. In the second, it is assumed by default.

The implicit **int** rule does not apply only to function return values (although that was its most common use). For example, the following function uses the implicit **int** rule for the type of its parameters:

```
/* Here, the return type defaults to int, and so do
   the types of a and b. */
f(register a, register b) {
  register c; /* c defaults to int, too */
```

```
    c = a + b;

    printf("%d", c);

    return c;
}
```

Here, the return type of **f( )** defaults to **int**. So do the types of the parameters, **a** and **b**, and the local variable **c**.

Remember, the "implicit **int**" rule is not supported by C++. It is, however, supported by C++ Builder when compiling C code. Even for C code, its use is not recommended.

Declaring Variable Length Parameter Lists

You can specify a function that has a variable number of parameters. The most common example is **printf( )**. To tell the compiler that an unknown number of arguments will be passed to a function, you must end the declaration of its parameters using three periods. For example, this prototype specifies that **func( )** will have at least two integer parameters and an unknown number (including 0) of parameters after that:

```
    int func(int a, int b, ...);
```

This form of declaration is also used by a function's definition.

Any function that uses a variable number of parameters must have at least one actual parameter. For example, this is incorrect:

```
    int func(...); /* illegal */
```

Returning Pointers

Although functions that return pointers are handled just like any other type of function, it is helpful to review some key concepts and look at an example.

Pointers are *neither* integers, *nor* unsigned integers. They are the memory addresses of a certain type of data. One reason for this distinction is that pointer arithmetic is relative to the base type. For example, if an integer pointer is incremented, it will contain a value that is 4 greater than its previous value (assuming four-byte integers). In general, each time a pointer is incremented (or decremented), it points to the next (or previous) item of its type. Since the length of different data types may differ, the compiler must know what type of data the pointer is pointing to. For this reason, a function that returns a pointer must declare explicitly what type of pointer it is returning. (The subject of pointer arithmetic is covered in detail in Chapter 6.)

For example, the following is a function that returns a pointer to the first occurrence of the character **c** in string **s**. If no match is found, a pointer to the null terminator is returned:

```
char *match(char c, char *s)
{
  while(c != *s && *s) s++;
  return(s);
}
```

Here is a short program that uses **match( )**:

```
#include <stdio.h>

char *match(char c, char *s);

int main(void)
{
  char s[80], *p, ch;

  gets(s);
  ch = getchar();
  p = match(ch, s);
  if(*p)   /* there is a match */
    printf("%s ", p);
  else
    printf("No match found.");

  return 0;
}
```

This program reads a string and then a character. It then searches for an occurrence of the character in the string. If the character is in the string, **p** will point to that character, and the program prints the string from the point of the match. When no match is found, **p** will be pointing to the null terminator, making ***p** false. In this case, the program displays "No match found".

Recursion

Functions can call themselves. A function is *recursive* if a statement in the body of the function calls the function that contains it. Sometimes called *circular definition*, recursion is the process of defining something in terms of itself.

A simple example is the function **factr( )**, which computes the factorial of an integer. The factorial of a number N is the product of all the whole numbers from 1 to N. For example, 3 factorial is $1 \times 2 \times 3$, or 6. Both **factr( )** and its iterative equivalent are shown here:

```
/* Compute the factorial of a number. */
int factr(int n)   /* recursive */
{
  int answer;

  if(n==1) return(1);
  answer = factr(n-1)*n;
  return(answer);
}

/* Compute the factorial of a number. */
int fact(int n)     /* non-recursive */
{
  int t, answer;

  answer = 1;
  for(t=1; t<=n; t++)
    answer=answer*(t);
  return(answer);
}
```

The operation of the nonrecursive **fact( )** should be clear. It uses a loop starting at 1 and ending at the number, and progressively multiplies each number by the moving product.

The operation of the recursive **factr( )** is a little more complex. When **factr( )** is called with an argument of 1, the function returns 1; otherwise it returns the product of **factr(n–1) * n**. To evaluate this expression, **factr( )** is called with **n–1**. This happens until **n** equals 1 and the calls to the function begin returning.

Computing the factorial of 2, the first call to **factr( )** causes a second call to be made with the argument of **1**. This call returns 1, which is then multiplied by 2 (the original **n** value). The answer is then 2. You might find it interesting to insert **printf( )** statements into **factr( )** to show the level and the intermediate answers of each call.

When a function calls itself, new local variables and parameters are allocated storage on the stack, and the function code is executed with these new variables from its beginning. A recursive call does not make a new copy of the function. Only the arguments are new. As each recursive call returns, the old local variables and parameters are removed from the stack and execution resumes at the point of the function call inside the function. Recursive functions could be said to "telescope" out and back.

Most recursive functions are not smaller than their iterative counterparts. The recursive versions of most routines may execute a bit more slowly than the iterative equivalents because of the added function calls; but this slightly increased overhead is not a significant concern for most situations. Many recursive calls to a function could cause a stack overrun. Because storage for function parameters and local variables is on the stack and each new call creates a new copy of these variables, the stack space could become exhausted. If this happens, a *stack overflow* occurs.

The main advantage to recursive functions is that they can be used to create versions of several algorithms that are clearer and simpler than their iterative equivalents. For example, the QuickSort sorting algorithm is quite difficult to implement in an iterative way. Some problems, especially artificial intelligence–related ones, also seem to lend themselves to recursive solutions. Finally, some people seem to think recursively more easily than iteratively.

When writing recursive functions, you must have a conditional statement, such as an **if**, somewhere to force the function to return without the recursive call being executed. If you don't, the function will never return once you call it. This is a very common error when writing recursive functions. Use **printf( )** and **getchar( )** liberally during development so that you can watch what is going on and abort execution if you see a mistake.

Pointers to Functions

A particularly confusing yet powerful feature is the *function pointer*. Even though a function is not a variable, it still has a physical location in memory that can be assigned to a pointer. The address assigned to the pointer is the entry point of the function. This pointer can then be used in place of the function's name. It also allows functions to be passed as arguments to other functions.

To understand how function pointers work, you must understand a little about how a function is compiled and called. As each function is compiled, source code is transformed into object code and an entry point is established. When a call is made to a function while your program is running, a machine language "call" is made to this entry point. Therefore, a pointer to a function actually contains the memory address of the entry point of the function.

The address of a function is obtained by using the function's name without any parentheses or arguments. (This is similar to the way an array's address is obtained by using only the array name without indexes.) For example, consider the following program, paying very close attention to the declarations:

```
#include <stdio.h>
#include <string.h>

void check(char *a, char *b, int (*cmp) (const char *, const char *));

int main(void)
{
  char s1[80], s2[80];
  int  (*p)(const char*, const char*);

  p = strcmp;  /* get address of strcmp() */

  gets(s1);
  gets(s2);

  check(s1, s2, p);
  return 0;
}

void check(char *a, char *b, int (*cmp) (const char *, const char *))
{
  printf("Testing for equality.\n");
  if(!(*cmp) (a, b)) printf("Equal");
  else printf("Not equal");
}
```

When the function **check( )** is called, two character pointers and one function pointer are passed as parameters. Inside the function **check( )**, the arguments are declared as character pointers and a function pointer. Notice how the function pointer is declared. You should use the same method when declaring other function pointers, except that the return type or parameters of the function can be different. The parentheses around the *cmp are necessary for the compiler to interpret this statement correctly.

When you declare a function pointer, you can still provide a prototype to it as the preceding program illustrates. In many cases, however, you won't know the names of the actual parameters, so you can leave them blank, or you can use any names you like.

Once inside **check( )**, you can see how the **strcmp( )** function is called. The statement

```
if(!(*cmp) (a, b)) printf("Equal");
```

performs the call to the function, in this case **strcmp( )**, which is pointed to by **cmp** with the arguments **a** and **b**. This statement also represents the general form of using a function pointer to call the function it points to. The parentheses are necessary around the ***cmp** because of C and C++'s precedence rules.

Actually, you can also just use **cmp** directly, if you like, as shown here:

```
if(!cmp(a, b)) printf("Equal");
```

This version also calls the function pointed to by **cmp**, but it uses the normal function syntax. However, using the **(*cmp)** form tips off anyone reading your code that a function pointer is being used to indirectly call a function, instead of calling a function named **cmp**.

It is possible to call **check( )** using **strcmp** directly, as shown here:

```
check(s1, s2, strcmp);
```

This statement would eliminate the need for an additional pointer variable.

You may be asking yourself why anyone would want to write a program this way. In this example, nothing is gained and significant confusion is introduced. However, there are times when it is advantageous to pass arbitrary functions to procedures or to keep an array of functions. The following helps illustrate a use of function pointers. When an interpreter is written, it is common for it to perform function calls to various support routines, such as the sine, cosine, and tangent functions. Instead of having a large **switch** statement listing all of these functions, you can use an array of function pointers with the function to call determined by some index. You can get the flavor of this type of use by studying the expanded version of the previous example. In this program, **check( )** can be made to check for either alphabetical equality or numeric equality by calling it with a different comparison function:

```
#include <stdio.h>
#include <ctype.h>
#include <string.h>
#include <stdlib.h>

void check(char *a, char *b, int (*cmp) (const char *, const char *));
int numcmp(const char *a, const char *b);
```

```
int main(void)
{
  char s1[80], s2[80];
  gets(s1);
  gets(s2);

  if(isalpha(*s1))
      check(s1, s2, strcmp);
  else
      check(s1, s2, numcmp);

   return 0;
}

void check(char *a, char *b, int (*cmp) (const char *, const char *))
{
  printf("Testing for equality.\n");
  if(!(*cmp) (a, b)) printf("Equal");
  else printf("Not equal");
}

int numcmp(const char *a, const char *b)
{
  if(atoi(a)==atoi(b)) return 0;
  else return 1;
}
```

Implementation Issues

When you create functions, you should remember a few important things that affect their efficiency and usability. These issues are the subject of this section.

Parameters and General-Purpose Functions

A general-purpose function is one that is used in a variety of situations, perhaps by many different programmers. Typically, you should not base general-purpose functions on global data. All the information a function needs should be passed through parameters. In the few cases in which this is not possible, you should use **static** variables.

Besides making your functions general-purpose, parameters keep your code readable and less susceptible to bugs caused by side effects.

Efficiency

Functions are the building blocks of C and C++, and crucial to the creation of all but the most trivial programs. Nothing said in this section should be construed otherwise. In certain specialized applications, however, you may need to eliminate a function and replace it with *in-line code*. In-line code is the equivalent of a function's statements used without a call to that function. In-line code should be substituted for function calls only when execution time is critical.

There are two reasons in-line code is faster than a function call. First, a "call" instruction takes time to execute. Second, arguments to be passed have to be placed on the stack, which also takes time. For almost all applications, this very slight increase in execution time is of no significance. But if it is, remember that each function call uses time that would be saved if the code in the function were placed in line. For example, here are two versions of a program that prints the square of the numbers from 1 to 10. The in-line version runs faster than the other because the function call takes time.

In-line

```
#include <stdio.h>

int main(void)

{

   int x;


   for(x=1; x<11; ++x)

     printf("%d", x*x);

   return 0;

}
```

Function Call

```
#include <stdio.h>

int sqr(int a);

int main(void)

{

  int x;


  for(x=1; x<11; ++x)

    printf("%d", sqr(x));

  return 0;

}

int sqr(int a)

{

  return a*a;

}
```

As you create programs, you must always weigh the cost of functions in terms of execution time against the benefits of increased readability and modifiability.

 In C++, the concept of inline functions is expanded and formalized. In fact, inline functions are an important component of the C++ language.

The
Complete
Reference

Borland
C++
Builder

Chapter 5

Arrays

115

A n *array* is a collection of variables of the same type that are referenced by a common name. A specific element in an array is accessed by an index. In C/C++ all arrays consist of contiguous memory locations. The lowest address corresponds to the first element; the highest address corresponds to the last element. Arrays can have from one to several dimensions. The most common array is the null-terminated *string*, which is simply an array of characters terminated by a null.

Arrays and pointers are closely related; a discussion of one usually refers to the other. This chapter focuses on arrays, while Chapter 6 looks closely at pointers. You should read both to understand fully these important constructs.

Single-Dimension Arrays

The general form of a single-dimension array declaration is

   type var_name[size];

Like other variables, arrays must be explicitly declared so that the compiler can allocate space for them in memory. Here, *type* declares the base type of the array, which is the type of each element in the array. *size* defines how many elements the array will hold and must be a positive integer. For a single-dimension array, the total size of an array in bytes is computed as shown here:

   *total bytes = sizeof(base type) * number of elements*

All arrays have 0 as the index of their first element. Therefore, when you write

```
char p[10];
```

you are declaring a character array that has 10 elements, **p[0]** through **p[9]**. For example, the following program loads an integer array with the numbers 0 through 9 and displays them:

```
#include <stdio.h>

int main(void)
{
  int x[10];  /* this reserves 10 integer elements */
  int t;
```

```
   for(t=0; t<10; ++t) x[t] = t;

   for(t=0; t<10; ++t) printf("%d ", x[t]);

   return 0;
}
```

C/C++ has no bounds checking on arrays. You could overwrite either end of an array and write into some other variable's data, or even into the program's code. It is the programmer's job to provide bounds checking where needed. For example, make certain that the character arrays that accept character input are long enough to accept the longest input.

Single-dimension arrays are essentially lists of information of the same type. For example, Figure 5-1 shows how array **a** appears in memory if it is declared as shown here and starts at memory location 1000:

```
char a[7];
```

Generating a Pointer to an Array

You can generate a pointer to the first element of an array by simply specifying the array name, without any index. For example, given

```
int sample[10];
```

you can generate a pointer to the first element by using the name **sample**. Thus, the following code fragment assigns **p** the address of the first element of **sample**:

```
int *p;
int sample[10];

p = sample;
```

You can also obtain the address of the first element of an array using the & operator. For example, **sample** and **&sample[0]** both produce the same results. However, in professionally written C/C++ code, you will almost never see **&sample[0]**.

Element	a[0]	a[1]	a[2]	a[3]	a[4]	a[5]	a[6]
Address	1000	1001	1002	1003	1004	1005	1006

Figure 5-1. *A seven-element character array beginning at location 1000*

Passing Single-Dimension Arrays to Functions

When passing single-dimension arrays to functions, call the function with just the array name (no index). This passes the address of the first element of the array to the function. It is not possible to pass the entire array as an argument; a pointer is automatically passed instead. For example, the following program fragment passes the address of **i** to **func1( )**:

```
int main(void)
{
  int i[10];

  func1(i);
  /*... */
  return 0;
}
```

If a function is to receive a single-dimension array, you may declare the formal parameter as a pointer, as a sized array, or as an unsized array. For example, to receive **i** into a function called **func1( )**, you could declare **func1( )** as

```
void func1(int *a)   /* pointer */
{
  /*...*/
}
```

or

```
void func1(int a[10]) /* sized array */
{
  /*...*/
}
```

or finally as

```
void func1(int a[]) /* unsized array */
{
  /*...*/
}
```

All three methods of declaration tell the compiler that an integer pointer is going to be received. In the first declaration a pointer is used; in the second the standard array declaration is employed. In the third declaration, a modified version of an array declaration simply specifies that an array of type **int** of some length is to be received. As far as the function is concerned, it doesn't matter what the length of the array actually is because C/C++ performs no bounds checking. In fact, as far as the compiler is concerned,

```
void func1(int a[32])
{
  /*...*/
}
```

also works because the compiler generates code that instructs **func1( )** to receive a pointer—it does not actually create a 32-element array.

Null-Terminated Strings

By far the most common use of the one-dimensional array is as a character string. C defines only one type of string, the *null-terminated string,* which is a null-terminated character array. (A null is zero.) Thus a null-terminated string contains the characters that compose the string followed by a null. Sometimes null-terminated strings are called *C-strings.* C++ also defines a string class, called **string**, which provides an object-oriented approach to string handling. It is described later in this book. Here, null-terminated strings are examined.

When declaring a character array that will hold a null-terminated string, you need to declare it to be one character longer than the largest string that it will hold. For example, to declare an array **s** that can hold a 10-character string, you would write

```
char s[11];
```

This statement makes room for the 10 characters as well as the null at the end of the string.

A *string constant* (also called a *string literal*) is a list of characters enclosed between double quotes. For example, here are two string constants:

```
"hello there"
"this is a test"
```

A string constant automatically creates a null-terminated string. It is not necessary to manually add the null to the end of string constants, because compiler does this for you.

C/C++ supports a wide range of string manipulation functions. The most common are listed here:

Name	Function
strcpy(*s1*, *s2*)	Copies *s2* into *s1*.
strcat(*s1*, *s2*)	Concatenates *s2* onto the end of *s1*.
strlen(*s1*)	Returns the length of *s1*.
strcmp(*s1*, *s2*)	Returns 0 if *s1* and *s2* are the same; less than 0 if *s1* < *s2*; greater than 0 if *s1* > *s2*.
strchr(*s1*, *ch*)	Returns a pointer to the first occurrence of *ch* in *s1*.
strstr(*s1*, *s2*)	Returns a pointer to the first occurrence of *s2* in *s1*.

These functions use the **<string.h>** header. (These and other string functions are discussed in detail in Part Two of this book.)

The following program illustrates the use of these string functions:

```
#include <string.h>
#include <stdio.h>

int main(void)
{
  char s1[80], s2[80];

  gets(s1); gets(s2);

  printf("lengths: %d %d\n", strlen(s1), strlen(s2));

  if(!strcmp(s1, s2)) printf("The strings are equal\n");

  strcat(s1, s2);
```

```
    printf("%s\n", s1);

    strcpy(s1, "This is a test.\n");
    printf(s1);
    if(strchr("hello", 'e')) printf("e is in hello\n");
    if(strstr("hi there", "hi")) printf("found hi");

    return 0;
}
```

If this program is run and the strings "hello" and "hello" are entered, the output is

```
lengths: 5 5
The strings are equal
hellohello
This is a test.
e is in hello
found hi
```

It is important to remember that **strcmp( )** returns false if the strings are equal, so be sure to use the **!** to reverse the condition, as shown in this example, if you are testing for equality.

Two-Dimensional Arrays

C/C++ supports multidimensional arrays. The simplest form of the multidimensional array is the two-dimensional array. A two-dimensional array is, essentially, an array of one-dimensional arrays. Two-dimensional arrays are declared using this general form:

type array_name[2nd dimension size][1st dimension size];

To declare a two-dimensional integer array **d** of size 10,20, you would write

```
int d[10][20];
```

Pay careful attention to the declaration. Some other computer languages use commas to separate the array dimensions, but C/C++ places each dimension in its own set of brackets.

Similarly, to access point 3,5 of array **d**, you would use

```
d[3][5]
```

In the following example, a two-dimensional array is loaded with the numbers 1 through 12, which is then displayed row by row:

```
#include <stdio.h>

int main(void)
{
  int t,i, num[3][4];

  /* load numbers */
  for(t=0; t<3; ++t)
    for(i=0; i<4; ++i)
      num[t][i] = (t*4)+i+1;

  /* display numbers */
  for(t=0; t<3; ++t) {
    for(i=0; i<4; ++i)
      printf("%d ", num[t][i]);
    printf("\n");
  }

  return 0;
}
```

In this example, **num[0][0]** has the value 1; **num[0][1]**, the value 2; **num[0][2]**, the value 3; and so on. The value of **num[2][3]** is 12.

Two-dimensional arrays are stored in a row-column matrix, where the left index indicates the row and the right index indicates the column. This means that the right index changes faster than the left when accessing the elements in the array in the order they are actually stored in memory. See Figure 5-2 for a graphic representation of a two-dimensional array in memory. In essence, the left index can be thought of as a "pointer" to the correct row.

The number of bytes of memory required by a two-dimensional array is computed using the following formula:

bytes = size of 1st index * size of 2nd index * sizeof (base-type)

Therefore, assuming 4-byte integers, an integer array with dimensions 10,5 would have $10 \times 5 \times 4$ or 200 bytes allocated.

When a two-dimensional array is used as an argument to a function, only a pointer to the first element is passed. However, a function receiving a two-dimensional array

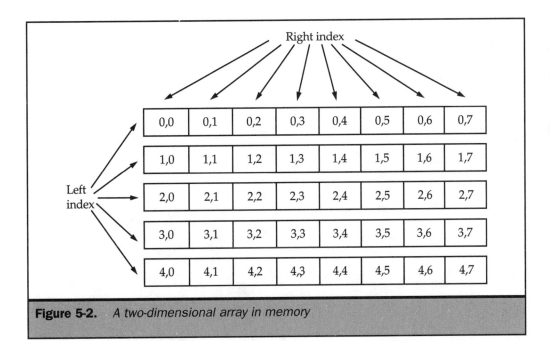

Figure 5-2.   *A two-dimensional array in memory*

as a parameter must minimally define the length of the right index, because the compiler needs to know the length of each row if it is to index the array correctly. For example, a function that will receive a two-dimensional integer array with dimensions 5,10 would be declared like this:

```
void func1(int x[][10])
{
    /*...*/
}
```

You can specify the left dimension as well, but it is not necessary. The compiler needs to know the size of the right dimension in order to work on statements such as

```
x[2][4]
```

inside the function. If the length of the rows is not known, it is impossible to know where the next row begins.

The following program uses a two-dimensional array to store the numeric grade for each student in a teacher's classes. The program assumes that the teacher has three classes and a maximum of 30 students per class. Notice how the array **grade** is accessed by each of the functions:

```
#include <conio.h>
#include <ctype.h>
#include <stdio.h>
#include <stdlib.h>

#define CLASSES  3
#define GRADES  30
int grade[CLASSES][GRADES];

void disp_grades(int g[][GRADES]), enter_grades(void);
int get_grade(int num);

int main(void)  /* class grades program */
{
  char ch;

  for(;;) {
    do {
      printf("(E)nter grades\n");
      printf("(R)eport grades\n");
      printf("(Q)uit\n");
      ch = toupper(getche());
    } while(ch!='E' && ch!='R' && ch!='Q');

    switch(ch) {
      case 'E':
        enter_grades();
        break;
      case 'R':
        disp_grades(grade);
        break;
      case 'Q':
        return 0;
    }
  }
}

/* Enter each student's grade. */
void enter_grades(void)
```

```
{
  int t, i;

  for(t=0; t<CLASSES; t++) {
    printf("Class # %d:\n", t+1);
    for(i=0; i<GRADES; ++i)
      grade[t][i] = get_grade(i);
  }
}

/* Actually input the grade. */
int get_grade(int num)
{
  char s[80];

  printf("enter grade for student # %d:\n", num+1);
  gets(s);
  return(atoi(s));
}

/* Display the class grades. */
void disp_grades(int g[][GRADES])
{
  int t, i;

  for(t=0; t<CLASSES; ++t) {
    printf("Class # %d:\n", t+1);
    for(i=0; i<GRADES; ++i)
      printf("grade for student #%d is %d\n",i+1, g[t][i]);
  }
}
```

Arrays of Strings

It is not uncommon in programming to use an array of strings. For example, the input processor to a database may verify user commands against a string array of valid commands. A two-dimensional character array is used to create an array of strings with the size of the left index determining the number of strings and the size of the right index specifying the maximum length of each string. This code fragment declares an array of 30 strings, each having a maximum length of 79 characters:

```
char str_array[30][80];
```

To access an individual string is quite easy: You simply specify only the left index. For example, this statement calls **gets( )** with the third string in **str_array**:

```
gets(str_array[2]);
```

This is functionally equivalent to

```
gets(&str_array[2][0]);
```

but the previous form is much more common in professionally written code.

To understand better how string arrays work, study the following short program, which uses a string array as the basis for a very simple text editor:

```
#include <stdio.h>

#define MAX 100
#define LEN 255

char text[MAX][LEN];

/* A very simple text editor. */
int main(void)
{
  register int t, i, j;

  for(t=0; t<MAX; t++) {
    printf("%d: ", t);
    gets(text[t]);
    if(!*text[t]) break; /* quit on blank line */
  }

  /* this displays the text one character at a time */
  for(i=0; i<t; i++) {
    for(j=0; text[i][j]; j++) putchar(text[i][j]);
    putchar('\n');
  }

  return 0;
}
```

This program inputs lines of text until a blank line is entered. Then it redisplays each line. For purposes of illustration, it displays the text one character at a time by indexing the first dimension. However, because each string in the array is null-terminated, the routine that displays the text could be simplified like this:

```
for(i=0; i<t; i++)
    printf("%s\n", text[i]);
```

Multidimensional Arrays

You can have arrays greater than two dimensions. The general form of a multidimensional array declaration is

type name[*size1*][*size2*][*size3*]. . .[*sizeN*];

Arrays of more than three dimensions are rarely used because of the large amount of memory required to hold them.

A point to remember about multidimensional arrays is that it takes the computer time to compute each index. This means that accessing an element in a multidimensional array will be slower than accessing an element in a single-dimension array.

When passing multidimensional arrays into functions, you must declare all but the leftmost dimension. For example, if you declare array **m** as

```
int m[4][3][6][5];
```

then a function, **func1( )**, that receives **m**, would look like this:

```
int func1(int d[][3][6][5])
{
   /*...*/
}
```

Of course, you can include the leftmost dimension if you like.

Indexing Pointers

Pointers and arrays are closely related. As you know, an array name without an index is a pointer to the first element in the array. For example, given this array,

```
char p[10];
```

the following statements are identical:

```
p

&p[0]
```

Put another way,

```
p == &p[0]
```

evaluates true because the address of the first element of an array is the same as the address of the array.

Conversely, a pointer can be indexed as if it were declared to be an array. For example:

```
int *p, i[10];
p = i;
p[5] = 100;   /* assign using index */
*(p+5) = 100; /* assign using pointer arithmetic */
```

Both assignment statements place the value 100 in the sixth element of **i**. The first statement indexes **p**; the second uses pointer arithmetic. Either way, the result is the same. (Pointers and pointer arithmetic are dealt with in detail in Chapter 6.)

The same holds true for arrays of two or more dimensions. For example, assuming that **a** is a 10-by-10 integer array, these two statements are equivalent:

```
a
&a[0][0]
```

Furthermore, the 0,4 element of **a** may be referenced either by array-indexing, **a[0][4]**, or by the pointer, ***((int *) a + 4)**. Similarly, element 1,2 is either **a[1][2]** or ***((int *) a + 12)**. In general, for any two-dimensional array:

a[j][k] is equivalent to **((base type *) a + (j * rowlength) + k)*

The cast of the pointer to the array into a pointer of its base type is necessary in order for the pointer arithmetic to operate properly. Pointers are sometimes used to access arrays because pointer arithmetic is often faster than array indexing. The gain in speed with pointers is the greatest when an array is being accessed sequentially. In this situation, the pointer may be incremented or decremented using the highly efficient increment and decrement operators. On the other hand, if the array is accessed in random order, then the pointer approach may not be any better than array-indexing.

A two-dimensional array can be reduced to a pointer to an array of one-dimensional arrays. Therefore, using a separate pointer variable is one easy way to access elements within a row of a two-dimensional array. The following function illustrates this technique. It prints the contents of the specified row for the global integer array **num**:

```c
int num[10][10];
  /*...*/
void pr_row(int j)
{
  int *p, t;

  p = (int *) &num[j][0]; /* get address of first
                             element in row j */
  for(t=0; t<10; ++t) printf("%d ", *(p+t));
}
```

This function can be generalized by making the calling arguments be the row, the row length, and a pointer to the first array element, as shown here:

```c
/* General */
void pr_row(int j, int row_dimension, int *p)
{
  int t;

  p = p + (j * row_dimension);
  for(t=0; t<row_dimension; ++t)
    printf("%d ", *(p+t));
}
```

Arrays greater than two dimensions may be reduced in a similar way. For example, a three-dimensional array can be reduced to a pointer to a two-dimensional array, which can be reduced to a pointer to a one-dimensional array. Generally, an N-dimensional array can be reduced to a pointer and an N – 1 dimensional array. This new array can be reduced again using the same method. The process ends when a single-dimension array is produced.

Allocated Arrays

In many programming situations it is impossible to know how large an array is needed. In addition, many types of programs need to use as much memory as is available, yet still run on machines having only minimal memory. A text editor or a database are examples of such programs. In these situations, it is not possible to use a predefined array because its dimensions are established at compile time and cannot be changed during execution. The solution is to create a *dynamic array*. A dynamic array uses memory from the region of free memory called the *heap* and is accessed by indexing a pointer to that memory. (Remember that any pointer can be indexed as if it were an array variable.)

In C you can dynamically allocate and free memory by using the standard library routines **malloc( )**, which allocates memory and returns a **void *** pointer to the start of it, and **free( )**, which returns previously allocated memory to the heap for possible reuse. The prototypes for **malloc( )** and **free( )** are

```
void *malloc(size_t num_bytes);
void free(void *p);
```

Both functions use the **<stdlib.h>** header. Here, *num_bytes* is the number of bytes requested. The type **size_t** is defined as an unsigned integer. If there is not enough free memory to fill the request, **malloc( )** returns a null. It is important that **free( )** be called only with a valid, previously allocated pointer; otherwise, damage could be done to the organization of the heap and possibly cause the program to crash.

The code fragment shown here allocates 1000 bytes of memory:

```
char *p;
p = malloc(1000); /* get 1000 bytes */
```

Here, **p** points to the first of 1000 bytes of free memory. Notice that no cast is used to convert the **void** pointer returned by **malloc( )** into the desired **char** pointer. Because **malloc( )** returns a **void** pointer, it can be assigned to any other type of pointer and is automatically converted into a pointer of the target type. However, it is important to understand that this automatic conversion *does not* occur in C++. In C++, an explicit type cast in needed when a **void** pointer is assigned to another type of pointer. Thus, in C++, the preceding assignment must be written as follows:

```
p = (char *) malloc(1000); /* get 1000 bytes */
```

As a general rule, in C++ you must use a type cast when assigning (or otherwise converting) one type of pointer into another. This is one of the fundamental differences between C and C++. Since type casts are needed for C++ and do no harm in C, this book will use them when allocating memory using **malloc( )**.

This example shows the proper way to use a dynamically allocated array to read input from the keyboard using **gets( )**:

```
/* Print a string backward using dynamic allocation. */
```

```
#include <stdlib.h>
#include <stdio.h>
#include <string.h>

int main(void)
{
  char *s;
  register int t;

  s = (char *) malloc(80);

  if(!s) {
    printf("Memory request failed.\n");
    exit(1);
  }

  gets(s);
  for(t=strlen(s)-1; t>=0; t--) putchar(s[t]);
  free(s);

  return 0;
}
```

As the program shows, **s** is tested prior to its first use to ensure that a valid pointer is returned by **malloc( )**. This is absolutely necessary to prevent accidental use of a null pointer. Notice how the pointer **s** is indexed as an array to print the string backward.

Array Initialization

C/C++ allows the initialization of arrays at the time of their declaration. The general form of array initialization is similar to that of other variables, as shown here:

type-specifier array_name[size1]. . .[sizeN] = { value-list };

The *value-list* is a comma-separated list of values that are type-compatible with *type-specifier*. The first value is placed in the first position of the array, the second value in the second position, and so on. The last entry in the list is not followed by a comma. Note that a semicolon follows the }.

Note *For compatibility with C89, array initializers must be constants.*

In the following example, a 10-element integer array is initialized with the numbers 1 through 10:

```
int i[10] = {1, 2, 3, 4, 5, 6, 7, 8, 9, 10};
```

This means that **i[0]** has the value 1 and **i[9]** has the value 10.

Character arrays that hold strings allow a shorthand initialization in the form

char *array_name*[*size*] = "*string*";

In this form of initialization, the null terminator is automatically appended to the string. For example, this code fragment initializes **str** to the phrase "hello":

```
char str[6] = "hello";
```

This is the same as writing

```
char str[6] = {'h', 'e', 'l', 'l', 'o', '\0'};
```

Notice that in this version you must explicitly include the null terminator. Because strings end with a null, you must make sure that the array you declare is long enough to include it. This is why **str** is six characters long even though "hello" is only five characters. When the string constant is used (as in the previous approach), the compiler automatically supplies the null terminator.

Multidimensional arrays are initialized in the same fashion as single-dimension ones. For example, the following initializes **sqrs** with the numbers 1 through 10 and their squares:

```
int sqrs[10][2] = {
   1, 1,
   2, 4,
   3, 9,
   4, 16,
   5, 25,
   6, 36,
   7, 49,
   8, 64,
   9, 81,
   10, 100
};
```

THE FOUNDATION OF C++

Here, **sqrs[0][0]** contains 1, **sqrs[0][1]** contains 1, **sqrs[1][0]** contains 2, **sqrs[1][1]** contains 4, and so forth.

When initializing a multidimensional array, you may add braces around the initializers for each dimension. This is called *subaggregate grouping*. For example, here is another way to write the preceding declaration:

```
int sqrs[10][2] = {
  {1, 1},
  {2, 4},
  {3, 9},
  {4, 16},
  {5, 25},
  {6, 36},
  {7, 49},
  {8, 64},
  {9, 81},
  {10, 100}
};
```

When using subaggregate grouping, if you don't supply enough initializers for a given group, the remaining members will be set to zero, automatically.

Unsized-Array Initializations

Imagine that you are using an array initialization to build a table of error messages as shown here:

```
char e1[12] = "Read Error\n";
char e2[13] = "Write Error\n";
char e3[18] = "Cannot Open File\n";
```

As you might guess, it is very tedious to count the characters in each message manually to determine the correct array dimensions. It is possible to let the compiler dimension the arrays automatically by using *unsized arrays*. If the size of the array is not specified in an array initialization statement, the compiler automatically creates an array big enough to hold all the initializers present. Using this approach, the message table becomes

```
char e1[] = "Read Error\n";
char e2[] = "Write Error\n";
char e3[] = "Cannot Open File\n";
```

Given these initializations, this statement

```
printf("%s has length %d\n", e2, sizeof e2);
```

prints

```
Write Error
has length 13
```

Aside from being less tedious, the unsized-array initialization method allows any of the messages to be changed without fear of accidentally counting incorrectly.

Unsized-array initializations are not restricted to only single-dimension arrays. For multidimensional arrays, you must specify all but the leftmost dimensions in order to allow the array to be properly indexed. (This is similar to specifying array parameters.) In this way, you can build tables of varying lengths and the compiler automatically allocates enough storage for them. For example, the declaration of **sqrs** as an unsized array is shown here:

```
int sqrs[][2] = {
   1, 1,
   2, 4,
   3, 9,
   4, 16,
   5, 25,
   6, 36,
   7, 49,
   8, 64,
   9, 81,
   10, 100
};
```

The advantage to this declaration over the sized version is that the table may be lengthened or shortened without changing the array dimensions.

A Tic-Tac-Toe Example

This chapter concludes with a longer example that illustrates many of the ways arrays can be manipulated using C/C++.

Two-dimensional arrays are commonly used to simulate board game matrices, as in chess and checkers. Although it is beyond the scope of this book to present a chess or checkers program, a simple tic-tac-toe program can be developed.

The tic-tac-toe matrix is represented using a 3-by-3 character array. You are "X" and the computer is "O". When you move, an "X" is placed in the specified position of the game matrix. When it is the computer's turn to move, it scans the matrix and puts its "O" in the first empty location of the matrix. (This makes for a fairly dull game—you might find it fun to spice it up a bit!) If the computer cannot find an empty location, it reports a draw game and exits. The game matrix is initialized to contain spaces at the start of the game. The tic-tac-toe program is shown here:

```c
#include <stdio.h>
#include <stdlib.h>

/* A simple game of Tic-Tac-Toe. */

#define SPACE ' '

char matrix[3][3] = {  /* the tic-tac-toe matrix */
  {SPACE, SPACE, SPACE},
  {SPACE, SPACE, SPACE},
  {SPACE, SPACE, SPACE}
};

void get_computer_move(void), get_player_move(void);
void disp_matrix(void);
char check(void);

int main(void)
{
  char done;

  printf("This is the game of Tic-Tac-Toe.\n");
  printf("You will be playing against the computer.\n");

  do {
    disp_matrix();          /* display the game board */
    get_player_move();      /* get your move */
    done = check();         /* see if winner */
    if(done!=SPACE) break;  /* winner! */
    get_computer_move();    /* get computer's move */
    done=check();           /* see if winner */
  } while(done==SPACE);
  if(done=='X') printf("You won!\n");
  else printf("I won!!!!\n");
```

```
    disp_matrix(); /* show final positions */

    return 0;
}

/* Input the player's move. */
void get_player_move(void)
{
  int x, y;

  printf("Enter coordinates for your X.\n");
  printf("Row? ");
  scanf("%d", &x);
  printf("Column? ");
  scanf("%d", &y);
  x--; y--;
  if(x<0 || y<0 || x>2 || y>2 || matrix[x][y]!=SPACE) {
    printf("Invalid move, try again.\n");
    get_player_move();
  }
  else matrix[x][y]='X';
}

/* Get the computer's move */
void get_computer_move(void)
{
  register int t;
  char *p;

  p = (char *) matrix;
  for(t=0; *p!=SPACE && t<9; ++t) p++;
  if(t==9)  {
    printf("draw\n");
    exit(0); /* game over */
  }
  else *p = 'O';
}
```

```c
/* Display the game board. */
void disp_matrix(void)
{
  int t;

  for(t=0; t<3; t++) {
    printf(" %c | %c | %c ", matrix[t][0],
      matrix[t][1], matrix [t][2]);
    if(t!=2) printf("\n---|---|---\n");
  }
   printf("\n");
}

/* See if there is a winner. */
char check(void)
{
  int t;
  char *p;

  for(t=0; t<3; t++) { /* check rows */
    p = &matrix[t][0];
    if(*p==*(p+1) && *(p+1)==*(p+2)) return *p;
  }

  for(t=0; t<3; t++) { /* check columns */
    p = &matrix[0][t];
    if(*p==*(p+3) && *(p+3)==*(p+6)) return *p;
  }

  /* test diagonals */
  if(matrix[0][0]==matrix[1][1] && matrix[1][1]==matrix[2][2])
    return matrix[0][0];

  if(matrix[0][2]==matrix[1][1] && matrix[1][1]==matrix[2][0])
    return matrix[0][2];

  return SPACE;
}
```

The array is initialized to contain spaces because a space is used to indicate to **get_player_move( )** and **get_computer_move( )** that a matrix position is vacant. The fact that spaces are used instead of nulls simplifies the matrix display function **disp_matrix( )** by allowing the contents of the array to be printed on the screen without any translations. Note that the routine **get_player_move( )** is recursive when an invalid location is entered. This is an example of how recursion can be used to simplify a routine and reduce the amount of code necessary to implement a function.

In the main loop, each time a move is entered the function **check( )** is called. This function determines if the game has been won and by whom. The **check( )** function returns an "X" if you have won, or an "O" if the computer has won. Otherwise, it returns a space. **check( )** works by scanning the rows, the columns, and then the diagonals looking for a winning configuration.

The routines in this example all access the array **matrix** differently. You should study them to make sure that you understand each array operation.

The Complete Reference

Borland
C++
Builder

Chapter 6

Pointers

The correct understanding and use of pointers is crucial to the successful C/C++ programming for four reasons:

1. Pointers provide the means by which functions can modify their calling arguments.
2. Pointers support dynamic allocation.
3. Pointers can improve the efficiency of certain routines.
4. Pointers provide support for dynamic data structures such as linked lists and binary trees.

Pointers are one of the strongest but also one of the most dangerous features in C/C++. For example, uninitialized or wild pointers can cause the system to crash. Perhaps worse, it is easy to use pointers incorrectly, causing bugs that are very difficult to find.

Because of their importance and their potential for abuse, this chapter examines the subject of pointers in detail.

Pointers Are Addresses

A *pointer* is a variable that holds a memory address. This address is the location of another object (typically, a variable) in memory. If one variable contains the address of another variable, the first variable is said to *point to* the second. For example, if a variable at location 1004 is pointed to by a variable at location 1000, location 1000 will contain the value 1004. This situation is illustrated in Figure 6-1.

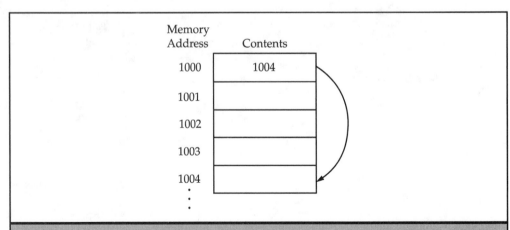

Figure 6-1.   *One variable pointing to another*

Pointer Variables

If a variable is going to be a pointer, it must be declared as such. A pointer declaration consists of a base type, an *, and the variable name. The general form for declaring a pointer variable is

type *name;

where *type* is any valid type (the pointer's base type), and *name* is the name of the pointer variable.

The base type of the pointer defines what type of variables the pointer can point to. Technically, any type of pointer can point anywhere in memory, but C/C++ assumes that what the pointer is pointing to is an object of its base type. Also, all pointer arithmetic is done relative to its base type, so the base type of a pointer is very important.

The Pointer Operators

There are two special pointer operators: * and &. These operators were introduced in Chapter 2. We will take a closer look at them here, beginning with a review of their basic operation.

The & is a unary operator that returns the memory address of its operand. For example,

```
p = &num;
```

places into **p** the memory address of the variable **num**. This address is the computer's internal location of the variable. It has nothing to do with the value of **num**. The operation of the & can be remembered as returning "the address of." Therefore, the preceding assignment statement could be read as "**p** receives the address of **num**."

For example, assume the variable **num** uses memory location 2000 to store its value. Also assume that **num** has a value of 100. Then, after the preceding assignment, **p** will have the value 2000.

The second operator, *, is the complement of &. It is a unary operator that returns the value of the variable located at the address that follows. For example, if **p** contains the memory address of the variable **num**,

```
q = *p;
```

places the value of **num** into **q**. Following through with this example, **q** has the value 100 because 100 is stored at location 2000, which is the memory address that was stored in **p**. The operation of the * can be remembered as "at address." In this case the statement could be read as "**q** receives the value at address **p**."

The following program illustrates the foregoing discussion:

```
#include <stdio.h>

int main(void)
{
  int num, q;
  int *p;

  num = 100; /* num is assigned 100 */
  p = &num;  /* p receives num's address */
  q = *p;    /* q is assigned num's value
                   indirectly through p */

  printf("%d", q); /* prints 100 */

  return 0;
}
```

The preceding program displays the value 100.

Unfortunately, the multiplication sign and the "at address" sign are the same, and the bitwise AND and the "address of" sign are the same. These operators have no relationship to each other. Both **&** and * have a higher precedence than the binary arithmetic operators.

You must make sure that your pointer variables always point to the correct type of data. For example, when you declare a pointer to be of type **int**, the compiler assumes that any address it holds points to an integer value. Because C allows you to assign any address to a pointer variable, the following code fragment compiles (although C++ Builder will issue a warning message) but does not produce the desired result.

```
#include <stdio.h>

int main(void)
{
  double x, y;
  int   *p;

  x = 100.123;

  p = &x;
  y = *p;
  printf("%f", y);   /* this will be wrong */
```

THE FOUNDATION
OF C++

```
      return 0;
   }
```

This does not assign the value of **x** to **y**. Because **p** is declared to be an integer pointer (and assuming 32-bit integers), only 4 bytes of information will be transferred to **y**, not the 8 that normally make up a **double**.

In C++, it is illegal to convert one type of pointer into another without the use of an explicit type cast. For this reason, the preceding program will not even compile if you try to compile it as a C++ (rather than as a C) program. However, the type of error described can still occur in C++ in a more roundabout manner.

Pointer Expressions

In general, expressions involving pointers conform to the same rules as any other C/C++ expression. This section will examine a few special aspects of pointer expressions.

Pointer Assignments

As with any variable, a pointer may be used on the right-hand side of assignment statements to assign its value to another pointer. For example:

```
#include <stdio.h>

int main(void)
{
   int x;
   int *p1, *p2;

   p1 = &x;
   p2 = p1;

   /* This will display the addresses held by
      p1 and p2. They will be the same.
   */
   printf("%p  %p", p1, p2);

   return 0;
}
```

Here, both **p1** and **p2** will contain the address of **x**.

Pointer Arithmetic

Only two arithmetic operations can be used on pointers: addition and subtraction. To understand what occurs in pointer arithmetic, let **p1** be a pointer to an integer with a current value of 2000, and assume that integers are 4 bytes long. After the expression

```
p1++;
```

the content of **p1** is 2004, not 2001! Each time **p1** is incremented, it points to the next integer. The same is true of decrements. For example,

```
p1--;
```

will cause **p1** to have the value 1996, assuming that it previously was 2000.

Generalizing from the preceding example, the following rules govern pointer arithmetic. Each time a pointer is incremented, it points to the memory location of the next element of its base type. Each time it is decremented, it points to the location of the previous element. When applied to character pointers, this will appear as "normal" arithmetic because characters are always 1 byte long. All other pointers will increase or decrease by the length of the data type they point to. This approach ensures that a pointer is always pointing to an appropriate element of its base type. Figure 6-2 illustrates this concept.

You are not limited to the increment and decrement operations, however. You may also add or subtract integers to or from pointers. The expression

```
p1 = p1 + 9;
```

makes **p1** point to the ninth element of **p1**'s type beyond the one it is currently pointing to.

Besides addition and subtraction of a pointer and an integer, the only other operation you can perform on a pointer is to subtract it from another pointer. For the most part, subtracting one pointer from another only makes sense when both pointers point to a common object, such as an array. The subtraction then yields the number of elements of the base type separating the two pointer values. Aside from these operations, no other arithmetic operations can be performed on pointers. You cannot multiply or divide pointers; you cannot add pointers; you cannot apply the bitwise shift and mask operators to them; and you cannot add or subtract type **float** or **double** to pointers.

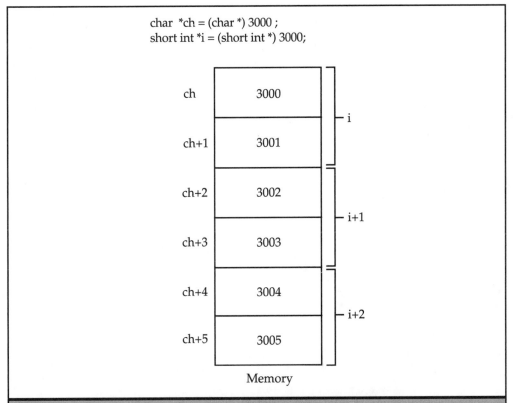

Figure 6-2. *All pointer arithmetic is relative to its base type. (Assume 2-byte short integers.)*

Pointer Comparisons

You can compare two pointers in a relational expression. For instance, given the pointers **p** and **q**, the following statement is perfectly valid:

```
if(p<q) printf("p points to lower memory than q\n");
```

Generally, pointer comparisons are useful only when two or more pointers are pointing to a common object. As an example, imagine that you are constructing a stack routine to hold integer values. A stack is a list that uses "first in, last out" accessing. It is often compared to a stack of plates on a table—the first one set down is the last one to be used. Stacks are used frequently in compilers, interpreters, spreadsheets, and other system-related software. To create a stack, you need two routines: **push( )** and **pop( )**. The **push( )** function puts values on the stack, and **pop( )** takes them off. In the following expample, the stack is held in the array **stack**, which is **STCKSIZE** elements long. The variable **tos** holds the memory address of the top of the stack and is used to prevent stack overflows and underflows. Once the stack has been initialized, **push( )** and **pop( )** can be used to access the stack. These routines are shown here with a simple **main( )** function to drive them:

```c
#include <stdio.h>
#include <stdlib.h>

#define STCKSIZE 50

void push(int i);
int pop(void);

int *p1, *tos, stack[STCKSIZE];

int main(void)
{
  int value;

  p1 =  stack; /* assign p1 the start of stack */
  tos = p1;  /* let tos hold top of stack */

  do {
    printf("Enter a number (-1 to quit, 0 to pop): ");
    scanf("%d", &value);
    if(value!=0) push(value);
    else printf("this is it %d\n", pop());
  } while(value!=-1);
  return 0;
}

void push(int i)
{
  p1++;
  if(p1==(tos + STCKSIZE)) {
    printf("stack overflow");
    exit(1);
  }
```

```
    *p1 = i;
}

int pop(void)
{
  if(p1==tos) {
    printf("stack underflow");
    exit(1);
  }
  p1--;
  return *(p1+1);
}
```

Both the **push( )** and **pop( )** functions perform a relational test on the pointer **p1** to detect limit errors. In **push( )**, **p1** is tested against the end of stack by adding **STCKSIZE** (the size of the stack) to **tos**. In **pop( )**, **p1** is checked against **tos** to be sure that a stack underflow has not occurred.

In **pop( )**, the parentheses are necessary in the **return** statement. Without them, the statement would look like

```
return *p1 + 1;
```

which would return the value at location **p1** plus 1, not the value of the location **p1+1**.

Dynamic Allocation and Pointers

Once compiled, all C/C++ programs organize the computer's memory into four regions: *program code, global data,* the *stack,* and the *heap.* The *heap* is an area of free memory that is managed by the dynamic allocation functions **malloc( )** and **free( )**. These functions were introduced in Chapter 5 in conjunction with arrays. Here we will examine them further, beginning with a review of their of their basic operation.

Note   *Although C++ still supports C's dynamic allocation functions, it also defines its own approach, which is based upon dynamic allocation operators. These are described in Part Three.*

The **malloc( )** function allocates memory and returns a pointer to the start of it. **free( )** returns previously allocated memory to the heap for possible reuse. The prototypes for **malloc( )** and **free( )** are

void *malloc(size_t *num_bytes*);
void free(void *p*);

Both functions use the **<stdlib.h>** header. Here, *num_bytes* is the number of bytes requested. If there is not enough free memory to fill the request, **malloc( )** returns a null. The type **size_t** is defined in **<stdlib.h>** and specifies an unsigned integer type that is capable of holding the largest amount of memory that may be allocated with a single call to **malloc( )**. It is important that **free( )** be called only with a valid, previously allocated pointer; otherwise, the organization of the heap could be damaged, which might cause a program crash.

The code fragment shown here allocates 25 bytes of memory:

```
char *p;
p = (char *) malloc(25);
```

After the assignment, **p** points to the first of 25 bytes of free memory. The cast to **char *** is not needed for C but is required for C++ programs. In C, if no type cast is used with **malloc( )**, the pointer type is converted automatically to the same type as the pointer variable on the left side of the assignment. In C++, such implicit pointer conversions are disallowed. Although not needed by C, the use of the type cast allows your C code to be compatible with C++. As another example, this fragment allocates space for 50 integers. It uses **sizeof** to ensure portability.

```
int *p;
p = (int *) malloc(50*sizeof(int));
```

Since the heap is not infinite, whenever you allocate memory it is imperative to check the value returned by **malloc( )** to make sure that it is not null before using the pointer. Using a null pointer may crash the computer. The proper way to allocate memory and test for a valid pointer is illustrated in this code fragment:

```
int *p;
if((p = (int *) malloc(100))==NULL) {
  printf("Out of memory.\n");
  exit(1);
}
```

The macro **NULL** is defined in **<stdlib.h>**. Of course, you can substitute some sort of error handler in place of **exit( )**. The point is that you do not want the pointer **p** to be used if it is null.

You should include the header **<stdlib.h>** at the top of any file that uses **malloc( )** and **free( )** because it contains their prototypes.

Understanding const Pointers

The **const** qualifier was introduced in Chapter 2, where it was used to create variables
that could not be changed (by the program) after they were created. However, there is
a second use of **const** that relates to pointers. The **const** qualifier can be used to prevent
the object pointed to by an argument to a function from being modified by that function.
That is, when a pointer is passed to a function, that function can modify the object
pointed to by the pointer. However, if the pointer is specified as **const** in the parameter
declaration, the function code won't be able to modify the object. For example, the
sp_to_dash( ) function in the following program prints a dash for each space in its
string argument. That is, the string "this is a test" will be printed as "this-is-a-test". The
use of **const** in the parameter declaration ensures that the code inside the function
cannot modify the object pointed to by the parameter.

```
#include <stdio.h>

void sp_to_dash(const char *str);

int main(void)
{
  sp_to_dash("this is a test");

  return 0;
}

void sp_to_dash(const char *str)
{
  while(*str) {
    if(*str == ' ') printf("%c", '-');
    else printf("%c", *str);
    str++;
  }
}
```

If you had written **sp_to_dash( )** in such a way that the string would be modified, it
would not compile. For example, if you had coded **sp_to_dash( )** as follows, you would
receive a compile-time error:

```
/* This is wrong. */
void sp_to_dash(const char *str)
```

```
{
  while(*str) {
    if(*str == ' ') *str = '-'; /* can't do this */
    printf("%c", *str);
    str++;
  }
}
```

Many functions in the standard library use **const** in their parameter declarations. Doing so ensures that no changes to the argument pointed to by a parameter will occur.

Pointers and Arrays

There is a close relationship between pointers and arrays. Consider this fragment:

```
char str[80], *p1;
p1 = str;
```

Here, **p1** has been set to the address of the first array element in **str**. If you wanted to access the fifth element in **str**, you could write

```
str[4]
```

or

```
*(p1+4)
```

Both statements return the fifth element. Remember, arrays start at 0, so a 4 is used to index **str**. You add 4 to the pointer **p1** to get the fifth element because **p1** currently points to the first element of **str**. (Recall that an array name without an index returns the starting address of the array, which is the first element.)

In essence, C/C++ allows two methods of accessing array elements. This is important because pointer arithmetic can be faster than array-indexing. Since speed is often a consideration in programming, the use of pointers to access array elements is very common.

To see an example of how pointers can be used in place of array-indexing, consider these two simplified versions of the **puts( )** standard library function—one with array-indexing and one with pointers. The **puts( )** function writes a string to the standard output device.

```
/* Use array. */
int puts(const char *s)
{
  register int t;

  for(t=0; s[t]; ++t) putchar(s[t]);
  return 1;
}

/* Use pointer. */
int puts(const char *s)
{
  while(*s) putchar(*s++);
  return 1;
}
```

Most professional C/C++ programmers would find the second version easier to read and understand. In fact, the pointer version is the way routines of this sort are commonly written.

Pointers to Character Arrays

String operations in C are usually performed by using pointers and pointer arithmetic because strings tend to be accessed in a sequential fashion.

For example, here is one version of the standard library function **strcmp( )** that uses pointers:

```
/* Use pointers. */
int strcmp(const char *s1, const char *s2)
{
  while(*s1)
    if(*s1-*s2)
      return *s1-*s2;
    else {
      s1++;
      s2++;
    }
  return 0; /* equal */
}
```

Remember, strings in C are terminated by a null, which is a false value. Therefore, a statement such as

```
while (*s1)
```

continues to iterate until the end of the string is reached. Here, **strcmp( )** returns 0 if **s1** is equal to **s2**. It returns less than 0 if **s1** is less than **s2**; otherwise, it returns greater than 0.

Most string functions resemble **strcmp( )** with regard to the way it uses pointers, especially where loop control is concerned. Using pointers is faster, more efficient, and often easier to understand than using array-indexing.

One common error that sometimes creeps in when using pointers is illustrated by the following program:

```
/* This program is incorrect. */

#include <stdio.h>
#include <string.h>

int main(void)
{
  char *p1, s[80];

  p1 = s;  /* assign p1 the starting address of s */
  do {
    printf("\nEnter string: ");
    gets(s);  /* read a string */

    /* print the decimal equivalent of each
       character */
    while(*p1) printf(" %d", *p1++);

  } while(strcmp(s, "done"));
  return 0;
}
```

Can you find the error in this program?

The problem is that **p1** is assigned the address of **s** only once—outside the loop. The first time through the loop, **p1** does point to the first character in **s**. However, in the second (and subsequent iterations), it continues from where it left off, because it is not reset to the start of the array **s**. The proper way to write this program is

```
/* This program is correct. */

#include <stdio.h>
#include <string.h>
```

```
int main(void)
{
  char *p1, s[80];

  do {
    p1 = s; /* assign p1 the starting address of s */
    printf("\nEnter string: ");
    gets(s);  /* read a string */

    /* print the decimal equivalent of each
       character */
    while(*p1) printf(" %d", *p1++);

  } while(strcmp(s, "done"));
  return 0;
}
```

Here, each time the loop iterates, **p1** is set to the start of string **s**.

Arrays of Pointers

Pointers can be arrayed like any other data type. The declaration for an **int** pointer array of size 10 is

```
int *x[10];
```

To assign the address of an integer variable called **var** to the third element of the array, you would write:

```
x[2] = &var;
```

To find the value of **var**, you would write

```
*x[2]
```

If you want to pass an array of pointers into a function, you can use the same method used for other arrays—simply call the function with the array name without any indexes. For example, a function that could receive array **x** would look like:

```
void display_array(int *q[])
{
```

```
int t;

for(t=0; t<10; t++)
  printf("%d ", *q[t]);
}
```

Remember, **q** is not a pointer to integers, but to an array of pointers to integers. Therefore it is necessary to declare the parameter **q** as an array of integer pointers as shown here. You cannot declare **q** simply as an integer pointer because that is not what it is.

A common use of pointer arrays is to hold pointers to error messages. You can create a function that outputs a message given its code number, as shown here:

```
void serror(int num)
{
  static char *err[] = {
    "Cannot Open File\n",
    "Read Error\n",
    "Write Error\n",
    "Media Failure\n"
  };

  printf("%s", err[num]);
}
```

As you can see, **printf( )** inside **serror( )** is called with a character pointer that points to one of the various error messages indexed by the error number passed to the function. For example, if **num** is passed a 2, the message "Write Error" is displayed.

As a point of interest, note that the command line argument **argv** is an array of character pointers.

Pointers to Pointers: Multiple Indirection

The concept of arrays of pointers is straightforward because the indexes keep the meaning clear. However, cases in which one pointer points to another can be very confusing. A pointer to a pointer is a form of *multiple indirection,* or a chain of pointers. Consider Figure 6-3.

In the case of a normal pointer, the value of the pointer is the address of the location that contains the value desired. In the case of a pointer to a pointer, the first pointer contains the address of the second pointer, which contains the address of the location that contains the value desired.

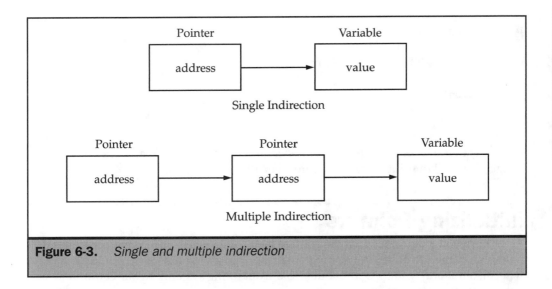

Figure 6-3.   *Single and multiple indirection*

Multiple indirection can be carried on to whatever extent desired, but there are few cases where using more than a pointer to a pointer is necessary, or even wise. Excessive indirection is difficult to follow and prone to conceptual errors. (Do not confuse multiple indirection with linked lists, which are used in databases.)

A variable that is a pointer to a pointer must be declared as such. This is done by placing an additional asterisk in front of its name. For example, this declaration tells the compiler that **newbalance** is a pointer to a pointer of type **float**.

```
float **newbalance;
```

It is important to understand that **newbalance** is not a pointer to a floating-point number but rather a pointer to a **float** pointer.

In order to access the target value indirectly pointed to by a pointer to a pointer, the asterisk operator must be applied twice, as is shown in this short example:

```
#include <stdio.h>

int main(void)
{
  int x, *p, **q;

  x = 10;
  p = &x;
```

```
   q = &p;

   printf("%d", **q); /* print the value of x */

   return 0;
}
```

Here, **p** is declared as a pointer to an integer, and **q** as a pointer to a pointer to an integer. The call to **printf( )** prints the number 10 on the screen.

Initializing Pointers

After a pointer is declared, but before it has been assigned a value, it may contain an unknown value. If you try to use the pointer prior to giving it a value, you probably will crash not only your program but also the operating system of your computer—a very nasty type of error!

By convention, a pointer that is pointing nowhere should be given the value null to signify that it points to nothing. However, just because a pointer has a null value does not make it "safe." If you use a null pointer on the left side of an assignment statement, you still risk crashing your program or operating system.

Because a null pointer is assumed to be unused, you can use the null pointer to make many of your pointer routines easier to code and more efficient. For example, you could use a null pointer to mark the end of a pointer array. If this is done, a routine that accesses that array knows that it has reached the end when the null value is encountered. This type of approach is illustrated by the **search( )** function shown here:

```
/* Look up a name. */
int search(char *p[], char *name)
{
  register int t;
  for(t=0; p[t]; ++t)
    if(!strcmp(p[t], name)) return t;

  return -1; /* not found */
}
```

The **for** loop inside **search( )** runs until either a match or a null pointer is found. Assuming the end of the array is marked with a null, the condition controlling the loop fails when it is reached.

It is common in professionally written programs to initialize strings. You saw an example of this in the **serror( )** function shown earlier. Another variation on this theme is the following type of string declaration:

```
char *p = "hello world\n";
```

As you can see, the pointer **p** is not an array. The reason this sort of initialization works has to do with the way the compiler operates. All C/C++ compilers create what is called a *string table,* which is used internally by the compiler to store the string constants used by the program. Therefore, this declaration statement places the address of "hello world" into the pointer **p**. Throughout the program **p** can be used like any other string. For example, the following program is perfectly valid:

```
#include <stdio.h>
#include <string.h>

char *p = "hello world\n";

int main(void)
{
  register int t;

  /* print the string forward and backwards */
  printf(p);
  for(t=strlen(p)-1; t>-1; t--) printf("%c", p[t]);
  return 0;
}
```

Pointers to Functions

In Chapter 4, you were introduced to a particularly confusing yet powerful feature, the *function pointer.* Even though a function is not a variable, it still has a physical location in memory that can be assigned to a pointer. A function's address is the entry point of the function. Because of this a function pointer can be used to call a function. In this section, we will take another look at the function pointer.

In certain types of programs, the user can select one option from a long list of possible actions. For example, in an accounting program, you may be presented with a menu that has 20 or more selections. Once the selection has been made, the routine that routes program execution to the proper function can be handled two ways. The most common way is to use a **switch** statement. However, in applications that demand the highest performance there is a better way. An array of pointers can be created with each pointer in the array containing the address of a function. The selection made by the user is decoded and used to index into the pointer array, causing the proper function to be executed. This method can be very fast—much faster than the **switch** method.

To see how an array of function pointers can be used as described, imagine that you are implementing a very simple inventory system that is capable of entering, deleting, and reviewing data, as well as exiting to the operating system. If the functions that perform these activities are called **enter( )**, **del( )**, **review( )**, and **quit( )**, respectively, the following fragment correctly initializes an array of function pointers to these functions:

```
void enter(void), del(void), review(void), quit(void);
int menu(void);

void (*options[])(void) = {
  enter,
  del,
  review,
  quit
} ;
```

Pay special attention to the way an array of function pointers is declared. Notice the placement of the parentheses and square brackets.

Although the actual inventory routines are not developed, the following program illustrates the proper way to execute the functions by using the function pointers. Notice how the **menu( )** function automatically returns the proper index into the pointer array.

```
#include <stdlib.h>
#include <stdio.h>
#include <conio.h>
#include <string.h>

void enter(void), del(void), review(void), quit(void);
int menu(void);

void (*options[])(void) = {
  enter,
  del,
  review,
  quit
} ;

int main(void)
{
  int i;

  i = menu(); /* get user's choice */

  (*options[i])();  /* execute it */
```

```
    return 0;

}

int menu(void)
{
  char ch;

  do {

    printf("1. Enter\n");
    printf("2. Delete\n");
    printf("3. Review\n");
    printf("4. Quit\n");
    printf("Select a number: ");
    ch = getche();
    printf("\n");
  } while(!strchr("1234", ch));
  return ch-49; /* convert to an integer equivalent */
}

void enter(void)
{
  printf("\nIn enter.");
}

void del(void)
{
  printf("\nIn del.");
}

void review(void)
{
  printf("\nIn review.");
}

void quit(void)
{
  printf("\nIn quit.");
  exit(0);
}
```

The program works like this. The menu is displayed, and the user enters the number of the selection desired. Since the number is in ASCII, 49 (the decimal value of 0) is subtracted from it in order to convert it into a binary integer. This value is then returned to **main( )** and is used as an index to **options**, the array of function pointers. Next, the call to the proper function is executed.

Using arrays of function pointers is very common, not only in interpreters and compilers but also in database programs, because often these programs provide a large number of options and efficiency is important.

Problems with Pointers

Nothing will get you into more trouble than a wild pointer! Pointers are a mixed blessing. They give you tremendous power and are necessary for many programs. But when a pointer accidentally contains a wrong value, it can be the most difficult bug to track down. The trouble is that the pointer itself is not the problem; the problem is that each time you perform an operation using it, you are reading or writing to some unknown piece of memory. If you read from it, the worst that can happen is that you get garbage. If you write to it, you might be writing over other pieces of your code or data. In either case, the problem might not show up until later in the execution of your program, and may lead you to look for the bug in the wrong place. There may be little or no evidence to suggest that the pointer is the problem.

Because pointer errors are so troublesome, you should do your best never to generate one. Toward this end, two of the more common errors are discussed here.

The classic example of a pointer error is the *uninitialized pointer*. For example:

```
/* This program is wrong. */

int main(void)
{
  int x, *p;

  x = 10;
  *p = x;

  return 0;
}
```

This program assigns the value 10 to some unknown memory location. The pointer **p** has never been given a value; therefore it contains an indeterminate (i.e., garbage) value. This type of problem often goes unnoticed when your program is very small because the odds are in favor of **p** containing a "safe" address—one that is not in your code, data, stack, heap, or operating system. However, as your program grows, so does the probability of **p** pointing into something vital. Eventually your program stops working. The solution to this sort of trouble is obvious: make sure that a pointer is always pointing at something valid before it is used. Although the mistake is easy to catch in this simple case, frequently uninitialized pointers (or, incorrectly initialized ones) occur in a way that is not as easy to find.

A second common error is caused by a simple misunderstanding of how to use a pointer. For example, this program is fundamentally wrong.

```c
#include <stdio.h>

/* This program is wrong. */
int main(void)
{
  int x, *p;

  x = 10;
  p = x;
  printf("%d", *p);

  return 0;
}
```

The call to **printf( )** does not print the value of **x**, which is 10, on the screen. It prints some unknown value because the assignment

```c
p = x;
```

is wrong. That statement has assigned the value 10 to the pointer **p**, which was supposed to contain an address, not a value. Fortunately, the error in this program is caught by C++ Builder. The compiler issues a warning message that tells you that a nonportable pointer conversion is taking place. This is your clue that a pointer error might have been made—which is the case in this example. To make the program correct, you should write

```c
p = &x;
```

Although C++ Builder reported a warning for the mistake in this program, you can't always count on it for help. These types of errors can occur in convoluted, roundabout ways that escape detection. So, be careful.

The fact that pointers can cause very tricky bugs if handled incorrectly is no reason to avoid using them. Simply be careful and make sure that you know where each pointer is pointing before using it.

THE FOUNDATION OF C++

Borland
C++
Builder

Chapter 7

Structures, Unions, and User-Defined Types

The C language gives you five ways to create a custom data type:

1. The *structure*, which is a grouping of variables under one name and is called a *compound* data type.(The terms *aggregate* or *conglomerate* are also commonly used.)
2. The *bit-field*, which is a variation on the structure and allows easy access to individual bits.
3. The *union*, which enables the same piece of memory to be defined as two or more different types of variables.
4. The *enumeration*, which is a list of named integer constants.
5. The **typedef** keyword, which defines a new name for an existing type.

C++ supports all of these and adds classes, which are described in Part Three. The other methods of creating custom data types are described here.

> **Note**
>
> *In C++, structures and unions have both object-oriented and non-object-oriented attributes. This chapter discusses only their C-like, non-object-oriented features. Their object-oriented qualities are described later in this book.*

Structures

A *structure* is a collection of variables that are referenced under one name, providing a convenient means of keeping related information together. A *structure declaration* forms a template that can be used to create structure objects. The variables that make up the structure are called *members* of the structure. (Structure members are also commonly referred to as *elements* or *fields*.)

Usually, the members of a structure are logically related. For example, the name and address information found in a mailing list is normally represented as a structure. The following code fragment declares a structure template that defines the name and address fields of such a structure. The keyword **struct** tells the compiler that a structure is being declared.

```
struct addr {
  char name[30];
  char street[40];
  char city[20];
  char state[3];
  char zip[11];
  int customer_num;
};
```

The declaration is terminated by a semicolon because a structure declaration is a statement. Also, the structure name **addr** identifies this particular data structure and is its type specifier. The structure name is often referred to as its *tag*.

At this point, *no variable has actually been declared.* Only the form of the data has been defined. To declare a variable with this structure, you would write

```
struct addr addr_info;
```

This declares a variable of type **addr** called **addr_info**. When you declare a structure, you are defining a compound variable type, not a variable. Not until you declare a variable of that type does one actually exist.

When a structure variable is declared, the compiler automatically allocates sufficient memory to accommodate all of its members. Figure 7-1 shows how **addr_info** appears in memory.

You may also declare one or more variables at the same time that you declare a structure. For example,

```
struct addr {
  char name[30];
  char street[40];
  char city[20];
  char state[3];
  char zip[11];
  int customer_num;
} addr_info, binfo, cinfo;
```

declares a structure type called **addr** and declares variables **addr_info**, **binfo**, and **cinfo** of that type.

It is important to understand that each structure variable that you create contains its own copies of the variables that make up the structure. For example, the **zip** field of **binfo** is separate and distinct from the **zip** field in **cinfo**. In fact, the only relationship that **binfo** and **cinfo** have with each other is that they are both instances of the same type of structure. There is no other linkage between the two.

name	30 bytes	
street	40 bytes	
city	20 bytes	addr_info
state	3 bytes	
zip	11 bytes	
customer_num	4 bytes	

Figure 7-1.   *The **addr_info** structure as it appears in memory*

If you need only one structure variable, the structure tag is not needed. This means that

```
struct {
  char name[30];
  char street[40];
  char city[20];
  char state[3];
  char zip[11];
  int customer_num;
} addr_info;
```

declares one variable named **addr_info** as defined by the structure preceding it.
The general form of a structure declaration is

```
struct tag {
  type member-name;
  type member-name;
  type member-name;
  
  .
  .
  .
} structure-variables;
```

The *tag* is the type name of the structure—not a variable name. The *structure-variables* are a comma-separated list of variable names. Remember, either *tag* or *structure-variables* is optional, but not both.

Accessing Structure Members

Individual structure members are accessed through the use of the . (usually called the "dot") operator. For example, the following code statement assigns the value 88 to the **customer_num** field of the structure variable **addr_info** declared earlier:

```
addr_info.customer_num = 88;
```

The structure variable name followed by a period and the member name references that individual element. All structure members are accessed in the same way. The general form is

structure-name.member-name

Therefore, to print the customer number to the screen, you could write

```
printf("%d", addr_info.customer_num);
```

This prints the customer number contained in the **customer_num** variable of the structure variable **addr_info**.

In the same fashion, the **addr_info.name** character array can be used with **gets( )** as shown here:

```
gets(addr_info.name);
```

This passes a character pointer to the start of **name**.

To access the individual characters of **addr_info.name**, you can index **name**. For example, you can print the contents of **addr_info.name** one character at a time by using this code:

```
register int t;
for(t=0; addr_info.name[t]; ++t) putchar(addr_info.name[t]);
```

Structure Assignments

The information contained in one structure can be assigned to another structure of the same type using a single assignment statement. That is, you do not need to assign the value of each member separately. The following program illustrates structure assignments.

```
#include <stdio.h>

int main(void)
{
  struct {
    int a;
    int b;
  } x, y;

  x.a = 10;
  x.b = 20;

  y = x; /* assign one structure to another */
  printf("Contents of y: %d %d.", y.a, y.b);

  return 0;
}
```

After the assignment, **y.a** and **y.b** will contain the values 10 and 20, respectively.

Arrays of Structures

Perhaps the most common use of structures is in *arrays of structures*. To declare an array of structures, you must first define a structure, and then declare an array variable of that type. For example, to declare a 100-element array of structures of type **addr**, which was declared earlier in this chapter, you would write

```
struct addr addr_info[100];
```

This creates 100 sets of variables that are organized as declared in the structure type **addr**.

To access a specific structure within the **addr_info** array, index the array variable name. For example, to print the ZIP code of the third structure, you would write

```
printf("%s", addr_info[2].zip);
```

Like all array variables, arrays of structures begin indexing at 0.

An Inventory Example

To help illustrate how structures and arrays of structures are used, consider a simple inventory program that uses an array of structures to hold the inventory information. The functions in this program interact with structures and their members in various ways to illustrate structure usage.

In this example, the information to be stored includes

- item name
- cost
- number on hand

You can define the basic data structure, called **inv**, to hold this information as

```
#define MAX 100

struct inv {
  char item[30];
  float cost;
  int on_hand;
} inv_info[MAX];
```

In the **inv** structure, **item** is used to hold each inventoried item's name. The **cost** member contains the item's cost, and **on_hand** represents the number of items currently available.

The first function needed for the program is **main( )**.

```
int main(void)
{
  char choice;

  init_list(); /* initialize the structure array */
  for(;;) {
    choice = menu_select();
    switch(choice) {
      case 1: enter();
        break;
      case 2: del();
        break;
      case 3: list();
        break;
      case 4: return 0;
    }
  }
}
```

In **main( )**, the call to **init_list( )** prepares the structure array for use by putting a null character into the first byte of each **item** field. The program assumes that a structure is not in use if the **item** field is empty. The **init_list( )** function is defined as follows.

```
/* Initialize the structure array. */
void init_list(void)
{
  register int t;

  for(t=0; t<MAX; ++t) inv_info[t].item[0] = '\0';
}
```

The **menu_select( )** function displays the option messages and returns the user's selection:

```
/* Input the user's selection. */
int menu_select(void)
{
  char s[80];
  int c;
```

```
  printf("\n");
  printf("1. Enter an item\n");
  printf("2. Remove an item\n");
  printf("3. List the inventory\n");
  printf("4. Quit\n");
  do {
    printf("\nEnter your choice: ");
    gets(s);
    c = atoi(s);
  } while(c<0 || c>4);
  return c;
}
```

The **enter( )** function prompts the user for input and places the information entered into the next free structure. If the array is full, the message "List Full" is printed on the screen. The function **find_free( )** searches the structure array for an unused element.

```
/* Input the inventory information. */
void enter(void)
{
  int slot;

  slot = find_free();
  if(slot == -1) {
    printf("\nList Full");
    return;
  }

  printf("Enter item: ");
  gets(inv_info[slot].item);

  printf("Enter cost: ");
  scanf("%f", &inv_info[slot].cost);

  printf("Enter number on hand: ");
  scanf("%d%*c",&inv_info[slot].on_hand);
}

/* Return the index of the first unused array
   location or -1 if no free locations exist.
*/
int find_free(void)
{
```

```
  register int t;

  for(t=0; inv_info[t].item[0] && t<MAX; ++t) ;
  if(t == MAX) return -1; /* no slots free */
  return t;
}
```

Notice that **find_free( )** returns a −1 if every structure array variable is in use. This is a "safe" number to use because there cannot be a −1 element of the **inv_info** array.

The **del( )** function requires the user to specify the number of the item that needs to be deleted. The function then puts a null character in the first character position of the **item** field.

```
/* Remove an item from the list. */
void del(void)
{
  register int slot;
  char s[80];

  printf("enter record #: ");
  gets(s);
  slot = atoi(s);
  if(slot >= 0 && slot < MAX) inv_info[slot].item[0] = '\0';
}
```

The final function the program needs is **list( )**. It prints the entire inventory list on the screen.

```
/* Display the list on the screen. */
void list(void)
{
  register int t;

  for(t=0; t<MAX; ++t) {
    if(inv_info[t].item[0]) {
      printf("Item: %s\n", inv_info[t].item);
      printf("Cost: %f\n", inv_info[t].cost);
      printf("On hand: %d\n\n", inv_info[t].on_hand);
    }
  }
  printf("\n\n");
}
```

The complete listing for the inventory program is shown here. If you have any doubts about your understanding of structures, you should enter this program into your computer and study its execution by making changes and watching their effects.

```c
/* A simple inventory program using an array of structures */

#include <stdio.h>
#include <stdlib.h>

#define MAX 100

struct inv {
  char item[30];
  float cost;
  int on_hand;
} inv_info[MAX];

void init_list(void), list(void), del(void);
void enter(void);
int menu_select(void), find_free(void);

int main(void)
{
  char choice;

  init_list(); /* initialize the structure array */
  for(;;) {
    choice = menu_select();
    switch(choice) {
      case 1: enter();
        break;
      case 2: del();
        break;
      case 3: list();
        break;
      case 4: return 0;
    }
  }
}

/* Initialize the structure array. */
void init_list(void)
```

```
{
  register int t;

  for(t=0; t<MAX; ++t) inv_info[t].item[0] = '\0';
}

/* Input the user's selection. */
int menu_select(void)
{
  char s[80];
  int c;

  printf("\n");
  printf("1. Enter an item\n");
  printf("2. Remove an item\n");
  printf("3. List the inventory\n");
  printf("4. Quit\n");
  do {
    printf("\nEnter your choice: ");
    gets(s);
    c = atoi(s);
  } while(c<0 || c>4);
  return c;
}

/* Input the inventory information. */
void enter(void)
{
  int slot;

  slot = find_free();
  if(slot == -1) {
    printf("\nList Full");
    return;
  }

  printf("Enter item: ");
  gets(inv_info[slot].item);

  printf("Enter cost: ");
  scanf("%f", &inv_info[slot].cost);
```

```
  printf("Enter number on hand: ");
  scanf("%d%*c", &inv_info[slot].on_hand);
}

/* Return the index of the first unused array
   location or -1 if no free locations exist.
*/
int find_free(void)
{
  register int t;

  for(t=0; inv_info[t].item[0] && t<MAX; ++t) ;
  if(t == MAX) return -1; /* no slots free */
  return t;
}

/* Remove an item from the list. */
void del(void)
{
  register int slot;
  char s[80];

  printf("enter record #: ");
  gets(s);
  slot = atoi(s);
  if(slot >= 0 && slot < MAX) inv_info[slot].item[0] = '\0';
}

/* Display the list on the screen. */
void list(void)
{
  register int t;

  for(t=0; t<MAX; ++t) {
    if(inv_info[t].item[0]) {
      printf("Item: %s\n", inv_info[t].item);
      printf("Cost: %f\n", inv_info[t].cost);
      printf("On hand: %d\n\n", inv_info[t].on_hand);
    }
  }
  printf("\n\n");
}
```

Passing Structures to Functions

So far, all structures and arrays of structures used in the examples have been assumed to be either global or defined within the function that uses them. In this section special consideration will be given to passing structures and their members to functions.

Passing Structure Members to Functions

When you pass a member of a structure to a function, you are actually passing the value of that member to the function. Therefore, you are passing a simple variable (unless, of course, that element is compound, such as an array of characters). For example, consider this structure:

```
struct fred {
  char x;
  int y;
  float z;
  char s[10];
} mike;
```

Here are examples of each member being passed to a function:

```
func(mike.x);     /* passes character value of x */
func2(mike.y);    /* passes integer value of y */
func3(mike.z);    /* passes float value of z */
func4(mike.s);    /* passes address of string s */
func(mike.s[2]); /* passes character value of s[2] */
```

If you wanted to pass the address of an individual structure member to achieve call-by-reference parameter passing, you would place the **&** operator before the structure name. For example, to pass the address of the elements in the structure **mike**, you would write

```
func(&mike.x);     /* passes address of character x */
func2(&mike.y);    /* passes address of integer y */
func3(&mike.z);    /* passes address of float z */
func4(mike.s);     /* passes address of string s */
func(&mike.s[2]); /* passes address of character s[2] */
```

Notice that the **&** operator precedes the structure name, not the individual member name. Note also that the array **s** already signifies an address, so that no **&** is required. However, when accessing a specific character in string **s**, as shown in the final example, the **&** is still needed.

Passing Entire Structures to Functions

When a structure is used as an argument to a function, the entire structure is passed using the standard call-by-value method. This means that any changes made to the contents of the structure inside the function to which it is passed do not affect the structure used as an argument.

When using a structure as a parameter, the most important thing to remember is that the type of the argument must match the type of the parameter. The best way to do this is to define a structure globally and then use its tag name to declare structure variables and parameters as needed. For example:

```c
#include <stdio.h>

/* declare a structure type */
struct struct_type {
  int a, b;
  char ch;
};

void f1(struct struct_type parm);

int main(void)
{
  struct struct_type arg;  /* declare arg */

  arg.a = 1000;
  f1(arg);

  return 0;
}

void f1(struct struct_type parm)
{
  printf("%d", parm.a);
}
```

This program prints the number 1000 on the screen. As you can see, both **arg** and **parm** are declared to be structures of type **struct_type**.

Structure Pointers

C/C++ allows pointers to structures in the same way it does to other types of variables. However, there are some special aspects to structure pointers that you must keep in mind.

Declaring a Structure Pointer

Structure pointers are declared by placing the * in front of a structure variable's name. For example, assuming the previously defined structure **addr**, the following declares **addr_pointer** to be a pointer to data of that type:

```
struct addr *addr_pointer;
```

Using Structure Pointers

To find the address of a structure variable, the **&** operator is placed before the structure's name. For example, given the following fragment,

```
struct bal {
  float balance;
  char name[80];
} person;

struct bal *p;  /* declare a structure pointer */
```

then

```
p = &person;
```

places the address of the structure **person** into the pointer **p**.

To access the members of a structure using a pointer to that structure, you must use the *arrow operator*. The arrow operator, −>, is formed using a minus sign and a greater-than symbol. For example, to reference the **balance** member using **p**, you would write

```
p->balance
```

To see how structure pointers can be used, examine this simple program that prints the hours, minutes, and seconds on the screen using a software timer. (The timing of the program is adjusted by changing the definition of **DELAY** to fit the speed of your computer.)

```c
/* Display a software timer. */

#include <stdio.h>
#include <conio.h>

#define DELAY 128000

struct my_time {
  int hours;
  int minutes;
  int seconds;
};

void update(struct my_time *t), display(struct my_time *t);
void mydelay(void);

int main(void)
{
  struct my_time systime;

  systime.hours = 0;
  systime.minutes = 0;
  systime.seconds = 0;

  for(;;) {
    update(&systime);
    display(&systime);
    if(kbhit()) return 0;
  }
}

void update(struct my_time *t)
{
  t->seconds++;
  if(t->seconds==60) {
    t->seconds = 0;
    t->minutes++;
  }
```

```
    if(t->minutes==60) {
      t->minutes = 0;
      t->hours++;
    }
    if(t->hours==24) t->hours = 0;
    mydelay();
}

void display(struct my_time *t)
{
  printf("%02d:", t->hours);
  printf("%02d:", t->minutes);
  printf("%02d\n", t->seconds);
}

void mydelay(void)
{
  long int t;

  for(t=1; t<DELAY; ++t) ;
}
```

A global structure called **my_time** is declared. Inside **main( )**, the structure variable called **systime,** of type **my_time,** is declared and initialized to 00:00:00. This means that **systime** is known directly only to the **main( )** function.

The functions **update( )**, which changes the time, and **display( )**, which prints the time, are passed the address of **systime**. In both functions the argument is declared to be a pointer to a structure of type **my_time**. Inside the functions, each structure element is actually referenced through a pointer. For example, to set the hours back to 0 when 24:00:00 is reached, this statement is used.

```
    if(t->hours==24) t->hours = 0;
```

This line of code tells the compiler to take the address of **t** (which points to **systime** in **main( )**) and assign 0 to its **hours** member.

Remember *Use the dot operator to access structure members when operating on the structure itself. Use the arrow operator when referencing a structure through a pointer.*

As a final example of using structure pointers, the following program illustrates how a general-purpose integer input function can be designed. The function **input_xy( )** allows you to specify the **x** and **y** coordinates at which a prompting message will be displayed and then inputs an integer value. To accomplish these things it uses the structure **xyinput**.

```c
/* A generalized input example using structure pointers. */

#include <stdio.h>
#include <conio.h>
#include <string.h>

struct xyinput {
  int x, y; /* screen location for prompt */
  char message[80]; /* prompting message */
  int i; /* input value */
} ;

void input_xy(struct xyinput *info);

int main(void)
{
  struct xyinput mess;

  mess.x = 10; mess.y = 10;
  strcpy(mess.message, "Enter an integer: ");
  clrscr();
  input_xy(&mess);
  printf("Your number squared is: %d.", mess.i*mess.i);

  return 0;
}

/* Display a prompting message at the specified location
   and input an integer value.
*/
void input_xy(struct xyinput *info)
{
  gotoxy(info->x, info->y);
  printf(info->message);
  scanf("%d", &info->i);
}
```

The program uses the functions **clrscr( )** and **gotoxy( )** to clear the screen and position the cursor, respectively. Both functions use the **<conio.h>** header file. A function like **input_xy( )** is useful when your program must input many pieces of information. (In fact, you might want to create several functions like **input_xy( )** that input other types of data.)

Arrays and Structures Within Structures

A member of a structure can be either simple or compound. A simple member is any of the built-in data types, such as integer or character. You have already seen a few compound elements. The character array used in **addr_info** is an example. Other compound data types are single- and multidimensional arrays of the other data types and structures.

A member of a structure that is an array is treated as you might expect from the earlier examples. For example, consider this structure:

```
struct x {
  int a[10][10]; /* 10 x 10 array of ints */
  float b;
} y;
```

To reference integer 3,7 in **a** of structure **y**, you would write

```
y.a[3][7]
```

When a structure is a member of another structure, it is called a *nested structure*. For example, here the structure **addr** is nested inside **emp**:

```
struct emp {
  struct addr address;
  float wage;
} worker;
```

Here, a structure **emp** has been declared as having two members. The first is the structure of type **addr**, which contains an employee's address. The other is **wage**, which holds the employee's wage. The following code fragment assigns $65,000 to the **wage** element of **worker** and 98765 to the **zip** field of **address**:

```
worker.wage = 65000.00;
strcpy(worker.address.zip,"98765");
```

As this example shows, the members of each structure are referenced from outermost to innermost (left to right).

Bit-Fields

Unlike most other computer languages, C/C++ has a built-in feature, called a *bit-field*, that allows access to a single bit. Bit-fields are useful for a number of reasons. Here are three:

1. If storage is limited, you can store several Boolean (true/false) variables in one byte.
2. Certain device interfaces transmit information encoded into bits within a single byte.
3. Certain encryption routines need to access the bits within a byte.

Although all these functions can be performed using the bitwise operators, a bit-field can add more structure to your code.

The method C/C++ uses to access bits is based on the structure. A bit-field is really just a special type of structure member that defines how long, in bits, the field is to be. The general form of a bit-field declaration is

```
struct struct-name {
    type name1 : length;
    type name2 : length;
       .
       .
       .
    type nameN : length;
}
```

Here, *type* is the type of the bit-field and *length* is the number of bits in the field. Also, *type* must be an integral type.

Here is a bit-field example:

```
struct device {
  unsigned int active : 1;
  unsigned int ready : 1;
  unsigned int xmt_error : 1;
} dev_code;
```

This structure defines three variables of 1 bit each. The structure variable **dev_code** might be used to decode information from the port of a tape drive, for example. Assuming a hypothetical tape drive, the following code fragment writes a byte of information to the tape and checks for errors using **dev_code** from the preceding code:

```
void wr_tape(char c)
{
  while(!dev_code.ready) rd(&dev_code); /* wait */
  wr_to_tape(c); /* write out byte */

  while(dev_code.active) rd(&dev_code); /* wait until info is written */
  if(dev_code.xmt_error) printf("Write Error");
}
```

Here, **rd( )** returns the status of the tape drive and **wr_to_tape( )** actually writes the data.

Figure 7-2 shows what the bit-field variable **dev_code** looks like in memory.

As you can see from the previous example, each bit-field is accessed using the dot operator. However, if the structure is referenced through a pointer, you must use the −> operator.

You do not have to name each bit-field. This makes it easy to reach the bit you want and pass up unused ones. For example, if the tape drive also returned an end-of-tape flag in bit 5, you could alter the structure **device** to accommodate this, as shown here.

```
struct device {
  unsigned active : 1;
  unsigned ready : 1;
  unsigned xmt_error : 1;
  unsigned : 2;
  unsigned EOT : 1;
} dev_code;
```

Bit-fields have certain restrictions. You cannot take the address of a bit-field variable. Bit-field variables cannot be arrayed. You cannot know, from machine to machine, whether the fields will run from right to left or from left to right; any code that uses bit-fields may have machine dependencies.

Finally, it is valid to mix other structure elements with bit-fields. For example,

```
struct emp {
  struct addr address;
  float pay;
  unsigned lay_off:1;   /* lay off or active */
  unsigned hourly:1;    /* hourly pay or wage */
  unsigned deductions:3; /* IRS deductions */
};
```

defines an employee record that uses only 1 byte to hold three pieces of information: the employee's status, whether the employee is salaried, and the number of deductions. Without the use of the bit-field, this information would have taken 3 bytes.

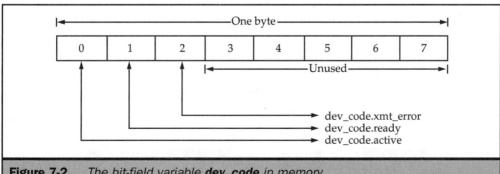

Figure 7-2. *The bit-field variable **dev_code** in memory*

Unions

A **union** is a memory location that is shared by several variables that are of different types. The **union** declaration is similar to that of a structure, as shown in this example:

```
union union_type {
  int i;
  char ch;
} ;
```

As with structures, you may declare a variable either by placing its name at the end of the definition or by using a separate declaration statement. To declare a **union** variable **cnvt** of type **union_type** using the definition just given, you would write

```
union union_type cnvt;
```

In **cnvt**, both integer **i** and character **ch** share the same memory location. Of course, for C++ Builder, **i** occupies 4 bytes and **ch** uses only 1. Figure 7-3 shows how **i** and **ch** share the same address. At any time, you can refer to the data stored in **cnvt** as either an integer or a character.

When a **union** is declared, the compiler automatically creates a variable large enough to hold the largest variable type in the **union**.

To access a **union** member, use the same syntax that you would use for structures: the dot and arrow operators. If you are operating on the **union** directly, use the dot operator. If the **union** variable is accessed through a pointer, use the arrow operator. For example, to assign the integer 10 to element **i** of **cnvt**, you would write

```
cnvt.i = 10;
```

Unions are used frequently when type conversions are needed because you can refer to the data held in the union in fundamentally different ways. For example, using a **union** you can easily create a function that writes the binary representation of an integer to a file, one byte at a time. For C++ Builder, which uses 32-bit integers, this means writing the four bytes that form the integer. Although there are many ways to

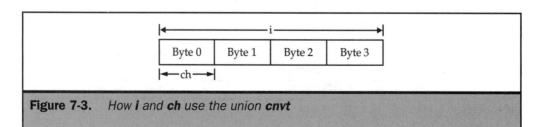

Figure 7-3. *How **i** and **ch** use the union **cnvt***

code such a function, here is one way to do it using a **union**. First, a **union** composed of one integer and a 4-byte character array is created:

```
union pw {
  int i;
  char ch[4];
};
```

This union will let you access the four bytes that make up an interger as four individual characters. Now, you can use **pw** to create the **write_int( )** function shown in the following program.

```
#include <stdio.h>
#include <stdlib>

union pw {
  int i;
  char ch[4];
};

int write_int(int num, FILE *fp);

int main()
{
  FILE *fp;

  fp = fopen("test.tmp", "w+");
  if(fp==NULL) {
    printf("Cannot open file.\n");
    exit(1);
  }
  write_int(1000, fp);
  fclose(fp);

  return 0;
}

/* write an integer using union */
int write_int(int num, FILE *fp)
{
  union pw wrd;

  wrd.i = num;
  putc(wrd.ch[0], fp); /* write first byte */
```

```
    putc(wrd.ch[1], fp); /* write second byte */
    putc(wrd.ch[2], fp); /* write third byte */
    return putc(wrd.ch[3], fp); /* writes last byte */
}
```

Although called with an integer, **write_int( )** uses the **union** to write all four bytes (remember you are dealing with 32-bit integers—4 bytes in total) of the integer to the disk file.

Enumerations

An *enumeration* is a set of named integer constants that specifies all the legal values that a variable of its type can have. Enumerations are common in everyday life. For example, an enumeration of the coins used in the United States is

penny, nickel, dime, quarter, half-dollar, dollar

Enumerations are defined by using the keyword **enum** to signal the start of an enumeration type. The general form is

enum *tag* { *enumeration-list* } *variable-list*;

Both the enumeration name *tag* and the *variable-list* are optional, but one of them must be present. The *enumeration-list* is a comma-separated list of identifiers. As with structures, the tag is used to declare variables of its type. The following fragment defines an enumeration called **coin** and declares **money** to be of that type:

```
enum coin { penny, nickel, dime, quarter,
            half_dollar, dollar};

enum coin money;
```

Given this definition and declaration, the following types of statements are perfectly valid:

```
money = dime;
if(money==quarter) printf("is a quarter\n");
```

The key point to understand about an enumeration is that each of the symbols stands for an integer value and can be used in any integer expression. For example,

```
printf("The value of quarter is %d ", quarter);
```

is perfectly valid.

Unless initialized otherwise, the value of the first enumeration symbol is 0, the second is 1, and so forth. Therefore,

```
printf("%d %d", penny, dime);
```

displays **0 2** on the screen.

It is possible to specify the value of one or more of the symbols by using an initializer. This is done by following the symbol with an equal sign and an integer value. Whenever an initializer is used, symbols that appear after it are assigned values greater than the previous initialization value. For example, the following assigns the value of 100 to **quarter**.

```
enum coin { penny, nickel, dime, quarter=100,
            half_dollar, dollar};
```

Now, the values of these symbols are

penny	0
nickel	1
dime	2
quarter	100
half_dollar	101
dollar	102

Using initializations, more than one element of an enumeration can have the same value.

A common misconception is that the symbols of an enumeration can be input and output directly, but this is not true. For example, the following code fragment will not perform as desired:

```
/* This will not work. */
money = dollar;
printf("%s", money);
```

Remember that the symbol **dollar** is simply a name for an integer; it is not a string. Hence, it is not possible for **printf( )** to display the string "dollar" using the value in

money. Likewise, you cannot give an enumeration variable a value using a string equivalent. That is, this code does not work:

```
/* This code will not work. */
money = "penny";
```

Actually, creating code to input and output enumeration symbols is quite tedious (unless you are willing to settle for their integer values). For example, the following code is needed to display, in words, the kind of coins that **money** contains:

```
switch(money) {
  case penny: printf("penny");
    break;
  case nickel: printf("nickel");
    break;
  case dime: printf("dime");
    break;
  case quarter: printf("quarter");
    break;
  case half_dollar: printf("half_dollar");
    break;
  case dollar: printf("dollar");
}
```

Sometimes, it is possible to declare an array of strings and use the enumeration value as an index to translate an enumeration value into its corresponding string. For example, this code also outputs the proper string:

```
char name[][12]={
  "penny",
  "nickel",
  "dime",
  "quarter",
  "half_dollar",
  "dollar"
};
/* ... */
printf("%s", name[money]);
```

Of course, this works only if no initializations are used, because the string array must be indexed starting at 0.

Since enumeration values must be converted manually to their human-readable string values for human I/O, they are most useful in routines that do not make such conversions. For example, an enumeration is commonly used to define a compiler's symbol table.

An Important Difference Between C and C++

There is an important difference between C and C++ as it relates to the type names of structures, unions, and enumerations. In C, to declare a structure, you would use the following statement

```
struct addr addr_info;
```

where **addr** is the *tag*. As you can see, the tag name **addr** is preceded with the keyword **struct**. However in C++, you can use this shorter form:

```
addr addr_info;    /* OK for C++, wrong for C */
```

Here, the keyword **struct** is not needed. In C++, once a structure has been declared, you can declare variables of its type using only the tag, without preceding it with the keyword **struct**. The reason for this difference is that in C, a structure's name does not define a complete type name. This is why C refers to this name as a tag. However, in C++, a structure's name is a complete type name and can be used by itself to define variables. Keep in mind, however, that it is still okay to use the C-style declaration in a C++ program. The preceding discussion also holds true for the use of **union** and **enum**.

Using sizeof to Ensure Portability

You have seen that structures and unions can be used to create variables of varying sizes, and that the actual size of these variables may change from machine to machine. The **sizeof** unary operator computes the size of any variable or type and can help eliminate machine-dependent code from your programs. It is especially useful where structures or unions are concerned.

For the discussion that follows, keep in mind that C++ Builder has the following sizes for these data types:

Type	Size in Bytes
char	1
short int	2
int	4
long int	4
float	4
double	8
long double	10

Therefore, the following code will print the numbers **1, 4, 4,** and **10** on the screen:

```
char ch;
int i;
float f;

printf("%d\n", sizeof ch);
printf("%d\n", sizeof i);
printf("%d\n", sizeof f);
printf("%d\n", sizeof(long double));
```

The size of a structure is equal to or greater than the sum of the sizes of its members. For example,

```
struct s {
  char ch;
  int i;
  float f;
} s_var;
```

Here, the sum of the sizes of the individual members is 9 (4+4+1). However, the actual size of **s_var** might be greater because the compiler is free to align data on word (or paragraph) boundaries. This means that the size of an aggregate data type (such as a structure) may be slightly larger than the sum of its parts. Manually adding up the lengths of the structure members, for example, may not yield its correct size. For C++

Builder, the size of **s_var** is 12, because of the reasons just stated. Therefore, for maximum portability, you should always use **sizeof** to determine the size of a structure variable.

Since the **sizeof** operator is a *compile-time* operator, all the information necessary to compute the size of any variable is known at compile time. This is especially meaningful for **union**s because the size of a union is always equal to the size of its largest member. For example, consider the following:

```
union u {
  char ch;
  int i;
  float f;
} u_var;
```

The **sizeof(u_var)** will be 4 bytes long. At run time, it does not matter what **u_var** is *actually* holding; all that matters is the size of the largest variable it can hold, because the **union** must be as large as its largest element.

typedef

C/C++ allows you to define new data type names using the **typedef** keyword. You are not actually creating a new data type; you are defining a new name for an existing type. This process can help make machine-dependent programs more portable; only the **typedef** statements need to be changed. It also can help you document your code by allowing descriptive names for the standard data types. The general form of the **typedef** statement is

typedef type newname;

where *type* is any existing data type and *newname* is the new name for this type. The new name you define is an addition to, not a replacement for, the existing type name.

For example, you could create a new name for **float** by using

```
typedef float balance;
```

This statement tells the compiler to recognize **balance** as another name for **float**. Next you could create a **float** variable using **balance**:

```
balance past_due;
```

Here, **past_due** is a floating-point variable of type **balance**, which is another word for **float**.

You can also use **typedef** to create names for more complex types. For example:

```
typedef struct {
  float due;
  int over_due;
  char name[40];
} client;  /* here client is the new type name */

client clist[NUM_CLIENTS]; /* define array of
                              structures of type client */
```

Using **typedef** can help make your code easier to read and more portable. But remember, you are *not* creating any new data types.

The Complete Reference

Chapter 8

Input, Output, Streams, and Files

The C language does not define any keywords that perform input or output. Instead, I/O is accomplished through library functions. C++ Builder supports three I/O systems:

- The ANSI/ISO Standard C I/O system
- The UNIX-like I/O system
- Several low-level, platform-specific I/O functions

With a few exceptions, this chapter discusses only the I/O system defined by the ANSI/ISO standard for C. The reason for this is twofold. First, the ANSI/ISO C I/O system is the most widely used. Second, it is fully portable to all platforms. The functions that compose the other two systems are covered in Part Two of this book.

This chapter presents an overview of the ANSI/ISO C I/O system and illustrates the way its core functions work together. The ANSI/ISO C I/O library contains a rich and diverse assortment of I/O routines—more than can be fully covered here. However, the functions in this chapter are sufficient for most circumstances. From this point forward, we will refer to the ANSI/ISO C I/O system as simply the *C I/O system*.

The prototypes and several predefined types and constants for the C I/O library functions are found in the file **<stdio.h>**.

C Versus C++ I/O

Because C forms the foundation for C++, there is sometimes confusion over how C's I/O system relates to C++. First, C++ supports the entire set of C I/O functions. Thus, if you will be porting C code to C++, you will not have to change all of the I/O routines right away. Second, C++ defines its own, object-oriented I/O system, which includes both I/O functions and I/O operators and completely duplicates the functionality of the C I/O system. If you are writing C++ programs, you should use the C++ I/O system (described in Part Three). For C code, you must use the standard C I/O system described in this chapter. However, even if you will be writing mostly C++ code, you will still want to be familiar with the C I/O system for these three reasons:

- For several years to come, C and C++ will coexist. Also, many programs will be hybrids of both C and C++ code. Further, many C programs will be upgraded into C++ programs. Thus, knowledge of both the C and the C++ I/O systems is necessary. For example, in order to change the C-based I/O functions into C++ object-oriented I/O functions, you will need to know how both the C and C++ I/O systems operate.

- An understanding of the basic principles behind the C I/O system helps you understand the C++ object-oriented I/O system. (Both share the same general concepts.)

■ In certain situations (for example, in very short, "throw-away" programs), it
may be easier to use C's non-object-oriented approach to I/O than it is to use
the object-oriented I/O defined by C++.

In addition, there is an unwritten rule that any C++ programmer must also be a
C programmer. If you don't know how to use the C I/O system, you will be limiting
your professional horizons.

Streams and Files

Fundamental to understanding the C (and C++) I/O system are the concepts of *streams*
and *files*. The C I/O system supplies a consistent interface to the programmer independent
of the actual device being accessed. That is, the C I/O system provides a level of abstraction
between the programmer and the hardware. This abstraction is called a *stream;* the
actual device is called a *file*. It is important to know how streams and files interact.

Streams

The C I/O system is designed to work with a wide variety of devices, including terminals,
disk drives, and tape drives. Even though each device is different, the I/O system
transforms each into a logical device called a *stream.* All streams behave similarly.
Because streams are largely device independent, the same function that can write to
a disk file can also write to another type of device, such as the console. There are two
types of streams: text and binary.

Text Streams

A *text stream* is a sequence of characters. Standard C states that a text stream is organized
into lines terminated by a newline character. However, the newline character is optional
on the last line. In a text stream, certain character translations may occur as required
by the host environment. For example, a newline may be converted to a carriage
return/linefeed pair. Therefore, there may not be a one-to-one relationship between the
characters that are written or read and those on the external device. Also, because of
possible translations, the number of characters written or read may not be the same as
the number that is stored on the external device.

Binary Streams

A *binary stream* is a sequence of bytes that have a one-to-one correspondence to those
on the external device. That is, no character translations occur. Also, the number of
bytes written or read is the same as the number on the external device. However, an
implementation-defined number of null bytes may be appended to a binary stream.
These null bytes might be used to pad the information so that it fills a sector on a disk,
for example.

Files

In C, a *file* is a logical concept that can be applied to everything from disk files to terminals or printers. You associate a stream with a specific file by performing an *open* operation. Once a file is open, information can be exchanged between it and your program.

Not all files have the same capabilities. For example, a disk file can support random access, while some printers cannot. This illustrates an important point about the C I/O system: All streams are the same, but all files are not.

If the file can support random access (also called *position requests*), opening that file initializes the *file position indicator* to the start of the file. As each character is read from or written to the file, the position indicator is incremented, ensuring progression through the file.

The smallest accessible portion of a disk is a sector. Information is written to or read from a disk one sector at a time. Thus, even if your program only needs a single byte of data, an entire sector of data will be read. This data is put into a region of memory called a *buffer* until it can be used by your program. When data is output to a disk file, it is buffered until a full sector's worth of information has been accumulated, at which point it is actually physically written to the file.

You disassociate a file from a specific stream using a *close* operation. Closing a stream causes any contents of its associated buffer to be written to the external device (it will be padded, if necessary, to fill out a complete sector). This process, generally called *flushing* the buffer, guarantees that no information is accidentally left in the disk buffer. All files are closed automatically when your program terminates normally by **main( )** returning to the operating system or by calling **exit( )**. However, it is better to actually close a file using **fclose( )** as soon as it is no longer needed because several events can prevent the buffer from being written to the disk file. For example, files are not written if a program terminates through a call to **abort( )**, if it crashes, or if the user turns the computer off before terminating the program.

At the beginning of a program's execution five predefined text streams are opened. They are **stdin**, **stdout**, **stderr**, **stdaux**, and **stdprn**, and they refer to the standard I/O devices connected to the system, as shown here:

Stream	Device
stdin	Keyboard
stdout	Screen
stderr	Screen
stdaux	First serial port
stdprn	Printer

THE FOUNDATION OF C++

The first three streams are defined by ANSI/ISO Standard C, and any code that uses them is fully portable. The last two are specific to C++ Builder and may not be portable to other compilers. Most operating systems allow I/O redirection, so routines that read or write to these streams can be redirected to other devices. (Redirection of I/O is the process whereby information that would normally go to one device is rerouted to another device by the operating system.) You should never try explicitly to open or close these files.

Each stream that is associated with a file has a file control structure of type **FILE**. This structure is defined in the header **<stdio.h>**. You must not make modifications to this structure.

If you are new to programming, C's separation of streams and files may seem unnecessary or contrived. Just remember that its main purpose is to provide a consistent interface. In C, you need only think in terms of streams and use only one file system to accomplish all I/O operations. The C I/O system automatically converts the raw input or output from each device into an easily managed stream.

The remainder of this chapter discusses the Standard C I/O system. It does so by dividing it into two parts: console I/O and file I/O. As you will see, these are different sides of the same coin. However, this somewhat artificial distinction makes it easier to discuss them.

Console I/O

Console I/O refers to operations that occur at the keyboard and screen of your computer. Because input and output to the console is such a common affair, a subsystem of the C I/O file system was created to deal exclusively with console I/O. Technically, these functions direct their operations to the standard input (**stdin**) and standard output (**stdout**) of the system. Thus, it is possible to redirect console I/O to other devices. However, in this chapter it is assumed that the standard input and the standard output have not been redirected.

 Neither the C nor C++ languages provide built-in support for graphic user interfaces such as Windows. When performing input or output in a Windows environment, you will need to use special functions defined by Windows itself.

Reading and Writing Characters

The simplest of the console I/O functions are **getchar( )**, which reads a character from the keyboard, and **putchar( )**, which prints a character to the screen. However, **getchar( )** has some significant limitations, which are described later. For this reason, most of the time you will substitute **getche( )** when you need to read a character. The

getche( ) function is defined by C++ Builder, not by ANSI/ISO Standard C. Although it is a common extension, it is not portable to all other environments. **getche( )** waits until a key is pressed and then returns its value. The key pressed is also *echoed* to the screen automatically. The prototypes for **getche( )** and **putchar( )** are shown here:

int getche(void); /* requires <conio.h> */
int putchar(int *ch*); /* requries <stdio.h> */

The **getche( )** function returns the character pressed. The **putchar( )** function returns *ch* if successful, or **EOF** if an error occurs. (**EOF** is a macro defined in **<stdio.h>** that stands for *end of file*.) Even though *ch* is declared as an integer, only the low-order byte is displayed on the screen. Similarly, even though **getche( )** returns an integer, the low-order byte will contain the character entered at the keyboard. The **getche( )** function requires the **<conio.h>** header file, which is not part of Standard C.

The following program inputs characters from the keyboard and prints them in reverse case. That is, uppercase prints as lowercase, and lowercase as uppercase. The program halts when a period is typed.

```
/* Case Switcher */
#include <conio.h>
#include <stdio.h>
#include <ctype.h>

int main(void) {
  char ch;

  do {
    ch = getche();
    if(islower(ch)) putchar(toupper(ch));
    else putchar(tolower(ch));
  } while (ch!='.'); /* use a period to stop*/
  return 0;
}
```

There are two important alternatives to **getche( )**. The first is **getchar( )**, mentioned earlier, which is the character input function defined by ANSI/ISO Standard C. The trouble with **getchar( )** is that it buffers input until a carriage return is entered. The reason for this is that the original UNIX systems line-buffered terminal input—that is, you had to enter a carriage return before anything you had just typed was actually sent to the computer. To be compatible with the UNIX implementation, many compilers, including C++ Builder, have implemented **getchar( )** so that it line-buffers input. This is quite annoying in today's interactive environments, and the use of **getchar( )** is not recommended. You may want to play with it a little to understand its effect better. However, this guide makes little use of **getchar( )**.

A second, more useful, variation on **getche( )** is **getch( )**, which operates like **getche( )** except that the character you type is not echoed to the screen. You can use this fact to create a rather humorous (if disconcerting) program to run on some unsuspecting user. The program, shown here, displays what appears to be a standard command prompt and waits for input. However, every character the user types is displayed as the next letter in the alphabet. That is, an "A" becomes "B", and so forth. To stop the program, press CTRL-A.

```
/* This program appears to act as a command-prompt gone wild. It
   displays the command prompt but displays every character
   the user types as the next letter in the alphabet.
*/

#include <stdio.h>
#include <conio.h>

int main(void)
{
  char ch;

  do {
    printf("C>");
    for(;;) {
      ch = getch(); /* read chars without echo */
      if(ch=='\r' || ch==1) {
        printf("\n");
        break;
      }
      putchar(ch+1);
    }
  } while(ch!=1) ; /* exit on control-A */

  return 0;
}
```

While this program is, obviously, just for fun, **getch( )** has many practical uses. For example, you could use it to input a password without echoing the password to the screen.

Reading and Writing Strings: gets( ) and puts( )

The next step up in console I/O are the functions **gets( )** and **puts( )**. They enable you to read and write strings of characters.

The **gets( )** function reads a string of characters entered at the keyboard and stores it at the address pointed to by its argument. You can type characters at the keyboard until you strike a carriage return. The carriage return does not become part of the string; instead, a null terminator is placed at the end, and **gets( )** returns. In fact, it is impossible to use **gets( )** to obtain a carriage return (you can use **getchar( )** and its variants, though). Typing mistakes can be corrected by using the backspace before pressing ENTER. The prototype for **gets( )** is:

char *gets(char *str);

where *str* is a character array. The **gets( )** function returns a pointer to *str*. For example, the following program reads a string into the array **str** and prints its length:

```
#include <stdio.h>
#include <string.h>

int main(void)
{
  char str[80];

  gets(str);
  printf("Length is %d", strlen(str));

  return 0;
}
```

There is a potential problem with **gets( )**. Using **gets( )**, it is possible to overrun the boundaries of its character array argument. This is because there is no way for **gets( )** to know when it has reached the limit of the array. For example, if you call **gets( )** with an array that is 40 bytes long and then enter 40 or more characters, you will have overrun the array. This will, obviously, cause problems and often lead to a system crash. As an alternative, you can use the **fgets( )** function described later in this chapter, which allows you to specify a maximum length. The only trouble with **fgets( )** is that it retains the newline character. If you don't want the newline, it must be removed manually.

The **puts( )** function writes its string argument to the screen followed by a newline. Its prototype is

int puts(const char *str);

Here, *str* is the string to display. The function returns nonnegative if successful and **EOF** on failure. It recognizes the same backslash codes as **printf( )**, such as \t for tab. A call to **puts( )** requires far less overhead than the same call to **printf( )** because **puts( )** outputs only a string of characters; it does not output numbers or do format conversions. It takes up less space and runs faster than **printf( )**. The following statement displays "hello".

```
puts("hello");
```

Table 8-1 summarizes the basic console I/O functions.

Formatted Console I/O

The C/C++ standard library contains two functions that perform formatted input and output on the built-in data types: **printf( )** and **scanf( )**. The term *formatted* refers to the fact that these functions can read and write data in various formats that are under your control. The **printf( )** function is used to write data to the console. The **scanf( )** function reads data from the keyboard. Both **printf( )** and **scanf( )** can operate on any of the built-in data types, including characters, strings, and numbers.

printf( )

The **printf( )** function has this prototype

int printf(const char *fmt_string, . . .);

Function	Operation
getchar( )	Reads a character from the keyboard; waits for carriage return.
getche( )	Reads a character with echo; does not wait for carriage return; not defined by Standard C, but a common extension.
getch( )	Reads a character without echo; does not wait for carriage return; not defined by Standard C, but a common extension.
putchar( )	Writes a character to the screen.
gets( )	Reads a string from the keyboard.
puts( )	Writes a string to the screen.

Table 8-1.   *The Basic Console I/O Functions*

The first argument, *fmt_string*, defines the way any subsequent arguments are displayed. It consists of two types of items. The first type is characters that will be printed on the screen. The second type contains format specifiers that define the way subsequent arguments are displayed. A format specifier begins with a percent sign and is followed by a format code. The format specifiers are shown in Table 8-2. There must be exactly the same number of arguments as there are format specifiers, and the format specifiers and arguments are matched in order from left to right. For example, this call to **printf( )**

```
printf("Hi %c %d %s", 'c', 10, "there!");
```

displays "Hi c 10 there!". The **printf( )** function returns the number of characters written or an **EOF** if an error occurs.

Code	Format
%c	Character
%d	Signed decimal integers
%i	Signed decimal integers
%e	Scientific notation (lowercase e)
%E	Scientific notation (uppercase E)
%f	Decimal floating point
%g	Uses %e or %f, whichever is shorter.
%G	Uses %E or %F, whichever is shorter.
%o	Unsigned octal
%s	String of characters
%u	Unsigned decimal integers
%x	Unsigned hexadecimal (lowercase letters)
%X	Unsigned hexadecimal (uppercase letters)
%p	Displays a pointer.
%n	The associated argument is an integer pointer into which the number of characters written so far is placed.
%%	Prints a % sign.

Table 8-2. *The **printf( )** Format Specifiers*

Printing Characters

To print an individual character, use **%c**. This causes its matching argument to be output, unmodified, to the screen.

To print a string, use **%s**.

Printing Numbers

You can use either **%d** or **%i** to display a signed integer in decimal format. These format specifiers are equivalent; both are supported for historical reasons.

To output an unsigned integer, use **%u**.

The **%f** format specifier displays numbers in floating point. The matching argument must be of type **double**.

The **%e** and **%E** specifiers tell **printf( )** to display a **double** argument in scientific notation. Numbers represented in scientific notation take this general form:

x.ddddddE+/-yy

If you want to display the letter E in uppercase, use the **%E** format; otherwise use **%e**.

You can tell **printf( )** to use either **%f** or **%e** by using the **%g** or **%G** format specifiers. This causes **printf( )** to select the format specifier that produces the shortest output. Where applicable, use **%G** if you want the E shown in uppercase; otherwise, use **%g**. The following program demonstrates the effect of the **%g** format specifier:

```
#include <stdio.h>

int main(void)
{
  double f;

  for(f=1.0; f<1.0e+10; f=f*10)
    printf("%g ", f);

  return 0;
}
```

It produces the following output.

```
1 10 100 1000 10000 100000 1e+06 1e+07 1e+08 1e+09
```

You can display unsigned integers in octal or hexadecimal format using **%o** and **%x**, respectively. Since the hexadecimal number system uses the letters A through F to represent the numbers 10 through 15, you can display these letters in either upper- or lowercase. For uppercase, use the **%X** format specifier; for lowercase, use **%x**, as shown here:

```
#include <stdio.h>

int main(void)
{
  unsigned num;

  for(num=0; num<=16; num++) {
    printf("%d ", num);    /* Integer */
    printf("%o ", num);    /* Octal */
    printf("%x ", num);    /* Hexidecimal - lowercase */
    printf("%X\n", num);   /* Hexidecimal - uppercase */
  }

  return 0;
}
```

Displaying an Address

If you want to display an address, use **%p**. This format specifier causes **printf( )** to display a machine address in a format compatible with the type of addressing used by the computer. The next program displays the address of **sample**:

```
#include <stdio.h>

int sample;

int main(void)
{
  printf("%p", &sample);

  return 0;
}
```

The %n Specifier

The **%n** format specifier is different from the others. Instead of telling **printf( )** to display something, it causes **printf( )** to load the integer variable pointed to by its corresponding argument with a value equal to the number of characters that have been output. In other words, the value that corresponds to the **%n** format specifier must be a pointer to a variable. After the call to **printf( )** has returned, this variable will hold the number of characters output, up to the point at which the **%n** was encountered. Examine this program to understand this somewhat unusual format code.

```
#include <stdio.h>

int main(void)
{
  int count;

  printf("this%n is a test\n", &count);
  printf("%d", count);

  return 0;
}
```

This program displays **this is a test** followed by the number **4**. The **%n** format specifier is used primarily to enable your program to perform dynamic formatting.

Format Modifiers

Many format specifiers can take modifiers that alter their meaning slightly. For example, you can specify a minimum field width, the number of decimal places, and left justification. The format modifier goes between the percent sign and the format code. These modifiers are discussed next.

The Minimum Field Width Specifier

An integer placed between the % sign and the format code acts as a *minimum field width specifier*. This pads the output with spaces to ensure that it reaches a certain minimum length. If the string or number is longer than that minimum, it will still be printed in full. The default padding is done with spaces. If you want to pad with 0's, place an 0 before the field width specifier. For example, **%05d** will pad a number of less than five digits with 0's so that its total length is five. The following program demonstrates the minimum field width specifier:

```
#include <stdio.h>

int main(void)
{
  double item;

  item = 10.12304;

  printf("%f\n", item);
  printf("%10f\n", item);
  printf("%012f\n", item);

  return 0;
}
```

This program produces the following output:

```
10.123040
 10.123040
00010.123040
```

The minimum field width modifier is most commonly used to produce tables in which the columns line up. For example, the next program produces a table of squares and cubes for the numbers between 1 and 19:

```c
#include <stdio.h>

int main(void)
{
  int i;

  /* display a table of squares and cubes */
  for(i=1; i<20; i++)
    printf("%8d %8d %8d\n", i, i*i, i*i*i);

  return 0;
}
```

A sample of its output is shown here:

```
   1         1         1
   2         4         8
   3         9        27
   4        16        64
   5        25       125
   6        36       216
   7        49       343
   8        64       512
   9        81       729
  10       100      1000
  11       121      1331
  12       144      1728
  13       169      2197
  14       196      2744
  15       225      3375
  16       256      4096
```

```
17      289     4913
18      324     5832
19      361     6859
```

The Precision Specifier

The *precision specifier* follows the minimum field width specifier (if there is one). It consists of a period followed by an integer. Its exact meaning depends upon the type of data to which it is applied.

When you apply the precision specifier to floating-point data using the **%f**, **%e**, or **%E** specifiers, it determines the number of decimal places displayed. For example, **%10.4f** displays a number at least ten characters wide with four decimal places. If you don't specify the precision, a default of six is used for **%e**, **%E** and **%f**. When the precision specifier is applied to **%g** or **%G**, it specifies the number of significant digits.

Applied to strings, the precision specifier specifies the maximum field length. For example, **%5.7s** displays a string at least five and not exceeding seven characters long. If the string is longer than the maximum field width, the end characters will be truncated.

When applied to integer types, the precision specifier determines the minimum number of digits that will appear for each number. Leading zeros are added to achieve the required number of digits.

The following program illustrates the precision specifier:

```
#include <stdio.h>

int main(void)
{
  printf("%.4f\n", 123.1234567);
  printf("%3.8d\n", 1000);
  printf("%10.15s\n", "This is a simple test.");

  return 0;
}
```

It produces the following output:

```
123.1235
00001000
This is a simpl
```

Justifying Output

By default, all output is right-justified. That is, if the field width is larger than the data printed, the data will be placed on the right edge of the field. You can force output to be left-justified by placing a minus sign directly after the %. For example, **%-10.2f** left-justifies a floating-point number with two decimal places in a 10-character field.

The following program illustrates left justification:

```c
#include <stdio.h>

int main(void)
{
  printf("......................\n");
  printf("right-justified:%8d\n", 100);
  printf("left-justified:%-8d\n", 100);

  return 0;
}
```

It produces the following output:

```
......................
right-justified:     100
left-justified:100
```

Handling Other Data Types

There are two format modifiers that allow **printf( )** to display **short** and **long** integers. These modifiers may be applied to the **d**, **i**, **o**, **u**, and **x** type specifiers. The **l** (*ell*) modifier tells **printf( )** that a **long** data type follows. For example, **%ld** means that a **long int** is to be displayed. The **h** modifier instructs **printf( )** to display a **short** integer. For instance, **%hu** indicates that the data is of type **short unsigned int**.

The **l** and **h** modifiers can also be applied to the **n** specifier, to indicate that the corresponding argument is a pointer to a long or short integer, respectively.

The **L** modifier may prefix the floating-point specifiers **e**, **f**, and **g** and indicates that a **long double** follows.

The * and # Modifiers

The **printf( )** function supports two additional modifiers to some of its format specifiers: * and #.

Preceding **g**, **G**, **f**, **E**, or **e** specifiers with a # ensures that there will be a decimal point even if there are no decimal digits. If you precede the **x** or **X** format specifier with a #, the hexadecimal number will be printed with a **0x** prefix. Preceding the **o** specifier with # causes the number to be printed with a leading zero. You cannot apply # to any other format specifiers.

Instead of constants, the minimum field width and precision specifiers can be provided by arguments to **printf( )**. To accomplish this, use an * as a placeholder. When the format string is scanned, **printf( )** will match the * to an argument in the order in which they occur. For example, in Figure 8-1, the minimum field width is 10, the precision is 4, and the value to be displayed is **123.3**.

The following program illustrates both # and *:

```c
#include <stdio.h>

int main(void)
{
  printf("%x %#x\n", 10, 10);
  printf("%*.*f", 10, 4, 123.3);

  return 0;
}
```

The following is produced:

```
a 0xa
  123.3000
```

scanf( )

The general-purpose console input routine is **scanf( )**. It reads all the built-in data types and automatically converts numbers into the proper internal format. It is much like the reverse of **printf( )**. The prototype for **scanf( )** is

int scanf(const char *fmt_string, . . .);

The *fmt_string* determines how values are read into the variables pointed to in the argument list.

The format string consists of three classifications of characters:

■ Format specifiers

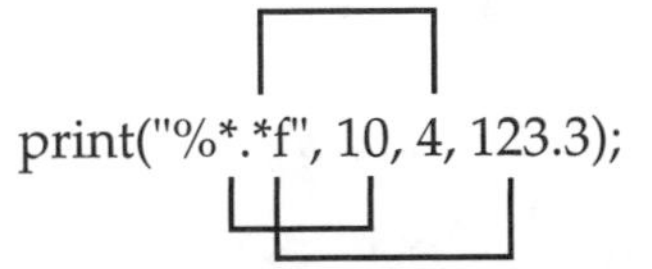

```
print("%*.*f", 10, 4, 123.3);
```

Figure 8-1.   *How the * is matched to its value*

- White-space characters
- Non-white-space characters

The **scanf( )** function returns the number of fields that are input. It returns **EOF** if a premature end of file is reached.

Format Specifiers

The input format specifiers are preceded by a % sign and tell **scanf( )** what type of data is to be read next. These codes are listed in Table 8-3. The format specifiers are matched, in order from left to right, with the arguments in the argument list.

Inputting Numbers

To read a decimal number, use the **%d** or **%i** specifiers.

To read a floating-point number represented in either standard or scientific notation, use **%e**, **%f**, or **%g**.

Code	Meaning
%c	Read a single character.
%d	Read a decimal integer.
%i	Read a decimal integer.
%e	Read a floating-point number.
%f	Read a floating-point number.
%g	Read a floating-point number.
%o	Read an octal number.
%s	Read a string.
%x	Read a hexadecimal number.
%p	Read a pointer.
%n	Receives an integer value equal to the number of characters read so far.
%u	Read an unsigned integer.
%[ ]	Scan for a set of characters.

Table 8-3.   The *scanf( )* Format Specifiers

You can use **scanf( )** to read integers in either octal or hexadecimal form by using the **%o** and **%x** format commands, respectively. The **%x** may be in either upper- or lowercase. Either way, you may enter the letters A through F in either case when entering hexadecimal numbers. The following program reads an octal and hexadecimal number:

```
#include <stdio.h>

int main(void)
{
  int i, j;

  scanf("%o%x", &i, &j);
  printf("%o %x", i, j);

  return 0;
}
```

The **scanf( )** function stops reading a number when the first nonnumeric character is encountered.

Inputting Unsigned Integers

To input an unsigned integer, use the **%u** format specifier. For example,

```
unsigned num;
scanf("%u", &num);
```

reads an unsigned number and puts its value into **num**.

Reading Individual Characters Using scanf( )

As explained earlier in this chapter, you can read individual characters using **getchar( )** or a derivative function. You can also use **scanf( )** for this purpose if you use the **%c** format specifier. However, like most implementations of **getchar( )**, **scanf( )** will generally line-buffer input when the **%c** specifier is used. This is the case with C++ Builder, too. Line-buffering makes **scanf( )** somewhat troublesome in an interactive environment.

Although spaces, tabs, and newlines are used as field separators when reading other types of data, when reading a single character, white-space characters are read like any other character. For example, with an input stream of "**x y**," this code fragment

```
scanf("%c%c%c", &a, &b, &c);
```

returns with the character **x** in **a**, a space in **b**, and the character **y** in **c**.

Reading Strings

The **scanf( )** function can be used to read a string from the input stream using the **%s** format specifier. The **%s** causes **scanf( )** to read characters until it encounters a white-space character. The characters that are read are put into the character array pointed to by the corresponding argument, and the result is null terminated. As it applies to **scanf( )**, a white-space character is either a space, a newline, a tab, a vertical tab, or a form feed. Unlike **gets( )**, which reads a string until a carriage return is typed, **scanf( )** reads a string until the first white space is entered. This means that you cannot use **scanf( )** to read a string like "this is a test" because the first space terminates the reading process. To see the effect of the **%s** specifier, try this program using the string "hello there".

```
#include <stdio.h>

int main(void)
{
  char str[80];

  printf("Enter a string: ");
  scanf("%s", str);
  printf("Here's your string: %s", str);

  return 0;
}
```

The program responds with only the "hello" portion of the string.

Inputting an Address

To input a memory address, use the **%p** format specifier. This specifier causes **scanf( )** to read an address in the format defined by the architecture of the CPU. For example, this program inputs an address and then displays what is at that memory address:

```
#include <stdio.h>

int main(void)
{
  char *p;

  printf("Enter an address: ");
  scanf("%p", &p);
  printf("Value at location %p is %c\n", p, *p);

  return 0;
}
```

The %n Specifier

The **%n** specifier instructs **scanf( )** to assign the number of characters read from the input stream at the point at which the **%n** was encountered to the variable pointed to by the corresponding argument.

Using a Scanset

The **scanf( )** function supports a general-purpose format specifier called a scanset. A *scanset* defines a set of characters. When **scanf( )** processes the scanset, it will input characters as long as those characters are part of the set defined by the scanset. The characters read will be assigned to the character array that is pointed to by the scanset's corresponding argument. You define a scanset by putting the characters to scan for inside square brackets. The beginning square bracket must be prefixed by a percent sign. For example, the following scanset tells **scanf( )** to read only the characters X, Y, and Z.

```
%[XYZ]
```

When you use a scanset, **scanf( )** continues to read characters and put them into the corresponding character array until it encounters a character that is not in the scanset. Upon return from **scanf( )**, this array will contain a null-terminated string that consists of the characters that have been read. To see how this works, try this program:

```
#include <stdio.h>

int main(void)
{
  int i;
  char str[80], str2[80];

  scanf("%d%[abcdefg]%s", &i, str, str2);
  printf("%d %s %s", i, str, str2);

  return 0;
}
```

Enter **123abcdtye** followed by ENTER. The program will then display **123 abcd tye**. Because the "t" is not part of the scanset, **scanf( )** stops reading characters into **str** when it encounters the "t." The remaining characters are put into **str2**.

You can specify a range inside a scanset using a hyphen. For example, this tells **scanf( )** to accept the characters "A" through "Z".

```
%[A-Z]
```

The use of the hyphen to describe a range is not defined by the ANSI/ISO C standard. However, it is nearly universally accepted.

You can specify more than one range within a scanset. For example, this program reads digits and then letters:

```
/* A scanset example using ranges. */
#include <stdio.h>

int main(void)
{
  char s1[80], s2[80];

  printf("Enter numbers, then some letters");
  scanf("%[0-9]%[a-zA-Z]", s1, s2);
  printf("%s %s", s1, s2);

  return 0;
}
```

You can specify an inverted set if the first character in the set is a caret (^). When the ^ is present, it instructs **scanf( )** to accept any character that *is not* defined by the scanset. Here, the previous program uses the ^ to invert the type of characters the scanset will read:

```
/* A scanset example using inverted ranges. */
#include <stdio.h>

int main(void)
{
  char s1[80], s2[80];

  printf("Enter non-numbers, then some non-letters");
  scanf("%[^0-9]%[^a-zA-Z]", s1, s2);
  printf("%s %s", s1, s2);

  return 0;
}
```

One important point to remember is that the scanset is case-sensitive. Therefore, if you want to scan for both uppercase and lowercase letters, they must be specified individually.

Discarding Unwanted White Space

A white-space character in the control string causes **scanf( )** to skip over one or more white-space characters in the input stream. A white-space character is either a space, a tab, a vertical tab, a form feed, or a newline. In essence, one white-space character in the control string causes **scanf( )** to read, but not store, any number (including zero) of white-space characters up to the first non-white-space character.

Non-White-Space Characters in the Control String

A non-white-space character in the control string causes **scanf( )** to read and discard matching characters in the input stream. For example, **"%d,%d"** causes **scanf( )** to read an integer, read and discard a comma, and then read another integer. If the specified character is not found, **scanf( )** terminates. If you wish to read and discard a percent sign, use %% in the control string.

You Must Pass scanf( ) Addresses

All the variables used to receive values through **scanf( )** must be passed by their addresses. This means that all arguments must be pointers. Recall that this is how C creates a call by reference, which allows a function to alter the contents of an argument. For example, to read an integer into the variable **count**, you would use the following **scanf( )** call:

```
scanf("%d", &count);
```

Strings will be read into character arrays, and the array name, without any index, is the address of the first element of the array. So, to read a string into the character array **str**, you would use

```
scanf("%s", str);
```

In this case, **str** is already a pointer and need not be preceded by the & operator.

Format Modifiers

As with **printf( )**, **scanf( )** allows a number of its format specifiers to be modified. The format specifiers can include a maximum field length modifier. This is an integer, placed between the % and the format specifier, that limits the number of characters read for that field. For example, to read no more than 20 characters into **str**, write

```
scanf("%20s", str);
```

If the input stream is greater than 20 characters, a subsequent call to input begins where this call leaves off. For example, if you enter

ABCDEFGHIJKLMNOPQRSTUVWXYZ

as the response to the **scanf( )** call in this example, only the first 20 characters, or up to the T, are placed into **str** because of the maximum field width specifier. This means that the remaining characters, UVWXYZ, have not yet been used. If another **scanf( )** call is made, such as

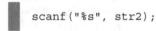

```
scanf("%s", str2);
```

the letters UVWXYZ are placed into **str2**. Input for a field may terminate before the maximum field length is reached if a white space is encountered. In this case, **scanf( )** moves on to the next field.

To read a long integer, put an **l** (*ell*) in front of the format specifier. To read a short integer, put an **h** in front of the format specifier. These modifiers can be used with the **d**, **i**, **o**, **u**, and **x** format codes.

By default, the **f**, **e**, and **g** specifiers instruct **scanf( )** to assign data to a **float**. If you put an **l** (*ell*) in front of one of these specifiers, **scanf( )** assigns the data to a **double**. Using an **L** tells **scanf( )** that the variable receiving the data is a **long double**.

Suppressing Input

You can tell **scanf( )** to read a field but not assign it to any variable by preceding that field's format code with an *. For example, given

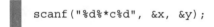

```
scanf("%d%*c%d", &x, &y);
```

you could enter the coordinate pair **10,10**. The comma would be correctly read, but not assigned to anything. Assignment suppression is especially useful when you need to process only a part of what is being entered.

The C File System

The file system is the part of the C I/O system that allows you to read and write disk files. It is composed of several interrelated functions. The most common are shown in Table 8-4. The header **<stdio.h>** must be included in any program in which these functions are used.

The header **<stdio.h>** provides the prototypes for the I/O functions and defines these three types: **size_t**, **fpos_t**, and **FILE**. The **size_t** type is an unsigned integer, as is **fpos_t**. The **FILE** type is discussed in the next section.

Name	Function
fopen( )	Opens a file.
fclose( )	Closes a file.
putc( )	Writes a character to a file.
fputc( )	Same as **putc( )**.
getc( )	Reads a character from a file.
fgetc( )	Same as **getc( )**.
fseek( )	Seeks to a specified byte in a file.
fprintf( )	Is to a file what **printf( )** is to the console.
fscanf( )	Is to a file what **scanf( )** is to the console.
feof( )	Returns true if end-of-file is reached.
ferror( )	Returns true if an error has occurred.
rewind( )	Resets the file position indictor to the beginning of the file.
remove( )	Erases a file.
fflush( )	Flushes a file.

Table 8-4.   *The Most Common C File System Functions*

The **<stdio.h>** header also defines several macros. The ones relevant to this chapter are **NULL**, **EOF**, **FOPEN_MAX**, **SEEK_SET**, **SEEK_CUR**, and **SEEK_END**. The **NULL** macro defines a null pointer. The **EOF** macro, generally defined as –1, is the value returned when an input function tries to read past the end of the file. **FOPEN_MAX** defines an integer value that determines the number of files that may be open at any one time. The other macros are used with **fseek( )**, which is the function that performs random access on a file.

The File Pointer

The file pointer is the common thread that unites the C file system. A *file pointer* is a pointer to information that defines various things about the file, including its name, status, and the current position of the file. In essence, the file pointer identifies a specific disk file and is used by the associated stream to direct the operation of the I/O functions. A file pointer is a pointer variable of type **FILE**. In order to read or write files, your program needs to use file pointers. To obtain a file pointer variable, use a statement like this:

```
FILE *fp;
```

Opening a File

The **fopen( )** function opens a stream for use, links a file with that stream, and then returns a **FILE** pointer to that stream. Most often (always for the purpose of this discussion) the file is a disk file. The **fopen( )** function has this prototype

FILE *fopen(const char *filename, const char *mode);

where *mode* points to a string containing the desired open status. The legal values for *mode* in C++ Builder are shown in Table 8-5. The *filename* must be a string of characters that provides a valid filename for the operating system and may include a path specification.

The **fopen( )** function returns a pointer of type **FILE**. This pointer identifies the file and is used by most other file system functions. It should never be altered by your code. The function returns a null pointer if the file cannot be opened.

As Table 8-5 shows, a file can be opened in either text or binary mode. In text mode, carriage return–linefeed sequences are translated into newline characters on input. On output, the reverse occurs: newlines are translated to carriage return–linefeeds. No such translations occur on binary files. When neither a **t** nor a **b** is specified in the *mode* argument, the text/binary status of the file is determined by the value of the global variable defined by C++ Builder called **_fmode**. By default, **_fmode** is set to **O_TEXT**, which is text mode. When set to **O_BINARY**, then files will be opened in binary mode. (These macros are defined in **<fcntl.h>**.) Of course, using a explicit **t** or **b** overrides the effects of the **_fmode** variable. Also, **_fmode** is specific to C++ Builder; it is not defined by the C I/O system.

Mode	Meaning
"r"	Open a file for reading. (Opened as text file by default, see discussion.)
"w"	Create a file for writing. (Opened as text file by default, see discussion.)
"a"	Append to a file. (Opened as text file by default, see discussion.)

Table 8-5. *The Legal Values for mode*

Mode	Meaning
"rb"	Open a binary file for reading.
"wb"	Create a binary file for writing.
"ab"	Append to a binary file.
"r+"	Open a file for read/write. (Open as text file by default, see discussion.)
"w+"	Create a file for read/write. (Open as text file by default, see discussion.)
"a+"	Append or create a file for read/write. (Open as text file by default, see discussion.)
"r+b"	Open a binary file for read/write.
"w+b"	Create a binary file for read/write.
"a+b"	Append or create a binary file for read/write.
"rt"	Open a text file for reading.
"wt"	Create a text file for writing.
"at"	Append to a text file.
"r+t"	Open a text file for read/write.
"w+t"	Create a text file for read/write.
"a+t"	Append or create a text file for read/write.

Table 8-5.   *The Legal Values for mode* (continued)

If you wish to open a file for writing with the name **test**, write:

```
FILE *fp;
fp = fopen("test", "w");
```

Here, **fp** is a variable of type **FILE ***. However, you usually see it written like this:

```
FILE *fp;
if((fp = fopen("test", "w"))==NULL) {
  printf("Cannot open file.\n");
```

```
    exit(1);
}
```

This method will detect any error in opening a file, such as a write-protected or full disk, before your program attempts to write to it. In general, you will always want to make sure that **fopen( )** succeeded before attempting any other operations on the file.

If you use **fopen( )** to open a file for output, then any preexisting file by that name will be destroyed and a new file will be created. If no file by that name exists, then one is created. If you want to add to the end of the file, you must use **a** (append) mode. If the file does not exist, it will be created. Opening a file for read operations requires an existing file. If no file exists, an error is returned. If a file is opened for read/write operations it is not erased if it exists; if no file exists, one is created.

Writing a Character

The C I/O system defines two equivalent functions that output a character: **putc( )** and **fputc( )**. (Actually, **putc( )** is implemented as a macro.) There are two identical functions simply to preserve compatibility with older versions of C. This book uses **putc( )**, but you can use **fputc( )** if you like.

The **putc( )** function is used to write characters to a stream that was previously opened for writing using the **fopen( )** function. The prototype for **putc( )** is

int putc(int *ch*, FILE **fp*);

where *fp* is the file pointer returned by **fopen( )** and *ch* is the character to be output. The file pointer tells **putc( )** which disk file to write to. For historical reasons, *ch* is defined as an **int**, but only the low-order byte is used.

If a **putc( )** operation is a success, it returns the character written. If **putc( )** fails, an **EOF** is returned.

Reading a Character

There are also two equivalent functions that input a character: **getc( )** and **fgetc( )**. Both are defined to preserve compatibility with older versions of C. This book uses **getc( )** (which is actually implemented as a macro), but you can use **fgetc( )** if you like.

The **getc( )** function is used to read characters from a stream opened in read mode by **fopen( )**. The prototype is

int getc(FILE **fp*);

where *fp* is a file pointer of type **FILE** returned by **fopen( )**. For historical reasons, **getc( )** returns an integer, but the high-order byte is 0.

The **getc( )** function returns an **EOF** when the end of the file has been reached, or if an error occurs. To read a text file to the end, you could use the following code:

```
do {
   ch = getc(fp);
} while(ch!=EOF);
```

Closing a File

The **fclose( )** function closes a stream that was opened by a call to **fopen( )**. It writes
any data still remaining in the disk buffer to the file and does a formal operating-
system–level close on the file. Failure to close a stream invites all kinds of trouble,
including lost data, destroyed files, and possible intermittent errors in your program.
fclose( ) frees the file control block associated with the stream and makes it available
for reuse. There is an operating system limit to the number of open files you can have
at any one time, so it may be necessary to close one file before opening another.

The **fclose( )** function has the prototype

int fclose(FILE *fp);

where *fp* is the file pointer returned by the call to **fopen( )**. A return value of 0 signifies
a successful close operation; an **EOF** is returned if an error occurs. Generally, **fclose( )**
will fail only when a diskette has been prematurely removed from the drive or if there
is no more space on the disk.

Using fopen( ), getc( ), putc( ), and fclose( )

The functions **fopen( )**, **getc( )**, **putc( )**, and **fclose( )** comprise a minimal set of file
routines. A simple example of using **putc( )**, **fopen( )**, and **fclose( )** is the following
program, **ktod**. It simply reads characters from the keyboard and writes them to a disk
file until a dollar sign is typed. The filename is specified from the command line. For
example, if you call this program **KTOD**, then typing **KTOD TEST** allows you to enter
lines of text into the file called **test**.

```
/* KTOD: A key to disk program. */

#include <stdio.h>
#include <stdlib.h>

int main(int argc, char *argv[])
{
  FILE *fp;
  char ch;

  if(argc!=2) {
```

```
    printf("You forgot to enter the filename.\n");
    exit(1);
  }

  if((fp=fopen(argv[1], "w")) == NULL) {
    printf("Cannot open file.\n");
    exit(1);
  }

  do {
    ch = getchar();
    putc(ch, fp);
  } while (ch != '$');

  fclose(fp);

  return 0;
}
```

The complementary program **DTOS** will read any text file and display the contents on the screen. You must specify the name of the file on the command line.

```
/* DTOS: A program that reads text files
         and displays them on the screen. */
#include <stdio.h>
#include <stdlib.h>

int main(int argc, char *argv[])
{
  FILE *fp;
  char ch;

  if(argc!=2) {
    printf("You forgot to enter the filename.\n");
    exit(1);
  }

  if((fp=fopen(argv[1], "r")) == NULL) {
    printf("Cannot open file.\n");
    exit(1);
  }
```

```
  ch = getc(fp);    /* read one character */

  while (ch!=EOF) {
    putchar(ch);  /* print on screen */
    ch = getc(fp);
  }

  fclose(fp);

  return 0;
}
```

Using feof( )

As stated earlier, the C file system can also operate on binary data. When a file is opened for binary input, an integer value equal to the **EOF** mark may be read. This would cause the routine just given to indicate an end-of-file condition even though the physical end of the file had not been reached. Also, **getc( )** returns **EOF** when it fails and when it reaches the end of the file. So to help resolve this ambiguity, C includes the function **feof( )**, which is used to determine the end of the file when reading binary data. It has this prototype:

int feof(FILE *fp);

where fp identifies the file. The **feof( )** function returns non-0 if the end of the file has been reached; otherwise, 0 is returned. Therefore, the following routine reads a binary file until the end-of-file mark is encountered:

```
while(!feof(fp)) ch = getc(fp);
```

This method can be applied to text files as well as binary files.

The following program copies a file of any type. Notice that the files are opened in binary mode and **feof( )** is used to check for the end of the file. (No error checking is performed on output, but in a real-world situation it would be a good idea. Try to add it as an exercise.)

```
/* This program will copy a file to another. */
#include <stdio.h>
#include <stdlib.h>

int main(int argc, char *argv[])
```

```
{
  FILE *in, *out;
  char ch;

  if(argc!=3) {
    printf("You forgot to enter a filename.\n");
    exit(1);
  }

  if((in=fopen(argv[1], "rb")) == NULL) {
    printf("Cannot open source file.\n");
    exit(1);
  }
  if((out=fopen(argv[2], "wb")) == NULL) {
    printf("Cannot open destination file.\n");
    exit(1);
  }

  /* This code actually copies the file. */
  while(!feof(in)) {
    ch = getc(in);
    if(!feof(in)) putc(ch, out);
  }

  fclose(in);
  fclose(out);

  return 0;
}
```

Working with Strings: fgets( ) and fputs( )

The C I/O system includes two functions that can read and write strings from and to streams: **fgets( )** and **fputs( )**. Their prototypes are

> int fputs(const char *str, FILE *fp);
> char *fgets(char *str, int length, FILE *fp);

The function **fputs( )** works much like **puts( )** except that it writes the string to the specified stream. The **fgets( )** function reads a string from the specified stream until either a newline character or *length* –1 characters have been read. If a newline is read, it will be part of the string (unlike **gets( )**). In either case, the resultant string will be null-terminated. The function returns *str* if successful and a null pointer if an error occurs.

As mentioned earlier in this chapter, you may want to use **fgets( )** as an alternative to **gets( )**. To do so, simply specify **stdin** as the file pointer. For example, this program reads up to 79 characters received from standard input.

```
#include <stdio.h>

int main(void)
{
  char s[80];

  printf("Enter a string: ");
  fgets(s, 80, stdin);
  printf("Here is your string: %s", s);

  return 0;
}
```

The advantage of using **fgets( )** over **gets( )** is that you can prevent the input array from being overrun. However, the array may contain the newline character.

fread( ) and fwrite( )

The C file system provides two functions, **fread( )** and **fwrite( )**, that allow the reading and writing of blocks of data. Their prototypes are

size_t fread(void *buffer, size_t num_bytes, size_t count, FILE *fp);
size_t fwrite(const void *buffer, size_t num_bytes, size_t count, FILE *fp);

In the case of **fread( )**, buffer is a pointer to a region of memory that receives the data read from the file. For **fwrite( )**, buffer is a pointer to the information to be written to the file. The length of each item, in bytes, to be read or written is specified by num_bytes. The argument count determines how many items (each being num_bytes in length) will be read or written. Finally, fp is a file pointer to a previously opened stream.

The **fread( )** function returns the number of items read. This value may be less than count if the end of the file is reached or an error occurs. The **fwrite( )** function returns the number of items written. This value will equal count unless an error occurs.

As long as the file has been opened for binary data, **fread( )** and **fwrite( )** can read and write any type of information. For example, this program writes a **float** to a disk file:

```
/* Write a floating point number to a disk file. */
#include <stdio.h>
#include <stdlib.h>
```

```
int main(void)
{
  FILE *fp;
  float f = 12.23;

  if((fp=fopen("test", "wb"))==NULL) {
    printf("Cannot open file.\n");
    exit(1);
  }

  fwrite(&f, sizeof(float), 1, fp);
  fclose(fp);
  return 0;
}
```

As this program illustrates, the buffer can be, and often is, simply a variable.

One of the most useful applications of **fread( )** and **fwrite( )** involves the reading and writing of blocks of data, such as arrays or structures. For example, this fragment writes the contents of the floating-point array **balance** to the file **balance** using a single **fwrite( )** statement. Next, it reads the array, using a single **fread( )** statement, and displays its contents.

```
#include <stdio.h>
#include <stdlib.h>

int main(void)
{
  register int i;
  FILE *fp;
  float balance[100];

  /* open for write */
  if((fp=fopen("balance", "wb"))==NULL) {
    printf("Cannot open file.\n");
    exit(1);
  }

  for(i=0; i<100; i++) balance[i] = (float) i;

  /* this saves the entire balance array in one step */
```

```
    fwrite(balance, sizeof balance, 1, fp);
    fclose(fp);

    /* zero array */
    for(i=0; i<100; i++) balance[i] = 0.0;

    /* open for read */
    if((fp=fopen("balance","rb"))==NULL) {
      printf("cannot open file\n");
      exit(1);
    }

    /* this reads the entire balance array in one step */
    fread(balance, sizeof balance, 1, fp);

    /* display contents of array */
    for(i=0; i<100; i++) printf("%f ", balance[i]);

    fclose(fp);
    return 0;
}
```

Using **fread( )** and **fwrite( )** to read or write complex data is more efficient than using repeated calls to **getc( )** and **putc( )**.

fseek( ) and Random Access I/O

You can perform random read and write operations using the buffered I/O system with the help of **fseek( )**, which sets the file position locator. Its prototype is

int fseek(FILE *fp, long *num_bytes*, int *origin*);

where *fp* is a file pointer returned by a call to **fopen( )**; *num_bytes*, a long integer, is the number of bytes from *origin* to seek to; and *origin* is one of the following macros (defined in **<stdio.h>**):

Origin	Macro Name
Beginning of file	SEEK_SET
Current position	SEEK_CUR
End of file	SEEK_END

The macros are defined as integer values with **SEEK_SET** being 0, **SEEK_CUR** being 1, and **SEEK_END** being 2. Therefore, to seek *num_bytes* from the start of the file, *origin* should be **SEEK_SET**. To seek from the current position use **SEEK_CUR**, and to seek from the end of the file use **SEEK_END**. The **fseek( )** function returns 0 when successful and a nonzero value if an error occurs.

For example, you could use the following code to read the 234th byte in a file called **test**:

```
int func1(void)
{
  FILE *fp;

  if((fp=fopen("test", "rb")) == NULL) {
    printf("Cannot open file.\n");
    exit(1);
  }

  fseek(fp, 234L, 0);
  return getc(fp);    /* read one character */
                      /* at 234th position */

  }
}
```

Another example that uses **fseek( )** is the following **DUMP** program, which lets you examine the contents in both ASCII and hexadecimal of any file you choose. You can look at the file in 128-byte "sectors" as you move about the file in either direction. To exit the program, type a **–1** when prompted for the sector. Notice the use of **fread( )** to read the file. At the end-of-file mark, less than **SIZE** number of bytes are likely to be read, so the number returned by **fread( )** is passed to **display( )**. (Remember that **fread( )** returns the number of items actually read.) Enter this program into your computer and study it until you are certain how it works:

```
/* DUMP: A simple disk look utility using fseek. */
#include <stdio.h>
#include <stdlib.h>
#include <ctype.h>

#define SIZE 128

void display(int numread);

char buf[SIZE];
void display();
```

```
int main(int argc, char *argv[])
{
  FILE *fp;
  int sector, numread;

  if(argc!=2) {
    printf("Usage: dump filename\n");
    exit(1);
  }

  if((fp=fopen(argv[1], "rb"))==NULL) {
    printf("Cannot open file.\n");
    exit(1);
  }

  do {
    printf("Enter sector: ");
    scanf("%d", &sector);
    if(sector >= 0) {
      if(fseek(fp, sector*SIZE, SEEK_SET)) {
        printf("seek error");
      }
      if((numread=fread(buf, 1, SIZE, fp)) != SIZE)
        printf("EOF reached.");

      display(numread);
    }
  } while(sector>=0);
  return 0;
}

/* Display the contents of a file. */
void display(int numread)
{
  int i, j;

  for(i=0; i<numread/16; i++) {
    for(j=0; j<16; j++) printf("%3X", buf[i*16+j]);
    printf("  ");
    for(j=0; j<16; j++) {
      if(isprint(buf[i*16+j])) printf("%c", buf[i*16+j]);
      else printf(".");
```

```
    }
    printf("\n");
  }
}
```

Notice that the library function **isprint( )** is used to determine which characters are printing characters. The **isprint( )** function returns true if the character is printable and false otherwise, and requires the use of the header file **<ctype.h>**, which is included near the top of the program. A sample output with **DUMP** used on itself is shown in Figure 8-2.

fprintf( ) and fscanf( )

In addition to the basic I/O functions, the buffered I/O system includes **fprintf( )** and **fscanf( )**. These functions behave exactly like **printf( )** and **scanf( )** except that they operate with disk files. The prototypes of **fprintf( )** and **fscanf( )** are

int fprintf(FILE *fp, const char *fmt_string, . . .);
int fscanf(FILE *fp, const char *fmt_string, . . .);

```
Enter sector: 0
 2F 2A 20 44 55 4D 50 3A 20 41 20 73 69 6D 70 6C   /* DUMP: A simpl
 65 20 64 69 73 6B 20 6C 6F 6F 6B 20 75 74 69 6C   e disk look util
 69 74 79 20 75 73 69 6E 67 20 66 73 65 65 6B 2E   ity using fseek.
 20 2A 2F  D  A 23 69 6E 63 6C 75 64 65 20 3C 73    */..#include <s
 74 64 69 6F 2E 68 3E  D  A 23 69 6E 63 6C 75 64   tdio.h>..#includ
 65 20 3C 73 74 64 6C 69 62 2E 68 3E  D  A 23 69   e <stdlib.h>..#i
 6E 63 6C 75 64 65 20 3C 63 74 79 70 65 2E 68 3E   nclude <ctype.h>
  D  A  D  A 23 64 65 66 69 6E 65 20 53 49 5A 45   ....#define SIZE
Enter sector: 1
 20 31 32 38  D  A  D  A 76 6F 69 64 20 64 69 73   128....void dis
 70 6C 61 79 28 69 6E 74 20 6E 75 6D 72 65 61 64   play(int numread
 29 3B  D  A  D  A 63 68 61 72 20 62 75 66 5B 53   );....char buf[S
 49 5A 45 5D 3B  D  A 76 6F 69 64 20 64 69 73 70   IZE];..void disp
 6C 61 79 28 29 3B  D  A  D  A 69 6E 74 20 6D 61   lay();....int ma
 69 6E 28 69 6E 74 20 61 72 67 63 2C 20 63 68 61   in(int argc, cha
 72 20 2A 61 72 67 76 5B 5D 29  D  A 7B  D  A 20   r *argv[])..{..
 20 46 49 4C 45 20 2A 66 70 3B  D  A 20 20 69 6E    FILE *fp;..  in
Enter sector: -1
```

Figure 8-2.   *Sample output from the dump program*

where *fp* is a file pointer returned by a call to **fopen( )**. Except for directing their output to the file defined by *fp*, they operate exactly like **printf( )** and **scanf( )** respectively.

Note
*Although **fprintf( )** and **fscanf( )** are often the easiest way to write and read assorted data to disk files, they are not always the most efficient. Because formatted ASCII data is being written just as it would appear on the screen (instead of in binary), you incur extra overhead with each call. If speed or file size is a concern, you should probably use **fread( )** and **fwrite( )**.*

Erasing Files

The **remove( )** function erases a file. Its prototype is

int remove(const char *filename);

It returns 0 upon success, non-0 if it fails.

This program uses **remove( )** to erase a file specified by the user.

```
/* A remove() example. */

#include <stdio.h>
#include <stdlib.h>

int main(void)
{
  char fname[80];

  printf("Name of file to remove: ");
  gets(fname);

  if(remove(fname)) {
    printf("Error removing file\n");
    exit(1);
  }

  return 0;
}
```

ferror( ) and rewind( )

The **ferror( )** function is used to determine whether a file operation has produced an error. The function **ferror( )** has this prototype

int ferror(FILE *fp)

where *fp* is a valid file pointer. It returns true if an error has occurred during the last file operation; it returns false otherwise. Because each file operation sets the error condition, **ferror( )** should be called immediately after each file operation; otherwise, an error may be lost.

The **rewind( )** function resets the file position locator to the beginning of the file specified as its argument. The prototype is

    void rewind(FILE *fp)

where *fp* is a valid file pointer.

The Console Connection

As mentioned at the start of this chapter, whenever a program starts execution, five streams are opened automatically. They are **stdin**, **stdout**, **stderr**, **stdaux**, and **stdprn**. Because these are file pointers, they may be used by any function in the C I/O system that uses a file pointer. For example, **putchar( )** could be defined as

```
int putchar(int c)
{
   return putc(c, stdout);
}
```

As this example illustrates, C makes little distinction between console I/O and file I/O. In essence, the console I/O functions are simply special versions of their parallel file functions that direct their operations to either **stdin** or **stdout**. The reason they exist is as a convenience to you, the programmer. In general, you may use **stdin**, **stdout**, and **stderr** as file pointers in any function that uses a variable of type **FILE ***.

In environments that allow redirection of I/O, **stdin** and **stdout** can be redirected. This means that they could refer to a device other than the keyboard and or screen. For example, consider this program:

```
#include <stdio.h>

int main(void)
{
   char str[80];

   printf("Enter a string: ");
   gets(str);
   printf(str);
```

```
    return 0;
}
```

Assume that this program is called TEST. If you execute TEST normally, it displays its prompt on the screen, reads a string from the keyboard, and displays that string on the display. However, either **stdin**, **stdout**, or both could be redirected to a file. For example, in a DOS or Windows environment, executing TEST like this:

```
TEST > OUTPUT
```

causes the output of TEST to be written to a file called OUTPUT. Executing TEST like this:

```
TEST < INPUT > OUTPUT
```

directs **stdin** to the file called INPUT and sends output to the file called OUTPUT.

As you can see, console I/O and file I/O are really just two slightly different ways of looking at the same thing.

The Complete Reference

Borland C++ Builder

Chapter 9

The Preprocessor and Comments

The source code for a C (or C++) program can include various instructions to the compiler. Although not actually part of the C/C++ language, these *preprocessor directives* expand the scope of its programming environment. This chapter examines the preprocessor. It also examines C++ Builder's built-in macros, and some additions made to the preprocessor by C++ Builder. The chapter ends with an examination of comments.

Standard C/C++ supports the following preprocessor directives:

#define	#elif	#else	#endif
#error	#if	#ifdef	#ifndef
#include	#line	#pragma	#undef

To these, C++ Builder adds **#import**.

All preprocessor directives begin with a # sign, and each preprocessing directive must be on its own line. For example,

```
/* Will not work! */
#include <stdio.h>  #include <stdlib.h>
```

will not work.

#define

The **#define** directive defines an identifier and a character sequence that will be substituted for the identifier each time it is encountered in the source file. The identifier is referred to as a *macro name* and the replacement process as *macro replacement*. The general form of the directive is

#define *macro-name character-sequence*

Notice that there is no semicolon in this statement. There can be any number of spaces between the identifier and the character sequence, but once it begins, it is terminated only by a newline.

For example, if you want to use the word **UP** for the value 1 and **DOWN** for the value 0, then you would use these two directives:

```
#define UP 1
#define DOWN 0
```

This causes the compiler to substitute a 1 or a 0 each time the name **UP** or **DOWN** is encountered in your source file. For example, the following prints "0 1 2" on the screen:

```
printf("%d %d %d", DOWN, UP, UP+1);
```

Once a macro name has been defined, it can be used as part of the definition of other macro names. For example, this code defines the values of **ONE**, **TWO**, and **THREE**:

```
#define ONE    1
#define TWO    ONE+ONE
#define THREE  ONE+TWO
```

Macro substitution is simply the replacement of an identifier with its associated string. Therefore, if you wanted to define a standard error message, you might write something like this:

```
#define E_MS "Standard error on input.\n"
/* ... */
printf(E_MS);
```

The compiler substitutes the string "Standard error on input.\n" when the identifier **E_MS** is encountered. To the compiler, the **printf( )** statement actually appears to be

```
printf("Standard error on input.\n");
```

No text substitutions occur if the identifier is within a quoted string. For example,

```
#define XYZ "this is a test"
/* ... */
printf("XYZ");
```

does not print "this is a test" but "XYZ".

If the string is longer than one line, you can continue it on the next line by placing a backslash at the end of the line, as shown in this example:

```
#define LONG_STRING "This is a very long \
string that is used as an example."
```

C/C++ programmers often use capital letters for defined identifiers. This convention helps anyone reading the program know at a glance that a macro substitution will take place. Also, it is usually best to put all **#define**s at the start of the file or in a separate header file rather than sprinkling them throughout the program.

The most common use of macro substitutions is to define names for "magic numbers" that occur in a program. For example, you may have a program that defines an array and has several routines that access that array. Instead of "hard-coding" the array's size with a constant, you can define a name that represents the size and use that name whenever the size of the array is needed. This way, if you need to change the size of the array, you will only need to change the **#define** statement and then recompile. All uses of the name will automatically be updated. For example:

```
#define MAX_SIZE 100
/* ... */
float balance[MAX_SIZE];
/* ... */
float temp[MAX_SIZE];
```

To change the size of both arrays, simply change the definition of **MAX_SIZE** and recompile.

The **#define** directive has another powerful feature: the macro name can have arguments. Each time the macro name is encountered, the arguments used in its definition are replaced by the actual arguments found in the program. This type of macro is called a *function-like macro*. For example:

```
#include <stdio.h>

#define MIN(a,b)   ((a)<(b)) ? (a) : (b)

int main(void)
{
    int x, y;

    x = 10;
    y = 20;
    printf("The minimum is: %d", MIN(x, y));

    return 0;
}
```

When this program is compiled, the expression defined by **MIN(a,b)** is substituted, except that x and y are used as the operands. That is, the **printf( )** statement looks like this after the substitution:

```
printf("The minimum is: %d",((x)<(y)) ? (x) : (y));
```

Be very careful how you define macros that take arguments; otherwise, there can be some surprising results. For example, examine this short program, which uses a macro to determine whether a value is even or odd:

```
/* This program will give the wrong answer. */

#include <stdio.h>

#define EVEN(a) a%2==0 ? 1 : 0

int main(void)
{
  if(EVEN(9+1)) printf("is even");
  else printf("is odd");

  return 0;
}
```

This program will not work correctly because of the way the macro substitution is made. When C++ Builder compiles this program, the **EVEN(9+1)** is expanded to

```
9+1%2==0 ? 1 : 0
```

As you may recall, the % (modulus) operator has higher precedence than the plus operator. This means that the % operation is first performed on the 1 and that result is added to 9, which (of course) does not equal 0. To fix the trouble, there must be parentheses around **a** in the macro definition of **EVEN**, as shown in this corrected version of the program:

```
#include <stdio.h>

#define EVEN(a) (a)%2==0 ? 1 : 0

int main(void)
{
  if(EVEN(9+1)) printf("is even");
  else printf("is odd");

  return 0;
}
```

Now, the **9+1** is evaluated prior to the modulus operation. In general, it is a good idea to surround macro parameters with parentheses to avoid troubles like the one just described.

The use of macro substitutions in place of real functions has one major benefit: it increases the execution speed of the code because there is no function call overhead. However, if the size of the macro is very large, this increased speed may be paid for with an increase in the size of the program because of duplicated code.

Note   *Although parameterized macros are a valuable feature, you will see in Part Three that C++ has a better way of creating in-line code that does not rely upon macros.*

#error

The **#error** directive forces the compiler to stop compilation. It is used primarily for debugging. The general form of the directive is

#error *error-message*

The *error-message* is not between double quotes. When the compiler encounters this directive, it displays an error message that has the following general form and then terminates compilation.

Fatal: *filename linenum*: Error directive: *error-message*

Here, *filename* is the name of the file in which the **#error** directive was found, *linenum* is the line number of the directive, and *error-message* is the message, itself.

#include

The **#include** directive tells the compiler to read another source file in addition to the one that contains the **#include** directive. The name of the additional source file must be enclosed between double quotes or angle brackets. For example, these two directives both instruct the compiler to read and compile the header for the standard I/O library functions:

```
#include "stdio.h"
#include <stdio.h>
```

The preceding two **#include** directives are the most commonly used ones; however, C++ Builder also supports the following:

#include *macro_name*

Here *macro_name* is a macro that once expanded has the proper header filename, including either the double quotes or the brackets.

Included files can have **#include** directives in them. This is referred to as *nested includes.* For example, this program, shown with its include files, includes a file that includes another file:

```
/* The program file: */
#include <stdio.h>

int main(void)
{
  #include "one"

  return 0;
}




/* Include file ONE: */
printf("This is from the first include file.\n");
#include "two"



/* Include file TWO: */
printf("This is from the second include file.\n");
```

If explicit path names are specified as part of the filename identifier, only those directories are searched for the included file. Otherwise, if the filename is enclosed in quotes, first the directory of the including file is searched (which is often the current working directory), then in the case of nested includes, the directories of any files that include the file are searched, and then the current working directory is searched. If the file is not found, the standard directories are searched.

If no explicit path names are specified and the filename is enclosed by angle brackets, the file is searched for in the standard directories. At no time is the current working directory searched.

Conditional Compilation Directives

There are several directives that allow you to selectively compile portions of your program's source code. This process is called *conditional compilation* and is used widely by commercial software houses that provide and maintain many customized versions of one program.

#if, #else, #elif, and #endif

The general idea behind the **#if** is that if the constant expression following the **#if** is true, the code that is between it and an **#endif** is compiled; otherwise, the code is skipped. The **#endif** is used to mark the end of an **#if** block.

The general form of **#if** is

#if *constant-expression*
   statement sequence
#endif

If the constant expression following the **#if** is true, the code that is between it and **#endif** is compiled; otherwise, the intervening code is skipped. For example:

```
/* A simple #if example. */
#include <stdio.h>

#define MAX 100
int main(void)
{
#if MAX>99
  printf("Compiled for array greater than 99.\n");
#endif
  return 0;
}
```

This program displays the message on the screen because, as defined in the program, **MAX** is greater than 99. This example illustrates an important point. The expression that follows the **#if** is *evaluated at compile time*. Therefore, it must contain only identifiers that have been previously defined and constants; no variables can be used.

The **#else** works in much the same way as the **else** that is part of the C/C++ language: it establishes an alternative if the **#if** fails. The previous example can be expanded as shown here:

```
/* A simple #if/#else example. */
#include <stdio.h>

#define MAX 10
int main(void)
{
```

```
#if MAX>99
  printf("Compiled for array greater than 99.\n");
#else
  printf("Compiled for small array.\n");
#endif
  return 0;
}
```

In this case, **MAX** is defined to be less than 99, so the **#if** portion of the code is not compiled. Instead, the **#else** alternative is compiled and the message "Compiled for small array." is displayed.

Notice that the **#else** is used to mark both the end of the **#if** block and the beginning of the **#else** block. This is necessary because there can be only one **#endif** associated with any **#if**.

The **#elif** directive means "else if" and establishes an if-else-if chain for multiple compilation options. The **#elif** is followed by a constant expression. If the expression is true, that block of code is compiled and no other **#elif** expressions are tested. Otherwise, the next block in the series is checked. The general form of the **#elif** is

#if *expression*
    statement sequence
#elif *expression 1*
    statement sequence
#elif *expression 2*
    statement sequence
#elif *expression 3*
    statement sequence
#elif *expression 4*
.
.
.
#elif *expression N*
    statement sequence
#endif

For example, the following fragment uses the value of **ACTIVE_COUNTRY** to define the currency sign:

```
#define US 0
#define ENGLAND 1
```

```
#define FRANCE 2

#define ACTIVE_COUNTRY US

#if ACTIVE_COUNTRY==US
  char currency[] = "dollar";
#elif ACTIVE_COUNTRY==ENGLAND
  char currency[] = "pound";
#else
  char currency[] = "franc";
#endif
```

#ifs and **#elif**s can be nested. When this occurs, each **#endif**, **#else**, or **#elif** is associated with the nearest **#if** or **#elif**. For example, the following is perfectly valid:

```
#if MAX>100
   #if SERIAL_VERSION
      int port = 198;
   #elif
      int port = 200;
   #endif
#else
   char out_buffer[100];
#endif
```

In C++ Builder, you can use the **sizeof** compile-time operator in an **#if** statement. For example, the next fragment determines whether a program is being compiled for a small or large arrays.

```
#if (sizeof(char *) == 2)
  printf("Program compiled for small array.");
#else
  printf("Program compiled for large array.");
#endif
```

#ifdef and #ifndef

Another method of conditional compilation uses the directives **#ifdef** and **#ifndef**, which mean "if defined" and "if not defined," respectively. The general form of **#ifdef** is

```
#ifdef macro-name
  statement sequence
#endif
```

If the *macro-name* has been previously defined in a **#define** statement, the statement sequence between the **#ifdef** and **#endif** is compiled.

The general form of **#ifndef** is

```
#ifndef macro-name
  statement sequence
#endif
```

If *macro-name* is currently undefined by a **#define** statement, the block of code is compiled.

Both the **#ifdef** and **#ifndef** can use an **#else** or an **#elif** statement. For example,

```
#include <stdio.h>

#define TED 10

int main(void)
{
#ifdef TED
  printf("Hi Ted\n");
#else
  printf("Hi anyone\n");
#endif
#ifndef RALPH
  printf("RALPH not defined\n");
#endif
  return 0;
}
```

prints "Hi Ted" and "RALPH not defined". However, if **TED** were not defined, "Hi anyone" would be displayed, followed by "RALPH not defined".

You can nest **#ifdef**s and **#ifndef**s in the same way as **#if**s.

#undef

The **#undef** directive removes a previously defined definition of the macro name that follows it. That is, it "undefines" a macro. Its general form is

```
#undef macro-name
```

For example:

```
#define LEN 100
#define WIDTH 100

char array[LEN][WIDTH];

#undef LEN
#undef WIDTH
/* at this point both LEN and WIDTH are undefined */
```

Both **LEN** and **WIDTH** are defined until the **#undef** statements are encountered.

The principal use of **#undef** is to allow macro names to be localized to only those sections of code that need them.

Using defined

In addition to **#ifdef**, there is a second way to determine if a macro name is defined. You can use the **#if** directive in conjunction with the **defined** compile-time operator. The **defined** operator has this general form:

defined *macro-name*

If *macro-name* is currently defined, then the expression is true. Otherwise, it is false. For example, to determine if the macro **MYFILE** is defined, you can use either of these two preprocessing commands:

```
#if defined MYFILE
```

or

```
#ifdef MYFILE
```

You may also precede **defined** with the **!** to reverse the condition. For example, the following fragment is compiled only if **DEBUG** is not defined.

```
#if !defined DEBUG
  printf("Final version!\n");
#endif
```

THE FOUNDATION
OF C++

One reason for **defined** is that it allows the existence of a macro name to be determined by a **#elif** statement.

#line

The **#line** directive is used to change the contents of _ _LINE_ _ and _ _FILE_ _, which are predefined identifiers in the compiler. _ _LINE_ _ contains the line number of the line currently being compiled, and _ _FILE_ _ contains the name of the source file being compiled. The basic form of the **#line** command is

#line *number "filename"*

where *number* is any positive integer and the optional *filename* is any valid file identifier. The line number becomes the new value of _ _LINE_ _. The filename becomes the new value of _ _FILE_ _. **#line** is primarily used for debugging and special applications.

For example, the following specifies that the line count will begin with 100. The **printf( )** statement displays the number 102 because it is the third line in the program after the **#line 100** statement.

```
#include <stdio.h>

#line 100                    /* reset the line counter */
int main(void)               /* line 100 */
{                            /* line 101 */
  printf("%d\n",__LINE__);   /* line 102 */

  return 0;
}
```

#pragma

The **#pragma** directive is defined by Standard C/C++ to be an implementation-defined directive that allows various instructions to be given to the compiler. The general form of the **#pragma** directive is

#pragma *name*

where *name* is the name of the **#pragma** directive.

C++ Builder supports these twenty-three **#pragma**s:

alignment	anon_struct	argsused
checkoption	codeseg	comment
defineonoption	exit	hdrfile
hdrstop	inline	intrinsic
link	message	nopushoptwarn
obsolete	option	pack
package	resource	startup
undefineonoption	warn	

Use the **alignment** pragma to show the current enumeration and alignment size. This information is displayed only in the C++ Builder IDE and only if the "Show general messages" option is set.

To enable the use of anonymous structures, specify the **anon_struct** directive.

The **argsused** directive must precede a function. It is used to prevent a warning message if an argument to the function that the **#pragma** precedes is not used in the body of the function.

To check if a compiler option is set, use the **checkoption** directive.

You can specify the segment, class, or group used by a function with the **codeseg** directive.

Using the **comment** directive, you can embed a comment into an output file, such as your program's **.obj** or **.exe** file.

The **defineonoption** directive allows you to define an alias to a command line option. The **undefineonoption** removes the alias.

The **exit** directive specifies one or more functions that will be called when the program terminates. The **startup** directive specifies one or more functions that will be called when the program starts running. They have these general forms:

#pragma exit *function-name priority*
#pragma startup *function-name priority*

The *priority* is an integer value between 64 and 255 (the values 0 through 63 are reserved). The priority determines the order in which the functions are called. If no priority is given, it defaults to 100. All startup and exit functions must be declared as shown here:

```
void f(void);
```

The following example defines a startup function called **start( )**.

```
#include <stdio.h>

void start(void);

#pragma startup start 65

int main(void)
{
  printf("In main\n");

  return 0;
}

void start(void)
{
  printf("In start\n");
}
```

The output from this program is shown here.

```
In start
In main
```

As this example shows, you must provide a function prototype for all exit and startup functions prior to the **#pragma** statement.

You can specify the name of the file that will be used to hold precompiled headers using the **hdrfile** directive. Its general form is

#pragma hdrfile *"fname.csm"*

where *fname* is the name of the file (the extension must be **.csm**).

The **hdrstop** directive tells C++ Builder to stop precompiling header files.

Another **#pragma** directive is **inline**. It has the general form

#pragma inline

This tells the compiler that in-line assembly code is contained in the program. For the fastest compile times, C++ Builder needs to know in advance that in-line assembly code is contained in a program.

Using C++ Builder, it is possible to tell the compiler to generate in-line code instead of an actual function call using the **intrinsic** directive. It has the general form

#pragma intrinsic *func-name*

where *func-name* is the name of the function that you want to in-line.

If you check the Inline Intrinsic Function option in the IDE or use the –Oi command line switch, C++ Builder automatically in-lines the following functions:

alloca	memcpy	strchr	strncat	strrchr
fabs	memset	strcmp	strncmp	rotl
memchr	stpcpy	strcpy	strncpy	rotr
memcmp	strcat	strlen	strnset	

You can override automatic in-lining by using this form of the **intrinsic** directive:

#pragma intrinsic –*func-name*

The **link** directive tells the compiler to add a file into the executable file. It has the general form:

#pragma link *"filename"*

where *filename* may include the path as well as the filename.

The **message** directive lets you specify a message within your program code that is displayed when the program is compiled. For example,

```
#include <stdio.h>

#pragma message This will be displayed.

int main(void)
{
   int i=10;

   printf("This is i: %d\n", i);
#pragma message This is also displayed.
   return 0;
}
```

When you compile the program, you will see the two **#pragma** messages displayed.

The **option** directive allows you to specify command line options within your program instead of actually specifying them on the command line. It has the general form

#pragma option *option-list*

For some options, the **option** directive must precede all declarations, including function prototypes. For this reason, it is a good idea to make it one of the first statements in your program.

The **option** directive also allows you to *push* options onto and *pop* options from a stack. These additional options are good for saving the options state before including any files that may alter the compiler options and then restoring the state afterward. When using the *push* and *pop* argument, you may receive a message indicating that the stack is not the same at the start of the file as it is at the end. To eliminate these warning messages, you should use the **nopushoptwarn** directive.

The **obsolete** directive takes this form:

#pragma obsolete *ident*

and will generate a warning message that *ident* is obsolete, if *ident* is found within the code after the **#pragma**.

The **pack** directive packs the code on a specific byte alignment.

The **package** directive is used to ensure that all the units in a packaged source file are initialized in order of their dependencies.

The **resource** directive marks the file as a form unit for use by the IDE.

The **warn** directive allows you to enable or disable various warning messages. It takes the form

#pragma warn *setting*

where *setting* specifies the warning option. These options are discussed later in this book.

#

The preprocessor directive consisting solely of a # followed by a newline is known as the *null directive.* Any line that begins with this single character is ignored by the compiler.

#import

C++ Builder supports the Microsoft-defined **#import** directive, which is used to import information from a type library. It is included only for Microsoft compatibility.

The # and ## Preprocessor Operators

C provides two preprocessor operators: # and ##. These operators are used in conjunction with **#define**.

The # operator causes the argument it precedes to be turned into a quoted string. For example, consider this program:

```
#include <stdio.h>

#define mkstr(s)   # s

int main(void)
{
  printf(mkstr(I like C++ Builder));

  return 0;
}
```

The preprocessor turns the line

```
printf(mkstr(I like C++ Builder));
```

into

```
printf("I like C++ Builder");
```

The ## operator is used to concatenate two tokens. For example:

```
#include <stdio.h>

#define concat(a, b)   a ## b

int main(void)
{
  int xy = 10;

  printf("%d", concat(x, y));

  return 0;
}
```

The preprocessor transforms

```
printf("%d", concat(x, y));
```

into

```
printf("%d", xy);
```

If these operators seem strange to you, keep in mind that they are not needed or used in most programs. They exist primarily to allow some special cases to be handled by the preprocessor.

Predefined Macro Names

Standard C specifies five built-in predefined macro names. They are

_ _LINE_ _
_ _FILE_ _
_ _DATE_ _
_ _TIME_ _
_ _STDC_ _

Standard C++ adds

_ _cplusplus

To these, C++ Builder defines these additional built-in macros:

_ _BCOPT_ _
_ _BCPLUSPLUS_ _
_ _BORLANDC_ _
_ _CDECL_ _
_CHAR_UNSIGNED
_ _CODEGUARD_ _
_ _CONSOLE_ _
_ CPPUNWIND
_ _DLL_ _
_ _FLAT_ _
_ _FUNC_ _
_M_IX86
_ _MSDOS_ _
_ _MT_ _
_ _PASCAL_ _

_ _TCPLUSPLUS_ _
_ _TEMPLATES_ _
_ _TLS_ _
_ _TURBOC_ _
_WCHAR_T
_WCHAR_T_DEFINED
_Windows
_ _WIN32_ _

The _ _**LINE**_ _ and _ _**FILE**_ _ macros were discussed in the **#line** discussion earlier in this chapter. The others are examined here.

The _ _**DATE**_ _ macro contains a string in the form *month/day/year* that is the date of the translation of the source file into object code.

The time at which the source code was compiled is contained as a string in _ _**TIME**_ _. The form of the string is *hour:minute:second*.

If the macro _ _**STDC**_ _ is defined, your program was compiled with ANSI C compliance checking turned on (–A compiler option). If this is not the case, _ _**STDC**_ _ is undefined. If your program is compiled as a C++ program, _ _**cplusplus**_ is defined as 1. Otherwise, it is not defined.

_ _**BCOPT**_ _ is defined if optimization is used.

If you are using C++ Builder, the macro _ _**BCPLUSPLUS**_ _ is defined if you compile your programs as a C++ program. It is undefined otherwise. Compiling a C++ program also causes _ _**TCPLUSPLUS**_ _ to be defined. Both these macros contain hexadecimal values that will increase with each new release of the compiler.

_ _**BORLANDC**_ _ contains the current version number (as specified in hexadecimal) of the compiler. For C++ Builder 5, the value is 0x0550.

The _ _**CDECL**_ _ macro is defined if the standard C calling convention is used—that is, if the Pascal option is not in use. If this is not the case, the macro is undefined (if defined, its value is 1).

If _**CHAR_UNSIGNED** is defined, the default character type is **unsigned**.

If the CodeGuard tool is used, _ _**CODEGUARD**_ _ will be defined.

When _ _**CONSOLE**_ _ is defined, the program is a console application.

If _ _**CPPUNWIND** is defined as 1, stack unwinding is enabled.

For C++ Builder, _ _**DLL**_ _ is defined as 1 when creating a DLL executable file. Otherwise, it is undefined.

The _ _**FLAT**_ _ macro is defined to 1 when your program is being compiled in flat 32-bit memory mode.

The name of the current function is found in the _ _**FUNC**_ _ macro.

The _**M_IX86** macro is always defined.

The _ _**MSDOS**_ _ macro is defined as an integer constant with a value 1.

The _ _**MT**_ _ macro is defined as 1 only if the multithreaded library is used.

The _ _**PASCAL**_ _ macro is defined as 1 only if the Pascal calling conventions are used to compile a program. If not, this macro is undefined.

When compiling for C++, _ _**TEMPLATES**_ _ is defined as 1. This indicates that templates are supported.

The _ _**TLS**_ _ macro is always defined as 1.

_ _**TURBOC**_ _ represents a hexadecimal value that is increased with each new release.

For C++ programs, _**WCHAR_T** and _**WCHAR_T_DEFINED** are defined as 1 to indicate that **wchar_t** is a built-in data type. They are not defined for C programs.

For C++ Builder, _**Windows** is defined if your program is compiled for use under Windows.

The _ _**WIN32**_ _ macro is always defined as 1.

For the most part, these built-in macros are used in fairly complex programming environments when several different versions of a program are developed or maintained.

Comments

In C, all comments begin with the character pair /* and end with */. There must be no spaces between the asterisk and the slash. The compiler ignores any text between the beginning and ending comment symbols. For example, this program prints only **hello** on the screen:

```
#include <stdio.h>

int main(void)
{
  printf("hello");
  /* printf("there"); */

  return 0;
}
```

Comments may be placed anywhere in a program, as long as they do not appear in the middle of keyword or identifier. That is, this comment is valid:

```
x = 10+ /* add the numbers */5;
```

while

```
swi/*this will not work*/tch(c) { ...
```

is incorrect because a keyword cannot contain a comment. However, you should not generally place comments in the middle of expressions because it obscures their meaning.

Comments may not be nested. That is, one comment may not contain another comment. For example, this code fragment causes a compile-time error:

```
/* this is an outer comment
  x = y/a;
  /* this is an inner comment - and causes an error */
*/
```

You should include comments whenever they are needed to explain the operation of the code. All but the most obvious functions should have a comment at the top that states what the function does, how it is called, and what it returns.

 C++ fully supports C-style comments. However, it also allows you to define a single-line comment. Single line comments begin with a // and end at the end of the line. Also, the new C99 standard for C allows //-style comments.

The Complete Reference

Borland C++ Builder

Part II

The C++ Builder Function Library

Part Two examines the function library included with C++ Builder. Chapter 10 begins with a discussion of linking, libraries, and headers. Chapters 11 through 19 describe the functions found in the library, with each chapter concentrating on a specific group.

The functions described here are available for use by both C and C++ programs. As you may know, the C++ language also defines a number of class libraries that may only be used by C++ programs. Several of the class libraries are described in Part Three, when C++ is discussed.

The
Complete
Reference

Borland
C++
Builder

Chapter 10

Linking, Libraries, and Headers

The creation of a C/C++ compiler involves two major efforts. The first is the construction of the compiler itself. The second is the creation of the function library. Because the C++ Builder library contains so many functions, it is safe to assume that it required a substantial programming effort. (Consider that even a description of these functions requires several hundred pages!) Every C or C++ program relies upon library functions to perform many of the tasks carried out by the program. Because of the fundamental role that the library plays in your program, it is important to have an overview of how the library works. Specifically, you need to understand the job the linker performs, how libraries differ from object files, and the role of headers. These items are examined here.

The Linker

The output of the compiler is a relocatable object file, and the output of the linker is an executable file. The role the linker plays is twofold. First, it physically combines the files specified in the link list into one program file. Second, it resolves external references and memory addresses. An external reference is created any time the code in one file refers to code found in another file. This may be through either a function call or a reference to a global variable. For example, when the two files shown here are linked together, File Two's reference to **count** must be resolved. It is the linker that "tells" the code in File Two where **count** will be found in memory.

File One:

```
int count;
void display(void);

int main(void)
{
  count = 10;
  display();
  return 0;
}
```

File Two:

```
#include <stdio.h>
extern int count;

void display(void)
{
```

```
    printf("%d", count);
}
```

In a similar fashion, the linker also "tells" File One where the function **display( )** is located so that it can be called.

When the compiler generates the object code for File Two, it substitutes a placeholder for the address of **count** because it has no way of knowing where **count** will be located in memory. The same sort of thing occurs when File One is compiled. The address of **display( )** is not known, so a placeholder is used. This process forms the basis for *relocatable code.* When the files are joined by the linker, the placeholders are replaced with relative addresses.

To better understand relocatable code, you must first understand *absolute code.* Although it is seldom used today, in the early days of computers, it was not uncommon for a program to be compiled to run at a specific memory location. When compiled in this way, all addresses are fixed at compile time. Because the addresses are fixed, the program can only be loaded into and executed in exactly one region of memory: the one for which it was compiled. *Relocatable code,* on the other hand, is compiled in such a way that the address information is not fixed. When making a relocatable object file, the linker assigns each call, jump, or global variable an offset. When the file is loaded into memory for execution, the loader automatically resolves the offsets into addresses that will work for the location in memory into which the program is being loaded. This means that a relocatable program can be loaded into and run from many different memory locations.

Library Files Versus Object Files

Although libraries are similar to object files, they have one crucial difference: not all the code in the library is added to your program. When you link a program that consists of several object files, all the code in each object file becomes part of the finished executable program. This happens whether the code is actually used or not. In other words, all object files specified at link time are "added together" to form the program. However, this is not the case with library files.

A library is a collection of functions. Unlike an object file, a library file stores the name of each function, the function's object code, and relocation information necessary to the linking process. When your program references a function contained in a library, the linker looks up that function and adds that code to your program. In this way, only functions that you actually use in your program are added to the executable file.

Since C++ Builder functions are contained in a library, only those actually used by your program will be included in your program's executable code. (If they were in object files, every program you wrote would be several hundred thousand bytes long!)

The Standard Library Versus C++ Builder Extensions

The ANSI/ISO standard for C defines both the form and the content of the C standard function library. Furthermore, C++ includes the entire C function library. Thus, every function in the C library is also a function in the C++ library. C++ Builder supplies all functions defined by the ANSI/ISO C89 and C++ standards. However, to allow the fullest use and control of the computer, C++ Builder contains additional functions that are not defined by Standard C or C++. Such extensions include a complete set of screen manipulation functions for console applications and directory management functions, for example. This book describes both the standard functions and the extended ones added by C++ Builder. As long as you will not be porting the programs you write to a new environment, it is perfectly fine to use these extended functions. However, if ANSI/ISO compliance is an issue, then you will want to use only those functions defined by the standard.

Headers

Many functions found in the C library work with their own specific data types and structures to which your program must have access. These structures and types are defined in *headers*, which for C++ Builder are contained in files supplied with the compiler. They must be included (using **#include**) in any file that uses the specific functions to which they refer. In addition, all functions in the library have their prototypes defined in a header. This is done for two reasons. First, in C++, all functions must be prototyped. Second, although technically an option in C, prototyping is strongly suggested because it provides a means of stronger type checking. In a C program, by including the headers that correspond to the standard functions used by your program, you can catch potential type-mismatch errors. For example, including **<string.h>**, the string function's header, causes the following code to produce a warning message when compiled.

```
#include <string.h>

char s1[20] = "hello ";
char s2[] = "there.";

int main(void)
{
  int p;

  p = strcat(s1, s2);
```

```
   return 0;
}
```

Because **strcat( )** is declared as returning a character pointer in its header, the compiler can now flag as a possible error the assignment of that pointer to the integer **p**.

Remember: although the inclusion of many headers is technically optional (yet advisable) in C, they must be included in all C++ programs. In the remaining chapters of Part Two, the description of each function will specify its header.

C++ Builder supplies a large number of headers. The headers for C++ Builder are located in its Include directory. In a standard installation, this will be Borland\CBuilder5\Include. Fortunately, most of the time your program will only need to include a few of the headers. Several of the more commonly used headers supplied with C++ Builder are shown in Table 10-1. Those headers defined by the ANSI/ISO Standard C/C++ are so indicated.

<alloc.h>	Dynamic allocation functions.
<assert.h>	Defines the **assert( )** macro (ANSI/ISO C/C++).
<conio.h>	Screen-handling functions.
<ctype.h>	Character-handling functions (ANSI/ISO C/C++).
<dir.h>	Directory-handling functions.
<dos.h>	DOS interfacing functions.
<errno.h>	Defines error codes (ANSI/ISO C/C++).
<fcntl.h>	Defines constants used by **open( )** function.
<float.h>	Defines implementation-dependent floating-point values (ANSI/ISO C/C++).
<io.h>	UNIX-like I/O routines.
<limits.h>	Defines various implementation-dependent limits (ANSI/ISO C/C++).
<locale.h>	Country- and language-specific functions (ANSI/ISO C/C++).

Table 10-1.   *Some Commonly Used Headers*

<math.h>	Various definitions used by the math library (ANSI/ISO C/C++).
<process.h>	**spawn( )** and **exec( )** functions.
<setjmp.h>	Nonlocal jumps (ANSI/ISO C/C++).
<share.h>	File sharing.
<signal.h>	Defines signal values (ANSI/ISO C/C++).
<stdarg.h>	Variable-length argument lists (ANSI/ISO C/C++).
<stddef.h>	Defines some commonly used constants (ANSI/ISO C/C++).
<stdio.h>	Declarations for standard I/O streams (ANSI/ISO C/C++).
<stdlib.h>	Miscellaneous declarations (ANSI/ISO C/C++).
<string.h>	String handling (ANSI/ISO C/C++).
<time.h>	System time functions (ANSI/ISO C/C++).

Table 10-1.   *Some Commonly Used Headers* (continued)

Macros in Headers

Many of the library functions are not actually functions at all but rather parameterized macro definitions contained in a header. Generally, this is of little consequence, but this distinction will be pointed out when discussing such "functions." If for some reason you wish to avoid the use of a standard macro, you can undefine it using the **#undef** preprocessing directive.

The
Complete
Reference

Borland
C++
Builder

Chapter 11

I/O Functions

C++ Builder's I/O library functions can be grouped into three major categories:

- The ANSI/ISO C I/O system
- The UNIX-like I/O system
- Several platform-specific I/O functions

This chapter describes the functions that compose the ANSI/ISO C I/O system (which are also supported by C++) and the UNIX-like I/O system. It also describes some of the platform-specific functions. Other platform-specific functions, such as those for direct screen output, are described in Chapter 18. The platform-specific functions relate mostly to the Windows environment, including its "DOS" environment.

For the ANSI/ISO C I/O system, the header **<stdio.h>** is required. For the UNIX-like routines, the header **<io.h>** is required. The platform-specific functions use headers such as **<conio.h>**.

Many of the I/O functions set the predefined global integer variable **errno** to an appropriate error code when an error occurs. This variable is declared in **<errno.h>**.

 The C++ I/O classes, functions, and operators are discussed in Part Three.

int access(const char *filename, int mode)

Description

The prototype for **access( )** is found in **<io.h>**.

The **access( )** function belongs to the UNIX-like file system and is not defined by the ANSI/ISO C/C++ standard. It is used to see if a file exists. It can also be used to tell whether the file is write-protected and if it can be executed. The name of the file in question is pointed to by *filename*. The value of *mode* determines exactly how **access( )** functions. The legal values are

Value	Checks for
0	File existence
1	Executable file
2	Write access
4	Read access
6	Read/write access

The **access( )** function returns 0 if the specified access is allowed; otherwise, it returns –1. Upon failure, the predefined global variable **errno** is set to one of these values:

ENOENT   File not found

EACCES   Access denied

Example

The following program checks to see if the file **TEST.TST** is present in the current working directory:

```
#include <stdio.h>
#include <io.h>

int main(void)
{
  if(!access("TEST.TST", 0))
    printf("File Present");
  else
    printf("File not Found");

  return 0;
}
```

Related Function

chmod( )

int chmod(const char *filename, int mode)

Description

The prototype for **chmod( )** is found in **<io.h>**.

The **chmod( )** function is not defined by the ANSI/ISO C/C++ standard. It changes the access mode of the file pointed to by *filename* to that specified by *mode*. The value of *mode* must be one or both of the macros **S_IWRITE** and **S_IREAD**, which correspond to write access and read access, respectively. To change a file's mode to read/write status, call **chmod( )** with *mode* set to **S_IWRITE | S_IREAD**. These macros are located in the **<sys\stat.h>** header file, which must be included before they can be used.

The **chmod( )** function returns 0 if successful and –1 if unsuccessful.

Example

This call to **chmod( )** attempts to set the file **TEST.TST** to read/write access:

```
if(!chmod("TEST.TST", S_IREAD | S_IWRITE))
  printf("File set to read/write access.");
```

Related Functions

access( ), **_chmod( )**

int chsize(int handle, long size)

Description

The prototype for **chsize( )** is found in **<io.h>**.

The **chsize( )** function is not defined by the ANSI/ISO C/C++ standard. It extends or truncates the file specified by *handle* to the value of *size*.

The **chsize( )** function returns 0 if successful. Upon failure, it returns –1 and **errno** is set to one of the following:

EACCES	Access denied
EBADF	Bad file handle
ENOSPC	Out of space

Example

This call to **chsize( )** attempts to change the size of **TEST.TST**.

```
/*
Assume that a file associated with handle
  has been opened.
*/

if(!chsize(handle, 256))
  printf("File size is now 256 bytes.");
```

Related Functions

open( ), **close( )**, **_creat( )**

void clearerr(FILE *stream)

Description

The prototype for **clearerr( )** is found in **<stdio.h>**.

The **clearerr( )** function is used to reset the file error flag pointed to by *stream* to 0 (off). The end-of-file indicator is also reset.

The error flags for each stream are initially set to 0 by a successful call to **fopen( )**. Once an error has occurred, the flags stay set until an explicit call to either **clearerr( )** or **rewind( )** is made.

File errors can occur for a wide variety of reasons, many of which are system dependent. The exact nature of the error can be determined by calling **perror( )**, which displays which error has occurred (see **perror( )**).

Example

This program copies one file to another. If an error is encountered, a message is printed and the error is cleared.

```
#include <stdio.h>
#include <stdlib.h>

int main(int argc, char *argv[])  /* copy one file to another */
{
  FILE *in, *out;
  char ch;

  if(argc!=3) {
    printf("You forgot to enter a filename\n");
    exit(0);
  }

  if((in=fopen(argv[1], "rb")) == NULL) {
    printf("Cannot open file.\n");
    exit(0);
  }
  if((out=fopen(argv[2],"wb")) == NULL) {
    printf("Cannot open file.\n");
    exit(0);
  }

  while(!feof(in)) {
    ch = getc(in);
    if(ferror(in)) {
```

```
        printf("Read Error");
        clearerr(in);
      } else {
        if(!feof(in)) putc(ch, out);
        if(ferror(out)) {
          printf("Write Error");
          clearerr(out);
        }
      }
    }
  }
  fclose(in);
  fclose(out);

  return 0;
}
```

Related Functions

feof( ), ferror( ), perror( )

int close(int fd)
int _rtl_close(int fd)

Description

The prototypes for **close( )** and **_rtl_close( )** are found in **<io.h>**.

The **close( )** function belongs to the UNIX-like file system and is not defined by the ANSI/ISO C/C++ standard. When **close( )** is called with a valid file descriptor, it closes the file associated with it and flushes the write buffers if applicable. (File descriptors are created through a successful call to **open( )** or **_creat( )** and do not relate to streams or file pointers.)

When successful, **close( )** returns a 0; if unsuccessful, it returns a –1. Although there are several reasons why you might not be able to close a file, the most common is the premature removal of the medium. For example, if you remove a diskette from the drive before the file is closed, an error will result.

The **_rtl_close( )** function works exactly like **close( )**.

Example

This program opens and closes a file using the UNIX-like file system:

```
#include <stdio.h>
#include <fcntl.h>
#include <sys\stat.h>
```

```
#include <io.h>
#include <stdlib.h>

int main(int argc, char *argv[])
{
  int fd;

  if((fd=open(argv[1], O_RDONLY))==-1) {
    printf("Cannot open file.");
    exit(1);
  }

  printf("File is existent.\n");

  if(close(fd))
    printf("Error in closing file.\n");

  return 0;
}
```

Related Functions

open( ), _creat( ), read( ), write( ), unlink( )

int _creat(const char *filename, int pmode)
int _rtl_creat(const char *filename, int attrib)
int creatnew(const char *filename, int attrib)
int creattemp(char *filename, int attrib)

Description

The prototypes for these functions are found in **<io.h>**.

The **_creat( )** function is part of the UNIX-like file system and is not defined by the ANSI/ISO C/C++ standard. Its purpose is to create a new file with the name pointed to by *filename* and to open it for writing. On success **_creat( )** returns a file descriptor that is greater than or equal to 0; on failure it returns a –1. (File descriptors are integers and do not relate to streams or file pointers.)

The value of *pmode* determines the file's access setting, sometimes called its *permission mode*. The value of *pmode* is highly dependent upon the execution environment. For C++ Builder, its values can be **S_IWRITE** or **S_IREAD**. If *pmode* is set to **S_IREAD**, a read-only file is created. If it is set to **S_IWRITE**, a writable file is created. You can OR these values together to create a read/write file.

If, at the time of the call to **_creat( )**, the specified file already exists, it is erased and all previous contents are lost unless the original file was write-protected.

The **_rtl_creat( )** function works like **_creat( )** but uses a DOS/Windows attribute byte. The *attrib* argument may be one of these macros:

FA_RDONLY	Set file to read only
FA_HIDDEN	Make hidden file
FA_SYSTEM	Mark as a system file

The **creatnew( )** function is the same as **_rtl_creat( )** except that if the file already exists on disk, **creatnew( )** returns an error and does not erase the original file.

The **creattemp( )** function is used to create a unique temporary file. You call **creattemp( )** with *filename* pointing to the path name ending with a backslash. Upon return, *filename* contains the name of a unique file. You must make sure that *filename* is large enough to hold the filename.

In the case of an error in any of these functions, **errno** is set to one of these values:

ENOENT	Path or file does not exist
EMFILE	Too many files are open
EACCES	Access denied
EEXIST	File exists (**creatnew( )** only)

Example
The following code creates a file called **test**:

```
#include <stdio.h>
#include <sys\stat.h>
#include <io.h>
#include <stdlib.h>

int main(void)
{
  int fd;

  if((fd=_creat("test", S_IWRITE))==-1) {
    printf("Cannot open file.\n");
    exit(1);
  }
```

```
/* ... */

  close(fd);  /* close the file */

  return 0;
}
```

Related Functions

open( ), close( ), read( ), write( ), unlink( ), eof( )

int dup(int handle)
int dup2(int old_handle, int new_handle)

Description

The prototypes for **dup( )** and **dup2( )** are found in **<io.h>**. The functions are not defined by ANSI/ISO C/C++

The **dup( )** function returns a new file descriptor that fully describes (i.e., duplicates) the state of the file associated with *handle*. It returns nonnegative on success; –1 on failure.

The **dup2( )** function duplicates *old_handle* as *new_handle*. If there is a file associated with *new_handle* prior to the call to **dup2( )**, it is closed. It returns 0 if successful, –1 when an error occurs. In the case of an error, **errno** is set to one of these values:

EMFILE	Too many files are open
EBADF	Bad file handle

Example

This fragment assigns **fp2** a new file descriptor:

```
FILE *fp, *fp2;
/* ... */
fp2 = dup(fp);
```

Related Functions

close( ), _creat( )

int eof(int fd)

Description

The prototype for **eof( )** is found in **<io.h>**.

The **eof( )** function is not defined by the ANSI/ISO C/C++ standard. When called with a valid file descriptor, **eof( )** returns 1 if the end of the file has been reached; otherwise, it returns a 0. If an error has occurred, it returns a –1 and **errno** is set to **EBADF** (bad file number).

Example

The following program displays a text file on the console using **eof( )** to determine when the end of the file has been reached.

```
#include <stdio.h>
#include <io.h>
#include <fcntl.h>
#include <stdlib.h>

int main(int argc, char *argv[])
{
  int fd;
  char ch;

  if((fd=open(argv[1], O_RDWR))==-1) {
    printf("Cannot open file.\n");
    exit(1);
  }

  while(!eof(fd)) {
    read(fd, &ch, 1);  /* read one char at a time */
    printf("%c", ch);
  }

  close(fd);

  return 0;
}
```

Related Functions

open( ), close( ), read( ), write( ), unlink( )

int fclose(FILE *stream)
int _fcloseall(void)

Description

The prototypes for **fclose( )** and **_fcloseall( )** are found in **<stdio.h>**.

The **fclose( )** function closes the file associated with *stream* and flushes its buffer. After an **fclose( )**, *stream* is no longer connected with the file and any automatically allocated buffers are deallocated.

If **fclose( )** is successful, a 0 is returned; otherwise, it returns an EOF. Trying to close a file that has already been closed is an error.

The **_fcloseall( )** function closes all open streams except **stdin**, **stdout**, **stdprn**, and **stderr**. It is not defined by the ANSI/ISO C/C++ standard. It returns EOF on error.

Example

The following code opens and closes a file:

```
#include <stdio.h>
#include <stdlib.h>

int main(void)
{
  FILE *fp;

  if((fp=fopen("test", "rb"))==NULL) {
    printf("Cannot open file.\n");
    exit(1);
  }

/* ... */

  if(fclose(fp))
    printf("File close error.\n");

  return 0;
}
```

THE C++ BUILDER
FUNCTION LIBRARY

Related Functions

fopen( ), freopen( ), fflush( )

FILE *fdopen(int handle, char *mode)

Description

The prototype for **fdopen( )** is found in **<stdio.h>**.

The **fdopen( )** function is not defined by the ANSI/ISO C/C++ standard. It returns a stream that shares the same file that is associated with *handle,* where *handle* is a valid file descriptor obtained through a call to one of the UNIX-like I/O routines. In essence, **fdopen( )** is a bridge between the ANSI/ISO stream-based file system and the UNIX-like file system. The value of *mode* must be the same as that of the mode that originally opened the file.

See **open( )** and **fopen( )** for details.

Related Functions

open( ), fopen( ), _creat( )

int feof(FILE *stream)

Description

The prototype for **feof( )** is found in **<stdio.h>**.

The **feof( )** macro checks the file position indicator to determine if the end of the file associated with *stream* has been reached. A non-0 value is returned if the file position indicator is at the end of the file; a 0 is returned otherwise.

Once the end of the file has been reached, subsequent read operations return **EOF** until either **rewind( )** is called or the file position indicator is moved using **fseek( )**.

The **feof( )** macro is particularly useful when working with binary files because the end-of-file marker is also a valid binary integer. You must make explicit calls to **feof( )** rather than simply testing the return value of **getc( )**, for example, to determine when the end of the file has been reached.

Example

This code fragment shows the proper way to read to the end of a binary file:

```
/*
Assume that fp has been opened as a binary file
  for read operations.
```

```
*/
while(!feof(fp)) getc(fp);
```

Related Functions

clearerr( ), ferror( ), perror( ), putc( ), getc( )

int ferror(FILE *stream)

Description

The prototype for the **ferror( )** macro is found in **<stdio.h>**.

The **ferror( )** function checks for a file error on the given *stream*. A return value of 0 indicates that no error has occurred, while a non-0 value indicates an error.

The error flags associated with *stream* stay set until either the file is closed, or **rewind( )** or **clearerr( )** is called.

Use the **perror( )** function to determine the exact nature of the error.

Example

The following code fragment aborts program execution if a file error occurs:

```
/*
Assume that fp points to a stream opened for write
  operations.
*/

while(!done) {
  putc(info,fp);
  if(ferror(fp)) {
    printf("File Error\n");
    exit(1);
  }
/* ... */
}
```

Related Functions

clearerr( ), feof( ), perror( )

int fflush(FILE *stream)

Description

The prototype for **fflush( )** is found in **<stdio.h>**.

If *stream* is associated with a file opened for writing, a call to **fflush( )** causes the contents of the output buffer to be physically written to the file. If *stream* points to an input file, the input buffer is cleared. In either case the file remains open.

A return value of 0 indicates success, while EOF means an error has occurred.

All buffers are automatically flushed upon normal termination of the program or when they are full. Closing a file flushes its buffer.

Example

The following code fragment flushes the buffer after each write operation.

```
/*
Assume that fp is associated with an output file.
*/
/* ... */
fwrite(buf, sizeof(data_type), 1, fp);
fflush(fp);
/* ... */
```

Related Functions

fclose( ), fopen( ), _flushall( ), fwrite( )

int fgetc(FILE *stream)

Description

The prototype for **fgetc( )** is found in **<stdio.h>**.

The **fgetc( )** function returns the next character from the input *stream* from the current position and increments the file position indicator.

If the end of the file is reached, **fgetc( )** returns **EOF**. However, since **EOF** is a valid integer value, when working with binary files you must use **feof( )** to check for end-of-file. If **fgetc( )** encounters an error, **EOF** is also returned. Again, when working with binary files you must use **ferror( )** to check for file errors.

Example

This program reads and displays the contents of a binary file:

```
#include <stdio.h>
#include <stdlib.h>

int main(int argc, char *argv[])
{
  FILE *fp;
  char ch;

  if((fp=fopen(argv[1], "r"))==NULL) {
    printf("Cannot open file.\n");
    exit(1);
  }

  while((ch=fgetc(fp))!=EOF) {
    printf("%c", ch);
  }
  fclose(fp);

  return 0;
}
```

Related Functions

fputc( ), **getc( )**, **putc( )**, **fopen( )**

int fgetchar(void)

Description

The prototype for **fgetchar( )** is found in **<stdio.h>**.

The **fgetchar( )** macro is defined as **fgetc(stdin)**. Refer to **fgetc( )** for details.

int *fgetpos(FILE *stream, fpos_t *pos)

Description

The prototype for **fgetpos( )** is found in **<stdio.h>**.

The **fgetpos( )** function stores the current location of the file pointer associated with *stream* in the variable pointed to by *pos*. The type **fpos_t** is defined in **<stdio.h>**.

If successful, **fgetpos( )** returns 0; upon failure, a value other than 0 is returned and **errno** is set to one of the following values:

EBADF	Bad file stream
EINVAL	Invalid argument

Example

This program uses **fgetpos( )** to display the current file position:

```
#include <stdio.h>
#include <stdlib.h>

int main(int argc, char *argv[])
{
  FILE *fp;
  long l;
  int  i;
  fpos_t *pos;  /* fpos_t is defined in stdio.h */
  pos = &l;

  if((fp=fopen(argv[1], "w+"))==NULL) {
    printf("Cannot open file.\n");
    exit(1);
  }

  for (i=0; i<10; i++)
    fputc('Z', fp);  /* write 10 Z's to the file */
  fgetpos(fp, pos);

  printf("We are now at position %ld in the file.", *pos);
  fclose(fp);

  return 0;
}
```

Related Functions

fsetpos( ), **fseek( )**, **ftell( )**

char *fgets(char *str, int num, FILE *stream)

Description

The prototype for **fgets( )** is found in **<stdio.h>**.

The **fgets( )** function reads up to *num*–1 characters from *stream* and places them into the character array pointed to by *str*. Characters are read until either a newline or an **EOF** is received or until the specified limit is reached. After the characters have been read, a null is placed in the array immediately after the last character read. A newline character will be retained and will be part of *str*.

If successful, **fgets( )** returns *str*; a null pointer is returned upon failure. If a read error occurs, the contents of the array pointed to by *str* are indeterminate. Because a null pointer is returned when either an error occurs or the end of the file is reached, you should use **feof( )** or **ferror( )** to determine what has actually happened.

Example

This program uses **fgets( )** to display the contents of the text file specified in the first command line argument:

```
#include <stdio.h>
#include <stdlib.h>

int main(int argc, char *argv[])
{
  FILE *fp;
  char str[128];

  if((fp=fopen(argv[1], "r"))==NULL) {
    printf("Cannot open file.\n");
    exit(1);
  }

  while(!feof(fp)) {
    if(fgets(str, 126, fp))
      printf("%s", str);
  }
  fclose(fp);

  return 0;
}
```

THE C++ BUILDER
FUNCTION LIBRARY

Related Functions

fputs( ), fgetc( ), gets( ), puts( )

long filelength(int handle)

Description

The prototype for **filelength( )** is found in **<io.h>**.

The **filelength( )** function is not defined by the ANSI/ISO C/C++ standard. It returns the length, in bytes, of the file associated with the file descriptor *handle*. Remember that the return value is of type **long**. If an error occurs, –1L is returned and **errno** is set to **EBADF**, which means bad file handle.

Example

This fragment prints the length of a file whose file descriptor is **fd**:

```
printf("The file is %ld bytes long.", filelength(fd));
```

Related Function

open( )

int fileno(FILE *stream)

Description

The prototype for the **fileno( )** macro is found in **<stdio.h>**.

The **fileno( )** function is not defined by the ANSI/ISO C/C++ standard. It is used to return a file descriptor to the specified stream.

Example

After this fragment has executed, **fd** is associated with the file pointed to by **stream**:

```
FILE *stream;
int fd;

if((stream=fopen("TEST", "r"))==NULL) {
  printf("Cannot open TEST file.\n");
  exit(1);
}

fd = fileno(stream);
```

Related Function

fdopen( )

int _flushall(void)

Description

The prototype for **_flushall( )** is found in **<stdio.h>**. It is not defined by the ANSI/ISO C/C++ standard.

A call to **_flushall( )** causes the contents of all the output buffers associated with file streams to be physically written to their corresponding files and all the input buffers to be cleared. All streams remain open.

The number of open streams is returned.

All buffers are automatically flushed upon normal termination of the program or when they are full. Also, closing a file flushes its buffer.

Example

The following code fragment flushes all buffers after each write operation:

```
/*
Assume that fp is associated with an output file.
*/
/* ... */
fwrite(buf,sizeof(data_type),1,fp);
_flushall();
```

Related Functions

fclose( ), fopen( ), _fcloseall( ), fflush( )

FILE *fopen(const char *fname, const char *mode)

Description

The prototype for **fopen( )** is found in **<stdio.h>**.

The **fopen( )** function opens a file whose name is pointed to by *fname* and returns the stream that is associated with it. The type of operations that are allowed on the file are defined by the value of *mode*. The legal values for *mode* are shown in Table 11-1. The parameter *fname* must be a string of characters that constitutes a valid filename and can include a path specification.

If **fopen( )** is successful in opening the specified file, a **FILE** pointer is returned. If the file cannot be opened, a null pointer is returned.

As Table 11-1 shows, a file can be opened in either text or binary mode. In text mode, carriage return, linefeed sequences are translated to newline characters on input. On output, the reverse occurs: newlines are translated to carriage return, linefeeds. No such translations occur on binary files.

Mode	Meaning
"r"	Open a file for reading. (Opened as text file by default, see discussion.)
"w"	Create a file for writing. (Opened as text file by default, see discussion.)
"a"	Append to a file. (Opened as text file by default, see discussion.)
"rb"	Open a binary file for reading.
"wb"	Create a binary file for writing.
"ab"	Append to a binary file.
"r+"	Open a file for read/write. (Open as text file by default, see discussion.)
"w+"	Create a file for read/write. (Open as text file by default, see discussion.)
"a+"	Append or create a file for read/write. (Open as text file by default, see discussion.)
"r+b"	Open a binary file for read/write.
"w+b"	Create a binary file for read/write.
"a+b"	Append or create a binary file for read/write.
"rt"	Open a text file for reading.
"wt"	Create a text file for writing.
"at"	Append to a text file.
"r+t"	Open a text file for read/write.
"w+t"	Create a text file for read/write.
"a+t"	Append or create a text file for read/write.

Table 11-1.   *Legal Values for mode*

If the *mode* string does not specify either a **b** (for binary) or a **t** (for text), the type of file opened is determined by the value of the built-in global variable **_fmode**. By default, **_fmode** is **O_TEXT**, which means text mode. It can be set to **O_BINARY**, which means binary mode. These macros are defined in **<fcntl.h>**.

One correct method of opening a file is illustrated by this code fragment:

```
FILE *fp;

if ((fp = fopen("test", "w"))==NULL) {
  printf("Cannot open file.\n");
  exit(1);
}
```

This method detects any error in opening a file, such as a write-protected or full disk, before attempting to write to it. A null, which is 0, is used because no file pointer ever has that value. **NULL** is defined in **<stdio.h>**.

If you use **fopen( )** to open a file for write operations, any preexisting file by that name is erased, and a new file is started. If no file by that name exists, one is created. If you want to add to the end of the file, you must use mode **a**. If the file does not exist, an error is returned. Opening a file for read operations requires an existing file. If no file exists, an error is returned. Finally, if a file is opened for read/write operations, it is not erased if it exists; however, if no file exists, one is created.

Example

This fragment opens a file called **test** for binary read/write operations:

```
FILE *fp;

if((fp=fopen("test", "r+b"))==NULL) {
  printf("Cannot open file.\n");
  exit(1);
}
```

Related Functions

fclose( ), fread( ), fwrite( ), putc( ), getc( )

int fprintf(FILE *stream, const char *format, arg-list)

Description

The prototype for **fprintf( )** is found in **<stdio.h>**.

The **fprintf( )** function outputs the values of the arguments that make up *arg-list* as specified in the *format* string to the stream pointed to by *stream*. The return value is the number of characters actually printed. If an error occurs, a negative number is returned.

The operations of the format control string and commands are identical to those in **printf( )**; see the **printf( )** function for a complete description.

Example

This program creates a file called **test** and writes the string "this is a test 10 20.01" into the file using **fprintf( )** to format the data:

```
#include <stdio.h>
#include <stdlib.h>

int main(void)
{
  FILE *fp;

  if((fp=fopen("test", "w"))==NULL) {
    printf("Cannot open file.\n");
    exit(1);
  }

  fprintf(fp, "this is a test %d %f", 10, 20.01);

  fclose(fp);

  return 0;
}
```

Related Functions

printf( ), fscanf( )

int fputc(int ch, FILE *stream)

Description

The prototype for **fputc( )** is found in **<stdio.h>**.

The **fputc( )** function writes the character *ch* to the specified stream at the current file position and then increments the file position indicator. Even though *ch* is declared to be an **int**, it is converted by **fputc( )** into an **unsigned char**. Because all character arguments are elevated to integers at the time of the call, you generally see character variables used as arguments. If an integer is used, the high-order byte is simply discarded.

The value returned by **fputc( )** is the value of the character written. If an error occurs, **EOF** is returned. For files opened for binary operations, **EOF** may be a valid character, and the function **ferror( )** must be used to determine whether an error has actually occurred.

Example

This function writes the contents of a string to the specified stream:

```
void write_string(char *str, FILE *fp)
{
  while(*str) if(!ferror(fp)) fputc(*str++, fp);
}
```

Related Functions

fgetc( ), fopen( ), fprintf( ), fread( ), fwrite( )

int fputchar(int ch)

Description

The prototype for **fputchar( )** is found in **<stdio.h>**.

The **fputchar( )** function writes the character *ch* to **stdout**. Even though *ch* is declared to be an **int**, it is converted by **fputchar( )** into an **unsigned char**. Because all character arguments are elevated to integers at the time of the call, you generally see character variables used as arguments. If an integer is used, the high-order byte is simply discarded. A call to **fputchar( )** is the functional equivalent of a call to **fputc(ch, stdout)**.

The value returned by **fputchar( )** is the value of the character written. If an error occurs, **EOF** is returned. For files opened for binary operations, **EOF** may be a valid character and the function **ferror( )** must be used to determine whether an error has actually occurred.

Example

This function writes the contents of a string to **stdout**:

```
void write_string(char *str)
{
  while(*str) if(!ferror(fp)) fputchar(*str++);
}
```

Related Functions

fgetc( ), fopen( ), fprintf( ), fread( ), fwrite( )

int fputs(const char *str, FILE *stream)

Description

The prototype for **fputs( )** is found in **<stdio.h>**.

The **fputs( )** function writes the contents of the string pointed to by *str* to the specified stream. The null terminator is not written.

The **fputs( )** function returns nonnegative on success, **EOF** on failure. If the stream is opened in text mode, certain character translations may take place. This means that there may not be a one-to-one mapping of the string onto the file. However, if it is opened in binary mode, no character translations occur and a one-to-one mapping exists between the string and the file.

Example

This code fragment writes the string "this is a test" to the stream pointed to by **fp**.

```
fputs("this is a test", fp);
```

Related Functions

fgets( ), gets( ), puts( ), fprintf( ), fscanf( )

size_t fread(void *buf, size_t size, size_t count, FILE *stream)

Description

The prototype for **fread( )** is found in **<stdio.h>**.

The **fread( )** function reads *count* number of objects—each object being *size* number of bytes in length—from the stream pointed to by *stream* and places them in the array pointed to by *buf*. The file position indicator is advanced by the number of bytes read.

The **fread( )** function returns the number of items actually read. If fewer items are read than are requested in the call, either an error has occurred or the end of the file has been reached. You must use **feof( )** or **ferror( )** to determine what has taken place.

If the stream is opened for text operations, then carriage return, linefeed sequences are automatically translated into newlines.

Example

This program reads ten floating-point numbers from a disk file called **test** into the array **bal**:

```
#include <stdio.h>
#include <stdlib.h>

int main(void)
{
  FILE *fp;
  float bal[10];

  if((fp=fopen("test", "rb"))==NULL) {
    printf("Cannot open file.\n");
    exit(1);
  }

  if(fread(bal, sizeof(float), 10, fp)!=10) {
    if(feof(fp)) printf("Premature end of file.");
    else printf("File read error.");
  }

  fclose(fp);

  return 0;
}
```

Related Functions

fwrite( ), fopen( ), fscanf( ), fgetc( ), getc( )

FILE *freopen(const char *fname, const char *mode, FILE *stream)

Description

The prototype for **freopen( )** is found in **<stdio.h>**.

The **freopen( )** function is used to associate an existing stream with a different file. The new file's name is pointed to by *fname*, the access mode is pointed to by *mode*, and the stream to be reassigned is pointed to by *stream*. The string *mode* uses the same format as **fopen( )**; a complete discussion is found in the **fopen( )** description.

When called, **freopen( )** first tries to close a file that is currently associated with *stream*. However, failure to achieve a successful closing is ignored, and the attempt to reopen continues.

The **freopen( )** function returns a pointer to *stream* on success and a null pointer otherwise.

The main use of **freopen( )** is to redirect the system-defined files **stdin**, **stdout**, and **stderr** to some other file.

Example

The program shown here uses **freopen( )** to redirect the stream **stdout** to the file called **OUT**. Because **printf( )** writes to **stdout**, the first message is displayed on the screen and the second is written to the disk file.

```
#include <stdio.h>
#include <stdlib.h>

int main(void)
{
  FILE *fp;

  printf("This will display on the screen\n");

  if((fp=freopen("OUT", "w", stdout))==NULL) {
    printf("Cannot open file.\n");
    exit(1);
  }

  printf("This will be written to the file OUT");
  fclose(fp);

  return 0;
}
```

Related Functions

fopen( ), fclose( )

int fscanf(FILE *stream, const char *format, arg-list)

Description

The prototype for **fscanf( )** is found in **<stdio.h>**.

The **fscanf( )** function works exactly like the **scanf( )** function except that it reads the information from the stream specified by *stream* instead of **stdin**. See the **scanf( )** function for details.

The **fscanf( )** function returns the number of arguments actually assigned values. This number does not include skipped fields. A return value of **EOF** means that an attempt was made to read past the end of the file.

Example
This code fragment reads a string and a **float** number from the stream **fp**:

```
char str[80];
float f;

fscanf(fp, "%s%f", str, &f);
```

Related Functions

scanf( ), **fprintf( )**

int fseek(FILE *stream, long offset, int origin)

Description
The prototype for **fseek( )** is found in **<stdio.h>**.

The **fseek( )** function sets the file position indicator associated with *stream* according to the values of *offset* and *origin*. Its main purpose is to support random I/O operations. The *offset* is the number of bytes from *origin* to make the new position. The *origin* is 0, 1, or 2, with 0 being the start of the file, 1 the current position, and 2 the end of the file. The following macros for *origin* are defined in **<stdio.h>**:

Name	Origin
SEEK_SET	Beginning of file
SEEK_CUR	Current position
SEEK_END	End-of-file

A return value of 0 means that **fseek( )** succeeded. A non-0 value indicates failure.

You can use **fseek( )** to move the position indicator anywhere in the file, even beyond the end. However, it is an error to attempt to set the position indicator before the beginning of the file.

The **fseek( )** function clears the end-of-file flag associated with the specified stream. Furthermore, it nullifies any prior **ungetc( )** on the same stream. (See **ungetc( )**.)

Example

The function shown here seeks to the specified structure of type **addr**. Notice the use of **sizeof** both to obtain the proper number of bytes to seek and to ensure portability.

```
struct addr {
char name[40];
  char street[40];
  char city[40];
  char state[3];
  char zip[10];
} info;

void find(long client_num)
{
  FILE *fp;

  if((fp=fopen("mail", "rb"))==NULL) {
    printf("Cannot open file.\n");
    exit(1);
  }

  /* find the proper structure */
  fseek(client_num*sizeof(struct addr), 0);

  /* read the data into memory */
  fread(&info, sizeof(struct addr), 1, fp);
  fclose(fp);
}
```

Related Functions

ftell( ), rewind( ), fopen( )

int fsetpos(FILE *stream, const fpos_t *pos)

Description

The prototype for **fsetpos( )** is found in **<stdio.h>**.

The **fsetpos( )** function sets the file pointer associated with *stream* to the location pointed to by *pos*. This value was set by a previous call to **fgetpos( )**. The type **fpos_t** is defined in **<stdio.h>**. It is capable of representing any file location.

If successful, **fsetpos( )** returns 0; upon failure, a value other than 0 is returned, and **errno** is also set to a non-0 value.

Example

This program uses **fsetpos( )** to reset the current file position to an earlier value:

```c
#include <stdio.h>
#include <stdlib.h>

int main(int argc, char *argv[])
{
  FILE *fp;
  long l;
  int  i;
  fpos_t *pos;  /* fpos_t is defined in stdio.h */
  pos = &l;

  if((fp=fopen(argv[1], "w+"))==NULL) {
    printf("Cannot open file.\n");
    exit(1);
  }

  for (i=0; i<10; i++)
    fputc('Y', fp);  /* write 10 Y's to the file */
  fgetpos(fp, pos);

  for (i=0; i<10; i++)
    fputc('Z', fp);  /* write 10 Z's to the file */
  fsetpos(fp, pos);  /* reset to the end of the Y's */

  fputc('A', fp);      /* replace first Z with an A. */
  fclose(fp);

  return 0;
}
```

Related Functions

fgetpos( ), **fseek( )**, **ftell( )**

FILE *_fsopen(const char *fname, const char *mode, int shflg)

Description

The prototype for **_fsopen( )** is found in **<stdio.h>**. You will also need to include **<share.h>**. This function is not defined by the ANSI/ISO C/C++ standard.

The **_fsopen( )** function opens a file whose name is pointed to by *fname* and returns a **FILE** pointer to the stream associated with it. The file is opened for shared-mode access using a network. It returns null if the file cannot be opened.

_fsopen( ) is similar to the standard library function **fopen( )** except that it is designed for use with networks to manage file sharing. The string pointed to by *mode* determines the type of operations that may be performed on the file. Its legal values are the same as for **fopen( )**. (Refer to **fopen( )** for details.)

The *shflg* parameter determines how file sharing will be allowed. It will be one of the following macros (defined in **<share.h>**):

shflg	Meaning
SH_COMPAT	Compatibility mode
SH_DENYRW	No reading or writing
SH_DENYWR	No writing
SH_DENYRD	No reading
SH_DENYNONE	Allow reading and writing
SH_DENYNO	Allow reading and writing

Example

This call to **_fsopen( )** opens a file called **TEST.DAT** for binary output and denies network input operations:

```
fp=_fsopen("TEST.DAT", "wb", SH_DENYRD);
```

Related Functions

fopen( ), sopen( )

int fstat(int handle, struct stat *statbuf)

Description

The prototype for **fstat( )** is found in **<sys\stat.h>**.

The function is not defined by the ANSI/ISO C/C++ standard. The **fstat( )** function fills the structure *statbuf* with information on the file associated with the file descriptor *handle*. Information on the contents of **stat** can be found in the file **<sys\stat.h>**.

Upon successfully filling the **stat** structure, 0 is returned. On error, −1 is returned and **errno** is set to **EBADF**.

Example

The following example opens a file, fills the **stat** structure, and prints out one of its fields:

```
#include <stdio.h>
#include <sys\stat.h>
#include <stdlib.h>

int main(void)
{
  FILE *fp;
  struct stat buff;

  if((fp=fopen("test", "rb"))==NULL) {
    printf("Cannot open file.\n");
    exit(1);
  }

  /* fill the stat structure */
  fstat(fileno(fp), &buff);

  printf("Size of the file is: %ld\n", buff.st_size);
  fclose(fp);

  return 0;
}
```

Related Functions

stat( ), **access( )**

long ftell(FILE *stream)

Description

The prototype for **ftell( )** is found in **<stdio.h>**.

The **ftell( )** function returns the current value of the file position indicator for the specified stream. This value is the number of bytes the indicator is from the beginning of the file.

The **ftell( )** function returns –1L when an error occurs. If the stream is incapable of random seeks—if it is the console, for instance—the return value is undefined.

Example

This code fragment returns the current value of the file position indicator for the stream pointed to by **fp**:

```
long i;
if((i=ftell(fp))==-1L) printf("A file error has occurred.\n");
```

Related Function

fseek( )

size_t fwrite(const void *buf, size_t size, size_t count, FILE *stream)

Description

The prototype for **fwrite( )** is found in **<stdio.h>**.

The **fwrite( )** function writes *count* number of objects—each object being *size* number of bytes in length—to the stream pointed to by *stream* from the array pointed to by *buf*. The file-position indicator is advanced by the number of bytes written.

The **fwrite( )** function returns the number of items actually written, which, if the function is successful, equals the number requested. If fewer items are written than are requested, an error has occurred.

If the stream is opened for text operations, then newlines characters are automatically translated into carriage return, linefeed sequences when the file is written.

Example

This program writes a **float** to the file **test**. Notice that **sizeof** is used both to determine the number of bytes in a **float** variable and to ensure portability.

```
#include <stdio.h>
#include <stdlib.h>

int main(void)
{
  FILE *fp;
  float f=12.23;

  if((fp=fopen("test", "wb"))==NULL) {
    printf("Cannot open file.\n");
    exit(1);
  }

  fwrite(&f, sizeof(float), 1, fp);

  fclose(fp);

  return 0;
}
```

Related Functions

fread( ), **fscanf( )**, **getc( )**, **fgetc( )**

int getc(FILE *stream)

Description

The prototype for **getc( )** is found in **<stdio.h>**.

The **getc( )** macro returns the next character from the current position in the input *stream* and increments the file position indicator. The character is read as an **unsigned char** that is converted to an integer.

If the end of the file is reached, **getc( )** returns **EOF**. However, since **EOF** is a valid integer value, when working with binary files you must use **feof( )** to check for the end of the file. If **getc( )** encounters an error, **EOF** is also returned. Remember that if you are working with binary files, you must use **ferror( )** to check for file errors.

Example

This program reads and displays the contents of a text file:

```
#include <stdio.h>
#include <stdlib.h>
```

```
int main(int argc, char *argv[])
{
  FILE *fp;
  char ch;

  if((fp=fopen(argv[1], "r"))==NULL) {
    printf("Cannot open file.\n");
    exit(1);
  }

  while((ch=getc(fp))!=EOF)
    printf("%c", ch);

  fclose(fp);

  return 0;
}
```

Related Functions

fputc( ), fgetc( ), putc( ), fopen( )

int getch(void)
int getche(void)

Description

The prototypes for **getch( )** and **getche( )** are found in **<conio.h>**.

The **getch( )** function returns the next character read from the console but does not echo that character to the screen.

The **getche( )** function returns the next character read from the console and echoes that character to the screen.

Neither function is defined by the ANSI/ISO C/C++ standard.

Example

This fragment uses **getch( )** to read the user's menu selection for a spelling checker program.

```
do {
  printf("1: Check spelling\n");
  printf("2: Correct spelling\n");
```

```
    printf("3: Look up a word in the dictionary\n");
    printf("4: Quit\n");

    printf("\nEnter your selection: ");
    choice = getch();
  } while(!strchr("1234", choice));
```

Related Functions

getc( ), getchar( ), fgetc( )

int getchar(void)

Description

The prototype for **getchar( )** is found in **<stdio.h>**.

The **getchar( )** macro returns the next character from **stdin**. The character is read as an **unsigned char** that is converted to an integer. If the end-of-file marker is read, **EOF** is returned.

The **getchar( )** macro is functionally equivalent to **getc(stdin)**.

Example

This program reads characters from **stdin** into the array **s** until a carriage return is entered and then displays the string.

```
#include <stdio.h>

int main(void)
{
  char s[256], *p;

  p = s;

  while((*p++=getchar())!='\n') ;
  *p = '\0';  /* add null terminator */
  printf(s);

  return 0;
}
```

THE C++ BUILDER
FUNCTION LIBRARY

Related Functions

fputc( ), fgetc( ), putc( ), fopen( )

char *gets(char *str)

Description

The prototype for **gets( )** is found in **<stdio.h>**.

The **gets( )** function reads characters from **stdin** and places them into the character array pointed to by *str*. Characters are read until a newline or an **EOF** is reached. The newline character is not made part of the string but is translated into a null to terminate the string.

If successful, **gets( )** returns *str*; if unsuccessful, it returns a null pointer. If a read error occurs, the contents of the array pointed to by *str* are indeterminate. Because a null pointer is returned when either an error has occurred or the end of the file is reached, you should use **feof( )** or **ferror( )** to determine what has actually happened.

There is no limit to the number of characters that **gets( )** will read; it is the programmer's job to make sure that the array pointed to by *str* is not overrun. When performing user input for real-world applications, a better choice is **fgets( )**.

Example

This program uses **gets( )** to read a filename:

```
#include <stdio.h>
#include <stdlib.h>

int main(void)
{
  FILE *fp;
  char fname[128];

  printf("Enter filename: ");
  gets(fname);

  if((fp=fopen(fname, "r"))==NULL) {
    printf("Cannot open file.\n");
    exit(1);
  }

/* ...*/
```

```
    fclose(fp);
    return 0;
}
```

Related Functions

fputs( ), fgetc( ), fgets( ), puts( )

int getw(FILE *stream)

Description

The prototype for **getw( )** is found in **<stdio.h>**.

The **getw( )** function is not defined by the ANSI/ISO C/C++ standard.

The **getw( )** function returns the next integer from *stream* and advances the file position indicator appropriately.

Because the integer read may have a value equal to **EOF**, you must use **feof( )** or **ferror( )** to determine when the end-of-file marker is reached or an error has occurred.

Example

This program reads integers from the file **inttest** and displays their sum.

```
#include <stdio.h>
#include <stdlib.h>

int main(void)
{
  FILE *fp;
  int sum = 0;

  if((fp=fopen("inttest", "rb"))==NULL) {
    printf("Cannot open file.\n");
    exit(1);
  }

  while(!feof(fp))
    sum = getw(fp)+sum;

  printf("The sum is %d", sum);
```

```
    fclose(fp);

    return 0;
}
```

Related Functions

putw( ), **fread( )**

int isatty(int handle)

Description

The prototype for **isatty( )** is found in **<io.h>**.

The function **isatty( )** is not defined by the ANSI/ISO C/C++ standard. It returns non-0 if *handle* is associated with a character device that is either a terminal, console, printer, or serial port; otherwise, it returns 0.

Example

This fragment reports whether the device associated with **fd** is a character device:

```
if(isatty(fd)) printf("is a character device");
else printf("is not a character device");
```

Related Function

open( )

int lock(int handle, long offset, long length)

Description

The prototype for **lock( )** is found in **<io.h>**.

The **lock( )** function is not defined by the ANSI/ISO C/C++ standard. It is used to lock a region of a file, thus preventing another program from using it until the lock is removed. To unlock a file use **unlock( )**. These functions provide control for file sharing in network environments.

The file to be locked is associated with *handle*. The portion of the file to be locked is determined by the starting *offset* from the beginning of the file and the *length*.

If **lock( )** is successful, 0 is returned. Upon failure, –1 is returned.

Example

This fragment locks the first 128 bytes of the file associated with **fd**:

```
lock(fd, 0, 128);
```

Related Functions

unlock( ), **sopen( )**

int locking(int handle, int mode, long length)

Description

The prototype for **locking( )** is in **<io.h>**. You must also include **<sys\locking.h>**.

The **locking( )** function is not defined by the ANSI/ISO C/C++ standard. It is used to lock a region of a shared file when using a network. Locking the file prevents other users from accessing it.

The *mode* parameter must be one of these macros:

Mode	Meaning
LK_LOCK	Lock the specified region. If the locking request fails, retry 10 times, once each second.
LK_RLCK	Same as LK_LOCK
LK_NBLCK	Lock the specified region. If the locking request fails, perform no retries.
LK_NBRLCK	Same as LK_NBLCK
LK_UNLCK	Unlock the specified region.

The handle of the file to lock is specified in *handle*. The file will be locked (or unlocked) beginning with the current position and extending *length* number of bytes.

The **locking( )** function returns 0 if successful and –1 otherwise. On failure, **errno** is set to one of these values:

EBADF	Bad file handle
EACCESS	Access denied
EDEADLOCK	File cannot be locked
EINVAL	Invalid argument

Example

This call to **locking( )** unlocks 10 bytes in the file described by **fd**:

```
if(locking(fd, LK_UNLOCK, 10)) {
// process error
}
```

Related Functions

lock( ), sopen( )

long lseek(int handle, long offset, int origin)

Description

The prototype for **lseek( )** is found in **<io.h>**.

The **lseek( )** function is part of the UNIX-like I/O system and is not defined by the ANSI/ISO C/C++ standard.

The **lseek( )** function sets the file position indicator to the location specified by *offset* and *origin* for the file specified by *handle*.

How **lseek( )** works depends on the values of *origin* and *offset*. The *origin* may be either 0, 1, or 2. The following chart explains how the *offset* is interpreted for each *origin* value:

Origin	Effect of Call to lseek( )
0	Count the offset from the start of the file
1	Count the offset from the current position
2	Count the offset from the end of the file

The following macros are defined in **<io.h>**. They can be used for a value of *origin* in order of 0 through 2.

SEEK_SET
SEEK_CUR
SEEK_END

The **lseek( )** function returns *offset* on success. Therefore, **lseek( )** will be returning a **long** integer. Upon failure, a −1L is returned and **errno** is set to one of these values;

EBADF	Bad file number
EINVAL	Invalid argument
ESPIPE	Seek attempted is illegal.

Example
The example shown here allows you to examine a file one sector at a time using the UNIX-like I/O system. You will want to change the buffer size to match the sector size of your system.

```
#include <stdio.h>
#include <fcntl.h>
#include <sys\stat.h>
#include <io.h>
#include <stdlib.h>

#define BUF_SIZE  128

/* read buffers using lseek() */
int main(int argc, char *argv[])
{
  char buf[BUF_SIZE+1], s[10];
  int fd, sector;

  buf[BUF_SIZE+1] = '\0'; /* null terminate buffer for printf */
  if((fd=open(argv[1], O_RDONLY | O_BINARY))==-1) { /* open for write */
    printf("Cannot open file.\n");
    exit(0);
  }
  do {
    printf("Buffer: ");
    gets(s);
```

```
    sector = atoi(s); /* get the sector to read */

    if(lseek(fd, (long)sector*BUF_SIZE,0)==-1L)
      printf("Seek Error\n");

    if(read(fd, buf, BUF_SIZE)==0) {
      printf("Read Error\n");
    }
    else {
      printf("%s\n", buf);
    }
  } while(sector > 0);
  close(fd);

  return 0;
}
```

Related Functions

read( ), write( ), open( ), close( )

int open(const char *filename, int access, unsigned mode)
int _rtl_open(const char *filename, int access)

Description

The prototypes for **open( )** and **_rtl_open( )** are found in **<io.h>**.

The **open( )** function is part of the UNIX-like I/O system and is not defined by the ANSI/ISO C/C++ standard.

Unlike the C/C++ I/O system, the UNIX-like system does not use file pointers of type **FILE**, but rather file descriptors of type **int**. The **open( )** function opens a file with the name *filename* and sets its access mode as specified by *access*. You can think of *access* as being constructed of a base mode of operation plus modifiers. The following base modes are allowed.

Base	Meaning
O_RDONLY	Open for read only
O_WRONLY	Open for write only
O_RDWR	Open for read/write

After selecting one of these values, you may **OR** it with one or more of the following access modifiers:

Access modifiers	Meaning
O_NDELAY	Not used; included for UNIX compatibility
O_APPEND	Causes the file pointer to be set to the end of the file before to each write operation
O_CREAT	If the file does not exist, creates it with its attribute set to the value of *mode*
O_TRUNC	If the file exists, truncates it to length 0 but retains its file attributes
O_EXCL	When used with O_CREAT, will not create output file if a file by that name already exists
O_BINARY	Opens a binary file
O_TEXT	Opens a text file

The *mode* argument is required only if the **O_CREAT** modifier is used. In this case, *mode* may be one of three values:

Mode	Meaning
S_IWRITE	Write access
S_IREAD	Read access
S_IWRITE	S_IREAD	Read/write access

A successful call to **open( )** returns a positive integer that is the file descriptor associated with the file. A return value of –1 means that the file cannot be opened, and **errno** is set to one of these values:

ENOENT	File does not exist
EMFILE	Too many open files
EACCES	Access denied
EINVACC	Access code is invalid

The function **_rtl_open( )** accepts a larger number of modifiers for the *access* parameter. These additional values are

Access Modifier	Meaning
O_NOINHERIT	File not passed to child programs
SH_COMPAT	Other open operations that use SH_COMPAT are allowed
SH_DENYRW	Only the current file descriptor has access to the file
SH_DENYWR	Only read access to the file allowed
SH_DENYRD	Only write access to the file allowed
SH_DENYNO	Allow other sharing options except SH_COMPAT

Example

You will usually see the call to **open( )** like this:

```
if((fd=open(filename, mode)) == -1)  {
printf("Cannot open file.\n");
   exit(1);
}
```

Related Functions

close( ), **read( )**, **write( )**

void perror(const char *str)

Description

The prototype for **perror( )** is found in **<stdio.h>**.

The **perror( )** function maps the value of the global **errno** onto a string and writes that string to **stderr**. If the value of *str* is not null, the string is written first, followed by a colon, and then the proper error message as determined by the value of **errno**.

Example

This program purposely generates a domain error by calling **asin( )** with an out-of-range argument. The output is "Program Error Test: Math argument".

```
#include <stdio.h>
#include <math.h>
#include <errno.h> /* contains declaration for errno */

int main(void)
```

```
{
  /* this will generate a domain error */
  asin(10.0);
  if(errno==EDOM)
    perror("Program Error Test");

  return 0;
}
```

Related Function
ferror( )

int printf (const char *format, arg-list)

Description
The prototype for **printf( )** is found in **<stdio.h>**.

The **printf( )** function writes to **stdout** the arguments that make up *arg-list* under the control of the string pointed to by *format.*

The string pointed to by *format* contains two types of items. The first type consists of characters that will be printed on the screen. The second type contains format specifiers that define the way the arguments are displayed. A format specifier consists of a percent sign followed by the format code. The format commands are shown in Table 11-2. There must be exactly the same number of arguments as there are format specifiers, and the format specifiers and arguments are matched in order. For example, this **printf( )** call

```
printf("Hi %c %d %s", 'c', 10, "there!");
```

displays **Hi c 10 there!**.

If there are insufficient arguments to match the format commands, the output is undefined. If there are more arguments than format commands, the remaining arguments are discarded.

The **printf( )** function returns the number of characters actually printed. A negative return value indicates an error.

The format commands may have modifiers that specify the field width, the precision, and left-justification. An integer placed between the percent sign and the format command acts as a *minimum field-width specifier,* padding the output with blanks or zeros to ensure that it is a minimum length. If the string or number is greater than that minimum, it will be printed in full. The default padding is done with spaces. For numeric values, if you wish to pad with zeros, place a zero before the field width specifier. For example, **%05d** pads a number of less than five digits with zeros so that its total length is five digits.

Code	Format
%c	Character
%d	Signed decimal integers
%i	Signed decimal integers
%e	Scientific notation (lowercase e)
%E	Scientific notation (uppercase E)
%f	Decimal floating point
%g	Uses %e or %f, whichever is shorter (if %g, uses lowercase e).
%G	Uses %E or %f, whichever is shorter (if %G, uses uppercase E).
%o	Unsigned octal
%s	String of characters
%u	Unsigned decimal integers
%x	Unsigned hexadecimal (lowercase letters)
%X	Unsigned hexadecimal (uppercase letters)
%p	Displays a pointer.
%n	Associated argument is a pointer to an integer into which is placed the number of characters written so far.
%%	Prints a % sign.

Table 11-2.   *printf( )* Format Commands

The effect of the *precision modifier* depends upon the type of format command being modified. To add a precision modifier, place a decimal point followed by the precision after the field-width specifier. For **e**, **E**, and **f** formats, the precision modifier determines the number of decimal places printed. For example, **%10.4f** displays a number at least ten characters wide with four decimal places. However, when used with the **g** or **G** specifier, the precision determines the maximum number of significant digits displayed.

When the precision modifier is applied to integers, it specifies the minimum number of digits that will be displayed. (Leading zeros are added, if necessary.)

When the precision modifier is applied to strings, the number following the period specifies the maximum field length. For example, **%5.7s** displays a string that is at least five characters long and does not exceed seven. If the string is longer than the maximum field width, the end characters are truncated.

By default, all output is right justified. That is, if the field width is larger than the data printed, the data will be placed on the right edge of the field. You can force the information to be left justified by placing a minus sign directly after the percent sign. For example, **%-10.2f** left justifies a floating-point number with two decimal places in a ten-character field.

There are two format modifiers that allow **printf( )** to display **short** and **long** integers. These specifiers may be applied to the **d**, **i**, **o**, **u**, **x**, and **X** type specifiers. The **l** specifier tells **printf( )** that a **long** data type follows. For example, **%ld** means that a **long int** is to be displayed. The **h** specifier instructs **printf( )** to display a **short int**. Therefore, **%hu** indicates that the data is of type **short unsigned int**.

An **L** can prefix the floating-point commands and indicates a **long double**.

The **n** format causes the number of characters written so far to be put into the integer variable pointed to by the argument corresponding to the **n** specifier. For example, this code fragment displays the number **15** after the line **this is a test**.

```
int i;

printf("this is a test %n", &i);
printf("%d", i);
```

You can apply the **l** modifier to the **n** specifiers to indicate that the corresponding argument points to a long integer. You can specify the **h** modifier to indicate the corresponding argument points to a short integer.

The **#** has a special meaning when used with some **printf( )** format specifiers. Preceding a **g**, **G**, **f**, **e** or **E** specifier with a **#** ensures that the decimal point will be present even if there are no decimal digits. If you precede the **x** format specifier with a **#**, the hexadecimal number will be printed with a **0x** prefix. When used with the **o** specifier, it causes a leading 0 to be printed. The **#** cannot be applied to any other format specifiers.

The minimum field width and precision specifiers may be provided by arguments to **printf( )** instead of by constants. To accomplish this, use an ***** as a placeholder. When the format string is scanned, **printf( )** will match ***** to arguments in the order in which they occur.

Example

This program displays the output shown in its comments:

```
#include <stdio.h>
```

```
int main(void)
{
  /* This prints "this is a test" left-justified
     in a 20-character field.
  */
  printf("%-20s", "this is a test");

  /* This prints a float with 3 decimal places in a
     10-character field. The output will be "    12.235".
  */
  printf("%10.3f", 12.234657);
  return 0;
}
```

Related Functions

scanf( ), fprintf( )

int putc(int ch, FILE *stream)

Description

The prototype for **putc( )** is found in **<stdio.h>**.

The **putc( )** macro writes the character contained in the least significant byte of *ch* to the output stream pointed to by *stream*. Because character arguments are elevated to integers at the time of the call, you can use character variables as arguments to **putc( )**.

If successful, **putc( )** returns the character written; it returns **EOF** if an error occurs. If the output stream has been opened in binary mode, **EOF** is a valid value for *ch*. This means that you must use **ferror( )** to determine whether an error has occurred.

Example

The following loop writes the characters in string **str** to the stream specified by **fp**. The null terminator is not written.

```
for(; *str; str++) putc(*str, fp);
```

Related Functions

fgetc( ), fputc( ), getchar( ), putchar( )

int putch(int ch)

Description

The prototype for **putch( )** is in **<conio.h>**. This function is not defined by the ANSI/ISO C/C++ standard.

The **putch( )** function displays the character specified in *ch* on the screen. This function writes directly to the screen and not to **stdout**. Therefore, no character translations are performed and no redirection will occur.

If successful, **putch( )** returns *ch*. On failure, **EOF** is returned.

Example

This outputs the character X to the screen:

```
putch('X');
```

Related Function

putchar( )

int putchar(int ch)

Description

The prototype for **putchar( )** is found in **<stdio.h>**.

The **putchar( )** macro writes the character contained in the least significant byte of *ch* to **stdout**. It is functionally equivalent to **putc(ch,stdout)**. Because character arguments are elevated to integers at the time of the call, you can use character variables as arguments to **putchar( )**.

If successful, **putchar( )** returns the character written; if an error occurs, it returns **EOF**. If the output stream has been opened in binary mode, **EOF** is a valid value for *ch*. This means that you must use **ferror( )** to determine if an error has occurred.

Example

The following loop writes the characters in string **str** to **stdout**. The null terminator is not written.

```
for(; *str; str++) putchar(*str);
```

Related Functions

fputchar( ), putc( )

int puts(const char *str)

Description

The prototype for **puts( )** is found in **<stdio.h>**.

The **puts( )** function writes the string pointed to by *str* to the standard output device. The null terminator is translated to a newline.

The **puts( )** function returns non-negative if successful and an **EOF** if unsuccessful.

Example

The following writes the string "this is an example" to **stdout**.

```
#include <stdio.h>
#include <string.h>

int main(void)
{
  char str[80];

  strcpy(str, "this is an example");
  puts(str);

  return 0;
}
```

Related Functions

putc( ), gets( ), printf( )

int putw(int i, FILE *stream)

Description

The prototype for **putw( )** is in **<stdio.h>**. The **putw( )** function is not defined by the ANSI/ISO C/C++ standard and may not be fully portable.

The **putw( )** function writes the integer *i* to *stream* at the current file position and increments the file pointer appropriately.

The **putw( )** function returns the value written. A return value of **EOF** means an error has occurred in the stream if it is in text mode. Because **EOF** is also a valid integer value, you must use **ferror( )** to detect an error in a binary stream.

Example

This code fragment writes the value 100 to the stream pointed to by **fp**:

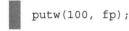
```
putw(100, fp);
```

Related Functions

getw( ), printf( ), fwrite( )

int read(int fd, void *buf, unsigned count)
int _rtl_read(int fd, void *buf, unsigned count)

Description

The prototypes for **read( )** and **_rtl_read( )** are found in **<io.h>**.

Neither the **read( )** nor the **_rtl_read( )** function is defined by the ANSI/ISO C/C++ standard. The **read( )** function is part of the UNIX-like I/O system. The **_rtl_read( )** function is specific to Borland C++ and the Windows operating system.

The **read( )** function reads *count* number of bytes from the file described by *fd* into the buffer pointed to by *buf*. The file position indicator is incremented by the number of bytes read. If the file is opened in text mode, character translations may take place.

The return value is the number of bytes actually read. This number will be smaller than *count* if an end-of-file marker is encountered or an error occurs before *count* number of bytes have been read. A value of –1 is returned if an error occurs, and a value of 0 is returned if an attempt is made to read at end-of-file. If an error occurs, then **errno** is set to one of these values:

EACCES	Access denied
EBADF	Bad file number

The difference between **read( )** and **_rtl_read( )** is that **read( )** removes carriage returns and returns **EOF** when a CTRL-Z is read from a text file. The **_rtl_read( )** function does not perform these actions.

Example

This program reads the first 100 bytes from the file **TEST.TST** into the array **buffer**:

```
#include <stdio.h>
#include <io.h>
#include <fcntl.h>
#include <stdlib.h>

int main(void)
{
  int fd;
  char buffer[100];

  if((fd=open("TEST.TST", O_RDONLY))==-1) {
    printf("Cannot open file.\n");
    exit(1);
  }

  if(read(fd, buffer, 100)!=100)
    printf("Possible read error.\n");

  return 0;
}
```

Related Functions

open( ), close( ), write( ), lseek( )

int remove(const char *fname)

Description

The prototype for **remove( )** is found in **<stdio.h>**.

The **remove( )** function erases the file specified by *fname*. It returns 0 if the file was successfully deleted and –1 if an error occurred. If an error occurs, then **errno** is set to one of these values:

ENOENT	File does not exist
EACCES	Access denied

Example

This program removes the file specified on the command line:

```
#include <stdio.h>

int main(int argc, char *argv[])
{
  if(remove(argv[1])==-1)
    printf("Remove Error\n");

  return 0;
}
```

Related Function

rename( )

int rename(const char *oldfname, const char *newfname)

Description

The prototype for **rename( )** is found in **<stdio.h>**.

The **rename( )** function changes the name of the file specified by *oldfname* to *newfname*. The *newfname* must not match any existing directory entry.

The **rename( )** function returns 0 if successful and non-0 if an error has occurred. If an error occurs, then **errno** is set to one of these values:

ENOENT	File does not exist
EEXIST	Filename already exists
ENOTSAM	Device not the same

Example

This program renames the file specified as the first command-line argument to that specified by the second command-line argument. Assuming the program is called **change**, a command line consisting of "change this that" will change the name of a file called **this** to **that**.

```
#include <stdio.h>
```

```
int main(int argc, char *argv[])
{
  if(rename(argv[1], argv[2])!=0)
    printf("Rename Error\n");

  return 0;
}
```

Related Function

remove( )

void rewind(FILE *stream)

Description

The prototype for **rewind( )** is found in **<stdio.h>**.

The **rewind( )** function moves the file position indicator to the start of the specified stream. It also clears the end-of-file and error flags associated with *stream*. It returns 0 if successful and non-0 otherwise.

Example

This function reads the stream pointed to by **fp** twice, displaying the file each time:

```
void re_read(FILE *fp)
{
  /* read once */
  while(!feof(fp)) putchar(getc(fp));

  rewind(fp);

  /* read twice */
  while(!feof(fp)) putchar(getc(fp));
}
```

Related Function

fseek( )

int _rtl_chmod (const char *filename, int get_set, int attrib)

Description

The prototype for **_rtl_chmod( )** is found in **<io.h>**.

The **_rtl_chmod( )** function is not defined by the ANSI/ISO C/C++ standard. It is used to read or set the attribute byte associated with the file pointed to by *filename*. If *get_set* is 0, **_rtl_chmod( )** returns the current file attribute and *attrib* is not used. If *get_set* is 1, the file attribute is set to the value of *attrib*. The *attrib* argument can be one of these constants, which are found in the **<dos.h>** header file.

FA_RDONLY	Set file to read only
FA_HIDDEN	Make hidden file
FA_SYSTEM	Mark as a system file
FA_LABEL	Make volume label
FA_DIREC	Make directory
FA_ARCH	Mark as archive

The **_rtl_chmod( )** function returns the file attribute if successful. Upon failure, it returns a –1 and sets **errno** to either **ENOENT** if the file does not exist or **EACCES** if access to the file is denied.

Example

This line of code sets the file **TEST.TST** to read only.

```
if(_rtl_chmod("TEST.TST", 1, FA_RDONLY)==FA_RDONLY)
printf("File set to read-only mode.");
```

Related Functions

chmod( ), **access( )**

int scanf(const char *format, arg-list)

Description

The prototype for **scanf( )** is in **<stdio.h>**. The **scanf( )** function is a general-purpose input routine that reads the stream **stdin**. It can read all the built-in data types and automatically convert them into the proper internal format. It is much like the reverse of **printf( )**.

The control string pointed to by *format* consists of three types of characters:

- Format specifiers
- White-space characters
- Non-white-space characters

The format specifiers are preceded by a percent sign and tell **scanf( )** what type of data is to be read next. These codes (including some non-standard ones added by C++ Builder) are listed in Table 11-3. For example, **%s** reads a string while **%d** reads an integer.

The format string is read left to right, and the format codes are matched, in order, with the arguments that make up the argument list.

A white-space character in the control string causes **scanf( )** to skip over one or more white-space characters in the input stream. A white-space character is either a space, a tab, or a newline. In essence, one white-space character in the control string causes **scanf( )** to read, but not store, any number (including zero) of white-space characters up to the first non-white-space character.

A non-white-space character causes **scanf( )** to read and discard a matching character. For example, **"%d,%d"** causes **scanf( )** to read an integer, read and discard a comma, and then read another integer. If the specified character is not found, **scanf( )** terminates.

All the variables used to receive values through **scanf( )** must be passed by their addresses. This means that all arguments must be pointers to the variables used as arguments. This is C's way of creating a call by reference, and it allows a function to alter the contents of an argument. For example, to read an integer into the variable **count**, you would use the following **scanf( )** call:

```
scanf("%d", &count);
```

Strings are read into character arrays, and the array name, without any index, is the address of the first element of the array. So, to read a string into the character array **address**, use

```
scanf("%s", address);
```

In this case, **address** is already a pointer and need not be preceded by the **&** operator.

Code	Meaning
%c	Read a single character
%d	Read a decimal integer
%D	Read a long integer (C++ Builder specific)
%i	Read a decimal integer
%I	Read a long integer (C++ Builder specific)
%e	Read a floating-point number
%E	Read a floating-point number
%f	Read a floating-point number
%g	Read a floating-point number
%G	Read a floating-point number
%o	Read an octal number
%O	Read an long octal number (C++ Builder specific)
%s	Read a string
%x	Read a hexadecimal number
%X	Read a hexadecimal number
%p	Read a pointer
%n	Receives an integer value equal to the number of characters read so far
%u	Read an unsigned integer
%U	Read an unsigned long integer (C++ Builder specific)
%[ ]	Scan for a set of characters
%%	Read a % sign

Table 11-3. *scanf( ) Format Codes*

THE C++ BUILDER
FUNCTION LIBRARY

The input data items must be separated by spaces, tabs, or newlines. Punctuation such as commas, semicolons, and the like do not count as separators. This means that

```
scanf("%d%d", &r, &c);
```

accepts an input of **10 20**, but fails with **10,20**. The **scanf( )** format specifiers are matched in order with the variables receiving the input in the argument list.

An * placed after the % and before the format specifier reads data of the specified type but suppresses its assignment. Thus,

```
scanf("%d%*c%d", &x, &y);
```

given the input **10/20** places the value 10 into **x**, discards the division sign, and gives **y** the value 20.

The format commands can specify a maximum field-length modifier. This is an integer placed between the % and the format specifier that limits the number of characters read for any field. For example, if you wish to read no more than 20 characters into **address**, you would write

```
scanf("%20s", address);
```

If the input stream were greater than 20 characters, a subsequent call to input would begin where this call left off. Input for a field may terminate before the maximum field length is reached if a white space is encountered. In this case, **scanf( )** moves on to the next field.

Although spaces, tabs, and newlines are used as field separators, they are read like any other character when reading a single character. For example, with an input stream of **"x y"**,

```
scanf("%c%c%c", &a, &b, &c);
```

returns with the character **x** in **a**, a space in **b**, and the character **y** in **c**.

Be careful: Any other characters in the control string—including spaces, tabs, and newlines—are used to match and discard characters from the input stream. Any character that matches is discarded. For example, given the input stream **"10t20"**,

```
scanf("%st%s", &x, &y);
```

places 10 into **x** and 20 into **y**. The **t** is discarded because of the **t** in the control string.

Another feature of **scanf( )** is called a *scanset*. A scanset defines a set of characters that will be read by **scanf( )** and assigned to the scanset's corresponding character array. You define a scanset by putting inside square brackets the characters you want to scan for. The beginning square bracket must be prefixed by a percent sign. For example, this scanset tells **scanf( )** to read only the characters **A**, **B**, and **C**:

```
% [ABC]
```

The argument corresponding to the scanset must be a pointer to a character array. When you use a scanset, **scanf( )** continues to read characters and put them into the array until a character that is not part of the scanset is encountered. (That is, a scanset reads only matching characters.) Upon return from **scanf( )**, the array will contain a null-terminated string.

You can specify an inverted set if the first character in the set is a ^ . When the ^ is present, it instructs **scanf( )** to accept any character that *is not* defined by the scanset.

You can specify a range using a hyphen. For example, this tells **scanf( )** to accept the letters "A" through "Z":

```
% [A-Z]
```

Remember that the scanset is case sensitive. Therefore, if you want to scan for both upper- and lowercase letters, you must specify them individually.

The **scanf( )** function returns a number equal to the number of fields that were successfully assigned values. This number does not include fields that were read but not assigned because the * modifier was used to suppress the assignment. **EOF** is returned if an error occurs before the first field is assigned.

Example

The operation of the following **scanf( )** statements are explained in their comments.

```
char str[80];
int i;

/* read a string and an integer */
scanf("%s%d", str, &i);

/* read up to 79 chars into str */
scanf("%79s", str);

/* skip the integer between the two strings */
scanf("%s%*d%s", str, &i, str);
```

Related Functions

printf( ), fscanf( )

void setbuf(FILE *stream, char *buf)

Description

The prototype to **setbuf( )** is found in **<stdio.h>**.

The **setbuf( )** function is used either to specify the buffer the specified stream will use or, if called with *buf* set to null, to turn off buffering. If a programmer-defined buffer is to be specified, it must be **BUFSIZ** characters long. **BUFSIZ** is defined in **<stdio.h>**.

The **setbuf( )** function returns no value.

Example

This following fragment associates a programmer-defined buffer with the stream pointed to by **fp**:

```
char buffer[BUFSIZ];
/* ... */
setbuf(fp,buffer);
```

Related Functions

fopen( ), fclose( ), setvbuf( )

int setmode(int handle, int mode)

Description

The prototype to **setmode( )** is found in **<io.h>**.

The **setmode( )** function is not defined by the ANSI/ISO C/C++ standard. It is used to reset the mode of an already open file given its file descriptor and the new mode desired. The only valid modes are **O_BINARY** and **O_TEXT**.

It returns 0 on success, –1 on error. If an error occurs, **errno** is set to **EINVAL** (invalid argument).

Example

This line of code sets the file associated with **fd** to text-only operation.

```
setmode(fd, O_TEXT)
```

Related Functions

open( ), _creat( )

int setvbuf(FILE *stream, char *buf, int mode, size_t size)

Description

The prototype for **setvbuf( )** is found in **<stdio.h>**.

The **setvbuf( )** function allows the programmer to specify the buffer, its size, and its mode for the specified stream. The character array pointed to by *buf* is used as *stream's* buffer for I/O operations. The size of the buffer is set by *size,* and *mode* determines how buffering will be handled. If *buf* is null, no buffering takes place.

The legal values of *mode* are **_IOFBF, _IONBF,** and **_IOLBF**. These are defined in **<stdio.h>**. When the mode is set to **_IOFBF**, full buffering takes place. This is the default setting. When set to **_IONBF**, the stream is unbuffered regardless of the value *buf.* If *mode* is **_IOLBF**, the stream is line-buffered, which means that the buffer is flushed each time a newline character is written for output streams; for input streams an input request reads all characters up to a newline. In either case, the buffer is also flushed when full.

The value of *size* must be greater than 0 and less than **UINT_MAX**, which is found in **<limits.h>**.

The **setvbuf( )** function returns 0 on success, non-0 on failure.

Example

This fragment sets the stream **fp** to line-buffered mode with a buffer size of 128:

```
#include <stdio.h>
char buffer[128];
/* ... */
setvbuf(fp, buffer, _IOLBF, 128);
```

Related Function

setbuf( )

int sopen(const char *filename, int access, int shflag, int mode)

Description

The prototype for **sopen( )** is found in **<io.h>**. The **sopen( )** macro is part of the UNIX-like file system and is not defined by ANSI/ISO C/C++.

The **sopen( )** macro opens a file for shared-mode access using a network. It is defined as

open(*filename*, (*access* | *shflag*), *mode*)

The **sopen( )** macro opens a file with the name *filename* and sets its access mode as specified by *access* and its share mode as specified by *shflag*. You can think of *access* as being constructed of a base mode of operation plus modifiers. The following base modes are allowed:

Base	Meaning
O_RDONLY	Open for read only
O_WRONLY	Open for write only
O_RDWR	Open for read/write

After selecting one of these values, you may **OR** it with one or more of the following access modifiers:

Modifiers	Meaning When Set
O_NDELAY	Not used; included for UNIX compatibility
O_APPEND	Causes the file pointer to be set to the end of the file before to each write operation
O_CREAT	If the file does not exist, it is created with its attribute set to the value of *mode*
O_TRUNC	If the file exists, it is truncated to length 0 but retains its file attributes
O_EXCL	When used with **O_CREAT**, will not create output file if a file by that name already exists
O_NOINHERIT	Child programs do not inherit the file
O_BINARY	Opens a binary file
O_TEXT	Opens a text file

The *shflag* argument defines the type of sharing allowed on this file and can be one of these values:

shflag	Meaning
SH_COMPAT	Compatibility mode
SH_DENYRW	No read or write
SH_DENYWR	No write
SH_DENYRD	No read
SH_DENYNONE	Allow read/write
SH_DENYNO	Allow read/write

The *mode* argument is required only if the **O_CREAT** modifier is used. In this case, *mode* can be one of these values:

Mode	Meaning
S_IWRITE	Write access
S_IREAD	Read access
S_IWRITE I S_IREAD	Read/write access

A successful call to **sopen( )** returns a positive integer that is the file descriptor associated with the file. A return value of –1 means that the file cannot be opened, and **errno** will be set to one of these values:

ENOENT	File does not exist
EMFILE	Too many open files
EACCES	Access denied
EINVACC	Invalid access code

Example

You will usually see the call to **sopen( )** like this:

```
if((fd=sopen(filename, access, shflag, mode)) ==-1)  {
printf("Cannot open file.\n");
  exit(1);
}
```

Related Functions

open( ), _rtl_open( ), close( )

int sprintf(char *buf, const char *format, arg-list)

Description

The prototype for **sprintf( )** is found in **<stdio.h>**.

The **sprintf( )** function is identical to **printf( )** except that the output generated is placed into the array pointed to by *buf*. See the **printf( )** function.

The return value is equal to the number of characters actually placed into the array.

Example

After this code fragment executes, **str** holds **one 2 3**:

```
char str[80];
sprintf(str, "%s %d %c", "one", 2, '3');
```

Related Functions

printf( ), fsprintf( )

int sscanf(char *buf, const char *format, arg-list)

Description

The prototype for **sscanf( )** is found in **<stdio.h>**.

The **sscanf( )** function is identical to **scanf( )** except that data is read from the array pointed to by *buf* rather than **stdin**. See **scanf( )**.

The return value is equal to the number of fields that were actually assigned values. This number does not include fields that were skipped through the use of the * format-command modifier. A value of 0 means that no fields were assigned, and **EOF** indicates that a read was attempted at the end of the string.

Example

This program prints the message **hello 1** on the screen:

```
#include <stdio.h>

int main(void)
{
```

```
    char str[80];
    int i;

    sscanf("hello 1 2 3 4 5", "%s%d", str, &i);
    printf("%s %d", str, i);

    return 0;
}
```

Related Functions

scanf( ), fscanf( )

int stat(char *filename, struct stat *statbuf)

Description

The prototype for **stat( )** is found in **<sys\stat.h>** It is not defined by ANSI/ISO C/C++.

The **stat( )** function fills the structure *statbuf* with information on the file associated with *filename*. The **stat** structure is defined in **sys\stat.h**.

Upon successfully filling the **stat** structure, 0 is returned. If unsuccessful, −1 is returned and **errno** is set to **ENOENT**.

Example

The following example opens a file, fills the **stat** structure, and prints out one of its fields:

```
#include <stdio.h>
#include <sys\stat.h>
#include <stdlib.h>

int main(void)
{
  FILE *fp;
  struct stat buff;

  if((fp=fopen("test", "rb"))==NULL) {
    printf("Cannot open file.\n");
    exit(1);
  }
```

```
/* fill the stat structure */
stat("test", &buff);

printf("Size of the file is: %ld\n", buff.st_size);
fclose(fp);

return 0;
}
```

Related Functions

fstat( ), access( )

long tell(int fd)

Description

The prototype for **tell( )** is found in **<io.h>**.

The **tell( )** function is part of the UNIX-like I/O system and is not defined by the ANSI/ISO C/C++ standard.

The **tell( )** function returns the current value of the file position indicator associated with the file descriptor *fd*. This value is the number of bytes the position indicator is from the start of the file. A return value of –1L indicates an error and **errno** is set to **EBADF** (bad file handle).

Example

This fragment prints the current value of the position indicator for the file described by **fd**:

```
long pos;
/* ... */
pos = tell(fd);
printf("Position indicator is %ld bytes from the start", pos);
```

Related Functions

lseek( ), open( ), close( ), read( ), write( )

FILE *tmpfile(void)

Description

The prototype for the **tmpfile( )** function is found in **<stdio.h>**.

The **tmpfile( )** function opens a temporary file for update and returns a pointer to the stream. The function automatically uses a unique filename to avoid conflicts with existing files.

The **tmpfile( )** function returns a null pointer on failure; otherwise it returns a pointer to the stream.

The temporary file created by **tmpfile( )** is automatically removed when the file is closed or when the program terminates.

Example

This fragment creates a temporary working file:

```
FILE *temp;

if(!(temp=tmpfile())) {
  printf("Cannot open temporary work file.\n");
  exit(1);
}
```

Related Function

tmpnam( )

char *tmpnam(char *name)

Description

The prototype for **tmpnam( )** is found in **<stdio.h>**.

The **tmpnam( )** function is defined by the ANSI/ISO C/C++ standard. It generates a unique filename and stores it in the array pointed to by *name*. The main purpose of **tmpnam( )** is to generate a temporary filename that is different from any other filename in the directory.

The function may be called up to **TMP_MAX** times, defined in **<stdio.h>**. Each time it generates a new temporary filename.

A pointer to *name* is returned. If *name* is null, a pointer to an internal string is returned.

Example

This program displays three unique temporary filenames:

```
#include <stdio.h>

int main(void)
{
```

```
    char name[40];
    int i;
    for(i=0; i<3; i++) {
      tmpnam(name);
      printf("%s ", name);
    }

    return 0;
}
```

Related Function

tmpfile( )

int ungetc(int ch, FILE *stream)

Description

The prototype for **ungetc( )** is found in **<stdio.h>**.

The **ungetc( )** function returns the character specified by the low-order byte of *ch* back into the input *stream*. This character is then returned by the next read operation on *stream*. A call to **fflush( )** or **fseek( )** undoes an **ungetc( )** operation and discards the character put back.

Only one character can be put back between subsequent read operations.

You cannot unget an **EOF**.

A call to **ungetc( )** clears the end-of-file flag associated with the specified stream. The value of the file position indicator for a text stream is undefined until all pushed-back characters are read, in which case it is the same as it was prior to the first **ungetc( )** call. For binary streams, each **ungetc( )** call decrements the file position indicator.

The return value is equal to *ch* on success and **EOF** on failure.

Example

This function reads words from the input stream pointed to by **fp**. The terminating character is returned to the stream for later use. For example, given input of **count/10**, the first call to **read_word( )** returns **count** and puts the **/** back on the input stream.

```
void read_word(FILE *fp, char *token)
{

  while(isalpha(*token=getc(fp))) token++;
```

```
    ungetc(fp, *token);
}
```

Related Function

getc( )

int ungetch(int ch)

Description

The prototype for **ungetch( )** is in **<conio.h>**. This function is not defined by the
ANSI/ISO C/C++ standard. It cannot be used in Windows programs.

The **ungetch( )** function returns the character specified in the low-order byte of *ch*
back into the console input buffer. This character is then returned by the next call to a
console input function. Only one character can be put back between subsequent input
operations.

The return value is equal to *ch* on success and **EOF** on failure.

Example

This program inputs a key, displays it, returns it to the input buffer, and reads and
displays it again:

```
#include <stdio.h>
#include <conio.h>

int main(void)
{
  char ch;

  ch = getch(); // get keypress
  putch(ch); // show the key
  ungetch(ch);  // return to buffer
  ch = getch(); // get same key again
  putch(ch); // show the key again

  return 0;
}
```

Related Function

ungetc( )

int unlink(const char *fname)

Description

The prototype to **unlink( )** is found in **<dos.h>**.

The **unlink( )** function is part of the UNIX-like I/O system and is not defined by the ANSI/ISO C/C++ standard.

The **unlink( )** function removes the specified file from the directory. It returns 0 on success and –1 on failure and sets **errno** to one of the following values:

Error	Meaning
ENOENT	Invalid path or filename
EACCES	Access denied

Example

This program deletes the file specified as the first command-line argument:

```c
#include <stdio.h>
#include <dos.h>

int main(int argc, char *argv[])
{
  if(unlink(argv[1])==-1)
    printf("Cannot remove file.");

  return 0;
}
```

Related Functions

open( ), close( )

int unlock(int handle, long offset, long length)

Description

The prototype for **unlock( )** is found **<io.h>**.

The **unlock( )** function is not defined by the ANSI/ISO C/C++ standard. It is used to unlock a portion of a locked file, thus allowing another program to use it until a new lock is placed on the file. To lock a file, use **lock( )**. These functions provide control for file sharing in network environments.

The file to be unlocked is associated with *handle.* The portion of the file to be unlocked is determined by the starting *offset* from the beginning of the file and the *length.*

If **unlock( )** is successful, 0 is returned. If it is unsuccessful, –1 is returned.

Example

This fragment unlocks the first 128 bytes of the file associated with **fd**:

```
unlock(fd, 0, 128);
```

Related Functions

lock( ), **sopen( )**

int vprintf(const char *format, va_list arg_ptr)
int vfprintf(FILE *stream, const char *format,
va_list arg_ptr)
int vsprintf(char *buf, const char *format, va_list arg_ptr)

Description

The prototypes for these functions require the files **<stdio.h>** and **<stdarg.h>**.

The functions **vprintf( )**, **vfprintf( )**, and **vsprintf( )** are functionally equivalent to **printf( )**, **fprintf( )**, and **sprintf( )**, respectively, except that the argument list has been replaced by a pointer to a list of arguments. This pointer must be of type **va_list**, which is defined in **<stdarg.h>**. See the proper related function. Also see **va_arg( )**, **va_start( )**, and **va_end( )** in Chapter 19 for further information.

Example

This fragment shows how to set up a call to **vprintf( )**. The call to **va_start( )** creates a variable-length argument pointer to the start of the argument list. This pointer must be used in the call to **vprintf( )**. The call to **va_end( )** clears the variable-length argument pointer.

```
#include <stdio.h>
#include <stdarg.h>
```

```
void print_message(char *, ...);

int main(void)
{
  print_message("Cannot open file %s","test");

  return 0;
}

void print_message( char *format, ...)
{
  va_list ptr; /* get an arg ptr */

  /* initialize ptr to point to the first argument after the
     format string
  */
  va_start(ptr, format);
  /* print out message */
  vprintf(format, ptr);
  va_end(ptr);
}
```

Related Functions

va_list( ), va_start( ), va_end( )

int vscanf(const char *format, va_list arg_ptr)
int vfscanf(FILE *stream, const char *format, va_list arg_ptr)
int vsscanf(const char *buf, const char *format, va_list arg_ptr)

Description

The prototypes for these functions require the files <stdio.h> and <stdarg.h>.

The functions **vscanf( )**, **vfscanf( )**, and **vsscanf( )** are functionally equivalent to **scanf( )**, **fscanf( )**, and **sscanf( )**, respectively, except that the argument list has been replaced by a pointer to a list of arguments. This pointer must be of type **va_list**, which is defined in **<stdarg.h>**. See the proper related function. Also see **va_arg( )**, **va_start( )**, and **va_end( )** in Chapter 19 for further information.

Example

This fragment shows how to set up a call to **vscanf( )**. The program reads two integers entered by the user. The call to **va_start( )** creates a variable-length argument pointer to the start of the argument list. It is this pointer that must be used in the call to **vscanf( )**. The call to **va_end( )** clears the variable-length argument pointer.

```c
#include <stdio.h>
#include <stdarg.h>

void read_int(int num, ...);

int main(void)
{
  int a, b;
  read_int(2, &a, &b);
  printf("%d %d", a, b);

  return 0;
}

void read_int(int num, ...)
{
  va_list ptr; /* get an arg ptr */

  /* initialize ptr to point to the first argument after the
     format string
  */
  va_start(ptr, num);

  printf("Enter %d integers: ", num);
  /* read ints */
  vscanf("%d %d", ptr);

  va_end(ptr);
}
```

Related Functions

va_list( ), va_start( ), va_end( )

int write(int handle, void *buf, int count)
int _rtl_write(int handle, void *buf, int count)

Description

The prototypes for **write( )** and **_rtl_write( )** are found in **<io.h>**.

The **write( )** function is part of the UNIX-like I/O system and is not defined by the ANSI/ISO C/C++ standard.

The **write( )** function writes *count* number of bytes to the file described by *handle* from the buffer pointed to by *buf*. The file position indicator is incremented by the number of bytes written. If the file is opened in text mode, linefeeds are automatically expanded to carriage return, linefeed combinations. However, **_rtl_write( )** does not perform this expansion.

The return value is the number of bytes actually written. This number may be smaller than *count* if an error is encountered. A value of –1 means an error has occurred, and **errno** is set to one of these values:

Value	Meaning
EACCES	Access denied
EBADF	Bad file number

Example

This program writes the 100 bytes from **buffer** to the file **test**.

```
#include <stdio.h>
#include <io.h>
#include <fcntl.h>
#include <stdlib.h>

int main(void)
{
  int fd;
  char buffer[100];
```

```
  if((fd=open("test", O_WRONLY))==-1) {
    printf("Cannot open file.\n");
    exit(1);
  }

  gets(buffer);

  if(write(fd, buffer, 100)!=100)
    printf("Write Error");
  close(fd);

  return 0;
}
```

Related Functions

read( ), close( ), lseek( )

The Complete Reference

Borland
C++
Builder

Chapter 12

String, Memory, and Character Functions

The C++ Builder library has a rich and varied set of string-, memory-, and character-handling functions. As they relate to these functions, a string is a null-terminated array of characters, memory is a block of contiguous RAM, and a character is a single byte value. The ANSI/ISO standard string functions require the header <string.h> to provide their prototypes. The ANSI/ISO standard memory manipulation functions also use **<string.h>**. In some cases, C++ Builder includes prototypes for these standard functions in **<mem.h>**, but you should use **<string.h>** for the greatest portability. C++ Builder also provides several nonstandard functions. Some of these are prototyped in **<string.h>**. Others are prototyped in **<mem.h>**. The character functions use **<ctype.h>** as their header.

Because C/C++ has no bounds checking on array operations, it is the programmer's responsibility to prevent an array overflow. Technically, if an array has overflowed, its behavior is undefined. In a practical sense, overflowing an array means that your program will seriously malfunction.

In C/C++, a *printable character* is one that can be displayed on screen. These are the characters between a space (0x20) and tilde (0xFE). *Control characters* have values between (0) and (0x1F) as well as DEL (0x7F). The ASCII characters are between 0 and 0x7F.

The character functions are declared to take an integer argument. While this is true, only the low-order byte is used by the function. Therefore, you are free to use a character argument because it is automatically elevated to **int** at the time of the call.

Several functions use the **size_t** data type. This type is defined in the various headers used by the functions described here and is an unsigned integer type.

int isalnum(int ch)

Description

The prototype for **isalnum( )** is found in **<ctype.h>**.

The **isalnum( )** macro returns non-0 if its argument is either a letter of the alphabet (upper- or lowercase) or a digit. If the character is not alphanumeric, 0 is returned.

Example

This program checks each character read from **stdin** and reports all alphanumeric ones:

```
#include <ctype.h>
#include <stdio.h>

int main(void)
{
  char ch;
```

```
   for(;;) {
      ch = getchar();
      if(ch==' ') break;
      if(isalnum(ch)) printf("%c is alphanumeric\n", ch);
   }

   return 0;
}
```

Related Functions

isalpha( ), isdigit( ), iscntrl( ), isgraph( ), isprint( ), ispunct( ), isspace( )

int isalpha(int ch)

Description

The prototype for **isalpha( )** is found in **<ctype.h>**.

The **isalpha( )** macro returns non-0 if *ch* is a letter of the alphabet (upper- or lowercase); otherwise, it returns 0.

Example

This program checks each character read from **stdin** and reports all those that are letters of the alphabet:

```
#include <ctype.h>
#include <stdio.h>

int main(void)
{
   char ch;

   for(;;) {
      ch = getchar();
      if(ch==' ') break;
      if(isalpha(ch)) printf("%c is a letter\n", ch);
   }

   return 0;
}
```

Related Functions

isalnum( ), isdigit( ), iscntrl( ), isgraph( ), isprint( ), ispunct( ), isspace( )

int isascii(int ch)

Description

The prototype for **isascii( )** is found in **<ctype.h>** and is not defined by the ANSI/ISO C/C++ standard.

The **isascii( )** macro returns non-0 if *ch* is in the range 0 through 0x7F; otherwise, it returns 0.

Example

This program checks each character read from **stdin** and reports all those that are defined by ASCII:

```
#include <ctype.h>
#include <stdio.h>

int main(void)
{
  char ch;

  for(;;) {
    ch = getchar();
    if(ch==' ') break;
    if(isascii(ch)) printf("%c is ASCII defined\n", ch);
  }

  return 0;
}
```

Related Functions

isalnum( ), isdigit( ), iscntrl( ), isgraph( ), isprint( ), ispunct( ), isspace( )

int iscntrl(int ch)

Description

The prototype for **iscntrl( )** is found in **<ctype.h>**.

The **iscntrl( )** macro returns non-0 if *ch* is between 0 and 0x1F or is equal to 0x7F (DEL); otherwise, it returns 0.

Example

This program checks each character read from **stdin** and reports all those that are control characters:

```
#include <ctype.h>
#include <stdio.h>

int main(void)
{
  char ch;

  for(;;) {
    ch = getchar();
    if(ch==' ') break;
    if(iscntrl(ch)) printf("%c is a control character\n", ch);
  }

  return 0;
}
```

Related Functions

isalnum( ), isdigit( ), isalpha( ), isgraph( ), isprint( ), ispunct( ), isspace( )

int isdigit(int ch)

Description

The prototype for **isdigit( )** is found in **<ctype.h>**.

The **isdigit( )** macro returns non-0 if *ch* is a digit, that is, 0 through 9; otherwise, it returns 0.

Example

This program checks each character read from **stdin** and reports all those that are digits:

```
#include <ctype.h>
#include <stdio.h>

int main(void)
```

```
{
  char ch;

  for(;;) {
    ch = getchar();
    if(ch==' ') break;
    if(isdigit(ch)) printf("%c is a digit\n", ch);
  }

  return 0;
}
```

Related Functions

isalnum( ), iscntrl( ), isalpha( ), isgraph( ), isprint( ), ispunct( ), isspace( )

int isgraph(int ch)

Description

The prototype for **isgraph( )** is found in **<ctype.h>**.

The **isgraph( )** macro returns non-0 if *ch* is any printable character other than a space; otherwise, it returns 0. Printable characters are in the range 0x21 through 0x7E.

Example

This program checks each character read from **stdin** and reports all those that are printable characters:

```
#include <ctype.h>
#include <stdio.h>

int main(void)
{
  char ch;

  for(;;) {
    ch = getchar();
    if(ch==' ') break;
    if(isgraph(ch)) printf("%c is a printing character\n", ch);
```

```
    }

    return 0;
}
```

Related Functions

isalnum( ), iscntrl( ), isalpha( ), isdigit( ), isprint( ), ispunct( ), isspace( )

int islower(int ch)

Description

The prototype for **islower( )** is found in **<ctype.h>**.

The **islower( )** macro returns non-0 if *ch* is a lowercase letter ("a" through "z"); otherwise, it returns 0.

Example

This program checks each character read from **stdin** and reports all those that are lowercase letters:

```
#include <ctype.h>
#include <stdio.h>

int main(void)
{
  char ch;

  for(;;) {
    ch = getchar();
    if(ch==' ') break;
    if(islower(ch)) printf("%c is lowercase\n", ch);
  }

  return 0;
}
```

Related Function

isupper( )

THE C++ BUILDER
FUNCTION LIBRARY

int isprint(int ch)

Description

The prototype for **isprint( )** is found in **<ctype.h>**.

The **isprint( )** macro returns non-0 if *ch* is a printable character, including a space; otherwise, it returns 0. The printable characters are in the range 0x20 through 0x7E.

Example

This program checks each character read from **stdin** and reports all those that are printable:

```
#include <ctype.h>
#include <stdio.h>

int main(void)
{
  char ch;

  for(;;) {
    ch = getchar();
    if(ch==' ') break;
    if(isprint(ch)) printf("%c is printable\n", ch);
  }

  return 0;
}
```

Related Functions

isalnum( ), iscntrl( ), isalpha( ), isdigit( ), isgraph( ), ispunct( ), isspace( )

int ispunct(int ch)

Description

The prototype for **ispunct( )** is found in **<ctype.h>**.

The **ispunct( )** macro returns non-0 if *ch* is a punctuation character or a space; otherwise, it returns 0.

Example

This program checks each character read from **stdin** and reports all those that are punctuation:

```
#include <ctype.h>
#include <stdio.h>

int main(void)
{
  char ch;

  for(;;) {
    ch = getchar();
    if(ch==' ') break;
    if(ispunct(ch)) printf("%c is punctuation\n", ch);
  }

  return 0;
}
```

Related Functions

isalnum( ), **iscntrl( )**, **isalpha( )**, **isdigit( )**, **isgraph( )**, **isspace( )**

int isspace(int ch)

Description

The prototype for **isspace( )** is found in **<ctype.h>**.

The **isspace( )** macro returns non-0 if *ch* is either a space, carriage return, horizontal tab, vertical tab, form feed, or newline character; otherwise, it returns 0.

Example

This program checks each character read from **stdin** and reports all those that are white-space characters:

```
#include <ctype.h>
#include <stdio.h>

int main(void)
{
  char ch;

  for(;;) {
    ch = getchar();
    if(ch=='.') break;
```

```
    if(isspace(ch)) printf("%c is white-space\n", ch);
  }

  return 0;
}
```

Related Functions

isalnum( ), iscntrl( ), isalpha( ), isdigit( ), isgraph( ), ispunct( )

int isupper(ch)

Description
The prototype for **isupper( )** is found in **<ctype.h>**.

The **isupper( )** macro returns non-0 if *ch* is an uppercase letter ("A" through "Z"); otherwise, it returns 0.

Example
This program checks each character read from **stdin** and reports all those that are uppercase letters:

```
#include <ctype.h>
#include <stdio.h>

int main(void)
{
  char ch;

  for(;;) {
    ch = getchar();
    if(ch==' ') break;
    if(isupper(ch)) printf("%c is upper-case\n", ch);
  }

  return 0;
}
```

Related Function

islower( )

int isxdigit(int ch)

Description

The prototype for **isxdigit( )** is found in **<ctype.h>**.

The **isxdigit( )** macro returns non-0 if *ch* is a hexadecimal digit; otherwise, it returns 0. A hexadecimal digit will be in one of these ranges: "A" through "F", "a" through "f", or "0" through "9".

Example

This program checks each character read from **stdin** and reports all those that are hexadecimal digits:

```
#include <ctype.h>
#include <stdio.h>

int main(void)
{
  char ch;

  for(;;) {
    ch = getchar();
    if(ch==' ') break;
    if(isxdigit(ch)) printf("%c is hexadecimal \n", ch);
  }

  return 0;
}
```

Related Functions

isalnum( ), iscntrl( ), isalpha( ), isdigit( ), isgraph( ), isspace( ), ispunct( )

void *memccpy(void *dest, const void *source, int ch, size_t count)

Description

The prototype for **memccpy( )** is found in both **<string.h>** and **<mem.h>** and is not defined by the ANSI/ISO C/C++ standard.

The **memccpy( )** function copies the contents of the memory pointed to by *source* into the memory pointed to by *dest*. The copy operation stops either when *count* number of bytes have been copied or after the first occurrence of *ch* has been copied. It returns a pointer to the end of *dest* if *ch* is found or null if *ch* is not part of *source*.

Example

After this fragment has executed, the word "**hello**" will be in array **out** because the space is used to terminate the copy operation:

```
char str[20], out[20];
strcpy(str, "hello there");
memccpy(out, str,' ', 20);
```

Related Functions

memcpy( ), strcpy( )

void *memchr(const void *buffer, int ch, size_t count)

Description

The prototype for the **memchr( )** function is found in both **<string.h>** and **<mem.h>**.

The **memchr( )** function searches *buffer* for the first occurrence of *ch* in the first *count* characters.

The **memchr( )** function returns a pointer to the first occurrence of *ch* in *buffer*, or a null pointer if *ch* is not found.

Example

This program prints " **is a test**" on the screen:

```
#include <stdio.h>
#include <string.h>

int main(void)
{
  void *p;

  p = memchr("this is a test", ' ', 14);
  printf((char *) p);

  return 0;
}
```

Related Functions

memmove( ), memcpy( )

int memcmp(const void *buf1, const void *buf2, size_t count)
int memicmp(const void *buf1, const void *buf2, size_t count)

Description

The prototype for the **memcmp( )** function is found in both **<string.h>** and **<mem.h>**. The **memicmp( )** function is not defined by the ANSI/ISO C/C++ standard.

The **memcmp( )** function compares the first *count* characters of the arrays pointed to by *buf1* and *buf2*. The comparison is done lexicographically.

The **memcmp( )** function returns an integer that is interpreted as indicated here:

Value	Meaning
Less than 0	*buf1* is less than *buf2*
0	*buf1* is equal to *buf2*
Greater than 0	*buf1* is greater than *buf2*

The **memicmp( )** function is identical to **memcmp( )** except that case is ignored when comparing letters.

Example

This program shows the outcome of a comparison of its two command line arguments:

```
#include <stdio.h>
#include <string.h>

int main(int argc, char *argv[])

{
  int outcome;
  size_t len, l1, l2;
```

```
  if(argc != 3) {
    printf("Use two command-line args.");
    return 1;
  }

  /* find the length of shortest */
  len = (l1=strlen(argv[1]))<(l2=strlen(argv[2])) ? l1:l2;

  outcome = memcmp(argv[1], argv[2], len);
  if(!outcome) printf("equal");
  else if(outcome<0) printf("First less than second.\n");
  else printf("First greater than second\n");

  return 0;
}
```

Related Functions

memcpy( ), memchr( ), strcmp( )

void *memcpy(void *dest, const void *source, size_t count)

Description

The prototype for **memcpy( )** is found in both **<string.h>** and **<mem.h>**.

The **memcpy( )** function copies *count* characters from the array pointed to by *source* into the array pointed to by *dest*. If the arrays overlap, the behavior of **memcpy( )** is undefined.

The **memcpy( )** function returns a pointer to *dest*.

Example

This program copies the contents of **buf1** into **buf2** and displays the result:

```
#include <stdio.h>
#include <string.h>
#define SIZE 80

int main(void)
{
  char buf1[SIZE], buf2[SIZE];
```

```
strcpy(buf1, "When, in the course of...");
memcpy(buf2, buf1, SIZE);
printf(buf2);

return 0;
}
```

Related Function

memmove( )

void *memmove(void *dest, const void *source, size_t count)

Description

The prototype for **memmove( )** is found in both **<string.h>** and **<mem.h>**.

The **memmove( )** function copies *count* characters from the array pointed to by *source* into the array pointed to by *dest*. If the arrays overlap, the copy takes place correctly, placing the correct contents into *dest* but leaving *source* modified.

The **memmove( )** function returns a pointer to *dest*.

Example

This program copies the contents of *str1* into *str2* and displays the result:

```
#include <stdio.h>
#include <string.h>

int main(void)
{
  char str1[40], str2[40];

  strcpy(str1, "Born to code in C/C++.");
  memmove(str2, str1, strlen(str1)+1);
  printf(str2);

  return 0;
}
```

Related Functions

memcpy( ), movmem( )

void *memset(void *buf, int ch, size_t count)

Description

The prototype for **memset( )** is found in both **<string.h>** and **<mem.h>**.

The **memset( )** function copies the low-order byte of *ch* into the first *count* characters of the array pointed to by *buf*. It returns *buf*.

The most common use of **memset( )** is to initialize a region of memory to some known value.

Example

This fragment first initializes to null the first 100 bytes of the array pointed to by *buf* and then sets the first 10 bytes to **X** and displays the string **XXXXXXXXXX**:

```
memset(buf, '\0', 100);
memset(buf, 'X', 10);
printf((char *) buf);
```

Related Functions

memcpy( ), memcmp( ), memmove( )

void movmem(const void *source, void *dest, unsigned count)

Description

The prototype for **movmem( )** is found in **<mem.h>**. The function **movmem( )** is not defined by the ANSI/ISO C/C++ standard.

The **movmem( )** function copies *count* characters from the array pointed to by *source* into the array pointed to by *dest*. If the arrays overlap, the copy takes place correctly, placing the correct contents into *dest* but leaving *source* modified.

The **movmem( )** function is equivalent to the **memmove( )** function except that the **movmem( )** function has no return value and is not defined by the ANSI/ISO C/C++ standard.

Related Functions

memcpy( ), memmove( )

void setmem(void *buf, unsigned count, char ch)

Description

The prototype for **setmem( )** is found in **<mem.h>**. The **setmem( )** function is not defined by the ANSI/ISO C/C++ standard.

The **setmem( )** function copies *ch* into the first *count* characters of the array pointed to by *buf*.

The **setmem( )** function is equivalent to the **memset( )** function except that the **setmem( )** function has no return value and is not defined by the ANSI/ISO C/C++ standard.

Related Functions

memcpy( ), memset( ), memmove( )

char *stpcpy(char *str1, const char *str2)

Description

The prototype for **stpcpy( )** is found in **<string.h>** and is not defined by the ANSI/ISO C/C++ standard.

The **stpcpy( )** function is used to copy the contents of *str2* into *str1*. *str2* must be a pointer to a null-terminated string. The **stpcpy( )** function returns a pointer to the end of *str1*.

Example

The following code fragment copies **hello** into string **str**:

```
char str[8];
stpcpy(str, "hello");
```

Related Function

strcpy( )

char *strcat(char *str1, const char *str2)

Description

The prototype for **strcat( )** is found in **<string.h>**.

The **strcat( )** function concatenates a copy of *str2* to *str1* and terminates *str1* with a null. The null terminator originally ending *str1* is overwritten by the first character of *str2*. The string *str2* is untouched by the operation.

The **strcat( )** function returns *str1*.

Remember that no bounds checking takes place, so it is the programmer's responsibility to ensure that *str1* is large enough to hold both its original contents and the contents of *str2*.

Example

This program appends the first string read from **stdin** to the second. For example, assuming the user enters **hello** and **there**, the program prints **therehello**.

```
#include <stdio.h>
#include <string.h>

int main(void)
{
  char s1[80], s2[80];

  gets(s1);
  gets(s2);

  strcat(s2, s1);
  printf(s2);

  return 0;
}
```

Related Functions

strchr( ), strcmp( ), strcpy( )

char *strchr(const char *str, int ch)

Description

The prototype for **strchr( )** is found in **<string.h>**.

The **strchr( )** function returns a pointer to the first occurrence of *ch* in the string pointed to by *str*. If no match is found, it returns a null pointer.

Example

This program prints the string " **is a test**":

```
#include <stdio.h>
#include <string.h>

int main(void)
{
  char *p;

  p = strchr("this is a test", ' ');
  printf(p);

  return 0;
}
```

Related Functions

strpbrk( ), strstr( ), strtok( ), strspn( )

int strcmp(const char *str1, const char *str2)

Description

The prototype for the **strcmp( )** function is found in **<string.h>**.

The **strcmp( )** function lexicographically compares two null-terminated strings and returns an integer based on the outcome, as shown here:

Value	Meaning
Less than 0	*str1* is less than *str2*
0	*str1* is equal to *str2*
Greater than 0	*str1* is greater than *str2*

Example

The following function can be used as a password-verification routine. It returns 0 on failure and 1 on success.

```
int password(void)
{
  char s[80];

  printf("Enter password: ");
  gets(s);
  if(strcmp(s, "pass")) {
    printf("Invalid password.\n");
    return 0;
  }
  return 1;
}
```

Related Functions

strchr( ), strcpy( ), strncmp( )

int strcoll(const char *str1, const char *str2)

Description

The prototype for the **strcoll( )** function is found in **<string.h>**.

The **strcoll( )** function is equivalent to the **strcmp( )** function except that the comparison is performed in accordance with the current locale, which is specified using **setlocale( )** function.

Related Functions

strncmp( ), stricmp( )

char *strcpy(char *str1, const char *str2)

Description

The prototype for **strcpy( )** is found in **<string.h>**.

The **strcpy( )** function is used to copy the contents of *str2* into *str1*; *str2* must be a pointer to a null-terminated string. The **strcpy( )** function returns a pointer to *str1*.

If *str1* and *str2* overlap, the behavior of **strcpy( )** is undefined.

Example

The following code fragment copies **hello** into string **str**.

```
char str[80];
strcpy(str, "hello");
```

Related Functions

strchr( ), strcmp( ), memcpy( ), strncmp( )

size_t strcspn(const char *str1, const char *str2)

Description

The prototype for the **strcspn( )** function is found in **<string.h>**.

The **strcspn( )** function returns the length of the initial substring of the string pointed to by *str1* that is made up of only those characters not contained in the string pointed to by *str2*. Stated differently, **strcspn( )** returns the index of the first character in the string pointed to by *str1* that matches any of the characters in the string pointed to by *str2*.

Example

This program prints the number **8**:

```
#include <stdio.h>
#include <string.h>

int main(void)
{
  int len;

  len = strcspn("this is a test", "ab");
  printf("%d", len);

  return 0;
}
```

Related Functions

strpbrk( ), strstr( ), strtok( ), strrchr( )

char *strdup(const char *str)

Description

The prototype for **strdup( )** is found in **<string.h>**. The **strdup( )** function is not defined by the ANSI/ISO C/C++ standard.

The **strdup( )** function allocates enough memory, via a call to **malloc( )**, to hold a duplicate of the string pointed to by *str* and then copies that string into the allocated region and returns a pointer to it.

Example

This fragment duplicates the string **str**.

```
char str[80], *p;
strcpy(str, "this is a test");
p = strdup(str);
```

Related Function

strcpy( )

char *_strerror(const char *str)

Description

The prototype for the **_strerror( )** function is found in **<stdio.h>** and **<string.h>**.

The **_strerror( )** function lets you display your own error message followed by a colon and the most recent error message generated by the program. It returns a pointer to the entire string.

The **_strerror( )** function is not defined by the ANSI/ISO C/C++ standard.

Example

This fragment prints a message stating that the function called **swap( )** encountered an error:

```
void swap()
{
  /* ... */
  if(error) printf(_strerror("Error in swap."));
```

Related Functions

perror( ), strerror( )

char *strerror(int num)

Description

The prototype for the **strerror( )** function is found in **<string.h>**.

The **strerror( )** function returns a pointer to the error message associated with an error number.

Example

This fragment prints the error message associated with the global variable **errno** if an error has occurred.

```
if(errno) printf(strerror(errno));
```

Related Functions

perror( ), _strerror( )

int stricmp(const char *str1, const char *str2)
int strcmpi(const char *str1, const char *str2)

Description

The prototypes for the **stricmp( )** function and **strcmpi( )** macro are found in **<string.h>**. Neither of these are defined by the ANSI/ISO C/C++ standard.

The **stricmp( )** function lexicographically compares two null-terminated strings while ignoring case; **strcmpi( )** is a macro that translates to a **stricmp( )** call.

Both functions return an integer based on the outcome, as shown here:

Value	Meaning
Less than 0	*str1* is less than *str2*
0	*str1* is equal to *str2*
Greater than 0	*str1* is greater than *str2*

Example

The following function compares the two filenames specified on the command line to determine if they are the same:

```
#include <stdio.h>
#include <string.h>

int main(int argc, char *argv[])
{

  if(argc != 3) {
    printf("Use two command-line args.");
    return 1;
  }

  if(!stricmp(argv[1], argv[2]))
    printf("The filenames are the same.\n");
  else
    printf("The filenames differ.\n");

  return 0;
}
```

Related Functions

strnchr( ), strcmp( ), strncpy( )

size_t strlen(const char *str)

Description

The prototype for **strlen( )** is found in **<string.h>**.

The **strlen( )** function returns the length of the null-terminated string pointed to by *str*. The null is not counted.

Example

This code fragment prints the number **5** on the screen:

```
strcpy(s, "hello");
printf("%d", strlen(s));
```

Related Functions

strchr( ), strcmp( ), memcpy( ), strncmp( )

char *strlwr(char *str)

Description

The prototype for **strlwr( )** is found in **<string.h>**. The **strlwr( )** function is not defined by the ANSI/ISO C/C++ standard.

The **strlwr( )** function converts the string pointed to by *str* to lowercase. It returns *str*.

Example

This program prints **this is a test** on the screen:

```
#include <stdio.h>
#include <string.h>

int main(void)
{
  char s[80];

  strcpy(s, "THIS IS A TEST");
  strlwr(s);
  printf(s);

  return 0;
}
```

Related Function

strupr( )

char *strncat(char *str1, const char *str2, size_t count)

Description

The prototype for the **strncat( )** function is found in **<string.h>**.

The **strncat( )** function concatenates no more than *count* characters of the string pointed to by *str2* to the string pointed to by *str1* and terminates *str1* with a null. The null terminator originally ending *str1* is overwritten by the first character of *str2*. The string *str2* is untouched by the operation.

The **strncat( )** function returns *str1*.

Remember, no bounds checking takes place, so it is the programmer's responsibility to ensure that *str1* is large enough to hold both its original contents and those of *str2*.

Example

This program appends the first string read from **stdin** to the second and prevents an array overflow from occurring in *str1*. For example, if the user enters **hello** and **there**, the program prints **therehello**:

```
#include <stdio.h>
#include <string.h>

int main(void)
{
  char s1[80], s2[80];
  size_t len;

  gets(s1);
  gets(s2);

  /* compute how many chars will actually fit */
  len = 79-strlen(s2);

  strncat(s2, s1, len);
  printf(s2);

  return 0;
}
```

Related Functions

strnchr( ), strncmp( ), strncpy( ), strcat( )

int strncmp(const char *str1, const char *str2, size_t count)
int strnicmp(const char *str1, const char *str2, size_t count)
int strncmpi(const char *str1, const char *str2, size_t count)

Description

The prototypes for the **strncmp( )** and **strnicmp( )** functions, and the **strncmpi( )** macro, are found in **<string.h>**. Of these, only **strncmp( )** is defined by the ANSI/ISO C/C++ standard.

The **strncmp( )** function lexicographically compares no more than *count* characters from the two null-terminated strings. The functions **strnicmp( )** and **strncmpi( )** perform the same comparison while ignoring case; **strncmpi( )** is a macro that translates to a **strnicmp( )** call.

All three functions return an integer based on the outcome, as shown here:

Value	Meaning
Less than 0	*str1* is less than *str2*
0	*str1* is equal to *str2*
Greater than 0	*str1* is greater than *str2*

If there are fewer than *count* characters in either string, the comparison ends when the first null is encountered.

Example

The following function compares the first eight characters of the two filenames specified on the command line to determine if they are the same:

```
#include <stdio.h>
#include <string.h>

int main(int argc, char *argv[])
{
```

```
if(argc != 3) {
  printf("Use two command-line args.");
  return 1;
}

if(!strnicmp(argv[1], argv[2], 8))
  printf("The filenames are the same.\n");
else
  printf("The filenames differ.\n");

return 0;
}
```

Related Functions

strnchr( ), strcmp( ), strncpy( )

char *strncpy(char *dest, const char *source, size_t count)

Description

The prototype for **strncpy( )** is found in **<string.h>**.

The **strncpy( )** function is used to copy up to *count* characters from the string pointed to by *source* into the string pointed to by *dest*. The *source* must be a pointer to a null-terminated string. The **strncpy( )** function returns a pointer to *dest*.

If *dest* and *source* overlap, the behavior of **strncpy( )** is undefined.

If the string pointed to by *source* has fewer than *count* characters, nulls are appended to the end of *dest* until *count* characters have been copied.

Alternately, if the string pointed to by *source* is longer than *count* characters, the resulting string pointed to by *dest* is not null-terminated.

Example

The following code fragment copies at most 79 characters of *str1* into *str2,* thus ensuring that no array boundary overflow will occur:

```
char str1[128], str2[80];
gets(str1);
strncpy(str2, str1, 79);
```

Related Functions

strchr( ), strncmp( ), memcpy( ), strncat( )

char *strnset(char *str, int ch, size_t count)

Description

The prototype for **strnset( )** is found in **<string.h>**.

The **strnset( )** function sets the first *count* characters in the string pointed to by *str* to the value of *ch*. It returns *str*.

Example

This fragment sets the first 10 characters of *str* to the value **x**:

```
strnset(str, 'x', 10);
```

Related Function

strset( )

char *strpbrk(const char *str1, const char *str2)

Description

The prototype to **strpbrk( )** is found in **<string.h>**.

The **strpbrk( )** function returns a pointer to the first character in the string pointed to by *str1* that matches any character in the string pointed to by *str2*. The null terminators are not included. If there are no matches, a null pointer is returned.

Example

This program prints the message **s is a test** on the screen:

```
#include <stdio.h>
#include <string.h>

int main(void)
{
  char *p;

  p = strpbrk("this is a test", " absj");
```

```
    printf(p);

    return 0;
}
```

Related Functions

strrchr( ), strstr( ), strtok( ), strspn( )

char *strrchr(const char *str, int ch)

Description

The prototype to **strrchr( )** is found in **<string.h>**.

The **strrchr( )** function returns a pointer to the last occurrence of the low-order byte of *ch* in the string pointed to by *str*. If no match is found, it returns a null pointer.

Example

This program prints the string **is a test**:

```
#include <stdio.h>
#include <string.h>

int main(void)
{
  char *p;

  p = strrchr("this is a test", 'i');
  printf(p);

  return 0;
}
```

Related Functions

strpbrk( ), strstr( ), strtok( ), strspn( )

char *strrev(char *str)

Description

The prototype for **strrev( )** is found in **<string.h>**. The **strrev( )** function is not defined by the ANSI/ISO C/C++ standard.

The **strrev( )** function reverses all characters, except the null terminator, in the string pointed to by *str*. It returns *str*.

Example

This program prints **hello** backward on the screen:

```
#include <stdio.h>
#include <string.h>

char s[] = "hello";

int main(void)
{
  strrev(s);
  printf(s);

  return 0;
}
```

Related Function

strset( )

char *strset(char *str, int ch)

Description

The prototype for **strset( )** is found in **<string.h>**. The **strset( )** function is not defined by the ANSI/ISO C/C++ standard.

The **strset( )** function sets all characters in the string pointed to by *str* to the value of *ch*. It returns *str*.

Example

This fragment fills the string *str* with the value **x**.

```
strset(str, 'x');
```

Related Function

strnset( )

size_t strspn(const char *str1, const char *str2)

Description

The prototype for **strspn( )** is found in **<string.h>**.

The **strspn( )** function returns the length of the initial substring of the string pointed to by *str1* that is made up of only those characters contained in the string pointed to by *str2*. Stated differently, **strspn( )** returns the index of the first character in the string pointed to by *str1* that does not match any of the characters in the string pointed to by *str2*.

Example

This program prints the number **8**:

```
#include <stdio.h>
#include <string.h>

int main(void)
{
  int len;

  len = strspn("this is a test", "siht ");
  printf("%d",len);

  return 0;
}
```

Related Functions

strpbrk( ), strstr( ), strtok( ), strrchr( )

char *strstr(const char *str1, const char *str2)

Description

The prototype for **strstr( )** is found in **<string.h>**.

The **strstr( )** function returns a pointer to the first occurrence in the string pointed to by *str1* of the string pointed to by *str2* (except *str2*'s null terminator). It returns a null pointer if no match is found.

Example

This program displays the message **is is a test**:

```
#include <stdio.h>
#include <string.h>

int main(void)
{
  char *p;

  p = strstr("this is a test", "is");
  printf(p);

  return 0;
}
```

Related Functions

strpbrk( ), **strspn( )**, **strtok( )**, **strrchr( )**, **strchr( )**, **strcspn( )**

char *strtok(char *str1, const char *str2)

Description

The prototype for **strtok( )** is in **<string.h>**.

The **strtok( )** function returns a pointer to the next token in the string pointed to by *str1*. The characters making up the string pointed to by *str2* are the delimiters that determine the token. A null pointer is returned when there is no token to return.

The first time **strtok( )** is called, *str1* is actually used in the call. Subsequent calls use a null pointer for the first argument. In this way the entire string can be reduced to its tokens.

It is important to understand that the **strtok( )** function modifies the string pointed to by *str1*. Each time a token is found, a null is placed where the delimiter was found. In this way **strtok( )** continues to advance through the string.

It is possible to use a different set of delimiters for each call to **strtok( )**.

Example

This program tokenizes the string **The summer soldier, the sunshine patriot** with spaces and commas as the delimiters.
The output is **The | summer | soldier | the | sunshine | patriot**.

```
#include <stdio.h>
#include <string.h>

int main(void)
{
  char *p;

  p = strtok("The summer soldier, the sunshine patriot"," ");
  printf(p);
  do {
    p=strtok('\0', ", ");
    if(p) printf("|%s", p);
  } while(p);

  return 0;
}
```

Related Functions

strpbrk( ), **strspn( )**, **strrchr( )**, **strchr( )**, **strcspn( )**

char *strupr(char *str)

Description

The prototype for **strupr( )** is found in **<string.h>**. The **strupr( )** function is not defined by the ANSI/ISO C/C++ standard.

The **strupr( )** function converts the string pointed to by *str* to uppercase. It returns *str*.

Example

This program prints **THIS IS A TEST** on the screen:

```
#include <stdio.h>
#include <string.h>

int main(void)
{
  char s[80];

  strcpy(s, "this is a test");
  strupr(s);
  printf(s);

  return 0;
}
```

Related Function

strlwr( )

size_t strxfrm(char *dest, const char *source, size_t count)

Description

The prototype for **strxfrm( )** is found in **<string.h>**.

The **strxfrm( )** function is used to copy up to *count* characters from the string pointed to by *source* into the string pointed to by *dest*. The *source* must be a pointer to a null-terminated string. In the process, any country-related items are transformed into the proper format for the current country. The **strxfrm( )** function returns the number of characters copied.

The **strxfrm( )** function is similar to the **strncpy( )** function.

Related Functions

strncpy( ), memcpy( ), strncat( )

int tolower(int ch)
int _tolower(int ch)

Description

The prototype for **tolower( )** and the definition of the macro **_tolower( )** are found in **<ctype.h>**. The _tolower( ) macro is not defined by the ANSI/ISO C/C++ standard.

The **tolower( )** function returns the lowercase equivalent of *ch* if *ch* is an uppercase letter; otherwise, it returns *ch* unchanged. The **_tolower( )** macro is equivalent, but should only be used when *ch* is an uppercase letter; otherwise, the results are undefined.

Example

This code fragment displays a **q**.

```
putchar(tolower('Q'));
```

Related Function

toupper( )

int toupper(int ch)
int _toupper(int ch)

Description

The prototype for **toupper( )** and the macro **_toupper( )** are found in **<ctype.h>**. The **_toupper( )** macro is not defined by the ANSI/ISO C/C++ standard.

The **toupper( )** function returns the uppercase equivalent of *ch* if *ch* is a letter; otherwise, it returns *ch* unchanged. The **_toupper( )** macro is equivalent but should only be used when *ch* is a lowercase letter; otherwise, the results are undefined.

Example

This displays an **A**.

```
putchar(toupper('a'));
```

Related Function

tolower( )

Borland
C++
Builder

Chapter 13

Mathematical Functions

T he ANSI/ISO C/C++ standard defines 22 mathematical functions that fall into the following categories:

- Trigonometric functions
- Hyperbolic functions
- Exponential and logarithmic functions
- Miscellaneous

C++ Builder implements all of these functions and includes several of its own. Many of the functions added by C++ Builder are **long double** versions of the standard functions. These C++ Builder–specific functions are also discussed here. Remember, however, that they are not defined by C89 or C++.

All the math functions require the header **<math.h>** to be included in any program using them. In addition to declaring the math functions, this header defines three macros called **EDOM**, **ERANGE**, and **HUGE_VAL**. If an argument to a math function is not in the domain for which it is defined, an implementation-defined value is returned and the global **errno** is set equal to **EDOM**. If a routine produces a result that is too large to be represented, an overflow happens. This causes the routine to return **HUGE_VAL** and **errno** is set to **ERANGE**, indicating a range error. (If the function returns a **long double**, then it returns **_LHUGE_VAL**.) If an underflow happens, the routine returns 0 and sets **errno** to **ERANGE**.

double acos(double arg)
long double acosl(long double arg)

Description

The prototype for **acos( )** is in **<math.h>**.

The **acos( )** function returns the arc cosine of *arg*. The argument to **acos( )** must be in the range –1 to 1; otherwise, a domain error occurs. The return value is in the range 0 to π and is in radians.

acosl( ) is the **long double** version of this function.

Example

This program prints the arc cosines, in one-tenth increments, of the values –1 through 1:

```
#include <stdio.h>
#include <math.h>

int main(void)
{
```

```
  double val = -1.0;

  do {
    printf("arc cosine of %f is %f\n", val, acos(val));
    val += 0.1;
  } while(val <= 1.0);

  return 0;
}
```

Related Functions

asin( ), **atan( )**, **atan2( )**, **sin( )**, **cos( )**, **tan( )**, **sinh( )**, **cosh( )**, **tanh( )**

double asin(double arg)
long double asinl(long double arg)

Description

The prototype for **asin( )** is in **<math.h>**.

The **asin( )** function returns the arc sine of *arg*. The argument to **asin( )** must be in the range –1 to 1; otherwise, a domain error occurs. Its return value is in the range $-\pi/2$ to $\pi/2$ and is in radians.

asinl( ) is the **long double** version of this function.

Example

This program prints the arc sines, in one-tenth increments, of the values –1 through 1:

```
#include <stdio.h>
#include <math.h>

int main(void)
{
  double val = -1.0;

  do {
    printf("arc sine of %f is %f\n", val, asin(val));
    val += 0.1;
  } while(val <= 1.0);
```

```
    return 0;
}
```

Related Functions

atan( ), atan2( ), sin( ), cos( ), tan( ), sinh( ), cosh( ), tanh( )

double atan(double arg)
long double atanl(long double arg)

Description

The prototype for **atan( )** is in **<math.h>**.

The **atan( )** function returns the arc tangent of *arg*. The return value is in radians and in the range $-\pi/2$ to $\pi/2$.

atanl( ) is the **long double** version of this function.

Example

This program prints the arc tangents, in one-tenth increments, of the values –1 through 1.

```
#include <stdio.h>
#include <math.h>

int main(void)
{
  double val = -1.0;

  do {
    printf("arc tangent of %f is %f\n", val, atan(val));
    val += 0.1;
  } while(val <= 1.0);

  return 0;
}
```

Related Functions

asin( ), acos( ), atan2( ), tan( ), cos( ), sin( ), sinh( ), cosh( ), tanh( )

double atan2(double y, double x)
long double atan2l(long double y, long double x)

Description

The prototype for **atan2( )** is in **<math.h>**.

The **atan2( )** function returns the arc tangent of y/x. It uses the signs of its arguments to compute the quadrant of the return value. The return value is in radians and in the range $-\pi$ to π.

atan2l( ) is the **long double** version of this function.

Example

This program prints the arc tangents, in one-tenth increments of y, from -1 through 1:

```
#include <stdio.h>
#include <math.h>

int main(void)
{
  double y = -1.0;

  do {
    printf("atan2 of %f is %f\n", y, atan2(y, 1.0));
    y += 0.1;
  } while(y <= 1.0);

  return 0;
}
```

Related Functions

asin( ), acos( ), atan( ), tan( ), cos( ), sin( ), sinh( ), cosh( ), tanh( )

double cabs(struct complex znum)
long double cabsl(struct _complexl znum)

Description

The prototype for **cabs( )** is in **<math.h>**. This macro is not defined by the ANSI/ISO C89/C++ standard.

The **cabs( )** macro returns the absolute value of a complex number. The structure **complex** is defined as

```
struct complex {
    double x;
    double y;
};
```

If an overflow occurs, **HUGE_VAL** is returned and **errno** is set to **ERANGE** (out of range).

cabsl( ) is the **long double** version of this macro and **_complexl** is the **long double** equivalent of **complex**.

Example

This code prints the absolute value of a complex number that has a real part equal to 1 and an imaginary part equal to 2:

```
#include <stdio.h>
#include <math.h>

int main(void)
{
  struct complex z;

  z.x = 1;
  z.y = 2;

  printf("%f", cabs(z));

  return 0;
}
```

Related Function

abs( )

double ceil(double num)
long double ceill(long double num)

Description

The prototype for **ceil( )** is in **<math.h>**.

The **ceil( )** function returns the smallest integer (represented as a **double**) not less than *num*. For example, given 1.02, **ceil( )** returns 2.0. Given –1.02, **ceil( )** returns –1.

ceill( ) is the **long double** version of **ceil( )**.

Example

This fragment prints the value **10** on the screen:

```
printf("%f", ceil(9.9));
```

Related Functions

floor( ), **fmod( )**

double cos(double arg)
long double cosl(long double arg)

Description

The prototype for **cos( )** is in **<math.h>**.

The **cos( )** function returns the cosine of *arg*. The value of *arg* must be in radians. The return value is in the range –1 to 1.

cosl( ) is the **long double** version of this function.

Example

This program prints the cosines, in one-tenth increments, of the values –1 through 1:

```
#include <stdio.h>
#include <math.h>

int main(void)
{
  double val = -1.0;

  do {
    printf("cosine of %f is %f\n", val, cos(val));
    val += 0.1;
  } while(val <= 1.0);

  return 0;
}
```

Related Functions

asin( ), acos( ), atan2( ), atan( ), tan( ), sin( ), sinh( ), cosh( ), tanh( )

double cosh(double arg)
long double coshl(long double arg)

Description

The prototype for **cosh( )** is in **<math.h>**.

The **cosh( )** function returns the hyperbolic cosine of *arg*.

coshl( ) is the **long double** version of this function.

Example

This program prints the hyperbolic cosines, in one-tenth increments, of the values −1 through 1:

```
#include <stdio.h>
#include <math.h>

int main(void)
{
  double val = -1.0;

  do {
    printf("hyperbolic cosine of %f is %f\n", val, cosh(val));
    val += 0.1;
  } while(val <= 1.0);

  return 0;
}
```

Related Functions

asin( ), acos( ), atan2( ), atan( ), tan( ), cos( ), sin( ), tanh( )

double exp(double arg)
long double expl(long double arg)

Description

The prototype for **exp( )** is in **<math.h>**.

The **exp( )** function returns the natural logarithm *e* raised to the *arg* power.

expl( ) is the **long double** version of **exp( )**.

Example

This fragment displays the value of *e* (rounded to **2.718282**).

```
printf("Value of e to the first: %f", exp(1.0));
```

Related Function

log( )

double fabs(double num)
long double fabsl(long double num)

Description

The prototype for **fabs( )** is in **<math.h>**.

The **fabs( )** function returns the absolute value of *num*.

fabsl( ) is the **long double** version of this function.

Example

This program prints **1.0 1.0** on the screen:

```
#include <stdio.h>
#include <math.h>

int main(void)
{
```

```
    printf("%1.1f %1.1f", fabs(1.0), fabs(-1.0));

    return 0;
}
```

Related Function

abs( )

double floor(double num)
long double floorl(long double num)

Description

The prototype for **floor( )** is in **<math.h>**.

The **floor( )** function returns the largest integer (represented as a **double**) that is not greater than *num*. For example, given 1.02, **floor( )** returns 1.0. Given −1.02, **floor( )** returns −2.0.

floor( ) is the **long double** version of this function.

Example

This fragment prints **10** on the screen:

```
    printf("%f", floor(10.9));
```

Related Function

fmod( )

double fmod(double x, double y)
long double fmodl(long double x, long double y)

Description

The prototype for **fmod( )** is in **<math.h>**.

The **fmod( )** function returns the remainder of x/y.

fmodl( ) is the **long double** version of this function.

Example

This program prints **1.0** on the screen, which represents the remainder of 10/3:

```c
#include <stdio.h>
#include <math.h>

int main(void)
{
  printf("%1.1f", fmod(10.0, 3.0));

  return 0;
}
```

Related Functions

ceil( ), **floor( )**, **fabs( )**

double frexp(double num, int *exp)
long double frexpl(long double num, int *exp)

Description

The prototype for **frexp( )** is in **<math.h>**.

The **frexp( )** function decomposes the number *num* into a mantissa in the range 0.5 to less than 1, and an integer exponent such that $num = mantissa * 2^{exp}$. The mantissa is returned by the function, and the exponent is stored at the variable pointed to by *exp*.

frexpl( ) is the **long double** version of this function.

Example

This code fragment prints **0.625** for the mantissa and **4** for the exponent:

```c
int e;
double f;

f = frexp(10.0, &e);
printf("%f %d", f, e);
```

Related Function

ldexp( )

double hypot(double x, double y)
long double hypotl(long double x, long double y)

Description

The prototype for **hypot( )** is in **<math.h>**. This function is not defined by the ANSI/ISO C89/C++ standard.

The **hypot( )** function returns the length of the hypotenuse of a right triangle given the lengths of the other two sides.

hypotl( ) is the **long double** version of this function.

Example

This code fragment prints the value **2.236068**:

```
printf("%f", hypot(2, 1));
```

double ldexp(double num, int exp)
long double ldexpl(long double num, int exp)

Description

The prototype for **ldexp( )** is in **<math.h>**.

The **ldexp( )** function returns the value of $num * 2^{exp}$. If overflow occurs, **HUGE_VAL** is returned.

ldexpl( ) is the **long double** version of this function.

Example

This program displays the number **4**:

```
#include <stdio.h>
#include <math.h>

int main(void)
{
  printf("%f", ldexp(1, 2));
```

```
    return 0;
}
```

Related Functions

frexp( ), modf( )

double log(double num)
long double logl(long double num)

Description
The prototype for **log( )** is in **<math.h>**.

The **log( )** function returns the natural logarithm for *num.* A domain error occurs if *num* is negative and a range error occurs if the argument is 0.

logl( ) is the **long double** version of this function.

Example
This program prints the natural logarithms for the numbers 1 through 10:

```
#include <stdio.h>
#include <math.h>

int main(void)
{
  double val = 1.0;

  do {
    printf("%f %f\n", val, log(val));
    val++;
  } while (val < 11.0);

  return 0;
}
```

Related Function

log10( )

double log10(double num)
long double log10l(long double num)

Description
The prototype for **log10( )** is in **<math.h>**.

The **log10( )** function returns the base 10 logarithm for *num*. A domain error occurs if *num* is negative, and a range error occurs if the argument is 0.

log10l( ) is the **long double** version of this function.

Example
This program prints the base 10 logarithms for the numbers 1 through 10:

```
#include <stdio.h>
#include <math.h>

int main(void)
{
  double val = 1.0;

  do {
    printf("%f %f\n", val, log10(val));
    val++;
  } while (val < 11.0);

  return 0;
}
```

Related Function

log( )

int _matherr(struct exception *err)
int _matherrl(struct _exceptionl *err)

Description
The prototype for **_matherr( )** is in **<math.h>**. This function is not defined by the ANSI/ISO C/C++ standard.

The _matherr( ) function allows you to create custom math error handling routines. The function must perform as follows. When the **_matherr( )** function can resolve a problem, it returns nonzero and no message is printed. Also, the **errno** built-in variable is not altered. However, if **_matherr( )** cannot resolve the problem, it returns zero, the appropriate error message is printed, and the value of **errno** is changed. By default, C++ Builder provides a version **_matherr( )** function that returns zero.

The _matherr( ) function is called with an argument of type **exception**, which is shown here.

```
struct exception {
  int type;
  char *name;
  double arg1, arg2;
  double retval;
};
```

The **type** element holds the type of the error that occurred. Its value will be one of the following values.

Symbol	Meaning
DOMAIN	Domain error
SING	Result is a singularity
OVERFLOW	Overflow error
UNDERFLOW	Underflow error
TLOSS	Total loss of significant digits

The **name** element holds a pointer to a string that holds the name of the function in which the error took place. The **arg1** and **arg2** elements hold the arguments to the function that caused the error. If the function takes only one argument, it will be in **arg1**. Finally, **retval** holds the default return value for **_matherr( )**. You can return a different value.

_matherrl is used with the **long double** math functions. The structure **_exceptionl** is the same as **_exception** except that the elements **arg1**, **arg2**, and **retval** are of type **long double**.

double modf(double num, double *i)
long double modfl(long double num, long double *i)

Description

The prototype for **modf( )** is in **<math.h>**.

The **modf( )** function decomposes *num* into its integer and fractional parts. It returns the fractional portion and places the integer part in the variable pointed to by *i*.

modfl( ) is the **long double** version of this function.

Example

This fragment prints **10** and **0.123** on the screen:

```
double i;
double f;

f = modf(10.123, &i);
printf("%f %f", i, f);
```

Related Functions

frexp( ), **ldexp( )**

double poly(double x, int n, double c[ ])
long double polyl(long double x, int n, long double c[ ])

Description

The prototype for **poly( )** is in **<math.h>**. This function is not defined by the ANSI/ISO C/C++ standard.

The **poly( )** function evaluates a polynomial in *x* of degree *n* with coefficients *c[0]* through *c[n]* and returns the result. For example, if *n=3*, the polynomial evaluated is

$$c[3]x^3 + c[2]x^2 + c[1]x + c[0]$$

polyl( ) is the **long double** version of this function.

Example

This program prints **47** on the screen.

```
#include <stdio.h>
#include <math.h>
```

```
int main(void)
{
  double c[2];

  c[1] = 2;
  c[0] = 45;
  printf("%f", poly(1, 2, c));

  return 0;
}
```

Related Function

hypot( )

double pow(double base, double exp)
long double powl(long double base, long double exp)

Description

The prototype for **pow( )** is in **<math.h>**.

The **pow( )** function returns *base* raised to the *exp* power ($base^{exp}$).

An overflow produces a range error. Domain errors may also occur.

powl( ) is the **long double** version of this function.

Example

This program prints the first 11 powers of 12.

```
#include <stdio.h>
#include <math.h>

int main(void)
{
  double x=12.0, y=0.0;

  do {
    printf("%f\n", pow(x, y));
    y++;
  } while(y<11);
```

```
   return 0;
}
```

Related Functions

exp( ), log( ), sqrt( ), pow10( )

double pow10(int n)
long double pow10l(int n)

Description

The prototype for **pow10( )** is in **<math.h>**. This function is not defined by the ANSI/ISO C/C++ standard.

The **pow10( )** function returns 10 raised to the power n. Overflow and underflow are the only possible errors.

pow10l( ) is the **long double** version of this function.

Example

This program prints the first 11 powers of 10:

```
#include <stdio.h>
#include <math.h>

int main(void)
{
   int x=0;

   while(x < 11)
     printf("%f\n", pow10(x++));

   return 0;
}
```

Related Functions

exp( ), log( ), sqrt( ), pow( )

double sin(double arg)
long double sinl(long double arg)

Description

The prototype to **sin( )** is in **<math.h>**.

The **sin( )** function returns the sine of *arg*. The value of *arg* must be in radians.

sinl( ) is the **long double** version of this function.

Example

This program prints the sines, in one-tenth increments, of the values –1 through 1:

```
#include <stdio.h>
#include <math.h>

int main(void)
{
  double val = -1.0;

  do {
    printf("sine of %f is %f\n", val, sin(val));
    val += 0.1;
  } while(val <= 1.0);

  return 0;
}
```

Related Functions

asin( ), acos( ), atan2( ), atan( ), tan( ), cos( ), sinh( ), cosh( ), tanh( )

double sinh(double arg)
long double sinhl(long double arg)

Description

The prototype for **sinhl( )** is in **<math.h>**.

The **sinh( )** function returns the hyperbolic sine of *arg*.

sinhl( ) is the **long double** version of this function.

THE C++ BUILDER
FUNCTION LIBRARY

Example

This program prints the hyperbolic sines, in one-tenth increments, of the values –1 through 1.

```
#include <stdio.h>
#include <math.h>

int main(void)
{
  double val = -1.0;

  do {
    printf("hyperbolic sine of %f is %f\n", val, sinh(val));
    val += 0.1;
  } while(val <= 1.0);

  return 0;
}
```

Related Functions

asin( ), acos( ), atan2( ), atan( ), tan( ), cos( ), tanh( ), cosh( )

double sqrt(double num)
long double sqrtl(long double num)

Description

The prototype for **sqrt( )** is in **<math.h>**.

The **sqrt( )** function returns the square root of *num*. If called with a negative argument, a domain error occurs.

sqrtl( ) is the **long double** version of this function.

Example

This fragment prints **4** on the screen:

```
printf("%f", sqrt(16.0));
```

Related Functions

exp( ), log( ), pow( )

double tan(double arg)
long double tanl(long double arg)

Description

The prototype for **tan( )** is in **<math.h>**.

The **tan( )** function returns the tangent of *arg*. The value of *arg* must be in radians.
tanl( ) is the **long double** version of this function.

Example

This program prints the tangent, in one-tenth increments, of the values –1 through 1:

```
#include <stdio.h>
#include <math.h>

int main(void)
{
  double val = -1.0;

  do {
    printf("tangent of %f is %f\n", val, tan(val));
    val += 0.1;
  } while(val <= 1.0);

  return 0;
}
```

Related Functions

asin( ), atan( ), atan2( ), cos( ), sin( ), sinh( ), cosh( ), tanh( )

double tanh(double arg)
long double tanhl(long double arg)

Description

The prototype for **tanh( )** is in **<math.h>**.

The **tanh( )** function returns the hyperbolic tangent of *arg*.
tanhl( ) is the **long double** version of this function.

Example

This program prints the hyperbolic tangent, in one-tenth increments, of the values –1 through 1:

```
#include <stdio.h>
#include <math.h>

int main(void)
{
  double val = -1.0;

  do {
    printf("Hyperbolic tangent of %f is %f\n", val, tanh(val));
    val += 0.1;
  } while(val <= 1.0);

  return 0;
}
```

Related Functions

asin( ), atan( ), atan2( ), cos( ), sin( ), cosh( ), sinh( )

Borland
C++
Builder

Chapter 14

Time, Date, and System-Related Functions

This chapter covers those functions that in one way or another are more system sensitive than others. Of the functions defined by the ANSI/ISO C/C++ standard, these include the time and date functions, which relate to the system by using its time and date information.

Also discussed in this chapter is a category of functions that allow a lower level of system control than is normal. With the popularity and advancement of GUI-type operating systems, like Windows and Linux, these types of functions are slowly being phased out by various compilers, including C++ Builder. However, several low-level functions are still available, and they are covered here for completeness. None of these low-level functions are defined by the ANSI/ISO C/C++ standard. Also, some of the low-level functions apply only to programs written for a DOS session when running Windows.

The functions that deal with the system time and date require the header **<time.h>** for their prototypes. This header also defines three types. The types **time_t** and **clock_t** are capable of representing the system time and date as a long integer. This is referred to as the *calendar time*. The structure type **tm** holds the date and time broken down into its elements. The **tm** structure is defined as shown here:

```
struct tm{
    int tm_sec;   /* seconds, 0-59 */
    int tm_min;   /* minutes, 0-59 */
    int tm_hour;  /* hours, 0-23 */
    int tm_mday;  /* day of the month, 1-31 */
    int tm_mon;   /* months since Jan, 0-11 */
    int tm_year;  /* years from 1900 */
    int tm_wday;  /* days since Sunday, 0-6 */
    int tm_yday;  /* days since Jan 1, 0-365 */
    int tm_isdst; /* daylight saving time indicator */
};
```

The value of **tm_isdst** will be positive if daylight saving time is in effect, 0 if it is not in effect, and negative if there is no information available. This form of the time and date is called the *broken-down time*.

C++ Builder also includes some nonstandard time and date functions that bypass the normal time and date system and interface more closely with DOS. The functions use structures of either type **time** or **date**, which are defined in **<dos.h>**. Their declarations are shown here.

```
struct date{
    int da_year; /* year */
    char da_day; /* day of month */
    char da_mon; /* month, Jan=1 */
};
```

```
struct time {
  unsigned char ti_min;  /* minutes */
  unsigned char ti_hour; /* hours */
  unsigned char ti_hund; /* hundredths of seconds */
  unsigned char ti_sec;  /* seconds */
};
```

The DOS interfacing functions require the header **<dos.h>**.

char *asctime(const struct tm *ptr)

Description
The prototype for **asctime( )** is in **<time.h>**.

The **asctime( )** function returns a pointer to a string representing the information stored in the structure pointed to by *ptr* that is converted into the following form:

day month date hours:minutes:seconds year

For example:

Thu Jan 25 12:05:34 2001

The structure pointer passed to **asctime( )** is generally obtained from either **localtime( )** or **gmtime( )**.

The buffer used by **asctime( )** to hold the formatted output string is a statically allocated character array and is overwritten each time the function is called. If you wish to save the contents of the string, it is necessary to copy it elsewhere.

Example
This program displays the local time defined by the system:

```
#include <stdio.h>
#include <time.h>

int main(void)
{
  struct tm *ptr;
  time_t lt;

  lt = time(NULL);
  ptr = localtime(&lt);
  printf(asctime(ptr));
```

```
   return 0;
}
```

Related Functions

localtime( ), gmtime( ), time( ), ctime( )

clock_t clock(void)

Description

The prototype for **clock( )** is in **<time.h>**.

The **clock( )** function returns the amount of time elapsed since the program that called **clock( )** started running. If a clock is not available, –1 is returned. To convert the return value to seconds, divide it by the macro **CLK_TCK**.

Example

This program times the number of seconds that it takes for the empty **for** loop to go from 0 to 500000:

```
#include <stdio.h>
#include <time.h>

int main(void)
{
  clock_t start, stop;
  unsigned long t;

  start = clock();
  for(t=0; t<500000L; t++);
  stop = clock();
  printf("Loop required %f seconds",
         (stop - start) / CLK_TCK);

  return 0;
}
```

Related Functions

localtime( ), gmtime( ), time( ), asctime( )

char *ctime(const time_t *time)

Description

The prototype for **ctime( )** is in **<time.h>**.

The **ctime( )** function returns a pointer to a string of the form

day month date hours:minutes:seconds year

given a pointer to the calendar time. The calendar time is generally obtained through a call to **time( )**. The **ctime( )** function is equivalent to

```
asctime(localtime(time))
```

The buffer used by **ctime( )** to hold the formatted output string is a statically allocated character array and is overwritten each time the function is called. If you wish to save the contents of the string, it is necessary to copy it elsewhere.

Example

This program displays the local time defined by the system:

```
#include <stdio.h>
#include <time.h>
#include <stddef.h>

int main(void)
{
  time_t lt;

  lt = time(NULL);
  printf(ctime(&lt));

  return 0;
}
```

Related Functions

localtime( ), gmtime( ), time( ), asctime( )

double difftime(time_t time2, time_t time1)

Description
The prototype for **difftime( )** is in **<time.h>**.

The **difftime( )** function returns the difference, in seconds, between *time1* and *time2*. That is, it returns *time2–time1*.

Example
This program times the number of seconds that it takes for the empty **for** loop to go from 0 to 500,000:

```
#include <stdio.h>
#include <time.h>
#include <stddef.h>

int main(void)
{
  time_t start,end;
  long unsigned int t;

  start = time(NULL);
  for(t=0; t<500000L; t++) ;
  end = time(NULL);
  printf("Loop required %f seconds", difftime(end, start));

  return 0;
}
```

Related Functions

localtime( ), gmtime( ), time( ), asctime( )

void disable(void)
void _disable(void)

Description

The prototypes for **disable( )** and **_disable( )** are in **<dos.h>**. These macros are not defined by the ANSI/ISO C/C++ standard.

The **disable( )** and **_disable( )** macros disable interrupts. The only interrupt that they allow is the NMI (nonmaskable interrupt). Use this function with care because many devices in the system use interrupts.

Related Functions

enable( ), geninterrupt( )

unsigned _dos_close(int fd)

Description

The prototype for **_dos_close( )** is in **<dos.h>**. This function is not defined by the ANSI/ISO C/C++ standard. This function is obsolete and not recommended for future code.

The **_dos_close( )** function closes the file specified by the file descriptor *fd*. The file must have been opened using a call to either **_dos_creat( )**, **_dos_open( )**, or **_dos_creatnew( )**. The function returns 0 if successful. Otherwise, non-0 is returned and **errno** is set to **EBADF** (bad file descriptor).

Example

This fragment closes the file associated with the file descriptor **fd**:

```
_dos_close(fd);
```

Related Functions

_dos_creat( ), **_dos_open( )**

unsigned _dos_creat(const char *fname, unsigned attr, int *fd)
unsigned _dos_creatnew(const char *fname, unsigned attr, int *fd)

Description

The prototypes for **_dos_creat( )** and **_dos_creatnew( )** are in **<dos.h>**. These functions are not defined by the ANSI/ISO C/C++ standard. These functions are obsolete and not recommended for future code.

The **_dos_creat( )** function creates a file by the name pointed to by *fname* with the attributes specified by *attr*. It returns a file descriptor to the file in the integer pointed to by *fd*. If the file already exists, it will be erased. The **_dos_creatnew( )** function is the same as **_dos_creat( )** except that if the file already exists, it will not be erased and **_dos_creatnew( )** will return an error.

The valid values for *attr* are shown here. (The macros are defined in **<dos.h>**.)

Macro	Meaning
_A_NORMAL	Normal file
_A_RDONLY	Read-only file
_A_HIDDEN	Hidden file
_A_SYSTEM	System file
_A_VOLID	Volume Label
_A_SUBDIR	Subdirectory
_A_ARCH	Archive byte set

Both functions return 0 if successful and non-0 on failure. On failure, **errno** will contain one of these values: **ENOENT** (file not found), **EMFILE** (too many open files), **EACCES** (access denied), or **EEXIST** (file already exists).

Example

This fragment opens a file called TEST.TST for output:

```
int fd;

if(_dos_creat("test.tst", _A_NORMAL, &fd))
  printf("Cannot open file.\n");
```

Related Function

_dos_open( )

void _dos_getdate(struct dosdate_t *d)
void _dos_gettime(struct dostime_t *t)

Description

The prototypes for **_dos_getdate( )** and **_dos_gettime( )** are in **<dos.h>**. These functions are not defined by the ANSI/ISO C/C++ standard. These functions are obsolete and not recommended for future code.

The **_dos_getdate( )** function returns the DOS system date in the structure pointed to by *d*. The **_dos_gettime( )** function returns the DOS system time in the structure pointed to by *t*.

The **dosdate_t** structure is defined like this:

```
struct dosdate_t {
  unsigned char day;
  unsigned char month;
  unsigned int year;
  unsigned char dayofweek;  /* Sunday is 0 */
};
```

The **dostime_t** structure is defined as shown here:

```
struct dostime_t {
  unsigned char hour;
  unsigned char minute;
  unsigned char second;
  unsigned char hsecond; /* hundredths of second */
};
```

Example

This displays the system time and date:

```
#include <stdio.h>
#include <dos.h>

int main(void)
{
  struct dosdate_t d;
  struct dostime_t t;
```

```
    _dos_getdate(&d);
    _dos_gettime(&t);

    printf("Time and date: %d:%d:%d, %d/%d/%d",
            t.hour, t.minute, t.second, d.month, d.day,
            d.year);

    return 0;
}
```

Related Functions

_dos_settime( ), _dos_setdate( )

unsigned _dos_getdiskfree(unsigned char drive, struct diskfree_t *dfptr)

Description

The prototype for **_dos_getdiskfree( )** is in **<dos.h>**. This function is not defined by the ANSI/ISO C/C++ standard. This function is obsolete and not recommended for future code.

The **_dos_getdiskfree( )** function returns the amount of free disk space in the structure pointed to by *dfptr* for the drive specified by *drive*. The drives are numbered from 1 beginning with A. You can specify the default drive by giving *drive* the value 0. The **diskfree_t** structure is defined like this:

```
struct diskfree_t {
  unsigned total_clusters;
  unsigned avail_clusters;
  unsigned sectors_per_cluster;
  unsigned bytes_per_sector;
};
```

The function returns 0 if successful. If an error occurs, it returns non-0 and **errno** is set to **EINVAL** (invalid drive).

Example

This program prints the number of free clusters available for use on drive C:

```
#include <dos.h>
#include <stdio.h>

int main(void)
{
  struct diskfree_t p;

  _dos_getdiskfree(3, &p); /* drive C */

  printf("Number of free clusters is %d.",
          p.avail_clusters);

  return 0;
}
```

Related Function

getdfree( )

void _dos_getdrive(unsigned *drive)

Description

The prototype for **_dos_getdrive( )** is in **<dos.h>**. This function is not defined by the ANSI/ISO C/C++ standard. This function is obsolete and not recommended for future code.

The **_dos_getdrive( )** function returns the number of the currently logged in disk drive in the integer pointed to by *drive*. Drive A is encoded as 1, drive B as 2, and so on.

Example

This fragment displays the current disk drive:

```
unsigned d;

_dos_getdrive(&d);
printf("drive is %c", d-1+'A');
```

Related Function

_dos_setdrive( )

unsigned _dos_getfileattr(const char *fname, unsigned *attrib)

Description

The prototype for **_dos_getfileattr( )** is in **<dos.h>**. This function is not defined by the ANSI/ISO C/C++ standard. This function is obsolete and not recommended for future code.

The **_dos_getfileattr( )** returns the attribute of the file specified by *fname* in the unsigned integer pointed to by *attrib*, which may be one or more of these values. (The macros are defined in **<dos.h>**.)

Macro	Meaning
_A_NORMAL	Normal file
_A_RDONLY	Read-only file
_A_HIDDEN	Hidden file
_A_SYSTEM	System file
_A_VOLID	Volume label
_A_SUBDIR	Subdirectory
_A_ARCH	Archive byte set

The **_dos_getfileattr( )** function returns 0 if successful; it returns non-0 otherwise. If failure occurs, **errno** is set to **ENOENT** (file not found).

Example

This fragment determines if the file TEST.TST is a normal file:

```
unsigned attr;

if(_dos_getfileattr("test.tst", &attr))
  printf("file error");

if(attr & _A_NORMAL) printf("File is normal.\n");
```

Related Function

_dos_setfileattr( )

unsigned _dos_getftime(int fd, unsigned *fdate, unsigned *ftime)

Description

The prototype for **_dos_getftime( )** is in **<dos.h>**. This function is not defined by the ANSI/ISO C/C++ standard. This function is obsolete and not recommended for future code.

The function **_dos_getftime( )** returns the time and date of creation for the file associated with file descriptor *fd* in the integers pointed to by *ftime* and *fdate*. The file must have been opened using either **_dos_open( )**, **_dos_creatnew( )**, or **_dos_creat( )**.

The bits in the object pointed to by *ftime* are encoded as shown here:

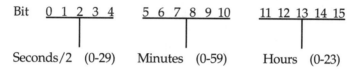

The bits in the object pointed to by *fdate* are encoded like this:

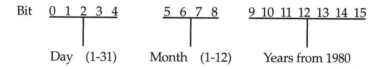

As indicated, the year is represented as the number of years from 1980. Therefore, if the year is 2000, the value of bits 9 through 15 will be 20. The **_dos_getftime( )** function returns 0 if successful. If an error occurs, non-0 is returned and **errno** is set to **EBADF** (bad file handle).

Example

This program prints the year the file TEST.TST was created:

```
#include <io.h>
#include <dos.h>
#include <fcntl.h>
#include <stdio.h>
#include <stdlib.h>

int main(void)
```

```
{
  struct {
    unsigned day: 5;
    unsigned month: 4;
    unsigned year: 7;
  } d;

  unsigned t;
  int fd;

  if(_dos_open("TEST.TST", O_RDONLY, &fd)) {
    printf("Cannot open file.\n");
    exit(1);
  }

  _dos_getftime(fd, (unsigned *) &d, &t);

  printf("Date of creation: %u", d.year+1980);

  return 0;
}
```

Related Function

_dos_setftime( )

unsigned _dos_open(const char *fname, unsigned mode, int *fd)

Description

The prototype for **_dos_open( )** is in **<dos.h>**. This function is not defined by the ANSI/ISO C/C++ standard. This function is obsolete and not recommended for future code.

The **_dos_open( )** function opens the file whose name is pointed to by *fname* in the mode specified by *mode* and returns a file descriptor to the file in the integer pointed to by *fd*.

The foundation values for the *mode* parameter are shown below. (These macros are defined in **<fcntl.h>**.)

Value	Meaning
O_RDONLY	Read only
O_WRONLY	Write only
O_RDWR	Read/write

You may add the following file sharing attributes to *mode* by ORing them to the foundation value. (These macros are defined in **<share.h>**.)

Value	Meaning
SH_COMPAT	Compatibility mode only
SH_DENYNO	Allow reading and writing
SH_DENYRD	Deny reading
SH_DENYRW	Deny reading and writing
SH_DENYWR	Deny writing

You may also specify that the file cannot be inherited by a child process by ORing the macro **O_NOINHERIT**. This macro is defined in **<fcntl.h>**.

The **_dos_open( )** function returns 0 if successful and non-0 on failure. If an error occurs, **errno** is set to one of these values:

EACCES	Access denied
EINVACC	Invalid access attempted
EMFILE	Too many open files
ENOENT	File not found

Example

This fragment opens a file called TEST.TST for read/write operations:

```
int fd;

if(_dos_open("test.tst", O_RDWR, &fd))
   printf("Error opening file.");
```

Related Functions

_dos_creat( ), _dos_creatnew( ), _dos_close( )

unsigned _dos_read(int fd, void *buf, unsigned count, unsigned *numread)

Description

The prototype for **_dos_read( )** is in **<dos.h>**. This function is not defined by the ANSI/ISO C/C++ standard. This function is obsolete and not recommended for future code.

The **_dos_read( )** function reads up to *count* bytes from the file specified by the file descriptor *fd* into the buffer pointed to by *buf*. The number of bytes actually read are returned in *numread*, which may be less than *count* if the end of the file is reached before the specified number of bytes have been input. The file must have been opened using a call to **_dos_creat( )**, **_dos_creatnew( )**, or **_dos_open( )**. Also, **_dos_read( )** treats all files as binary.

Upon success, **_dos_read( )** returns 0; non-0 on failure. On failure, **errno** is set to either **EACCES** (access denied) or **EBADF** (bad file handle). Also, when a failure occurs, the return value is determined by DOS and you will need DOS technical documentation to determine the exact nature of the error, if one should occur.

Example

This fragment reads up to 128 characters from the file described by **fd**:

```
int fd;
unsigned count
char *buf[128];
   .
   .
   .
if(_dos_read(fd, buf, 128, &count))
  printf("Error reading file.\n");
```

Related Function

_dos_write( )

unsigned _dos_setdate(struct dosdate_t *d)
unsigned _dos_settime(struct dostime_t *t)

Description

The prototypes for **_dos_setdate( )** and **_dos_settime( )** are in **<dos.h>**. These functions are not defined by the ANSI/ISO C/C++ standard. These functions are obsolete and not recommended for future code.

The **_dos_setdate( )** function sets the DOS system date as specified in the structure pointed to by *d*. The **_dos_settime( )** function sets the DOS system time as specified in the structure pointed to by *t*.

The **dosdate_t** structure is defined like this:

```
struct dosdate_t {
  unsigned char day;
  unsigned char month;
  unsigned int year;
  unsigned char dayofweek;   /* Sunday is 0 */
};
```

The **dostime_t** structure is defined as shown here:

```
struct dostime_t {
  unsigned char hour;
  unsigned char minute;
  unsigned char second;
  unsigned char hsecond; /* hundredths of second */
};
```

Both functions return 0 if successful. On failure they return a non-0 DOS error code and **errno** is set to **EINVAL** (invalid time or date).

Example

The following program sets the system time to 10:10:10.0.

```
struct dostime_t t;

t.hour = 10;
```

```
t.minute  = 10;
t.second  = 10;
t.hsecond = 0;

_dos_settime(&t);
```

Related Functions

_dos_gettime( ), _dos_getdate( )

void _dos_setdrive(unsigned drive, unsigned *num)

Description

The prototype for **_dos_setdrive( )** is in **<dos.h>**. This function is not defined by the ANSI/ISO C/C++ standard. This function is obsolete and not recommended for future code.

The **_dos_setdrive( )** function changes the current disk drive to the one specified by *drive*. Drive A corresponds to 1, drive B to 2, and so on. The number of drives in the system is returned in the integer pointed to by *num*.

Example

This fragment makes drive C the current drive:

```
unsigned num;

_dos_setdrive(3, &num);
```

Related Function

_dos_getdrive( )

unsigned _dos_setfileattr(const char *fname, unsigned attrib)

Description

The prototype for **_dos_setfileattr( )** is in **<dos.h>**. This function is not defined by the ANSI/ISO C/C++ standard. This function is obsolete and not recommended for future code.

The **_dos_setfileattr( )** sets the attributes of the file specified by *fname* to that specified by *attrib,* which must be one (or more) of these values. When using more than one, OR them together. (The macros are defined in **<dos.h>**.)

Macro	Meaning
_A_NORMAL	Normal file
_A_RDONLY	Read-only file
_A_HIDDEN	Hidden file
_A_SYSTEM	System file
_A_VOLID	Volume label
_A_SUBDIR	Subdirectory
_A_ARCH	Archive byte set

The **_dos_setfileattr( )** function returns 0 if successful; it returns non-0 otherwise. If failure occurs, **errno** is set to **ENOENT** (invalid file).

Example

This fragment sets the file TEST.TST to read only:

```
unsigned attr;

attr = _A_RDONLY;

if(_dos_setfileattr("test.tst", attr))
  printf("File Error");
```

Related Function

_dos_getfileattr( )

unsigned _dos_setftime(int fd, unsigned fdate, unsigned ftime)

Description

The prototype for **_dos_setftime( )** is in **<dos.h>**. This function is not defined by the ANSI/ISO C/C++ standard. This function is obsolete and not recommended for future code.

The **_dos_setftime( )** sets the date and time of the file specified by *fd,* which must be a valid file descriptor obtained through a call to **_dos_open( )**, **_dos_creat( )**, or **_dos_creatnew( )**.

The bits in *ftime* are encoded as shown here:

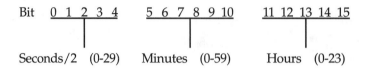

Bit   0 1 2 3 4   5 6 7 8 9 10   11 12 13 14 15

Seconds/2   (0-29)   Minutes   (0-59)   Hours   (0-23)

The bits in *fdate* are encoded like this:

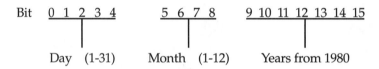

Bit   0 1 2 3 4   5 6 7 8   9 10 11 12 13 14 15

Day   (1-31)   Month   (1-12)   Years from 1980

As indicated, the year is represented as the number of years from 1980. Therefore, to set the year to 2002, the value of bits 9 through 15 must be 22. The **_dos_setftime( )** function returns 0 if successful. If an error occurs, non-0 is returned and **errno** is set to **EBADF** (bad file handle).

Example

This changes the year of the file's creation date to 2002:

```
#include <stdio.h>
#include <io.h>
#include <dos.h>
#include <fcntl.h>
#include <stdlib.h>

int main(void)
{
  struct dt {
    unsigned day: 5;
    unsigned month: 4;
    unsigned year: 7;
  } ;
```

```
union {
  struct dt date_time;
  unsigned u;
} d;

unsigned t;
int fd;

if(_dos_open("TEST.TST", O_RDWR, &fd)) {
  printf("Cannot open file.\n");
  exit(1);
}

_dos_getftime(fd, &d.u, &t);
d.date_time.year = 22;

_dos_setftime(fd, d.u, t);

return 0;
}
```

THE C++ BUILDER
FUNCTION LIBRARY

Related Function

_dos_getftime( )

long dostounix(struct date *d, struct time *t)

Description
The prototype for **dostounix( )** is in **<dos.h>**. This function is not defined by the ANSI/ISO C/C++ standard.

The function **dostounix( )** returns the system time as returned by **gettime( )** and **getdate( )** into a form compatible with the UNIX time format.

Example
See **getdate( )** for an example.

Related Functions

unixtodos( ), ctime( ), time( )

unsigned _dos_write(int fd, void *buf, unsigned count, unsigned *numwritten)

Description

The prototype for **_dos_write( )** is in **<dos.h>**. This function is not defined by the ANSI/ISO C/C++ standard. This function is obsolete and not recommended for future code.

The **_dos_write( )** function writes up to *count* bytes to the file specified by the file descriptor *fd* from the buffer pointed to by *buf*. The number of bytes actually written are returned in *numwritten*, which may be less than requested if the disk becomes full. All files are treated as binary, and no character translations will occur.

Upon success, **_dos_write( )** returns 0; it returns non-0 on failure. The return value is determined by DOS and you will need DOS technical documentation to determine the nature of the error, if one should occur. Also, if an error occurs, **errno** will be set to either **EACCES** (access denied) or **EBADF** (bad file handle).

Example

This fragment writes 128 characters from the file described by **fd**:

```
int fd;
unsigned count
char *buf[128];
   .
   .
   .
if(_dos_write(fd, buf, 128, &count))
  printf("Error writing file.");
```

Related Function

_dos_read( )

void enable(void)
void _enable(void)

Description

The prototypes for **enable( )** and **_enable( )** are in **<dos.h>**. These functions are not defined by the ANSI/ISO C/C++ standard.

The **enable( )** and **_enable( )** functions enable interrupts.

Related Functions

disable( ), geninterrupt( )

void ftime(struct timeb *time)

Description

The prototype for **ftime( )** is in **<sys\timeb.h>**. This function is not defined by the ANSI/ISO C/C++ standard.

The **ftime( )** function fills the **timeb** structure with system time information. Specifically, it retrieves the elapsed time in seconds since January 1, 1970 (GMT), the fractional part of any elapsed second in milliseconds, the difference between GMT and local time in minutes, and whether daylight saving time is in effect.

The **timeb** structure looks like this:

```
struct timeb {
  long time; /* time in seconds from Jan. 1, 1970 */
  short millitm; /* milliseconds */
  short timezone; /* difference between GMT and local time */
  short dstflag; /* non-0 if daylight saving time is in effect */
};
```

Example

This program displays the number of seconds that have elapsed since January 1, 1970, Greenwich mean time:

```
#include <stdio.h>
#include <sys\timeb.h>

int main(void)
{
  struct timeb lt;

  ftime(&lt);
  printf("%ld seconds %d milliseconds.",lt.time,lt.millitm);

  return 0;
}
```

Related Functions

localtime( ), gmtime( ), ctime( ), asctime( )

void geninterrupt(int intr)

Description

The prototype for **geninterrupt( )** is in **<dos.h>**. This function is not defined by the ANSI/ISO C/C++ standard.

The **geninterrupt( )** macro generates a software interrupt. The number of the interrupt generated is determined by the value of *intr*. Given the nature of Windows and its protection of low-level access, this function fits best in device drivers.

Related Functions

enable( ), disable( )

void getdate(struct date *d)
void gettime(struct time *t)

Description

The prototypes for **getdate( )** and **gettime( )** are in **<dos.h>**. These functions are not defined by the ANSI/ISO C/C++ standard.

The **getdate( )** function fills the **date** structure pointed to by *d* with the DOS form of the current system date. The **gettime( )** function fills the **time** structure pointed to by *t* with the DOS form of the current system time.

Example

This converts the DOS version of time and date into the form that can be used by the standard ANSI/ISO C/C++ time and date routines and displays the time and date on the screen:

```
#include <stdio.h>
#include <time.h>
#include <dos.h>

int main(void)
{
  time_t t;
  struct time dos_time;
  struct date dos_date;
  struct tm *local;

  getdate(&dos_date);
  gettime(&dos_time);

  t = dostounix(&dos_date, &dos_time);
```

```
    local = localtime(&t);
    printf("time and date: %s", asctime(local));

    return 0;
}
```

Related Functions

settime( ), setdate( )

void getdfree(unsigned char drive, struct dfree *dfptr)

Description

The prototype for **getdfree( )** is in **<dos.h>**. This function is not defined by the ANSI/ISO C/C++ standard.

The **getdfree( )** function assigns information about the amount of free disk space to the structure pointed to by *dfptr* for the drive specified by *drive*. The drives are numbered from 1 beginning with drive A. You can specify the default drive by calling **getdfree( )** with a value of 0. The **dfree** structure is defined like this:

```
struct dfree {
  unsigned df_avail; /* unused clusters */
  unsigned df_total; /* total number of clusters */
  unsigned df_bsec;  /* number of bytes per sector */
  unsigned df_sclus; /* number of sectors per cluster */
};
```

If an error occurs, the **df_sclus** field is set to –1.

Example

This program prints the number of free clusters available for use on drive C:

```
#include <stdio.h>
#include <dos.h>

int main(void)
{
  struct dfree p;

  getdfree(3, &p); /* drive C */

  printf("Number of free clusters is %d.", p.df_avail);
```

```
    return 0;
}
```

Related Function

_dos_getdiskfree( )

int getftime(int handle, struct ftime *ftptr)

Description

The prototype for **getftime( )** is in **<io.h>**. This function is not defined by the ANSI/ISO C/C++ standard.

The function **getftime( )** returns time and date of creation for the file associated with *handle*. The information is loaded into the structure pointed to by *ftptr*. The bit-field structure **ftime** is defined like this:

```
struct ftime {
  unsigned ft_tsec:  5; /* seconds */
  unsigned ft_min:   6; /* minutes */
  unsigned ft_hour:  5; /* hours */
  unsigned ft_day:   5; /* days */
  unsigned ft_month: 4; /* month */
  unsigned ft_year:  7; /* year from 1980 */
};
```

The **getftime( )** function returns 0 if successful. If an error occurs, -1 is returned and **errno** is set to either **EINVFNC** (invalid function number), **EBADF** (bad file number), or **EACCES** (access denied).

Example

This program prints the year the file TEST.TST was created:

```
#include <stdio.h>
#include <io.h>
#include <dos.h>
#include <fcntl.h>
#include <stdlib.h>

int main(void)
{
  struct ftime p;
  int fd;
```

```
   if((fd=open("TEST.TST", O_RDONLY))==-1) {
     printf("Cannot open file.\n");
    exit(1);
   }

   getftime(fd, &p);

   printf("%d", p.ft_year + 1980);

   return 0;
}
```

Related Functions

open( ), **_dos_open( )**

struct tm *gmtime(const time_t *time)

Description

The prototype for **gmtime( )** is in **<time.h>**.

The **gmtime( )** function returns a pointer to the broken-down form of *time* in the form of a **tm** structure. The time is represented in Greenwich mean time. The *time* value is generally obtained through a call to **time( ).**

The structure used by **gmtime( )** to hold the broken-down time is statically allocated and is overwritten each time the function is called. If you wish to save the contents of the structure, it is necessary to copy it elsewhere.

Example

This program prints both the local time and the Greenwich mean time of the system:

```
#include <stdio.h>
#include <time.h>
#include <stddef.h>

/* print local and GM time */
int main(void)
{
  struct tm *local, *gm;
  time_t t;

  t = time(NULL);
  local = localtime(&t);
  printf("Local time and date: %s", asctime(local));
```

```
    gm = gmtime(&t);
    printf("Greenwich mean time and date: %s", asctime(gm));

    return 0;
}
```

Related Functions

localtime( ), time( ), asctime( )

int kbhit(void)

Description

The prototype for **kbhit( )** is in **<conio.h>**. This function is not defined by the ANSI/ISO C/C++ standard.

The **kbhit( )** function returns true if a key has been pressed on the keyboard. It returns 0 otherwise. In no situation is the key removed from the input buffer.

Example

This fragment loops until a key is pressed:

```
    while(!kbhit());  /* wait for keypress */
```

Related Functions

getch( ), getche( )

struct tm *localtime(const time_t *time)

Description

The prototype for **localtime( )** is in **<time.h>**

The **localtime( )** function returns a pointer to the broken-down form of *time* in the form of a **tm** structure. The time is represented in local time. The *time* value is generally obtained through a call to **time( )**.

The structure used by **localtime( )** to hold the broken-down time is statically allocated and is overwritten each time the function is called. To save the contents of the structure, it is necessary to copy it elsewhere.

Example

This program prints both the local time and the Greenwich mean time of the system:

```
include <stdio.h>
#include <time.h>
#include <stddef.h>

/* Print local and Greenwich mean time. */
int main(void)
{
  struct tm *local, *gm;
  time_t t;

  t = time(NULL);
  local = localtime(&t);
  printf("Local time and date: %s", asctime(local));
  gm = gmtime(&t);
  printf("Greenwich mean time and date: %s", asctime(gm));

  return 0;
}
```

Related Functions

gmtime( ), **time( )**, **asctime( )**

time_t mktime(struct tm *p)

Description

The prototype for **mktime( )** is in **<time.h>**.

The **mktime( )** function converts the time pointed to by *p* into calendar time.

The **mktime( )** returns the time as a value of type **time_t**. If no time information is available, then –1 is returned.

Example

This program displays the day of the week for the given year, month, and day:

```
#include <stdio.h>
#include <time.h>

int main(void)
{
  struct tm t;

  t.tm_year = 90;  /* year 1990   */
  t.tm_mon  = 1;   /* month - 1 */
  t.tm_mday =  7;
```

```
    mktime(&t);
    printf("The day of the week is %d", t.tm_wday);

    return 0;
}
```

Related Functions

localtime( ), time( ), asctime( )

void setdate(struct date *d)
void settime(struct time *t)

Description

The prototypes for **setdate( )** and **settime( )** are in **<dos.h>**. These functions are not defined by the ANSI/ISO C/C++ standard.

The **setdate( )** function sets the DOS system date as specified in the structure pointed to by *d*. The **settime( )** function sets the DOS system time as specified in the structure pointed to by *t*.

Example

The following code fragment sets the system time to 10:10:10.0.

```
struct time t;

t.ti_hour = 10;
t.ti_min  = 10;
t.ti_sec  = 10;
t.ti_hund = 0;

settime(&t);
```

Related Functions

gettime( ), getdate( )

int setftime(int handle, struct ftime *t)

Description

The prototype for **setftime( )** is found in **<io.h>**. This function is not defined by the ANSI/ISO C/C++ standard.

The **setftime( )** function is used to set the date and time associated with a disk file. It changes the date and time of the file linked to *handle* using the information found in the structure pointed to by *t*. The **ftime** structure is shown here:

```
struct ftime {
  unsigned ft_tsec:  5; /* seconds */
  unsigned ft_min:   6; /* minutes */
  unsigned ft_hour:  5; /* hours */
  unsigned ft_day:   5; /* days */
  unsigned ft_month: 4; /* month */
  unsigned ft_year:  7; /* year from 1980 */
}
```

Since a file's date and time are generally used to indicate the time of the file's last modification, you should use **setftime( )** carefully.

If **setftime( )** is successful, 0 is returned. If an error occurs, –1 is returned and **errno** is set to one of the following:

EINVFNC	Invalid function number
EACCES	Access denied
EBADF	Bad file handle

Example

This line of code sets the file to the date and time specified in the **ftime** structure:

```
setftime(fd, &t);
```

Related Function

getftime( )

void sleep(unsigned time)

Description

The prototype for **sleep( )** is in **<dos.h>**. This function is not defined by the ANSI/ISO C/C++ standard. This function is obsolete and not recommended for future code.

The **sleep( )** function suspends program execution for *time* number of seconds.

Example

This program waits 10 seconds between messages:

```
#include <stdio.h>
#include <dos.h>

int main(void)
{
  printf("hello");
  sleep(10);
  printf(" there");

  return 0;
}
```

Related Function

time( )

int stime(time_t *t)

Description

The prototype for **stime( )** is in **<time.h>**. This function is not defined by the ANSI/ISO C/C++ standard.

The **stime( )** function sets the current system time to the value pointed to by *t*. This value must specify the time as the number of seconds since January 1, 1970, Greenwich mean time.

The **stime( )** function always returns 0.

Related Functions

settime( ), gettime( ), time( )

char *_strdate(char *buf)
char *_strtime(char *buf)

Description

The prototypes for **_strdate( )** and **_strtime( )** are in **<time.h>**. These functions are not defined by the ANSI/ISO C/C++ standard.

The **_strdate( )** function converts the system date into a string and copies it into the character array pointed to by *buf*. The date will have the form *MM/DD/YY*. The array pointed to by *buf* must be at least 9 characters long. **_strdate( )** returns *buf*.

The **_strtime( )** function converts the system time into a string and copies it into the array pointed to by *buf*. The time will have this form: *HH:MM:SS*. The array pointed to by *buf* must be at least 9 characters long. **_strtime( )** returns a pointer to *buf*.

Example

This program displays the current system time and date:

```
#include <stdio.h>
#include <time.h>

int main(void)
{
  char str[9];

  _strtime(str);
  printf("Time: %s", str);

  _strdate(str);
  printf(", Date: %s", str);

  return 0;
}
```

Related Functions

time( ), clock( )

size_t strftime(char *str, size_t maxsize, char const *fmt, const struct tm *time)

Description

The prototype for **strftime( )** is in **<time.h>**. It stores time and date information, along with other information, into the string pointed to by *str* according to the format commands found in the string pointed to by *fmt* and using the time specified in *time*. A maximum of *maxsize* characters will be placed into *str*.

The **strftime( )** function works a little like **sprintf( )** in that it recognizes a set of format commands that begin with the percent sign (%) and it places its formatted output into a string. The format commands are used to specify the exact way various time and date information is represented in *str*. Any other characters found in the format string are placed into *str* unchanged. The time and date displayed are in local time. The format commands are shown in Table 14-1. Notice that many of the commands are case sensitive.

The **strftime( )** function returns the number of characters placed in the string pointed to by *str*, or 0 if an error occurs.

Example

Assuming that **ltime** points to a structure that contains 10:00:00 AM, Jan 18, 2001, then this fragment will print "It is now 10 AM".

```
strftime (str, 100, "It is now %H %p", ltime)
printf(str);
```

Related Functions

time( ), localtime( ), gmtime( )

time_t time(time_t *time)

Description

The prototype for **time( )** is in **<time.h>**.

The **time( )** function returns the current calendar time of the system.

Command	Replaced by
%a	Abbreviated weekday name
%A	Full weekday name
%b	Abbreviated month name
%B	Full month name
%c	Standard date and time string
%d	Day-of-month as decimal (1–31)
%H	Hour, range (0–23)
%I	Hour, range (1–12)
%j	Day-of-year as decimal (1–366)
%m	Month as decimal (1–12)
%M	Minute as decimal (0–59)
%p	Locale's equivalent of AM or PM
%S	Second as decimal (0–60)
%U	Week-of-year, Sunday being first day (0–53)
%w	Weekday as decimal (0–6, Sunday being 0)
%W	Week-of-year, Monday being first day (0–53)
%x	Standard date string
%X	Standard time string
%y	Year in decimal without century (00–99)
%Y	Year including century as decimal
%Z	Time zone name
%%	The percent sign

Table 14-1.   *The ANSI/ISO Defined **strftime( )** Format Commands*

The **time( )** function can be called either with a null pointer or with a pointer to a variable of type **time_t**. If the latter is used, then the argument is also assigned the calendar time.

Example

This program displays the local time defined by the system:

```
#include <stdio.h>
#include <time.h>

int main(void)
{
  struct tm *ptr;
  time_t lt;

  lt = time(NULL);
  ptr = localtime(&lt);
  printf(asctime(ptr));

  return 0;
}
```

Related Functions

localtime( ), gmtime( ), strftime( ), ctime( )

void tzset(void)

Description

The prototype for **tzset( )** is in **<time.h>**. This function is not defined by the ANSI/ISO C/C++ standard.

The **tzset( )** function sets C++ Builder's built-in variables **_daylight** (daylight saving time indicator), **_timezone** (time zone number), and **_tzname** (time zone name) using the environmental variable **TZ**. Since the ANSI/ISO C/C++ standard time functions provide complete access and control over the system time and date, there is no reason to use **tzset( )**. The **tzset( )** function is included for UNIX compatibility.

void unixtodos(long utime, struct date *d, struct time *t)

Description

The prototype for **unixtodos( )** is in **<dos.h>**. This function is not defined by the ANSI/ISO C/C++ standard.

The **unixtodos( )** function converts the UNIX-like time format into a DOS format. The UNIX and ANSI standard time formats are the same. The *utime* argument holds the UNIX time format. The structures pointed to by *d* and *t* are loaded with the corresponding DOS date and time.

Example

This converts the time contained in **timeandday** into its corresponding DOS format:

```
struct time t;
struct date d;

unixtodos(timeandday, &d, &t)
```

Related Function

dostounix( )

The
Complete
Reference

Borland
C++
Builder

Chapter 15

Dynamic Allocation

There are two primary ways in which your program can store information in the main memory of the computer. The first uses *global* and *local variables*—including arrays, structures, and classes. In the case of global and static local variables, the storage is fixed throughout the run time of your program. For local variables, storage is allocated on the stack. Although these variables are implemented efficiently in C++ Builder, they require the programmer to know in advance the amount of storage needed for every situation.

The second way information can be stored is through the use of C++ Builder's dynamic allocation system. In this method, storage for information is allocated from the free memory area as it is needed and returned to free memory when it has served its purpose. The free memory region lies between your program's permanent storage area and the stack. This region, called the *heap*, is used to satisfy a dynamic allocation request.

One advantage of dynamically allocated memory is that the same memory can be used for several different things in the course of a program's execution. Because memory can be allocated for one purpose and freed when that use has ended, it is possible for another part of the program to use the same memory for something else at a different time. Another advantage of dynamically allocated storage is that it enables the creation of linked lists, binary trees, and other dynamic data structures.

At the core of C's dynamic allocation system are the functions **malloc( )** and **free( )**, which are part of the standard library. Each time a **malloc( )** memory request is made, a portion of the remaining free memory is allocated. Each time a **free( )** memory release call is made, memory is returned to the system.

 C++ *also defines two dynamic allocation operators called* ***new*** *and* ***delete***. *These are discussed in Part Three of this book. For C++ code, you will normally use the allocation operators and not the C-based functions described in this chapter. However, C++ does fully support the C dynamic allocation functions.*

Standard C/C++ defines only four functions for the dynamic allocation system: **calloc( )**, **malloc( )**, **free( )**, and **realloc( )**. The header used by the dynamic allocation functions is **<stdlib.h>**. However, C++ Builder lets you use either **<stdlib.h>** or **<alloc.h>**. This guide uses **<stdlib.h>** because it is portable. C++ Builder also includes several nonstandard dynamic allocation fucntions. These require the headers **<alloc.h>**, or **<malloc.h>**. You should pay special attention to which header is used with each function.

void *alloca(size_t size)

Description

The prototype for **alloca( )** is in **<malloc.h>**. This function is not defined by the ANSI/ISO C/C++ standard.

The **alloca( )** function allocates *size* bytes of memory from the system stack (not the heap) and returns a character pointer to it. A null pointer is returned if the allocation request cannot be honored.

Memory allocated using **alloca( )** is automatically released when the function that called **alloca( )** returns. This means that you should never use a pointer generated by **alloca( )** as an argument to **free( )**.

*For technical reasons, to ensure that the stack is not corrupted, any function that executes a call to **alloca( )** must contain at least one local variable that is assigned a value.*

Example

The following program allocates 80 bytes from the stack using **alloca( )**.

```
#include <malloc.h>
#include <stdio.h>
#include <stdlib.h>

int main(void)
{
  char *str;

  if(!(str = (char *) alloca(80))) {
    printf("Allocation error.");
    exit(1);
  }
  /* ... */
  return 0;
}
```

Related Function

malloc( )

void *calloc(size_t num, size_t size)

Description

The prototype for **calloc( )** is in **<stdlib.h>**.

The **calloc( )** function returns a pointer to the allocated memory. The amount of memory allocated is equal to *num*size* where *size* is in bytes. That is, **calloc( )** allocates sufficient memory for an array of *num* objects of *size* bytes.

The **calloc( )** function returns a pointer to the first byte of the allocated region. If there is not enough memory to satisfy the request, a null pointer is returned. It is always important to verify that the return value is not a null pointer before attempting to use the pointer.

Example

This function returns a pointer to a dynamically allocated array of 100 **float**s:

```
#include <stdlib.h>
#include <stdio.h>

float *get_mem(void)
{
  float *p;

  p = (float *) calloc(100, sizeof(float));
  if(!p) {
    printf("Allocation failure.");
    exit(1);
  }
  return p;
}
```

Related Functions

malloc( ), **realloc( )**, **free( )**

void free(void *ptr)

Description

The prototype for **free( )** is in **<stdlib.h>**.

The **free( )** function returns the memory pointed to by *ptr* back to the heap. This makes the memory available for future allocation.

It is imperative that **free( )** be called only with a pointer that was previously obtained using one of these dynamic allocation functions: **malloc( )**, **realloc( )**, or **calloc( )**. Using an invalid pointer in the call most likely will destroy the memory-management mechanism and cawuse a system crash.

Example

This program first allocates room for strings entered by the user and then frees them:

```
#include <stdlib.h>
#include <stdio.h>

int main(void)
{
  char *str[100];
  int i;

  for(i=0; i<100; i++) {
    if((str[i]=(char *)malloc(128))==NULL) {
      printf("Allocation error.");
      exit(0);
    }
    gets(str[i]);
  }

  /* now free the memory */
  for(i=0; i<100; i++) free(str[i]);

  return 0;
}
```

Related Functions

malloc( ), realloc( ), calloc( )

int heapcheck(void)

Description

The prototype for **heapcheck( )** is in **<alloc.h>**. This function is not defined by the ANSI/ISO C/C++ standard, and is specific to C++ Builder.

The **heapcheck( )** function examines the heap for errors and returns one of these values:

Value	Meaning
_HEAPOK	No errors
_HEAPEMPTY	No heap present
_HEAPCORRUPT	Error found in the heap

Example

This fragment illustrates how to check the heap for errors:

```
if(heapcheck() == _HEAPOK)
  printf("Heap is correct.");
else
  printf("Error in heap.");
```

Related Functions

heapwalk( ), heapchecknode( )

int heapcheckfree(unsigned fill)

Description

The prototype for **heapcheckfree( )** is in **<alloc.h>**. This function is not defined by the ANSI/ISO C/C++ standard, and is specific to C++ Builder.

The **heapcheckfree( )** function verifies that the free area is filled with the specified value *fill* and returns one of these values:

Value	Meaning
_HEAPOK	No errors
_HEAPEMPTY	No heap present
_HEAPCORRUPT	Error found in the heap
_BADVALUE	A value other than *fill* was found

Example

The following code illustrates how to check the heap for the specified value after filling the heap with that value.

```
int status;

heapfillfree(1);
status = heapcheckfree(1)

if(status == _HEAPOK)
  printf("Heap is filled correctly.\n");
else
  if(status == _BADVALUE)
    printf("Heap not filled with correct value.\n");
```

Related Functions

heapfillfree( ), heapchecknode( )

int heapchecknode(void *ptr)

Description

The prototype for **heapchecknode( )** is in **<alloc.h>**. This function is not defined by the ANSI/ISO C/C++ standard, and is specific to C++ Builder.

The **heapchecknode( )** function checks the status of a single node in the heap pointed to by *ptr* and returns one of these values:

Value	Meaning
_BADNODE	The specified node could not be located
_FREEENTRY	The specified node is free memory
_HEAPCORRUPT	Error found in the heap
_HEAPEMPTY	No heap present
_USEDENTRY	The specified node is being used

If either function is called with a pointer to a node that has been freed, **_BADNODE** could be returned because adjacent free memory is sometimes merged.

Example

The following code illustrates how to check a node on the heap.

```
#include <stdio.h>
#include <stdlib.h>
#include <alloc.h>

int main(void)
{
  char *ptr;
  int status;

  if((ptr = (char *) malloc(10)) == NULL)
    exit(1);

  status = heapchecknode(ptr);

  if(status == _USEDENTRY)
    printf("Node is being used.\n");
```

```
    else
      printf("Error in heap.\n");

    free(ptr);

    return 0;
  }
```

Related Functions

heapcheck( ), heapcheckfree( )

int _heapchk(void)

Description

The prototype for **_heapchk( )** is in **<malloc.h>**. This function is not defined by the ANSI/ISO C/C++ standard.

The **_heapchk( )** function checks the heap. It returns one of these values:

Value	Meaning
_HEAPOK	No errors
_HEAPEMPTY	No heap present
_HEAPBADNODE	Error found in the heap

Related function

heapcheck( )

int heapfillfree(unsigned fill)

Description

The prototype for **heapfillfree( )** is in **<alloc.h>**. This function is not defined by the ANSI/ISO C/C++ standard and is specific to C++ Builder.

The **heapfillfree( )** function fills the free blocks of memory in the heap with *fill*. You may want to use this function to give allocated memory a known initial value.

This function returns one of these values:

Value	Meaning
_HEAPOK	No errors
_HEAPEMPTY	No heap present
_HEAPCORRUPT	Error found in the heap

Example

This code fragment illustrates how to fill the heap with a desired value:

```
int status;

status = heapfillfree(0);
if(status == _HEAPOK)
  printf("Heap is correct.");
else
  printf("Error in heap.");
```

Related Functions

heapcheckfree( ), _heapset( )

int _heapmin(void)

Description

The prototype for **_heapmin( )** is in **<malloc.h>**. This function is not defined by the ANSI/ISO C/C++ standard.

The **_heapmin( )** function releases unallocated portions of the heap so that it can be used by other processes. That is, it "minimizes" the heap. It returns 0 if successful and −1 on failure.

Related Function

free( )

int _heapset(unsigned fill)

Description

The prototype for **_heapset( )** is in **<malloc.h>**. This function is not defined by the ANSI/ISO C/C++ standard.

The **_heapset( )** function fills unallocated blocks of memory in the heap with *fill*. (Only the low-order byte of *fill* is used.) The function returns one of these values.

Value	Meaning
_HEAPOK	No errors
_HEAPEMPTY	No heap present
_HEAPBADNODE	Error found in the heap

Related Functions

heapcheckfree( ), **heapfillfree( )**

int heapwalk(struct heapinfo *hinfo)
int _rtl_heapwalk(_HEAPINFO *hinfo)

Description

The prototype for **heapwalk( )** is in **<alloc.h>**. The prototype for **_rtl_heapwalk( )** is in **<malloc.h>**. These functions are not defined by the ANSI/ISO C/C++ standard and are specific to C++ Builder.

The **heapwalk( )** function fills the structure pointed to by *hinfo*. Each call to **heapwalk( )** steps to the next node in the heap and obtains information for that node. When there are no more nodes on the heap, **_HEAPEND** is returned. If there is no heap, **_HEAPEMPTY** is returned. Each time a valid block is examined, **_HEAPOK** is returned.

The **heapinfo** structure contains four fields: two pointers to blocks, the size of the block, and a flag that is set if the block is being used. This structure is shown here:

```
struct heapinfo {
  void *ptr; /* pointer to block */
  void *ptr2;/* pointer to block */
  unsigned int size; /* size of block, in bytes */
  int in_use; /* set if block is in use */
};
```

Before the first call is made, you must set *ptr* field to **NULL**.

Because of the way C++ Builder organizes the dynamic allocation system, the size of an allocated block of memory is slightly larger than the amount requested when it is allocated.

This function assumes the heap is not corrupted. Always call **heapcheck( )** before beginning a walk through the heap.

The **_rtl_heapwalk( )** function is similar to **heapwalk( )** except that it uses the following structure.

```
typedef struct _heapinfo {
  int *_pentry; /* pointer to block */
  int *__pentry;/* pointer to block */
  size_t _size; /* size of block */
  int _useflag; /* contains _USEDENTRY if block is in use --
                   contains _FREEENTRY if not in use */
} _HEAPINFO;
```

In addition to the values returned by **heapwalk( )**, **_rtl_heapwal( )** can also return **_HEAPBADNODE** (error found in heap) or **_HEAPBADPTR** (**_pentry** is invalid).

Example

This program walks through the heap, printing the size of each allocated block:

```
#include <stdio.h>
#include <stdlib.h>
#include <alloc.h>

int main(void)
{
  struct heapinfo hinfo;
  char *p1, *p2;

  if((p1 = (char *) malloc(80)) == NULL)
    exit(1);

  if((p2 = (char *) malloc(20)) == NULL)
    exit(1);

  if(heapcheck() < 0) { /* always check heap before walk */
    printf("Heap corrupt.");
    exit(1);
  }

  hinfo.ptr = NULL;  /* set ptr to null before first call */
```

```
/* examine first block */
if(heapwalk(&hinfo) == _HEAPOK)
  printf("Size of p1's block is %d\n", hinfo.size);

/* examine second block */
if(heapwalk(&hinfo) == _HEAPOK)
  printf("Size of p2's block is %d\n", hinfo.size);

free(p1);
free(p2);

return 0;
}
```

Related Function

heapcheck( )

void *malloc(size_t size)

Description

The prototype for **malloc( )** is in **<stdlib.h>**.

The **malloc( )** function returns a pointer to the first byte of a region of memory *size* bytes long that has been allocated from the heap. If there is insufficient memory in the heap to satisfy the request, **malloc( )** returns a null pointer. It is always important to verify that the return value is not a null pointer before attempting to use the pointer. Attempting to use a null pointer usually causes a system crash.

Example

This function allocates sufficient memory to hold structures of type **addr**:

```
#include <stdlib.h>

struct addr {
  char name[40];
  char street[40];
  char city[40];
  char state[3];
  char zip[10];
```

```
};
/* ... */
struct addr *get_struct(void)
{
  struct addr *p;

  if(!(p=(struct addr *)malloc(sizeof(addr)))) {
    printf("Allocation error.");
    exit(0);
  }
  return p;
}
```

Related Functions

free( ), **realloc( )**, **calloc( )**

void *realloc(void *ptr, size_t newsize)

Description

The prototype for **realloc( )** is in **<stdlib.h>**.

The **realloc( )** function changes the size of the allocated memory pointed to by *ptr* to that specified by *newsize*. The value of *newsize* specified in bytes can be greater or less than the original. A pointer to the memory block is returned because it may be necessary for **realloc( )** to move the block to increase its size. If this occurs, the contents of the old block are copied into the new block and no information is lost.

If there is not enough free memory in the heap to allocate *newsize* bytes, a null pointer is returned.

Example

The following program allocates 17 characters of memory, copies the string "this is 16 chars" into them, and then uses **realloc( )** to increase the size to 18 in order to place a period at the end.

```
#include <stdlib.h>
#include <stdio.h>
#include <string.h>

int main(void)
{
```

```
char *p;

p = (char *) malloc(17);
if(!p) {
  printf("Allocation error.");
  exit(1);
}

strcpy(p, "This is 16 chars");

p = (char *) realloc(p,18);
if(!p) {
  printf("Allocation error.");
  exit(1);
}

strcat(p, ".");
printf(p);
free(p);

return 0;
}
```

Related Functions

free( ), malloc( ), calloc( )

The
Complete
Reference

Borland
C++
Builder

Chapter 16

Directory Functions

C++ Builder has a number of directory-manipulation functions in its library. Although none of these functions is defined by the ANSI/ISO C/C++ standard, they are included to allow easy access to directories.

int chdir(const char *path)

Description

The prototype for **chdir( )** is in **<dir.h>**. This function is not defined by the ANSI/ISO C/C++ standard.

The **chdir( )** function makes the directory whose path name is pointed to by *path* the current directory. The path name may include a drive specifier. The directory must exist.

If successful, **chdir( )** returns 0.

If unsuccessful, it returns −1 and sets **errno** to **ENOENT** (invalid path name).

Example

This fragment makes the WP\FORMLET directory on drive C the current working directory:

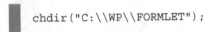

```
chdir("C:\\WP\\FORMLET");
```

Related Functions

mkdir( ), rmdir( )

int _chdrive(int drivenum)

Description

The prototype for **_chdrive( )** is in **<direct.h>**. This function is not defined by the ANSI/ISO C/C++ standard.

The **_chdrive( )** function changes the currently logged-in drive to the one specified by *drivenum*, with A being 1, B being 2, and so on.

The **_chrdrive( )** function returns 0 if successful. Otherwise, −1 is returned.

Example

This changes the currently logged in drive to C.

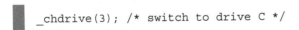

```
_chdrive(3); /* switch to drive C */
```

Related Functions

setdrive( ), getdrive( )

void closedir(DIR *ptr)
DIR *opendir(char *dirname)
struct dirent *readdir(DIR *ptr)
void rewinddir(DIR *ptr)

Description

The prototypes for **closedir( )**, **opendir( )**, **readdir( )**, and **rewinddir( )** are found in **<dirent.h>**. These functions are not defined by the ANSI/ISO C/C++ standard. These functions are included for UNIX compatibility.

The **closedir( )** function closes a directory that was previously opened using **opendir( )**. The **opendir( )** function opens a directory stream and returns a pointer to a structure of type **DIR**, which maintains information about the directory. You should not modify the contents of this structure. The **closedir( )** function closes the directory stream pointed to by *ptr*.

The **readdir( )** function returns the name of the next file in the directory. That is, **readdir( )** reads the contents of the directory a file at a time. The parameter *ptr* must point to a directory stream opened by **opendir( )**. The **dirent** structure is shown here.

```
struct dirent
{
  char d_name[260];
};
```

Therefore, **d_name** contains the name of the next file in the directory after a call to **readdir( )** has returned.

The **rewinddir( )** function causes the directory pointed to by *ptr* (and previously obtained using **opendir( )**) to return to the start (that is, to the first entry in the specified directory). This allows the directory to be reread.

The **closedir( )** function returns 0 if successful; it returns −1 otherwise. On failure, it also sets **errno** to **EBADF** (invalid directory). The **opendir( )** function returns null if the directory cannot be opened and **errno** is set to either **ENOENT** (directory not found) or **ENOMEM** (insufficient memory). The **readdir( )** function returns null when the end of the directory is reached.

Because these functions are primarily included for compatibility with UNIX (and better ways exist under Windows to access directories), no examples are given.

Related Functions

findfirst( ), findnext( )

unsigned _dos_findfirst(const char *fname, int attr, struct find_t *ptr)
unsigned _dos_findnext(struct find_t *ptr)

Description

The prototypes for **_dos_findfirst( )** and **_dos_findnext( )** are in **<dos.h>**. These functions are not defined by the ANSI/ISO C/C++ standard. These functions are obsolete and not recommended for future code.

The **_dos_findfirst( )** function searches for the first filename that matches that pointed to by *fname*. The filename may include both a drive specifier and a path name. Also, the filename may include the wildcard characters * and ?. If a match is found, the structure pointed to by *ptr* is filled with information about the file.

The **find_t** structure is defined like this:

```
struct find_t {
  long reserved;
  long size;               /* size in bytes */
  unsigned long attrib;    /* attribute of file */
  unsigned wr_time;        /* last time file was written to */
  unsigned wr_date;        /* last date file was written to */
  char name[MAXPATH];      /* filename */
};
```

The *attrib* parameter determines what type of files will be found by **_dos_findfirst( )**. The *attrib* can be one or more of the following macros (defined in **<dos.h>**):

Macro	Meaning
_A_NORMAL	Normal file
_A_RDONLY	Read-only file
_A_HIDDEN	Hidden file
_A_SYSTEM	System file
_A_VOLID	Volume label
_A_SUBDIR	Subdirectory
_A_ARCH	Archive bit set

The **_dos_findnext( )** function continues a search started by **_dos_findfirst( )**. The buffer pointed to by *ptr* must be the one used in the call to **_dos_findfirst( )**.

Both the **_dos_findfirst( )** and **_dos_findnext( )** functions return 0 on success and non-0 on failure or when no more matches are found. On failure, **errno** will be set to **ENOENT** (file not found).

Example

This program displays all normal files and their sizes in the current directory with a .C extension.

```
#include <dos.h>
#include <stdio.h>

int main(void)
{
  struct find_t f;
  register int done;

  done = _dos_findfirst("*.c", _A_NORMAL, &f);
  while(!done) {
    printf("%s %ld\n", f.name, f.size);
    done = _dos_findnext(&f);
  }

  return 0;
}
```

Related Functions

findfirst( ), findnext( )

int findfirst(const char *fname, struct ffblk *ptr, int attrib)
int findnext(struct ffblk *ptr)

Description

The prototypes for **findfirst( )** and **findnext( )** are in **<dir.h>**. However, you also need to include the **<dos.h>** header, which contains macros that can be used as values for *attrib*. These functions are not defined by the ANSI/ISO C/C++ standard.

The **findfirst( )** function searches for the first filename that matches that pointed to by *fname*. The filename may include both a drive specifier and a path name. The filename may also include the wildcard characters * and ?. If a match is found, the structure pointed to by *ptr* is filled with information about the file.

The **ffblk** structure is defined like this:

```
struct ffblk {
  long ff_reserved;          /* reserved */
  long ff_fsize;             /* size in bytes */
  unsigned long ff_attrib;   /* attributes of file */
  unsigned ff_ftime;         /* creation time */
  unsigned ff_fdate;         /* creation date */
  char ff_name[MAXPATH];     /* file name */
};
```

The *attrib* parameter determines the type of files to be found by **findfirst( )**. If *attrib* is 0, all types of files that match the desired filename are acceptable. To cause a more selective search, *attrib* can be one the following macros:

Macro	Meaning
FA_RDONLY	Read-only file
FA_HIDDEN	Hidden file
FA_SYSTEM	System file
FA_LABEL	Volume label
FA_DIREC	Subdirectory
FA_ARCH	Archive bit set

The **findnext( )** function continues a search started by **findfirst( )**.

Both the **findfirst( )** and **findnext( )** functions return 0 on success and −1 on failure. On failure, **errno** is set to **ENOENT** (filename not found). **_doserrno** is set to either **ENMFILE** (no more files in directory) or **ENOENT**.

Example

This program displays all files with a .CPP extension (and their sizes) in the current working directory:

```
#include <stdio.h>
#include <dos.h>
#include <dir.h>

int main(void)
{
  struct ffblk f;
  register int done;
```

```
  done = findfirst("*.cpp", &f, 0);
  while(!done) {
    printf("%s %ld\n", f.ff_name, f.ff_fsize);
    done = findnext(&f);
  }

  return 0;
}
```

Related Function

fnmerge( )

void fnmerge(char *path, const char *drive, const char *dir, const char *fname, const char *ext)
int fnsplit(const char *path, char *drive, char *dir, char *fname, char *ext)

Description

The prototypes for **fnmerge( )** and **fnsplit( )** are in **<dir.h>**. These functions are not defined by the ANSI/ISO C/C++ standard.

The **fnmerge( )** function constructs a filename from the specified individual components and puts that name into the string pointed to by *path*. For example, if *drive* is C:, *dir* is \CBuilder5\, *fname* is TEST, and *ext* is .C, the filename produced is C:\CBuilder5\TEST.C.

The **fnsplit( )** decomposes the filename pointed to by *path* into its component parts. The array size needed for each parameter is shown here, along with a macro defined in **<dir.h>** that can be used in place of the actual number:

Parameter	Size	Macro Name
path	260	MAXPATH
drive	3	MAXDRIVE
dir	256	MAXDIR
fname	256	MAXFILE
ext	256	MAXEXT

The **fnsplit( )** function puts the colon after the drive specifier in the string pointed to by *drive*. It puts the period preceding the extension into the string pointed to by *ext*. Leading and trailing backslashes are retained.

The two functions **fnmerge( )** and **fnsplit( )** are complementary—the output from one can be used as input to the other.

The **fnsplit( )** function returns an integer than has five flags encoded into it. The flags have these macro names associated with them (defined in **<dir.h>**):

Macro Name	Meaning When Set
EXTENSION	Extension present
FILENAME	Filename present
DIRECTORY	Directory path present
DRIVE	Drive specifier present
WILDCARDS	One or more wildcard characters present

To determine if a flag is set, AND the flag macro with the return value and test the result. If the result is 1, the flag is set; otherwise, it is cleared.

Example

This program illustrates how **fnmerge( )** encodes a filename. Its output is "C:TEST.C":

```
#include <stdio.h>
#include <dir.h>

int main(void)
{
  char path[MAXPATH];
  fnmerge(path, "C:", "", "TEST", ".C");
  printf(path);

  return 0;
}
```

Related Functions

findfirst( ), **findnext( )**

char *_fullpath(char *fpath, const char *rpath, int len)

Description

The prototype for **_fullpath( )** is in **<stdlib.h>**. This function is not defined by the ANSI/ISO C/C++ standard.

The **_fullpath( )** function constructs a full path name given a relative path name. The relative path name is pointed to by *rpath*. The full path name is put into the array pointed to by *fpath*. The size of the array pointed to by *fpath* is specified by *len*. If *fpath* is null, then an array will be dynamically allocated. (In this case, the array must be freed manually using **free( )**.)

The **_fullpath( )** function returns a pointer to *fpath*, or null if an error occurs.

Example

This program displays the full path to the \INCLUDE directory.

```
#include <stdio.h>
#include <stdlib.h>

int main(void)
{
  char fpath[_MAX_PATH];

  _fullpath(fpath, "\\INCLUDE", _MAX_PATH);

  printf("Full path: %s\n", fpath);

  return 0;
}
```

Related Functions

_makepath( ), mkdir( ), getcwd( )

int getcurdir(int drive, char *dir)

Description

The prototype for **getcurdir( )** is in **<dir.h>**. This function is not defined by the ANSI/ISO C/C++ standard.

The **getcurdir( )** function copies the name of the current working directory of the drive specified in *drive* into the string pointed to by *dir*. A 0 value for *drive* specifies the default drive. For drive A, use 1; for B, use 2; and so on.

The string pointed to by *dir* must be at least **MAXDIR** bytes in length. **MAXDIR** is a macro defined in **<dir.h>**. The directory name will not contain the drive specifier and will not include leading backslashes.

The **getcurdir( )** function returns 0 if successful, −1 on failure.

Example

The following program prints the current directory on the default drive:

```
#include <stdio.h>
#include <dir.h>

int main(void)
{
  char dir[MAXDIR];

  getcurdir(0, dir);
  printf("Current directory is %s", dir);

  return 0;
}
```

Related Function

getcwd( )

char *getcwd(char *dir, int len)

Description

The prototype for **getcwd( )** is in **<dir.h>**. This function is not defined by the ANSI/ISO C/C++ standard.

The **getcwd( )** function copies the full path name (up to *len* characters) of the current working directory into the string pointed to by *dir*. An error occurs if the full path name is longer than *len* characters. The **getcwd( )** function returns a pointer to *dir*.

If **getcwd( )** is called with *dir*'s value being null, **getcwd( )** automatically allocates a buffer using **malloc( )** and returns a pointer to this buffer. You can free the memory allocated by **getcwd( )** using **free( )**.

On failure, **getcwd( )** returns null and **errno** is set to either **ENODEV** (nonexistent device), **ENOMEM** (insufficient memory), or **ERANGE** (out-of-range).

Example

This program prints the full path name of the current working directory:

```
#include <stdio.h>
#include <dir.h>

int main(void)
{
  char dir[MAXDIR];

  getcwd(dir, MAXDIR);
  printf("Current directory is %s", dir);

  return 0;
}
```

Related Function

getcurdir( )

char *_getdcwd(int drive, char *path, int len)

Description

The prototype for **_getdcwd( )** is in **<direct.h>**. This function is not defined by the ANSI/ISO C/C++ standard.

The **_getdcwd( )** function obtains the path name of the current directory of the drive specified by *drive,* with A being 1, B being 2, and so on. (The default drive is specified as 0.) It copies the path name into the array pointed to by *path.* The size of *path* is specified by *len.* If *path* is null, then an array will be dynamically allocated. (In this case, the array must be freed manually using **free( )**.)

The **_getdcwd( )** function returns *path.* On failure, a null pointer is returned and **errno** contains either **ENOMEM** (insufficient memory) or **ERANGE** (path name exceeds array size).

Example

This program displays the current directory of drive D.

```
#include <stdio.h>
#include <direct.h>

int main(void)
{
  char path[MAXPATH];
```

```
    _getdcwd(4, path, MAXPATH);
    printf("Current directory of drive D is %s\n", path);

    return 0;
}
```

Related Functions

mkdir( ), chdir( ), _fullpath( )

int getdisk(void)

Description

The prototype for **getdisk( )** is in **<dir.h>**. This function is not defined by the ANSI/ISO C/C++ standard.

The **getdisk( )** function returns the number of the current drive. Drive A corresponds to 0, drive B is 1, and so on.

Example

This program displays the name of the current drive:

```
#include <stdio.h>
#include <dir.h>

int main(void)
{
  printf("Current drive is %c", getdisk()+'A');

  return 0;
}
```

Related Functions

setdisk( ), getcwd( )

int _getdrive(void)

Description

The prototype for **_getdrive( )** is in **<dos.h>**. This function is not defined by the ANSI/ISO C/C++ standard.

The **_getdrive( )** function returns the number of the current drive, with A being 1, B being 2, and so on.

Example

This statement displays the number of the current drive.

```
printf("Current drive is %d.", _getdrive());
```

Related Functions

getcwd( )

void _makepath(char *pname, const char *drive, const char *directory, const char *fname, cont char *extension)

Description

The prototype for **_makepath( )** is in **<stdlib.h>**. This function is not defined by the ANSI/ISO C/C++ standard.

The **_makepath( )** function constructs a full path name from the elements specified in its parameters and places the result in the array pointed to by *pname*. The drive is specified in the string pointed to by *drive*. The directory (along with any subdirectories) is specified in the string pointed to by *directory*. The filename is pointed to by *fname*, and the extension is pointed to by *extension*. Any of these strings may be empty.

Example

This program constructs a full path name from its elements. Next, it displays the path and then dissects it into its components using **_splitpath( )**, which is the complement to **_makepath( )**.

```
#include <stdio.h>
#include <stdlib.h>

int main(void)
{
  char fpath[_MAX_PATH];
  char fname[_MAX_FNAME];
  char dir[_MAX_DIR];
  char drive[_MAX_DRIVE];
  char ext[_MAX_EXT];
```

```
   _makepath(fpath, "B:", "MYDIR", "MYFILE", "DAT");
   printf("%s\n", fpath);

   _splitpath(fpath, drive, dir, fname, ext);
   printf("%s %s %s %s\n", drive, dir, fname, ext);

   return 0;
}
```

Related Functions

_splitpath( ), fnmerge( ), fnsplit( )

int mkdir(const char *path)

Description

The prototype for **mkdir( )** is in **<dir.h>**. This function is not defined by the ANSI/ISO C/C++ standard.

The **mkdir( )** function creates a directory using the path name pointed to by *path*.

The **mkdir( )** function returns 0 if successful. If unsuccessful, it returns −1 and sets **errno** to either **EACCES** (access denied) or **ENOENT** (invalid path name).

Example

This program creates a directory called FORMLET:

```
#include <dir.h>

int main(void)
{
   mkdir("FORMLET");

   return 0;
}
```

Related Function

rmdir( )

char *mktemp(char *fname)

Description

The prototype for **mktemp( )** is in **<dir.h>**. This function is not defined by the ANSI/ISO C/C++ standard.

The **mktemp( )** function creates a unique filename and copies it into the string pointed to by *fname*. When you call **mktemp( )**, the string pointed to by *fname* must contain six "X"s followed by a null terminator. The **mktemp( )** function transforms that string into a unique filename. It does not create the file, however.

If successful, **mktemp( )** returns a pointer to *fname*; otherwise, it returns a null.

Example

This program displays a unique filename:

```
#include <stdio.h>
#include <dir.h>

char fname[7] = "XXXXXX";

int main(void)
{
  mktemp(fname);
  printf(fname);

  return 0;
}
```

Related Functions

findfirst( ), findnext( )

int rmdir(const char *path)

Description

The prototype for **rmdir( )** is in **<dir.h>**. This function is not defined by the ANSI/ISO C/C++ standard.

The **rmdir( )** function removes the directory whose path name is pointed to by *path*. To be removed, a directory must be empty, must not be the current directory, and must not be the root.

If **rmdir( )** is successful, 0 is returned. Otherwise, −1 is returned and **errno** is set to either **EACCES** (access denied) or **ENOENT** (invalid path name).

Example

This removes the directory called FORMLET:

```
#include <stdio.h>
#include <dir.h>
int main(void)
{
  if(!rmdir("FORMLET")) printf("FORMLET removed.\n");

  return 0;
}
```

Related Function

mkdir( )

char *searchpath(const char *fname)

Description

The prototype for **searchpath( )** is in **<dir.h>**. This function is not defined by the ANSI/ISO C/C++ standard.

The **searchpath( )** function tries to find the file whose name is pointed to by *fname* using the PATH environmental variable. If it finds the file, it returns a pointer to the entire path name. This string is statically allocated and is overwritten by each call to **searchpath( )**. If the file cannot be found, a null is returned.

Example

This program displays the path name for the file BCC32.EXE:

```
#include <stdio.h>
#include <dir.h>

int main(void)
{
  printf(searchpath("BCC32.EXE"));

  return 0;
}
```

Related Function

mktemp( )

int setdisk(int drive)

Description

The prototype for **setdisk( )** is in **<dir.h>**. This function is not defined by the ANSI/ISO C/C++ standard.

The **setdisk( )** function sets the current drive to that specified by *drive*. Drive A corresponds to 0, drive B to 1, and so on. It returns the total number of drives in the system.

Example

This program switches to drive A and reports the total number of drives in the system:

```
#include <stdio.h>
#include <dir.h>

int main(void)
{
  printf("%d drives", setdisk(0));

  return 0;
}
```

Related Function

getdisk( )

void _splitpath(const char *fpath, char *drive, char *directory char *fname, char *extension)

Description

The prototype for **_splitpath( )** is in **<stdlib.h>**. This function is not defined by the ANSI/ISO C/C++ standard.

The **_splitpath( )** function dissects the full path name specified in the string pointed to by *fpath*. The drive letter is put in the string pointed to by *drive*. The directory (and any subdirectories) is put in the string pointed to by *directory*. The filename is put in the string pointed to by *fname* and the extension is put in the string pointed to by *extension*. The minimum size of the arrays pointed to by these parameters is shown here.

Parameter	Size	Macro Name
fpath	260	_MAX_PATH
drive	3	_MAX_DRIVE
directory	256	_MAX_DIR
fname	256	_MAX_FNAME
extension	256	_MAX_EXT

Example

This program displays the elements of this full path: C:\MYDIR\MYFILE.DAT.

```
#include <stdio.h>
#include <stdlib.h>

int main(void)
{
  char fname[_MAX_FNAME];
  char dir[_MAX_DIR];
  char drive[_MAX_DRIVE];
  char ext[_MAX_EXT];

  _splitpath("C:\\MYDIR\\MYFILE.DAT", drive, dir, fname, ext);
  printf("%s %s %s %s\n", drive, dir, fname, ext);

  return 0;
}
```

Related Functions

_makepath( ), fnsplit( ), fnmerge( )

Borland
C++
Builder

Chapter 17

Process Control
Functions

This chapter covers a number of functions that are used to control the way a program executes, terminates, or invokes the execution of another program. Aside from **abort( )**, **atexit( )**, and **exit( )**, none of the functions described here is defined by the ANSI/ISO C/C++ standard. However, all allow your program greater flexibility in its execution.

The process control functions have their prototypes in **<process.h>**. However, those functions defined by the ANSI/ISO C/C++ standard also have their prototypes in the **<stdlib.h>** header file.

void abort(void)

Description
The prototype for **abort( )** is in **<process.h>** and **<stdlib.h>**.

The **abort( )** function causes immediate termination of a program. No files are flushed. It returns a value of 3 to the calling process (usually the operating system).

The primary use of **abort( )** is to prevent a runaway program from closing active files.

Example
This program terminates if the user enters an "A":

```
#include <process.h>
#include <conio.h>

int main(void)
{
  for(;;)
    if(getch()=='A') abort();

  return 0;
}
```

Related Functions

exit( ), atexit( )

int atexit(void (*func)(void))

Description
The prototype for **atexit( )** is in **<stdlib.h>**.

The **atexit( )** function establishes the function pointed to by *func* as the function to be called upon normal program termination. That is, the specified function is called at the end of a program run. The act of establishing the function is referred to as *registration*.

The **atexit( )** function returns 0 if the function is registered as the termination function, and non-0 otherwise.

Up to 32 termination functions can be established. They are called in the reverse order of their establishment: first in, last out.

Example
This program prints **Hello there!** on the screen:

```
#include <stdio.h>
#include <stdlib.h>

/* Example using atexit(). */
int main(void)
{
  void done();

  if(atexit(done)) printf("Error in atexit().");

  return 0;
}

void done()
{
  printf("Hello there!");
}
```

Related Functions

exit( ), **abort( )**

**unsigned long _beginthread(void (*func)(void *),
    unsigned stksize, void *arglist)**
**unsigned long _beginthreadex(void *secattr,
    unsigned stksize, unsigned (*start)(void *),
    void *arglist, unsigned createflags,
    unsigned *threadID)**
**unsigned long _beginthreadNT(void (*func)(void *),
    unsigned stksize, void *arglist,
    void *secattr, unsigned createflags,
    unsigned *threadID);**

Description

The prototypes for these functions are in **<process.h>**. These functions are not defined by the ANSI/ISO C/C++ standard.

The **_beginthread** group of functions is used for multithreaded programming. A multithreaded program contains two or more parts that can run concurrently. Each part of such a program is called a *thread,* and each defines a separate path of execution.

Each of these three functions do the same thing, create and execute threads. For each **_beginthread** function, *func* is the name of the function that serves as the entry point to the new thread of execution, *stksize* specifies the size of the stack for the thread, which must be a multiple of 4096, and *arglist* is a pointer to information passed to the thread and can be **NULL**. In addition, the **_beginthreadex( )** and **_beginthreadNT( )** functions take these additional parameters: *secattr, createflags,* and *threadID*. The *secattr* parameter is a pointer to the **SECURITY_ATTRIBUTES** structure, which is defined like this:

```
typedef struct _SECURITY_ATTRIBUTES
{
    DWORD nLength;
    LPVOID lpSecurityDescriptor;
    BOOL bInheritHandle;
} SECURITY_ATTRIBUTES;
```

If *secattr* is set to **NULL**, then default security is used. The *createflags* parameter indicates that the thread should be executed immediately. It can also be set to **CREATE_SUSPENDED**, which causes the thread to be suspended until resumed. The *threadID* parameter points to a variable that receives the thread identifier.

When successful, the **beginthread** functions return the handle to the thread. On failure, they return −1 and set **errno** to one of the following values.

Macro	Meaning
EAGAIN	There are too many threads opened
EINVAL	Bad request
ENOMEM	Not enough free memory to create/execute the thread

Example

The follow program starts and executes 10 threads. It needs to be compiled using the −tWM options in order to execute.

```
#include <stdio.h>
#include <stddef.h>
#include <process.h>
#include <conio.h>

void ThreadToRun(void *);

int main(void)
{
  int i;
  unsigned long thread;

  for(i = 1; i < 10; i++)
  {
    thread = _beginthread(ThreadToRun, 4096, (void *)i);
    if((long)thread == -1)
    {
      printf("Error creating thread number %d\n", i);
      exit(1);
    }
    printf("Thread %d created with an ID of %uld.\n", i, thread);
```

```
    }

    printf("Press any key to exit...\n");
    getch();

    return 0;
}

void ThreadToRun(void *num)
{
    printf("Running thread %d with an ID of %ld\n",
            (int)num, _threadid);
    _endthread();
}
```

Related Function

_endthread( )

void _c_exit(void)
void _cexit(void)

Description

The prototypes for **_c_exit( )** and **_cexit( )** are in **<process.h>**. These functions are not defined by the ANSI/ISO C/C++ standard.

The **_c_exit( )** function performs the same actions as **_exit( )** except that the program is not terminated.

The **_cexit( )** function performs the same actions as **exit( )** except that the program is not terminated. However, all files are closed and all buffers are flushed and any termination functions are executed.

Example

This statement performs program shutdown procedures, except that the program is not terminated.

```
    _cexit();
```

Related Functions

exit( ), _exit( ), atexit( )

void _endthread(void)
void _endthreadex(unsigned threadvalue)

Description

The prototypes for these functions are in **<process.h>**. These functions are not defined by the ANSI/ISO C/C++ standard.

The **endthread** group of functions is used for terminating a thread created by one of the **_beginthread( )** functions described earlier.

The **_endthreadex( )** function returns the value in *threadvalue* to the calling process.

Example

See the **_beginthread( )** function for an example.

Related Functions

_beginthread( ), _beginthreadex( )

int execl(char *fname, char *arg0, . . ., char *argN, NULL)
int execle(char *fname, char *arg0, . . ., char *argN, NULL, char *envp[ ])
int execlp(char *fname, char *arg0, . . ., char *argN, NULL)
int execlpe(char *fname, char *arg0, . . ., char *argN, NULL, char *envp[ ])
int execv(char *fname, char *arg[ ])
int execve(char *fname, char *arg[ ], char *envp[ ])
int execvp(char *fname, char *arg[ ])
int execvpe(char *fname, char *arg[ ], char *envp[ ])

Description

The prototypes for these functions are in **<process.h>**. These functions are not defined by the ANSI/ISO C/C++ standard.

The **exec** group of functions is used to execute another program. This other program, called the *child process*, is loaded over the one that contains the **exec** call. The name of the file that contains the child process is pointed to by *fname*. Any arguments to the child process are pointed to either individually by *arg0* through *argN* or by the array *arg[ ]*. An environment string must be pointed to by *envp[ ]*. (The arguments are pointed to by **argv** in the child process.)

If no extension or period is part of the string pointed to by *fname,* a search is first made for a file by that name. If that fails, the .EXE extension is added and the search is tried again. If that fails, the .COM extension is added and the search is tried again. When an extension is specified, only an exact match will satisfy the search. Finally, if a period but no extension is present, a search is made for only the file specified by the left side of the filename.

The exact way the child process is executed depends on which version of **exec** you use. You can think of the **exec** function as having different suffixes that determine its operation. A suffix can consist of either one or two characters.

Functions that have a **p** in the suffix search for the child process in the directories specified by the PATH command. If a **p** is not in the suffix, only the current directory is searched.

An **l** in the suffix specifies that pointers to the arguments to the child process will be passed individually. Use this method when passing a fixed number of arguments. Notice that the last argument must be **NULL**. (**NULL** is defined in **<stdio.h>**.)

A **v** in the suffix means that pointers to the arguments to the child process will be passed in an array. This is the way you must pass arguments when you do not know in advance how many there will be or when the number of arguments may change during the execution of your program. Typically, the end of the array is signaled by a null pointer.

An **e** in the suffix specifies that one or more environmental strings will be passed to the child process. The *envp* parameter is an array of string pointers. Each string pointed to by the array must have the form

environment-variable = value

The last pointer in the array must be **NULL**. If the first element in the array is **NULL**, the child retains the same environment as the parent.

It is important to remember that files open at the time of an **exec** call are also open in the child program.

When successful, the **exec** functions return no value. On failure, they return −1 and set **errno** to one of the following values.

Macro	Meaning
EACCES	Access to child process file denied
EMFILE	Too many open files
ENOENT	File not found
ENOEXEC	Format of **exec** is invalid
ENOMEM	Not enough free memory to load child process

Example

The first of the following programs invokes the second, which displays its arguments. Remember, both programs must be in separate files.

```
/* First file - parent */

#include <stdio.h>
#include <process.h>
#include <stdlib.h>

int main(void)
{
  execl("test.exe", "test.exe", "hello", "10", NULL);

  return 0;
}


/* Second file - child */
#include <stdio.h>
#include <stdlib.h>

int main(int argc, char *argv[])
{
  printf("This program is executed with these command line ");
  printf("arguments: ");
  printf(argv[1]);
  printf(" %d", atoi(argv[2]));
  return 0;
}
```

Related Function

The **spawn** family of functions.

void exit(int status)
void _exit(int status)

Description

The prototypes for **exit( )** and **_exit( )** are in **<process.h>** and **<stdlib.h>**.

The **exit( )** function causes immediate, normal termination of a program. The value of *status* is passed to the calling process. By convention, if the value of *status* is 0, normal program termination is assumed. A non-0 value can be used to indicate an implementation-defined error. You can also use the macros **EXIT_SUCCESS** and **EXIT_FAILURE** as values for *status*. They indicate normal and abnormal termination, respectively. Calling **exit( )** flushes and closes all open files and calls any program termination functions registered using **atexit( )**.

The **_exit( )** program does not close any files, flush any buffers, or call any termination functions. This function is not defined by the ANSI/ISO C/C++ standard.

Example

This function performs menu selection for a mailing-list program. If **Q** is pressed, the program is terminated.

```
char menu(void)
{
  char ch;

  do {
    printf("Enter names (E)");
    printf("Delete name (D)");
    printf("Print (P)");
    printf("Quit (Q)");
  } while(!strchr("EDPQ", toupper(ch)));
  if(ch=='Q') exit(0);
  return ch;
}
```

Related Functions

atexit( ), **abort( )**

int getpid(void)

Description

The prototypes for this function is in **<process.h>**. This function is not defined by the ANSI/ISO C/C++ standard.

The **getpid( )** function returns the process ID for the calling process.

Example

The following code returns the current process ID.

```
#include <stdio.h>
#include <process.h>
#include <conio.h>

int main()
{
    printf("This program PID = %d\n", getpid());

    return 0;
}
```

**int spawnl(int mode, char *fname, char *arg0, . . .,
    char *argN, NULL)**
**int spawnle(int mode, char *fname, char *arg0, . . .,
    char *argN, NULL, char *envp[ ])**
**int spawnlp(int mode, char *fname, char *arg0, . . .,
    char *argN, NULL)**
**int spawnlpe(int mode, char *fname, char *arg0, . . .,
    char *argN, NULL, char *envp[ ])**
int spawnv(int mode, char *fname, char *arg[ ])
int spawnve(int mode, char *fname, char *arg[ ], char *envp[ ])
int spawnvp(int mode, char *fname, char *arg[ ])
int spawnvpe(int mode, char *fname, char *arg[ ], char *envp[ ])

Description

The prototypes for these functions are in **<process.h>**. These functions are not defined by the ANSI/ISO C/C++ standard.

The **spawn** group of functions is used to execute another program. This other program, the *child process*, does not necessarily replace the parent program (unlike the child process executed by the **exec** group of functions). The name of the file that contains the child process is pointed to by *fname*. The arguments to the child process, if any, are pointed to either individually by *arg0* through *argN* or by the array *arg[]*. If you pass an environment string, it must be pointed to by *envp[ ]*. (The arguments will be pointed to by **argv** in the child process.) The *mode* parameter determines how the child process will be executed. It can have one of these values (defined in **<process.h>**).

Macro	Execution Mode
P_WAIT	Suspends parent process until the child has finished executing
P_NOWAIT	Executes both the parent and the child concurrently. The ID of the child process is returned to the parent.
P_NOWAITO	Same as P_NOWAIT except that the child process ID is not returned to the parent.
P_DETACH	Same as P_NOWAITO except that the child executes as a background process.
P_OVERLAY	Replaces the parent process in memory

If you use the **P_WAIT** option, when the child process terminates, the parent process is resumed at the line after the call to **spawn**.

If no extension or period is part of the string pointed to by *fname*, a search is made for a file by that name. If that fails, then a .EXE extension is tried. If that fails, the .COM extension is added and the search is tried again. If that fails, then a .BAT extension is tried. If an extension is specified, only an exact match satisfies the search. If a period but no extension is present, a search is made for only the file specified by the left side of the filename.

The exact way the child process is executed depends on which version of **spawn** you use. You can think of the **spawn** function as having different suffixes that determine its operation. A suffix can consist of either one or two characters.

Those functions that have a **p** in the suffix search for the child process in the directories specified by the PATH command. If a **p** is not in the suffix, only the current directory is searched.

An **l** in the suffix specifies that pointers to the arguments to the child process will be passed individually. Use this method when passing a fixed number of arguments. Notice that the last argument must be **NULL**. (**NULL** is defined in **<stdio.h>**.)

A **v** in the suffix means that pointers to the arguments to the child process will be passed in an array. This is the way you must pass arguments when you do not know in advance how many there will be or when the number of arguments may change during the execution of your program. Typically, the end of the array is signaled by a null pointer.

An **e** in the suffix specifies that one or more environmental strings will be passed to the child process. The *envp[ ]* parameter is an array of string pointers. Each string pointed to by the array must have the form:

environment-variable = value

The last pointer in the array must be **NULL**. If the first element in the array is **NULL**, the child retains the same environment as the parent.

It is important to remember that files open at the time of a **spawn** call are also open in the child process.

When successful, the spawned functions return 0. On failure, they return −1 and set **errno** to one of the following values:

Macro	Meaning
EINVAL	Bad argument
E2BIG	Too many arguments
ENOENT	File not found
ENOEXEC	Format of **spawn** is invalid
ENOMEM	Not enough free memory to load child process

A spawned process can spawn another process. The level of nested spawns is limited by the amount of available RAM and the size of the programs.

Example

The first of the following programs invokes the second, which displays its arguments and invokes a third program. After the third program terminates, the second is resumed. When the second program terminates, the parent program is resumed. Remember that the three programs must be in separate files.

```
/* Parent process */
#include <stdio.h>
#include <process.h>

int main(void)
{
  printf("In parent\n");
  spawnl(P_WAIT, "test.exe", "test.exe", "hello", "10", NULL);
  printf("In parent\n");

  return 0;
}



/* First child */
```

```
#include <stdio.h>
#include <stdlib.h>
#include <process.h>

int main(int argc, char *argv[])
{
  printf("First child process executing ");
  printf("with these command line arguments: ");
  printf(argv[1]);
  printf(" %d\n", atoi(argv[2]));
  spawnl(P_WAIT, "test2.exe", "test2.exe", NULL);
  printf("In first child process.\n");
  return 0;
}


/* Second child */
#include <stdio.h>
int main(void)
{
  printf("In second child process.\n");
  return 0;
}
```

Related Functions

The **exec** family of functions.

int wait(int *status)

Description

The prototype for this function is in **<process.h>**. This function is not defined by the ANSI/ISO C/C++ standard.

The **wait( )** function causes a program to wait until a child process has completed. The value returned by the child process will be stored in the variable pointed to by *status*. If you don't need the status code, specify **NULL** for *status*. The status code is interpreted as follows.

If the child process ends without error, bits 0–7 will be zero and bits 8–15 will contain the value being returned from the child process. If the other application ends because of an error (or a user-break), then these two sections of bits are reversed. Bits 8–15 will be zero and bits 0–7 will hold a value that indicates the cause of the error.

It will be 1 if the child process was aborted, 2 if a protection error occurred, and 3 if the user (or some other external event) terminated the program.

The **wait( )** method returns the child's process ID if the child application ends normally. Otherwise, it returns −1 and sets **errno** to **ECHILD** or **EINTR**.

Related Functions

The **exec** and **spawn** families of functions.

The
Complete
Reference

Borland
C++
Builder

Chapter 18

Screen-Based
Text Functions

The ANSI/ISO C/C++ standard doesn't define any screen-based text functions that take advantage of the various capabilities of the modern computer display environment, such as cursor positioning, setting of foreground and background colors, and clearing the screen. The reason these types of functions are not standardized is that the capabilities of diverse hardware environments preclude standardization across a wide range of machines. However, C++ Builder provides extensive screen support for the DOS-style environment available under Windows. If you will be using this environment and not be porting your code to a different compiler, you should feel free to use these screen-based functions.

None of the functions described in this chapter relate to or can be used for Windows GUI programming. Graphical output in Windows is accomplished through the use of API (application program interface) functions provided by Windows. The functions described in this chapter relate only to a DOS session run under Windows.

The prototypes and header information for the screen-based text functions are in **<conio.h>**. None of the functions described in this chapter are defined by the ANSI/ISO C/C++ standard.

Central to the screen-based text functions is the concept of the *window*. As the term is used here, "window" does not refer to a GUI window provided by Windows, but rather the active part of the DOS-like screen within which output is displayed. A window can be as large as the entire screen, as it is by default, or as small as your specific needs require. In general, all output is contained within the active window. That is, output that would extend beyond the boundaries of a window is automatically clipped.

It is important to understand that most of the text functions are window relative. For example, the **gotoxy( )** cursor location function sends the cursor to the specified *x,y* position relative to the window, not the screen. Of course, by default, the window is the entire screen. One last point: the upper-left corner is location 1,1.

char *cgets(char *inpstr)

Description

The prototype for **cgets( )** is in <conio.h>.

The **cgets( )** function reads a string and stores it in the array pointed to by *inpstr*. The string is stored beginning at *inpstr*[2]. Before the call, *inpstr*[0] must contain the maximum number of characters that the string pointed to by *inpstr* can store. On return, *inpstr*[1] contains the number of characters actually read.

The **cgets( )** function returns a pointer to the start of the string, which is at *inpstr*[2].

Example

This program reads a string using **cgets( )**.

```
#include <conio.h>

int main(void)
{
  char holdstr[12];
  char *inpstr;

  holdstr[0] = 10;  /* Only allow 10 characters */
  cprintf("Enter a string: ");
  inpstr = cgets(holdstr);
  cprintf("\r\nThe string:  \"%s\"  contains %d characters.\n",
          inpstr, holdstr[1]);

  return 0;
}
```

Related Functions

getch( ), gets( )

void clreol(void)
void clrscr(void)

Description

The prototypes for **clreol( )** and **clrscr( )** are in **<conio.h>**.

The **clreol( )** function clears from the current cursor position to the end of the line in the active text window. The cursor position remains unchanged.

The **clrscr( )** function clears the entire active text window and locates the cursor in the upper-left corner (1,1).

Example

This program illustrates **clreol( )** and **clrscr( )**:

```
#include <conio.h>

int main(void)
{
  register int i;

  gotoxy(10, 10);
```

```
   cprintf("This is a test of the clreol() function.");
   getch();
   gotoxy(10, 10);
   clreol();

   for(i=0; i<20; i++) cprintf("Hello there\n\r");
   getch();

   /* clear the screen */
   clrscr();

   return 0;
}
```

Related Functions

delline( ), window( )

int cprintf(const char *fmt, . . .)

Description

The prototype for **cprintf( )** is in **<conio.h>**.

The **cprintf( )** function works like the **printf( )** function except that it writes to the current text window instead of **stdout**. Its output may not be redirected, and it automatically prevents the boundaries of the window from being overrun. See the **printf( )** function for details.

The **cprintf( )** function does not translate the newline (\n) into the linefeed, carriage return pair as does the **printf( )** function, so it is necessary to manually insert a carriage return (\r) where desired.

The **cprintf( )** function returns the number of characters actually printed. A negative return value indicates that an error has taken place.

Example

This program displays the output shown in its comments:

```
#include <conio.h>

int main(void)
{
   /* This prints "this is a test" left justified
```

```
     in 20 character field.
  */
  cprintf("%-20s", "this is a test");

  /* This prints a float with 3 decimal places in a 10
     character field. The output will be "    12.235".
  */
  cprintf("%10.3f\n\r", 12.234657);

  return 0;
}
```

Related Functions

cscanf( ), cputs( )

int cputs(const char *str)

Description

The prototype for **cputs( )** is in **<conio.h>**.

The **cputs( )** function outputs the string pointed to by *str* to the current text window. Its output cannot be redirected, and it automatically prevents the boundaries of the window from being overrun.

It returns the last character written if successful and **EOF** if unsuccessful.

Example

This program creates a window and uses **cputs( )** to write a line longer than will fit in the window. The line is automatically wrapped at the end of the window instead of spilling over into the rest of the screen.

```
#include <conio.h>

void border(int, int, int, int);

int main(void)
{
  clrscr();
  /* create first window */
  window(3, 2, 40, 9);
  border(3, 2, 40, 9);
```

```
      gotoxy(1,1);
      cputs("This line will be wrapped at the end of the window.");
      getche();

      return 0;
}

/* Draws a border around a text window. */
void border(int startx, int starty, int endx, int endy)
 {
   register int i;

   gotoxy(1, 1);
   for(i=0; i<=endx-startx; i++)
     putch('-');

   gotoxy(1, endy-starty);
   for(i=0; i<=endx-startx; i++)
     putch('-');

   for(i=2; i<endy-starty; i++) {
     gotoxy(1, i);
     putch('|');
     gotoxy(endx-startx+1, i);
     putch('|');
   }
}
```

Related Functions

cprintf( ), window( )

int cscanf(char *fmt, . . .)

Description

The prototype for **cscanf( )** is in **<conio.h>**.

The **cscanf( )** function works like the **scanf( )** function except that it reads the information from the console instead of **stdin**. It cannot be redirected. See the **scanf( )** function for details.

The **cscanf( )** function returns the number of arguments that are actually assigned values. This number does not include skipped fields. The **cscanf( )** function returns the value **EOF** if an attempt is made to read past end-of-file.

Example

This code fragment reads a string and a **float** number from the console:

```
char str[80];
float f;

cscanf("%s%f", str, &f);
```

Related Functions

scanf( ), **cprintf( )**, **sscanf( )**

void delline(void)

Description

The prototype for **delline( )** is in **<conio.h>**.

The **delline( )** function deletes the line in the active window that contains the cursor. All lines below the deleted line are moved up to fill the void. Remember that if the current window is smaller than the entire screen, only the text inside the window is affected.

Example

This program prints 24 lines on the screen and then deletes line 3:

```
#include <conio.h>

int main(void)
{
  register int i;

  clrscr();

  for(i=0; i<24; i++) cprintf("line %d\n\r", i);
  getch();
  gotoxy(1, 4);
  delline();
```

```
    getch();

    return 0;
}
```

Related Functions

clreol( ), insline( )

int gettext(int left, int top, int right, int bottom, void *buf)

Description

The prototype for **gettext( )** is in **<conio.h>**.

The **gettext( )** function copies the text from a rectangle with upper-left corner coordinates *left,top* and lower-right corner coordinates *right,bottom* into the buffer pointed to by *buf.* The coordinates are screen, not window, relative.

The amount of memory needed to hold a region of the screen is computed by the formula **num_bytes = rows × columns × 2**. The reason you must multiply the number of rows times the number of columns by 2 is that each character displayed on the screen requires 2 bytes of storage: 1 for the character itself and 1 for its attributes.

The function returns 1 on success and 0 on failure.

Example

This fragment copies a region of the screen into the memory pointed to by **buf**:

```
buf = (char *)malloc(10 * 10 *2);
gettext(10, 10, 20, 20, buf);
```

Related Functions

puttext( ), movetext( )

void gettextinfo(struct text_info *info)

Description

The prototype for **gettextinfo( )** is in **<conio.h>**.

The **gettextinfo( )** function obtains the current text settings and returns them in the structure pointed to by *info.* The **text_info** structure is declared as shown here.

```
struct text_info {
  unsigned char winleft;      /* upper left  */
  unsigned char wintop;       /* coordinates */
  unsigned char winright;     /* lower right */
  unsigned char winbottom;    /* coordinates */
  unsigned char attribute;    /* current attributes */
  unsigned char normattr;     /* normal attributes */
  unsigned char currmode;     /* active video mode */
  unsigned char screenheight; /* screen */
  unsigned char screenwidth;  /* dimensions */
  unsigned char curx;         /* current X and */
  unsigned char cury;         /* Y cursor location */
};
```

Example

This fragment obtains the current text settings.

```
struct text_info i;
gettextinfo(&i);
```

Related Function

textmode( )

void gotoxy(int x, int y)

Description

The prototype for **gotoxy( )** is in **<conio.h>**.

The **gotoxy( )** function sends the text screen cursor to the location specified by *x,y*. If either or both of the coordinates are invalid, no action takes place.

Example

This program prints **X**s diagonally across the screen:

```
#include <conio.h>

int main(void)
{
  register int i, j;
```

```
clrscr();
/* print diagonal Xs */
for(i=1, j=1; j<24; i+=3, j++) {
  gotoxy(i, j);
  cprintf("X");
}
 getche();
 clrscr();

 return 0;
}
```

Related Functions

wherex( ), wherey( )

void highvideo(void)

Description

The prototype for **highvideo( )** is in <conio.h>.

After a call to **highvideo( )**, characters written to the screen are displayed in high-intensity video.

Example

This fragment turns on high-intensity output:

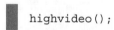

```
highvideo();
```

Related Functions

lowvideo( ), normvideo( )

void insline(void)

Description

The prototype for **insline( )** is in <conio.h>.

The **insline( )** function inserts a blank line at the current cursor position. All lines below the cursor move down. This function operates relative to the current text window.

Example

The following program illustrates the use of **insline( )**.

```c
#include <conio.h>

int main(void)
{
  register int i;

  clrscr();

  for(i=1; i<24; i++) {
    gotoxy(1, i);
    cprintf("This is line %d\n\r", i);
  }
  getche();
  gotoxy(1, 10);
  insline();
  getch();

  return 0;
}
```

Related Function

delline( )

void lowvideo(void)

Description

The prototype for **lowvideo( )** is in **<conio.h>**.

After a call to **lowvideo( )**, characters written to the screen are displayed in low-intensity video.

Example

This fragment turns on low-intensity output:

```c
lowvideo();
```

Related Functions

highvideo( ), normvideo( )

int movetext(int left, int top, int right, int bottom, int newleft, int newtop)

Description

The prototype for **movetext( )** is in **<conio.h>**.

The **movetext( )** function moves the portion of a text screen with the upper-left corner at *left,top* and lower-right corner at *right,bottom* to the region of the screen that has *newleft,newtop* as the coordinates of its upper-left corner. This function is screen, not window, relative.

The **movetext( )** function returns 0 if one or more coordinates are out of range and non-0 otherwise.

Example

This fragment moves the contents of the rectangle with upper-left corner coordinates of 1,1 and lower-right corner coordinates of 8,8 to 10,10:

```
movetext(1, 1, 8, 8, 10, 10);
```

Related Function

gettext( )

void normvideo(void)

Description

The prototype for **normvideo( )** is in **<conio.h>**.

After a call to **normvideo( )**, characters written to the screen are displayed in normal-intensity video.

Example

This fragment turns on normal-intensity output:

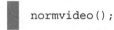

```
normvideo();
```

Related Functions

highvideo( ), lowvideo( )

int puttext(int left, int top, int right, int bottom, void *buf)

Description

The prototype for **puttext( )** is in **<conio.h>**.

The **puttext( )** function copies text previously saved by **gettext( )** from the buffer pointed to by *buf* into the region with upper-left and lower-right corners specified by *left,top* and *right,bottom*.

The **puttext( )** function uses screen-absolute, not window-relative, coordinates. It returns 0 if the coordinates are out of range, non-0 otherwise.

Example

This fragment copies a region of the screen into the memory pointed to by *buf* and puts that text in a new location:

```
buf = (char *) malloc(10 * 10 *2);
gettext(10, 10, 20, 20, buf);
puttext(0, 0, 30, 30, buf);
```

Related Functions

gettext( ), movetext( )

void textattr(int attr)

Description

The prototype for **textattr( )** is in **<conio.h>**.

The **textattr( )** function sets both the foreground and background colors in a text screen at one time. The value of *attr* represents an encoded form of the color information, as shown here.

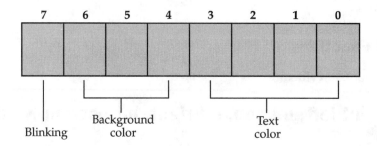

If bit 7 is set, the text blinks. Bits 6 through 4 determine the background color. Bits 3 through 0 set the color for the text. The easiest way to encode the background color into the attribute byte is to multiply the number of the color you desire by 16 and then OR that with the text color. For example, to create a green background with blue text you would use **GREEN * 16 | BLUE**. To cause the text to blink, OR the text color, background color, and **BLINK** (128) together.

Example

This fragment displays the text in red with a blue background:

```
textattr(RED | BLUE*16);
```

Related Functions

textbackground( ), textcolor( )

void textbackground(int color)

Description

The prototype for **textbackground( )** is in **<conio.h>**.

The **textbackground( )** function sets the background text color. The valid colors are shown here along with their macro names (defined in **<conio.h>**):

Macro	Integer Equivalent
BLACK	0
BLUE	1
GREEN	2

Macro	Integer Equivalent
CYAN	3
RED	4
MAGENTA	5
BROWN	6
LIGHTGRAY	7

The new background color takes effect after the call to **textbackground( )**. The background of characters currently on the screen is not affected.

Example

This fragment sets the background color to cyan.

```
textbackground(CYAN);
```

Related Function

textcolor( )

void textcolor(int color)

Description

The prototype of **textcolor( )** is in **<conio.h>**.

The **textcolor( )** function sets the color in which characters are displayed. It can also be used to specify blinking characters. The valid values for *color* are shown here, along with their macro names (defined in **<conio.h>**):

Macro	Integer Equivalent
BLACK	0
BLUE	1
GREEN	2
CYAN	3
RED	4
MAGENTA	5
BROWN	6

Macro	Integer Equivalent
LIGHTGRAY	7
DARKGRAY	8
LIGHTBLUE	9
LIGHTGREEN	10
LIGHTCYAN	11
LIGHTRED	12
LIGHTMAGENTA	13
YELLOW	14
WHITE	15
BLINK	128

The color of characters on the screen is not changed by **textcolor( )**; it affects only those written after **textcolor( )** has executed.

Example
This fragment displays subsequent output in blinking characters:

```
textcolor(BLINK);
```

Related Function

textattr( )

void textmode(int mode)

Description
The prototype for **textmode( )** is in **<conio.h>**.

The **textmode( )** function changes the video mode of a text screen. The argument *mode* must be one of the values shown in the following table. You can use either the integer value or the macro name (the macros are defined in **<conio.h>**):

Macro Name	Integer Equivalent	Description
BW40	0	40-column black and white
C40	1	40-column color
BW80	2	80-column black and white

Macro Name	Integer Equivalent	Description
C80	3	80-column color
MONO	7	80-column monochrome
C4350	64	43-line EGA or 50-line VGA
LASTMODE	−1	Previous mode

After a call to **textmode( )**, the screen is reset and all text screen attributes are returned to their default settings.

Example

This fragment puts the video hardware into 80-column color mode:

```
textmode(C80);
```

Related Function

gettextinfo( )

int wherex(void)
int wherey(void)

Description

The prototypes for **wherex( )** and **wherey( )** are in **<conio.h>**.

The **wherex( )** and **wherey( )** functions return the current x and y cursor coordinates relative to the current text window.

Example

This fragment loads the variables **xpos** and **ypos** with the current x,y coordinates:

```
int xpos, ypos;

xpos = wherex();
ypos = wherey();
```

Related Function

gotoxy( )

void window(int left, int top, int right, int bottom)

Description
The prototype for **window( )** is in **<conio.h>**.

The **window( )** function creates a rectangular text window with upper-left and lower-right coordinates specified by *left,top* and *right,bottom*. If any coordinate is invalid, **window( )** takes no action. Once a call to **window( )** has been successfully completed, all references to location coordinates are interpreted relative to the window, not the screen.

Example
This fragment creates a window and writes a line of text at location 2,3 inside that window:

```
window(10, 10, 60, 15);
gotoxy(2, 3);
cprintf("at location 2, 3");
```

Related Function

clrscr( )

Borland
C++
Builder

Chapter 19

Miscellaneous
Functions

The functions discussed in this chapter are those that don't fit easily in any other category. They include various conversions, variable-length argument processing, sorting, and random number generators.

Many of the functions covered here require the use of the header **<stdlib.h>**. This header defines two types: **div_t** and **ldiv_t**, which are the types of the structures returned by **div( )** and **ldiv( )**, respectively. Also defined are **size_t**, which is the unsigned value that is returned by **sizeof**, and **wchar_t**, which is the data type of wide characters. These macros are also defined:

Macro	Meaning
NULL	A null pointer.
RAND_MAX	The maximum value that can be returned by the **rand( )** function.
EXIT_FAILURE	The value returned to the calling process if program termination is unsuccessful.
EXIT_SUCCESS	The value returned to the calling process if program termination is successful.
MB_CUR_MAX	Maximum number of bytes in a multibyte character.

Some functions require a different header, which will be discussed for those functions.

int abs(int num)

Description

The prototype for **abs( )** is in both **<stdlib.h>** and **<math.h>**. For maximum portability, use **<stdlib.h>**.

The **abs( )** function returns the absolute value of the integer *num*.

Example

This program converts a user-entered number into its absolute value:

```
#include <stdio.h>
#include <stdlib.h>

int main(void)
{
```

```
char num[80];

gets(num);
printf("Absolute value is %d.\n", abs(atoi(num)));

return 0;
}
```

Related Function

labs( )

void assert(int exp)

Description

The prototype for **assert( )** is in **<assert.h>**.

The **assert( )** macro writes error information to **stderr** and aborts program execution if the expression *exp* evaluates to 0. Otherwise, **assert( )** does nothing. The output of the function is in this general form:

Assertion failed: *exp*, file *<file >*, line *<linenum >*

The **assert( )** macro is generally used to help verify that a program is operating correctly; the expression is devised so that it evaluates true only when no errors have taken place.

It is not necessary to remove the **assert( )** statements from the source code once a program is debugged, because if the macro **NDEBUG** is defined (as anything) before the **<assert.h>** header is included, the **assert( )** macros are ignored.

Example

This code fragment is used to test whether the data read from a serial port is ASCII (that is, that it does not use the 8th bit):

```
ch = read_port ();
assert(!(ch & 128)); /* check bit 8 */
```

Related Function

abort( )

double atof(const char *str)
long double _atold(const char *str)

Description

The prototypes for **atof( )** and **_atold( )** are in **<stdlib.h>** and **<math.h>**. For compatibility with the ANSI/ISO C/C++ standard, use **<stdlib.h>**.

The **atof( )** function converts the string pointed to by *str* into a **double** value. The string must contain a valid floating-point number. If this is not the case, 0 is returned and **errno** is set to **ERANGE**.

The number can be terminated by any character that cannot be part of a valid floating-point number. This includes white space, punctuation (other than periods), and characters other than "E" or "e". This means that if **atof( )** is called with "100.00HELLO", the value 100.00 is returned.

_atold( ) is the **long double** version of **atof( )**.

Example

This program reads two floating-point numbers and displays their sum:

```
#include <stdio.h>
#include <stdlib.h>

int main(void)
{
  char num1[80], num2[80];

  printf("Enter first number: ");
  gets(num1);
  printf("Enter second number: ");
  gets(num2);
  printf("The sum is: %f", atof(num1)+atof(num2));

  return 0;
}
```

Related Functions

atoi( ), **atol( )**

int atoi(const char *str)

Description

The prototype for **atoi( )** is in **<stdlib.h>**.

The **atoi( )** function converts the string pointed to by *str* into an **int** value. The string must contain a valid integer number. If this is not the case, 0 is returned.

The number can be terminated by any character that cannot be part of an integer number. This includes white space, punctuation, and other nondigit characters. This means that if **atoi( )** is called with **123.23**, the integer value 123 is returned and the 0.23 ignored.

Example

This program reads two integer numbers and displays their sum:

```
#include <stdio.h>
#include <stdlib.h>

int main(void)
{
  char num1[80], num2[80];

  printf("Enter first number: ");
  gets(num1);
  printf("Enter second number: ");
  gets(num2);
  printf("The sum is: %d", atoi(num1)+atoi(num2));

  return 0;
}
```

Related Functions

atof( ), atol( )

long atol(const char *str)

Description

The prototype for **atol( )** is in **<stdlib.h>**.

The **atol( )** function converts the string pointed to by *str* into a **long int** value. The string must contain a valid **long** integer number. If this is not the case, 0 is returned.

The number can be terminated by any character that cannot be part of an integer number. This includes white space, punctuation, and other nondigit characters. This means that if **atol( )** is called with **123.23**, the integer value 123 is returned and the 0.23 ignored.

Example

This program reads two **long** integer numbers and displays their sum:

```
#include <stdio.h>
#include <stdlib.h>

int main(void)
{
  char num1[80], num2[80];

  printf("Enter first number: ");
  gets(num1);
  printf("Enter second number: ");
  gets(num2);
  printf("The sum is: %ld", atol(num1)+atol(num2));

  return 0;
}
```

Related Functions

atof( ), atoi( )

void *bsearch(const void *key, const void *base, size_t num, size_t size, int (*compare)(const void *, const void *))

Description

The prototype for **bsearch( )** is in **<stdlib.h>**.

The **bsearch( )** function performs a binary search on the sorted array pointed to by *base* and returns a pointer to the first member that matches the key pointed to by *key*. The number of elements in the array is specified by *num*, and the size (in bytes) of each element is described by *size*.

The type **size_t** is defined as an **unsigned int** in **<stdlib.h>**.

The function pointed to by *compare* compares an element of the array with the key. The form of the *compare* function must be

func_name(const void *arg1, const void *arg2)

It must return the following values:

If *arg1* is less than *arg2*, return less than 0.

If *arg1* is equal to *arg2*, return 0.

If *arg1* is greater than *arg2*, return greater than 0.

The array must be sorted in ascending order with the lowest address containing the lowest element.
If the array does not contain the key, a null pointer is returned.

Example
This program reads characters entered at the keyboard and determines whether they belong to the alphabet:

```
#include <stdio.h>
#include <stdlib.h>
#include <ctype.h>

char *alpha="abcdefghijklmnopqrstuvwxyz";
int comp(const void *, const void *);

int main(void)
{
  char ch;
  char *p;

  do {
    printf("Enter a character: ");
    scanf("%c%*c", &ch);
    ch = tolower(ch);
    p = (char *) bsearch(&ch, alpha, 26, 1, comp);
    if(p) printf("is in alphabet\n");
    else printf("is not in alphabet\n");
  } while(p);

  return 0;
}
```

```
/* Compare two characters. */
int comp(const void *ch, const void *s)
{
   return *(char *)ch - *(char *)s;
}
```

Related Function

qsort( )

unsigned int _clear87(void)

Description

The prototype for **_clear87( )** is in **<float.h>**. This function is not defined by the ANSI/ISO C/C++ standard.

The **_clear87( )** function resets the 80x87 hardware floating-point coprocessor's status word. The function returns the previous status word.

You must have an 80x87 math coprocessor installed in your system in order to use any of the 80x87-based functions.

Related Function

_status87( )

unsigned int _control87(unsigned fpword, unsigned fpmask)

Description

The prototype for **_control87( )** is in **<float.h>**. This function is not defined by the ANSI/ISO C/C++ standard.

The **_control87( )** function returns or modifies the value of the 80x87 control word that controls the behavior of the chip. You must have an 80x87 math coprocessor installed in the computer before using this function.

The parameter *fpmask* determines which bits of the control word will be modified. Each bit in *fpmask* corresponds with each bit in *fpword* and the bits in the floating-point control word. If the bit in *fpmask* is non-0, the control word at the corresponding bit position is set to the value of the corresponding position in *fpword*.

The **_control87( )** function returns the modified control word. However, if *fpmask* contains 0, the control word is unchanged, and the current value of the control word is returned.

For a complete description of what each bit controls, consult the header file **<float.h>**.

Related Functions

_clear87( ), **_fpreset( )**

div_t div(int numerator, int denominator)

Description

The prototype for **div( )** is in **<stdlib.h>**.

The **div( )** function returns the quotient and the remainder of the operation *numerator/denominator*.

The structure type **div_t** is defined in **<stdlib.h>** and has these two fields.

```
int quot;  /* the quotient */
int rem;   /* the remainder */
```

Example

This program displays the quotient and the remainder of 10/3:

```
#include <stdio.h>
#include <stdlib.h>

int main(void)
{
  div_t n;

  n = div(10,3);
  printf("Quotient and remainder: %d %d\n", n.quot, n.rem);

  return 0;
}
```

Related Function

ldiv( )

char *ecvt(double value, int ndigit, int *dec, int *sign)

Description

The prototype for **ecvt( )** is in **<stdlib.h>**. This function is not defined by the ANSI/ISO C/C++ standard.

The **ecvt( )** function converts *value* into a string *ndigit* long. After the call, the value of the variable pointed to by *dec* indicates the position of the decimal point. If the decimal point is to the left of the number, the number pointed to by *dec* is negative. The decimal point is not actually stored in the string. If *value* is positive, *sign* is 0. If the number is negative, *sign* is non-0.

The **ecvt( )** function returns a pointer to a static data area that holds the string representation of the number.

Example

This call converts the number 10.12 into a string:

```
int decpnt, sign;
char *out;

out = ecvt(10.12, 5, &decpnt, &sign);
```

Related Functions

fcvt( ), gcvt( )

void _ _emit_ _(unsigned char arg, . . .)

Description

There is no prototype for _ _ **emit_ _( )** because C++ Builder automatically handles this function. This function is not defined by the ANSI/ISO C/C++ standard.

The _ _**emit_ _( )** function is used to insert one or more values directly into the executable code of your program at the point at which _ _**emit_ _( )** is called. These values generally will be x86 machine instructions. If a value fits into a byte, it is treated as a byte quantity. Otherwise, it is treated as a word quantity. You can pass _ _**emit_ _( )** byte or word values only.

You must be an expert assembly language programmer to use _ _**emit_ _( )**. If you insert incorrect values, your program will crash.

char *fcvt(double value, int ndigit, int *dec, int *sign)

Description

The prototype for **fcvt( )** is in **<stdlib.h>**. This function is not defined by the ANSI/ISO C/C++ standard.

The **fcvt( )** function is the same as **ecvt( )** except that the output is rounded to the number of digits specified by *ndigit.*

The **fcvt( )** function returns a pointer to a static data area that holds the string representation of the number.

Example

This call converts the number 10.12 into a string:

```
int decpnt, sign
char *out;

out = fcvt(10.12, 5, &decpnt, &sign);
```

Related Functions

ecvt( ), gcvt( )

void _fpreset(void)

Description

The prototype for **_fpreset( )** is in **<float.h>**. This function is not defined by the ANSI/ISO C/C++ standard.

The **_fpreset( )** function resets the floating-point arithmetic system. You may need to reset the floating-point routines after a **system( )**, **exec( )**, **spawn( )**, or **signal( )** function executes. Refer to the user manuals for specific details.

Example

This fragment ensures that the floating-point arithmetic routines are reset after **system( )** returns:

```
/* compute and print payroll checks */
system("payroll");
_fpreset();
```

THE C++ BUILDER
FUNCTION LIBRARY

Related Function

_status87( )

char *gcvt(double value, int ndigit, char *buf)

Description

The prototype for **gcvt( )** is in **<stdlib.h>**. This function is not defined by the ANSI/ISO C/C++ standard.

The **gcvt( )** function converts *value* into a string *ndigit* long. The converted string is stored in the array pointed to by *buf* in FORTRAN F-format if possible. If not, it uses the E-format as defined for **printf( )**. A pointer to *buf* is returned.

Example

This call converts the number 10.12 into a string:

```
char buf [80]
gcvt(10.12, 5, buf);
```

Related Functions

fcvt( ), ecvt( )

char *getenv(const char *name)

Description

The prototype for **getenv( )** is in **<stdlib.h>**.

The **getenv( )** function returns a pointer to environmental information associated with the string pointed to by *name* in the environmental information table. The string returned must never be changed by the program.

The environment of a program can include such things as path names and devices online. The exact meaning of this data is defined by the operating system.

If a call is made to **getenv( )** with an argument that does not match any of the environmental data, a null pointer is returned.

Example

The following fragment returns a pointer to the **PATH** list.

```
p = getenv("PATH");
```

Related Functions

putenv( ), **system( )**

char *getpass(const char *str)

Description

The prototype for **getpass( )** is in **<conio.h>**. This function is not defined by the ANSI/ISO C/C++ standard.

After displaying the prompt *str* on the screen, the **getpass( )** function returns a pointer to a null-terminated string of not more than eight characters. This string is statically allocated by **getpass( )** and is overwritten each time the function is called. If you want to save the string, you must copy it elsewhere. Keystrokes are not echoed when the password is entered.

Example

This function waits until the proper password is entered:

```
#include <conio.h>
#include <string.h>

void pswd (char *pw)
{
  char *input;

  do {
    input = getpass("Enter your password:");
  }while (strcmp("starbar", input));

  printf("You're in!");
}
```

unsigned getpid(void)

Description

The prototype for **getpid( )** is in **<process.h>**. This function is not defined by the ANSI/ISO C/C++ standard.

The **getpid( )** function returns the process ID number associated with a program.

Example

This fragment displays the process ID number:

```
printf("The process ID of this program is %d\n", getpid());
```

char *itoa(int num, char *str, int radix)

Description

The prototype for **itoa( )** is in **<stdlib.h>**. This function is not defined by the ANSI/ISO C/C++ standard.

The **itoa( )** function converts the integer *num* into its string equivalent and places the result in the string pointed to by *str*. The base of the output string is determined by *radix*, which can be in the range 2 through 36.

The **itoa( )** function returns a pointer to *str*. There is no error return value. Be sure to call **itoa( )** with a string of sufficient length to hold the converted result. The maximum length needed is 33 bytes.

Example

This program displays the value of 1423 in hexadecimal (**58f**):

```
#include <stdio.h>
#include <stdlib.h>

int main(void)
{
  char p[17];

  itoa(1423, p, 16);
  printf(p);

  return 0;
}
```

Related Functions

atoi( ), **sscanf( )**

long labs(long num)

Description

The prototype for **labs( )** is in **<stdlib.h>** and **<math.h>**. For the ANSI/ISO C/C++ standard compatibility, use **<stdlib.h>**.

The **labs( )** function returns the absolute value of the **long int** *num*.

Example

This function converts the user-entered numbers into their absolute values:

```
#include <stdio.h>
#include <stdlib.h>

long int get_labs()
{
  char num[80];

  gets(num);

  return labs(atol(num));
}
```

Related Function

abs( )

ldiv_t ldiv(long numerator, long denominator)

Description

The prototype for **ldiv( )** is in **<stdlib.h>**.

The **ldiv( )** function returns the quotient and the remainder of the operation *numerator/denominator*.

The structure type **ldiv_t** is defined in **<stdlib.h>** and has these two fields:

```
long quot;  /*the quotient*/
long rem;   /* the remainder */
```

Example

This program displays the quotient and the remainder of 100000L/3L:

```
#include <stdio.h>
#include <stdlib.h>

int main(void)
{
  ldiv_t n;

  n = ldiv(100000L,3L);
  printf("Quotient and remainder: %ld %ld.\n", n.quot, n.rem);

  return 0;
}
```

Related Function

div( )

void *lfind(const void *key, const void *base, size_t *num, size_t size, int (*compare)(const void *, const void *)

void *lsearch(const void *key, void *base, size_t *num, size_t size, int (*compare)(const void *, const void *))

Description

The prototypes for **lfind( )** and **lsearch( )** are in **<stdlib.h>**. These functions are not defined by the ANSI/ISO C/C++ standard.

The **lfind( )** and **lsearch( )** functions perform a linear search on the array pointed to by *base* and return a pointer to the first element that matches the key pointed to by *key*. The number of elements in the array is pointed to by *num*, and the size (in bytes) of each element is described by *size*.

The function pointed to by *compare* compares an element of the array with the key. The form of the *compare* function must be

int *func_name*(const void *arg1, const void *arg2)

It must return the following values:

If *arg1* does not equal *arg2*, return non-0.

If *arg1* is equal to *arg2*, return 0.

The array being searched does not have to be sorted. If the array does not contain the key, a null pointer is returned.

The difference between **lfind( )** and **lsearch( )** is that if the item being searched for does not exist in the array, **lsearch( )** adds it to the end of the array; **lfind( )** does not.

Example

This program reads characters entered at the keyboard and determines whether they belong to the alphabet:

```c
#include <stdlib.h>
#include <ctype.h>
#include <stdio.h>

char *alpha="abcdefghijklmnopqrstuvwxyz";

int comp(const void *, const void *);

int main(void)
{
  char ch;
  char *p;
  size_t num=26;

  do {
    printf("Enter a character: ");
    scanf("%c%*c", &ch);
    ch = tolower(ch);

    p = (char *) lfind(&ch, alpha, &num, 1, comp);

    if(p) printf("is in alphabet\n");
    else printf("is not in alphabet\n");
  } while(p);

  return 0;
}

/* Compare two characters. */
int comp(const void *ch, const void *s)
{
```

THE C++ BUILDER
FUNCTION LIBRARY

```
    return *(char *)ch - *(char *)s;
}
```

Related Function

qsort( )

struct lconv *localeconv(void)

Description

The prototype for **localeconv( )** is in **<locale.h>**. It returns a pointer to a structure of type **lconv**, which contains various items of country-specific environmental information relating to the way numbers are formatted. The **lconv** structure is organized as shown here.

```
struct lconv {
  char *decimal_point;     /* decimal point character
                              for non-monetary values */
  char *thousands_sep;     /* thousands separator
                              for non-monetary values */
  char *grouping;          /* specifies grouping for
                              non-monetary values */
  char int_curr_symbol;    /* international currency symbol */
  char *currency_symbol;   /* local currency symbol */
  char *mon_decimal_point; /* decimal point character
                              for monetary values */
  char *mon_thousands_sep; /* thousands separator
                              for monetary values */
  char *mon_grouping;      /* specifies grouping for
                              monetary values */
  char *positive_sign;     /* positive value indicator
                              for monetary values */
  char *negative_sign;     /* negative value indicator
                              for monetary values */
  char int_frac_digits;    /* number of digits displayed
                              to the right of the decimal
                              point for monetary values
                              displayed using international
                              format */
  char frac_digits;        /* number of digits displayed
```

```
                                     to the right of the decimal
                                     point for monetary values
                                     displayed using local format */
      char p_cs_precedes;        /* 1 if currency symbol precedes
                                     positive value,
                                     0 if currency symbol
                                     follows value */
      char p_sep_by_space;       /* 1 if currency symbol is
                                     separated from value by a
                                     space, 0 otherwise */
      char n_cs_precedes;        /* 1 if currency symbol precedes
                                     a negative value, 0 if
                                     currency symbol follows value */
      char n_sep_by_space;       /* 1 if currency symbol is
                                     separated from a negative
                                     value by a space, 0 if
                                     currency symbol follows value */
      char p_sign_posn;          /* indicates position of positive
                                     value symbol */
      char n_sign_posn;          /* indicates position of negative
                                     value symbol */
    }
```

Related Function

setlocale( )

void longjmp(jmp_buf envbuf, int val)

Description

The prototype for **longjmp( )** is in **<setjmp.h>**.

The **longjmp( )** instruction causes program execution to resume at the point of the last call to **setjmp( )**. These two functions create a way to jump between functions.

The **longjmp( )** function operates by resetting the stack to the state defined in *envbuf*, which must have been set by a prior call to **setjmp( )**. This causes program execution to resume at the statement following the **setjmp( )** invocation. That is, the computer is "tricked" into thinking that it never left the function that called **setjmp( )**. (As a somewhat graphic explanation, the **longjmp( )** function "warps" across time and [memory] space to a previous point in your program without having to perform the normal function-return process.)

The buffer *envbuf* is of type **jmp_buf**, which is defined in the header **<setjmp.h>**. The buffer must have been set through a call to **setjmp( )** prior to calling **longjmp( )**.

The value of *val* becomes the return value of **setjump( )** and can be interrogated to determine where the long jump came from. The only value not allowed is 0.

It is important to understand that the **longjmp( )** function must be called before the function that called **setjmp( )** returns. If not, the result is technically undefined. (Actually, a crash will almost certainly occur.)

By far, the most common use of **longjmp( )** is to return from a deeply nested set of routines when a catastrophic error occurs.

Example

This program prints **1 2 3**:

```
#include <stdio.h>
#include <setjmp.h>
#include <stdlib.h>

jmp_buf ebuf;
void f2(void);

int main(void)
{
  int i;

  printf("1 ");
  i = setjmp(ebuf);
  if ( i !=0 ) {
     printf("%d",i);
     exit(1);
  }
  f2();

  return 0;
}

void f2(void)
{
  printf("2 ");
  longjmp(ebuf, 3);
}
```

Related Function

setjmp( )

char *ltoa(long num, char *str, int radix)
char *ultoa(unsigned long num, char *str, int radix)

Description
The prototype for **ltoa( )** and **ultoa( )** are in **<stdlib.h>**. These functions are not defined by the ANSI/ISO C/C++ standard.

The **ltoa( )** function converts the **long** integer *num* into its string equivalent and places the result in the string pointed to by *str*. The base of the output string is determined by *radix*, which must be in the range 2 through 36. The **ultoa( )** function performs the same conversion, but on an **unsigned long** integer.

The **ltoa( )** and **ultoa( )** functions return a pointer to *str*. There is no error return value. Be sure *str* is of sufficient length to hold the converted result. The longest array you need is 34 bytes.

Example
This program displays the value of 1423 in hexadecimal (**58f**):

```
#include <stdio.h>
#include <stdlib.h>

int main(void)
{
  char p[34];

  ltoa(1423, p, 16);
  printf(p);

  return 0;
}
```

Related Functions

itoa( ), sscanf( )

unsigned long _lrotl(unsigned long l, int i)
unsigned long _lrotr(unsigned long l, int i)

Description

The prototypes for **_lrotl( )** and **_lrotr( )** are in **<stdlib.h>**. These functions are not defined by the ANSI/ISO C/C++ standard.

The **_lrotl( )** and **_lrotr( )** functions rotate the bits of the **long** value *l, i* number of bits to the left or right, respectively, and return the result. When a rotate is performed, bits rotated off one end are inserted onto the other end. For example, given the value

1111 0000 0000 1111 1111 0000 1010 0101

rotating it left by one bit, produces the value

1110 0000 0001 1111 1110 0001 0100 1011

Example

The following program shows the effect of left and right rotation.

```
#include <stdio.h>
#include <stdlib.h>

int main(void)
{
  unsigned long l = 1;
  printf("1 rotated left 2 bits = %ld\n", _lrotl(1,2));
  l=16;
  printf("16 rotated right 2 bits = %ld\n", _lrotr(1,2));

  return 0;
}
```

Related Functions

_rotl( ), _rotr( )

max(x,y)
min(x,y)

Description

The **max( )** and **min( )** macros are defined in **<stdlib.h>**. These functions are not defined by the ANSI/ISO C/C++ standard.

The **max( )** macro returns the larger of the two values and the **min( )** returns the smaller of the two values. The **max( )** and **min( )** macros return the same type as passed to them; both arguments passed must be of the same type.

Example

This program illustrates the **min( )** and **max( )** macros:

```
#include <stdlib.h>
#include <stdio.h>

int main (void)
{
  printf("max of 10, 20 is %d\n", max (10, 20));
  printf("min of 10, 20 is %d\n", min (10, 20));

  return 0;
}
```

int mblen(const char *str, size_t size)

Description

The prototype for **mblen( )** is in **<stdlib.h>**.

This function returns the length of a multibyte character pointed to by *str*. Only the first *size* number of characters are examined.

If *str* is null, then **mblen( )** determines if multibyte characters have state-dependent encodings. In this case, it returns nonzero if they do and zero if they do not.

Example

This statement displays the length of the multibyte character pointed to by **mb**.

```
printf("%d", mblen(mb, 2));
```

Related Functions

mbtowc( ), **wctomb( )**

size_t mbstowcs(wchar_t *out, const char *in, size_t size)

Description

The prototype for **mbstowcs( )** is in **<stdlib.h>**.

The **mbstowcs( )** converts the multibyte string pointed to by *in* into a wide character string and puts that result in the array pointed to by *out*. Only *size* number of bytes will be stored in *out*.

The **mbstowcs( )** function returns the number of multibyte characters that are converted. If an error occurs, the function returns−1.

Example

This statement converts the first four characters in the multibyte string pointed to by **mb** and puts the result in **wstr**.

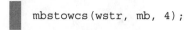

```
mbstowcs(wstr, mb, 4);
```

Related Functions

wcstombs( ), **mbtowc( )**

int mbtowc(wchar_t *out, const char *in, size_t size)

Description

The prototype for **mbtowc( )** is in **<stdlib.h>**.

The **mbtowc( )** function converts the multibyte character in the array pointed to by *in* into its wide character equivalent and puts that result in the array pointed to by *out*. Only *size* number of characters will be examined.

This function returns the number of bytes that are put into *out*. −1 is returned if an error occurs.

If *in* is null, then **mbtowc( )** returns non-0 if multibyte characters have state dependencies. If they do not, 0 is returned.

Example

This statement converts the multibyte character in **mbstr** into its equivalent wide character and puts the result in the object pointed to by **wstr**. (Only the first 2 bytes of **mbstr** are examined.)

```
mbtowc(wstr, mbstr, 2);
```

Related Functions

mblen( ), wctomb( )

int putenv(const char *evar)

Description

The prototype for **putenv( )** is in **<stdlib.h>**. This function is not defined by the ANSI/ISO C/C++ standard.

The **putenv( )** function defines an environmental variable. It returns 0 if successful, −1 if unsuccessful. Refer to **getenv( )** and to your operating system manual for information about environmental variables.

Related Function

getenv( )

void qsort(void *base, size_t num, size_t size, int (*compare) (const void *, const void *))

Description

The prototype for **qsort( )** is in **<stdlib.h>**.

The **qsort( )** function sorts the array pointed to by *base* using a *quicksort*, a general-purpose sorting algorithm (developed by C.A.R. Hoare). Upon termination, the array is sorted. The number of elements in the array is specified by *num*, and the size (in bytes) of each element is described by *size*.

The function pointed to by *compare* compares an element of the array with the key. The form of the *compare* function must be

int *func_name*(const void *arg1*, const void *arg2*)

It must return the following values:

If *arg1* is less than *arg2*, return less than 0.

If *arg1* is equal to *arg2*, return 0.

If *arg1* is greater than *arg2*, return greater than 0.

The array is sorted into ascending order with the lowest address containing the lowest element.

Example

This program sorts a list of integers and displays the result:

```
#include <stdio.h>
#include <stdlib.h>

int num[10] = {
  1,3,6,5,8,7,9,6,2,0
};

int comp(const int *, const int *);

int main(void)
{
  int i;

  printf("Original array: ");
  for(i=0; i<10; i++) printf("%d ",num[i]);
  printf("\n");

  qsort(num, 10, sizeof(int),
        (int (*)(const void *, const void *)) comp);

  printf("Sorted array: ");
  for(i=0; i<10; i++) printf("%d ", num[i]);

  return 0;
}

/* compare the integers */
int comp(const int *i, const int *j)
{
  return *i - *j;
}
```

Related Function

bsearch( )

int raise(int signal)

Description

The prototype for **raise( )** is in **<signal.h>**. The **raise( )** function sends the signal specified by *signal* to the currently executing program.

The following signals are defined in **<signal.h>**:

Macro	Meaning
SIGABRT	Termination error
SIGBREAK	User pressed CTRL-Break
SIGFPE	Floating-point error
SIGILL	Bad instruction
SIGINT	User pressed CTRL-C
SIGSEGV	Illegal memory access
SIGTERM	Terminate program
SIGUSR1, SIGUSR2, SIGUSR3	User-defined signals

On success, **raise( )** returns 0.

You will often use this function in conjunction with the **signal( )** function.

Example

This program raises the **SIGTERM** signal, which causes **myhandler( )** to be executed:

```
#include <signal.h>
#include <stdio.h>
#include <stdlib.h>

void myhandler(int);

int main(void)
{
  signal(SIGTERM, myhandler);
  raise(SIGTERM);
  printf("This line will not be executed.\n");

  return 0;
}
```

THE C++ BUILDER
FUNCTION LIBRARY

```
void myhandler(int notused)
{
  printf("Program terminated.\n");
  exit(1);
}
```

Related Function

signal( )

int rand(void)

Description

The prototype for **rand( )** is in **<stdlib.h>**.

The **rand( )** function generates a sequence of pseudorandom numbers. Each time it is called it returns an integer between 0 and **RAND_MAX**.

Example

This program displays ten pseudorandom numbers:

```
#include <stdio.h>
#include <stdlib.h>

int main(void)
{
  int i;

  for(i=0; i<10; i++)
    printf("%d ", rand());

  return 0;
}
```

Related Function

srand( )

int random(int num)
void randomize(void)

Description

The prototypes for **random( )** and **randomize( )** are in **<stdlib.h>**. These functions are not defined by the ANSI/ISO C/C++ standard.

The **random( )** macro returns a random number in the range 0 through *num* −1.

The **randomize( )** macro initializes the random number generator to some random value. It uses the **time( )** function, so you should include **<time.h>** in any program that uses **randomize( )**.

Example

This program prints ten random numbers between 0 and 24:

```
#include <time.h>
#include <stdio.h>
#include <stdlib.h>

int main(void)
{
  int i;

  randomize();
  for(i=0; i<10; i++) printf("%d ", random(25));

  return 0;
}
```

Related Functions

rand( ), srand( )

unsigned short _rotl(unsigned short val, int num)
unsigned short _rotr(unsigned short val, int num)

Description

The prototypes for **_rotl( )** and **_rotr( )** are in **<stdlib.h>**. These functions are not defined by the ANSI/ISO C/C++ standard.

The **_rotl( )** and **_rotr( )** functions rotate the bits of the value *val, num* number of bits to the left or right, respectively, and return the result. When a rotate is performed, bits rotated off one end are inserted onto the other end. For example, given the value

1111 0000 0000 1111

rotating it left by one bit produces the value

1110 0000 0001 1111

Example
The following program prints the value of 64 after it is rotated left and it is rotated right:

```
#include <stdio.h>
#include <stdlib.h>

int main(void)
{
  unsigned val = 64;

  printf("Rotated left 2 bits = %d\n", _rotl(val,2));
  printf("Rotated right 2 bits = %d\n", _rotr(val,2));

  return 0;
}
```

Related Functions

_lrotl( ), _lrotr( )

void _setcursortype(int type)

Description
The prototype for **_setcursortype( )** is in **<conio.h>**. This function is not defined by the ANSI/ISO C/C++ standard.

The **_setcursortype( )** function changes how the cursor is displayed. It can be called with one of three macros (defined in **<conio.h>**). Calling **_setcursortype( )** with **_NOCURSOR** turns off the cursor. Using **_SOLIDCURSOR** makes a block cursor, and **_NORMALCURSOR** creates an underscore cursor.

Example

This fragment changes the cursor type to a block:

```
_setcursortype(_SOLIDCURSOR);
```

int setjmp(jmp_buf envbuf)

Description

The prototype for **setjmp( )** is in **<setjmp.h>**.

The **setjmp( )** function saves the contents of the system stack in the buffer *envbuf* for later use by **longjmp( )**.

The **setjmp( )** function returns zero upon invocation. However, when **longjmp( )** executes, it passes an argument (always nonzero) to **setjmp( )**, which appears to be **setjmp( )**'s return value.

See **longjmp( )** for additional information.

Example

This program prints **1 2 3**:

```
#include <stdio.h>
#include <setjmp.h>
#include <stdlib.h>

jmp_buf ebuf;
void f2(void);

int main(void)
{
  int i;

  printf("1 ");
  i = setjmp(ebuf);
  if(i != 0) {
    printf("%d",i);
    exit(1);
  }
  f2();
```

```
    return 0;
  }

void f2(void)
{
  printf("2 ");
  longjmp(ebuf, 3);
}
```

Related Function

longjmp( )

void _searchenv(const char *fname, const char *ename, char *fpath)

Description

The prototype for **_searchenv( )** is in **<stdlib.h>**. The function is not defined by the ANSI/ISO C/C++ standard.

The **_searchenv( )** searches for the file whose name is pointed to by *fname* using the path defined by the environmental name pointed to by *ename.* If the file is found, its full path is put into the string pointed to by *fpath.*

Example

This program searches for the specified file using the specified path. If it finds the file, it displays the full path.

```
#include <stdio.h>

int main(int argc, char *argv[])
{
  char fpath[64];

  if(argc!=3) {
    printf("Usage: FINDFILE <fname> <ename>");
    return 1;
  }

  _searchenv(argv[1], argv[2], fpath);
```

```
/* fpath will contain path if file is found */
if(*fpath) printf("Path: %s", fpath);

return 0;
}
```

Related Function

searchpath( )

char *setlocale(int type, const char *locale)

Description

The prototype for **setlocale( )** is in **<locale.h>**. This function allows certain parameters that are sensitive to the geopolitical location of a program's execution to be queried or set. For example, in Europe, the comma is used in place of the decimal point.

If *locale* is null, then **setlocale( )** returns a pointer to the current localization string. Otherwise, **setlocale( )** attempts to use the specified localization string to set the locale parameters as specified by *type*.

At the time of the call, *type* must be one of the following macros:

LC_ALL
LC_COLLATE
LC_CTYPE
LC_MONETARY
LC_NUMERIC
LC_TIME

LC_ALL refers to all localization categories. **LC_COLLATE** affects the operation of the **strcoll( )** function. **LC_CTYPE** alters the way the character functions work. **LC_MONETARY** determines the monetary format. **LC_NUMERIC** changes the decimal-point character for formatted input/output functions. Finally, **LC_TIME** determines the behavior of the **strftime( )** function.

The **setlocale( )** function returns a pointer to a string associated with the *type* parameter. It returns null if an error occurs.

Related Functions

localeconv( ), time( ), strcoll( ), strftime( )

void (*set_new_handler(void (* newhand)( )))( )

Description

The prototype for **set_new_handler( )** is in **<new.h>**. This function is not defined by the ANSI/ISO C/C++ standard.

The **set_new_handler( )** function allows you to determine which function is called when a **new** memory allocation request fails. The address of this function is passed in *newhand*. To deactivate your function and return to the default processing of allocation request failures, call **set_new_handler( )** with *newhand* being **NULL**.

In general, you should not use this function. Its use is highly specialized and no example is given.

void (*signal (int signal, void (*sigfunc) (int func)))(int)

Description

The prototype for **signal( )** is in **<signal.h>**.

The **signal( )** function tells C++ Builder to execute the function pointed to by *sigfunc* if *signal* is received.

The value for *func* must be one of the following macros, defined in **<signal.h>**, or the address of a function you created:

Macro	Meaning
SIG_DFL	Use default signal handling
SIG_IGN	Ignore the signal

If you create your own function, it is executed each time the specified signal is received.

The following signals are defined in **<signal.h>**. These are the values that can be given to *signal*.

Macro	Meaning
SIGABRT	Termination error
SIGBREAK	User pressed CTRL-Break
SIGFPE	Floating-point error
SIGILL	Bad instruction
SIGINT	User pressed CTRL-C
SIGSEGV	Illegal memory access

Macro	Meaning
SIGTERM	Terminate program
SIGUSR1, SIGUSR2, SIGUSR3	User-defined signals

On success, **signal( )** returns the address of the previously defined function for the specified signal. On error, **SIG_ERR** is returned, and **errno** is set to **EINVAL**.

Example

This line causes the function **myint( )** to be called if CTRL-C is pressed:

```
signal(SIGINT, myint);
```

Related Function

raise( )

void srand(unsigned seed)

Description

The prototype for **srand( )** is in **<stdlib.h>**.

The **srand( )** function is used to set a starting point for the sequence generated by **rand( )**. (The **rand( )** function returns pseudorandom numbers.)

The **srand( )** function allows multiple program runs using different sequences of pseudorandom numbers.

Example

This program uses the system time to initialize the **rand( )** function randomly by using **srand( )**.

```
#include <stdio.h>
#include <stdlib.h>
#include <time.h>

/* Seed rand with the system time
   and display the first 10 numbers.
*/
int main(void)
```

```
{
  int i, stime;
  long ltime;

  /* get the current calendar time */

  ltime = time(NULL);
  stime = (unsigned int) ltime/2;
  srand(stime);
  for(i=0; i<10; i++) printf("%d ", rand());

  return 0;
}
```

Related Function

rand( )

unsigned int _status87(void)

Description

The prototype for **_status87( )** is in **<float.h>**. This function is not defined by the ANSI/ISO C/C++ standard.

The **_status87( )** function returns the value of the floating-point status word. You must have an 80x87 math coprocessor installed in the computer before using this function.

Related Functions

_clear87( ), _fpreset( )

double strtod(const char *start, char **end)
long double _strtold(const char *start, char **end)

Description

The **strtod( )** function converts the string representation of a number stored in the string pointed to by *start* into a **double** and returns the result. Its prototype is in **<stdlib.h>**.

The **strtod( )** function works as follows: First, any leading white space in the string pointed to by *start* is stripped. Next, each character that makes up the number is read. Any character that cannot be part of a floating-point number stops the process. This includes white space, punctuation other than periods, and characters other than "E" or "e". Finally, *end* is set to point to the remainder, if any, of the original string. This means that if **strtod( )** is called with **100.00 Pliers**, the value 100.00 is returned and *end* points to the space that precedes "Pliers".

If a conversion error occurs, **strtod( )** returns either **HUGE_VAL** for overflow, or −**HUGE_VAL** for underflow. If no conversion could take place, 0 is returned.

_strtold( ) is the **long double** version of this function.

Example

This program reads floating-point numbers from a character array:

```
#include <stdio.h>
#include <stdlib.h>
#include <ctype.h>

int main(void)
{
  char *end, *start="100.00 pliers 200.00 hammers";

  end = start;
  while(*start) {
    printf("%f, ",strtod(start, &end));
    printf("Remainder: %s\n", end);
    start = end;
    /* move past the non-digits */
    while(!isdigit(*start) && *start) start++;
  }

  return 0;
}
```

The output is

```
100.000000, Remainder: pliers 200.00 hammers
200.000000, Remainder: hammers
```

Related Function

atof( )

long strtol(const char *start, char **end, int radix)
unsigned long strtoul(const char *start, char **end, int radix)

Description

The prototypes for **strtol( )** and **strtoul( )** are in **<stdlib.h>**.

The **strtol( )** function converts the string representation of a number stored in the string pointed to by *start* into a **long int** and returns the result. The **strtoul( )** function performs the same conversion, but the result is an **unsigned long**. The base of the number is determined by *radix*. If *radix* is 0, the base is determined by rules that govern constant specification. If *radix* is other than 0, it must be in the range 2 through 36.

The **strtol( )** and **strtoul( )** functions work as follows: First, any leading white space in the string pointed to by *start* is stripped. Next, each character that makes up the number is read. Any character that cannot be part of a **long** integer number stops this process. This includes white space, punctuation, and nondigit characters. Finally, *end* is set to point to the remainder, if any, of the original string. This means that if **strtol( )** is called with **100 Pliers**, the value 100L is returned and *end* points to the space that precedes "Pliers".

If a conversion error occurs, the return value is **LONG_MAX** for overflow, or **LONG_MIN** for underflow, or **ULONG_MAX** for **strtoul( )**. If no conversion could take place, 0 is returned.

Example

This function reads base 10 numbers from standard input and returns their **long** equivalents:

```
#include <stdio.h>
#include <stdlib.h>

long int read_long()
{
  char start[80], *end;

  printf("Enter a number: ");
  gets(start);
  return strtol(start, &end, 10);
}
```

Related Function

atol( )

void swab(char *source, char *dest, int num)

Description

The prototype for **swab( )** is in **<stdlib.h>**. This function is not defined by the ANSI/ISO C/C++ standard.

The **swab( )** function copies *num* bytes from the string pointed to by *source* into the string pointed to by *dest,* switching the position of each even/odd pair of bytes as it goes.

Example

This fragment prints **iH**:

```
char dest[3];

swab("Hi", dest, 2);
printf(dest);
```

int system(const char *str)

Description

The prototype for **system( )** is in **<stdlib.h>**.

The **system( )** function passes the string pointed to by *str* as a command to the command processor of the operating system and returns the exit status of the command. A command processor must be present to execute the command.

Example

This program displays the contents of the current working directory:

```
#include <stdlib.h>

int main(void)
{
  system("dir");

  return 0;
}
```

Related Functions

spawn( ), **exec( )**

int toascii(int ch)

Description

The prototype for **toascii( )** is in **<ctype.h>**. This function is not defined by the ANSI/ISO C/C++ standard.

The **toascii( )** function clears all but the lower 7 bits in *ch* and returns the result.

Example

This fragment clears all but the lower 7 bits of the character input from the keyboard.

```
int ch;
ch = getche():
ch = toascii(ch);
```

Related Functions

tolower( ), **toupper( )**

unsigned umask(unsigned access)

Description

The prototype for **umask( )** is in **<io.h>**. This function is not defined by the ANSI/ISO C/C++ standard.

The **umask( )** function modifies the access attribute of a file opened by either **open( )** or **_creat( )**. The attribute specified in *access* is removed from the access attribute. The *access* parameter must be one of these two values (which may also be ORed together):

Macro	Meaning
S_IWRITE	File is writable
S_IREAD	File is readable

The **umask( )** function returns the previous access permission mask.

Example

This statement causes subsequent files to be opened as write-only.

```
umask(S_IREAD);
```

Related Functions

_creat(), open(), fopen()

int utime(char *fname, struct utimbuf *t)

Description

The prototype for **utime( )** is in **<utime.h>**. This function is not defined by the ANSI/ISO C/C++ standard.

The **utime( )** function changes the creation (or last modification) time of the file whose name is pointed to by *fname*. The new time is specified by the structure pointed to by *t*. The **utimbuf** structure is defined like this:

```
struct utimbuf {
  time_t actime;
  time_t modtime;
};
```

If *t* is null, then the file's creation time is set to the current system time.

The **utime( )** function returns 0 if successful. If an error occurs, −1 is returned and **errno** is set to one of these values:

EACCES	Access denied
EMFILE	Too many files are open
ENOENT	Nonexistent file

Example

This program sets the specified file's creation time to the current time of the system. (This is a simple version of the common TOUCH utility program.)

```
#include <utime.h>
#include <stdio.h>

int main(int argc, char *argv[])
{
  if(argc!=2) {
    printf("Usage: SETTIME <fname>");
    return 1;
  }
```

```
/* set to current system time */
utime(argv[1], NULL);

return 0;
}
```

Related Functions

time( ), **asctime( )**, **gmtime( )**

void va_start(va_list argptr, last_parm)
void va_end(va_list argptr)
type va_arg(va_list argptr, type)

Description

The prototypes for these macros are in **<stdarg.h>**.

The **va_arg( )**, **va_start( )**, and **va_end( )** macros work together to allow a variable number of arguments to be passed to a function. The most common example of a function that takes a variable number of arguments is **printf( )**. The type **va_list** is defined by **<stdarg.h>**.

The general procedure for creating a function that can take a variable number of arguments is as follows: The function must have at least one known parameter, but can have more, prior to the variable parameter list. The rightmost known parameter is called the *last_parm*. The name of the *last_parm* is used as the second parameter in a call to **va_start( )**. Before any of the variable-length parameters can be accessed, the argument pointer *argptr* must be initialized through a call to **va_start( )**. After that, parameters are returned via calls to **va_arg( )** with *type* being the type of the next parameter. Finally, once all the parameters have been read and prior to returning from the function, a call to **va_end( )** must be made to ensure that the stack is properly restored. If **va_end( )** is not called, a program crash is very likely.

Example

This program uses **sum_series( )** to return the sum of a series of numbers. The first argument contains a count of the number of arguments to follow. In this example, the first five elements of the following series are summed

$$\frac{1}{2} + \frac{1}{4} + \frac{1}{8} + \frac{1}{16} \dots + \frac{1}{2^n}$$

The output displayed is **Sum of series is 0.968750**.

```c
/* Variable length argument example - sum a series.*/

#include <stdio.h>
#include <stdarg.h>

double sum_series(int, ...);

int main(void)
{
  double d;

  d = sum_series(5, 0.5, 0.25, 0.125, 0.0625, 0.03125);
  printf("Sum of series is %f\n",d);

  return 0;
}

double sum_series(int num, ...)
{
  double sum = 0.0, t;
  va_list argptr;

  /* initialize argptr */
  va_start(argptr, num);

  /* sum the series */
  for(; num; num--) {
   t = va_arg(argptr,double);
   sum += t;
  }

  /* do orderly shutdown */
  va_end(argptr);
  return sum;
}
```

Related Function

vprintf( )

size_t wcstombs(char *out, const wchar_t *in, size_t size)

Description

The prototype for **wcstombs( )** is in **<stdlib.h>**.

The **wcstombs( )** converts the wide character string pointed to by *in* into its multibyte equivalent and puts the result in the string pointed to by *out*. Only the first *size* bytes of *in* are converted. Conversion stops before that if the null terminator is encountered.

If successful, **wcstombs( )** returns the number of bytes converted. On failure, −1 is returned.

Related Functions

wctomb( ), mbstowcs( )

int wctomb(char *out, wchar_t in)

Description

The prototype for **wctomb( )** is in **<stdlib.h>**.

The **wctomb( )** converts the wide character in *in* into its multibyte equivalent and puts the result in the string pointed to by *out*. The array pointed to by *out* must be at least **MB_CUR_MAX** characters long.

If successful, **wctomb( )** returns the number of bytes contained in the multibyte character. On failure, −1 is returned.

If *out* is NULL, then **wctomb( )** returns non-0 if the multibyte character has state dependencies and 0 if it does not.

Related Functions

wcstombs( ), mbtowc( )

The Complete Reference

Borland
C++
Builder

Part III

C++

Part One examined the C subset of C++. Part Three describes those features of the language specific to C++. That is, it discusses those features of C++ that it does not have in common with C. Because many of the C++ features are designed to support object-oriented programming (OOP), Part Three also provides a discussion of its theory and merits. We will begin with an overview of C++.

Chapter 20

An Overview of C++

Put simply, C++ is an *object-oriented* programming language. The object-oriented features of C++ are interrelated, so it is important to have a general understanding of these features before attempting to learn the details. The purpose of this chapter is to provide an overview of the key concepts embodied in C++. The rest of Part Three closely examines specific C++ features.

The Origins of C++

C++ began as an expanded version of C. The C++ extensions were first invented by Bjarne Stroustrup in 1979 at Bell Laboratories in Murray Hill, New Jersey. He initially called the new language "C with Classes." However, in 1983 the name was changed to C++.

Although C was one of the most liked and widely used professional programming languages in the world, the invention of C++ was necessitated by one major programming factor: increasing complexity. Over the years, computer programs have become larger and more complex. Even though C is an excellent programming language, it has its limits. In C, once a program exceeds somewhere around 25,000 lines of code, it becomes so complex that it is difficult to grasp as a totality. The purpose of C++ is to allow this barrier to be broken. The essence of C++ is to allow the programmer to comprehend and manage larger, more complex programs.

Most additions made by Stroustrup to C support object-oriented programming, sometimes referred to as OOP. (See the next section for a brief explanation of object-oriented programming.) Stroustrup states that some of C++'s object-oriented features were inspired by another object-oriented language called Simula67. Therefore, C++ represents the blending of two powerful programming methods.

Since C++ was first invented, it has undergone three major revisions, with each adding to and altering the language. The first revision was in 1985, and the second in 1990. The third occurred during the standardization of C++. Several years ago, work began on a standard for C++. Toward that end a joint ANSI (American National Standards Institute) and ISO (International Standards Organization) standardization committee was formed. The first draft of the proposed standard was created on January 25, 1994. In that draft, the ANSI/ISO C++ committee kept the features first defined by Stroustrup and added some new ones as well. But, in general, this initial draft reflected the state of C++ at the time.

Soon after the completion of the first draft of the C++ standard, an event occurred that caused the language to be greatly expanded: the creation of the Standard Template Library (STL) by Alexander Stepanov. The STL is a set of generic routines that you can use to manipulate data. It is both powerful and elegant. But it is also quite large. Subsequent to the first draft, the committee voted to include the STL in the specification for C++. The addition of the STL expanded the scope of C++ well beyond its original definition. While important, the inclusion of the STL, among other things, slowed the standardization of C++.

It is fair to say that the standardization of C++ took far longer than any one had expected when it began. In the process many new features were added to the language and many small changes were made. In fact, the version of C++ defined by the C++ committee is much larger and more complex than Stroustrup's original design. However, the standard is now complete. The final draft was passed out of committee on November 14, 1997. The final version was adopted as the ANSI/ISO Standard for C++ late in 1998. C++ Builder implements the ANSI/ISO Standard for C++.

What Is Object-Oriented Programming?

Object-oriented programming is a powerful way of approaching the job of programming. Programming methodologies have changed dramatically since the invention of the computer in order to accommodate the increasing complexity of programs. For example, when computers were first invented, programming was done by toggling in the binary machine instructions using the front panel. As long as programs were just a few hundred instructions long, this approach worked. As programs grew, assembly language was invented so that a programmer could deal with larger, increasingly complex programs using symbolic representations of the machine instructions.

Eventually high-level languages were introduced that gave the programmer more tools with which to handle complexity. The first widely used language was FORTRAN. While FORTRAN was a very impressive first step, it is hardly a language that encourages clear and easily understood programs.

The 1960s gave birth to *structured* programming—the method encouraged by languages such as C and Pascal. For the first time, with structured languages it was possible to write moderately complex programs fairly easily. However, even using structured programming methods, once a project reaches a certain size, its complexity becomes too difficult for a programmer to manage.

At each milestone in the development of programming, techniques and tools were created to allow the programmer to deal with increasingly greater complexity. Each step of the way, the new approach took the best elements of the previous methods and moved forward. Prior to the invention of OOP, many projects were nearing (or exceeding) the point where the structured approach no longer worked. To solve this problem, object-oriented programming was invented.

Object-oriented programming took the best ideas of structured programming and combined them with several new concepts. The result was a different way of organizing a program. In the most general sense, a program can be organized in one of two ways: around its code (what is happening) or around its data (who is being affected). Using only structured programming techniques, programs are typically organized around code. This approach can be thought of as "code acting on data." For example, a program written in a structured language such as C is defined by its functions, any of which may operate on any type of data used by the program.

Object-oriented programs work the other way around. They are organized around data, with the key principle being "data controlling access to code." In an object-oriented language, you define the data and the routines that are permitted to act on that data. Thus, a data type defines precisely what sort of operations can be applied to that data.

To support the principles of object-oriented programming, all OOP languages have three traits in common: encapsulation, polymorphism, and inheritance. Let's examine each.

Encapsulation

Encapsulation is the mechanism that binds together code and the data it manipulates, and keeps both safe from outside interference and misuse. In an object-oriented language, code and data may be combined in such a way that a self-contained "black box" is created. When code and data are linked together in this fashion, an *object* is created. In other words, an object is the device that supports encapsulation.

Within an object, code, data, or both may be *private* to that object or *public*. Private code or data is known to and accessible only by another part of the object. That is, private code or data may not be accessed by a piece of the program that exists outside the object. When code or data is public, other parts of your program may access it even though it is defined within an object. Typically, the public parts of an object are used to provide a controlled interface to the private elements of the object.

For all intents and purposes, an object is a variable of a user-defined type. It may seem strange at first to think of an object, which links both code and data, as a variable. However, in object-oriented programming, this is precisely the case. When you define an object, you are implicitly creating a new data type.

Polymorphism

Object-oriented programming languages support *polymorphism,* which is characterized by the phrase "one interface, multiple methods." In simple terms, polymorphism is the attribute that allows one interface to be used with a general class of actions. The specific action selected is determined by the exact nature of the situation. A real-world example of polymorphism is a thermostat. No matter what type of furnace your house has (gas, oil, electric, etc.), the thermostat works the same way. In this case, the thermostat (which is the interface) is the same no matter what type of furnace (method) you have. For example, if you want a 70-degree temperature, you set the thermostat to 70 degrees. It doesn't matter what type of furnace actually provides the heat.

This same principle can also apply to programming. For example, you might have a program that defines three different types of stacks. One stack is used for integer values, one for character values, and one for floating-point values. Because of polymorphism, you can create three sets of functions called **push( )** and **pop( )**—one set for each type of data. The general concept (interface) is that of pushing and popping data onto and from a stack. The functions define the specific ways (methods) this is done for each type of data. When you push data on the stack, it is the type of the data that will determine which specific version of the **push( )** function will be called.

Polymorphism helps reduce complexity by allowing the same interface to be used to specify a general class of actions. It is the compiler's job to select the *specific action* (i.e., method) as it applies to each situation. You, the programmer, don't need to do this selection manually. You need only remember and utilize the general interface.

The first object-oriented programming languages were interpreters, so polymorphism was supported at run time. However, because C++ is a compiled language, polymorphism is supported at both run time and compile time.

Inheritance

Inheritance is the process by which one object can acquire the properties of another object. This is important because it supports the concept of *classification.* If you think about it, most knowledge is made manageable by hierarchical classifications. For example, a Red Delicious apple is part of the *apple* class, which in turn is part of the *fruit* class, which is under the larger *food* class. Without the use of classifications, each object would have to define all of its characteristics explicitly. Using classifications, an object need only define those qualities that make it unique within its class. It is the inheritance mechanism that makes it possible for one object to be a specific instance of a more general case.

Some C++ Fundamentals

Since C++ is a superset of C, most C programs are C++ programs as well. (There are a few minor differences between C and C++ that will prevent certain types of C programs from being compiled by a C++ compiler. These differences will be discussed later in this book.) You can write C++ programs that look just like C programs, but you won't be taking full advantage of C++'s capabilities. Further, although C++ allows you to write C-like programs, most C++ programmers use a style and certain features that are unique to C++. Since it is important to use C++ to its full potential, this section introduces a few of these features before moving on to the "meat" of C++.

Let's begin with an example. Examine this C++ program:

```
#include <iostream>
using namespace std;

int main()
{
  int i;
  char str[80];
```

```
   cout << "I like C++ Builder.\n";  // this is a single-line comment
   /* you can still use C-style comments, too */

   // input a number using >>
   cout << "Enter a number: ";
   cin >> i;

   // now, output a number using <<
   cout << "Your number is " << i << "\n";

   // read a string
   cout << "Enter a string: ";
   cin >> str;
   // print it
   cout << str;

   return 0;
}
```

As you can see, this program looks different from the average C program. To begin, notice that the header **<iostream>** is included, not **<stdio.h>**. The **<iostream>** header is defined by C++ and supports the C++ I/O operations. Notice one other thing: there is no **.h** extension to the name **<iostream>**. The reason is that **<iostream>** is a modern, C++-style header, which does not use the **.h** extension.

The next line is

```
using namespace std;
```

This tells the compiler to use the **std** namespace. *Namespaces* are a relatively recent addition to C++. A namespace creates a declarative region in which various program elements can be placed. Namespaces help in the organization of large programs. The **using** statement informs the compiler that you want to use the **std** namespace. This is the namespace in which the entire Standard C++ library is declared. By using the **std** namespace, you simplify access to the standard library. The programs in Part One and Part Two, which use only the C subset, don't need a namespace statement because the C library functions are also available in the default, global namespace.

Note *Since both the new-style headers and namespaces are relatively recent additions to C++, you may encounter older code that does not use them. This will be especially likely if you are porting code developed under an older compiler.*

Now let's examine the declaration of **main( )**, which is defined like this

```
int main()
```

rather than the

```
int main(void)
```

that many of the programs in the preceding parts of this book have used. The reason for this is that in C++, an empty parameter list is the same as one specified as **void**. That is, the preceding two ways to declare **main( )** are the same as far as C++ is concerned. In C++, the use of **void** to indicate an empty parameter list is still permitted, but it is redundant. Since it's not needed, none of the C++ programs shown in this part of the book will use **void** to indicate an empty parameter list.

The following line introduces several C++ features:

```
cout << "I like C++ Builder.\n";   // this is a single line comment
```

This line has two parts. First, the statement

```
cout << "I like C++ Builder.\n";
```

displays "I like C++ Builder." on the screen followed by a carriage return, linefeed combination. In C++, the << has an expanded role. It is still the left-shift operator, but when it is used as shown in this example, it is also an output operator. The word **cout** is an identifier that is linked to the screen. Like C, C++ supports I/O redirection, but for the sake of discussion, we can assume that **cout** refers to the screen. You can use **cout** and the << to output any of the built-in data types plus strings of characters.

It is important to note that you can still use **printf( )** or any other of C's I/O functions, but most programmers feel that using **cout <<** is more in the spirit of C++. More generally, a C++ program can use any library function supported by C++ Builder—including those defined by C. (These functions are described in Part Two of this book.) However, in cases where C++ provides an alternative approach, it should usually be used instead of a C-like library function (although there is no rule that enforces this).

The second part of the line is a C++-style comment. In C++, two types of comments are supported. First, you can use a C-like /*...*/ comment, which works the same in C++ as it does in C. Second, you can define a *single-line comment* using //. When you start a comment using //, whatever follows is ignored by the compiler until the end of the line is reached. In general, use C-like comments when creating multiline comments and use single-line comments when only a short comment is needed.

Next, the program prompts the user for a number. The number is read from the keyboard using this statement:

```
cin >> i;
```

In C++, the **>>** operator retains its right-shift meaning, but when used as shown, it causes **i** to be given a value read from the keyboard. The identifier **cin** refers to the keyboard. In general you can use **cin >>** to load a variable of any of the basic data types or a string.

Although this fact is not illustrated by the program, you are free to use any of C's input functions, such as **scanf( )**, instead of using **cin >>**. However, as with **cout**, the vast majority of programmers feel that **cin >>** is more in the spirit of C++.

Another interesting line in the program is shown here:

```
cout << "Your number is " << i << "\n";
```

This code displays the following phrase (assuming **i** has the value 100):

```
Your number is 100
```

followed by a carriage return and linefeed. In general, you can run together as many **<<** output operations as you want.

The rest of the program demonstrates how you can read and write a string using **cin >>** and **cout <<**. When inputting a string, **cin >>** stops reading when the first white-space character is encountered. This is similar to the way the standard C function **scanf( )** works when inputting a string.

C++ Programs Use the .CPP Extension

Like all C++ compilers, C++ Builder can compile both C and C++ programs. In general, if a program ends in .CPP it is compiled as a C++ program. If it ends in .C, it is compiled as a C program. Therefore, the simplest way to cause C++ Builder to compile your C++ program as a C++ program is to give it the .CPP extension. This is important because attempting to compile a C++ program *as if it were a C program* will cause compilation errors.

Note   *For information on compiling C++ programs, see Part 4.*

A Closer Look at Headers and Namespaces

As explained earlier, C++ went through many changes before being standardized in 1998. In the course of these changes, many features were added to the language. Of these, two affect the way nearly all programs are written: modern-style headers and **namespace** statements. As they are relatively new additions to C++, old-style, prestandard C++ supports neither of them. Of course, there are millions and millions of lines of existing, old-style code. For the sake of compatibility with this older code, most C++ compilers, including C++ Builder, continue to support the old approach. However, for new code, you should use the modern approach, as the code in this book does.

Since the key differences between old-style and modern code involve headers and the **namespace** statement, a brief discussion of these features is warranted at this time. This discussion is especially important if you will be bringing older code up-to-date.

Modern-Style Headers

As you know, when you use a library function in a program, you must include its header file. This is done using the **#include** statement. For example, in C, to include the header file for the I/O functions, you include **stdio.h** with a statement like this:

```
#include <stdio.h>
```

Here, **stdio.h** is (for all practical purposes) the name of the file used by the I/O functions, and the preceding statement causes that file to be included in your program. The key point is that this **#include** statement almost always specifies *a file*.

When C++ was first invented and for several years after that, it used the same style of headers that C uses. That is, it used *header files.* In fact, Standard C++ still supports C-style headers for header files that you create and for backward compatibility. However, Standard C++ created a new kind of header that is used by the Standard C++ library. The new style headers *do not* specify filenames. Instead, they simply specify standard identifiers that may be mapped to files by the compiler but need not be. The new-style C++ headers are an abstraction that simply guarantees that the appropriate prototypes and definitions required by the C++ library have been declared.

Since the new-style headers are not filenames, they do not have a **.h** extension. They consist solely of the header name contained between angle brackets. For example, here are some of the new-style headers supported by C++.

<iostream> <fstream> <vector> <string>

Like the old-style headers, the new-style headers are included using the **#include** statement.

It is important to understand that ANSI/ISO Standard C++ does not support the older, **.h** headers. Thus, a program that uses an old-style header is technically nonstandard. As mentioned, C++ Builder supports the old-style headers for the sake of compatibility with older code, but for new code you should use the modern headers.

Because C++ includes the entire C function library, it still supports the standard C-style header files associated with that library. That is, header files such as **<stdio.h>** or **<ctype.h>** are still available. However, Standard C++ also defines new-style headers that you can use in place of these header files. The C++ versions of the C standard headers simply add a **c** prefix to the filename and drop the **.h**. For example, the C++ new-style header for **<math.h>** is **<cmath>**. The one for **<string.h>** is **<cstring>**. Although it is currently permissible to include a C-style header file when using C library functions, this approach is deprecated by Standard C++ (that is, it is not recommended). For this reason, Part Three of this book will use modern C++ headers in all **#include** statements.

Namespaces

When you include a modern C++ header in your program, the contents of that header are contained in the **std** namespace. As mentioned, a *namespace* is simply a declarative region. The purpose of a namespace is to localize the names of identifiers to avoid name collisions. Elements declared in one namespace are separate from elements declared in another. Originally, the names of the C++ library functions, etc., were simply put into the global namespace (as they are in C). However, with the advent of the ANSI/ISO C++ standard and the modern-style headers, the contents of the headers are in the **std** namespace. We will look at namespaces in detail later in this book. For now, you won't need to worry about them because the statement

```
using namespace std;
```

brings the **std** namespace into visibility (i.e., it puts **std** into the global namespace).

One other point: for the sake of compatibility, when a C++ program includes a C header, such as **<stdio.h>**, its contents are put into the global namespace. This allows a C++ compiler to compile C-subset programs.

Introducing C++ Classes

The **class** is at the root of C++. Before you can create an object in C++, you must first define its general form using the keyword **class**. A **class** is similar syntactically to a structure. As an example, this **class** defines a type called **queue**, which will be used to implement a queue:

```
// This creates the class queue.
class queue {
  int q[100];
  int sloc, rloc;
public:
  void init();
  void qput(int i);
  int qget();
};
```

A **class** can contain private as well as public parts. By default, all items defined in the **class** are private. For example, the variables **q, sloc,** and **rloc** are private, meaning they cannot be accessed by any function that is not a member of the **class**. This is how encapsulation is achieved—access to certain items of data is tightly controlled by keeping them private. Although not shown in this example, you can also define private functions, which can only be called by other members of the **class**.

To make parts of a **class** public (accessible to other parts of your program), you must declare them after the **public** keyword. All variables or functions defined after **public** are accessible by all other functions in the program. Generally, the rest of your program accesses an object through its **public** functions. Although you can have **public** variables, you should try to limit or eliminate their use. Instead, you should make all data private and control access to it through **public** functions. Thus, public functions provide the interface to your class's private data. This helps preserve encapsulation. One other point: Notice that the **public** keyword is followed by a colon.

The functions **init( )**, **qput( )**, and **qget( )** are called *member functions* because they are part of the **class queue**. The variables **sloc, rloc,** and **q** are called *member variables* (or *data members*). Only member functions have access to the private members of the **class** in which they are declared. Thus, only **init( )**, **qput( )**, and **qget( )** have access to **sloc, rloc,** and **q**.

Once you have defined a **class**, you can create an object of that type using the **class** name. In essence, the **class**'s name becomes a new data type specifier. For example, this code creates an object called **intqueue** of type **queue**:

```
queue intqueue;
```

You can also create objects when defining a **class** by putting the variable names after the closing curly brace, in exactly the same way as you do with a structure.

The general form of a **class** declaration is

class *class-name* {
    private data and functions
public:
    public data and functions
} *object-list;*

Of course, the *object-list* may be empty.

Inside the declaration of **queue**, prototypes to the member functions are used. In C++, when you need to tell the compiler about a function, you must use its full prototype form. Further, in C++, all functions must be prototyped. Prototypes are not optional, as they are in C.

When it comes time to actually code a function that is a member of a class, you must tell the compiler to which class the function belongs. For example, here is one way to code the **qput( )** function:

```
void queue::qput(int i)
{
  if(sloc==99) {
    cout << "Queue is full.\n";
    return;
  }
  sloc++;
  q[sloc] = i;
}
```

The **::** is called the *scope resolution operator.* Essentially, it tells the compiler that this version of **qput( )** belongs to the **queue** class or, put differently, that this **qput( )** is in **queue**'s scope. In C++, several different classes can use the same function names. The compiler knows which function belongs to which class because of the scope resolution operator and the class name.

To call a member function from a part of your program that is not a member of the class, you must use an object's name and the dot operator. For example, this fragment calls **init( )** for object **a**:

```
queue a, b;

a.init();
```

It is very important to understand that **a** and **b** are two separate objects. This means that initializing **a** does not cause **b** to be initialized. The only relationship **a** has with **b** is that they are objects of the same type. Further, **a**'s copies of **sloc**, **rloc**, and **q** are completely separate from **b**'s.

Only when a member function is called by code that does not belong to the **class** must the object name and the dot operator be used. Otherwise, one member function can call another member function directly, without using the dot operator. Also, a member function can refer directly to member variables without the use of the dot operator.

The program shown here demonstrates all the pieces of **queue** class.

```
#include <iostream>
using namespace std;

// This creates the class queue.
class queue {
  int q[100];
  int sloc, rloc;
public:
  void init();
  void qput(int i);
  int qget();
};

void queue::init()
{
  rloc = sloc = 0;
}

void queue::qput(int i)
{
  if(sloc==99) {
    cout << "Queue is full.\n";
    return;
  }
  sloc++;
  q[sloc] = i;
}

int queue::qget()
{
  if(rloc == sloc) {
    cout << "Queue underflow.\n";
    return 0;
```

```
    }
    rloc++;
    return q[rloc];
}

int main()
{
  queue a, b;   // create two queue objects

  // now, access the queues through their member functions
  a.init();
  b.init();

  a.qput(10);
  b.qput(19);

  a.qput(20);
  b.qput(1);

  cout << a.qget() << " ";
  cout << a.qget() << " ";
  cout << b.qget() << " ";
  cout << b.qget() << "\n";

  return 0;
}
```

Remember that the private members of an object are accessible only by functions that are also members of that object. For example, the statement

```
a.rloc = 0;
```

could not be in the **main( )** function of the previous program because **rloc** is private.

Note   *By convention, in most C programs the **main( )** function is the first function in the program. However, in the **queue** program the member functions of **queue** are defined before the **main( )** function. While there is no rule that dictates this (they could be defined anywhere in the program), this is the most common approach used when writing C++ code. (In fact, classes and the member functions associated with them are usually contained in a header file.)*

Function Overloading

One way that C++ achieves polymorphism is through the use of *function overloading*. In C++, two or more functions can share the same name as long as their parameter declarations are different. In this situation, the functions that share the same name are said to be *overloaded*. For example, consider this program:

```
#include <iostream>
using namespace std;

// sqr_it is overloaded three ways
int sqr_it(int i);
double sqr_it(double d);
long sqr_it(long l);

int main()
{
  cout << sqr_it(10) << "\n";
  cout << sqr_it(11.0) << "\n";
  cout << sqr_it(9L) << "\n";

  return 0;
}

// Define sqr_it for ints.
int sqr_it(int i)
{
  cout << "Inside the sqr_it() function that uses ";
  cout << "an integer argument.\n";

  return i*i;
}

// Overload sqr_it for doubles.
double sqr_it(double d)
{
  cout << "Inside the sqr_it() function that uses ";
  cout << "a double argument.\n";

  return d*d;
}
```

```
// Overload sqr_it again, this time for longs.
long sqr_it(long l)
{
  cout << "Inside the sqr_it() function that uses ";
  cout << "a long argument.\n";

  return l*l;
}
```

This program creates three similar but different functions called **sqr_it( )**, each of which returns the square of its argument. As the program illustrates, the compiler knows which function to use in each case because of the type of the argument. The value of overloaded functions is that they allow related sets of functions to be accessed using a common name. In a sense, function overloading lets you create a generic name for an operation; the compiler resolves which function is actually needed to perform the operation.

Function overloading is important because it can help manage complexity. To understand how, consider this example. C++ Builder contains the functions **itoa( )**, **ltoa( )**, and **ultoa( )** in its standard library. Collectively, these functions convert different types of numbers (integers, long integers, and unsigned integers) into their string equivalents. Even though these functions perform almost identical actions, in C three different names must be used to represent these tasks, which makes the situation more complex than it actually is. Even though the underlying concept of each function is the same, the programmer has three things to remember. However, in C++ it is possible to use the same name, such as **numtoa( )**, for all three functions. Thus, the name **numtoa( )** represents the *general action* that is being performed. It is left to the compiler to choose the *specific* version for a particular circumstance; the programmer need only remember the general action being performed. Therefore, by applying polymorphism, three things to remember are reduced to one. If you expand the concept, you can see how polymorphism can help you manage very complex programs.

A more practical example of function overloading is illustrated by the following program. There are no library functions that prompt the user for input and then wait for a response, but it is possible to create one. This program creates three functions called **prompt( )** that perform this task for data of types **int**, **double**, and **long**:

```
#include <iostream>
using namespace std;

void prompt(char *str, int *i);
void prompt(char *str, double *d);
void prompt(char *str, long *l);
```

```
int main()
{
  int i;
  double d;
  long l;

  prompt("Enter an integer: ", &i);
  prompt("Enter a double: ", &d);
  prompt("Enter a long: ", &l);

  cout << i << " " << d << " " << l;

  return 0;
}

// Prompt for an int.
void prompt(char *str, int *i)
{
  cout << str;
  cin >> *i;
}

// Prompt for a double.
void prompt(char *str, double *d)
{
  cout << str;
  cin >> *d;
}

// Prompt for a long.
void prompt(char *str, long *l)
{
  cout << str;
  cin >> *l;
}
```

You can use the same name to overload unrelated functions, but you should not. For example, you could use the name **sqr_it( )** to create functions that return the square of an **int** and the square root of a **double**. However, these two operations are fundamentally different, and applying function overloading in this manner defeats its purpose. In practice, you should only overload closely related operations.

Operator Overloading

Another way that polymorphism is achieved in C++ is through *operator overloading*. For example, in C++ you can use the **<<** and **>>** operators to perform console I/O operations. This is possible because in the **<iostream>** header, these operators are overloaded. When an operator is overloaded, it takes on an additional meaning relative to a certain class. However, it still retains all of its old meanings.

In general, you can overload C++'s operators by defining what they mean relative to a specific class. For example, think back to the **queue** class developed earlier in this chapter. It is possible to overload the **+** operator relative to objects of type **queue** so that it appends the contents of one queue to another. However, the **+** still retains its original meaning relative to other types of data.

Because operator overloading is, in practice, somewhat more complicated than function overloading, examples are deferred until Chapter 22, when the subject is covered in detail.

Inheritance

Inheritance is one of the major traits of an object-oriented programming language. In C++, inheritance is supported by allowing one class to incorporate another class into its declaration. Inheritance allows a hierarchy of classes to be built, moving from most general to most specific. The process involves first defining a *base class*, which defines those qualities common to all objects to be derived from the base. The base class represents the most general description. The classes derived from the base are usually referred to as *derived classes*. A derived class includes all features of the generic base class and then adds qualities specific to itself. To demonstrate how this process works, the next example creates classes that categorize different types of vehicles.

To begin, here is a class, called **road_vehicle**, that very broadly defines vehicles that travel on the road. It stores the number of wheels a vehicle has and the number of passengers it can carry.

```
class road_vehicle {
  int wheels;
  int passengers;
public:
  void set_wheels(int num);
  int get_wheels();
  void set_pass(int num);
  int get_pass();
};
```

We can now use this broad definition of a road vehicle to define specific objects. For example, this declares a class called **truck** using **road_vehicle**.

```
class truck : public road_vehicle {
  int cargo;
public:
  void set_cargo(int size);
  int get_cargo();
  void show();
};
```

Notice how **road_vehicle** is inherited. The general form for inheritance is:

class *new-class-name* : *access inherited-class* {
    // body of new class
}

Here, *access* is optional, but if present it must be either **public**, **private**, or **protected**. You will learn more about these options in Chapter 23. For now, all inherited classes will use **public**, which means that all the **public** elements of the ancestor are also **public** in the class that inherits it. Therefore, in the example, members of the class **truck** have access to the member functions of **road_vehicle** just as if they had been declared inside **truck**. However, the member functions of **truck** *do not* have access to the private elements of **road_vehicle**.

The following program illustrates inheritance by creating two subclasses of **road_vehicle**: **truck** and **automobile**:

```
#include <iostream>
using namespace std;

class road_vehicle {
  int wheels;
  int passengers;
public:
  void set_wheels(int num);
  int get_wheels();
  void set_pass(int num);
  int get_pass();
};

// Extend road_vehicle for trucks.
class truck : public road_vehicle {
  int cargo;
public:
  void set_cargo(int size);
  int get_cargo();
```

```
  void show();
};

enum type {car, van, wagon};

// Extend road_vehicle for cars.
class automobile : public road_vehicle {
  enum type car_type;
public:
  void set_type(enum type t);
  enum type get_type();
  void show();
};

void road_vehicle::set_wheels(int num)
{
  wheels = num;
}

int road_vehicle::get_wheels()
{
  return wheels;
}

void road_vehicle::set_pass(int num)
{
  passengers = num;
}

int road_vehicle::get_pass()
{
  return passengers;
}

void truck::set_cargo(int num)
{
  cargo = num;
}

int truck::get_cargo()
{
  return cargo;
```

```
}

void truck::show()
{
  cout << "Wheels: " << get_wheels() << "\n";
  cout << "Passengers: " << get_pass() << "\n";
  cout << "Cargo capacity in cubic feet: " << cargo << "\n";
}

void automobile::set_type(enum type t)
{
  car_type = t;
}

enum type automobile::get_type()
{
  return car_type;
}

void automobile::show()
{
  cout << "Wheels: " << get_wheels() << "\n";
  cout << "Passengers: " << get_pass() << "\n";
  cout << "Type: ";
  switch(get_type()) {
    case van: cout << "Van\n";
      break;
    case car: cout << "Car\n";
      break;
    case wagon: cout << "Wagon\n";
  }
}

int main()
{
  truck t1, t2;
  automobile c;

  t1.set_wheels(18);
  t1.set_pass(2);
  t1.set_cargo(3200);
```

```
     t2.set_wheels(6);
     t2.set_pass(3);
     t2.set_cargo(1200);

     t1.show();
     t2.show();

     c.set_wheels(4);
     c.set_pass(6);
     c.set_type(van);
     c.show();

     return 0;
}
```

As this program illustrates, the major advantage of inheritance is that you can create a base classification that can be incorporated into more specific classes. In this way, each object can represent its own classification precisely.

Notice that both **truck** and **automobile** include member functions called **show( )**, which display information about each object. This is another aspect of polymorphism. Since each **show( )** is linked with its own class, the compiler can easily tell which one to call in any circumstance.

Constructors and Destructors

It is not unusual for some part of an object to require initialization before it can be used. For example, think back to the **queue** class developed earlier in this chapter. Before **queue** could be used, the variables **rloc** and **sloc** had to be set to 0 using the function **init( )**. Because the requirement for initialization is so common, C++ allows objects to initialize themselves when they are created. This automatic initialization is performed through the use of a constructor.

A *constructor* is a special function that is a member of a class and has the same name as that class. For example, here is how the **queue** class looks when converted to use a constructor function for initialization:

```
// This creates the class queue.
class queue {
   int q[100];
   int sloc, rloc;
public:
```

```
    queue();  // constructor
    void qput(int i);
    int qget();
};
```

Notice that the constructor **queue( )** has no return type specified. In C++, constructors cannot return values.

The **queue( )** function is coded like this:

```
// This is the constructor function.
queue::queue()
{
  sloc = rloc = 0;
  cout << "Queue initialized.\n";
}
```

Keep in mind that the message "Queue initialized." is output as a way to illustrate the constructor. In actual practice, most constructors will not output or input anything. They will simply perform various initializations.

An object's constructor is automatically called when the object is created. This means that it is called when the object's declaration is executed. There is an important distinction between a C-like declaration statement and a C++ declaration. In C, variable declarations are, loosely speaking, passive and resolved mostly at compile time. Put differently, in C, variable declarations are not thought of as being executable statements. However, in C++, variable declarations are active statements that are, in fact, executed at run time. One reason for this is that an object declaration may need to call a constructor, thus causing the execution of a function. Although this difference may seem subtle and largely academic at this point, it has some important implications relative to variable initialization, as you will see later.

An object's constructor is called once for global or **static** local objects. For local objects, the constructor is called each time the object declaration is encountered.

The complement of the constructor is the *destructor*. In many circumstances, an object needs to perform some action or actions when it is destroyed. Local objects are created when their block is entered and destroyed when the block is left. Global objects are destroyed when the program terminates. There are many reasons why a destructor may be needed. For example, an object may need to deallocate memory that it had previously allocated. In C++, it is the destructor that handles deactivation. The destructor has the same name as the constructor but is preceded by a ~. The following is an example of **queue** that uses a constructor and a destructor. (Keep in mind that the **queue** class does not require a destructor, so the one shown here is just for illustration.)

```
// This creates the class queue.
class queue {
  int q[100];
  int sloc, rloc;
public:
  queue();  // constructor
  ~queue(); // destructor
  void qput(int i);
  int qget();
};

// This is the constructor function.
queue::queue()
{
  sloc = rloc = 0;
  cout << "Queue initialized.\n";
}

// This is the destructor function.
queue::~queue()
{
  cout << "Queue destroyed.\n";
}
```

To see how constructors and destructors work, here is a new version of the **queue** sample program from earlier in this chapter:

```
#include <iostream>
using namespace std;

// This creates the class queue.
class queue {
  int q[100];
  int sloc, rloc;
public:
  queue();  // constructor
  ~queue(); // destructor
  void qput(int i);
  int qget();
};

// This is the constructor function.
```

```
queue::queue()
{
  sloc = rloc = 0;
  cout << "Queue initialized.\n";
}

// This is the destructor function.
queue::~queue()
{
  cout << "Queue destroyed.\n";
}

void queue::qput(int i)
{
  if(sloc==99) {
    cout << "Queue is full.\n";
    return;
  }
  sloc++;
  q[sloc] = i;
}

int queue::qget()
{
  if(rloc == sloc) {
    cout << "Queue underflow.\n";
    return 0;
  }
  rloc++;
  return q[rloc];
}

int main()
{
  queue a, b;  // create two queue objects

  a.qput(10);
  b.qput(19);

  a.qput(20);
  b.qput(1);
```

```
cout << a.qget() << " ";
cout << a.qget() << " ";
cout << b.qget() << " ";
cout << b.qget() << "\n";

return 0;
}
```

This program displays the following:

```
Queue initialized.
Queue initialized.
10 20 19 1
Queue destroyed.
Queue destroyed.
```

The C++ Keywords

There are 63 keywords currently defined by Standard C++. These are shown in
Table 20-1. Remember that you cannot use any of the keywords as names for variables
or functions. C++ Builder also defines a few special-purpose, nonstandard keywords,
such as _ _rtti and _ _classid, which can be used in nonportable programs.

asm	auto	bool	break
case	catch	char	class
const	const_cast	continue	default
delete	do	double	dynamic_cast
else	enum	explicit	export
extern	false	float	for
friend	goto	if	inline
int	long	mutable	namespace
new	operator	private	protected
public	register	reinterpret_cast	return

Table 20-1. *The Standard C++ Keywords*

short	signed	sizeof	static
static_cast	struct	switch	template
this	throw	true	try
typedef	typeid	typename	union
unsigned	using	virtual	void
volatile	wchar_t	while	

Table 20-1.   *The Standard C++ Keywords* (continued)

Two New Data Types

In looking at the list of keywords in Table 20-1, you may have noticed **bool** and **wchar_t**. The **bool** data type is capable of holding a Boolean value. Objects of type **bool** may have only the values **true** and **false**. The values **true** and **false** are also keywords that are part of the C++ language. Values of type **bool** are automatically elevated to integers when used in a non-Boolean expression. Although C++ defines the **bool** data type, it still fully supports the fundamental concept of nonzero values being true and zero being false.

The type **wchar_t** holds wide characters. They are used to represent the character sets of languages that have more than 255 characters. The **wchar_t** is supported in C as a defined type using **typedef**. In C++, it has become a keyword.

Now that you have been introduced to many of C++'s major features, the remaining chapters in this section will examine C++ in detail.

C++

The Complete Reference

Borland
C++
Builder

Chapter 21

A Closer Look at Classes and Objects

lasses and objects are two of C++'s most important features. This chapter examines them and related issues in detail.

Parameterized Constructors

It is possible to pass arguments to constructors. Typically, these arguments are used to initialize an object when it is created. To create a parameterized constructor, simply add parameters to it the way you would to any other function. When you define the constructor's body, use the parameters to initialize the object. For example, it is possible to enhance the **queue** class that ended the previous chapter to accept an argument that will act as the queue's ID number. First, **queue** is changed to look like this:

```
// This creates the class queue.
class queue {
  int q[100];
  int sloc, rloc;
  int who; // holds the queue's ID number
public:
  queue(int id);  // parameterized constructor
  ~queue(); // destructor
  void qput(int i);
  int qget();
};
```

The variable **who** is used to hold an ID number that identifies the queue. Its value is determined by the argument passed to **id** when a variable of type **queue** is created. The **queue( )** constructor function now looks like this:

```
// This is the constructor function.
queue::queue(int id)
{
  sloc = rloc = 0;
  who = id;
  cout << "Queue " << who << " initialized\n";
}
```

To pass an argument to the constructor, you must specify its value when an object is declared. C++ has two ways to accomplish this. The first method is shown here.

```
queue a = queue(101);
```

This calls the **queue** class's constructor directly, passing the value 101 to it. The object returned by the constructor is assigned to **a**.

The second method is shorter and more to the point. In this method, the argument or arguments must follow the object's name and be enclosed in parentheses. This code accomplishes the same thing as the previous declaration:

```
queue a(101);
```

Since this method is used by virtually all C++ programmers, it is used by this book nearly exclusively.

The general form of passing arguments to constructor functions is

class-type obj(arg-list);

Here, *arg-list* is a comma-separated list of arguments that are passed to the constructor.

The following version of the **queue** program demonstrates passing arguments to constructor functions:

```
#include <iostream>
using namespace std;

// This creates the class queue.
class queue {
  int q[100];
  int sloc, rloc;
  int who; // holds the queue's ID number
public:
  queue(int id);  // parameterized constructor
  ~queue(); // destructor
  void qput(int i);
  int qget();
};

// This is the constructor function.
queue::queue(int id)
{
  sloc = rloc = 0;
  who = id;
  cout << "Queue " << who << " initialized.\n";
}

// This is the destructor function.
```

```
queue::~queue()
{
  cout << "Queue " << who << " destroyed.\n";
}

void queue::qput(int i)
{
  if(sloc==99) {
    cout << "Queue is full.\n";
    return;
  }
  sloc++;
  q[sloc] = i;
}

int queue::qget()
{
  if(rloc == sloc) {
    cout << "Queue underflow.\n";
    return 0;
  }
  rloc++;
  return q[rloc];
}

int main()
{
  queue a(1), b(2);  // create two queue objects

  a.qput(10);
  b.qput(19);

  a.qput(20);
  b.qput(1);

  cout << a.qget() << " ";
  cout << a.qget() << " ";
  cout << b.qget() << " ";
  cout << b.qget() << "\n";

  return 0;
}
```

This program produces the following output:

```
Queue 1 initialized.
Queue 2 initialized.
10 20 19 1
Queue 2 destroyed.
Queue 1 destroyed.
```

As you can see by looking at **main( )**, the queue associated with **a** is given the ID number 1, and the queue associated with **b** is given the number 2.

Although the **queue** example passes only a single argument when an object is created, it is possible to pass several. Here, for example, objects of type **widget** are passed two values:

```
#include <iostream>
using namespace std;

class widget {
  int i;
  int j;
public:
  widget(int a, int b);
  void put_widget();
} ;

widget::widget(int a, int b)
{
  i = a;
  j = b;
}

void widget::put_widget()
{
  cout << i << " " << j << "\n";
}

int main()
{
  widget x(10, 20), y(0, 0);

  x.put_widget();
  y.put_widget();
```

```
    return 0;
}
```

This program displays

```
10 20
0 0
```

Constructors with One Parameter: A Special Case

If a constructor has only one parameter, then there is a third way to pass an initial value to that constructor. For example, consider the following short program.

```
#include <iostream>
using namespace std;

class X {
  int a;
public:
  X(int j) { a = j; }
  int geta() { return a; }
};

int main()
{
  X ob = 99; // passes 99 to j

  cout << ob.geta(); // outputs 99

  return 0;
}
```

Here, the constructor for **X** takes one parameter. Pay special attention to how **ob** is declared in **main( )**. In this form of initialization, 99 is automatically passed to the **j** parameter in the **X( )** constructor. That is, this statement

```
X ob = 99; // passes 99 to j
```

is handled by the compiler as if it were written like this:

```
X ob = X(99);
```

In general, any time that you have a constructor that requires only one argument, you can use either *ob(i)* or *ob = i* to initialize an object. The reason for this is that whenever you create a constructor that takes one argument, you are also implicitly creating a conversion from the type of that argument to the type of the class.

Remember that the alternative shown here applies only to constructors that have exactly one parameter.

Friend Functions

It is possible for a nonmember function to have access to the private members of a class by declaring it as a **friend** of the class. For example, here **frd( )** is declared to be a **friend** of the class **cl**:

```
class cl {
  // ...
public:
  friend void frd();
  // ...
};
```

As you can see, the keyword **friend** precedes the entire function declaration.

One reason that **friend** functions are allowed in C++ is to accommodate situations in which, for the sake of efficiency, two classes must share the same function. To see an example, consider a program that defines two classes called **line** and **box**. The class **line** contains all necessary data and code to draw a horizontal dashed line of any specified length, beginning at a specified *x,y* coordinate using a specified color. The **box** class contains all code and data to draw a box at the specified upper-left and lower-right coordinates in a specified color. Both classes use the **same_color( )** function to determine whether a line and a box are drawn in the same color. These classes are declared as shown here:

```
class line;

class box {
  int color; // color of box
  int upx, upy; // upper left corner
  int lowx, lowy; // lower right corner
public:
  friend int same_color(line l, box b);
  void set_color(int c);
  void define_box(int x1, int y1, int x2, int y2);
  void show_box();
```

```
} ;

class line {
  int color; // color of line
  int startx, starty; // coordinates
  int len; // length
public:
  friend int same_color(line l, box b);
  void set_color(int c);
  void define_line(int x, int y, int l);
  void show_line();
} ;
```

The **same_color( )** function, which is a member of neither class but a **friend** of both, returns true if both the **line** object and the **box** object, which form its arguments, are drawn in the same color; it returns 0 otherwise. The **same_color( )** function is defined as:

```
// Return true if line and box have same color.
int same_color(line l, box b)
{
  if(l.color==b.color) return 1;
  return 0;
}
```

As you can see, the **same_color( )** function needs access to the private members of both **line** and **box** to perform its task efficiently. Being a **friend** of each class grants it this access privilege. Further, notice that because **same_color( )** is not a member, no scope resolution operator or class name is used in its definition. (Remember that **public** functions can be created to return the colors of both **line** and **box**, and any function could have compared their colors. However, such an approach requires extra function calls, which in some cases is inefficient.)

Notice the empty declaration of **line** at the start of the **class** declarations. Since **same_color( )** in **box** refers to **line** before **line** is declared, **line** must be forward referenced. If this is not done, the compiler will not know about **line** when it is encountered in the declaration of **box**. In C++, a forward reference to a class is simply the keyword **class** followed by the type name of the class.

Here is a program that demonstrates the **line** and **box** classes and illustrates how a **friend** function can access the private members of a class. (This program must be run in a console session under Windows.)

```
#include <iostream>
#include <conio.h>
using namespace std;

class line;

class box {
  int color; // color of box
  int upx, upy; // upper left corner
  int lowx, lowy; // lower right corner
 public:
  friend int same_color(line l, box b);
  void set_color(int c);
  void define_box(int x1, int y1, int x2, int y2);
  void show_box();
} ;

class line {
  int color; // color of line
  int startx, starty; // coordinates
  int len; // length
public:
  friend int same_color(line l, box b);
  void set_color(int c);
  void define_line(int x, int y, int l);
  void show_line();
} ;

// Return true if line and box have same color.
int same_color(line l, box b)
{
  if(l.color==b.color) return 1;
  return 0;
}

void box::set_color(int c)
{
  color = c;
}

void line::set_color(int c)
```

```
{
  color = c;
}

void box::define_box(int x1, int y1, int x2, int y2)
{
  upx = x1;
  upy = y1;
  lowx = x2;
  lowy = y2;
}

void box::show_box()
{
  int i;

  textcolor(color);

  gotoxy(upx, upy);
  for(i=upx; i<=lowx; i++) cprintf("-");

  gotoxy(upx, lowy-1);
  for(i=upx; i<=lowx; i++) cprintf("-");

  gotoxy(upx, upy);
  for(i=upy; i<=lowy; i++) {
    cprintf("|");
    gotoxy(upx, i);
  }

  gotoxy(lowx, upy);
  for(i=upy; i<=lowy; i++) {
    cprintf("|");
    gotoxy(lowx, i);
  }
}

void line::define_line(int x, int y, int l)
{
  startx = x;
```

```
    starty = y;
    len = l;
}

void line::show_line()
{
    int i;

    textcolor(color);

    gotoxy(startx, starty);

    for(i=0; i<len; i++) cprintf("-");
}

int main()
{
    box b;
    line l;

    b.define_box(10, 10, 15, 15);
    b.set_color(3);
    b.show_box();

    l.define_line(2, 2, 10);
    l.set_color(2);
    l.show_line();

    if(!same_color(l, b)) cout << "Not the same.\n";
    cout << "\nPress a key.";
    getch();

    // now, make line and box the same color
    l.define_line(2, 2, 10);
    l.set_color(3);
    l.show_line();

    if(same_color(l, b)) cout << "Are the same color.\n";

    return 0;
}
```

Notice that **same_color( )** is not called on an object, using the dot operator. As a **friend**, it cannot be called on an object the way a member function is. Usually, **friend** functions are passed the objects that they will operate on, as is the case with **same_color( )**.

There are two important restrictions that apply to **friend** functions. First, a derived class does not inherit **friend** functions. Second, **friend** functions may not have a storage-class specifier. That is, they may not be declared as **static** or **extern**.

Default Function Arguments

C++ allows a function to assign a default value to a parameter when no argument corresponding to that parameter is specified in a call to that function. The default value is specified in a manner syntactically similar to a variable initialization. For example, this declares **f( )** as taking one integer variable that has a default value of 1:

```
void f(int i = 1)
{
  // ...
}
```

Now, **f( )** can be called one of two ways, as these examples show.

```
f(10);  // pass an explicit value
f();    // let function use default
```

The first call passes the value 10 to **i**. The second call gives **i** the default value 1.

Default arguments in C++ enable a programmer to manage greater complexity. In order to handle the widest variety of situations, a function frequently contains more parameters than are required for its most common use. When using default arguments, you need only specify arguments that are not the defaults in that particular situation.

To better understand the reason for default arguments, let's develop a practical example. One useful function, called **xyout( )**, is shown here:

```
//Output a string at specified X,Y location.
void xyout(char *str, int x = 0, int y = 0)
{
  if(!x) x = wherex();
  if(!y) y = wherey();
  gotoxy(x, y);
  cout << str;
}
```

This function displays the string pointed to by **str** beginning at the *x,y* location defined by **x** and **y**. However, if neither **x** nor **y** are specified, the string is output at the current *x,y* location. (You can think of this function as an advanced version of **puts( )**.) The functions **wherex( )**, **wherey( )**, and **gotoxy( )** are part of C++ Builder's library. The **wherex( )** and **wherey( )** functions return the current *x* and *y* coordinates, respectively. The current *x* and *y* coordinates define where the following output operation will begin. The **gotoxy( )** function moves the cursor to the specified *x,y* location. (Chapter 18 discusses the screen control functions in depth.)

The following short program demonstrates how to use **xyout( )**. (This program must be run in a console session in Windows.)

```cpp
#include <iostream>
#include <conio.h>
using namespace std;

void xyout(char *str, int x=0, int y=0)
{
  if(!x) x = wherex();
  if(!y) y = wherey();
  gotoxy(x, y);
  cout << str;
}

int main()
{
  xyout("hello", 10, 10);
  xyout(" there");
  xyout("I like C++", 40);   // this is still on line 10

  xyout("This is on line 11.\n", 1, 11);
  xyout("This follows on line 12.\n");
  xyout("This follows on line 13.");

  return 0;
}
```

Look closely at how **xyout( )** is called inside **main( )**. This program produces output similar to that shown in Figure 21-1. As this program illustrates, although it is sometimes useful to specify the exact location where text will be displayed, often, you simply can continue on from the point at which the last output occurred. By using default arguments, you can use the same function to accomplish both goals—there is no need for two separate functions.

```
          hello there                    I like C++
    This is on line 11.
    This follows on line 12.
    This follows on line 13.
```

Figure 21-1.   *Sample output from the **xyout( )** program*

Notice that in **main( )**, **xyout( )** is called with either three, two, or one arguments. When the function is called with only one argument, both **x** and **y** default. However, when it is called with two arguments, only **y** defaults. There is no way to call **xyout( )** with **x** defaulting and **y** being specified. More generally, when a function is called, all arguments are matched to their respective parameters in order from left to right. Once all existing arguments have been matched, any remaining, default arguments are used.

When creating functions that have default argument values, the default values must be specified only once, and this must be the first time the function is declared within the file. For example, if **xyout( )** is defined after **main( )**, the default arguments must be declared in **xyout( )**'s prototype, but the values are not repeated in **xyout( )**'s definition. The following program illustrates this:

```cpp
#include <iostream>
#include <conio.h>
using namespace std;

void xyout(char *str, int x = 0, int y = 0);

int main()
{
  xyout("hello", 10, 10);
  xyout(" there");
  xyout("I like C++", 40);   // this is still on line 10

  xyout("This is on line 11.\n", 1, 11);
  xyout("This follows on line 12.\n");
  xyout("This follows on line 13.");

  return 0;
}
```

```
/* Since x and y's defaults have already been specified
   in xyout()'s prototype, they cannot
   be repeated here.
*/
void xyout(char *str, int x, int y)
{
  if(!x) x = wherex();
  if(!y) y = wherey();
  gotoxy(x, y);
  cout << str;
}
```

If you try specifying new or even the same default values in **xyout( )**'s definition, the compiler will display an error and not compile your program.

Even though default arguments cannot be redefined, each version of an overloaded function can specify different default arguments.

When defining parameters, it is important to understand that all parameters that take default values must appear to the right of those that do not. That is, you cannot specify a nondefaulting parameter once you have defined a parameter that takes a default value. For example, it would have been incorrect to define **xyout( )** as:

```
// wrong!
void xyout(int x = 0, int y = 0, char *str)
```

Here is another incorrect attempted use of default parameters.

```
// wrong !
int f(int i, int j=10, int k)
```

Once the default parameters begin, no nondefaulting parameter may occur in the list.

You can also use default parameters in an object's constructor. For example, here is a slightly different version of the **queue( )** constructor function, shown earlier in this chapter.

```
/* This is the constructor function that uses
   a default value. */
queue::queue(int id=0)
{
```

```
    sloc = rloc = 0;
    who = id;
    cout << "Queue " << who << " initialized.\n";
}
```

In this version, if an object is declared without any initializing values, **id** defaults to 0. For example,

```
queue a, b(2);
```

creates two objects, **a** and **b**. The **id** value of **a** is 0 and **b** is 2.

Using Default Arguments Correctly

Although default arguments can be a very powerful tool when used correctly, they can be misused. Default arguments should allow a function to perform its job efficiently and easily while still allowing considerable flexibility. Toward this end, default arguments should represent a common usage of the function. It should be the exception, not the rule, for the user of your function to specify other arguments. One other important guideline you should follow when using default arguments is this: No default argument should cause a harmful or destructive action. Put differently, the accidental use of a default argument should not cause a catastrophe.

Classes and Structures Are Related

In C++ the **struct** has some expanded capabilities compared to its C counterpart. In C++, **class**es and **struct**s are closely related. In fact, with one exception, they are interchangeable because the C++ **struct** can include data and the code that manipulates that data in the same way that a **class** can. Structures may also contain constructor and destructor functions. The only difference is that by default the members of a **class** are **private**, while by default the members of a **struct** are **public**. According to the formal C++ syntax, a **struct** defines a class type. Consider this program:

```
#include <iostream>
using namespace std;

struct cl {
  int get_i(); // these are public
  void put_i(int j); // by default
private:
```

```
    int i;
} ;

int cl::get_i()
{
  return i;
}

void cl::put_i(int j)
{
  i = j;
}

int main()
{
  cl s;

  s.put_i(10);
  cout << s.get_i();

  return 0;
}
```

This simple program defines a structure type called **cl** in which **get_i( )** and **put_i( )** are **public** and **i** is **private**. Notice that a **struct** uses the keyword **private** to introduce the **private** members of the structure.

The following program shows an equivalent program using a **class** instead of a **struct**.

```
#include <iostream>
using namespace std;

class cl {
  int i; // private by default
public:
  int get_i();
  void put_i(int j);
} ;

int cl::get_i()
{
  return i;
```

```
}

void cl::put_i(int j)
{
  i = j;
}

int main()
{
  cl s;

  s.put_i(10);
  cout << s.get_i();

  return 0;
}
```

For the most part, C++ programmers use **class** when defining an object that contains both code and data. They use **struct** when defining a data-only object. (That is, **struct** is usually used in a way that is compatible with C-style structures.) However, from time to time you will see C++ code that uses the expanded capabilities of structures.

Unions and Classes Are Related

Just as structures and classes are related in C++, unions are also related to classes. A *union* is essentially a structure in which all elements are stored in the same location. A union can contain constructor and destructor functions as well as member and **friend** functions. As in a structure, **union** members are public by default. For example, the following program uses a union to display the characters that make up the low- and high-order bytes of a short integer (which is 2 bytes long for C++ Builder):

```
#include <iostream>
using namespace std;

union u_type {
  u_type(short int a);   // public by default
  void showchars();
  short int i;
  char ch[2];
};
```

```
// constructor
u_type::u_type(short int a)
{
  i = a;
}

// Show the characters that compose an int.
void u_type::showchars()
{
  cout << ch[0] << " ";
  cout << ch[1] << "\n";
}

int main()
{
  u_type u(1000);

  u.showchars();

  return 0;
}
```

It is important to understand that like a structure, a union declaration in C++ defines a class type. This means that the principles of encapsulation are preserved.

There are several restrictions that must be observed when you use C++ unions. First, a **union** cannot inherit any other classes of any type. Further, a **union** cannot be a base **class**. A **union** cannot have virtual member functions. (Virtual functions are discussed in Chapter 23.) No **static** variables can be members of a **union**. A **union** cannot have as a member any object that overloads the = operator. A reference member cannot be used. Finally, no object can be a member of a **union** if the object has an explicit constructor or destructor.

Anonymous Unions

There is a special type of **union** in C++ called an *anonymous union.* An anonymous union does not include a type name, and no variables of the union can be declared. Instead, an anonymous union tells the compiler that its member variables are to share the same location. However, the variables themselves are referred to directly, without the normal dot operator syntax. Here is a short example using an anonymous union.

```
#include <iostream>
```

```
using namespace std;

int main()
{
  // This declares an anonymous union.
  union {  // no tag name
    int i;
    char ch[4];
  } ;  // no variables specified

  /* Now reference i and ch without referencing
     a union name or dot or arrow operators.
  */
  i = 88;
  cout << i << " " << ch[0];

  return 0;
}
```

As you can see, the elements of the union are referenced as if they had been declared as normal local variables. In fact, relative to your program, that is exactly how you will use them. Further, even though they are defined within a **union** declaration, they are at the same scope level as any other local variable within the same block. This implies that the names of the members of an anonymous union must not conflict with other identifiers known within the same scope.

All restrictions involving **union**s apply to anonymous ones, with these additions. First, the elements contained within an anonymous union must be data. No member functions are allowed. Anonymous unions cannot contain **private** or **protected** elements. Finally, global anonymous unions must be specified as **static**.

Remember, just because C++ gives unions greater power and flexibility does not mean that you have to use it. In cases where you simply need a C-style union you are free to use one in that manner. However, in cases where you can encapsulate a union along with the routines that manipulate it, you add considerable structure to your program.

Inline Functions

Although it does not pertain specifically to object-oriented programming, a very useful feature of C++ is the *inline function*. An inline function is a function whose code is expanded in line at the point at which it is called instead of actually being called. This is much like a parameterized function-like macro in C, but more flexible. There are two ways to create an inline function. The first is to use the **inline** modifier. For example, to create an inline function called **f** that returns an **int** and takes no parameters, you must declare it like this:

```
inline int f()
{
  // ...
}
```

The general form of **inline** is

inline *function_declaration*

The **inline** modifier precedes all other aspects of a function's declaration.

The reason for inline functions is efficiency. Every time a function is called, a series of instructions must be executed to set up the function call, including pushing any arguments onto the stack, and returning from the function. In some cases, many CPU cycles are used to perform these procedures. However, when a function is expanded in line, no such overhead exists, and the overall speed of your program increases. However, in cases where the inline function is large, the overall size of your program also increases. For this reason, the best inline functions are those that are very small. Larger functions should be left as normal functions.

As an example, the following program uses **inline** to inline the calls to **get_i( )** and **put_i( )**:

```
#include <iostream>
using namespace std;

class cl {
  int i;
public:
  int get_i();
  void put_i(int j);
} ;

inline int cl::get_i()
{
  return i;
}

inline void cl::put_i(int j)
{
```

```
    i = j;
}

int main()
{
  cl s;

  s.put_i(10);
  cout << s.get_i();

  return 0;
}
```

If you compile this version of the program and compare it to a compiled version of the program in which **inline** is removed, the inline version is several bytes smaller. Also, calls to **get_i( )** and **put_i( )** will execute faster. Remember, however, that if **get_i( )** and **put_i( )** had been very large functions, then the inline version of the program would have been larger than its noninline version, but it would still have run faster.

It is important to understand that, technically, **inline** is a *request*, not a *command*, to the compiler to generate inline code. There are various situations that can prevent the compiler from complying with the request. For example, some compilers will not inline a function if it contains a loop, a **switch**, or a **goto**. C++ Builder will not inline a function that uses an exception or that has a parameter of a class type that defines a destructor. It will also not inline functions that return objects that contain destructors.

Creating Inline Functions Inside a Class

The second way to create an inline function is to define the code to a function *inside* a **class** declaration. Any function that is defined inside a **class** declaration is automatically made into an inline function, if possible. It is not necessary to precede its declaration with the keyword **inline**. For example, the previous program can be rewritten as shown here:

```
#include <iostream>
using namespace std;

class cl {
  int i;
public:
  // automatic inline functions
  int get_i() { return i; }
```

```
   void put_i(int j) { i = j; }
} ;

int main()
{
  cl s;

  s.put_i(10);
  cout << s.get_i();

  return 0;
}
```

Notice the way the function code is arranged. For very short functions, this arrangement reflects common C++ style. However, you could also write them as shown here:

```
class cl {
   int i;
public:
   // automatic inline functions
   int get_i()
   {
     return i;
   }

   void put_i(int j)
   {
      i = j;
   }
} ;
```

In professionally written C++ code, short functions like those illustrated in the example are commonly defined inside the **class** declaration. This convention is followed in most of the C++ examples in this book.

Passing Objects to Functions

Objects can be passed to functions in just the same way that any other type of variable can. Objects are passed to functions through the use of the standard call-by-value mechanism. This means that a copy of an object is made when it is passed to a function.

However, the fact that a copy is created means, in essence, that another object is created. This raises the question of whether the object's constructor function is executed when the copy is made and whether the destructor function is executed when the copy is destroyed. The answer to these two questions may surprise you. To begin, here is an example:

```
#include <iostream>
using namespace std;

class myclass {
   int i;
public:
   myclass(int n);
   ~myclass();
   void set_i(int n) { i=n; }
   int get_i() { return i; }
};

myclass::myclass(int n)
{
   i = n;
   cout << "Constructing " << i << "\n";
}

myclass::~myclass()
{
   cout << "Destroying " << i << "\n";
}

void f(myclass ob);

int main()
{
   myclass o(1);

   f(o);
   cout << "This is i in main: ";
   cout << o.get_i() << "\n";

   return 0;
}

void f(myclass ob)
{
```

```
    ob.set_i(2);

    cout << "This is local i: " << ob.get_i();
    cout << "\n";
}
```

This program produces this output:

```
Constructing 1
This is local i: 2
Destroying 2
This is i in main: 1
Destroying 1
```

Notice that two calls to the destructor are executed, but only one call is made to the constructor. As the output illustrates, the constructor is not called when the copy of **o** (in **main( )**) is passed to **ob** (within **f( )**). The reason that the constructor is not called when the copy of the object is made is easy to understand. When you pass an object to a function, you want the current state of that object. If the constructor is called when the copy is created, initialization will occur, possibly changing the object. Thus, the constructor cannot be executed when the copy of an object is generated in a function call.

Although the constructor is not called when an object is passed to a function, it is necessary to call the destructor when the copy is destroyed. (The copy is destroyed like any other local variable, when the function terminates.) Remember, the copy of the object *does* exist as long as the function is executing. This means that the copy could be performing operations that will require a destructor to be called when the copy is destroyed. For example, it is perfectly valid for the copy to allocate memory that must be freed when it is destroyed. For this reason, the destructor must be executed when the copy is destroyed.

To summarize: When a copy of an object is generated because it is passed to a function, the object's constructor is not called. However, when the copy of the object inside the function is destroyed, its destructor is called.

By default, when a copy of an object is made, a bitwise copy occurs. This means that the new object is an exact duplicate of the original. The fact that an exact copy is made can, at times, be a source of trouble. Even though objects are passed to functions by means of the normal call-by-value parameter passing mechanism which, in theory, protects and insulates the calling argument, it is still possible for a side effect to occur that may affect, or even damage, the object used as an argument. For example, if an object used as an argument allocates memory and frees that memory when it is destroyed, then its local copy inside the function will free the same memory when its destructor is called. This will leave the original object damaged and effectively useless. As you will see later in this book, it is possible to prevent this type of problem by defining the copy operation relative to your own classes by creating a special type of constructor called a *copy constructor* (see Chapter 26).

Returning Objects

A function may return an object to the caller. For example, this is a valid C++ program:

```
#include <iostream>
using namespace std;

class myclass {
  int i;
public:
  void set_i(int n) { i=n; }
  int get_i() { return i; }
};

myclass f();  // return object of type myclass

int main()
{
  myclass o;

  o = f();
  cout << o.get_i() << "\n";

  return 0;
}

myclass f()
{
  myclass x;

  x.set_i(1);
  return x;
}
```

When an object is returned by a function, a temporary object is automatically created, which holds the return value. It is this object that is actually returned by the function. After the value has been returned, this object is destroyed. The destruction of this temporary object may cause unexpected side effects in some situations. For example, if the object returned by the function has a destructor that frees dynamically allocated memory, that memory will be freed even though the object that is receiving the return value is still using it. As you will see later in this book, there are ways to overcome this problem that involve overloading the assignment operator and defining a copy constructor.

Object Assignment

Assuming that both objects are of the same type, you can assign one object to another. This causes the data of the object on the right side to be copied into the data of the object on the left. For example, this program displays **this is ob2's i: 99**:

```
#include <iostream>
using namespace std;

class myclass {
  int i;
public:
  void set_i(int n) { i=n; }
  int get_i() { return i; }
};

int main()
{
  myclass ob1, ob2;

  ob1.set_i(99);
  ob2 = ob1; // assign data from ob1 to ob2

  cout << "this is ob2's i: " << ob2.get_i();

  return 0;
}
```

By default, all data from one object is assigned to the other by use of a bit-by-bit copy. However, it is possible to overload the assignment operator and define some other assignment procedure (see Chapter 22).

Arrays of Objects

You can create arrays of objects in the same way that you create arrays of any other data types. For example, the following program establishes a class called **display** that

holds information about various video display options. Inside **main( )**, an array of
three **display** objects is created, and the objects that make up the elements of the array
are accessed using the normal indexing procedure.

```cpp
// An example of arrays of objects.

#include <iostream>
using namespace std;

enum resolution { r640x480, r800x600, r1024x768 };
enum coloroption { c16, c256, cHighColor, cTrueColor };

class display {
  coloroption coption; // color option
  resolution res; // resolution
public:
  void set_coloropt(coloroption opt) { coption = opt; }
  coloroption get_coloropt() { return coption; }
  void set_res(resolution r) { res = r; }
  resolution get_res() { return res; }
} ;

char options[4][20] = {
  "16 Colors",
  "256 Colors",
  "High Color (16 bit)",
  "True Color (32 bit)"
} ;

char resvals[3][20] = {
  "640 x 480",
  "800 x 600",
  "1024 x 768"
} ;

int main()
{
  display monitors[3];
  register int i;

  monitors[0].set_coloropt(c16);
  monitors[0].set_res(r640x480);
```

```
    monitors[1].set_coloropt(cTrueColor);
    monitors[1].set_res(r640x480);

    monitors[2].set_coloropt(c256);
    monitors[2].set_res(r1024x768);

    for(i=0; i<3; i++) {
      cout << options[monitors[i].get_coloropt()] << " ";
      cout << "with resolution of " <<
           resvals[monitors[i].get_res()];
      cout << "\n";
    }

    return 0;
}
```

This program produces the following output:

```
16 Colors with resolution of 640 x 480
True Color (32 bit) with resolution of 640 x 480
256 Colors with resolution of 1024 x 768
```

Although not related to arrays of objects, notice how the two-dimensional character arrays **options** and **resvals** are used to convert between an enumerated value and its equivalent character string. In all enumerations that do not contain explicit initializations, the first constant has the value 0, the second 1, and so on. Therefore, the value returned by **get_coloropt( )** can be used to index the **options** array, causing the appropriate name to be printed. Likewise, the value returned by **get_res( )** can be used to index **resvals** to obtain a string representing the resolution.

Multidimensional arrays of objects are indexed in precisely the same way as arrays of other types of data.

Initializing Arrays of Objects

If a class defines a parameterized constructor, you can initialize each object in an array by specifying an initialization list as you do for other types of arrays. However, the exact form of the initialization list will be decided by the number of parameters required by the object's constructor. For objects whose constructors take only one parameter, you can simply specify a list of initial values, using the normal array-initialization syntax. Each value in the list is passed, in order, to the constructor function as each element in the array is created. For example, here is a program that initializes an array:

```cpp
#include <iostream>
using namespace std;

class cl {
  int i;
public:
  cl(int j) { i=j; }  // constructor
  int get_i() { return i; }
};

int main()
{
  cl ob[3] = {1, 2, 3};  // initializers
  int i;

  for(i=0; i<3; i++)
    cout << ob[i].get_i() << "\n";

  return 0;
}
```

This program displays the numbers **1**, **2**, and **3** on the screen.

If an object's constructor requires two or more arguments, then you will have to use the slightly different initialization form shown here.

```cpp
#include <iostream>
using namespace std;

class cl {
  int h;
  int i;
public:
  cl(int j, int k) { h=j; i=k; } // constructor
  int get_i() { return i; }
  int get_h() { return h; }
};

int main()
```

```
{
  cl ob[3] = {
    cl(1, 2),
    cl(3, 4),
    cl(5, 6)
  };  // initializers

  int i;

  for(i=0; i<3; i++) {
    cout << ob[i].get_h();
    cout << ", ";
    cout << ob[i].get_i() << "\n";
  }

  return 0;
}
```

In this example, **cl**'s constructor has two parameters and, therefore, requires two
arguments. This means that the "shorthand" initialization format cannot be used.
Instead, use the "long form" shown in the example. (Of course, you may use the long
form in cases where the constructor requires only one argument, too. It is just that the
short form is easier to use when only one argument is required.)

Creating Initialized Versus Uninitialized Arrays

A special case occurs if you intend to create both initialized and uninitialized arrays of
objects. Consider the following **class**.

```
class cl {
  int i;
public:
  cl(int j) { i=j; }
  int get_i() { return i; }
};
```

Here, the constructor function defined by **cl** requires one parameter. This implies
that any array declared of this type must be initialized. That is, it precludes this
array declaration:

```
cl a[9]; // error, constructor requires initializers
```

The reason that this statement isn't valid (as **cl** is currently defined) is that it implies that **cl** has a parameterless constructor because no initializers are specified. However, as it stands, **cl** does not have a parameterless constructor. Because there is no valid constructor that corresponds to this declaration, the compiler will report an error. To solve this problem, you need to overload the constructor, adding one that takes no parameters. In this way, arrays that are initialized and those that are not initialized are both allowed. For example, here is an improved version of **cl**:

```
class cl {
  int i;
public:
  cl() { i=0; }  // called for non-initialized arrays
  cl(int j) { i=j; }  // called for initialized arrays
  int get_i() { return i; }
};
```

Given this **class**, both of the following statements are permissible:

```
cl a1[3] = { 3, 5, 6 }; // initialized
cl a2[34]; // uninitialized
```

Pointers to Objects

In C you can access a structure directly or through a pointer to that structure. Similarly, in C++ you can refer to an object either directly (as has been the case in all preceding examples) or by using a pointer to that object. Pointers to objects are among C++'s most important features.

To access a member of an object when using the actual object itself, you use the dot (.) operator. To access a specific member of an object through a pointer to the object, you must use the arrow operator (–>). The use of the dot and arrow operators for objects is the same as their use for structures and unions.

You declare an object pointer using the same declaration syntax as you do for any other type of data. The following program creates a simple class called **P_example** and defines an object of that class called **ob** and a pointer for an object of type **P_example** called **p**. It then illustrates how to access **ob** directly and indirectly using a pointer.

```
// A simple example using an object pointer.

#include <iostream>
using namespace std;
```

```
class P_example {
  int num;
public:
  void set_num(int val) { num = val; }
  void show_num();
};

void P_example::show_num()
{
  cout << num << "\n";
}

int main()
{
  P_example ob, *p; // declare an object and pointer to it

  ob.set_num(1); // access ob directly
  ob.show_num();
  p = &ob; // assign p the address of ob
  p->show_num();   // access ob using pointer

  return 0;
}
```

Notice that the address of **ob** is obtained using the **&** (address of) operator in the same way the address is obtained for any type of variable.

When a pointer is incremented or decremented, it is increased or decreased in such a way that it will always point to the next element of its base type. The same thing occurs when a pointer to an object is incremented or decremented: the next object is pointed to. The following example modifies the preceding program so that **ob** is a two-element array of type **P_example**. Notice how **p** is incremented and decremented to access the two elements in the array.

```
// Incrementing an object pointer
#include <iostream>
using namespace std;

class P_example {
  int num;
public:
  void set_num(int val) { num = val; }
```

```
   void show_num();
};

void P_example::show_num()
{
  cout << num << "\n";
}

int main()
{
  P_example ob[2], *p;

  ob[0].set_num(10);  // access objects directly
  ob[1].set_num(20);

  p = &ob[0];  // obtain pointer to first element
  p->show_num(); // show value of ob[0] using pointer

  p++;  // advance to next object
  p->show_num(); // show value of ob[1] using pointer

  p--;  // retreat to previous object
  p->show_num(); // again show value of ob[0]

  return 0;
}
```

The output from this program is **10, 20, 10**.

The
Complete
Reference

Borland
C++
Builder

Chapter 22

Function and Operator Overloading

hapter 20 introduced two of C++'s most important features, function overloading and operator overloading. This chapter explores these topics in detail. In the course of the discussion, other related topics are also examined.

Overloading Constructor Functions

Although they perform a unique service, constructor functions are not much different from other types of functions, and they too can be overloaded. As the last example in the preceding chapter showed, to overload a class's constructor, simply declare the various forms it will take. As you will see, in many cases there is a significant advantage to be gained by providing overloaded constructors.

Let's begin with an example. The following program declares a class called **timer** that acts as a countdown timer (such as a darkroom timer). When an object of type **timer** is created, it is given an initial time value. When the **run( )** function is called, the timer counts down to 0 and then rings the bell. In this example, the constructor is overloaded to allow the time to be specified in seconds as either an integer or a string, or in minutes and seconds by specifying two integers.

This program makes use of the **clock( )** library function, which returns the number of system clock ticks since the program began running. Dividing this value by the macro **CLK_TCK** converts the return value of **clock( )** into seconds. Both the prototype for **clock( )** and the definition of **CLK_TCK** are found in the header **<time.h>**.

```
#include <iostream>
#include <cstdlib>
#include <ctime>
using namespace std;

class timer{
  int seconds;
public:
  // seconds specified as a string
  timer(char *t) { seconds = atoi(t); }

  // seconds specified as integer
  timer(int t) { seconds = t; }

  // time specified in minutes and seconds
  timer(int min, int sec) { seconds = min*60 + sec; }

  void run();
} ;
```

```
void timer::run()
{
  clock_t t1, t2;

  t1 = t2 = clock()/CLK_TCK;
  while(seconds) {
    if(t1/CLK_TCK+1 <= (t2=clock())/CLK_TCK) {
        seconds--;
        t1 = t2;
    }
  }
  cout << "\a"; // ring the bell
}

int main()
{
  timer a(10), b("20"), c(1, 10);

  a.run(); // count 10 seconds
  b.run(); // count 20 seconds
  c.run(); // count 1 minute, 10 seconds

  return 0;
}
```

As you can see, when **a**, **b**, and **c** are created inside **main( )** they are given initial values using the three different methods supported by the overloaded constructor functions. Each approach causes the appropriate constructor to be used and initializes all three variables properly.

In the program just shown, you may see little value in overloading a constructor function, because you could simply decide on a single way to specify the time. However, if you were creating a library of classes for someone else to use, you might want to supply constructors for the most common forms of initialization, allowing the programmer to choose the most appropriate form for his or her application. The next section shows another advantage that is gained by overloading a constructor function.

Note   *C++ defines a special type of overloaded constructor, called a copy constructor, that allows you to determine how objects are copied under certain circumstances. Copy constructors are discussed later in this book.*

Localizing Variables

Before continuing with the discussion of overloaded constructors, an important difference between the way local variables can be declared in C versus the way they can be declared in C++ needs to be explained. In C you must declare all local variables used within a block at the start of that block. You cannot declare a variable in a block after an "action" statement has occurred. For example, in C, this fragment is incorrect:

```c
/* Incorrect in C */
void f()
{
  int i;
  i = 10;
  int j;
  /* ... */
}
```

Because the statement **i=10** falls between the declaration of **i** and that of **j**, a C compiler will flag an error and refuse to compile this function. In C++, however, this fragment is perfectly acceptable and will compile without error. In C++, a local variable can be declared at any point within a block. Furthermore, it is known only to code that comes after it within that block.

Here is an example program that shows how local variables can be declared anywhere within a block when using C++.

```cpp
#include <iostream>
#include <cstring>
using namespace std;

int main()
{
  int i;
  i = 10;

  int j = 100; // perfectly legal in C++

  cout << i*j << "\n";

  cout << "Enter a string: ";
  char str[80];   // also legal in C++
  cin >> str;

  // display the string in reverse order
  int k;  // in C++, declare k where it is needed
```

```
  k = strlen(str);
  k--;
  while(k>=0) {
    cout << str[k];
    k--;
  }

  return 0;
}
```

Since much of the philosophy behind C++ is the encapsulation of code and data, it makes sense that you can declare variables close to where they are used instead of only at the beginning of the block. Here, the declarations of **i** and **j** are separated simply for illustration. However, you can see how the localization of **k** to its relevant code helps encapsulate that routine. Declaring variables close to the point where they are used helps you avoid accidental side effects. This feature of C++ is also helpful when creating objects, as the next section illustrates.

Localizing the Creation of Objects

The fact that local variables can be declared at any point within a block of code has significant implications for the creation of objects. In real-world programs, you often need to create objects that are initialized using values known only during the execution of your program. Being able to create an object after those values are known can be quite helpful because it prevents you from having to first create an uninitialized object and then later, set its values.

To see the advantages of declaring local objects near their point of first use, consider this version of the **timer** program. In it, two objects, **b** and **c**, are constructed using information furnished at run time, just prior to their use. It also further illustrates the benefit of overloading constructors to accept different forms of initializations.

```
#include <iostream>
#include <cstdlib>
#include <ctime>
using namespace std;

class timer{
  int seconds;
public:
  // seconds specified as a string
  timer(char *t) { seconds = atoi(t); }
```

```cpp
  // seconds specified as integer
  timer(int t) { seconds = t; }

  // time specified in minutes and seconds
  timer(int min, int sec) { seconds = min*60 + sec; }

  void run();
} ;

void timer::run()
{
  clock_t t1, t2;

  t1 = t2 = clock()/CLK_TCK;
  while(seconds) {
    if(t1/CLK_TCK+1 <= (t2=clock())/CLK_TCK) {
        seconds--;
        t1 = t2;
    }
  }
  cout << "\a"; // ring the bell
}

int main()
{
  timer a(10);
  a.run();

  cout << "Enter number of seconds: ";
  char str[80];
  cin >> str;
  timer b(str); // initialize at runtime using a string
  b.run();

  cout << "Enter minutes and seconds: ";
  int min, sec;
  cin >> min >> sec;
  timer c(min, sec);  /* initialize at runtime
                          using minutes and seconds */
  c.run();

  return 0;
}
```

Here, object **a** is constructed using an integer constant. However, objects **b** and **c** are constructed using information entered by the user. Thus, they are not declared until that information is known. Also, both **b** and **c** are constructed using the type of data available at the point of their creation. For **b**, this is a string representing seconds. For **c**, this is two integers describing minutes and seconds. By allowing various initialization formats, you need not perform any unnecessary conversions from one form to another when initializing an object. You also more easily allow objects to be constructed near their point of first use.

Function Overloading and Ambiguity

When overloading functions, it is possible to produce a type of error with which you may not be familiar. You can create a situation in which the compiler is unable to choose between two (or more) overloaded functions. When this happens, the situation is said to be *ambiguous*. Ambiguous statements are errors, and programs containing ambiguity will not compile.

By far the main cause of ambiguity involves C++'s automatic type conversions. C++ automatically attempts to convert the arguments used to call a function into the type of arguments expected by the function. For example, consider this fragment:

```
int myfunc(double d);
  // ...
cout << myfunc('c');  // not an error, conversion applied
```

As the comment indicates, this is not an error because C++ automatically converts the character **c** into its **double** equivalent. In C++, very few type conversions of this sort are actually disallowed. Although automatic type conversions are convenient, they are also a prime cause of ambiguity. For example, consider the following program:

```
#include <iostream>
using namespace std;

float myfunc(float i);
double myfunc(double i);

int main()
{
  cout << myfunc(10.1) << " "; // unambiguous, calls myfunc(double)
  cout << myfunc(10);  // ambiguous

  return 0;
```

```
}

float myfunc(float i)
{
  return i;
}

double myfunc(double i)
{
  return -i;
}
```

Here, **myfunc( )** is overloaded so that it can take arguments of either type **float** or type **double**. In the unambiguous line, **myfunc(double)** is called because, unless explicitly specified as **float**, all floating-point constants in C++ are automatically of type **double**. Hence, that call is unambiguous. However, when **myfunc( )** is called using the integer 10, ambiguity is introduced because the compiler has no way of knowing whether it should be converted to a **float** or to a **double**. This causes an error message to be displayed, and the program will not compile.

As preceding example illustrates, it is not the overloading of **myfunc( )** relative to **double** and **float** that causes the ambiguity. Rather, it is the specific call to **myfunc( )** using an indeterminate type of argument that causes the confusion. Put differently, the error is not caused by the overloading of **myfunc( )**, but by the specific invocation.

Here is another example of ambiguity caused by C++'s automatic type conversions:

```
#include <iostream>
using namespace std;

char myfunc(unsigned char ch);
char myfunc(char ch);

int main()
{
  cout << myfunc('c');  // this calls myfunc(char)
  cout << myfunc(88) << " "; // ambiguous

  return 0;
}

char myfunc(unsigned char ch)
{
  return ch-1;
```

```
}

char myfunc(char ch)
{
  return ch+1;
}
```

In C++, **unsigned char** and **char** are *not* inherently ambiguous. However, when **myfunc( )** is called by using the integer 88, the compiler does not know which function to call. That is, should 88 be converted into a **char** or an **unsigned char**?

Another way you can cause ambiguity is by using default arguments in overloaded functions. To see how, examine this program:

```
#include <iostream>
using namespace std;

int myfunc(int i);
int myfunc(int i, int j=1);

int main()
{
  cout << myfunc(4, 5) << " ";  // unambiguous
  cout << myfunc(10);  // ambiguous

  return 0;
}

int myfunc(int i)
{
  return i;
}

int myfunc(int i, int j)
{
  return i*j;
}
```

Here, in the first call to **myfunc( )**, two arguments are specified; therefore, no ambiguity is introduced and **myfunc(int i, int j)** is called. However, when the second call to **myfunc( )** is made, ambiguity occurs because the compiler does not know whether to call the version of **myfunc( )** that takes one argument or to apply the default to the version that takes two arguments.

Finding the Address of an Overloaded Function

As you saw in Part One, you can assign the address of a function to a pointer and then call that function through the pointer. This process is straightforward when the function is not overloaded. However, when the function *is* overloaded, this process is a little more complex. To understand why, first consider this statement, which assigns the address of some function called **myfunc( )** to a pointer called **p**:

```
p = myfunc;
```

If **myfunc( )** is not overloaded, there is one and only one function called **myfunc( )**, and the compiler has no difficulty assigning its address to **p**. However, if **myfunc( )** is overloaded, how does the compiler know which function's address to assign to **p**? The answer is that it depends upon how **p** is declared. For example, consider this program:

```cpp
#include <iostream>
using namespace std;

int myfunc(int a);
int myfunc(int a, int b);

int main()
{
   int (*fp)(int a);   // pointer to int xxx(int)

   fp = myfunc;   // points to myfunc(int)
   cout << fp(5);

   return 0;
}

int myfunc(int a)
{
   return a;
}

int myfunc(int a, int b)
{
   return a*b;
}
```

As the program illustrates, **fp** is declared as a pointer to a function that returns an integer and that takes one integer argument. C++ uses this information to select the **myfunc(int a)** version of **myfunc( )**. Had **fp** been declared like this:

```
int (*fp) (int a, int b);
```

then **fp** would have been assigned the address of the **myfunc(int a, int b)** version of **myfunc( )**.

To review: When you assign the address of an overloaded function to a function pointer, it is the declaration of the pointer that determines which function's address is assigned. Further, the declaration of the function pointer must exactly match one and only one of the overloaded function's declarations.

The this Pointer

Before moving on to operator overloading, it is necessary for you to learn about another of C++'s keywords, **this**, which is an essential ingredient for many overloaded operators.

Each time a member function is called, it is automatically passed a pointer to the object that invoked it. You can access this pointer using **this**. Thus, the **this** pointer is an *implicit* parameter to all member functions. (**friend** functions do not have a **this** pointer.) For example, given

```
ob.f();
```

the function **f( )** is automatically passed a **this** pointer, which points to **ob**.

As you know, a member function can access the data of its class directly. For example, given the following class:

```
class cl {
  int i;
  // ...
};
```

a member function can assign **i** the value 10 using this statement:

```
i = 10;
```

Actually, this statement is shorthand for the statement

```
this->i = 10;
```

To see how the **this** pointer works, examine this short program:

```
#include <iostream>
using namespace std;

class cl {
  int i;
public:
  void load_i(int val) { this->i = val; } // same as i = val
  int get_i() { return this->i; } // same as return i
} ;

int main()
{
  cl o;

  o.load_i(100);
  cout << o.get_i();

  return 0;
}
```

This program displays the number **100**.

While the preceding example is trivial—in fact, no one would actually use the **this** pointer in this way—the following section shows one reason why the **this** pointer is so important.

Operator Overloading

A feature of C++ that is related to function overloading is *operator overloading*. With very few exceptions, most of C++'s operators can be given special meanings relative to specific classes. For example, a class that defines a linked list might use the + operator to add an object to the list. Another class might use the + operator in an entirely different way. When an operator is overloaded, none of its original meaning is lost. It simply means that a new operation relative to a specific class is defined. Therefore, overloading the + to handle a linked list does not cause its meaning relative to integers (that is, addition) to be changed.

Operator functions will usually be either members or **friend**s of the class for which they are being used. Although very similar, there are some differences between the way a member operator function is overloaded and the way a **friend** operator function is overloaded. In this section, only member functions will be overloaded. Later in this chapter, you will see how to overload **friend** operator functions.

To overload an operator, you must define what that operation means relative to the class that it is applied to. To do this, you create an **operator** function, which defines its action. The general form of a member **operator** function is

type classname ::operator#(*arg-list*)
{
  // operation defined relative to the class
}

Here, the operator that you are overloading is substituted for the # and *type* is the type of value returned by the specified operation. To facilitate its use in larger expressions, the return value of an operator often is of the same type as the class for which the operator is being overloaded (although it could be of any type you choose). The specific nature of *arg-list* is determined by several factors, as you will soon see.

To see how operator overloading works, let's start with a simple example that creates a class called **three_d** that maintains the coordinates of an object in three-dimensional space. This program overloads the **+** and **=** operators relative to the **three_d** class:

```
#include <iostream>
using namespace std;

class three_d {
  int x, y, z; // 3-d coordinates
public:
  three_d operator+(three_d t);
  three_d operator=(three_d t);

  void show() ;
  void assign(int mx, int my, int mz);
} ;

// Overload the +.
three_d three_d::operator+(three_d t)
{
  three_d temp;

  temp.x = x+t.x;
  temp.y = y+t.y;
  temp.z = z+t.z;
  return temp;
}

// Overload the =.
```

```cpp
three_d three_d::operator=(three_d t)
{
  x = t.x;
  y = t.y;
  z = t.z;
  return *this;
}

// Show X, Y, Z coordinates.
void three_d::show()
{
  cout << x << ", ";
  cout << y << ", ";
  cout << z << "\n";
}

// Assign coordinates.
void three_d::assign(int mx, int my, int mz)
{
  x = mx;
  y = my;
  z = mz;
}

int main()
{
  three_d a, b, c;

  a.assign(1, 2, 3);
  b.assign(10, 10, 10);

  a.show();
  b.show();

  c = a+b;   // now add a and b together
  c.show();

  c = a+b+c; // add a, b and c together
  c.show();

  c = b = a;   // demonstrate multiple assignment
  c.show();
```

```
   b.show();

   return 0;
}
```

This program produces the following output:

```
1, 2, 3
10, 10, 10
11, 12, 13
22, 24, 26
1, 2, 3
1, 2, 3
```

As you examine this program, you may be surprised to see that both operator functions have only one parameter each, even though they overload binary operations. This is because, when a binary operator is overloaded using a member function, only one argument is explicitly passed to it. The other argument is implicitly passed using the **this** pointer. Thus, in the line

```
temp.x = x + t.x;
```

the **x** refers to **this –>x**, which is the **x** associated with the object that invoked the operator function. In all cases, it is the object on the left side of an operation that causes the call to the operator function. The object on the right side is passed to the function.

In general, when using a member function, no parameters are needed when overloading a unary operator, and only one parameter is required when overloading a binary operator. (You cannot overload the **?** ternary operator.) In either case, the object that causes the activation of the operator function is implicitly passed through the **this** pointer.

To understand how operator overloading works, let's examine the preceding program carefully, beginning with the overloaded operator **+**. When two objects of type **three_d** are operated on by the **+** operator, the magnitudes of their respective coordinates are added together, as shown in the **operator+( )** function associated with this class. Notice, however, that this function does not modify the value of either operand. Instead, an object of type **three_d**, which contains the result of the operation, is returned by the function. To understand why the **+** operation does not change the contents of either object, think about the standard arithmetic **+** operation as applied like this: 10+12. The outcome of this operation is 22, but neither 10 nor 12 is changed by it. Although there is no rule that states that an overloaded operator cannot alter the value of one of its operands, it usually makes sense for the overloaded operator to stay consistent with its original meaning. Further, related to the **three_d** class, we don't want the + to alter the contents of an operand.

Another key point about how the + operator is overloaded is that it returns an object of type **three_d**. Although the function could have returned any valid C++ type, the fact that it returns a **three_d** object allows the + operator to be used in more complicated expressions, such as **a+b+c**. Here, **a+b** generates a result that is of type **three_d**. This value can then be added to **c**. Had any other type of value been generated by **a+b**, it could not have been added to **c**.

Contrasting with the + operator, the assignment operator does, indeed, cause one of its arguments to be modified. (This is, after all, the very essence of assignment.) Since the **operator=( )** function is called by the object that occurs on the left side of the assignment, it is this object that is modified by the assignment operation. Of course, even the assignment operation must return a value because the assignment operation produces the value that occurs on the right side. Thus, to allow statements like

```
a = b = c = d;
```

it is necessary for **operator =( )** to return the object pointed to by **this**, which will be the object that occurs on the left side of the assignment statement. Doing so allows a chain of assignments to be made.

You can also overload unary operators, such as **++** or **– –**. As stated earlier, when overloading a unary operator using a member function, no object is explicitly passed to the operator function. Instead, the operation is performed on the object that generates the call to the function through the implicitly passed **this** pointer. For example, here is an expanded version of the previous example program that defines the increment operation for objects of type **three_d**.

```
#include <iostream>
using namespace std;

class three_d {
  int x, y, z; // 3-d coordinates
public:
  three_d operator+(three_d op2);  // op1 is implied
  three_d operator=(three_d op2);  // op1 is implied
  three_d operator++(); // op1 is also implied here

  void show() ;
  void assign(int mx, int my, int mz);
} ;

// Overload the +.
```

```
three_d three_d::operator+(three_d op2)
{
  three_d temp;

  temp.x = x+op2.x;  // these are integer additions
  temp.y = y+op2.y;  // and the + retains its original
  temp.z = z+op2.z;  // meaning relative to them
  return temp;
}

// Overload the =.
three_d three_d::operator=(three_d op2)
{
  x = op2.x; // these are integer assignments
  y = op2.y; // and the = retains its original
  z = op2.z; // meaning relative to them
  return *this;
}

// Overload a unary operator.
three_d three_d::operator++()
{
  x++;
  y++;
  z++;
  return *this;
}

// Show X, Y, Z coordinates.
void three_d::show()
{
  cout << x << ", ";
  cout << y << ", ";
  cout << z << "\n";
}

// Assign coordinates.
void three_d::assign(int mx, int my, int mz)
{
  x = mx;
  y = my;
  z = mz;
```

```
    }

    int main()
    {
        three_d a, b, c;

        a.assign(1, 2, 3);
        b.assign(10, 10, 10);

        a.show();
        b.show();

        c = a+b;   // now add a and b together
        c.show();

        c = a+b+c; // add a, b and c together
        c.show();

        c = b = a;  // demonstrate multiple assignment
        c.show();
        b.show();

        ++c;   // increment c
        c.show();
        return 0;
    }
```

In early versions of C++, it was not possible to determine whether an overloaded **++** or **- -** preceded or followed its operand. For example, assuming some object called **O**, these two statements were identical:

```
O++;

++O;
```

However, later versions of C++ provide a means of differentiating between a prefix or postfix increment or decrement operation. To accomplish this, your program must define two versions of the **operator++( )** function. One is defined as shown in the foregoing program. The other is declared like this:

```
loc operator++(int x);
```

If the **++** precedes its operand, then the **operator++( )** function is called. If the **++** follows its operand, then the **operator++(int x)** is called and **x** has the value 0.

The action of an overloaded operator as applied to the class for which it is defined need not have any relationship to that operator's default use with C++'s built-in types. For example, the **<<** and **>>** as applied to **cout** and **cin** have little in common with the same operators applied to integer types. However, for the purpose of structure and readability of your code, an overloaded operator should reflect, when possible, the spirit of the operator's original use. For example, the **+** relative to **three_d** is conceptually similar to the **+** relative to integer types. There is little benefit, for example, in defining the **+** operator relative to a particular class in such a way that it acts more like you would expect the **| |** operator to perform. While you can give an overloaded operator any meaning you like, it is best, for clarity, to relate its new meaning to its original meaning.

Some restrictions to overloading operators also apply. First, you cannot alter the precedence of any operator. Second, you cannot alter the number of operands required by the operator, although your **operator( )** function could choose to ignore an operand. Finally, except for the **=**, overloaded operators are inherited by any derived classes. Each class must define explicitly its own overloaded **=** operator if one is needed. Of course, a derived class is free to overload any operator relative to itself—including those overloaded by its base class.

The only operators you cannot overload are

    . :: .* ?

Friend Operator Functions

It is possible for an operator function to be a **friend** of a class rather than a member. As you learned earlier in this chapter, since **friend** functions are *not* members of a class, they do not have the implied argument **this**. Therefore, when a **friend** is used to overload an operator, both operands are passed when overloading binary operators and a single operand is passed when overloading unary operators. The only operators that cannot use **friend** functions are **=**, **( )**, **[]**, and **–>**. The rest can use either member or **friend** functions to implement the specified operation relative to its class. For example, here is a modified version of the preceding program using a **friend** instead of a member function to overload the **+** operator:

```
#include <iostream>
using namespace std;

class three_d {
  int x, y, z; // 3-d coordinates
public:
  friend three_d operator+(three_d op1, three_d op2);
  three_d operator=(three_d op2);  // op1 is implied
```

C++

```
    three_d operator++(); // op1 is implied here, too

    void show() ;
    void assign(int mx, int my, int mz);
} ;

// This is now a friend function.
three_d operator+(three_d op1, three_d op2)
{
  three_d temp;

  temp.x = op1.x + op2.x;  // these are integer additions
  temp.y = op1.y + op2.y;  // and the + retains its original
  temp.z = op1.z + op2.z;  // meaning relative to them
  return temp;
}

// Overload the =.
three_d three_d::operator=(three_d op2)
{
  x = op2.x; // these are integer assignments
  y = op2.y; // and the = retains its original
  z = op2.z; // meaning relative to them
  return *this;
}

// Overload a unary operator.
three_d three_d::operator++()
{
  x++;
  y++;
  z++;
  return *this;
}

// Show X, Y, Z coordinates.
void three_d::show()
{
  cout << x << ", ";
  cout << y << ", ";
  cout << z << "\n";
```

```
}

// Assign coordinates.
void three_d::assign(int mx, int my, int mz)
{
  x = mx;
  y = my;
  z = mz;
}
int main()
{
  three_d a, b, c;

  a.assign(1, 2, 3);
  b.assign(10, 10, 10);

  a.show();
  b.show();

  c = a+b;  // now add a and b together
  c.show();

  c = a+b+c; // add a, b and c together
  c.show();

  c = b = a;  // demonstrate multiple assignment
  c.show();
  b.show();

  ++c;  // increment c
  c.show();

  return 0;
}
```

As you can see by looking at **operator+( )**, now both operands are passed to it. The left operand is passed in **op1** and the right operand in **op2**.

In many cases, there is no benefit to using a **friend** function instead of a member function when overloading an operator. However, there is one situation in which you must use a **friend** function. As you know, a pointer to an object that invokes a member operator function is passed in **this**. In the case of binary operators, this is a pointer to the object on the left. This works as long as the object on the left defines the specified operation. For example, assuming an object called **Ob**, which has assignment and addition defined for it, this is a valid statement:

```
Ob = Ob + 10; // will work
```

Since the object **Ob** is on the left of the + operator, it invokes its overloaded operator function, which (presumably) is capable of adding an integer value to some element of **Ob**. However, this statement doesn't work:

```
Ob = 10 + Ob; // won't work
```

The reason this statement does not work is that the object on the left of the + operator is an integer, which is a built-in type for which no operation involving an integer and an object of **Ob**'s type is defined.

You can use built-in types on the left side of an operation if the + is overloaded using two **friend** functions. In this case, the operator function is explicitly passed both arguments and it is invoked like any other overloaded function, according to the types of its arguments. One version of the + operator function handles *object + integer* and the other handles *integer + object*. Overloading the + (or any other binary operator) using a **friend** allows a built-in type to occur on the left or right side of the operator. The following program shows how to accomplish this:

```cpp
#include <iostream>
using namespace std;

class CL {
public:
  int count;
  CL operator=(int i);
  friend CL operator+(CL ob, int i);
  friend CL operator+(int i, CL ob);
};

CL CL::operator=(int i)
{
  count = i;
  return *this;
}
```

```cpp
// This handles ob + int.
CL operator+(CL ob, int i)
{
  CL temp;

  temp.count = ob.count + i;
  return temp;
}

// This handles int + ob.
CL operator+(int i, CL ob)
{
  CL temp;

  temp.count = ob.count + i;
  return temp;
}

int main()
{
  CL obj;
  obj = 10;
  cout << obj.count << " "; // outputs 10

  obj = 10 + obj; // add object to integer
  cout << obj.count << " "; // outputs 20

  obj = obj + 12; // add integer to object
  cout << obj.count;        // outputs 32

  return 0;
}
```

As you can see, the **operator+( )** function is overloaded twice to accommodate the two ways in which an integer and an object of type **CL** can occur in the addition operation.

Although you can use a **friend** function to overload a unary operator, such as **++**, you first need to know about another feature of C++, called the reference, which is the subject of the next section.

References

C++ contains a feature that is related to the pointer. This feature is called a reference. A *reference* is essentially an implicit pointer that acts as another name for an object.

Reference Parameters

By default, C and C++ pass arguments to a function using call-by-value. Passing an argument using call-by-value causes a copy of that argument to be used by the function and prevents the argument used in the call from being modified by the function. In C (and optionally in C++), when a function needs to be able to alter the values of the variables used as arguments, the parameters must be explicitly declared as pointer types and the function must operate on the calling variables using the * pointer operator. For example, the following program implements a function called **swap( )**, which exchanges the values of its two integer arguments:

```
#include <iostream>
using namespace std;

void swap(int *a, int *b);

int main()
{
  int x, y;

  x = 99;
  y = 88;

  cout << x << " " << y << "\n";

  swap(&x, &y); // exchange their values

  cout << x << " " << y << "\n";

  return 0;
}

// C-like, explicit pointer version of swap().
void swap(int *a, int *b)
{
  int t;

  t = *a;
  *a = *b;
```

```
    *b = t;
}
```

When calling **swap( )**, the variables used in the call must be preceded by the **&** operator in order to produce a pointer to each argument. This is the way that a call-by-reference is generated in C. However, even though C++ still allows this syntax, it supports a cleaner, more transparent method of generating a call-by-reference using a *reference parameter*.

In C++, it is possible to tell the compiler to automatically generate a call-by-reference rather than a call-by-value for one or more parameters of a particular function. This is accomplished by preceding the parameter name in the function's declaration with the **&**. For example, here is a function called **f( )** that takes one reference parameter of type **int**.

```
void f(int &f)
{
    f = rand(); // this modifies the calling argument
}
```

Notice that the statement

```
f = rand();
```

does not use the * pointer operator. When you declare a reference parameter, the C++ compiler automatically knows that it is an implicit pointer and dereferences it for you.

Each time **f( )** is called, it is automatically passed the *address* of its argument. For example, given this fragment

```
int val;

f(val);   // get random value
printf("%d", val);
```

the address of **val**, not its value, is passed to **f( )**. Thus, **f( )** can modify the value of **val**. Notice that it is not necessary to precede **val** with the **&** operator when **f( )** is called. The compiler automatically passes **val**'s address.

To see reference parameters in actual use, the **swap( )** function is rewritten using references. Look carefully at how **swap( )** is declared and called:

```
#include <iostream>
using namespace std;
```

```
void swap(int &a, int &b); // declare as reference parameters

int main()
{
  int x, y;

  x = 99;
  y = 88;

  cout << x << " " << y << "\n";

  swap(x, y); // exchange their values

  cout << x << " " << y << "\n";

  return 0;
}

/* Here, swap() is defined as using call-by-reference,
   not call-by-value. */
void swap(int &a, int &b)
{
  int t;

  t = a;
  a = b;  // this swaps x
  b = t;  // this swaps y
}
```

Again, notice that by making **a** and **b** reference parameters, there is no need to precede the arguments of **swap( )** with the **&** operator or to apply the ***** inside **swap( )** when the values are exchanged. In fact, it would be an error to do so. Remember that the compiler automatically generates the addresses of the arguments used to call **swap( )** and automatically dereferences **a** and **b**.

There are several restrictions that apply to reference variables:

1. You cannot reference a reference variable. That is, you cannot take its address.

2. You cannot create arrays of references.

3. You cannot create a pointer to a reference.

4. References are not allowed on bit-fields.

Passing References to Objects

In Chapter 21 it was explained that when an object is passed as an argument to a function, a copy of that object is made. When the function terminates, the copy's destructor is called. If for some reason you do not want a copy to be made or the destructor function to be called, simply pass the object by reference. When you pass by reference, no copy of the object is made. This means that no object used as a parameter is destroyed when the function terminates, and the parameter's destructor is not called. For example, try this program:

```cpp
#include <iostream>
using namespace std;

class cl {
  int id;
public:
  int i;
  cl(int i);
  ~cl();
  void neg(cl &o) {o.i = -o.i;}
};

cl::cl(int num)
{
  cout << "Constructing " << num << "\n";
  id = num;
}

cl::~cl()
{
  cout << "Destructing " << id << "\n";
}

int main()
{
  cl o(1);

  o.i = 10;
  o.neg(o);
  cout << o.i << "\n";

  return 0;
}
```

Here is the output of this program:

```
Constructing 1
-10
Destructing 1
```

As you can see, only one call is made to **cl**'s destructor function. Had **o** been passed by value, a second object would have been created inside **neg( )**, and the destructor would have been called a second time when that object was destroyed at the time **neg( )** terminated.

When passing parameters by reference, remember that changes to the object inside the function affect the calling object.

Returning References

A function can return a reference. This has the rather startling effect of allowing a function to be used on the left side of an assignment statement! For example, consider this simple program:

```cpp
#include <iostream>
using namespace std;

char &replace(int i);  // return a reference
char s[80] = "Hello There";

int main()
{

  replace(5) = 'X'; // assign X to space after Hello
  cout << s;

  return 0;
}

char &replace(int i)
{
  return s[i];
}
```

This program replaces the space between **Hello** and **There** with an **X**. That is, the program displays **HelloXThere**. Take a look at how this is accomplished.

As shown, **replace( )** is declared as returning a reference to a character array. As **replace( )** is coded, it returns a reference to the element of **s** that is specified by its argument **i**. The reference returned by **replace( )** is then used in **main( )** to assign to that element the character **X**.

Independent References

Even though references are included in C++ primarily to support call-by-reference parameter passing and to act as a return value from a function, it is possible to declare a stand-alone reference variable. This is called an *independent reference*. However, independent reference variables are seldom a good idea because they tend to confuse and destructure your program. With these reservations in mind, we will take a short look at them here.

Since a reference variable must point to some object, an independent reference must be initialized when it is declared. Generally, this means that it will be assigned the address of a previously declared variable. Once this is done, the reference variable can be used anywhere that the variable it references can. In fact, there is virtually no distinction between the two. For example, consider this program:

```cpp
#include <iostream>
using namespace std;

int main()
{
  int j, k;
  int &i = j; // independent reference to j

  j = 10;
  cout << j << " " << i; // outputs 10 10

  k = 121;
  i = k; // copies k's value into j -- not k's address
  cout << "\n" << j;   // outputs 121

  return 0;
}
```

This program displays the following output:

```
10 10
121
```

The address pointed to by the reference variable **i** is fixed and cannot be changed. Thus, when the statement **i = k** is evaluated, it is **k**'s value that is copied into **j** (referenced by **i**), not its address. For another example, **i++** does *not* cause **i** to point to a new address. Instead, **k** is increased by 1.

You can also use an independent reference to point to a constant. For example, the following is valid.

```
void f() {
  int &i = 100;
  // ...
}
```

In this case, C++ Builder generates a temporary object that has the value 100 and **i** references that object.

As stated earlier, in general it is not a good idea to use independent references because they are not necessary and tend to confuse your code.

A Matter of Style

When declaring pointer and reference variables, some C++ programmers use a unique coding style that associates the * or the & with the type name and not the variable. For example, here are two functionally equivalent declarations.

```
int& p; // & associated with type
int &p; // & associated with variable
```

Associating the * or & with the type name reflects the desire of some programmers for C++ to contain a separate pointer or reference type. However, the trouble with associating the & or * with the type name rather than the variable is that, according to the formal C++ syntax, neither the & nor the * is distributive over a list of variables. Thus, misleading declarations are easily created. For example, the following declaration creates *one, not two*, integer pointers. Here, **b** is declared as an integer (not an integer pointer) because, as specified by the C++ syntax, when used in a declaration the * (or &) is linked to the individual variable that it precedes, not to the type that it follows.

```
int* a, b;
```

The trouble with this declaration is that the visual message suggests that both **a** and **b** are pointer types, even though, in fact, only **a** is a pointer. This visual confusion misleads not only novice C++ programmers, but occasionally old pros, too.

It is important to understand that, as far as the C++ compiler is concerned, it doesn't matter whether you write **int *p** or **int* p**. Thus, if you prefer to associate the * or & with the type rather than the variable, feel free to do so. However, to avoid confusion, this book will continue to associate the * and the & with the variables that they modify rather than their types.

Using a Reference to Overload a Unary Operator

Now that you have learned about references, you will see how to use them to allow a **friend** function to overload a unary operator. To begin, think back to the original version of the overloaded **++** operator relative to the **three_d** class. It is shown here for your convenience:

```
// Overload a unary operator.
three_d three_d::operator++()
{
  x++;
  y++;
  z++;
  return *this;
}
```

As you know, each member function has as an implicit argument a pointer to itself that is referred to inside the member function using the keyword **this**. For this reason, when overloading a unary operator using a member function, no argument is explicitly declared. The only argument needed in this situation is the implicit pointer to the object that activated the call to the overloaded operator function. Since **this** is a pointer to the object, any changes made to the object's data affect the object that generates the call to the operator function. Unlike member functions, a **friend** function does not receive a **this** pointer and therefore cannot reference the object that activated it. For this reason, trying to create a **friend operator++( )** function as shown here does not work:

```
// THIS WILL NOT WORK
three_d operator++(three_d op1)
{
```

```
    op1.x++;
    op1.y++;
    op1.z++;
    return op1;
}
```

This function does not work because a *copy* of the object that activated the call to **operator++( )** is passed to the function in parameter **op1**. Thus, the changes inside **operator++( )** do not affect the called object.

The way to use a **friend** when overloading a unary **++** or **– –** is to use a reference parameter. In this way the compiler knows in advance that it must generate the address of the invoking object when it calls the operator function. Here is the entire **three_d** program, using a **friend operator++( )** function:

```
// This version uses a friend operator++() function.
#include <iostream>
using namespace std;

class three_d {
  int x, y, z; // 3-d coordinates
public:
  friend three_d operator+(three_d op1, three_d op2);
  three_d operator=(three_d op2);   // op1 is implied
  // use a reference to overload the ++
  friend three_d operator++(three_d &op1);

  void show() ;
  void assign(int mx, int my, int mz);
} ;

// This is now a friend function.
three_d operator+(three_d op1, three_d op2)
{
  three_d temp;

  temp.x = op1.x + op2.x;  // these are integer additions
  temp.y = op1.y + op2.y;  // and the + retains its original
  temp.z = op1.z + op2.z;  // meaning relative to them
  return temp;
}
```

```
// Overload the =.
three_d three_d::operator=(three_d op2)
{
  x = op2.x; // these are integer assignments
  y = op2.y; // and the = retains its original
  z = op2.z; // meaning relative to them
  return *this;
}

/* Overload a unary operator using a friend function.
   This requires the use of a reference parameter. */
three_d operator++(three_d &op1)
{
  op1.x++;
  op1.y++;
  op1.z++;
  return op1;
}

// Show X, Y, Z coordinates.
void three_d::show()
{
  cout << x << ", ";
  cout << y << ", ";
  cout << z << "\n";
 }

// Assign coordinates.
void three_d::assign(int mx, int my, int mz)
{
  x = mx;
  y = my;
  z = mz;
}

int main()
{
  three_d a, b, c;
  a.assign(1, 2, 3);
  b.assign(10, 10, 10);

  a.show();
```

```
     b.show();

     c = a+b;   // now add a and b together
     c.show();

     c = a+b+c; // add a, b and c together
     c.show();

     c = b = a;   // demonstrate multiple assignment
     c.show();
     b.show();

     ++c;   // increment c
     c.show();

     return 0;
}
```

> **Remember** *In general, you should use member functions to implement overloaded operators. **friend** functions are allowed in C++ mostly to handle some special-case situations.*

Overloading [ ]

Aside from the few operators mentioned earlier, you can overload any other C++ operator. Most of the time you will need to overload only the standard operators, such as the arithmetic, relational, or logical. However, there is one rather "exotic" operator that is often useful to overload: [ ], the array subscripting operator. In C++, the [ ] is considered a binary operator when you are overloading it. The [ ] must be overloaded by a member function. You cannot use a **friend** function. The general form of an **operator[ ]( )** function is shown here:

type class-name::operator[ ](int *i*)
{
// . . .
}

Technically, the parameter does not have to be of type **int**, but an **operator[ ]( )** function is typically used to provide array subscripting, and as such, an integer value is generally used.

Given an object called **O**, the expression

O[3]

translates into this call to the **operator[ ]( )** function:

```
operator[] (3)
```

That is, the value of the expression within the subscripting operator is passed to the **operator[ ]( )** function in its explicit parameter. The **this** pointer will point to **O**, the object that generated the call.

In the following program, **atype** declares an array of three integers. Its constructor function initializes each member of the array to the specified values. The overloaded **operator[ ]( )** function returns the value of the array as indexed by the value of its parameter.

```
#include <iostream>
using namespace std;

class atype {
  int a[3];
public:
  atype(int i, int j, int k) {
    a[0] = i;
    a[1] = j;
    a[2] = k;
  }
  int operator[] (int i) { return a[i]; }
};

int main()
{
  atype ob(1, 2, 3);

  cout << ob[1];   // displays 2

  return 0;
}
```

You can design the **operator[ ]( )** function in such a way that the **[ ]** can be used on both the left and right sides of an assignment statement. To do this, simply specify the return value of **operator[ ]( )** as a reference. The following program makes this change and shows its use:

```
#include <iostream>
using namespace std;
```

```
class atype {
  int a[3];
public:
  atype(int i, int j, int k) {
    a[0] = i;
    a[1] = j;
    a[2] = k;
  }
  int &operator[](int i) { return a[i]; }
};

int main()
{
  atype ob(1, 2, 3);

  cout << ob[1];  // displays 2
  cout << " ";

  ob[1] = 25;  // [] on left of =
  cout << ob[1];  // now displays 25

  return 0;
}
```

Because **operator[ ]( )** now returns a reference to the array element indexed by **i**, it can be used on the left side of an assignment to modify an element of the array. (Of course, it may still be used on the right side as well.)

One advantage of being able to overload the [ ] operator is that it allows a means of implementing safe array indexing in C++. As you know, in C++, it is possible to overrun (or underrun) an array boundary at run time without generating a run-time error message. However, if you create a class that contains the array, and allow access to that array only through the overloaded [ ] subscripting operator, then you can intercept an out-of-range index. For example, this program adds a range check to the preceding program and proves that it works:

```
// A safe array example.
#include <iostream>
#include <cstdlib>
using namespace std;

class atype {
```

```
    int a[3];
public:
  atype(int i, int j, int k) {
    a[0] = i;
    a[1] = j;
    a[2] = k;
  }
  int &operator[](int i);
};

// Provide range checking for atype.
int &atype::operator[](int i)
{
  if(i<0 || i> 2) {
    cout << "Boundary Error\n";
    exit(1);
  }
  return a[i];
}

int main()
{
  atype ob(1, 2, 3);

  cout << ob[1];  // displays 2
  cout << " ";

  ob[1] = 25;  // [] appears on left
  cout << ob[1];  // displays 25

  ob[3] = 44; // generates runtime error, 3 out-of-range
  return 0;
}
```

In this program, when the statement

```
ob[3] = 44;
```

executes, the boundary error is intercepted by **operator[ ]( )**, and the program is terminated before any damage can be done. (In actual practice, some sort of error-handling function would be called to deal with the out-of-range condition; the program would not have to terminate.)

Applying Operator Overloading

This chapter concludes by designing and implementing a small string class. As you may know, Standard C++ provides a powerful, full-featured string class called **string** (which is discussed later in this book). The purpose of this chapter is not to develop an alternative to this class. Instead, it is give you insight into how any new data type can be easily added and integrated into the C++ environment through the use of operator overloading. The creation of a string class is the quintessential example of this process. In the past, many programmers honed their object-oriented skills developing their own personal string classes. To conclude this chapter, we will do the same.

Before beginning, it is useful to understand why string classes are important. A string class is a useful alternative to the null-terminated strings that are used by C++ by default. While it is true that null-terminated strings are powerful, elegant, and efficient, there are many times when you need to use a string but don't need an extremely high level of efficiency. In these cases, working with a null-terminated string can be a tiresome chore. One of the problems with null-terminated strings is that they are not fully integrated into C++'s type system. For example, they cannot be acted upon by operators. However, when you create a string class, you can overload the standard operators so that they can also be applied to strings. This allow strings to be manipulated using the normal expression syntax.

To begin, the following class declares the type **str_type**:

```
#include <iostream>
#include <cstring>
using namespace std;

class str_type {
  char string[80];
public:
  str_type(char *str = "\0") { strcpy(string, str); }


  str_type operator+(str_type str); // concatenate
  str_type operator=(str_type str); // assign

  // output the string
  void show_str() { cout << string; }
} ;
```

Here, **str_type** declares one string in its private portion. For the sake of this example, no string can be longer than 80 bytes. The class has one constructor function that can be used to initialize the array **string** with a specific value or assign it a null string in the absence of any initializer. It also declares two overloaded operators that perform concatenation and assignment. Finally, it declares the function **show_str( )**, which outputs **string** to the screen. The overloaded operator functions are shown here:

```
// Concatenate two strings.
str_type str_type::operator+(str_type str) {
  str_type temp;

  strcpy(temp.string, string);
  strcat(temp.string, str.string);
  return temp;
}

// Assign one string to another.
str_type str_type::operator=(str_type str) {
  strcpy(string, str.string);
  return *this;
}
```

Given these definitions, the following **main( )** illustrates their use:

```
int main()
{
  str_type a("Hello "), b("There"), c;

  c = a + b;
  c.show_str();

  return 0;
}
```

This program outputs **Hello There** on the screen. It first concatenates **a** with **b** and then assigns this value to **c**.

Keep in mind that both the **=** and the **+** are defined only for objects of type **str_type**. For example, this statement is invalid because it tries to assign object **a** a null-terminated string:

```
a = "this is currently wrong";
```

However, the **str_type** class can be enhanced to allow such a statement. To expand the types of operations supported by the **str_type** class so that you can assign null-terminated strings to **str_type** objects or concatenate a null-terminated string with a **str_type** object, you need to overload the + and = operations a second time. First, the class declaration is changed, as shown here:

```
class str_type {
  char string[80];
public:
  str_type(char *str = "\0") { strcpy(string, str); }

  str_type operator+(str_type str); // concatenate objects
  str_type operator+(char *str);   /* concatenate object with
                                       a string */

  str_type operator=(str_type str); /* assign object to
                                        object */
  char *operator=(char *str); // assign string to object

  void show_str() { cout << string; }
} ;
```

Next, the overloaded **operator+( )** and **operator =( )** are implemented, as shown here:

```
// Assign a string to an object.
str_type str_type::operator=(char *str)
{
  str_type temp;

  strcpy(string, str);
  strcpy(temp.string, string);
  return temp;
}

// Add a string to an object.
str_type str_type::operator+(char *str)
{
  str_type temp;

  strcpy(temp.string, string);
  strcat(temp.string, str);
  return temp;
}
```

Look carefully at these functions. Notice that the right-side argument is not an object of type **str_type** but rather a pointer to a character array—that is, a null-terminated string. However, notice that both functions return an object of type **str_type**. Although the functions could, in theory, have returned some other type, it makes the most sense to return an object, since the targets of these operations are also objects. The advantage to defining string operations that accept null-terminated strings as the right-side operand is that it allows some statements to be written in a natural way. For example, these are now valid statements:

```
str_type a, b, c;
a = "hi there";  // assign an object a string
c = a + " George";  // concatenate an object with a string
```

The following program incorporates the additional meanings for the + and = operators and illustrates their use.

```
// Expanding the string type.
#include <iostream>
#include <cstring>
using namespace std;

class str_type {
  char string[80];
public:
  str_type(char *str = "\0") { strcpy(string, str); }

  str_type operator+(str_type str);
  str_type operator+(char *str);

  str_type operator=(str_type str);
  str_type operator=(char *str);

  void show_str() { cout << string; }
} ;

str_type str_type::operator+(str_type str) {
  str_type temp;

  strcpy(temp.string, string);
  strcat(temp.string, str.string);
  return temp;
```

C++

```
}

str_type str_type::operator=(str_type str) {
  strcpy(string, str.string);
  return *this;
}

str_type str_type::operator=(char *str)
{
  str_type temp;

  strcpy(string, str);
  strcpy(temp.string, string);
  return temp;
}

str_type str_type::operator+(char *str)
{
  str_type temp;

  strcpy(temp.string, string);
  strcat(temp.string, str);
  return temp;
}

int main()
{
  str_type a("Hello "), b("There"), c;

  c = a + b;
  c.show_str();
  cout << "\n";

  a = "to program in because";
  a.show_str();
  cout << "\n";

  b = c = "C++ is fun";
  c = c+" "+a+" "+b;
  c.show_str();

  return 0;
}
```

This program displays the following on the screen:

```
Hello There
to program in because
C++ is fun to program in because C++ is fun
```

On your own, try creating other string operations. For example, you might try defining the – so that it performs a substring deletion. For example, if object **A**'s string is "This is a test" and object **B**'s string is "is", then **A–B** yields "th a test". In this case, all occurrences of the substring are removed from the original string.

Chapter 23

Inheritance,
Virtual Functions,
and Polymorphism

Two of the cornerstones of OOP are inheritance and polymorphism. Inheritance is important because it allows the creation of hierarchical classifications. Using inheritance, you can create a general class that defines traits common to a set of related items. This class can then be inherited by other, more specific classes, each adding only those things that are unique to the derived class. Inheritance was introduced in Chapter 20. It is examined in detail, here.

Inheritance is also important for another reason: it is used to support run-time polymorphism. Polymorphism is sometimes characterized by the phrase "one interface, multiple methods." This means that a general class of operations can be accessed in the same fashion even though the specific actions associated with each operation may differ.

In C++, polymorphism is supported both at run time and at compile time. Operator and function overloading are examples of compile-time polymorphism. However, as powerful as operator and function overloading are, they cannot perform all tasks required by a true, object-oriented language. Therefore, C++ also allows run-time polymorphism through the use of derived classes (i.e., inheritance) and virtual functions, both of which are discussed in this chapter.

Inheritance and the Access Specifiers

In this section we will explore the interplay between C++'s access specifiers and inheritance. Before beginning, let's review terminology. A class that is inherited by another class is called the *base class*. Sometimes it is also referred to as the *parent class* or the *superclass*. The class that does the inheriting is called the *derived class*, sometimes called the *child class* or *subclass*. This book uses the terms *base* and *derived* because they are the traditional terms.

Understanding the Access Specifiers

In C++, a class can categorize its members into three classifications: **public**, **private**, or **protected**. A **public** member can be accessed by any other function in the program. A **private** member can be accessed only by member or **friend** functions of its class. A **protected** member is similar to a **private** member, except where inheritance is concerned.

When one class inherits another class, all **public** members of the base class become **public** members of the derived class and are, therefore, accessible to the derived class. However, all **private** members of the base class remain private to that class and are inaccessible to the derived class. For example, in the following fragment

```
class X {
  int i;
  int j;
public:
```

```
  void get_ij();
  void put_ij();
} ;

class Y : public X {
  int k;
public:
  int get_k();
  void make_k();
} ;
```

Class **Y** inherits and can access **X**'s **public** functions **get_ij( )** and **put_ij( )**, but it cannot access **i** or **j** because they are **private** to **X**. In all cases, a **private** member remains private to the class in which it is declared. Thus, **private** members cannot participate in inheritance.

The fact that private members cannot be inherited gives rise to an interesting question: What if you want to keep a member private, but allow its use by derived classes? The answer is the keyword **protected**. A **protected** member acts just like a **private** one except for one important difference: When a **protected** member is inherited, the derived class has access to it. Thus, specifying a member as **protected** allows you to make it available within a class hierarchy but prevent its access from outside that hierarchy. For example,

```
class X {
protected:
  int i;
  int j;
public:
  void get_ij();
  void put_ij();
} ;

class Y : public X {
  int k;
public:
  int get_k();
  void make_k();
} ;
```

Here, **Y** has access to **i** and **j** even though they are still inaccessible to the rest of the program. When you make an element **protected**, you restrict its access, but you allow this access to be inherited. When an member is **private**, access is not inherited.

One other point about **private**, **protected**, and **public**. These keywords can appear in any order and any number of times in the declaration of a class. For example, this code is perfectly valid:

```
class my_class {
protected:
  int i;
  int j;
public:
  void f1();
  void f2();
protected:
  int a;
public:
  int b;
} ;
```

However, it is usually considered good form to have only one heading for each access specifier inside each **class** or **struct** declaration.

Base Class Access Control

How a base class is inherited by a derived class affects the access status of the inherited members. As you know, the general form for inheriting a class is

```
class class-name : access class-name {
  // ...
};
```

Here, *access* determines how the derived class is inherited, and it must be either **private**, **public**, or **protected**. (It can also be omitted, in which case **public** is assumed if the base class is a structure; or **private** if the base class is a class.) If *access* is **public**, all **public** and **protected** members of the base class become **public** and **protected** members of the derived class, respectively. If *access* is **private**, all **public** and **protected** members of the base class become **private** members of the derived class. If *access* is **protected**, all **public** and **protected** members of the base class become **protected** members of the derived class. To understand the ramifications of these conversions, let's work through an example. Consider the following program:

```
#include <iostream>
using namespace std;

class X {
protected:
```

```
    int i;
    int j;
public:
  void get_ij() {
    cout << "Enter two numbers: ";
    cin >> i >> j;
  }
  void put_ij() { cout << i << " " << j << "\n"; }
} ;

// In Y, i and j of X become protected members.
class Y : public X {
  int k;
public:
  int get_k() { return k; }
  void make_k() { k = i*j; }
} ;

/* Z has access to i and j of X, but not to
   k of Y, since it is private. */
class Z : public Y {
public:
  void f();
} ;

// i and j are accessible here
void Z::f()
{
  i = 2; // ok
  j = 3; // ok
}

int main()
{
  Y var;
  Z var2;

  var.get_ij();
  var.put_ij();

  var.make_k();
  cout << var.get_k();
  cout << "\n";
```

```
    var2.f();
    var2.put_ij();

    return 0;
}
```

Since **Y** inherits **X** as **public**, the **protected** elements of **X** become **protected** elements of **Y**, which means that they can be inherited by **Z** and this program compiles and runs correctly. However, changing **X**'s status in **Y** to **private**, as shown in the following program, causes **Z** to be denied access to **i** and **j**, and the functions **get_ij( )** and **put_ij( )** that access them, because they have been made **private** in **Y**.

```cpp
#include <iostream>
using namespace std;

class X {
protected:
  int i;
  int j;
public:
  void get_ij() {
    cout << "Enter two numbers: ";
    cin >> i >> j;
  }
  void put_ij() { cout << i << " " << j << "\n"; }
} ;

// Now, i and j are converted to private members of Y.
class Y : private X {
  int k;
public:
  int get_k() { return k; }
  void make_k() { k = i*j; }
} ;

/* Because i and j are private in Y, they
   cannot be inherited by Z. */
class Z : public Y {
public:
  void f();
} ;
```

```
// This function no longer works.
void Z::f()
{
// i = 2;  i and j are no longer accessible
// j = 3;
}

int main()
{
  Y var;
  Z var2;

// var.get_ij();  no longer accessible
// var.put_ij();  no longer accessible

  var.make_k();
  cout << var.get_k();
  cout << "\n";

  var2.f();
// var2.put_ij();  no longer accessible

  return 0;
}
```

When **X** is inherited as **private** in **Y**'s declaration, it causes **i, j, get_ij( )**, and **put_ij( )** to be treated as **private** in **Y**, which means they cannot be inherited by **Z**; thus, **Z**'s class can no longer access them.

Constructors and Destructors in Derived Classes

When using derived classes, it is important to understand how and when constructors and destructors are executed in both the base and derived classes. Let's begin with constructors.

It is possible for a base class and a derived class to each have a constructor function. (In fact, in the case of a multilayered class hierarchy, it is possible for all involved classes to have constructors, but we will start with the simplest case.) When a base class contains a constructor, that constructor is executed before the constructor in the derived class. For example, consider this short program:

```
#include <iostream>
using namespace std;
```

```
class Base {
public:
  Base() { cout << "\nBase created\n"; }
};

class D_class1 : public Base {
public:
  D_class1() { cout << "D_class1 created\n"; }
};

int main()
{
  D_class1 d1;

  // do nothing but execute constructors
  return 0;
}
```

This program creates an object of type **D_class1**. It displays this output:

```
Base created
D_class1 created
```

Here, **d1** is an object of type **D_class1**, which is derived using **Base**. Thus, when **d1** is created, first **Base( )** is executed, then **D_class1( )** is called.

It makes sense for constructors to be called in the same order in which the derivation takes place. Because the base class has no knowledge of the derived class, any initialization it needs to perform is separate from and possibly prerequisite to any initialization performed by the derived class, so it must be executed first.

On the other hand, a destructor function in a derived class is executed before the destructor in the base. The reason for this is also easy to understand. Since the destruction of a base class object implies the destruction of the derived class object, the derived object's destructor must be executed before the base object is destroyed. This program illustrates the order in which constructors and destructors are executed:

```
#include <iostream>
using namespace std;

class Base {
public:
  Base() { cout << "\nBase created\n"; }
```

```
  ~Base() { cout << "Base destroyed\n\n"; }
};

class D_class1 : public Base {
public:
  D_class1() { cout << "D_class1 created\n"; }
  ~D_class1() { cout << "D_class1 destroyed\n"; }
};

int main()
{
  D_class1 d1;

  cout << "\n";

  return 0;
}
```

This program produces the following output:

```
Base created
D_class1 created

D_class1 destroyed
Base destroyed
```

As you know, it is possible for a derived class to be used as a base class in the creation of another derived class. When this happens, constructors are executed in the order of their derivation and destructors in the reverse order. For example, consider this program, which uses **D_class1** to derive **D_class2**:

```
#include <iostream>
using namespace std;

class Base {
public:
  Base() { cout << "\nBase created\n"; }
  ~Base() { cout << "Base destroyed\n\n"; }
};

class D_class1 : public Base {
public:
```

```
    D_class1() { cout << "D_class1 created\n"; }
    ~D_class1() { cout << "D_class1 destroyed\n"; }
};

class D_class2 : public D_class1 {
public:
    D_class2() { cout << "D_class2 created\n"; }
    ~D_class2() { cout << "D_class2 destroyed\n"; }
};

int main()
{
  D_class1 d1;
  D_class2 d2;

  cout << "\n";

  return 0;
}
```

The program produces this output:

```
Base created
D_class1 created

Base created
D_class1 created
D_class2 created

D_class2 destroyed
D_class1 destroyed
Base destroyed

D_class1 destroyed
Base destroyed
```

As you can see, each derived constructor is called before its base class's constructor. The reverse is true for the destructors.

Remember *Constructors are called in order of derivation. Destructors are called in reverse order.*

Multiple Inheritance

It is possible for one class to inherit the attributes of two or more classes at the same time. To accomplish this, use a comma-separated inheritance list in the derived class's base class list. The general form is

class *derived-class-name* : *base-class list*
{
// ...
};

For example, in this program **Z** inherits both **X** and **Y**.

```cpp
#include <iostream>
using namespace std;

class X {
protected:
  int a;
public:
  void make_a(int i) { a = i; }
};

class Y {
protected:
  int b;
public:
  void make_b(int i) { b = i; }
} ;

// Z inherits both X and Y
class Z : public X, public Y {
public:
  int make_ab() { return a*b; }
} ;

int main()
{
  Z i;

  i.make_a(10);
  i.make_b(12);
  cout << i.make_ab();
```

```
    return 0;
}
```

In this example, **Z** inherits both **X** and **Y**. This means that it has access to the **public** and **protected** portions of both **X** and **Y**.

In the preceding example, neither **X**, **Y**, nor **Z** contained constructor functions. However, the situation is more complex when a base class contains a constructor function. For example, let's change the preceding example so that the classes **X**, **Y**, and **Z** each have a constructor.

```
#include <iostream>
using namespace std;

class X {
protected:
  int a;
public:
  X() {
    a = 10;
    cout << "Initializing X\n";
  }
};

class Y {
protected:
  int b;
public:
  Y() {
    cout << "Initializing Y\n";
    b = 20;
  }
};

// Z inherits both X and Y
class Z : public X, public Y {
public:
  Z() { cout << "Initializing Z\n"; }
  int make_ab() { return a*b; }
};
```

```
int main()
{
  Z i;

  cout << i.make_ab();

  return 0;
}
```

When this program runs, it displays the following:

```
Initializing X
Initializing Y
Initializing Z
200
```

Notice that the base classes are constructed in the order they appear from left to right in **Z**'s declaration.

In general, when a list of base classes is used, the constructors are called in order from left to right. Destructors are called in order from right to left.

Passing Parameters to a Base Class

So far, none of the examples of inheritance have included a base class constructor that used parameters. As long as no base class constructor requires arguments, a derived class need not do anything special. However, when a base class constructor requires arguments, your derived classes must explicitly handle this situation by passing the necessary arguments to the base class. To accomplish this, you will use an extended form of the constructor function within the derived class that passes arguments to the constructor function of the base class. This extended form is shown here:

derived-constructor(arg-list) : base1(arg-list), base2(arg-list), . . ., baseN(arg-list)
{
  // ...
}

Here, *base1* through *baseN* are the names of the base classes inherited by the derived class. Notice that the colon is used to separate the derived class's constructor function from the argument lists of the base classes. The argument lists associated with the base classes can consist of constants, global variables, or the parameters to the derived class's constructor function. Since an object's initialization occurs at run time, you can use as an argument any identifier that is defined within the current scope.

C++

The following program illustrates how to pass arguments to the base classes of a derived class by modifying the preceding program:

```cpp
#include <iostream>
using namespace std;

class X {
protected:
  int a;
public:
  X(int i) { a = i; }
};

class Y {
protected:
  int b;
public:
  Y(int i) { b = i; }
} ;

// Z inherits both X and Y
class Z : public X, public Y {
public:
  /* Initialize X and Y via Z's constructor.
     Notice that Z does not actually use x or y
     itself, but it could, if it so chooses. */
  Z(int x, int y) : X(x), Y(y)
  {
    cout << "Initializing\n";
  }
  int make_ab() { return a*b; }
} ;

int main()
{
  Z i(10, 20);

  cout << i.make_ab();

  return 0;
}
```

Notice how the constructor **Z** does not actually use its parameters directly. Instead, in this example, they are simply passed along to the constructor functions for **X** and **Y**. There is no reason, however, that **Z** could not use these or other arguments.

Pointers and References to Derived Types

Before moving on to virtual functions and polymorphism, it is necessary to explain a unique attribute of pointers and references that provides their foundation. We will begin with pointers. In general, a pointer of one type cannot point to an object of a different type. However, there is an important exception to this rule that relates only to derived classes. In C++, a base class pointer can point to an object of a class derived from that base. For example, assume that you have a base type called **B_class** and a type called **D_class**, that is derived from **B_class**. In C++, any pointer declared as type **B_class *** can also a point to an object of type **D_class**. For example, given

```
B_class *p;   // pointer to object of type B_class
B_class B_ob; // object of type B_class
D_class D_ob; // object of type D_class
```

the following is perfectly valid:

```
p = &B_ob; // p points to object of type B_class

p = &D_ob; /* p points to object of type D_class,
              which is an object derived from B_class. */
```

Using **p**, all elements of **D_ob** inherited from **B_ob** can be accessed. However, elements specific to **D_ob** cannot be referenced using **p** (unless a type cast is employed). This is because the pointer only "knows" about the members of its base type even though it can point to derived types.

For a concrete example that uses base class pointers, consider this short program, which defines a base class called **B_class** and a derived class called **D_class**. The derived class implements a simple automated telephone book.

```
// Using pointers on derived class objects.

#include <iostream>
#include <cstring>
using namespace std;

class B_class {
```

C++

```
    char name[80];
public:
  void put_name(char *s) { strcpy(name, s); }
  void show_name() { cout << name << " "; }
} ;

class D_class : public B_class {
  char phone_num[80];
public:
  void put_phone(char *num) {
    strcpy(phone_num, num);
  }
  void show_phone() { cout << phone_num << "\n"; }
};

int main()
{
  B_class *p;
  B_class B_ob;

  D_class *dp;
  D_class D_ob;

  p = &B_ob;   // address of base

  // Access B_class via pointer.
  p->put_name("Thomas Edison");

  // Access D_class via base pointer.
  p = &D_ob;
  p->put_name("Albert Einstein");

  // Show that each name went into proper object.
  B_ob.show_name();
  D_ob.show_name();
  cout << "\n";

  /* Since put_phone and show_phone are not part of the
     base class, they are not accessible via the base
     pointer p and must be accessed either directly,
     or, as shown here, through a pointer to the
```

```
    derived type.
*/
dp = &D_ob;
dp->put_phone("555 555-1234");
p->show_name(); // either p or dp can be used in this line
dp->show_phone();

return 0;
}
```

In this example, the pointer **p** is defined as a pointer to **B_class**. However, it can point to an object of the derived class **D_class** and can be used to access those elements of the derived class that are defined by the base class. Remember that a base pointer cannot access those elements specific to the derived class without the use of a type cast. This is why **show_phone( )** is accessed using the **dp** pointer, which is a pointer to the derived class.

If you want to access elements defined by a derived type using a base type pointer, you must cast it into a pointer of the derived type. For example, this line of code calls the **show_phone( )** function of **D_ob**:

```
((D_class *)p)->show_phone();
```

The outer set of parentheses are necessary to associate the cast with **p** and not with the return type of **show_phone( )**. While there is technically nothing wrong with casting a pointer in this manner, it is best avoided because it simply adds confusion to your code.

While a base pointer can be used to point to any type of derived object, the reverse is not true. That is, you cannot use a pointer to a derived class to access an object of the base type.

One final point: a pointer is incremented and decremented relative to its base type. Therefore, when a pointer to a base class is pointing to a derived class, incrementing or decrementing it does *not* make it point to the next object of the derived class. Therefore, you should consider it invalid to increment or decrement a pointer when it is pointing to a derived object.

References to Derived Types

Similar to the action of pointers just described, a base class reference can be used to refer to an object of a derived type. The most common application of this is found in function parameters. A base class reference parameter can receive objects of the base class as well as any other type derived from that base. You will see an example of this, shortly.

Virtual Functions

Run-time polymorphism is achieved through the use of derived types and virtual functions. In short, a *virtual function* is a function that is declared as **virtual** in a base class and redefined in one or more derived classes. Virtual functions are special because when one is called through a base-class pointer (or reference) to an object of a derived class, C++ determines which function to call *at run time* according to the type of object *pointed to*. Thus, when different objects are pointed to, different versions of the virtual function are executed. A class that contains one or more virtual functions is called a *polymorphic class*.

A virtual function is declared as **virtual** inside the base class by preceding its declaration with the keyword **virtual**. However, when a virtual function is redefined by a derived class, the keyword **virtual** need not be repeated (although it is not an error to do so).

As a first example of virtual functions, examine this short program:

```
// A short example that uses virtual functions.
#include <iostream>
using namespace std;

class Base {
public:
  virtual void who() { // specify a virtual function
    cout << "Base\n";
  }
};

class first_d : public Base {
public:
  void who() { // define who() relative to first_d
    cout << "First derivation\n";
  }
};

class second_d : public Base {
public:
  void who() { // define who() relative to second_d
    cout << "Second derivation\n";
  }
};
```

```
int main()
{
  Base base_obj;
  Base *p;
  first_d first_obj;
  second_d second_obj;

  p = &base_obj;
  p->who();  // access Base's who

  p = &first_obj;
  p->who(); // access first_d's who

  p = &second_obj;
  p->who();  // access second_d's who

  return 0;
}
```

This program produces the following output:

```
Base
First derivation
Second derivation
```

Let's examine the program in detail to understand how it works.

In **Base**, the function **who( )** is declared as **virtual**. This means that the function can be redefined by a derived class. Inside both **first_d** and **second_d**, **who( )** is redefined relative to each class. Inside **main( )**, four variables are declared. The first is **base_obj**, which is an object of type **Base**; **p**, which is a pointer to **Base** objects; and **first_obj** and **second_obj**, which are objects of the two derived classes. Next, **p** is assigned the address of **base_obj**, and the **who( )** function is called. Since **who( )** is declared as **virtual**, C++ determines at run time which version of **who( )** is referred to by the type of object pointed to by **p**. In this case, it is an object of type **Base**, so the version of **who( )** declared in **Base** is executed. Next, **p** is assigned the address of **first_obj**. (Remember that a base class pointer can point to an object of a derived class.) Now when **who( )** is called, C++ again examines the type of object pointed to by **p** to determine what version of **who( )** to call. Since **p** points to an object of type **first_d**, that version of **who( )** is used. Likewise, when **p** is assigned the address of **second_obj**, the version of **who( )** declared inside **second_d** is executed.

The most common way that a base class reference is used to call a virtual function is through a function parameter. For example, consider the following variation on the preceding program.

```cpp
/* Here, a base class reference is used to access
a virtual function. */
#include <iostream>
using namespace std;

class Base {
public:
  virtual void who() { // specify a virtual function
    cout << "Base\n";
  }
};

class first_d : public Base {
public:
  void who() { // define who() relative to first_d
    cout << "First derivation\n";
  }
};

class second_d : public Base {
public:
  void who() { // define who() relative to second_d
    cout << "Second derivation\n";
  }
};

// Use a base class reference parameter.
void show_who(Base &r) {
  r.who();
}

int main()
{
  Base base_obj;
  first_d first_obj;
  second_d second_obj;

  show_who(base_obj);    // access Base's who
  show_who(first_obj);   // access first_d's who
```

```
    show_who(second_obj); // access second_d's who

    return 0;
}
```

This program produces the same output as its preceding version. In this example, the function **show_who( )** defines a reference parameter of type **Base**. Inside **main( )**, the function is called using objects of type **Base**, **first_d**, and **second_d**. Inside **show_who( )**, the specific version of **who( )** that is called is determined by the type of object being referenced when the function is called.

The key point to using virtual functions to achieve run-time polymorphism is that you must access those functions through the use of a base class pointer or reference. Although it is legal to call a virtual function just as you call any other "normal" function, by applying the dot operator to an object, it is only when a virtual function is called through a base class pointer (or reference) that run-time polymorphism is achieved.

At first glance, the redefinition of a virtual function in a derived class looks like a special form of function overloading. But this is not the case, and the term *overloading* is not applied to virtual function redefinition because several differences exist. First, the prototypes for virtual functions must match. As you know, when overloading normal functions, the number and type of parameters must differ. However, when redefining a virtual function, these elements must be unchanged. If the prototypes of the functions differ, then the function is simply considered overloaded, and its virtual nature is lost. Also, if only the return types of the function differ, an error occurs. (Functions that differ only in their return types are inherently ambiguous.) Another restriction is that a virtual function must be a nonstatic member, not a **friend**, of the class for which it is defined. However, a virtual function can be a **friend** of another class. Also, destructor functions can be virtual, but constructors cannot.

Because of the restrictions and differences between overloading normal functions and redefining virtual functions, the term *overriding* is used to describe the virtual function redefinition.

Once a function is declared as **virtual**, it stays virtual no matter how many layers of derived classes it passes through. For example, if **second_d** is derived from **first_d** instead of **Base**, as shown in the following example, **who( )** is still virtual, and the proper version is still correctly selected:

```
// Derive from first_d, not Base
class second_d : public first_d {
public:
  void who() { // define who() relative to second_d
    cout << "Second derivation\n";
  }
};
```

When a derived class does not override a virtual function, then the version of the function in the base class is used. For example, try this version of the preceding program:

```cpp
#include <iostream>
using namespace std;

class Base {
public:
  virtual void who() {
    cout << "Base\n";
  }
};

class first_d : public Base {
public:
  void who() {
    cout << "First derivation\n";
  }
};

class second_d : public Base {
// who() not defined
};

int main()
{
  Base base_obj;
  Base *p;
  first_d first_obj;
  second_d second_obj;

  p = &base_obj;
  p->who();  // access Base's who()

  p = &first_obj;
  p->who(); // access first_d's who()

  p = &second_obj;
  p->who();  /* access Base's who() because
                second_d does not redefine it */
```

```
    return 0;
}
```

This program now outputs the following:

```
Base
First derivation
Base
```

Keep in mind that inherited characteristics are hierarchical. To illustrate this point, imagine that in the preceding example **second_d** is derived from **first_d** instead of **Base**. When **who( )** is referenced relative to an object of type **second_d** (in which **who( )** is not defined) it is the version of **who( )** declared inside **first_d** that is called, since it is the class closest to **second_d**. In general, when a class does not override a virtual function, C++ uses the first definition that it finds in reverse order of derivation.

Why Virtual Functions?

As stated at the start of this chapter, virtual functions in combination with derived types allow C++ to support run-time polymorphism. Polymorphism is essential to object-oriented programming because it allows a generalized class to specify those functions that will be common to any derivative of that class, while allowing a derived class to specify the exact implementation of those functions. In other words, the base class dictates the general *interface* that any object derived from that class will have, but it lets the derived class define the actual *method*. This is why the phrase "one interface, multiple methods" is often used to describe polymorphism.

Part of the key to successfully applying polymorphism is understanding that base and derived classes form a hierarchy that moves from greater to lesser generalization (base to derived). Hence, when used correctly, the base class provides all elements that a derived class can use directly plus the basis for those functions that the derived class must implement on its own.

Having a consistent interface with multiple implementations is important because it helps the programmer handle increasingly complex programs. For example, when you develop a program, all objects you derive from a particular base class are accessed in the same general way, even if the specific actions vary from one derived class to the next. This means that you need to remember only one interface rather than several. Further, the separation of interface and implementation allows the creation of *class libraries*, which can be provided by a third party. If these libraries are implemented correctly, they provide a common interface that you can use to derive your own specific classes.

C++

To get an idea of the power of the "one interface, multiple methods" concept, examine this short program. It creates a base class called **figure**. This class is used to store the dimensions of various two-dimensional objects and to compute their areas. The function **set_dim( )** is a standard member function because its operation is common to all derived classes. However, **show_area( )** is declared as **virtual** because the way the area of each object is computed varies. The program uses **figure** to derive two specific classes, called **square** and **triangle**.

```cpp
#include <iostream>
using namespace std;

class figure {
protected:
  double x, y;
public:
  void set_dim(double i, double j) {
    x = i;
    y = j;
  }
  virtual void show_area() {
    cout << "No area computation defined ";
    cout << "for this class.\n";
  }
} ;

class triangle : public figure {
  public:
    void show_area() {
      cout << "Triangle with height ";
      cout << x << " and base " << y;
      cout << " has an area of ";
      cout << x * 0.5 * y << ".\n";
    }
};

class square : public figure {
  public:
    void show_area() {
      cout << "Square with dimensions ";
      cout << x << "x" << y;
      cout << " has an area of ";
      cout << x * y << ".\n";
```

```
      }
};

int main()
{
    figure *p;   /* create a pointer to base type */
    triangle t;   /* create objects of derived types */
    square s;

    p = &t;
    p->set_dim(10.0, 5.0);
    p->show_area();
    p = &s;
    p->set_dim(10.0, 5.0);
    p->show_area();

    return 0;
}
```

As you can see by examining this program, the interface to both **square** and **triangle** is the same even though both provide their own methods for computing the area of each of their objects.

Given the declaration for **figure**, it is possible to derive a class called **circle** that computes the area of a circle given its radius. To do so, you must create a new derived type that computes the area of a circle. The power of virtual functions is based in the fact that you can easily derive a new type that shares the same common interface as other related objects. For example, here is one way to do it:

```
class circle : public figure {
public:
    void show_area() {
      cout << "Circle with radius ";
      cout << x;
      cout << " has an area of ";
      cout <<  3.14 * x * x;
    }
};
```

Before trying to use **circle**, look closely at the definition of **show_area( )**. Notice that it uses only the value of **x**, which is assumed to hold the radius. (Remember that the area of a circle is computed using the formula πR^2.) However, the function **set_dim( )**

as defined in **figure** assumes that it will be passed not just one, but two values. Since **circle** does not require this second value, what is the best course of action?

There are two ways to resolve this problem. First, you can call **set_dim( )** using a dummy value as the second parameter when using a **circle** object. This has the disadvantage of being sloppy as well as requiring you to remember a special exception, which violates the "one interface, many methods" approach.

A better way to resolve this problem is to give the **y** parameter inside **set_dim( )** a default value. In this way, when calling **set_dim( )** for a circle, you need specify only the radius. When calling **set_dim( )** for a triangle or a square, you would specify both values. The expanded program is shown here:

```cpp
#include <iostream>
using namespace std;

class figure {
protected:
  double x, y;
public:
  void set_dim(double i, double j=0) {
    x = i;
    y = j;
  }
  virtual void show_area() {
    cout << "No area computation defined ";
    cout << "for this class.\n";
  }
} ;

class triangle : public figure {
  public:
    void show_area() {
      cout << "Triangle with height ";
      cout << x << " and base " << y;
      cout << " has an area of ";
      cout << x * 0.5 * y << ".\n";
    }
};

class square : public figure {
  public:
    void show_area() {
      cout << "Square with dimensions ";
```

```
            cout << x << "x" << y;
            cout << " has an area of ";
            cout << x *  y << ".\n";
        }
};

class circle : public figure {
  public:
    void show_area() {
      cout << "Circle with radius ";
      cout << x;
      cout << " has an area of ";
      cout << 3.14 * x * x;
    }
} ;

int main()
{
  figure *p;  /* create a pointer to base type */
  triangle t;  /* create objects of derived types */
  square s;
  circle c;

  p = &t;
  p->set_dim(10.0, 5.0);
  p->show_area();

  p = &s;
  p->set_dim(10.0, 5.0);
  p->show_area();

  p = &c;
  p->set_dim(9.0);
  p->show_area();

  return 0;
}
```

This example also points out that when defining base classes it is important to be as flexible as possible. Don't give your program unnecessary restrictions.

Pure Virtual Functions and Abstract Types

When a virtual function that is not overridden in a derived class is called for an object of that derived class, the version of the function as defined in the base class is used. However, in many circumstances there is no meaningful definition of a virtual function inside the base class. For example, in the base class **figure**, used in the preceding example, the definition of **show_area( )** is simply a placeholder. It does not compute and display the area of any type of object. There are two ways you can handle this situation. One way is to simply have it report a warning message, as shown in the example. While this approach can be useful in certain situations, it is not appropriate for all circumstances. There can be virtual functions that must be defined by the derived class in order for the derived class to have any meaning. For example, the **class triangle** has no meaning if **show_area( )** is not defined. In this sort of case, you want some method to ensure that a derived class does, indeed, define all necessary functions. C++'s solution to this problem is the pure virtual function.

A *pure* virtual function is a function declared in a base class that has no definition relative to the base. Since it has no definition relative to the base, any derived type must define its own version—it cannot simply use the version defined in the base. To declare a pure virtual function, use this general form:

virtual *type func_name(parameter list)* = 0;

where *type* is the return type of the function and *func_name* is the name of the function. For example, in the following version of **figure**, **show_area( )** is a pure virtual function:

```
class figure {
double x, y;
public:
  void set_dim(double i, double j=0) {
    x = i;
    y = j;
  }
  virtual void show_area() = 0; // pure
} ;
```

By declaring a virtual function as pure, you force any derived class to define its own implementation. If a class fails to do so, a compile-time error results. For example, if you try to compile this modified version of the **figure** program, in which the definition for **show_area( )** has been removed from the **circle** class, you will see an error message:

```
/*
```

```
This program will not compile because the class
   circle does not override show_area().
*/
#include <iostream>
using namespace std;

class figure {
protected:
  double x, y;
public:
  void set_dim(double i, double j) {
    x = i;
    y = j;
  }
  virtual void show_area() = 0; // pure
} ;

class triangle : public figure {
  public:
    void show_area() {
      cout << "Triangle with height ";
      cout << x << " and base " << y;
      cout << " has an area of ";
      cout << x * 0.5 * y << ".\n";
    }
};

class square : public figure {
  public:
    void show_area() {
      cout << "Square with dimensions ";
      cout << x << "x" << y;
      cout << " has an area of ";
      cout << x *  y << ".\n";
    }
};

class circle : public figure {
// no definition of show_area() will cause an error
};

int main()
```

```
{
  figure *p;  // create a pointer to base type
  circle c;   // attempt to create a circle -- ERROR
  triangle t; // create objects of derived types
  square s;

  p = &t;
  p->set_dim(10.0, 5.0);
  p->show_area();

  p = &s;
  p->set_dim(10.0, 5.0);
  p->show_area();

  return 0;
}
```

If a class has at least one pure virtual function, that class is said to be *abstract*. Abstract classes have one important feature: There can be no objects of that class. Instead, an abstract class must be used only as a base that other classes will inherit. The reason that an abstract class cannot be used to declare an object is that one or more of its member functions have no definition. However, even if the base class is abstract, you still can use it to declare pointers or references, which are needed to support run-time polymorphism.

Early Versus Late Binding

There are two terms that are commonly used when discussing object-oriented programming languages: early binding and late binding. Relative to C++, these terms refer to events that occur at compile time and events that occur at run time, respectively.

In object-oriented terms, *early binding* means that an object is bound to its function call at compile time. That is, all information necessary to determine a function call is known when the program is compiled. Examples of early binding include standard function calls, overloaded function calls, and overloaded operator function calls. The principal advantage to early binding is efficiency—it is both faster and often requires less memory than late binding. Its disadvantage is a lack of flexibility.

Late binding means that an object is bound to its function call only at run time, not before. Late binding is achieved in C++ by using virtual functions and derived types. The advantage to late binding is that it allows greater flexibility. It can be used to support a common interface while allowing various objects that use that interface to define their own implementations. Further, it can be used to help you create class libraries, which can be reused and extended.

Whether your program uses early or late binding depends on what your program is designed to do. (Actually, most large programs use a combination of both.) Late binding is one of C++'s most powerful additions to the C language. However, the price you pay for this power is that your program will run slightly slower. Therefore, it is best to use late binding only when it adds to the structure and manageability of your program. Keep in mind that the loss of performance is small, so when the situation calls for late binding, you should most definitely use it.

C++

The Complete Reference

Borland
C++
Builder

Chapter 24

The C++ I/O
Class Library

This chapter presents an overview of the C++ I/O class library. It also discusses how to overload the << and >> operators so that you can input or output objects of classes that you design. C++'s I/O system is very large and it isn't possible to cover every class, function, or feature here, but this chapter introduces you to those that are most important and commonly used.

Why C++ Has Its Own I/O System

Since the I/O system inherited from C is extremely rich, flexible, and powerful, you might be wondering why C++ defines yet another system. The answer is that C's I/O system knows nothing about objects. Therefore, for C++ to provide complete support for object-oriented programming, it was necessary to create an I/O system that could operate on user-defined objects. In addition to support for objects, there are several benefits to using C++'s I/O system even in programs that don't make extensive (or any) use of user-defined objects. Frankly, for all new code, you should use the C++ I/O system. The C I/O is supported by C++ only for compatibility.

Old Versus Modern C++ I/O

There are currently two versions of the C++ object-oriented I/O library in use: the older one that is based upon the original specifications for C++ and the newer one defined by the ANSI/ISO standard for C++. The old I/O library is supported by the header file **<iostream.h>**. The new I/O library is supported by the header **<iostream>**. For the most part the two libraries appear the same to the programmer. This is because the new I/O library is, in essence, simply an updated and improved version of the old one. In fact, the vast majority of differences between the two occur beneath the surface, in the way that the libraries are implemented—not in how they are used.

From the programmer's perspective, there are two main differences between the old and new C++ I/O libraries. First, the new I/O library contains a few additional features and defines some new data types. Thus, the new I/O library is essentially a superset of the old one. Nearly all programs originally written for the old library will compile without substantive changes when the new library is used. Second, the old-style I/O library was in the global namespace. The new-style library is in the **std** namespace. (Recall that the **std** namespace is used by all of the Standard C++ libraries.) Since the old-style I/O library is now obsolete, this book describes only the new I/O library, but most of the information is applicable to the old I/O library as well.

C++ Builder supports both the old and new style approaches to I/O. Thus, you can use C++ Builder to maintain older code. For new code, however, you should use the new style I/O because it complies with the ANSI/ISO standard for C++.

C++ Streams

The C and C++ I/O systems have one important thing in common: they both operate on streams, which are discussed in Part One of this book. The fact that C and C++ streams are similar means that what you already know about streams is completely applicable to C++.

The C++ Predefined Streams

Like C, C++ contains several predefined streams that are opened automatically when your C++ program begins execution. They are **cin**, **cout**, **cerr**, and **clog**. As you know, **cin** is the stream associated with standard input and **cout** is the stream associated with standard output. The streams **cerr** and **clog** are used for error output. The difference between **cerr** and **clog**, which are both linked to standard output, is that **cerr** is not buffered, so any data sent to it is immediately output. Alternatively, **clog** is buffered, and output is written only when a buffer is full.

By default, the C++ standard streams are linked to the console, but they can be redirected to other devices or files by your program. Also, they can be redirected by the operating system.

The C++ Stream Classes

As mentioned, Standard C++ provides support for its I/O system in **<iostream>**. In this header, a rather complicated set of class hierarchies is defined that supports I/O operations. The I/O classes begin with a system of template classes. Templates are discussed in Chapter 25, but here is a brief description. A *template class* defines the form of a class without fully specifying the data upon which it will operate. Once a template class has been defined, specific instances of a template class can be created. As it relates to the I/O library, Standard C++ creates two specializations of the I/O template classes: one for 8-bit characters and another for wide characters. This book will use only the 8-bit character classes, since they are by far the most common. But the same techniques apply to both.

The C++ I/O system is built upon two related, but different, template class hierarchies. The first is derived from the low-level I/O class called **basic_streambuf**. This class supplies the basic, low-level input and output operations, and provides the underlying support for the entire C++ I/O system. Unless you are doing advanced I/O programming, you will not need to use **basic_streambuf** directly. The class hierarchy that you will most commonly be working with is derived from **basic_ios**. This is a high-level I/O class that provides formatting, error-checking, and status information related to stream I/O. (A base class for **basic_ios** is called **ios_base**, which defines several nontemplate traits used by **basic_ios**.) **basic_ios** is used as a base for several derived classes, including **basic_istream**, **basic_ostream**, and **basic_iostream**. These classes are used to create streams capable of input, output, and input/output, respectively.

As explained, the I/O library creates two specializations of the template class hierarchies just described: one for 8-bit characters and one for wide characters. Here is a list of the mapping of template class names to their character and wide-character versions.

Template Class	Character-Based Class	Wide-Character-Based Class
basic_streambuf	streambuf	wstreambuf
basic_ios	ios	wios
basic_istream	istream	wistream
basic_ostream	ostream	wostream
basic_iostream	iostream	wiostream
basic_fstream	fstream	wfstream
basic_ifstream	ifstream	wifstream
basic_ofstream	ofstream	wofstream

The character-based names will be used throughout the remainder of this book, since they are the names that you will usually use in your programs. They are also the same names that were used by the old I/O library. This is why the old and new I/O libraries are compatible at the source code level.

One last point: The **ios** class contains many member functions and variables that control or monitor the fundamental operation of a stream. It will be referred to frequently. Just remember that if you include **<iostream>** in your program, you will have access to this important class.

Creating Your Own Inserters and Extractors

In the preceding four chapters, member functions were created in order to output or input a class's data, often called something like **show_data( )** or **get_data( )**. While there is nothing technically wrong with this approach, C++ provides a much better way of performing I/O operations on classes by overloading the << and >> operators.

In the language of C++, the << operator is referred to as the *insertion* operator because it inserts characters into a stream. Likewise, the >> operator is called the *extraction* operator because it extracts characters from a stream. The operator functions that overload the insertion and extraction operators are generally called *inserters* and *extractors*, respectively.

The insertion and extraction operators are already overloaded (in **<iostream>**) to perform stream I/O on any of C++'s built-in types. This section explains how to define these operators relative to classes that you define.

Creating Inserters

C++ provides an easy way to create inserters for classes that you create. This simple example creates an inserter for the **three_d** class (first defined in Chapter 22):

```
class three_d {
public:
  int x, y, z; // 3-d coordinates
  three_d(int a, int b, int c) { x=a; y=b; z=c; }
} ;
```

To create an inserter function for an object of type **three_d**, you must define what an insertion operation means relative to the class **three_d**. To do this, you must overload the **<<** operator, as shown here:

```
// Display X, Y, Z coordinates (three_d's inserter).
ostream &operator<<(ostream &stream, three_d obj)
{
  stream << obj.x << ", ";
  stream << obj.y << ", ";
  stream << obj.z << "\n";
  return stream; // return the stream
}
```

Many of the features in this function are common to all inserter functions. First, notice that it is declared as returning a reference to an object of type **ostream**. This is necessary to allow several insertion operations to be performed in a single statement. Next, the function has two parameters. The first is the reference to the stream that occurs on the left side of the **<<** operator; the second parameter is the object that occurs on the right side. Inside the function, the three values contained in an object of type **three_d** are output, and **stream** is returned. Here is a short program that demonstrates the inserter:

```
#include <iostream>
using namespace std;

class three_d {
public:
```

```
     int x, y, z; // 3-d coordinates
     three_d(int a, int b, int c) { x=a; y=b; z=c; }
   } ;

   // Display X, Y, Z coordinates - three_d inserter.
   ostream &operator<<(ostream &stream, three_d obj)
   {
     stream << obj.x << ", ";
     stream << obj.y << ", ";
     stream << obj.z << "\n";
     return stream;   // return the stream
   }

   int main()
   {
     three_d a(1, 2, 3), b(3, 4, 5), c(5, 6, 7);

     cout << a << b << c;

     return 0;
   }
```

If you eliminate the code that is specific to the **three_d** class you are left with the general form of an inserter function, as shown here:

```
ostream &operator<<(ostream &stream, class_type obj )
{
// type specific code goes here
return stream; // return the stream
}
```

What an inserter function actually does is up to you. Just make sure that you return *stream*. Also, it is perfectly acceptable—indeed, it is common—for the *obj* parameter to be a reference, rather than an object. The advantage of passing a reference to the object being output is twofold. First, if the object is quite large, it will save time to pass only its address. Second, it prevents the object's destructor from being called when the inserter returns.

You might wonder why the **three_d** inserter function was not coded like this:

```
// Limited version - don't use.
ostream &operator<<(ostream &stream, three_d obj)
{
  cout << obj.x << ", ";
```

```
   cout << obj.y << ", ";
   cout << obj.z << "\n";
   return stream;  // return the stream
}
```

In this version, the **cout** stream is hard-coded into the function. Remember that the **<<** operator can be applied to any stream. Therefore, you must use the stream passed to the function if it is to work correctly in all cases.

In the **three_d** inserter program, the overloaded inserter function is not a member of **three_d**. In fact, neither inserter nor extractor functions can be members of a class. This is because when an operator function is a member of a class, the left operand (implicitly passed using the **this** pointer) is an object of the class that generated the call to the operator function. There is no way to change this. However, when overloading inserters, the left argument is a stream and the right argument is an object of the class. Therefore, overloaded inserters cannot be member functions.

The fact that inserters must not be members of the class on which they are defined to operate raises a serious question: How can an overloaded inserter access the private elements of a class? In the previous program, the variables **x**, **y**, and **z** were made public so that the inserter could access them. But, hiding data is an important part of object-oriented programming, and forcing all data to be public is inconsistent with the object-oriented approach. However, there is a solution: An inserter can be a friend of a class. As a friend of the class, it has access to private data. To see an example of this, the **three_d** class and sample program are reworked here, with the overloaded inserter declared as a **friend**.

```
#include <iostream>
using namespace std;

class three_d {
  int x, y, z; // 3-d coordinates - - now private
public:
  three_d(int a, int b, int c) { x=a; y=b; z=c; }
  friend ostream &operator<<(ostream &stream, three_d obj);
} ;

// Display X, Y, Z coordinates - three_d inserter.
ostream &operator<<(ostream &stream, three_d obj)
{
  stream << obj.x << ", ";
  stream << obj.y << ", ";
  stream << obj.z << "\n";
```

```
    return stream;   // return the stream
}

int main()
{
  three_d a(1, 2, 3), b(3, 4, 5), c(5, 6, 7);

  cout << a << b << c;

  return 0;
}
```

Notice that the variables **x**, **y**, and **z** are now private to **three_d** but can still be accessed directly by the inserter. Making inserters (and extractors) friends of the classes for which they are defined preserves the encapsulation principle of object-oriented programming.

Overloading Extractors

To overload an extractor, use the same general approach as when overloading an inserter. For example, this extractor inputs 3-D coordinates. Notice that it also prompts the user.

```
// Get three dimensional values - extractor.
istream &operator>>(istream &stream, three_d &obj)
{
  cout <<
    "Enter X Y Z values, separating each with a space: ";
  stream >> obj.x >> obj.y >> obj.z;
  return stream;
}
```

Extractors must return a reference to an object of type **istream**. Also, the first parameter must be a reference to an object of type **istream**. The second parameter is a reference to the variable that will be receiving input. Because it is a reference, the second argument can be modified when information is input.

The general form of an extractor is

```
istream &operator>>(istream &stream, class_type &obj )
{
 // put your extractor code here
 return stream;
}
```

Here is a program that demonstrates the extractor for objects of type **three_d**.

```cpp
#include <iostream>
using namespace std;

class three_d {
  int x, y, z; // 3-d coordinates
public:
  three_d(int a, int b, int c) {x=a; y=b; z=c;}
  friend ostream &operator<<(ostream &stream, three_d obj);
  friend istream &operator>>(istream &stream, three_d &obj);
} ;

// Display X, Y, Z coordinates - inserter.
ostream &operator<<(ostream &stream, three_d obj)
{
  stream << obj.x << ", ";
  stream << obj.y << ", ";
  stream << obj.z << "\n";
  return stream; // return the stream
}

// Get three dimensional values - extractor.
istream &operator>>(istream &stream, three_d &obj)
{
  cout <<
    "Enter X Y Z values, separating each with a space: ";
  stream >> obj.x >> obj.y >> obj.z;
  return stream;
}

int main()
{
  three_d a(1, 2, 3);

  cout << a;
  cin >> a;
  cout << a;

  return 0;
}
```

Like inserters, extractor functions cannot be members of the class they are designed to operate upon. As shown in the example, they can be friends, or simply independent functions.

Except for the fact that you must return a reference to an object of type **istream**, you can do anything you like inside an extractor function. However, for the sake of structure and clarity, it is best to limit the actions of an extractor to the input operation.

Formatting I/O

As you know, using **printf( )** you can control the format of information displayed on the screen. For example, you can specify field widths and left- or right-justification. You can also accomplish the same type of formatting using C++'s approach to I/O. There are two ways to format output. The first uses member functions of the **ios** class. The second uses a special type of function called a *manipulator*. We will begin by looking at formatting using the member functions of **ios**.

Formatting Using the ios Member Functions

Each stream has associated with it a set of format flags that control the way information is formatted. The **ios** class declares a bitmask enumeration called **fmtflags** in which the following values are defined. (Technically, these values are defined within **ios_base**, which, as explained earlier, is a base class for **ios**.)

adjustfield	basefield	boolalpha	dec
fixed	floatfield	hex	internal
left	oct	right	scientific
showbase	showpoint	showpos	skipws
unitbuf	uppercase		

The values defined by this enumeration are used to set or clear flags that control some of the ways information is formatted by a stream. The following describes each flag.

When the **skipws** flag is set, leading white-space characters (spaces, tabs, and newlines) are discarded when performing input on a stream. When **skipws** is cleared, white-space characters are not discarded.

When the **left** flag is set, output is left justified. When **right** is set, output is right justified. When the **internal** flag is set, a numeric value is padded to fill a field by inserting spaces between any sign or base character. If none of these flags is set, output is right justified by default.

By default, numeric values are output in decimal. However, it is possible to change the number base. Setting the **oct** flag causes output to be displayed in octal. Setting the **hex** flag causes output to be displayed in hexadecimal. To return output to decimal, set the **dec** flag.

Setting **showbase** causes the base of numeric values to be shown. For example, if the conversion base is hexadecimal, the value 1F will be displayed as 0x1F.

By default, when scientific notation is displayed, the **e** is in lowercase. Also, when a hexadecimal value is displayed, the **x** is in lowercase. When **uppercase** is set, these characters are displayed in uppercase.

Setting **showpos** causes a leading plus sign to be displayed before positive values.

Setting **showpoint** causes a decimal point and trailing zeros to be displayed for all floating-point output—whether needed or not.

By setting the **scientific** flag, floating-point numeric values are displayed using scientific notation. When **fixed** is set, floating-point values are displayed using normal notation. When neither flag is set, the compiler chooses an appropriate method.

When **unitbuf** is set, the buffer is flushed after each insertion operation.

When **boolalpha** is set, Booleans can be input or output using the keywords **true** and **false**.

Since it is common to refer to the **oct**, **dec**, and **hex** fields, they can be collectively referred to as **basefield**. Similarly, the **left**, **right**, and **internal** fields can be referred to as **adjustfield**. Finally, the **scientific** and **fixed** fields can be referenced as **floatfield**.

To set a flag, use the **setf( )** function, whose most common form is shown here:

fmtflags setf(fmtflags *flags*);

This function returns the stream's previous format flag settings and turns on those flags specified by *flags*. All other flags are unaffected. For example, to turn on the **showbase** flag, you can use the following statement.

```
stream.setf(ios::showbase);
```

Here, **stream** can be any stream you want to affect.

The following program turns on both the **showpos** and **scientific** flags for **cout**:

```
#include <iostream>
using namespace std;

int main()
{
  cout.setf(ios::showpos);
  cout.setf(ios::scientific);
  cout << 123 << " " << 123.23 << " ";

  return 0;
}
```

The output produced by this program is

```
+123 +1.232300e+02
```

You can OR together as many flags as you like in a single call. For example, you can change the program so that only one call is made to **setf( )** by ORing together **scientific** and **showpos**, as shown here.

```
cout.setf(ios::scientific | ios::showpos);
```

To turn off a flag, use the **unsetf( )** function. Its prototype is shown here:

void unsetf(fmtflags *flags*);

It turns off those flags specified by *flags.*

Sometimes it is useful to know the current flag settings. You can retrieve the current flag values using this form of the **flags( )** function:

fmtflags flags( );

This function returns the current value of the flags associated with the invoking stream.

The following form of **flags( )** sets the flag values to those specified by *flags* and returns the previous flag values:

fmtflags flags(fmtflags *flags*);

To see how **flags( )** and **unsetf( )** work, examine this program. It includes a function called **showflags( )** that displays the state of the flags.

```
#include <iostream>
using namespace std;

void showflags (long f);

int main ()
{
  long f;

  f = cout.flags ();

  showflags (f);
  cout.setf (ios::showpos);
  cout.setf (ios::scientific);
```

```
   f = cout.flags();
   showflags(f);

   cout.unsetf(ios::scientific);

   f = cout.flags();
   showflags(f);

   return 0;
}

void showflags(long f)
{
   long i;

   for(i=0x4000; i; i = i >> 1)
     if(i & f) cout << "1 ";
     else cout << "0 ";

   cout << "\n";
}
```

When run, the program produces this output:

```
0 0 1 0 0 0 0 0 0 0 0 0 0 1 0
0 0 1 1 0 0 1 0 0 0 0 0 0 1 0
0 0 1 1 0 0 0 0 0 0 0 0 0 1 0
```

In addition to the formatting flags, you can also set a stream's field width, the fill character, and the number of digits displayed after a decimal point, using these functions:

streamsize width(streamsize *len*);
char fill(char *ch*);
streamsize precision(streamsize *num*);

The **width( )** function returns the stream's current field width and sets the field width to *len*. By default the field width varies, depending upon the number of characters it takes to hold the data. The **fill( )** function returns the current fill character, which is a space by default, and makes the current fill character the same as *ch*. The fill character is the character used to pad output to fill a specified field width. The **precision( )** function returns the number of digits displayed after a decimal point and sets that value to *num*. The **streamsize** type is defined as some form of integer.

Here is a program that demonstrates these three functions:

```
#include <iostream>
using namespace std;

int main()
{
  cout.setf(ios::showpos);
  cout.setf(ios::scientific);
  cout << 123 << " " << 123.23 << "\n";

  cout.precision(2); // two digits after decimal point
  cout.width(10);   // in a field of ten characters
  cout << 123 << " " << 123.23 << "\n";

  cout.fill('#');   // fill using #
  cout.width(10);   // in a field of ten characters
  cout << 123 << " " << 123.23;

  return 0;
}
```

The program displays this output:

```
+123 +1.232300e+02
      +123 +1.23e+02
######+123 +1.23e+02
```

Remember, each stream maintains its own set of format flags. Changing the flag settings of one stream does not affect another stream.

Using Manipulators

The C++ I/O system includes a second way to alter the format parameters of a stream. This way uses special functions called *manipulators*, which can be included in an I/O expression. The standard manipulators are shown in Table 24-1. To use the manipulators that take parameters, you must include **<iomanip>** in your program.

Manipulator	Purpose	Input/Output
boolalpha	Turns on **boolalpha** flag.	Input/Output
dec	Turns on **dec** flag.	Input/Output
endl	Output a newline character and flush the stream.	Output
ends	Output a null.	Output
fixed	Turns on **fixed** flag.	Output
flush	Flush a stream.	Output
hex	Turns on **hex** flag.	Input/Output
internal	Turns on **internal** flag.	Output
left	Turns on **left** flag.	Output
noboolalpha	Turns off **boolalpha** flag.	Input/Output
noshowbase	Turns off **showbase** flag.	Output
noshowpoint	Turns off **showpoint** flag.	Output
noshowpos	Turns off **showpos** flag.	Output
noskipws	Turns off **skipws** flag.	Input
nounitbuf	Turns off **unitbuf** flag.	Output
nouppercase	Turns off **uppercase** flag.	Output
oct	Turns on **oct** flag.	Input/Output
resetiosflags(fmtflags *f*)	Turn off the flags specified in *f*.	Input/Output
right	Turns on **right** flag.	Output
scientific	Turns on **scientific** flag.	Output
setbase(int *base*)	Set the number base to *base*	Input/Output
setfill(int *ch*)	Set the fill character to *ch*	Output

Table 24-1. *The C++ I/O Manipulators*

C++

Manipulator	Purpose	Input/Output
setiosflags(fmtflags *f*)	Turn on the flags specified in *f*	Input/Output
setprecision(int *p*)	Set the number of digits of precision.	Output
setw(int *w*)	Set the field width to *w*	Output
showbase	Turns on **showbase** flag.	Output
showpoint	Turns on **showpoint** flag.	Output
showpos	Turns on **showpos** flag.	Output
skipws	Turns on **skipws** flag.	Input
unitbuf	Turns on **unitbuf** flag.	Output
uppercase	Turns on **uppercase** flag.	Output
ws	Skip leading white space.	Input

Table 24-1.   *The C++ I/O Manipulators* (continued)

A manipulator can be used as part of an I/O expression. Here is an example program that uses manipulators to change the format of output:

```cpp
#include <iostream>
#include <iomanip>
using namespace std;

int main()
{
  cout << setiosflags(ios::fixed);
  cout << setprecision(2) << 1000.243 << endl;
  cout << setw(20) << "Hello there.";

  return 0;
}
```

It produces this output.

```
1000.24
Hello there.
```

Notice how the manipulators occur in the chain of I/O operations. Also, notice that
when a manipulator does not take an argument, such as **endl** in the example, it is not
followed by parentheses. This is because the address of the manipulator is passed to
the overloaded **<<** operator.

This program uses **setiosflags( )** to set **cout**'s **scientific** and **showpos** flags:

```
#include <iostream>
#include <iomanip>
using namespace std;

main()
{
  cout << setiosflags(ios::showpos);
  cout << setiosflags(ios::scientific);
  cout << 123 << " " << 123.23;

  return 0;
}
```

The following program uses **ws** to skip any leading white space when inputting a
string into **s**.

```
#include <iostream>
using namespace std;

int main()
{
  char s[80];

  cin >> ws >> s;
  cout << s;
}
```

Creating Your Own Manipulator Functions

In addition to overloading the insertion and extraction operators, you can further
customize C++'s I/O system by creating your own manipulator functions. Custom
manipulators are important for two main reasons. First, you can consolidate a sequence
of several separate I/O operations into one manipulator. For example, it is not uncommon
to have situations in which the same sequence of I/O operations occurs frequently
within a program. In these cases you can use a custom manipulator to perform these
actions, thus simplifying your source code and preventing accidental errors. A custom

manipulator can also be important when you need to perform I/O operations on a nonstandard device. For example, you might use a manipulator to send control codes to a special type of printer or to an optical recognition system.

Custom manipulators are a feature of C++ that supports OOP, but they also can benefit programs that aren't object oriented. As you will see, custom manipulators can help make any I/O-intensive program clearer and more efficient.

As you know, there are two basic types of manipulators: those that operate on input streams and those that operate on output streams. In addition to these two broad categories, there is a secondary division: those manipulators that take an argument and those that don't. Here, the creation of parameterless manipulators is described, since they are the most common type of custom manipulator.

All parameterless manipulator output functions have this skeleton:

```
ostream &manip-name(ostream &stream)
{
// your code here
return stream;
}
```

Here, *manip-name* is the name of the manipulator. It is important to understand that even though the manipulator has as its single argument a reference to the stream upon which it is operating, no argument is used when the manipulator is inserted in an output operation.

The following program creates a manipulator called **setup( )** that turns on left-justification, sets the field width to 10, and specifies the dollar sign as the fill character.

```
#include <iostream>
#include <iomanip>
using namespace std;

ostream &setup(ostream &stream)
{
  stream.setf(ios::left);
  stream << setw(10) << setfill('$');
  return stream;
}

int main()
{
  cout << 10 << " " << setup << 10;

  return 0;
}
```

All parameterless manipulator input functions have this general form:

```
istream &manip-name(istream &stream)
{
// your code here
return stream;
}
```

For example, this program creates the **prompt( )** manipulator, which displays a prompting message and then switches numeric input to hexadecimal:

```
#include <iostream>
#include <iomanip>
using namespace std;

istream &prompt(istream &stream)
{
  cin >> hex;
  cout << "Enter number using hex format: ";

  return stream;
}

int main()
{
  int i;

  cin >> prompt >> i;
  cout << i;

  return 0;
}
```

It is crucial that your manipulator return the stream. If this is not done, then your manipulator cannot be used in a larger I/O statement.

As you work with C++, you will find that custom manipulators can help streamline your I/O statements.

File I/O

C++ supports an extensive file I/O system. Although the end result is the same, C++'s approach to file I/O differs somewhat from the C I/O system discussed earlier. For this reason, you should pay special attention to this section.

In order to perform file I/O, you must include the header **<fstream>** in your program. It defines several important classes and values.

Opening and Closing a File

In C++, a file is opened by linking it to a stream. There are three types of streams: input, output, and input/output. To open an input stream, you must declare the stream to be of class **ifstream**. To open an output stream, it must be declared as class **ofstream**. Streams that will perform both input and output operations must be declared as class **fstream**. For example, this fragment creates one input stream, one output stream, and one stream capable of both input and output:

```
ifstream in;  // input
ofstream out; // output
fstream both; // input and output
```

Once you have created a stream, one way to associate it with a file is by using **open( )**. This function is a member of each of the three stream classes. The prototype for each is shown here:

void ifstream::open(const char *filename,
                ios::openmode mode = ios::in);

void ofstream::open(const char *filename,
                ios::openmode mode = ios::out | ios::trunc);

void fstream::open(const char *filename,
                ios::openmode mode = ios::in | ios::out);

Here, *filename* is the name of the file; it can include a path specifier. The value of *mode* determines how the file is opened. It must be one or more of the values defined by **openmode**, which is an enumeration defined by **ios** (through its base clase **ios_base**).

ios::app
ios::ate
ios::binary
ios::in
ios::out
ios::trunc

You can combine two or more of these values by ORing them together.

Including **ios::app** causes all output to that file to be appended to the end. This value can be used only with files capable of output. Including **ios::ate** causes a seek to the end of the file to occur when the file is opened. Although **ios::ate** causes an initial seek to end-of-file, I/O operations can still occur anywhere within the file.

The **ios::in** value specifies that the file is capable of input. The **ios::out** value specifies that the file is capable of output.

The **ios::binary** value causes a file to be opened in binary mode. By default, all files are opened in text mode. In text mode, various character translations may take place, such as carriage return, linefeed sequences being converted into newlines. However, when a file is opened in binary mode, no such character translations will occur. Understand that any file, whether it contains formatted text or raw data, can be opened in either binary or text mode. The only difference is whether character translations take place.

The **ios::trunc** value causes the contents of a preexisting file by the same name to be destroyed, and the file is truncated to zero length. When creating an output stream using **ofstream**, any preexisting file by that name is automatically truncated.

The preceding versions of **open( )** are the ones defined by the ANSI/ISO standard for C++. C++ builder supports these versions. However, to each it adds a third parameter, which specifies a UNIX permission code, which defaults to normal access. Since this code is nonstandard, it is not used or described here.

The following fragment opens a normal output file.

```
ofstream out;
out.open("test", ios::out);
```

However, you will seldom see **open( )** called as shown, because the *mode* parameter provides default values for each type of stream. As their prototypes show, for **ifstream**, *mode* defaults to **ios::in**, for **ofstream** it is **ios::out | ios::trunc**, and for **fstream**, it is **ios::in | ios::out**. Therefore, the preceding statement will usually look like this:

```
out.open("test"); // defaults to output and normal file
```

If **open( )** fails, the stream will evaluate to false when used in a Boolean expression. Therefore, before using a file, you should test to make sure that the open operation succeeded. You can do so by using a statement like this:

```
if(!mystream) {
cout << "Cannot open file.\n";
  // handle error
}
```

Although it is entirely proper to open a file by using the **open( )** function, most of the time you will not do so because the **ifstream**, **ofstream**, and **fstream** classes have constructor functions that automatically open the file. The constructor functions have the same parameters and defaults as the **open( )** function. Therefore, you will most commonly see a file opened as shown here:

```
ifstream mystream("myfile"); // open file for input
```

C++ Builder also supplies an extra, nonstandard, parameter to the stream constructors which specifies a UNIX permission code. This parameter defaults to normal access. Since this parameter is nonstandard, it is not described here.

As stated, if for some reason the file cannot be opened, the value of the associated stream variable will evaluate to false. Therefore, whether you use a constructor function to open the file or an explicit call to **open( )**, you will want to confirm that the file has actually been opened by testing the value of the stream.

You can also check to see if you have successfully opened a file by using the **is_open( )** function, which is a member of **fstream**, **ifstream**, and **ofstream**. It has this prototype.

```
bool is_open( );
```

It returns true if the stream is linked to an open file and false otherwise. For example, the following checks if **mystream** is currently open.

```
if(!mystream.is_open()) {
cout << "File is not open.\n";
  // . . .
```

To close a file, use the member function **close( )**. For example, to close the file linked to a stream called **mystream**, use this statement:

```
mystream.close();
```

The **close( )** function takes no parameters and returns no value.

Reading and Writing Text Files

To read from or write to a text file, you simply use the **<<** and **>>** operators with the stream you opened. For example, the following program writes an integer, a floating-point value, and a string to a file called TEST.

```
#include <iostream>
#include <fstream>
using namespace std;
```

```
int main()
{
  ofstream out("test");
  if(!out) {
    cout << "Cannot open file.\n";
    return 1;
    }

  out << 10 << " " << 123.23 << "\n";
  out << "This is a short text file.\n";

  out.close();

  return 0;
}
```

The following program reads an integer, a floating-point number, and a string from the file created by the preceding program:

```
#include <iostream>
#include <fstream>
using namespace std;

int main()
{
  int i;
  float f;
  char str[80];

  ifstream in("test");
  if(!in) {
    cout << "Cannot open file.\n";
    return 1;
  }

  in >> i;
  in >> f;
  in >> str;

  cout << i << " " << f << " " << "\n";
  cout << str;
```

```
    in.close();
    return 0;
}
```

When reading text files using the >> operator, keep in mind that certain character translations occur. For example, white-space characters are omitted. If you want to prevent any character translations, you must use C++'s binary I/O functions, discussed in the next section.

Unformatted and Binary I/O

While reading and writing formatted text files is very easy, it is not always the most efficient way to handle files. Also, there will be times when you need to store unformatted (raw) binary data, not text. The functions that allow you to do this are described here.

When performing binary operations on a file, be sure to open it using the **ios::binary** mode specifier. Although the unformatted file functions will work on files opened for text mode, some character translations may occur. Character translations negate the purpose of binary file operations.

Before beginning our examination of unformatted I/O, it is important to clarify an important concept. For many years, I/O in C and C++ was thought of as *byte-oriented*. This is because a **char** is equivalent to a byte and the only types of streams available were **char** streams. However, with the advent of wide characters (of type **wchar_t**) and their attendant streams, we can no longer say that C++ I/O is byte-oriented. Instead, we must say that it is *character-oriented*. Of course, **char** streams are still byte-oriented and we can continue to think in terms of bytes, especially when operating on nontextual data. But the equivalence between a byte and a character can no longer be taken for granted.

All of the streams used in this book are **char** streams, since they are by far the most common. They also make unformatted file handling easier because a **char** stream establishes a one-to-one correspondence between bytes and characters, which is a benefit when reading or writing blocks of binary data.

Using get( ) and put( )

One way that you can read and write unformatted data is by using the member functions **get( )** and **put( )**. These functions operate on characters. That is, **get( )** will read a character and **put( )** will write a character. Of course, if you have opened the file for binary operations and are operating on a **char** (rather a **wchar_t** stream), then these functions read and write bytes of data.

The **get( )** function has many forms, but the most commonly used version is shown here along with **put( )**:

istream &get(char &*ch*);
ostream &put(char *ch*);

The **get( )** function reads a single character from the associated stream and puts that value in *ch*. It returns a reference to the stream. The **put( )** function writes *ch* to the stream and returns a reference to the stream.

Note   *Remember, when working with binary files, be sure to open them using the ios::binary mode specifier.*

This program displays the contents of any file on the screen. It uses the **get( )** function.

```
#include <iostream>
#include <fstream>
using namespace std;

int main(int argc, char *argv[])
{
  char ch;

  if(argc!=2) {
    cout << "Usage: PR <filename>\n";
    return 1;
  }

  ifstream in(argv[1], ios::in | ios::binary);
  if(!in) {
    cout << "Cannot open file.\n";
    return 1;
  }

  while(in) { // in will be null when eof is reached
    in.get(ch);
    cout << ch;
  }
  in.close();

  return 0;
}
```

When **in** reaches the end of the file it will become null, causing the **while** loop to stop.

There is a more compact way to code the loop that reads and displays a file, as shown here:

```
while(in.get(ch))
  cout << ch;
```

This works because **get( )** returns the stream **in**, and **in** will be null when the end of the file is encountered.

This program uses **put( )** to write a string that includes non-ASCII characters to a file.

```
#include <iostream>
#include <fstream>
using namespace std;

int main()
{
  char *p = "hello there\n\r\xfe\xff";

  ofstream out("test", ios::out | ios::binary);
  if(!out) {
    cout << "Cannot open file.\n";
    return 1;
  }

  while(*p) out.put(*p++);
  out.close();

  return 0;
}
```

Using read( ) and write( )

The second way to read and write binary data uses C++'s **read( )** and **write( )** member functions. The prototypes for two of their most commonly used forms are

> istream &read(char *buf*, streamsize *num*);
> ostream &write(const char *buf*, streamsize *num*);

The **read( )** function reads *num* bytes from the associated stream and puts them in the buffer pointed to by *buf*. The **write( )** function writes *num* bytes to the associated stream from the buffer pointed to by *buf*. **streamsize** is some form of integer that is capable of holding the number of characters that can be transferred in any one I/O operation.

The following program writes and then reads an array of integers:

```
#include <iostream>
#include <fstream>
using namespace std;

int main()
```

```
{
  int n[5] = {1, 2, 3, 4, 5};
  register int i;

  ofstream out("test", ios::out | ios::binary);
  if(!out) {
    cout << "Cannot open file.\n";
    return 1;
  }

  out.write((char *) &n, sizeof n);
  out.close();

  for(i=0; i<5; i++) // clear array
    n[i] = 0;

  ifstream in("test", ios::in | ios::binary);
  in.read((char *) &n, sizeof n);

  for(i=0; i<5; i++) // show values read from file
    cout << n[i] << " ";
  in.close();

  return 0;
}
```

Note that the type casts inside the calls to **read( )** and **write( )** are necessary when operating on a buffer that is not defined as a character array.

If the end of the file is reached before *num* characters have been read, **read( )** simply stops and the buffer contains as many characters as were available. You can find out how many characters have been read using another member function called **gcount( )**, which has this prototype:

streamsize gcount( );

It returns the number of characters read by the last binary input operation.

Detecting EOF

You can detect when the end of the file is reached using the member function **eof( )**, which has the prototype

bool eof( );

It returns true when the end of the file has been reached; otherwise, it returns false.

Random Access

In C++'s I/O system, you perform random access using the **seekg( )** and **seekp( )** functions. Their most common forms are

istream &seekg(off_type *offset*, seekdir *origin*);
ostream &seekp(off_type *offset*, seekdir *origin*);

Here, **off_type** is an integer type defined by **ios** that is capable of containing the largest valid value that *offset* can have. **seekdir** is an enumeration defined by **ios** that determines how the seek will take place.

The C++ I/O system manages two pointers associated with each file. One is the *get pointer*, which specifies where in the file the next input operation will occur. The other is the *put pointer*, which specifies where in the file the next output operation will occur. Each time an input or an output operation takes place, the appropriate pointer is automatically advanced. However, using the **seekg( )** and **seekp( )** functions, it is possible to access the file in a nonsequential fashion.

The **seekg( )** function moves the associated file's current get pointer *offset* number of bytes from the specified *origin*, which must be one of these three values:

Value	Meaning
ios::beg	Beginning of file
ios::cur	Current location
ios::end	End of file

The **seekp( )** function moves the associated file's current put pointer *offset* number of bytes from the specified *origin*, which must be one of the same three values.

This program demonstrates the **seekp( )** function. It allows you to specify a filename on the command line followed by the specific byte in the file you want to change. It then writes an "X" at the specified location. Notice that the file must be opened for read/write operations.

```
#include <iostream>
#include <fstream>
#include <cstdlib>
using namespace std;

int main(int argc, char *argv[])
{
  if(argc!=3) {
    cout << "Usage: CHANGE <filename> <byte>\n";
    return 1;
```

```
  }

  fstream out(argv[1], ios::in | ios::out | ios::binary);
  if(!out) {
    cout << "Cannot open file.\n";
    return 1;
  }

  out.seekp(atoi(argv[2]), ios::beg);

  out.put('X');
  out.close();

  return 0;
}
```

The next program uses **seekg( )** to display the contents of a file beginning with the location you specify on the command line:

```
#include <iostream>
#include <fstream>
#include <cstdlib>
using namespace std;

int main(int argc, char *argv[])
{
  char ch;

  if(argc!=3) {
    cout << "Usage: NAME <filename> <starting location>\n";
    return 1;
  }

  ifstream in(argv[1], ios::in | ios::binary);
  if(!in) {
    cout << "Cannot open file.\n";
    return 1;
  }

  in.seekg(atoi(argv[2]), ios::beg);

  while(in.get(ch))
```

```
     cout << ch;

  in.close();

  return 0;
}
```

You can determine the current position of each file pointer using these functions:

pos_type tellg( );
pos_type tellp( );

Here, **pos_type** is a type defined by **ios** that is capable of holding the largest value that either function can return.

You can use the values returned by **tellg( )** and **tellp( )** as arguments to the following forms of **seekg( )** and **seekp( )**, respectively.

istream &seekg(pos_type *pos*);

ostream &seekp(pos_type *pos*);

These functions allow you to save the current file location, perform other file operations, and then reset the file location to its previously saved location.

As you have seen, C++'s I/O system is both powerful and flexible. Although this chapter discusses some of the most commonly used classes and functions, C++ includes several others. For example, you will want to explore the **getline( )** function (defined by **istream**) and the various overloaded forms of the I/O functions described in this chapter.

The Complete Reference

Borland
C++
Builder

Chapter 25

Templates, Exceptions, and RTTI

This chapter discusses several of C++'s most advanced features: templates, exceptions, run-time type ID (RTTI), and the casting operators.

Using a template, it is possible to create *generic functions* and *generic classes*. In a generic function or class, the type of data upon which the function or class operates is specified as a parameter. Thus, you can use one function or class with several different types of data without having to explicitly recode specific versions for different data types.

Exception handling allows you to handle run-time errors in a structured and controlled manner. The principal advantage of exception handling is that it automates much of the error-handling code that previously had to be implemented "by hand" in any large program.

Run-time type identification (RTTI) lets you determine the actual type of an object at run time. You can also test if an object is of a particular type or if two objects are of the same type.

Also discussed in this chapter are four casting operators: **const_cast**, **dynamic_cast**, **reinterpret_cast**, and **static_cast**. These casting operators give you fine-grained control over type casting.

Generic Functions

A generic function defines a general set of operations that will be applied to various types of data. Using this mechanism, the same general procedure can be applied to a wide range of data. As you probably know, many algorithms are logically the same no matter what type of data is being operated upon. For example, the Quicksort sorting algorithm is the same whether it is applied to an array of integers or an array of **float**s. It is just that the type of the data being sorted is different. By creating a generic function, you can define, independent of any data, the nature of the algorithm. Once this is done, the compiler automatically generates the correct code for the type of data that is actually used when you execute the function. In essence, when you create a generic function you are creating a function that can automatically overload itself.

A generic function is created with the keyword **template**. The normal meaning of the word "template" accurately reflects its use in C++. It is used to create a template (or framework) that describes what a function will do, leaving it to the compiler to fill in the details, as needed. The general form of a **template** function definition is shown here:

```
template <class Ttype> ret-type func-name(parameter list)
{
    // body of function
}
```

Here, *Ttype* is a placeholder name for a data type used by the function. This name can be used within the function definition. However, it is only a placeholder that the compiler will automatically replace with an actual data type when it creates a specific version of the function.

Here is a short example that creates a generic function that swaps the values of the two variables with which it is called. Because the general process of exchanging two values is independent of the type of the variables, it is a good choice to be made into a generic function.

```cpp
// Function template example.
#include <iostream>
using namespace std;

// This is a function template.
template <class X> void swapargs(X &a, X &b)
{
  X temp;

  temp = a;
  a = b;
  b = temp;
}

int main()
{
  int i=10, j=20;
  float x=10.1, y=23.3;
  char a='x', b='z';

  cout << "Original i, j: " << i << ' ' << j << endl;
  cout << "Original x, y: " << x << ' ' << y << endl;
  cout << "Original a, b: " << a << ' ' << b << endl;

  swapargs(i, j); // swap integers
  swapargs(x, y); // swap floats
  swapargs(a, b); // swap chars

  cout << "Swapped i, j: " << i << ' ' << j << endl;
  cout << "Swapped x, y: " << x << ' ' << y << endl;
  cout << "Swapped a, b: " << a << ' ' << b << endl;

  return 0;
}
```

C++

Let's look closely at this program. The line:

```
template <class X> void swapargs(X &a, X &b)
```

tells the compiler two things: that a template is being created and that a generic definition is beginning. Here, **X** is a generic type that is used as a placeholder. After the **template** portion, the function **swapargs( )** is declared, using **X** as the data type of the values that will be swapped. In **main( )**, the **swapargs( )** function is called using three different types of data: integers, **float**s, and **char**s. Because **swapargs( )** is a generic function, the compiler automatically creates three versions of **swapargs( )**—one that will exchange integer values, one that will exchange floating-point values, and one that will swap characters.

A Function with Two Generic Types

You can define more than one generic data type in the **template** statement, using a comma-separated list. For example, this program creates a generic function that has two generic types:

```
#include <iostream>
using namespace std;

template <class type1, class type2>
void myfunc(type1 x, type2 y)
{
  cout << x << ' ' << y << endl;
}

int main()
{
  myfunc(10, "hi");
  myfunc(0.23, 10L);

  return 0;
}
```

In this example, the placeholder types **type1** and **type2** are replaced by the compiler with the data types **int** and **char *** and **double** and **long**, respectively, when the compiler generates the specific instances of **myfunc( )** within **main( )**. Remember: When you create a generic function, you are, in essence, allowing the compiler to generate as many different versions of that function as necessary to handle the various ways that your program calls that function.

Explicitly Overloading a Generic Function

Even though a template function overloads itself as needed, you can explicitly overload one, too. If you overload a generic function, then that overloaded function overrides (or "hides") the generic function relative to that specific version. For example, consider this version of **swapargs( )**:

```cpp
// Overriding a template function.
#include <iostream>
using namespace std;

template <class X> void swapargs(X &a, X &b)
{
  X temp;

  temp = a;
  a = b;
  b = temp;
}

// This overrides the generic version of swap().
void swapargs(int &a, int &b)
{
  int temp;

  temp = a;
  a = b;
  b = temp;
  cout << "Inside overloaded swapargs(int &, int &).\n";
}

int main()
{
  int i=10, j=20;
  float x=10.1, y=23.3;
  char a='x', b='z';

  cout << "Original i, j: " << i << ' ' << j << endl;
  cout << "Original x, y: " << x << ' ' << y << endl;
  cout << "Original a, b: " << a << ' ' << b << endl;
```

```
    swapargs(i, j); // this calls the explicitly overloaded swapargs()
    swapargs(x, y); // swap floats
    swapargs(a, b); // swap chars

    cout << "Swapped i, j: " << i << ' ' << j << endl;
    cout << "Swapped x, y: " << x << ' ' << y << endl;
    cout << "Swapped a, b: " << a << ' ' << b << endl;

    return 0;
}
```

As the comments indicate, when **swapargs(i, j)** is called, it invokes the explicitly overloaded version of **swapargs( )** defined in the program. Thus, the compiler does not generate this version of the generic **swapargs( )** function because the generic function is overridden by the explicit overloading.

Recently, a new-style syntax was introduced to denote the explicit specialization of a function. This new method uses the **template** keyword. For example, using the new-style specialization syntax, the overloaded **swapargs( )** function from the preceding program looks like this:

```
// Use new-style specialization syntax
template<> void swapargs<int>(int &a, int &b)
{
  int temp;

  temp = a;
  a = b;
  b = temp;
  cout << "Inside specialized swapargs(int &, int &).\n";
}
```

As you can see, the new-style syntax uses the **template<>** construct to indicate specialization. The type of data for which the specialization is being created is placed inside the angle brackets following the function name. This same syntax is used to specialize any type of generic function. While there is no advantage to using one specialization syntax over the other, the new-style is probably a better approach for the long term.

Manual overloading of a template, as shown in this example, allows you to specially tailor a version of a generic function to accommodate a special situation. In general, however, if you need to have different versions of a function for different data types, you should use overloaded functions rather than templates.

Overloading a Function Template

In addition to creating explicit, overloaded versions of a generic function, you can also overload the **template** specification itself. To do so, simply create another version of the template that differs from any others in its parameter list. For example:

```
// Overload a function template declaration.
#include <iostream>
using namespace std;

// First version of f() template.
template <class X> void f(X a)
{
  cout << "Inside f(X a)\n a = " << a << endl;
}

// Second version of f() template.
template <class X, class Y> void f(X a, Y b)
{
  cout << "Inside f(X a, Y b)\n a = " << a << "\n b = " << b << endl;
}

int main()
{
  f(10);     // calls f(X)
  f(10, 20); // calls f(X, Y)

  return 0;
}
```

Here, the template for **f( )** is overloaded to accept either one or two parameters.

Generic Function Restrictions

Generic functions are similar to overloaded functions except that they are more restrictive. When functions are overloaded, you can have different actions performed within the body of each function. But a generic function must perform the same general action for all versions—only the type of data may differ. For example, in the following program, the overloaded functions could *not* be replaced by a generic function because they do not do the same thing.

```
#include <iostream>
#include <cmath>
using namespace std;

void myfunc(int i)
{
  cout << "value is: " << i << "\n";
}

void myfunc(double d)
{
  double intpart;
  double fracpart;

  fracpart = modf(d, &intpart);
  cout << "Fractional part: " << fracpart;
  cout << "\n";
  cout << "Integer part: " << intpart;
}

int main()
{
  myfunc(1);
  myfunc(12.2);

  return 0;
}
```

Generic Classes

In addition to generic functions, you can also define a generic class. When you do this, you create a class that defines all algorithms used by that class, but the actual type of data being manipulated will be specified as a parameter when objects of that class are created.

Generic classes are useful when a class contains generalizable logic. For example, the same algorithm that maintains a queue of integers will also work for a queue of characters. Also, the same mechanism that maintains a linked list of mailing addresses will also maintain a linked list of auto part information. By using a generic class, you can create a class that will maintain a queue, a linked list, and so on for any type of data. The compiler will automatically generate the correct type of object according to the type you specify when the object is created.

The general form of a generic class declaration is shown here.

```
template <class Ttype> class class-name {
  // ...
}
```

Here, *Ttype* is the placeholder type name that will be specified when a class is instantiated. If necessary, you may define more than one generic data type using a comma-separated list.

Once you have created a generic class, you create a specific instance of that class using the following general form:

class-name <type> ob;

Here, *type* is the type name of the data that the class will be operating upon.

Member functions of a generic class are, themselves, automatically generic. They need not be explicitly specified as such using **template**.

In the following program, a generic **stack** class is created that implements a standard last-in, first-out stack. Thus, it can be used to provide a stack for any type of object. In the example shown here, a character stack, an integer stack, and a floating-point stack are created.

```cpp
// Demonstrate a generic stack class.
#include <iostream>
using namespace std;

const int SIZE = 100;

// This creates the generic class stack.
template <class SType> class stack {
  SType stck[SIZE];
  int tos;
public:
  stack();
  ~stack();
  void push(SType i);
  SType pop();
};

// stack's constructor function.
template <class SType> stack<SType>::stack()
{
```

```
  tos = 0;
  cout << "Stack Initialized\n";
}

/* stack's destructor function.
   This function is not required.  It is included
   for illustration only. */
template <class SType> stack<SType>::~stack()
{
  cout << "Stack Destroyed\n";
}

// Push an object onto the stack.
template <class SType> void stack<SType>::push(SType i)
{
  if(tos==SIZE) {
    cout << "Stack is full.\n";
    return;
  }
  stck[tos] = i;
  tos++;
}

// Pop an object off the stack.
template <class SType> SType stack<SType>::pop()
{
  if(tos==0) {
    cout << "Stack underflow.\n";
    return 0;
  }
  tos--;
  return stck[tos];
}

int main()
{
  stack<int> a; // create integer stack
  stack<double> b; // create a double stack
  stack<char> c; // create a character stack
```

```
    int i;

    // use the integer and double stacks
    a.push(1);
    b.push(99.3);
    a.push(2);
    b.push(-12.23);

    cout << a.pop() << " ";
    cout << a.pop() << " ";
    cout << b.pop() << " ";
    cout << b.pop() << "\n";

    // demonstrate the character stack
    for(i=0; i<10; i++) c.push((char) 'A'+i);
    for(i=0; i<10; i++) cout << c.pop();
    cout << "\n";

    return 0;
}
```

As you can see, the declaration of a generic class is similar to that of a generic function. The generic data type is used in the class declaration and in its member functions. It is not until an object of the stack is declared that the actual data type is determined. When a specific instance of **stack** is declared, the compiler automatically generates all the necessary functions and data to handle the actual data. In this example, three different types of stacks are declared. (One for **int**s, one for **double**s, and one for **char**s.) Pay special attention to these declarations:

```
stack<int> a; // create integer stack
stack<double> b; // create a double stack
stack<char> c; // create a character stack
```

Notice how the desired data type is passed inside the angle brackets. By changing the type of data specified when **stack** objects are created, you can change the type of data stored in that stack. For example, you could create another stack that stores character pointers by using this declaration:

```
stack<char *> chrptrstck;
```

You can also create stacks to store data types that you create. For example, suppose you want to store address information using this structure:

```
struct addr {
  char name[40];
  char street[40];
  char city[30];
  char state[3];
  char zip[12];
}
```

Then, to use **stack** to generate a stack that will store objects of type **addr**, use a declaration like this:

```
stack<addr> obj;
```

An Example with Two Generic Data Types

A template class can have more than one generic data type. Simply declare all the data types required by the class in a comma-separated list within the **template** specification. For example, the following short example creates a class that uses two generic data types.

```
/* This example uses two generic data types in a
   class definition.
*/
#include <iostream>
using namespace std;

template <class Type1, class Type2> class myclass
{
  Type1 i;
  Type2 j;
public:
  myclass(Type1 a, Type2 b) { i = a; j = b; }
  void show() { cout << i << ' ' << j << '\n'; }
};

int main()
{
  myclass<int, double> ob1(10, 0.23);
  myclass<char, char *> ob2('X', "This is a test");
```

```
    ob1.show(); // show int, double
    ob2.show(); // show char, char *

    return 0;
}
```

This program produces the following output:

```
10 0.23
X This is a test
```

The program declares two types of objects. **ob1** uses **int** and **double** data. **ob2** uses a character and a character pointer. For both cases, the compiler automatically generates the appropriate data and functions to accommodate the way the objects are created.

Template functions and classes give you unprecedented power to create reusable code. When you have a generalizable routine, consider making it into a template. Once you have fully debugged and tested it, you can employ it over and over again, in different situations, without having to incur additional development overhead. However, resist the temptation to make everything into a generic function or class. Using templates where they do not apply renders your code both confusing and misleading.

Exception Handling

Exception handling allows you to manage run-time errors in an orderly fashion. Using C++ exception handling, your program can automatically invoke an error-handling routine when an error occurs. The principal advantage of exception handling is that it automates much of the error-handling code that previously had to be coded "by hand" in any large program.

Exception Handling Fundamentals

C++ exception handling is built upon three keywords: **try**, **catch**, and **throw**. In the most general terms, program statements that you want to monitor for exceptions are contained in a **try** block. If an exception (i.e., an error) occurs within the **try** block, it is thrown (using **throw**). The exception is caught, using **catch**, and processed. The following discussion elaborates upon this general description.

As stated, any statement that throws an exception must have been executed from within a **try** block. (Functions called from within a **try** block may also throw an exception.) Any exception must be caught by a **catch** statement that immediately follows the **try** statement that throws the exception. The general form of **try** and **catch** are shown here.

```
try {
  // try block
}
catch (type1 arg) {
  // catch block
}
catch (type2 arg) {
  // catch block
}
catch (type3 arg) {
  // catch block
}
    .
    .
    .
catch (typeN arg) {
  // catch block
}
```

The **try** block must contain that portion of your program that you want to monitor for errors. This can be as short as a few statements within one function or as all-encompassing as enclosing the **main( )** function code within a **try** block (which effectively causes the entire program to be monitored).

When an exception is thrown, it is caught by its corresponding **catch** statement, which processes the exception. There can be more than one **catch** statement associated with a **try**. Which **catch** statement is used is determined by the type of the exception. That is, if the data type specified by a **catch** matches that of the exception, then that **catch** statement is executed (and all others are bypassed). When an exception is caught, *arg* will receive its value. Any type of data may be caught, including classes that you create. If no exception is thrown (that is, no error occurs within the **try** block), then no **catch** statement is executed.

The general form of the **throw** statement is shown here.

throw *exception*;

throw must be executed either from within the **try** block, proper, or from any function called (directly or indirectly) from within the **try** block. *exception* is the value thrown.

If you throw an exception for which there is no applicable **catch** statement, an abnormal program termination may occur. Throwing an unhandled exception causes the **terminate( )** function to be invoked. By default, **terminate( )** calls **abort( )** to stop your program. However, you may specify your own handlers if you like, using **set_terminate( )**.

Here is a simple example that shows the way C++ exception handling operates.

```
// A simple exception handling example.
#include <iostream>
using namespace std;

int main()
{
  cout << "Start\n";

  try { // start a try block
    cout << "Inside try block\n";
    throw 100; // throw an error
    cout << "This will not execute";
  }
  catch (int i) { // catch an error
    cout << "Caught an exception -- value is: ";
    cout << i << "\n";
  }

  cout << "End";

  return 0;
}
```

This program displays the following output:

```
Start
Inside try block
Caught an exception -- value is: 100
End
```

Look carefully at this program. As you can see, there is a **try** block containing three statements and a **catch(int i)** statement that processes an integer exception. Within the **try** block, only two of the three statements will execute: the first **cout** statement and the **throw**. Once an exception has been thrown, control passes to the **catch** expression and the **try** block is terminated. That is, **catch** is *not* called. Rather, program execution is transferred to it. (The program's stack is automatically reset as needed to accomplish this.) Thus, the **cout** statement following the **throw** will never execute.

Usually, the code within a **catch** statement attempts to remedy an error by taking appropriate action. If the error can be fixed, then execution will continue with the statements following the **catch**. However, sometimes an error cannot be fixed and a **catch** block will terminate the program with a call to **exit( )** or **abort( )**.

As mentioned, the type of the exception must match the type specified in a **catch** statement. In the preceding example, for example, if you change the type in the **catch** statement to **double**, then the exception will not be caught and abnormal termination will occur. This change is shown here.

```cpp
// This example will not work.
#include <iostream>
using namespace std;

int main()
{
  cout << "Start\n";

  try { // start a try block
    cout << "Inside try block\n";
    throw 100; // throw an error
    cout << "This will not execute";
  }
  catch (double i) { // Won't work for an int exception
    cout << "Caught an exception -- value is: ";
    cout << i << "\n";
  }

  cout << "End";

  return 0;
}
```

This program produces the following output because the integer exception will not be caught by the **catch(double i)** statement.

```
Start
Inside try block

Abnormal program termination
```

An exception can be thrown from a statement that is outside a **try** block as long as it is within a function that is called from within the **try** block. For example, this is a valid program.

```
/* Throwing an exception from a function outside the
   try block.
*/
#include <iostream>
using namespace std;

void Xtest(int test)
{
  cout << "Inside Xtest, test is: " << test << "\n";
  if(test) throw test;
}

int main()
{
  cout << "Start\n";

  try { // start a try block
    cout << "Inside try block\n";
    Xtest(0);
    Xtest(1);
    Xtest(2);
  }
  catch (int i) { // catch an error
    cout << "Caught an exception -- value is: ";
    cout << i << "\n";
  }

  cout << "End";

  return 0;
}
```

This program produces the following output:

```
Start
Inside try block
Inside Xtest, test is: 0
Inside Xtest, test is: 1
Caught an exception -- value is: 1
End
```

C++

A **try** block can be localized to a function. When this is the case, each time the function is entered, the exception handling relative to that function is reset. For example, examine this program.

```
#include <iostream>
using namespace std;

// A try/catch can be inside a function other than main().
void Xhandler(int test)
{
  try{
    if(test) throw test;
  }
  catch(int i) {
    cout << "Caught Exception #: " << i << '\n';
  }
}

int main()
{
  cout << "Start\n";

  Xhandler(1);
  Xhandler(2);
  Xhandler(0);
  Xhandler(3);

  cout << "End";

  return 0;
}
```

This program displays this output:

```
Start
Caught Exception #: 1
Caught Exception #: 2
Caught Exception #: 3
End
```

As you can see, three exceptions are thrown. After each exception, the function returns. When the function is called again, the exception handling is reset.

It is important to understand that the code associated with a **catch** statement will be executed only if it catches an exception. Otherwise, execution simply bypasses the **catch** statement.

Catching Class Types

An exception can be of any type, including class types that you create. Actually, in real-world programs, most exceptions will be class types rather than built-in types. Perhaps the most common reason that you will want to define a class type for an exception is to create an object that describes the error that occurred. This information can be used by the exception handler to help it process the error. The following example demonstrates this.

```cpp
// Catching class type exceptions.
#include <iostream>
#include <cstring>
using namespace std;

class MyException {
public:
  char str_what[80];
  int what;

  MyException() { *str_what = 0; what = 0; }

  MyException(char *s, int e) {
    strcpy(str_what, s);
    what = e;
  }
};

int main()
{
  int i;

  try {
    cout << "Enter a positive number: ";
    cin >> i;
    if(i<0)
```

```
        throw MyException("Not Positive", i);
    }
    catch (MyException e) { // catch an error
      cout << e.str_what << ": ";
      cout << e.what << "\n";
    }

    return 0;
}
```

This program produces the following output:

```
Enter a positive number: -20
Not Positive: -20
```

The program prompts the user for a positive number. If a negative number is entered, an object of the class **MyException** is created that describes the error. Thus, **MyException** encapsulates information about the error. This information is then used by the exception handler. In general, you will want to create exception classes that will encapsulate information about an error to enable the exception handler to respond effectively.

Using Multiple catch Statements

As stated, you can have more than one **catch** associated with a **try**. In fact, it is common to do so. However, each **catch** must catch a different type of exception. For example, this program catches both integers and strings.

```
#include <iostream>
using namespace std;

// Different types of exceptions can be caught.
void Xhandler(int test)
{
  try{
    if(test) throw test;
    else throw "Value is zero";
  }
  catch(int i) {
    cout << "Caught Exception #: " << i << '\n';
```

```
  }
  catch(char *str) {
    cout << "Caught a string: ";
    cout << str << '\n';
  }
}

int main()
{
  cout << "Start\n";

  Xhandler(1);
  Xhandler(2);
  Xhandler(0);
  Xhandler(3);

  cout << "End";

  return 0;
}
```

This program produces the following output:

```
Start
Caught Exception #: 1
Caught Exception #: 2
Caught a string: Value is zero
Caught Exception #: 3
End
```

As you can see, each **catch** statement responds only to its own type.

In general, **catch** expressions are checked in the order in which they occur in a program. Only a matching statement is executed. All other **catch** blocks are ignored.

Handling Derived-Class Exceptions

You need to be careful how you order your **catch** statements when trying to catch exception types that involve base and derived classes because a **catch** clause for a base class will also match any class derived from that base. Thus, if you want to catch exceptions of both a base class type and a derived class type, put the derived class first in the **catch** sequence. If you don't do this, the base class **catch** will also catch all derived classes. For example, consider the following program.

```
// Catching derived classes.
#include <iostream>
using namespace std;

class B {
};

class D: public B {
};

int main()
{
  D derived;

  try {
    throw derived;
  }
  catch(B b) {
    cout << "Caught a base class.\n";
  }
  catch(D d) {
    cout << "This won't execute.\n";
  }

  return 0;
}
```

Here, because **derived** is an object that has **B** as a base class, it will be caught by the first **catch** clause and the second clause will never execute. C++ Builder will flag this condition with a warning message. To fix this condition, reverse the order of the **catch** clauses.

Exception Handling Options

There are several additional features and nuances to C++ exception handling that make it easier and more convenient to use. These attributes are discussed here.

Catching All Exceptions

In some circumstances you will want an exception handler to catch all exceptions instead of just a certain type. This is easy to accomplish. Simply use this form of **catch**.

```
catch(...) {
    // process all exceptions
}
```

Here, the ellipsis matches any type of data. The following program illustrates **catch(...)**.

```cpp
// This example catches all exceptions.
#include <iostream>
using namespace std;

void Xhandler(int test)
{
  try{
    if(test==0) throw test; // throw int
    if(test==1) throw 'a'; // throw char
    if(test==2) throw 123.23; // throw double
  }
  catch(...) { // catch all exceptions
    cout << "Caught One!\n";
  }
}

int main()
{
  cout << "Start\n";

  Xhandler(0);
  Xhandler(1);
  Xhandler(2);

  cout << "End";

  return 0;
}
```

This program displays the following output.

```
Start
Caught One!
Caught One!
Caught One!
End
```

As you can see, all three **throw**s were caught using the one **catch** statement.

Restricting Exceptions

When a function is called from within a **try** block, you can restrict what type of exceptions that function can throw. In fact, you can also prevent that function from throwing any exceptions whatsoever. To accomplish these restrictions, you must add a **throw** clause to a function definition. The general form of this is shown here.

ret-type func-name(arg-list) throw(*type-list*)
{
   // ...
}

Here, only those data types contained in the comma-separated *type-list* may be thrown by the function. Throwing any other type of expression will cause abnormal program termination. If you don't want a function to be able to throw *any* exceptions, then use an empty list.

Attempting to throw an exception that is not supported by a function will cause the **unexpected( )** function to be called. Generally, this function, in turn, calls **terminate( )**. You can specify your own unexpected exception handler using **set_unexpected( )**.

The following program shows how to restrict the types of exceptions that can be thrown from a function.

```
// Restricting function throw types.
#include <iostream>
using namespace std;

// This function can only throw ints, chars, and doubles.
void Xhandler(int test) throw(int, char, double)
{
  if(test==0) throw test; // throw int
  if(test==1) throw 'a'; // throw char
  if(test==2) throw 123.23; // throw double
}
```

```
int main()
{
  cout << "start\n";

  try{
    Xhandler(0); // also, try passing 1 and 2 to Xhandler()
  }
  catch(int i) {
    cout << "Caught an integer\n";
  }
  catch(char c) {
    cout << "Caught char\n";
  }
  catch(double d) {
    cout << "Caught double\n";
  }

  cout << "end";

  return 0;
}
```

In this program, the function **Xhandler( )** may throw only **int, char,** and **double** exceptions. If it attempts to throw any other type of exception, then an abnormal program termination will occur. (Specifically, the **unexpected( )** function will be called.) To see an example of this, remove **int** from the list and retry the program.

A function can be restricted only in what types of exceptions it throws outside of itself. That is, a **try** block *within* a function can throw any type of exception so long as it is caught *within* that function. The restriction applies only when throwing an exception outside of the function.

The following change to **Xhandler( )** prevents it from throwing any exceptions.

```
// This function can throw NO exceptions!
void Xhandler(int test) throw()
{
  /* The following statements no longer work.  Instead,
     they will cause an abnormal program termination. */
  if(test==0) throw test;
  if(test==1) throw 'a';
  if(test==2) throw 123.23;
}
```

Rethrowing an Exception

If you want to rethrow an expression from within an exception handler, you may do so by calling **throw**, by itself, with no exception. This causes the current exception to be passed on to an outer **try/catch** sequence. The most likely reason for doing so is to allow multiple handlers access to the exception. For example, perhaps one exception handler manages one aspect of an exception and a second handler copes with another. An exception can only be rethrown from within a **catch** block (or from any function called from within that block). When you rethrow an exception, it will not be recaught by the same **catch** statement. It will propogate to the next **catch** statement. The following program illustrates rethrowing an exception. It rethrows a **char *** exception.

```
// Example of "rethrowing" an exception.
#include <iostream>
using namespace std;

void Xhandler()
{
  try {
    throw "hello"; // throw a char *
  }
  catch(char *) { // catch a char *
    cout << "Caught char * inside Xhandler\n";
    throw ; // rethrow char * out of function
  }
}

int main()
{
  cout << "Start\n";

  try{
    Xhandler();
  }
  catch(char *) {
    cout << "Caught char * inside main\n";
  }

  cout << "End";

  return 0;
}
```

This program displays this output:

```
Start
Caught char * inside Xhandler
Caught char * inside main
End
```

Understanding terminate( ) and unexpected( )

As mentioned earlier, **terminate( )** and **unexpected( )** are called when something goes wrong during the exception handling process. These functions are supplied by the Standard C++ Library. Their prototypes are shown here:

> void terminate( );
> void unexpected( );

These functions require the header **<exception>**.

The **terminate( )** function is called whenever the exception handling subsystem fails to find a matching **catch** statement for an exception. It is also called if your program attempts to rethrow an exception when no exception was originally thrown. The **terminate( )** function is also called under various other, more obscure circumstances. For example, such a circumstance could occur when, in the process of unwinding the stack because of an exception, a destructor for an object being destroyed throws an exception. In general, **terminate( )** is the handler of last resort when no other handlers for an exception are available. By default, **terminate( )** calls **abort( )**.

The **unexpected( )** function is called when a function attempts to throw an exception that is not allowed by its **throw** list. By default, **unexpected( )** calls **terminate( )**.

Setting the Terminate and Unexpected Handlers

The **terminate( )** and **unexpected( )** functions simply call other functions to actually handle an error. As just explained, by default **terminate( )** calls **abort( )**, and **unexpected( )** calls **terminate( )**. Thus, by default, both functions halt program execution when an exception handling error occurs. However, you can change the functions that are called by **terminate( )** and **unexpected( )**. Doing so allows your program to take full control of the exception handling subsystem. To change the terminate handler, use **set_terminate( )**, shown here:

> terminate_handler set_terminate(terminate_handler *newhandler*);

Here, *newhandler* is a pointer to the new terminate handler. The function returns a pointer to the old terminate handler. The new terminate handler must be of type **terminate_handler**, which is defined like this:

> typedef void (*terminate_handler) ( );

The only thing that your terminate handler must do is stop program execution. It must not return to the program or resume it in any way.

To change the unexpected handler, use **set_unexpected( )**, as shown here:

unexpected_handler set_unexpected(unexpected_handler *newhandler*);

Here, *newhandler* is a pointer to the new unexpected handler. The function returns a pointer to the old unexpected handler. The new unexpected handler must be of type **unexpected_handler**, which is defined like this:

typedef void (*unexpected_handler) ( );

This handler may itself throw an exception, stop the program, or call **terminate( )**. However, it must not return to the program.

Both **set_terminate( )** and **set_unexpected( )** require the header **<exception>**. Here is an example that defines its own **terminate( )** handler.

```cpp
// Set a new terminate handler.
#include <iostream>
#include <cstdlib>
#include <exception>
using namespace std;

void my_Thandler() {
  cout << "Inside new terminate handler\n";
  abort();
}

int main()
{
  // set a new terminate handler
  set_terminate(my_Thandler);

  try {
    cout << "Inside try block\n";
    throw 100; // throw an error
  }
  catch (double i) { // won't catch an int exception
    // ...
  }

  return 0;
}
```

The output from this program is shown here.

```
Inside try block
Inside new terminate handler

Abnormal program termination
```

The uncaught_exception( ) Function

The C++ exception handling subsystem supplies one other function that you may find useful: **uncaught_exception( )**. Its prototype is shown here:

bool uncaught_exception( );

This function returns **true** if an exception has been thrown but not yet caught. Once caught, the function returns **false**.

Applying Exception Handling

Exception handling is designed to provide a structured means by which your program can handle abnormal events. This implies that the error handler must do something rational when an error occurs. For example, consider the following simple program. It inputs two numbers and divides the first by the second. It uses exception handling to manage a divide-by-zero error.

```cpp
#include <iostream>
using namespace std;

void divide(double a, double b);

int main()
{
  double i, j;

  do {
    cout << "Enter numerator (0 to stop): ";
    cin >> i;
    cout << "Enter denominator: ";
    cin >> j;
    divide(i, j);
  } while(i != 0);
```

```
    return 0;
}

void divide(double a, double b)
{
  try {
    if(!b) throw b; // check for divide-by-zero
    cout << "Result: " << a/b << endl;
  }
  catch (double b) {
    cout << "Can't divide by zero.\n";
  }
}
```

While the preceding program is a very simple example, it does illustrate the essential nature of exception handling. Since division by zero is illegal, the program cannot continue if a zero is entered for the second number. In this case, the exception is handled by not performing the division (which would have caused abnormal program termination) and by notifying the user of the error. The program then reprompts the user for two more numbers. Thus, the error has been handled in an orderly fashion and the user may continue on with the program. The same basic concepts will apply to more complex applications of exception handling.

Exception handling is especially useful for exiting from a deeply nested set of routines when a catastrophic error occurs. In this regard, C++'s exception handling is designed to replace the rather clumsy C-based **setjmp( )** and **longjmp( )** functions.

The key point about using exception handling is to provide an orderly means of handling errors. This means rectifying the situation, if possible.

Run-Time Type Identification (RTTI)

Using run-time type identification, you can determine the type of an object during program execution. To obtain an object's type, use **typeid**. You must include the header **<typeinfo>** in order to use **typeid**. Its general form is shown here.

typeid(*object*)

Here, *object* is the object whose type you will be obtaining. **typeid** returns a reference to an object of type **type_info** that describes the type of object defined by *object*. The **type_info** class defines the following public members:

```
bool operator==(const type_info & ob ) const;
bool operator!=(const type_info & ob ) const;
bool before(const type_info & ob ) const;
const char *name( ) const;
```

The overloaded **==** and **!=** provide for the comparison of types. The **before( )** function returns true if the invoking object is before the object used as a parameter in collation order. (This function is mostly for internal use only. Its return value has nothing to do with inheritance or class hierarchies.) The **name( )** function returns a pointer to the name of the type.

When **typeid** is applied to a base class pointer of a polymorphic class, it will automatically return the type of the object being pointed to, which might be a class derived from that base. (Remember, a polymorphic class is one that contains at least one virtual function.) Thus, using **typeid**, you can determine at run time the type of the object that is being pointed to by a base class pointer. The following program demonstrates this principle.

```cpp
// An example that uses typeid.
#include <iostream>
#include <typeinfo>
using namespace std;

class BaseClass {
  int a, b;
  virtual void f() {}; // make BaseClass polymorphic
};

class Derived1: public BaseClass {
  int i, j;
};

class Derived2: public BaseClass {
  int k;
};

int main()
{
  int i;
  BaseClass *p, baseob;
  Derived1 ob1;
  Derived2 ob2;
```

```
   // First, display type name of a built in type.
   cout << "Typeid of i is ";
   cout << typeid(i).name() << endl;

   // Demonstrate typeid with polymorphic types.
   p = &baseob;
   cout << "p is pointing to an object of type ";
   cout << typeid(*p).name() << endl;

   p = &ob1;
   cout << "p is pointing to an object of type ";
   cout << typeid(*p).name() << endl;

   p = &ob2;
   cout << "p is pointing to an object of type ";
   cout << typeid(*p).name() << endl;

   return 0;
}
```

The output produced by this program is shown here.

```
Typeid of i is int
p is pointing to an object of type BaseClass
p is pointing to an object of type Derived1
p is pointing to an object of type Derived2
```

As mentioned, when **typeid** is applied to a base class pointer of a polymorphic type, the type of object pointed to will be determined at run time, as the output produced by the program shows. For an experiment, comment out the virtual function **f( )** in **BaseClass** and observe the results.

Run-time type identification is not something that every program will use. However, when working with polymorphic types, it allows you to know what type of object is being operated upon in any given situation.

Casting Operators

Although C++ still fully supports the traditional casting operator, it defines four additional casting operators. They are **const_cast**, **dynamic_cast**, **reinterpret_cast**, and **static_cast**. Their general forms are shown here.

const_cast<*target-type*> (*expr*)
dynamic_cast<*target-type*> (*expr*)
reinterpret_cast<*target-type*> (*expr*)
static_cast<*target-type*> (*expr*)

Here, *target-type* specifies the target type of the cast and *expr* is the expression being cast to the new type.

The **const_cast** operator is used to explicitly override **const** and/or **volatile** in a cast. The target type must be the same as the source type except for the alteration of its **const** or **volatile** attributes. The most common use of **const_cast** is to remove **const**-ness.

dynamic_cast performs a run-time cast that verifies the validity of the cast. If the cast cannot be made, the cast fails and the expression evaluates to null. Its main use is for performing casts on polymorphic types. For example, given two polymorphic classes B and D, with D derived from B, a **dynamic_cast** can always cast a D* pointer into a B* pointer. A **dynamic_cast** can cast a B* pointer into a D* pointer only if the object being pointed to *actually is* a D*. In general, **dynamic_cast** will succeed if the attempted polymorphic cast is permitted (that is, if the target type can legally apply to the type of object being cast). If the cast cannot be made, then **dynamic_cast** evaluates to null.

The **static_cast** operator performs a nonpolymorphic cast. For example, it can be used to cast a base class pointer into a derived class pointer. It can also be used for any standard conversion. No run-time checks are performed The **reinterpret_cast** operator changes one type into a fundamentally different type. For example, it can be used to change a pointer into an integer. A **reinterpret_cast** should be used for casting inherently incompatible pointer types.

Only **const_cast** can cast away **const**-ness. That is, neither **dynamic_cast**, **static_cast**, nor **reinterpret_cast** can alter the **const**-ness of an object.

The following program demonstrates the use of **dynamic_cast**.

```
#include <iostream>
using namespace std;

#define NUM_EMPLOYEES 4

class employee {
public:
  employee() { cout << "Constructing employee\n"; }
  virtual void print() = 0;
};

class programmer : public employee {
public:
  programmer() { cout << "Constructing programmer\n"; }
```

```
      void print() { cout << "Printing programmer object\n"; }
    };

    class salesperson : public employee {
    public:
      salesperson() { cout << "Constructing salesperson\n"; }
      void print() { cout << "Printing salesperson object\n"; }
    };

    class executive : public employee {
    public:
      executive() { cout << "Constructing executive\n"; }
      void print() { cout << "Printing executive object\n"; }
    };

    int main() {
      programmer prog1, prog2;
      executive ex;
      salesperson sp;

      // Initialize the array of employees
      employee *e[NUM_EMPLOYEES];
      e[0] = &prog1;
      e[1] = &sp;
      e[2] = &ex;
      e[3] = &prog2;

      // See which ones are programmers.
      for(int i = 0; i < NUM_EMPLOYEES; i++) {
        programmer *pp = dynamic_cast<programmer*>(e[i]);
        if(pp) {
          cout << "Is a programmer\n";
          pp->print();
        }
        else {
          cout << "Not a programmer\n";
        }
      }
    }
```

The array **e** contains pointers to the four employees. The **dynamic_cast** operator is used to identify which of these are programmers. If the **dynamic_cast** operator returns a null, that employee is not a programmer. Otherwise, the **print( )** function for that object is invoked.

The output produced by this program is shown here:

```
Constructing employee
Constructing programmer
Constructing employee
Constructing programmer
Constructing employee
Constructing executive
Constructing employee
Constructing salesperson
Is a programmer
Printing programmer object
Not a programmer
Not a programmer
Is a programmer
Printing programmer object
```

The following program demonstrates the use of **reinterpret_cast**.

```cpp
// An example that uses reinterpret_cast.
#include <iostream>
using namespace std;

int main()
{
  int i;
  char *p = "This is a string";

  i = reinterpret_cast<int> (p); // cast pointer to integer

  cout << i;

  return 0;
}
```

One final point: Although the traditional casting operator can handle a wide variety of casts, the casting operators just described give you more control over casting. This finer-grained control can be a great benefit in today's type-rich programming environments, such as Windows.

The Complete Reference

Borland
C++
Builder

Chapter 26

Miscellaneous
C++ Topics

T his chapter discusses several aspects of C++ not covered in the previous chapters. It also looks at some differences between C and C++, as well as some design philosophy.

Dynamic Allocation Using new and delete

As you know, C uses the functions **malloc( )** and **free( )** (among others) to dynamically allocate memory and to free dynamically allocated memory. However, C++ contains two operators that perform the functions of allocating and freeing memory in a more efficient and easier-to-use way. The operators are **new** and **delete**. Their general forms are

pointer_var = new *var_type* ;
delete *pointer_var* ;

Here, *pointer_var* is a pointer of type *var_type*. The **new** operator allocates sufficient memory to hold a value of type *var_type* and returns an address to it. Any data type can be allocated using **new**. The **delete** operator frees the memory pointed to by *pointer_var*.

If an allocation request cannot be filled, the **new** operator throws an exception of type **bad_alloc**. If your program does not catch this exception, then your program will be terminated. While this default behavior is fine for short sample programs, in real-world programs that you write, you should catch this exception and process it in some rational manner. To watch for this exception, you must include **<new>** in your program.

The actions of **new** on failure as just described are specified by ANSI/ISO Standard C++ and correctly implemented by C++ Builder. The trouble is that not all compilers, especially older ones, will have implemented **new** in compliance with Standard C++. When C++ was first invented, **new** returned null on failure. Later, this was changed such that **new** caused an exception on failure. Finally, it was decided that a **new** failure will generate an exception by default, but that a null pointer could be returned instead, as an option. Thus, **new** has been implemented differently, at different times, by compiler manufacturers. If you are updating old code, or porting code from another environment, you will need to check all uses of **new** very carefully.

Because of the way dynamic allocation is managed, you must use **delete** only with a pointer to memory that was allocated using **new**. Using **delete** with any other type of address will cause serious problems.

There are several advantages to using **new** instead of **malloc( )**. First, **new** automatically computes the size of the type being allocated. You don't have to make use of the **sizeof** operator, which saves you some effort. More important, it prevents the wrong amount of memory from being accidentally allocated. Second, it automatically returns the correct pointer type—you don't need to use a type cast. Third, as you will soon see, it is possible to initialize the object being allocated using **new**. Finally, it is possible to overload **new** (and **delete**) relative to classes you create, or globally.

Here is a simple example of **new** and **delete**. Notice how a **try/catch** block is used to monitor for an allocation failure.

```
#include <iostream>
#include <new>
using namespace std;

int main()
{
  int *p;

  try {
    p = new int; // allocate memory for int
  } catch (bad_alloc xa) {
    cout << "Allocation failure.\n";
    return 1;
  }

  *p = 20; // assign that memory the value 20
  cout << *p; // prove that it works by displaying value

  delete p; // free the memory

  return 0;
}
```

This program assigns to **p** an address in memory that is large enough to hold an integer. It then assigns that memory the value 20 and displays the contents of that memory on the screen. Finally, it frees the dynamically allocated memory.

As stated, you can initialize the memory using the **new** operator. To do this, specify the initial value inside parentheses after the type name. For example, this program uses initialization to give the memory pointed to by **p** the value 99:

```
#include <iostream>
#include <new>
using namespace std;

int main()
{
  int *p;

  try {
```

```
    p = new int (99);  // initialize with 99
  } catch(bad_alloc xa) {
    cout << "Allocation failure.\n";
    return 1;
  }

  cout << *p;
  delete p;

  return 0;
}
```

You can allocate arrays using **new**. The general form for a single-dimension array is

pointer_var = new *var_type* [*size*];

Here, *size* specifies the number of elements in the array. There is one important restriction to remember when allocating an array: you cannot initialize it.

When you free a dynamically allocated array, you must use this form of **delete:**

delete [ ] *pointer_var*;

Here, the [ ] informs **delete** that an array is being released.

The following program allocates a 10-element array of **float**s, assigns the array the values 100 to 109, and displays the contents of the array on the screen:

```
#include <iostream>
#include <new>
using namespace std;

int main()
{
  float *p;
  int i;

  try {
    p = new float [10]; // get a 10-element array
  } catch(bad_alloc xa) {
    cout << "Allocation failure.\n";
    return 1;
  }

  // assign the values 100 through 109
```

```
for(i=0; i<10; i++) p[i] = 100.00 + i;

// display the contents of the array
for(i=0; i<10; i++)  cout << p[i] << " ";

delete [] p; // delete the entire array

return 0;
}
```

Allocating Objects

As stated, you can allocate memory for any valid type. This includes objects. A dynamically created object acts just like any other object. When it is created, its constructor (if it has one) is called. When the object is freed, its destructor is executed. For example, in this program, **new** allocates memory for an object of type **three_d:**

```
#include <iostream>
#include <new>
using namespace std;

class three_d {
public:
  int x, y, z; // 3-d coordinates
  three_d(int a, int b, int c);
  ~three_d() { cout << "Destructing\n"; }
} ;

three_d::three_d(int a, int b, int c)
{
  cout << "Constructing\n";
  x = a;
  y = b;
  z = c;
}

// Display X, Y, Z coordinates - three_d inserter.
ostream &operator<<(ostream &stream, three_d &obj)
{
  stream << obj.x << ", ";
  stream << obj.y << ", ";
  stream << obj.z << "\n";
```

```
      return stream;   // return the stream
}

int main()
{
  three_d *p;

  try {
    p = new three_d (5, 6, 7);
  } catch(bad_alloc xa) {
    cout << "Allocation failure.\n";
    return 1;
  }

  cout << *p;
  delete p;

  return 0;
}
```

When you run the program, you will see that **three_d**'s constructor is called when **new** is encountered and that its destructor function is called when **delete** is reached. Also note that the initializers are automatically passed to the constructor by **new**.

Here is an example that allocates an array of objects of type **three_d**.

```
#include <iostream>
#include <new>
using namespace std;

class three_d {
public:
  int x, y, z; // 3-d coordinates
  three_d(int a, int b, int c) ;
  three_d(){ x=y=z=0; cout << "Constructing\n"; } // needed for arrays
  ~three_d() { cout << "Destructing\n"; }
};

three_d::three_d(int a, int b, int c)
{
  cout << "Constructing\n";
```

```
    x = a;
    y = b;
    z = c;
}

// Display X, Y, Z coordinates - three_d inserter.
ostream &operator<<(ostream &stream, three_d &obj)
{
  stream << obj.x << ", ";
  stream << obj.y << ", ";
  stream << obj.z << "\n";
  return stream;  // return the stream
}

int main()
{
  three_d *p;
  int i;

  try {
    p = new three_d [10];
  } catch (bad_alloc xa) {
    cout << "Allocation failure.\n";
    return 1;
  }

  for(i=0; i<10; i++) {
    p[i].x = 1;
    p[i].y = 2;
    p[i].z = 3;
  }

  for(i=0; i<10; i++) cout << *p;
  delete [] p;

  return 0;
}
```

Notice that a second constructor has been added to the **three_d** class. Because allocated arrays cannot be initialized, a constructor that does not have any parameters is needed. If you don't supply this constructor, a compile-time message will be displayed.

Another Way to Watch for Allocation Failure

As mentioned, when C++ was first invented, the **new** operator did not throw an exception when an allocation error occurred. Instead, it returned null (just like C's **malloc( )** function). If you want to have **new** work this way instead of throwing an exception, call the **new** function as shown here:

   p_var = new(nothrow) *type;*

Here, *p_var* is a pointer variable of *type*. The **nothrow** form of **new** works like the original version of **new** from years ago. Since it returns null on failure, it can be "dropped into" older code without having to add exception handling. However, for new code, exceptions provide a better alternative. To use the **nothrow** option, you must include the header **<new>**.

The following program shows this alternative approach to using **new**.

```
// Demonstrate nothrow version of new.
#include <iostream>
#include <new>
using namespace std;

int main()
{
  int *p, i;

  p = new(nothrow) int[32]; // use nothrow option
  if(!p) {
    cout << "Allocation failure.\n";
    return 1;
  }

  for(i=0; i<32; i++) p[i] = i;
  for(i=0; i<32; i++) cout << p[i] << " ";

  delete [] p; // free the memory

  return 0;
}
```

As this program demonstrates, when using this approach you must check the pointer returned by **new** after each allocation request.

Overloading new and delete

It is possible to overload **new** and **delete**. You might want to do this to use some special allocation method. For example, you may want allocation routines that automatically begin using a disk file as virtual memory when the heap has been exhausted. Whatever the reason, it is a very simple matter to overload these operators.

The skeletons for the functions that overload **new** and **delete** are

```
void *operator new(size_t size)
{
  // perform allocation
  return pointer_to_memory;
}

void operator delete(void *p)
{
  // free memory pointed to by p
}
```

The parameter *size* will contain the number of bytes needed to hold the object being allocated. This value is automatically obtained for you. The overloaded **new** function must return a pointer to the memory that it allocates or throw a **bad_alloc** exception if an allocation error occurs. Beyond these constraints, the overloaded **new** function can do anything else you require. When you allocate an object using **new** (whether your own version or not), the object's constructor is automatically called.

The **delete** function receives a pointer to the region of memory to free. It must then release the memory pointed to by that pointer. When an object is deleted, its destructor function is automatically called.

The **new** and **delete** operators can be overloaded globally so that all uses of these operators call your custom versions. They can also be overloaded relative to one or more classes. Let's begin with an example of overloading **new** and **delete** relative to a class. For the sake of simplicity, no new allocation scheme will be used. Instead, the overloaded operators will simply invoke the standard library functions **malloc( )** and **free( )**. (In your own application, you may, of course, implement any alternative allocation scheme you like.)

To overload the **new** and **delete** operators for a class, simply make the overloaded operator functions class members. For example, here the **new** and **delete** operators are overloaded for the **loc** class:

```
#include <iostream>
#include <cstdlib>
#include <new>
using namespace std;
```

```
class loc {
  int longitude, latitude;
public:
  loc() {}
  loc(int lg, int lt) {
    longitude = lg;
    latitude = lt;
  }

  void show() {
    cout << longitude << " ";
    cout << latitude << "\n";
  }

  void *operator new(size_t size);
  void operator delete(void *p);
};

// new overloaded relative to loc.
void *loc::operator new(size_t size)
{
  void *p;

  cout << "In overloaded new.\n";
  p =  malloc(size);
  if(!p) {
    bad_alloc ba;
    throw ba;
  }
  return p;
}

// delete overloaded relative to loc.
void loc::operator delete(void *p)
{
  cout << "In overloaded delete.\n";
  free(p);
}

int main()
{
  loc *p1, *p2;
```

```
    try {
      p1 = new loc (10, 20);
    } catch (bad_alloc xa) {
      cout << "Allocation error for p1.\n";
      return 1;
    }

    try {
      p2 = new loc (-10, -20);
    } catch (bad_alloc xa) {
      cout << "Allocation error for p2.\n";
      return 1;;
    }

    p1->show();
    p2->show();

    delete p1;
    delete p2;

    return 0;
}
```

Output from this program is shown here.

```
In overloaded new.
In overloaded new.
10 20
-10 -20
In overloaded delete.
In overloaded delete.
```

You can overload **new** and **delete** globally by overloading these operators outside of any class declaration. When **new** and **delete** are overloaded globally, C++'s default **new** and **delete** are ignored and the new operators are used for all allocation requests. Of course, if you have defined any version of **new** and **delete** relative to one or more classes, then the class-specific versions are used when allocating objects of the class for which they are defined. In other words, when **new** or **delete** are encountered, the compiler first checks to see whether they are defined relative to the class they are operating on. If so, those specific versions are used. If not, C++ uses the globally defined **new** and **delete**. If these have been overloaded, the overloaded versions are used.

To see an example of overloading **new** and **delete** globally, examine this program:

```
#include <iostream>
#include <cstdlib>
#include <new>
using namespace std;

class loc {
  int longitude, latitude;
public:
  loc() {}
  loc(int lg, int lt) {
    longitude = lg;
    latitude = lt;
  }

  void show() {
    cout << longitude << " ";
    cout << latitude << "\n";
  }
};

// Global new
void *operator new(size_t size)
{
  void *p;

  p = malloc(size);
  if(!p) {
    bad_alloc ba;
    throw ba;
  }
  return p;
}

// Global delete
void operator delete(void *p)
{
  free(p);
}
```

```
int main()
{
  loc *p1, *p2;
  float *f;

  try {
    p1 = new loc (10, 20);
  } catch (bad_alloc xa) {
    cout << "Allocation error for p1.\n";
    return 1;
  }

  try {
    p2 = new loc (-10, -20);
  } catch (bad_alloc xa) {
    cout << "Allocation error for p2.\n";
    return 1;
  }

  try {
    f = new float; // uses overloaded new, too
  } catch (bad_alloc xa) {
    cout << "Allocation error for f.\n";
    return 1;
  }

  *f = 10.10F;
  cout << *f << "\n";

  p1->show();
  p2->show();

  delete p1;
  delete p2;
  delete f;

  return 0;
}
```

Run this program to prove to yourself that the built-in **new** and **delete** operators have indeed been overloaded.

Overloading new and delete for Arrays

If you want to be able to allocate arrays of objects using your own allocation system, you will need to overload **new** and **delete** a second time. To allocate and free arrays, you must use these forms of **new** and **delete**.

```
void *operator new[ ](size_t size)
{
  // perform allocation — throw bad_alloc on failure
  return pointer_to_memory;
}

void operator delete[ ](void *p)
{
  // free memory pointed to by p
}
```

When allocating an array, the constructor for each object in the array is automatically called. When freeing an array, each object's destructor is automatically called. You do not have to provide explicit code to accomplish these actions.

The following program allocates and frees an object and an array of objects of type **loc**.

```cpp
#include <iostream>
#include <cstdlib>
#include <new>
using namespace std;

class loc {
  int longitude, latitude;
public:
  loc() { longitude = latitude = 0; }
  loc(int lg, int lt) {
    longitude = lg;
    latitude = lt;
  }

  void show() {
    cout << longitude << " ";
    cout << latitude << "\n";
  }
```

```
  void *operator new(size_t size);
  void operator delete(void *p);

  void *operator new[](size_t size);
  void operator delete[](void *p);
};

// new overloaded relative to loc.
void *loc::operator new(size_t size)
{
  void *p;

  cout << "In overloaded new.\n";
  p = malloc(size);
  if(!p) {
    bad_alloc ba;
    throw ba;
  }
  return p;
}

// delete overloaded relative to loc.
void loc::operator delete(void *p)
{
  cout << "In overloaded delete.\n";
  free(p);
}

// new overloaded for loc arrays.
void *loc::operator new[](size_t size)
{
  void *p;

  cout << "Using overload new[].\n";
  p = malloc(size);
  if(!p) {
    bad_alloc ba;
    throw ba;
  }
```

```
    return p;
}

// delete overloaded for loc arrays.
void loc::operator delete[](void *p)
{
  cout << "Freeing array using overloaded delete[]\n";
  free(p);
}

int main()
{
  loc *p1, *p2;
  int i;

  try {
    p1 = new loc (10, 20); // allocate an object
  } catch (bad_alloc xa) {
    cout << "Allocation error for p1.\n";
    return 1;
  }

  try {
    p2 = new loc [10]; // allocate an array
  } catch (bad_alloc xa) {
    cout << "Allocation error for p2.\n";
    return 1;
  }

  p1->show();

  for(i=0; i<10; i++)
    p2[i].show();

  delete p1; // free an object
  delete [] p2; // free an array

  return 0;
}
```

static Class Members

Both function and data members of a class can be made **static**. This section explains the consequences of each.

static Data Members

The keyword **static** can be applied to members of a class. Its meaning in this context is similar to its original C-like meaning. When you declare a member of a class as **static**, you are telling the compiler that no matter how many objects of the class are created, there is only one copy of the **static** member. A **static** member is *shared* by all objects of the class. All **static** data is initialized to zero when the first object of its class is created and if no other initialization is specified.

When you declare a **static** data member within a class, you are *not* defining it. (That is, you are not allocating storage for it.) Instead, you must provide a global definition for it elsewhere, outside the class. You do this by redeclaring the **static** variable, using the scope resolution operator to identify which class it belongs to. This is necessary for storage to be allocated for the **static** variable.

To understand the usage and effect of a **static** data member, consider this program:

```
#include <iostream>
using namespace std;

class shared {
  static int a;
  int b;
public:
  void set(int i, int j) { a=i; b=j; }
  void show();
} ;

int shared::a; // define a

void shared::show()
{
  cout << "This is static a: " << a;
  cout << "\nThis is non-static b: " << b;
  cout << "\n";
}
```

```
int main()
{
  shared x, y;

  x.set(1, 1); // set a to 1
  x.show();

  y.set(2, 2); // change a to 2
  y.show();

  x.show(); /* Here, a has been changed for both x and y
                  because a is shared by both objects. */

  return 0;
}
```

The program displays the following output when run.

```
This is static a: 1
This is non-static b: 1
This is static a: 2
This is non-static b: 2
This is static a: 2
This is non-static b: 1
```

Notice that the integer **a** is declared both inside **shared** and outside of it. As mentioned earlier, this is necessary because the declaration of **a** inside **shared** does not allocate storage.

As a convenience, older versions of C++ did not require the second declaration of a static member variable. However, this convenience gave rise to serious inconsistencies, and it was eliminated several years ago. Nonetheless, you may still find older C++ code that does not redeclare static member variables. In these cases, you will need to add the required definitions.

static Member Functions

You can also have **static** member functions. **static** member functions cannot refer directly to nonstatic data and nonstatic functions declared in their class. This is because a **static** member function does not have a **this** pointer; it has no way of knowing which object's nonstatic data to access. For example, if there are two objects of a class that contains a **static** function called **f( )** and if **f( )** attempts to access a nonstatic variable called **var**, defined by its class, which copy of **var** is being referred to? The compiler has no way of knowing. This is why **static** functions can access only other **static** functions or data directly. Also, a **static** function cannot be virtual or declared as **const** or **volatile**. A **static** function can be called either by using an object of its class or by using the class name and the scope resolution operator. Remember, even when called using an object, the function is still not passed a **this** pointer.

The following short program illustrates one of the many ways you can use **static** functions. It is not uncommon for an object to require access to some scarce resource, such as a shared file in a network. As the program illustrates, the use of **static** data and functions provides a method by which an object can check on the status of the resource and access it if it is available.

```cpp
#include <iostream>
using namespace std;

enum access_t {shared, in_use, locked, unlocked};

// a scarce resource control class
class access {
  static enum access_t acs;
  // ...
public:
  static void set_access(enum access_t a) { acs = a; }
  static enum access_t get_access()
  {
    return acs;
  }
  // ...
};

enum access_t access::acs; // define acs

int main()
{
  access  obj1, obj2;

  access::set_access(locked); // call using class name

  // ... intervening code

  // see if obj2 can access resource
  if(obj2.get_access()==unlocked) { // call using object
```

```
      access::set_access(in_use);   // call using class name
      cout << "Access resource.\n";
   }
   else cout << "Locked out.\n";

   // ...

   return 0;
}
```

When you run this program, **Locked out.** is displayed. Notice that **set_access( )** is called using the class name and the scope resolution operator. The function **get_access( )** is called using an object and the dot operator. Either form may be used when calling a **static** member function and both forms have the same effect. You might want to play with the program a little to make sure you understand the effect of **static** on both data and functions.

As stated, **static** functions can directly access only other **static** functions or **static** data within the same class. To prove this, try compiling this version of the program:

```
// This program contains an error and will not compile.
#include <iostream>
using namespace std;

enum access_t {shared, in_use, locked, unlocked};

// a scarce resource control class
class access {
  static enum access_t acs;
  int i;  // non-static
  // ...
public:
  static void set_access(enum access_t a) { acs = a; }
  static enum access_t get_access()
  {
    i = 100; // this will not compile
    return acs;
  }
  // ...
};

enum access_t access::acs; // define acs
```

```
int main()
{
  access  obj1, obj2;

  access::set_access(locked); // call using class name

  // ... intervening code

  // see if obj2 can access resource
  if(obj2.get_access()==unlocked) { // call using object
    access::set_access(in_use); // call using class name
    cout << "Access resource.\n";
  }
  else cout << "Locked out.\n";

  // ...
  return 0;
}
```

This program does not compile because **get_access( )** is attempting to access a
nonstatic variable.

You may not see an immediate need for **static** members, but as you continue to
write programs in C++, you will find them very useful in certain situations because
they allow you to avoid the use of global variables.

Virtual Base Classes

As you know, in C++, the **virtual** keyword is used to declare **virtual** functions that
will be overridden by a derived class. However, **virtual** also has another use that
enables you to specify *virtual base classes*. To understand what a virtual base class is
and why the keyword **virtual** has a second meaning, let's begin with the short,
incorrect program shown here:

```
// This program contains an error and will not compile.
#include <iostream>
using namespace std;

class base {
public:
  int i;
};
```

```
// d1 inherits base.
class d1 :  public base {
public:
  int j;
};

// d2 inherits base.
class d2 : public base {
public:
  int k;
};

/* d3 inherits both d1 and d2. This means that there
   are two copies of base in d3! */
class d3 : public d1, public d2 {
public:
  int m;
};

int main()
{
  d3 d;

  d.i = 10;  // this is ambiguous, which i???
  d.j = 20;
  d.k = 30;
  d.m = 40;


  // also ambiguous, which i???
  cout << d.i << " ";
  cout << d.j << " " << d.k << " ";
  cout << d.m;

  return 0;
}
```

As the comments in the program indicate, both **d1** and **d2** inherit **base**. However, **d3** inherits both **d1** and **d2**. This means there are two copies of **base** present in an object of type **d3**. Therefore, in an expression like

```
d.i = 20;
```

which **i** is being referred to? The one in **d1** or the one in **d2**? Since there are two copies of **base** present in object **d**, there are two **d.i**'s. As you can see, the statement is inherently ambiguous.

There are two ways to remedy the preceding program. The first is to apply the scope resolution operator to **i** and manually select one **i**. For example, this version of the program does compile and run as expected:

```cpp
#include <iostream>
using namespace std;

class base {
public:
  int i;
};

// d1 inherits base.
class d1 :  public base {
public:
  int j;
};

// d2 inherits base.
class d2 : public base {
public:
  int k;
};

/* d3 inherits both d1 and d2. This means that there
   are two copies of base in d3! */
class d3 : public d1, public d2 {
public:
  int m;
};

int main()
{
  d3 d;

  d.d2::i = 10; // scope resolved, using d2's i
  d.j = 20;
  d.k = 30;
  d.m = 40;
```

C++

```
    // scope resolved, using d2's i
    cout << d.d2::i << " ";
    cout << d.j << " " << d.k << " ";
    cout << d.m;

    return 0;
}
```

By applying the ::, the program has manually selected **d2**'s version of **base**. However, this solution raises a deeper issue: What if only one copy of **base** is actually required? Is there some way to prevent two copies from being included in **d3**? The answer, as you probably have guessed, is yes. And this solution is achieved by using virtual base classes.

When two or more classes are derived from a common base class, you can prevent multiple copies of the base class from being present in a class derived from those classes by declaring the base class as **virtual** when it is inherited. For example, here is another version of the example program in which **d3** contains only one copy of **base**:

```
#include <iostream>
using namespace std;

class base {
public:
  int i;
};

// d1 inherits base as virtual.
class d1 : virtual public base {
public:
  int j;
};

// d2 inherits base as virtual.
class d2 : virtual public base {
public:
  int k;
};
```

```
/* d3 inherits both d1 and d2. However, now there is
   only one copy of base in d3. */
class d3 : public d1, public d2 {
public:
  int m;
};

int main()
{
  d3 d;

  d.i = 10; // no longer ambiguous
  d.j = 20;
  d.k = 30;
  d.m = 40;

  cout << d.i << " "; // no longer ambiguous
  cout << d.j << " " << d.k << " ";
  cout << d.m;

  return 0;
}
```

As this examples shows, the keyword **virtual** precedes the rest of the inherited class's specification. Now that both **d1** and **d2** have inherited **base** as **virtual**, any multiple inheritance involving them will cause only one copy of **base** to be present. Therefore, in **d3**, there is only one copy of **base**, so **d.i = 10** is perfectly valid and unambiguous.

One further point to keep in mind: Even though both **d1** and **d2** specify **base** as **virtual**, **base** is still present in any objects of either type. For example, the following sequence is perfectly valid:

```
// define a class of type d1
d1 myclass;

myclass.i = 100;
```

Virtual base classes and normal ones differ only when an object inherits the base more than once. If virtual base classes are used, only one base class is present in the object. Otherwise, multiple copies will be found.

const Member Functions and mutable

Class member functions may be declared as **const**, which causes **this** to be treated as a **const** pointer. Thus, a **const** function cannot modify the object that invokes it. Also, a **const** object may not invoke a non**const** member function. However, a **const** member function can be called by either **const** or non**const** objects.

To specify a member function as **const**, use the form shown in the following example.

```
class X {
  int some_var;
public:
  int f1() const; // const member function
};
```

As you can see, the **const** follows the function's parameter declaration.

The purpose of declaring a member function as **const** is to prevent it from modifying the object that invokes it. For example, consider the following program.

```
/*
Demonstrate const member functions.
   This program won't compile.
*/
#include <iostream>
using namespace std;

class Demo {
  int i;
public:
  int geti() const {
    return i; // ok
  }

  void seti(int x) const {
    i = x; // error!
  }
};

int main()
{
  Demo ob;

  ob.seti(1900);
```

```
    cout << ob.geti();

    return 0;
}
```

This program will not compile because **seti( )** is declared as **const**. This means that it is not allowed to modify the invoking object. Since it attempts to change **i**, the program is in error. In contrast, since **geti( )** does not attempt to modify **i**, it is perfectly acceptable.

Sometimes there will be one or more members of a class that you want a **const** function to be able to modify even though you don't want the function to be able to modify any of its other members. You can accomplish this through the use of **mutable**. It overrides **const**ness. That is, a **mutable** member can be modified by a **const** member function. For example,

```
// Demonstrate mutable.
#include <iostream>
using namespace std;

class Demo {
  mutable int i;
  int j;
public:
  int geti() const {
    return i; // ok
  }

  void seti(int x) const {
    i = x; // now, OK.
  }

/* The following function won't compile.
  void setj(int x) const {
    j = x; // Still Wrong!
  }
*/
};

int main()
{
  Demo ob;
```

```
    ob.seti(1900);
    cout << ob.geti();

    return 0;
}
```

Here, **i** is specified as **mutable**, so it may be changed by the **seti( )** function. However, **j** is not **mutable** and **setj( )** is unable to modify its value.

Volatile Member Functions

Class member functions may be declared as **volatile**, which causes **this** to be treated as a **volatile** pointer. To specify a member function as **volatile**, use the form shown in the following example.

```
class X {
public:
   void f2(int a) volatile; // volatile member function
};
```

Using the asm Keyword

In C++ Builder, you can embed assembly language directly into your program by using the **asm** keyword. The **asm** keyword has three slightly different general forms:

asm *instruction ;*
asm *instruction newline*
asm {
   instruction sequence
}

Here, *instruction* is any valid assembly language instruction. Unlike any other C++ Builder statement, an **asm** statement does not have to end with a semicolon; it can end with either a semicolon or a newline. To use embedded assembly code, you will need to have TASM32.EXE (Borland's assembler) installed on your computer.

> **Note**   *A thorough working knowledge of assembly language programming is required to use the **asm** statement. If you are not proficient at assembly language, it is best to avoid using it because nasty errors may result.*

Linkage Specification

In C++ you can specify how a function is linked. By default, functions are linked as C++ functions. By using a *linkage specification,* however, you can cause a function to be linked as a different type of language function. The general form of a linkage specifier is

extern *"language " function-prototype*

where *language* denotes the desired language. In C++ Builder, *language* must be either C or C++, but other implementations may allow other language types.

This program causes **myCfunc( )** to be linked as a C function:

```
#include <iostream>
using namespace std;

extern "C" void myCfunc(void);

int main()
{
  myCfunc();

  return 0;
}

// This will link as a C function.
void myCfunc(void)
{
  cout << "This links as a C function.\n";
}
```

Note *The **extern** keyword is a necessary part of the linkage specification. Further, the linkage specification must be global; it cannot be used inside a function.*

You can specify more than one function at a time by using this form of the linkage specification:

extern *"language " {*
  prototypes
}

Linkage specifications are rare; you will probably not need to use one.

C++

The .* and ->* Operators

The .* and ->* are called *pointer-to-member* operators. Their job is to allow you to "point to" a member of a class, generically, rather than to a specific instance of that member within some object. These two operators are needed because a pointer to a member does not fully define an address. Instead, it provides an offset at which that member can be found within any object of its class. Since member pointers are not true pointers, the normal . and -> operators cannot be used. Instead, the .* and ->* operators must be employed.

Let's begin with an example. The following program displays the summation of the number 7. It accesses the function **sum_it( )** and the variable **sum** using member pointers.

```cpp
#include <iostream>
using namespace std;

class myclass {
public:
  int sum;
  void myclass::sum_it(int x);
};

void myclass::sum_it(int x) {
  int i;

  sum = 0;
  for(i=x; i; i--) sum += i;
}

int main()
{
  int myclass::*dp;   // pointer to an integer class member
  void (myclass::*fp)(int x); // pointer to member function
  myclass c;

  dp = &myclass::sum;   // get address of data
  fp = &myclass::sum_it; // get address of function

  (c.*fp)(7);   // compute summation of 7
  cout << "summation of 7 is " << c.*dp;

  return 0;
}
```

Inside **main( )**, this program creates two member pointers: **dp**, which points to the variable **sum**, and **fp**, which points to the function **sum_it( )**. Note carefully the syntax of each declaration. The scope resolution operator is used to specify which class is being referred to. The program also creates an object of **myclass** called **c**.

The program then obtains the addresses of **sum** and **sum_it( )**. As stated earlier, these "addresses" are really just offsets into an object of **myclass** where **sum** and **sum_it( )** are found. Next, the program uses a function pointer **fp** to call the **sum_it( )** function of **c**. The extra parentheses are necessary in order to correctly associate the **.*** operator. Finally, the summed value is displayed by accessing **c**'s **sum** through **dp**.

When you are accessing a member of an object using an object or a reference, you must use the **.*** operator. However, if you are using a pointer to the object, you need to use the **->*** operator, as illustrated in this version of the preceding program:

```
#include <iostream>
using namespace std;

class myclass {
public:
  int sum;
  void myclass::sum_it(int x);
};

void myclass::sum_it(int x) {
  int i;

  sum = 0;
  for(i=x; i; i--) sum += i;
}

int main()
{
  int myclass::*dp;  // pointer to an integer class member
  void (myclass::*fp)(int x); // pointer to member function
  myclass *c, d; // c is now a pointer to an object

  c = &d; // give c the address of an object

  dp = &myclass::sum;  // get address of data
  fp = &myclass::sum_it; // get address of function

  (c->*fp)(7);  // now, use ->* to call function
  cout << "summation of 7 is " << c->*dp; // use ->*
```

```
   return 0;
}
```

In this version, **c** is now a pointer to an object of type **myclass**, and the ->* operator is used to access **sum** and **sum_it( )**.

Creating Conversion Functions

Sometimes you will create a class that you want to be able to freely mix in an expression with other types of data. While overloaded operator functions can provide a means of mixing types, sometimes a simple conversion is all that you want. In these cases, you can use a type conversion function to convert your class into a type compatible with that of the rest of the expression. The general form of a type conversion function is

operator *type* ( ) {return *value* ;}

Here, *type* is the target type that you are converting your class to and *value* is the value of the class after conversion. A conversion function must be a member of the class for which it is defined.

To illustrate how to create a conversion function, let's use the **three_d** class once again. Suppose you want to be able to convert an object of type **three_d** into an integer so that it can be used in an integer expression. Further, the conversion will take place by using the product of the three dimensions. To accomplish this, you use a conversion function that looks like this:

```
operator int() { return x * y * z; }
```

Here is a program that illustrates how the conversion function works:

```
#include <iostream>
using namespace std;

class three_d {
  int x, y, z; // 3-d coordinates
public:
  three_d(int a, int b, int c) { x=a; y=b, z=c; }
```

```
    three_d operator+(three_d op2) ;
    friend ostream &operator<<(ostream &stream, three_d &obj);

    operator int() { return x*y*z; }
} ;

// Display X, Y, Z coordinates - three_d inserter.
ostream &operator<<(ostream &stream, three_d &obj)
{
  stream << obj.x << ", ";
  stream << obj.y << ", ";
  stream << obj.z << "\n";
  return stream;  // return the stream
}

three_d three_d::operator+(three_d op2)
{
  three_d temp(0, 0, 0);

  temp.x = x+op2.x;  // these are integer additions
  temp.y = y+op2.y;  // and the + retains its original
  temp.z = z+op2.z;  // meaning relative to them
  return temp;
}

int main()
{
  three_d a(1, 2, 3), b(2, 3, 4), c(0, 0, 0);

  cout << a << b;

  cout <<  b+100; // displays 124 because of conversion to int
  cout << "\n";

  c = a+b; // adds two objects
  cout << c;

  return 0;
}
```

This program displays the output

```
1, 2, 3
2, 3, 4
124
3, 5, 7
```

As the program illustrates, when a **three_d** object is used in an integer expression, such as **cout << b+100**, the conversion function is applied to the object. In this specific case, the conversion function returns the value 24, which is then added to 100. However, when no conversion is needed, as in **c = a+b**, the conversion function is not called.

Remember that you can create different conversion functions to meet different needs. You could define one that converts to **double** or **long**, for example. Each is applied automatically.

Copy Constructors

By default, when one object is used to initialize another, C++ performs a bitwise copy. That is, an identical copy of the initializing object is created in the target object. Although this is perfectly adequate for many cases—and generally exactly what you want to happen—there are situations in which a bitwise copy cannot be used. One of the most common situations in which you must avoid a bitwise copy is when an object allocates memory when it is created. For example, assume two objects, A and B, of the same class called *ClassType*, which allocates memory when creating objects, and assume that A is already in existence. This means that A has already allocated its memory. Further, assume that A is used to initialize B, as shown here.

ClassType B = A;

If a bitwise copy is performed, then B will be an exact copy of A. This means that B will be using the same piece of allocated memory that A is using, instead of allocating its own. Clearly, this is not the desired outcome. For example, if *ClassType* includes a destructor that frees the memory, then the same piece of memory will be freed twice when A and B are destroyed!

The same type of problem can occur in two additional ways: first, when a copy of an object is made when it is passed as an argument to a function; and second, when a temporary object is created as a return value from a function. (Remember, temporary objects are automatically created to hold the return value of a function, and they may also be created in certain other circumstances.)

To solve the type of problem just described, C++ allows you to create a *copy constructor*, which the compiler uses when one object is used to initialize another. When a copy constructor exists, the bitwise copy is bypassed. The general form of a copy constructor is

classname (const *classname &o*) {
  // body of constructor
}

Here, *o* is a reference to the object on the right side of the initialization. It is permissible for a copy constructor to have additional parameters as long as they have default arguments defined for them. However, in all cases the first parameter must be a reference to the object doing the initializing.

It is important to understand that C++ defines two distinct types of situations in which the value of one object is given to another. The first is assignment. The second is initialization, which can occur in three ways:

- when one object explicitly initializes another, such as in a declaration
- when a copy of an object is made to be passed to a function
- when a temporary object is generated (most commonly, as a return value)

The copy constructor applies only to initializations. For example, assuming a class called **myclass**, and that **y** is an object of type **myclass**, each of the following statements involves initialization.

```
myclass x = y; // y explicitly initializating x
func(y);       // y passed as a parameter
y = func();    // y receiving a temporary, return object
```

Following is an example where an explicit copy constructor is needed. This program creates a very simple "safe" integer array type that prevents array boundaries from being overrun. Storage for each array is allocated by the use of **new**, and a pointer to the memory is maintained within each array object.

```
/* This program creates a "safe" array class.  Since space
   for the array is allocated using new, a copy constructor
   is provided to allocate memory when one array object is
   used to initialize another.
*/
#include <iostream>
#include <new>
```

```cpp
#include <cstdlib>
using namespace std;

class array {
  int *p;
  int size;
public:
  array(int sz) {
    try {
      p = new int[sz];
    } catch (bad_alloc xa) {
      cout << "Allocation Failure\n";
      exit(EXIT_FAILURE);
    }
    size = sz;
  }
  ~array() { delete [] p; }

  // copy constructor
  array(const array &a);

  void put(int i, int j) {
    if(i>=0 && i<size) p[i] = j;
  }
  int get(int i) {
    return p[i];
  }
};

// Copy Constructor
array::array(const array &a) {
  int i;

  try {
    p = new int[a.size];
  } catch (bad_alloc xa) {
    cout << "Allocation Failure\n";
    exit(EXIT_FAILURE);
  }
  for(i=0; i<a.size; i++) p[i] = a.p[i];
}
```

```
int main()
{
  array num(10);
  int i;

  for(i=0; i<10; i++) num.put(i, i);
  for(i=9; i>=0; i--) cout << num.get(i);
  cout << "\n";

  // create another array and initialize with num
  array x(num); // invokes copy constructor
  for(i=0; i<10; i++) cout << x.get(i);

  return 0;
}
```

When **num** is used to initialize **x**, the copy constructor is called, memory for the new array is allocated and stored in **x.p**, and the contents of **num** are copied to **x**'s array. In this way, **x** and **num** have arrays that have the same values, but each array is separate and distinct. (That is, **num.p** and **x.p** do not point to the same piece of memory.) If the copy constructor had not been created, the default bitwise initialization would have resulted in **x** and **num** sharing the same memory for their arrays. (That is, **num.p** and **x.p** would have, indeed, pointed to the same location.)

The copy constructor is called only for initializations. For example, this sequence does not call the copy constructor defined in the preceding program:

```
array a(10);
// ...
array b(10);

b = a; // does not call copy constructor
```

In this case, **b = a** performs the assignment operation. If = is not overloaded (as it is not here), a bitwise copy will be made. Therefore, in some cases, you may need to overload the = operator as well as create a copy constructor to avoid problems.

Granting Access

When a base class is inherited as **private**, all public and protected members of that class become private members of the derived class. However, in certain circumstances, you may want to restore one or more inherited members to their original access specification.

For example, you might want to grant certain public members of the base class public status in the derived class even though the base class is inherited as **private**. You have two ways to accomplish this. First, you can use a **using** statement, and this is the preferred way. The **using** statement, designed primarily to support namespaces, is discussed later in this chapter. The second way to restore an inherited member's access specification is to employ an *access declaration* within the derived class. Access declarations are currently supported by ANSI/ISO Standard C++, but they are deprecated. This means that they should not be used for new code. Since there are still many existing programs that use access declarations, they will be examined here.

An access declaration takes this general form:

base-class::member;

The access declaration is put under the appropriate access heading in the derived class's declaration. Notice that no type declaration is required (or, indeed, allowed) in an access declaration.

To see how an access declaration works, let's begin with this short fragment:

```
class base {
public:
   int j; // public in base
};

// Inherit base as private.
class derived: private base {
public:

   // here is access declaration
   base::j; // make j public again
   .
   .
   .
};
```

Because **base** is inherited as **private** by **derived**, the public member **j** is made a private member of **derived**. However, by including

```
base::j;
```

as the access declaration under **derived**'s **public** heading, **j** is restored to its public status.

You can use an access declaration to restore the access rights of public and protected members. However, you cannot use an access declaration to raise or lower a member's access status. For example, a member declared as private to a base class cannot be made public by a derived class. (If C++ allowed this to occur, it would destroy its encapsulation mechanism!)

The following program illustrates the access declaration: Notice how this program uses access declarations to restore **j**, **seti( )**, and **geti( )** to **public** status.

```
#include <iostream>
using namespace std;

class base {
  int i; // private to base
public:
  int j, k;
  void seti(int x) { i = x; }
  int geti() { return i; }
};

// Inherit base as private.
class derived: private base {
public:
  /* The next three statements override
     base's inheritance as private and restore j,
     seti(), and geti() to public access. */
  base::j; // make j public again - but not k
  base::seti; // make seti() public
  base::geti; // make geti() public

// base::i; // illegal, you cannot elevate access

  int a; // public
};

int main()
{
  derived ob;

//ob.i = 10; // illegal because i is private in derived

  ob.j = 20; // legal because j is made public in derived
//ob.k = 30; // illegal because k is private in derived

  ob.a = 40; // legal because a is public in derived
  ob.seti(10);
```

C++

```
cout << ob.geti() << " " << ob.j << " " << ob.a;

return 0;
}
```

Access declarations are supported in C++ to accommodate those situations in which most of an inherited class is intended to be made private, but a few members are to retain their public or protected status.

*ANSI/ISO Standard C++ still allows access declarations, but they are deprecated. This means that they are allowed for now, but they might not be supported in the future. Instead, the standard suggests achieving the same effect by applying the **using** keyword.*

Namespaces

Namespaces were briefly introduced earlier in this book. They are a relatively recent addition to C++. Their purpose is to localize the names of identifiers to avoid name collisions. In the C++ programming environment, there has been an explosion of variable, function, and class names. Prior to the invention of namespaces, all of these names competed for slots in the global namespace, and many conflicts arose. For example, if your program defined a function called **abs( )**, it could (depending upon its parameter list) override the standard library function **abs( )** because both names would be stored in the global namespace. Name collisions were compounded when two or more third-party libraries were used by the same program. In this case, it was possible—even likely—that a name defined by one library would conflict with the same name defined by the other library. The situation can be particularly troublesome for class names. For example, if your program defines a class call **ThreeDCircle** and a library used by your program defines a class by the same name, a conflict will arise.

The creation of the **namespace** keyword was a response to these problems. Because it localizes the visibility of names declared within it, a namespace allows the same name to be used in different contexts without conflicts arising. Perhaps the most noticeable beneficiary of **namespace** is the C++ standard library. Prior to **namespace**, the entire C++ library was defined within the global namespace (which was, of course, the only namespace). Since the addition of **namespace**, the C++ library is now defined within its own namespace, called **std**, which reduces the chance of name collisions. You can also create your own namespaces within your program to localize the visibility of any names that you think may cause conflicts. This is especially important if you are creating class or function libraries.

Namespace Fundamentals

The **namespace** keyword allows you to partition the global namespace by creating a declarative region. In essence, a **namespace** defines a scope. The general form of **namespace** is shown here.

```
namespace name {
  // declarations
}
```

Anything defined within a **namespace** statement is within the scope of that namespace.

Here is an example of a **namespace**. It localizes the names used to implement a simple countdown counter class. In the namespace are defined the **counter** class, which implements the counter, and the variables **upperbound** and **lowerbound**, which contain the upper and lower bounds that apply to all counters.

```
namespace CounterNameSpace {
  int upperbound;
  int lowerbound;

  class counter {
      int count;
    public:
      counter(int n) {
        if(n <= upperbound) count = n;
        else count = upperbound;
      }

      void reset(int n) {
        if(n <= upperbound) count = n;
      }

      int run() {
        if(count > lowerbound) return count--;
        else return lowerbound;
      }
  };
}
```

Here, **upperbound**, **lowerbound**, and the class **counter** are part of the scope defined by the **CounterNameSpace** namespace.

Inside a namespace, identifiers declared within that namespace can be referred to directly, without any namespace qualification. For example, within **CounterNameSpace**, the **run( )** function can refer directly to **lowerbound** in the statement

```
if(count > lowerbound) return count--;
```

However, since **namespace** defines a scope, you need to use the scope resolution operator to refer to objects declared within a namespace from outside that namespace. For example, to assign the value 10 to **upperbound** from code outside **CounterNameSpace** you must use this statement.

```
CounterNameSpace::upperbound = 10;
```

Or, to declare an object of type **counter** from outside **CounterNameSpace** you will use a statement like this:

```
CounterNameSpace::counter ob;
```

In general, to access a member of a namespace from outside its namespace, precede the member's name with the name of the namespace followed by the scope resolution operator.

Here is a program that demonstrates the use of the **CounterNamespace**.

```
// Demonstrate a namespace.
#include <iostream>
using namespace std;

namespace CounterNameSpace {
   int upperbound;
   int lowerbound;

   class counter {
      int count;
    public:
      counter(int n) {
         if(n <= upperbound) count = n;
         else count = upperbound;
      }

      void reset(int n) {
         if(n <= upperbound) count = n;
```

```
      }

      int run() {
        if(count > lowerbound) return count--;
        else return lowerbound;
      }
  };
}

int main()
{
  CounterNameSpace::upperbound = 100;
  CounterNameSpace::lowerbound = 0;

  CounterNameSpace::counter ob1(10);
  int i;

  do {
    i = ob1.run();
    cout << i << " ";
  } while(i > CounterNameSpace::lowerbound);
  cout << endl;

  CounterNameSpace::counter ob2(20);

  do {
    i = ob2.run();
    cout << i << " ";
  } while(i > CounterNameSpace::lowerbound);
  cout << endl;

  ob2.reset(100);
  CounterNameSpace::lowerbound = 90;
  do {
    i = ob2.run();
    cout << i << " ";
  } while(i > CounterNameSpace::lowerbound);

  return 0;
}
```

Notice that the declaration of a **counter** object and the references to **upperbound** and **lowerbound** are qualified by **CounterNameSpace**. However, once an object of type **counter** has been declared, it is not necessary to further qualify it or any of its members. Thus, **ob1.run( )** can be called directly; the namespace has already been resolved.

using

As you can imagine, if your program includes frequent references to the members of a namespace, having to specify the namespace and the scope resolution operator each time you need to refer to one quickly becomes a tedious chore. The **using** statement was invented to alleviate this problem. The **using** statement has these two general forms:

using namespace *name*;

using *name::member*;

In the first form, *name* specifies the name of the namespace you want to access. All of the members defined within the specified namespace are brought into view (i.e., they become part of the current namespace) and may be used without qualification. In the second form, only a specific member of the namespace is made visible. For example, assuming **CounterNameSpace** as shown previously, the following **using** statements and assignments are valid.

```
using CounterNameSpace::lowerbound; // only lowerbound is visible
lowerbound = 10; // OK because lowerbound is visible

using namespace CounterNameSpace; // all members are visible
upperbound = 100; // OK because all members are now visible
```

The following program illustrates **using** by reworking the counter example from the previous section.

```
// Demonstrate using.
#include <iostream>
using namespace std;

namespace CounterNameSpace {
  int upperbound;
  int lowerbound;

  class counter {
    int count;
  public:
    counter(int n) {
```

```
      if(n <= upperbound) count = n;
      else count = upperbound;
    }

    void reset(int n) {
      if(n <= upperbound) count = n;
    }

    int run() {
      if(count > lowerbound) return count--;
      else return lowerbound;
    }
  };
}

int main()
{
  // use only upperbound from CounterNameSpace
  using CounterNameSpace::upperbound;

  // now, no qualification needed to set upperbound
  upperbound = 100;

  // qualification still needed for lowerbound, etc.
  CounterNameSpace::lowerbound = 0;

  CounterNameSpace::counter ob1(10);
  int i;

  do {
    i = ob1.run();
    cout << i << " ";
  } while(i > CounterNameSpace::lowerbound);
  cout << endl;

  // now, use entire CounterNameSpace
  using namespace CounterNameSpace;

  counter ob2(20);

  do {
    i = ob2.run();
```

```
    cout << i << " ";
  } while(i > lowerbound);
  cout << endl;

  ob2.reset(100);
  lowerbound = 90;
  do {
    i = ob2.run();
    cout << i << " ";
  } while(i > lowerbound);

  return 0;
}
```

The program illustrates one other important point: using one namespace does not override another. When you bring a namespace into view, it simply adds its names to whatever other namespaces are currently in effect. Thus, by the end of the program both **std** and **CounterNameSpace** have been added to the global namespace.

Unnamed Namespaces

There is a special type of namespace, called an *unnamed namespace*, that allows you to create identifiers that are unique within a file. Unnamed namespaces are also called *anonymous namespaces*. They have this general form:

namespace {
  // declarations
}

Unnamed namespaces allow you to establish unique identifiers that are known only within the scope of a single file. That is, within the file that contains the unnamed namespace, the members of that namespace may be used directly, without qualification. But outside the file, the identifiers are unknown.

Unnamed namespaces eliminate the need for certain uses of the **static** storage class modifier. As explained in Chapter 2, one way to restrict the scope of a global name to the file in which it is declared, is to use **static**. For example, consider the following two files that are part of the same program.

File One

```
static int k;
void f1() {
  k = 99; // OK
}
```

File Two

```
extern int k;
void f2() {
  k = 10; // error
}
```

Because **k** is defined in File One, it may be used in File One. In File Two, **k** is specified as **extern**, which means that its name and type are known but that **k**, itself, is not actually defined. When these two files are linked, the attempt to use **k** within File Two results in an error because there is no definition for **k**. By preceding **k** with **static** in File One, its scope is restricted to that file and it is not available to File Two.

While **static** global declarations are still allowed in C++, a better way to accomplish this is to use an unnamed namespace. For example,

File One

```
namespace {
  int k;
}
void f1() {
  k = 99; // OK
}
```

File Two

```
extern int k;
void f2() {
  k = 10; // error
}
```

Here, **k** is also restricted to File One. The use of the unnamed namespace rather than **static** is recommended for new code.

Some Namespace Options

There may be more than one namespace declaration of the same name. This allows a namespace to be split over several files or even separated within the same file. For example,

```
#include <iostream>
using namespace std;

namespace NS {
  int i;
}

// ...

namespace NS {
  int j;
}

int main()
{
  NS::i = NS::j = 10;
```

```
    // refer to NS specifically
    cout << NS::i * NS::j << "\n";

    // use NS namespace
    using namespace NS;

    cout << i * j;

    return 0;
}
```

This program produces the following output.

```
100
100
```

Here, **NS** is split into two pieces. However, the contents of each piece are still within the same namespace, i.e., **NS**.

A namespace must be declared outside of all other scopes. This means that you cannot declare namespaces that are localized to a function, for example. There is, however, one exception: a namespace can be nested within another. Consider this program:

```
#include <iostream>
using namespace std;

namespace NS1 {
  int i;
  namespace NS2 { // a nested namespace
    int j;
  }
}

int main()
{
  NS1::i = 19;
  // NS2::j = 10; Error, NS2 is not in view
  NS1::NS2::j = 10; // this is right

  cout << NS1::i << " "<<  NS1::NS2::j << "\n";
```

```
// use NS1
using namespace NS1;

/* Now that NS1 is in view, NS2 can be used to
   refer to j. */
cout << i * NS2::j;

return 0;
}
```

This program produces the following output.

```
19 10
190
```

Here, the namespace **NS2** is nested within **NS1**. Thus, when the program begins, to refer to **j**, you must qualify it with both the **NS1** and **NS2** namespaces. **NS2** by itself is insufficient. After the statement

```
using namespace NS1;
```

executes, you can refer directly to **NS2**, since the **using** statement brings **NS1** into view.

Typically, you will not need to create namespaces for most small to medium-sized programs. However, if you will be creating libraries of reusable code or if you want to ensure the widest portability, then consider wrapping your code within a namespace.

The std Namespace

C++ defines its entire library in its own namespace called **std**. This is the reason that most of the C++ programs in this book include the following statement.

```
using namespace std;
```

This causes the **std** namespace to be brought into the current namespace, which gives you direct access to the names of the functions and classes defined within the library without having to qualify each one with **std::**.

Of course, you can explicitly qualify each name with **std::** if you like. For example, the following program does not bring the library into the global namespace.

```
// Use explicit std:: qualification.
```

```
#include <iostream>

int main()
{
  int val;

  std::cout << "Enter a number: ";

  std::cin >> val;

  std::cout << "This is your number: ";
  std::cout << std::hex << val;

  return 0;
}
```

Here, **cout, cin**, and the manipulator **hex** are explicitly qualified by their namespace. That is, to write to standard output, you must specify **std::cout**; to read from standard input, you must use **std::cin;** and the **hex** manipulator must be referred to as **std::hex**.

You may not want to bring the standard C++ library into the global namespace if your program will be making only limited use of it. However, if your program contains hundreds of references to library names, then including **std** in the current namespace is far easier than qualifying each name individually.

If you are using only a few names from the C++ library, it may make more sense to specify a **using** statement for each individually. The advantage to this approach is that you can still use those names without an **std::** qualification but you will not be bringing the entire standard library into the global namespace. For example,

```
// Bring only a few names into the global namespace.
#include <iostream>

// gain access to cout, cin, and hex
using std::cout;
using std::cin;
using std::hex;

int main()
{
  int val;

  cout << "Enter a number: ";
```

```
    cin >> val;
    cout << "This is your number: ";
    cout << hex << val;
    return 0;
}
```

Here, **cin**, **cout**, and **hex** may be used directly, but the rest of the **std** namespace has not been brought into view.

As explained, the original C++ library was defined in the global namespace. If you will converting older C++ programs (including those developed using earlier versions of Borland's C++ compiler), then you will need to either include a **using namespace std** statement or qualify each reference to a library member with **std::**. This is especially important if you are replacing old **.h** header files with the modern headers. Remember, the old **.h** headers put their contents into the global namespace. The modern headers put their contents into the **std** namespace.

Explicit Constructors

The keyword **explicit** is used to create "nonconverting constructors." For example, given the following class

```
class MyClass {
int i;
public:
  MyClass(int j) {i = j;}
  // ...
};
```

MyClass objects can be declared as shown here:

```
MyClass ob1(1);
MyClass ob2 = 10;
```

In this case, the statement

```
MyClass ob2 = 10;
```

is automatically converted into the form

```
MyClass ob2(10);
```

However, by declaring the **MyClass** constructor as **explicit**, this automatic conversion will not be supplied. Here is **MyClass** shown using an **explicit** constructor.

```
class MyClass {
int i;
public:
  explicit MyClass(int j) {i = j;}
  // ...
};
```

Now, only constructors of the form

```
MyClass ob(110);
```

will be allowed.

typename and export

Recently, two keywords were added to C++ that relate specifically to templates: **typename** and **export**. Both play specialized roles in C++ programming. Each is briefly examined.

The **typename** keyword has two uses. First, it can be substituted for the keyword **class** in a template declaration. For example, the **swapargs( )** template function could be specified like this:

```
template <typename X> void swapargs(X &a, X &b)
{
  X temp;

  temp = a;
  a = b;
  b = temp;
}
```

Here, **typename** specifies the generic type **X**. There is no difference between using **class** and using **typename** in this context.

The second use of **typename** is to inform the compiler that a name used in a template declaration is a type name rather than an object name. For example,

```
typename X::Name someObject;
```

ensures that **X::Name** is treated as a type name.

The **export** keyword can precede a **template** declaration. Currently, for C++ Builder, it has no effect.

Differences Between C and C++

For the most part, C++ is a superset of C, and virtually all C programs are also C++ programs. However, a few differences do exist, the most important of which are discussed here.

One of the most important yet subtle differences between C and C++ is the fact that in C, a function declared like this:

```
int f();
```

says *nothing* about any parameters to that function. That is, when there is nothing specified between the parentheses following the function's name, in C this means that nothing is being stated, one way or the other, about any parameters to that function. It might have parameters and it might not have parameters. However, in C++, a function declaration like this means that the function does *not* have parameters. That is, in C++, these two declarations are equivalent:

```
int f();

int f(void);
```

In C++, the **void** is optional. Many C++ programmers include the **void** as a means of making it completely clear to anyone reading the program that a function does not have any parameters, but this is technically unnecessary.

In C++, all functions must be prototyped. This is an option in C (although good programming practice suggests full prototyping be used in a C program).

A small, but potentially important, difference between C and C++ is that in C, a character constant is automatically elevated to an integer. In C++, it is not.

In C, it is not an error to declare a global variable several times, even though it is bad programming practice. In C++, this is an error.

In C, an identifier will have at least 31 significant characters. In C++, all characters are considered significant. However, from a practical point of view, extremely long identifiers are unwieldy and are seldom needed.

In C, although unusual, you can call **main( )** from within a program. In C++, this is not allowed.

In C, you cannot take the address of a **register** variable. In C++, you can.

In C, if no type specifier is present in some types of declaration statements, the type **int** is assumed. This "default-to-int" rule does not apply to C++. The "default-to-int" rule has also been dropped from the C99 standard.

In C++, local variables can be declared anywhere within a block. In C, they must be declared at the start of a block, before any "action" statements occur.

The
Complete
Reference

Borland
C++
Builder

Chapter 27

The Standard Template Library and the string Class

This chapter explores what is considered by many to be the most important new feature added to C++ in recent years: the Standard Template Library. The inclusion of the *standard template library*, or *STL*, was one of the major efforts that took place during the standardization of C++. The STL provides general-purpose, templatized classes and functions that implement many popular and commonly used algorithms and data structures. For example, it includes support for vectors, lists, queues, and stacks. It also defines various routines that access them. Because the STL is constructed from template classes, the algorithms and data structures can be applied to nearly any type of data.

The STL is a complex piece of software engineering that uses some of C++'s most sophisticated features. To understand and use the STL, you must have a complete understanding of the C++ language, including pointers, references, and templates. Frankly, the template syntax that describes the STL can seem quite intimidating— although it looks more complicated than it actually is. While there is nothing in this chapter that is any more difficult than the material in the rest of this book, don't be surprised or dismayed if you find the STL confusing at first. Just be patient, study the examples, and don't let the unfamiliar syntax override the STL's basic simplicity.

The purpose of this chapter is to present an overview of the STL, including its design philosophy, organization, and constituents, along with the programming techniques needed to use it. Because the STL is a large library, it is not possible to discuss all of its features here.

This chapter also describes one of C++'s most important classes: **string**. The **string** class defines a string data type that allows you to work with character strings much as you do with other data types: using operators. The **string** class is closely related to the STL, so it makes sense to discuss both in this chapter.

An Overview of the STL

Although the Standard Template Library is large and its syntax is, at times, rather intimidating, it is actually quite easy to use once you understand how it is constructed and what elements it employs. Therefore, before looking at any code examples, an overview of the STL is warranted.

At the core of the Standard Template Library are three foundational items: *containers*, *algorithms*, and *iterators*. These items work in conjunction with one another to provide off-the-shelf solutions to a variety of programming problems.

Containers

Containers are objects that hold other objects. There are several different types of containers. For example, the **vector** class defines a dynamic array, **deque** creates a double-ended queue, and **list** provides a linear list. These containers are called *sequence containers* because in STL terminology, a sequence is a linear list. In addition to the basic containers, the STL also defines *associative containers* that allow efficient retrieval of values according to keys. For example, a **map** provides access to values with unique keys. Thus, a **map** stores a key/value pair and allows a value to be retrieved given its key.

Each container class defines a set of functions that may be applied to the container. For example, a list container includes functions that insert, delete, and merge elements. A stack includes functions that push and pop values.

Algorithms

Algorithms act on containers. They provide the means by which you will manipulate the contents of containers. Their capabilities include initializing, sorting, searching, and transforming the contents of containers. Many algorithms operate on a *range* of elements within a container.

Iterators

Iterators are objects that act, more or less, like pointers. They give you the ability to cycle through the contents of a container in much the same way that you would use a pointer to cycle through an array. There are five types of iterators:

Iterator	Access Allowed
Random Access	Store and retrieve values. Elements may be accessed randomly.
Bidirectional	Store and retrieve values. Forward and backward moving.
Forward	Store and retrieve values. Forward moving only.
Input	Retrieve, but not store, values. Forward moving only.
Output	Store, but not retrieve, values. Forward moving only.

In general, an iterator that has greater access capabilities can be used in place of one that has lesser capabilities. For example, a forward iterator can be used in place of an input iterator.

Iterators are handled just like pointers. You can increment and decrement them. You can apply the * operator to them. Iterators are declared using the **iterator** type defined by the various containers.

The STL also supports *reverse iterators*. Reverse iterators are either bidirectional or random-access iterators that move through a sequence in the reverse direction. Thus, if a reverse iterator points to the end of a sequence, incrementing that iterator will cause it to point one element before the end.

When referring to the various iterator types in template descriptions, this book will use the following terms.

Term	Represents
BiIter	Bidirectional iterator
ForIter	Forward iterator
InIter	Input iterator
OutIter	Output iterator
RandIter	Random-access iterator

Other STL Elements

In addition to containers, algorithms, and iterators, the STL relies upon several other standard components for support. Chief among these are allocators, predicates, comparison functions, and function objects.

Each container has defined for it an *allocator*. Allocators manage memory allocation for a container. The default allocator is an object of class **allocator**, but you can define your own allocators if needed by specialized applications. For most uses, the default allocator is sufficient.

Several of the algorithms and containers use a special type of function called a *predicate*. There are two variations of predicates: unary and binary. A unary predicate takes one argument. A binary predicate has two arguments. These functions return true/false results. But the precise conditions that make them return true or false are defined by you. For the rest of this chapter, when a unary predicate function is required, it will be notated using the type **UnPred**. When a binary predicate is required, the type **BinPred** will be used. In a binary predicate, the arguments are always in the order of *first, second*. For both unary and binary predicates, the arguments will contain values of the type of objects being stored by the container.

Some algorithms and classes use a special type of binary predicate that compares two elements. Comparison functions return true if their first argument is less than their second. Comparison functions will be notated using the type **Comp**.

In addition to the headers required by the various STL classes, the C++ standard library includes the **<utility>** and **<functional>** headers, which provide support for the STL. For example, in **<utility>** is defined the template class **pair**, which can hold a pair of values. We will make use of **pair** later in this chapter.

The templates in **<functional>** help you to construct objects that define **operator( )**. These are called *function objects*, and they may be used in place of function pointers in many places. Several predefined function objects are declared within **<functional>**. They are shown here.

plus	minus	multiplies	divides	modulus
negate	equal_to	not_equal_to	greater	greater_equal
less	less_equal	logical_and	logical_or	logical_not

Perhaps the most widely used function object is **less**, which determines when one object is less than another. Function objects can be used in place of actual function pointers in the STL algorithms described later. Using function objects rather than function pointers allows the STL to generate more efficient code.

Two other entities that populate the STL are *binders* and *negators*. A binder binds an argument to a function object. A negator returns the complement of a predicate.

One final term to know is *adaptor*. In STL terms, an adaptor transforms one thing into another. For example, the container **queue** (which creates a standard queue) is an adaptor for the **deque** container.

The Container Classes

As explained, containers are the STL objects that actually store data. The containers defined by the STL are shown in Table 27-1. Also shown are the headers necessary to use each container. The **string** class, which manages character strings, is also a container, but it is discussed later in this chapter.

Since the names of the generic placeholder types in a template class declaration are arbitrary, the container classes declare **typedef**ed versions of these types. This makes the type names concrete. Some of the most common **typedef** names are shown here.

size_type	Some type of integer.
reference	A reference to an element.
const_reference	A **const** reference to an element.
iterator	An iterator.
const_iterator	A **const** iterator.
reverse_iterator	A reverse iterator.
const_reverse_iterator	A **const** reverse iterator.
value_type	The type of a value stored in a container.
allocator_type	The type of the allocator.
key_type	The type of a key.
key_compare	The type of a function that compares two keys.
value_compare	The type of a function that compares two values.

Container	Description	Required Header
bitset	A set of bits.	<bitset>
deque	A double-ended queue.	<deque>
list	A linear list.	<list>
map	Stores key/value pairs in which each key is associated with only one value.	<map>
multimap	Stores key/value pairs in which one key may be associated with two or more values.	<map>
multiset	A set in which each element is not necessarily unique.	<set>
priority_queue	A priority queue.	<queue>
queue	A queue.	<queue>
set	A set in which each element is unique.	<set>
stack	A stack.	<stack>
vector	A dynamic array.	<vector>

Table 27-1.   *The Containers Defined by the STL*

General Theory of Operation

Although the internal operation of the STL is quite sophisticated, to use the STL is actually quite easy. First, you must decide on the type of container that you wish to use. Each offers certain benefits and trade-offs. For example, a **vector** is very good when a random-access, array-like object is required and not too many insertions or deletions are required. A **list** offers low-cost insertion and deletion but trades away speed. A **map** provides an associative container but, of course, incurs additional overhead.

Once you have chosen a container, you will use its member functions to add elements to the container, access or modify those elements, and delete elements. Except for **bitset**, a container will automatically grow as needed when elements are added to it and shrink when elements are removed.

Elements can be added to and removed from a container in a number of different ways. For example, both the sequence containers (**vector**, **list**, and **deque**) and the associative containers (**map**, **multimap**, **set**, and **multiset**) provide member functions called **insert( )**, which inserts elements into a container, and **erase( )**, which removes elements from a container. The sequence containers also provide **push_back( )** and **pop_back( )**, which add an element to or remove an element from the end, respectively. These functions are probably the most common way that individual elements are added to or removed from a sequence container. The **list** and **deque** containers also include **push_front( )** and **pop_front( )**, which add and remove elements from the start of the container.

One of the most common ways to access the elements within a container is through an iterator. The sequence containers and the associative containers provide the member functions **begin( )** and **end( )**, which return iterators to the start and end of the container, respectively. These iterators are very useful when accessing the contents of a container. For example, to cycle through a container you can obtain an iterator to its beginning using **begin( )** and then increment that iterator until its value is equal to **end( )**.

The associative containers provide the function **find( )**, which is used to locate an element in an associative container given its key. Since associative containers link a key with its value, **find( )** is the way that most elements in such a container are located.

Since a **vector** is a dynamic array, it also supports the standard array-indexing syntax for accessing its elements.

Once you have a container that holds information, it can be manipulated using one or more algorithms. The algorithms not only allow you to alter the contents of a container in some prescribed fashion, but they also let you transform one type of sequence into another.

In the following sections, you will learn to apply these general techniques to three representative containers: **vector**, **list**, and **map**. Once you understand how these containers work, you will have no trouble using the others.

Vectors

Perhaps the most general-purpose of the containers is **vector**. The **vector** class supports a dynamic array. This is an array that can grow as needed. As you know, in C++ the size of an array is fixed at compile time. While this is by far the most efficient way to implement arrays, it is also the most restrictive because the size of the array cannot be adjusted at run time to accommodate changing program conditions. A vector solves this problem by allocating memory as needed. Although a vector is dynamic, you can still use the standard array subscript notation to access its elements.

The template specification for **vector** is shown here.

```
template <class T, class Allocator = allocator<T> > class vector
```

Here, **T** is the type of data being stored and **Allocator** specifies the allocator, which defaults to the standard allocator. **vector** has the following constructors.

explicit vector(const Allocator &*a* = Allocator( ));

explicit vector(size_type *num*, const T &*val* = T ( ),
    const Allocator &*a* = Allocator( ));

vector(const vector<T, Allocator> &*ob*);

template <class InIter> vector(InIter *start*, InIter *end*,
    const Allocator &*a* = Allocator( ));

The first form constructs an empty vector. The second form constructs a vector that has *num* elements with the value *val*. The value of *val* may be allowed to default. The third form constructs a vector that contains the same elements as *ob*. The fourth form constructs a vector that contains the elements in the range specified by the iterators *start* and *end*.

For maximum flexibility (and portability to other STL implementations), any object that will be stored in a **vector** should define a default constructor. It should also define one or more relational operators, especially the < and = =. The relational operators are used by various parts of the STL. All of the built-in types automatically satisfy these requirements.

Although the template syntax looks rather complex, there is nothing difficult about declaring a vector. Here are some examples:

```
vector<int> iv;           // create zero-length int vector
vector<char> cv(5);       // create 5-element char vector
vector<char> cv(5, 'x');  // initialize a 5-element char vector
vector<int> iv2(iv);      // create int vector from an int vector
```

The following comparison operators are defined for **vector**.

==, <, <=, !=, >, >=

The subscripting operator [ ] is also defined for **vector**. This allows you to access the elements of a vector using standard array subscripting notation.

Several of the member functions defined by **vector** are shown in Table 27-2. Some of the most commonly used member functions are **size( )**, **begin( )**, **end( )**, **push_back( )**, **insert( )**, and **erase( )**. The **size( )** function returns the current size of the vector. This function is quite useful because it allows you to determine the size of a vector at run time. Remember, vectors will increase in size as needed, so the size of a vector must be determined during execution, not during compilation.

The **begin( )** function returns an iterator to the start of the vector. The **end( )** function returns an iterator to the end of the vector. As explained, iterators are similar to pointers,

Member	Description
reference back( ); const_reference back( ) const;	Returns a reference to the last element in the vector.
iterator begin( ); const_iterator begin( ) const;	Returns an iterator to the first element in the vector.
void clear( );	Removes all elements from the vector.
bool empty( ) const;	Returns true if the invoking vector is empty and false otherwise.
iterator end( ); const_iterator end( ) const;	Returns an iterator to the end of the vector.
iterator erase(iterator *i*);	Removes the element pointed to by *i*. Returns an iterator to the element after the one removed.
iterator erase(iterator *start*, iterator *end*);	Removes the elements in the range *start* to *end*. Returns an iterator to the element after the last element removed.
reference front( ); const_reference front( ) const;	Returns a reference to the first element in the vector.
iterator insert(iterator *i*, const T &*val*);	Inserts *val* immediately before the element specified by *i*. An iterator to the element is returned.
void insert(iterator *i*, size_type *num*, const T & *val*)	Inserts *num* copies of *val* immediately before the element specified by *i*.
template <class InIter> void insert(iterator *i*, InIter *start*, InIter *end*);	Inserts the sequence defined by *start* and *end* immediately before the element specified by *i*.
reference operator[ ] (size_type *i*) const; const_reference operator[ ] (size_type *i*) const;	Returns a reference to the element specified by *i*.
void pop_back( );	Removes the last element in the vector.
void push_back (const T &*val*);	Adds an element with the value specified by *val* to the end of the vector.
size_type size( ) const;	Returns the number of elements currently in the vector.

Table 27-2. *Some Commonly Used Member Functions Defined by* ***vector***

and it is through the use of the **begin( )** and **end( )** functions that you obtain an iterator to the beginning and end of a vector.

The **push_back( )** function puts a value onto the end of the vector. If necessary, the vector is increased in length to accommodate the new element. You can also add elements to the middle using **insert( )**. A vector can also be initialized. In any event, once a vector contains elements, you can use array subscripting to access or modify those elements. You can remove elements from a vector using **erase( )**.

One other point: Since **vector** implements a dynamic array, notice that the [ ] array subscript operator is overloaded. This operator allows you to access the elements in a vector using the standard array notation.

Here is a short example that illustrates the basic operation of a vector.

```
// Demonstrate a vector.
#include <iostream>
#include <vector>
#include <cctype>
using namespace std;

int main()
{
  vector<char> v(10); // create a vector of length 10
  unsigned int i;

  // display original size of v
  cout << "Size = " << v.size() << endl;

  // assign the elements of the vector some values
  for(i=0; i<10; i++) v[i] = i + 'a';

  // display contents of vector
  cout << "Current Contents:\n";
  for(i=0; i<v.size(); i++) cout << v[i] << " ";
  cout << "\n\n";

  cout << "Expanding vector\n";
  /* put more values onto the end of the vector,
     it will grow as needed */
  for(i=0; i<10; i++) v.push_back(i + 10 + 'a');

  // display current size of v
  cout << "Size now = " << v.size() << endl;

  // display contents of vector
  cout << "Current contents:\n";
  for(i=0; i<v.size(); i++) cout << v[i] << " ";
  cout << "\n\n";
```

```
// change contents of vector
for(i=0; i<v.size(); i++) v[i] = toupper(v[i]);
cout << "Modified Contents:\n";
for(i=0; i<v.size(); i++) cout << v[i] << " ";
cout << endl;

return 0;
}
```

The output of this program is shown here.

```
Size = 10
Current Contents:
a b c d e f g h i j

Expanding vector
Size now = 20
Current contents:
a b c d e f g h i j k l m n o p q r s t

Modified Contents:
A B C D E F G H I J K L M N O P Q R S T
```

Let's look at this program carefully. In **main( )**, a character vector called **v** is created with an initial capacity of 10. That is, **v** initially contains 10 elements. This is confirmed by calling the **size( )** member function. Next, these 10 elements are initialized to the characters 'a' through 'j' and the contents of **v** are displayed. Notice that the standard array subscripting notation is employed. Next, 10 more elements are added to the end of **v** using the **push_back( )** function. This causes **v** to grow in order to accommodate the new elements. As the output shows, its size after these additions is 20. Finally, the values of **v**'s elements are altered using standard subscripting notation.

There is one other point of interest in this program. Notice that the loops that display the contents of **v** use as their target value **v.size( )**. One of the advantages that vectors have over arrays is that it is possible to find the current size of a vector. As you can imagine, this is quite useful in a variety of situations.

Accessing a Vector Through an Iterator

As you know, arrays and pointers are tightly linked in C++. An array can be accessed either through subscripting or through a pointer. The parallel to this in the STL is the link between vectors and iterators. You can access the members of a vector using subscripting or through the use of an iterator. The following example shows how.

```
// Access the elements of a vector through an iterator.
#include <iostream>
#include <vector>
#include <cctype>
using namespace std;

int main()
{
  vector<char> v(10); // create a vector of length 10
  vector<char>::iterator p; // create an iterator
  int i;

  // assign elements in vector a value
  p = v.begin();
  i = 0;
  while(p != v.end()) {
    *p = i + 'a';
    p++;
    i++;
  }

  // display contents of vector
  cout << "Original contents:\n";
  p = v.begin();
  while(p != v.end()) {
    cout << *p << " ";
    p++;
  }
  cout << "\n\n";

  // change contents of vector
  p = v.begin();
  while(p != v.end()) {
    *p = toupper(*p);
    p++;
  }

  // display contents of vector
  cout << "Modified Contents:\n";
```

```
  p = v.begin();
  while(p != v.end()) {
    cout << *p << " ";
    p++;
  }
  cout << endl;

  return 0;
}
```

The output from this program is:

```
Original contents:
a b c d e f g h i j

Modified Contents:
A B C D E F G H I J
```

In the program, notice how the iterator **p** is declared. The type **iterator** is defined by the container classes. Thus, to obtain an iterator for a particular container, you will use a declaration similar that shown in the example: simply qualify **iterator** with the name of the container. In the program, **p** is initialized to point to the start of the vector by using the **begin( )** member function. This function returns an iterator to the start of the vector. This iterator can then be used to access the vector one element at a time by incrementing it as needed. This process is directly parallel to the way a pointer can be used to access the elements of an array. To determine when the end of the vector has been reached, the **end( )** member function is employed. This function returns an iterator to the location that is one past the last element in the vector. Thus, when **p** equals **v.end( )**, the end of the vector has been reached.

Inserting and Deleting Elements in a Vector

In addition to putting new values on the end of a vector, you can insert elements into the middle using the **insert( )** function. You can also remove elements using **erase( )**. The following program demonstrates **insert( )** and **erase( )**.

```
// Demonstrate insert and erase.
#include <iostream>
#include <vector>
using namespace std;
```

```
int main()
{
  vector<char> v(10);
  vector<char> v2;
  char str[] = "<Vector>";
  unsigned int i;

  // initialize v
  for(i=0; i<10; i++) v[i] = i + 'a';

  // copy characters in str into v2
  for(i=0; str[i]; i++) v2.push_back(str[i]);

  // display original contents of vector
  cout << "Original contents of v:\n";
  for(i=0; i<v.size(); i++) cout << v[i] << " ";
    cout << "\n\n";

  vector<char>::iterator p = v.begin();
  p += 2; // point to 3rd element

  // insert 10 X's into v
  v.insert(p, 10, 'X');

  // display contents after insertion
  cout << "Size after inserting X's = " << v.size() << endl;
  cout << "Contents after insert:\n";
  for(i=0; i<v.size(); i++) cout << v[i] << " ";
  cout << "\n\n";

  // remove those elements
  p = v.begin();
  p += 2; // point to 3rd element
  v.erase(p, p+10); // remove next 10 elements

  // display contents after deletion
  cout << "Size after erase = " << v.size() << endl;
  cout << "Contents after erase:\n";
  for(i=0; i<v.size(); i++) cout << v[i] << " ";
  cout << "\n\n";
```

```
   // Insert v2 into v
   v.insert(p, v2.begin(), v2.end());
   cout << "Size after v2's insertion = ";
   cout << v.size() << endl;
   cout << "Contents after insert:\n";
   for(i=0; i<v.size(); i++) cout << v[i] << " ";
   cout << endl;

   return 0;
}
```

This program produces the following output.

```
Original contents of v:
a b c d e f g h i j

Size after inserting X's = 20
Contents after insert:
a b X X X X X X X X X X c d e f g h i j

Size after erase = 10
Contents after erase:
a b c d e f g h i j

Size after v2's insertion = 18
Contents after insert:
a b < V e c t o r > c d e f g h i j
```

This program demonstrates two forms of **insert( )**. The first time it is used, it inserts 10 X's into **v**. The second time, it inserts the contents of a second vector, **v2**, into **v**. This second use is the most interesting. It takes three iterator arguments. The first specifies the point at which the insertion will occur within the invoking container. The last two point to the beginning and ending of the sequence to be inserted.

Storing Class Objects in a Vector

Although the preceding examples have only stored objects of the built-in types in a vector, **vector**s are not limited to this. They can store any type of objects, include those of classes that you create. Here is an example that uses a **vector** to store objects that hold the daily temperature highs for a week. Notice that **DailyTemp** defines the default constructor and that overloaded versions of < and = = are provided. While C++ Builder does not require them to be defined for this example, they are needed for many other STL operations. Thus, it is a good idea to define them for all objects that will be operated on by the STL. Doing so also ensures maximum portability to other STL implementations.

```cpp
// Store a class object in a vector.
#include <iostream>
#include <vector>
#include <cstdlib>
using namespace std;

class DailyTemp {
  int temp;
public:
  DailyTemp() { temp = 0; }
  DailyTemp(int x) { temp = x; }

  DailyTemp &operator=(int x) {
   temp = x; return *this;
  }

  double get_temp() { return temp; }
};

bool operator<(DailyTemp a, DailyTemp b)
{
  return a.get_temp() < b.get_temp();
}

bool operator==(DailyTemp a, DailyTemp b)
{
  return a.get_temp() == b.get_temp();
}

int main()
{
  vector<DailyTemp> v;
  unsigned int i;

  for(i=0; i<7; i++)
    v.push_back(DailyTemp(60 + rand()%30));
```

```
cout << "Fahrenheit temperatures:\n";
for(i=0; i<v.size(); i++)
  cout << v[i].get_temp() << " ";

cout << endl;

// convert from Fahrenheit to Celsius
for(i=0; i<v.size(); i++)
  v[i] = (v[i].get_temp()-32) * 5/9 ;

cout << " Celsius temperatures:\n";
for(i=0; i<v.size(); i++)
  cout << v[i].get_temp() << " ";

return 0;
}
```

The output from this program is shown here. Your output may be slightly different due to the use of the **rand( )** function.

```
Fahrenheit temperatures:
70 62 70 76 67 75 85
Celsius temperatures:
21 16 21 24 19 23 29
```

Vectors offer great power, safety, and flexibility. But they are less efficient than normal arrays. Thus, for most programming tasks, normal arrays will still be your first choice, but watch for situations in which the benefits of using a **vector** outweigh the costs.

Lists

The **list** class supports a bidirectional, linear list. Unlike a vector, which supports random access, a list can be accessed sequentially only. Since lists are bidirectional, they may be accessed front to back or back to front.

A **list** has this template specification

template <class T, class Allocator = allocator<T> > class list

Here, **T** is the type of data stored in the list. The allocator is specified by **Allocator**, which defaults to the standard allocator. It has the following constructors.

explicit list(const Allocator &*a* = Allocator( ));

explicit list(size_type *num*, const T &*val* = T ( ),
            const Allocator &*a* = Allocator( ));

list(const list<T, Allocator> &*ob*);

Member	Description
reference back( ); const_reference back( ) const;	Returns a reference to the last element in the list.
iterator begin( ); const_iterator begin( ) const;	Returns an iterator to the first element in the list.
void clear( );	Removes all elements from the list.
bool empty( ) const;	Returns true if the invoking list is empty and false otherwise.
iterator end( ); const_iterator end( ) const;	Returns an iterator to the end of the list.
iterator erase(iterator *i*);	Removes the element pointed to by *i*. Returns an iterator to the element after the one removed.
iterator erase(iterator *start*, iterator *end*);	Removes the elements in the range *start* to *end*. Returns an iterator to the element after the last element removed.
reference front( ); const_reference front( ) const;	Returns a reference to the first element in the list.
iterator insert(iterator *i*, const T &*val*);	Inserts *val* immediately before the element specified by *i*. An iterator to the element is returned.

void insert(iterator *i*,
            size_type *num*,
            const T &*val*)
	Inserts *num* copies of *val* immediately before the element specified by *i*.

template <class InIter>
    void insert(iterator *i*,
        InIter *start*, InIter *end*);
	Inserts the sequence defined by *start* and *end* immediately before the element specified by *i*.

void merge(list<T,
        Allocator> &*ob*);
template <class Comp>
    void merge(<list<T,
        Allocator> &*ob*,
        Comp *cmpfn*);
	Merges the ordered list contained in *ob* with the ordered invoking list. The result is ordered. After the merge, the list contained in *ob* is empty. In the second form, a comparison function can be specified that determines when one element is less than another.

Table 27-3.   *Some Commonly Used **list** Member Functions*

Member	Description
void pop_back( );	Removes the last element in the list.
void pop_front( );	Removes the first element in the list.
void push_back(const T &*val*);	Adds an element with the value specified by *val* to the end of the list.
void push_front(const T &*val*);	Adds an element with the value specified by *val* to the front of the list.
void remove(const T &*val*);	Removes elements with the value *val* from the list.
void reverse( );	Reverses the invoking list.
size_type size( ) const;	Returns the number of elements currently in the list.

void sort( );
template <class Comp>
    void sort(Comp *cmpfn*);
	Sorts the list. The second form sorts the list using the comparison function *cmpfn* to determine when one element is less than another.

void splice(iterator *i*, list<T, Allocator> &*ob*);	The contents of *ob* are inserted into the invoking list at the location pointed to by *i*. After the operation, *ob* is empty.
void splice(iterator *i*, list<T, Allocator> &*ob*, iterator *el*);	The element pointed to by *el* is removed from the list *ob* and stored in the invoking list at the location pointed to by *i*.
void splice(iterator *i*, list<T, Allocator> &*ob*, iterator *start*, iterator *end*);	The range defined by *start* and *end* is removed from *ob* and stored in the invoking list beginning at the location pointed to by *i*.

Table 27-3. *Some Commonly Used **list** Member Functions* (continued)

C++

```
template <class InIter>list(InIter start, InIter end,
                  const Allocator &a = Allocator( ));
```

The first form constructs an empty list. The second form constructs a list that has *num* elements with the value *val*, which can be allowed to default. The third form constructs a list that contains the same elements as *ob*. The fourth form constructs a list that contains the elements in the range specified by the iterators *start* and *end*.

The following comparison operators are defined for **list**:

==, <, <=, !=, >, >=

Some of the commonly used **list** member functions are shown in Table 27-3. Like a vector, an element may be put into a list by using the **push_back( )** function. You can put an element on the front of the list by using **push_front( )**. An element can also be inserted into the middle of a list by using **insert( )**. Two lists may be joined using **splice( )**. One list may be merged into another using **merge( )**.

For maximum flexibility and portability, an object that will be held in a list should define a default constructor. It should also define the various comparison operators.

Here is a simple example of a **list**.

```
// List basics.
#include <iostream>
#include <list>
using namespace std;

int main()
{
  list<int> lst; // create an empty list
  int i;

  for(i=0; i<10; i++) lst.push_back(i);

  cout << "Size = " << lst.size() << endl;

  cout << "Contents: ";
  list<int>::iterator p = lst.begin();
  while(p != lst.end()) {
    cout << *p << " ";
    p++;
  }
  cout << "\n\n";

  // change contents of list
  p = lst.begin();
  while(p != lst.end()) {
    *p = *p + 100;
    p++;
  }

  cout << "Contents modified: ";
  p = lst.begin();
  while(p != lst.end()) {
    cout << *p << " ";
    p++;
  }

  return 0;
}
```

The output produced by this program is shown here.

```
Size = 10
Contents:  0 1 2 3 4 5 6 7 8 9

Contents modified: 100 101 102 103 104 105 106 107 108 109
```

This program creates a list of integers. First, an empty **list** object is created. Next, ten integers are put into the list. This is accomplished using the **push_back( )** function, which puts each new value on the end of the existing list. Next, the size of the list and the list, itself, are displayed. The list is displayed via an iterator, using the following code.

```
list<int>::iterator p = lst.begin();
while(p != lst.end()) {
  cout << *p << " ";
  p++;
}
```

Here, the iterator **p** is initialized to point to the start of the list. Each time through the loop, **p** is incremented, causing it to point to the next element. The loop ends when **p** points to the end of the list. This code is essentially the same as was used to cycle through a vector using an iterator. Loops like this are common in STL code and the fact that the same constructs can be used to access different types of containers is part of the power of the STL.

Understanding end( )

Now is a good time to explain a somewhat unexpected attribute of the **end( )** container function. **end( )** does not return a pointer to the last element in a container. Instead, it returns a pointer *one past* the last element. Thus, the last element in a container is pointed to by **end( ) – 1**. This feature allows you to write very efficient algorithms that cycle through all of the elements of a container, including the last one, using an iterator. When the iterator has the same value as the one returned by **end( )**, you know that all elements have been accessed. However, you must keep this feature in mind, since it may seem a bit counterintuitive. For example, consider the following program, which displays a list forward and backward.

```
// Understanding end().
#include <iostream>
#include <list>
using namespace std;
```

```
int main()
{
  list<int> lst; // create an empty list
  int i;

  for(i=0; i<10; i++) lst.push_back(i);

  cout << "List printed forward:\n";
  list<int>::iterator p = lst.begin();
  while(p != lst.end()) {
    cout << *p << " ";
    p++;
  }
  cout << "\n\n";

  cout << "List printed backward:\n";
  p = lst.end();
  while(p != lst.begin()) {
    p--; // decrement pointer before using
    cout << *p << " ";
  }

  return 0;
}
```

The output produced by this program is shown here.

```
List printed forward:
0 1 2 3 4 5 6 7 8 9

List printed backward:
9 8 7 6 5 4 3 2 1 0
```

The code that displays the list in the forward direction is the same as we have been using. But pay special attention to the code that displays the list in reverse order. The iterator **p** is initially set to the end of the list through the use of the **end( )** function. Since **end( )** returns an iterator to an object that is one past the last object actually stored in the list, **p** must be decremented before it is used. This is why **p** is decremented before the **cout** statement inside the loop, rather than after. Remember: **end( )** does not return a pointer to the last object in the list; it returns a pointer that is one past the last value in the list.

push_front( ) Versus push_back( )

You can build a list by adding elements either to the end of the list or to the start of the list. So far, we have been adding elements to the end by using **push_back( )**. To add elements to the start, use **push_front( )**. For example,

```
/* Demonstrating the difference between
   push_back() and push_front(). */
#include <iostream>
#include <list>
using namespace std;

int main()
{
  list<int> lst1, lst2;
  int i;

  for(i=0; i<10; i++) lst1.push_back(i);
  for(i=0; i<10; i++) lst2.push_front(i);

  list<int>::iterator p;

  cout << "Contents of lst1:\n";
  p = lst1.begin();
  while(p != lst1.end()) {
    cout << *p << " ";
    p++;
  }
  cout << "\n\n";

  cout << "Contents of lst2:\n";
  p = lst2.begin();
  while(p != lst2.end()) {
    cout << *p << " ";
    p++;
  }
```

```
    return 0;
}
```

The output produced by this program is shown here.

```
Contents of lst1:
0 1 2 3 4 5 6 7 8 9

Contents of lst2:
9 8 7 6 5 4 3 2 1 0
```

Since **lst2** is built by putting elements onto its front, the resulting list is in the reverse order of **lst1**, which is built by putting elements onto its end.

Sort a List

A list can be sorted by calling the **sort( )** member function. The following program creates a list of random integers and then puts the list into sorted order.

```cpp
// Sort a list.
#include <iostream>
#include <list>
#include <cstdlib>
using namespace std;

int main()
{
  list<int> lst;
  int i;

  // create a list of random integers
  for(i=0; i<10; i++)
    lst.push_back(rand());

  cout << "Original contents:\n";
  list<int>::iterator p = lst.begin();
  while(p != lst.end()) {
    cout << *p << " ";
    p++;
  }
  cout << endl << endl;
```

```
// sort the list
lst.sort();

cout << "Sorted contents:\n";
p = lst.begin();
while(p != lst.end()) {
  cout << *p << " ";
  p++;
}

return 0;
}
```

Here is sample output produced by the program.

```
Original contents:
41 18467 6334 26500 19169 15724 11478 29358 26962 24464

Sorted contents:
41 6334 11478 15724 18467 19169 24464 26500 26962 29358
```

Merging One List with Another

One ordered list can be merged with another. The result is an ordered list that contains the contents of the two original lists. The new list is stored in the invoking list, and the second list is left empty. The next example merges two lists. The first contains the even numbers between 0 and 9. The second contains the odd numbers. These lists are then merged to produce the sequence 0 1 2 3 4 5 6 7 8 9.

```
// Merge two lists.
#include <iostream>
#include <list>
using namespace std;

int main()
{
  list<int> lst1, lst2;
  int i;

  for(i=0; i<10; i+=2) lst1.push_back(i);
```

```
    for(i=1; i<11; i+=2) lst2.push_back(i);

    cout << "Contents of lst1:\n";
    list<int>::iterator p = lst1.begin();
    while(p != lst1.end()) {
      cout << *p << " ";
      p++;
    }
    cout << endl << endl;

    cout << "Contents of lst2:\n";
    p = lst2.begin();
    while(p != lst2.end()) {
      cout << *p << " ";
      p++;
    }
    cout << endl << endl;

    // now, merge the two lists
    lst1.merge(lst2);
    if(lst2.empty())
      cout << "lst2 is now empty\n";

    cout << "Contents of lst1 after merge:\n";
    p = lst1.begin();
    while(p != lst1.end()) {
      cout << *p << " ";
      p++;
    }

    return 0;
}
```

The output produced by this program is shown here.

```
Contents of lst1:
0 2 4 6 8

Contents of lst2:
1 3 5 7 9
```

```
lst2 is now empty
Contents of lst1 after merge:
0 1 2 3 4 5 6 7 8 9
```

One other thing to notice about this example is the use of the **empty( )** function. It returns true if the invoking container is empty. Since **merge( )** removes all of the elements from the list being merged, it will be empty after the merge is completed, as the program output confirms.

Storing Class Objects in a List

Here is an example that uses a list to store objects of type **myclass**. Notice that the <, >, !=, and == are overloaded for objects of type **myclass**. The only one of these actually required by this example is <. The others are implemented for the sake of illustration (and to help ensure portability to other STL implementations). In general, the STL uses these operators to determine the ordering and equality of objects in a container. Even though a list is not an ordered container, it still needs a way to compare elements when searching, sorting, or merging.

```cpp
// Store class objects in a list.
#include <iostream>
#include <list>
#include <cstring>
using namespace std;

class myclass {
  int a, b;
  int sum;
public:
  myclass() { a = b = 0; }
  myclass(int i, int j) {
    a = i;
    b = j;
    sum = a + b;
  }
  int getsum() { return sum; }

  friend bool operator<(const myclass &o1,
                        const myclass &o2);
  friend bool operator>(const myclass &o1,
```

C++

```
                         const myclass &o2);
  friend bool operator==(const myclass &o1,
                         const myclass &o2);
  friend bool operator!=(const myclass &o1,
                         const myclass &o2);
};

bool operator<(const myclass &o1, const myclass &o2)
{
  return o1.sum < o2.sum;
}

bool operator>(const myclass &o1, const myclass &o2)
{
  return o1.sum > o2.sum;
}

bool operator==(const myclass &o1, const myclass &o2)
{
  return o1.sum == o2.sum;
}

bool operator!=(const myclass &o1, const myclass &o2)
{
  return o1.sum != o2.sum;
}

int main()
{
  int i;

  // create first list
  list<myclass> lst1;
  for(i=0; i<10; i++) lst1.push_back(myclass(i, i));

  cout << "First list: ";
  list<myclass>::iterator p = lst1.begin();
  while(p != lst1.end()) {
    cout << p->getsum() << " ";
    p++;
  }
  cout << endl;
```

```
// create a second list
list<myclass> lst2;
for(i=0; i<10; i++) lst2.push_back(myclass(i*2, i*3));

cout << "Second list: ";
p = lst2.begin();
while(p != lst2.end()) {
  cout << p->getsum() << " ";
  p++;
}
cout << endl;

// now, merge lst1 and lst2
lst1.merge(lst2);

// display merged list
cout << "Merged list: ";
p = lst1.begin();
while(p != lst1.end()) {
  cout << p->getsum() << " ";
  p++;
}

return 0;
}
```

The program creates two lists of **myclass** objects and displays the contents of each list. It then merges the two lists and displays the result. The output from this program is shown here.

```
First list: 0 2 4 6 8 10 12 14 16 18
Second list: 0 5 10 15 20 25 30 35 40 45
Merged list: 0 0 2 4 5 6 8 10 10 12 14 15 16 18 20 25 30 35 40 45
```

Maps

The **map** class supports an associative container in which unique keys are mapped with values. In essence, a key is simply a name that you give to a value. Once a value has been stored, you can retrieve it by using its key. Thus, in its most general sense a map is a list of key/value pairs. The power of a map is that you can look up a value given its key. For example, you could define a map that uses a person's name as its key and stores that person's telephone number as its value. Associative containers are becoming more popular in programming.

As mentioned, a map can hold only unique keys. Duplicate keys are not allowed. To create a map that allows nonunique keys, use **multimap**.

The **map** container has the following template specification.

template <class Key, class T, class Comp = less<Key>,
         class Allocator = allocator<pair<const Key, T> > > class map

Here, **Key** is the data type of the keys, **T** is the data type of the values being stored (mapped), and **Comp** is a function that compares two keys. This defaults to the standard **less( )** utility function object. **Allocator** is the allocator (which defaults to **allocator**).

A **map** has the following constructors.

explicit map(const Comp &*cmpfn* = Comp( ),
             const Allocator &*a* = Allocator( ));

map(const map<Key, T, Comp, Allocator> &*ob*);

template <class InIter> map(InIter *start*, InIter *end*,
             const Comp &*cmpfn* = Comp( ), const Allocator &*a* = Allocator( ));

The first form constructs an empty map. The second form constructs a map that contains the same elements as *ob*. The third form constructs a map that contains the elements in the range specified by the iterators *start* and *end*. The function specified by *cmpfn*, if present, determines the ordering of the map.

In general, any object used as a key should define a default constructor and overload any necessary comparison operators.

The following comparison operators are defined for **map**.

==, <, <=, !=, >, >=

Several of the **map** member functions are shown in Table 27-4. In the descriptions, **key_type** is the type of the key, and **value_type** represents **pair<Key, T>**.

Key/value pairs are stored in a map as objects of type **pair**, which has this template specification.

```
template <class Ktype, class Vtype> struct pair {
  typedef Ktype first_type; // type of key
  typedef Vtype second_type; // type of value
  Ktype first; // contains the key
  Vtype second; // contains the value

  // constructors
```

Member	Description
iterator begin( ); const_iterator begin( ) const;	Returns an iterator to the first element in the map.
void clear( );	Removes all elements from the map.
size_type count(const key_type &k) const;	Returns the number of times *k* occurs in the map (1 or zero).
bool empty( ) const;	Returns true if the invoking map is empty and false otherwise.
iterator end( ); const_iterator end( ) const;	Returns an iterator to the end of the list.
void erase(iterator *i*);	Removes the element pointed to by *i*.
void erase(iterator *start*, iterator *end*);	Removes the elements in the range *start* to *end*.
size_type erase(const key_type &k)	Removes from the map elements that have keys with the value *k*.
iterator find(const key_type &k); const_iterator find (const key_type &k) const;	Returns an iterator to the specified key. If the key is not found, then an iterator to the end of the map is returned.
iterator insert(iterator *i*, const value_type &*val*);	Inserts *val* at or after the element specified by *i*. An iterator to the element is returned.
template <class InIter> void insert(InIter *start*, InIter *end*)	Inserts a range of elements.
pair<iterator, bool> insert(const value_type &*val*);	Inserts *val* into the invoking map. An iterator to the element is returned. The element is inserted only if it does not already exist. If the element was inserted, pair<iterator, true> is returned. Otherwise, pair<iterator, false> is returned.
mapped_type& operator[ ] (const key_type &*i*)	Returns a reference to the element specified by *i*. If this element does not exist, it is inserted.
size_type size( ) const;	Returns the number of elements currently in the list.

Table 27-4.   *Several Commonly Used **map** Member Functions*

```
pair();
pair(const Ktype &k, const Vtype &v);
template<class A, class B> pair(const<A, B> &ob);
```

```
    ~pair();
}
```

As the comments suggest, the value in **first** contains the key and the value in **second** contains the value associated with that key.

You can construct a pair using one of **pair**'s constructors or by using **make_pair( )**, which constructs a **pair** object based upon the types of the data used as parameters. **make_pair( )** is a generic function that has this prototype.

template <class *Ktype*, class *Vtype*>
        pair<*Ktype*, *Vtype*> make_pair(const *Ktype* &k, const *Vtype* &v);

As you can see, it returns a **pair** object consisting of values of the types specified by *Ktype* and *Vtype*. The advantage of **make_pair( )** is that the types of the objects being stored are determined automatically by the compiler rather than being explicitly specified by you.

The following program illustrates the basics of using a map. It stores key/value pairs that show the mapping between the uppercase letters and their ASCII character codes. Thus, the key is a character and the value is an integer. The key/value pairs stored are

A   65

B   66

C   67

and so on. Once the pairs have been stored, you are prompted for a key (i.e., a letter between A and Z) and the ASCII code for that letter is displayed.

```cpp
// A simple map demonstration.
#include <iostream>
#include <map>
using namespace std;

int main()
{
  map<char, int> m;
  int i;

  // put pairs into map
  for(i=0; i<26; i++) {
    m.insert(pair<char, int>('A'+i, 65+i));
```

```
    }

    char ch;
    cout << "Enter key: ";
    cin >> ch;

    map<char, int>::iterator p;

    // find value given key
    p = m.find(ch);
    if(p != m.end())
      cout << "Its ASCII value is  " << p->second;
    else
      cout << "Key not in map.\n";

    return 0;
}
```

Notice the use of the **pair** template class to construct the key/value pairs. The data types specified by **pair** must match those of the **map** into which the pairs are being inserted.

Once the map has been initialized with keys and values, you can search for a value given its key by using the **find( )** function. **find( )** returns an iterator to the matching element or to the end of the map if the key is not found. When a match is found, the value associated with the key is contained in the **second** member of **pair**.

In the preceding example, key/value pairs were constructed explicitly, using **pair<char, int>**. While there is nothing wrong with this approach, it is often easier to use **make_pair( )**, which constructs a pair object based upon the types of the data used as parameters. For example, assuming the previous program, this line of code will also insert key/value pairs into **m**.

```
    m.insert(make_pair((char)('A'+i), 65+i));
```

Here, the cast to **char** is needed to override the automatic conversion to **int** when i is added to 'A'. Otherwise, the type determination is automatic.

Storing Class Objects in a Map

As with all of the containers, you can use a map to store objects of types that you create. For example, the next program creates a simple phone directory. That is, it creates a map of names with their numbers. To do this, it creates two classes called **name** and **number**. Since a map maintains a sorted list of keys, the program also defines the < operator for objects of type **name**. In general, you must define the < operator for any classes that you will use as the key. You may also need to implement other comparison operators, depending upon what elements of the STL you will be using (and for maximum portability).

```cpp
// Use a map to create a phone directory.
#include <iostream>
#include <map>
#include <cstring>
using namespace std;

class name {
  char str[40];
public:
  name() { strcpy(str, ""); }
  name(char *s) { strcpy(str, s); }
  char *get() { return str; }

};

// Must define less than relative to name objects.
bool operator<(name a, name b)
{
    return strcmp(a.get(), b.get()) < 0;
}

class phoneNum {
  char str[80];
public:
  phoneNum() { strcmp(str, ""); }
  phoneNum(char *s) { strcpy(str, s); }
  char *get() { return str; }
};


int main()
{
  map<name, phoneNum> directory;

 // put names and numbers into map
  directory.insert(pair<name, phoneNum>(name("Tom"),
                  phoneNum("555-4533")));
```

```
      directory.insert(pair<name, phoneNum>(name("Chris"),
                        phoneNum("555-9678")));
      directory.insert(pair<name, phoneNum>(name("John"),
                  phoneNum("555-8195")));
      directory.insert(pair<name, phoneNum>(name("Rachel"),
                        phoneNum("555-0809")));

      // given a name, find number
      char str[80];
      cout << "Enter name: ";
      cin >> str;

      map<name, phoneNum>::iterator p;

      p = directory.find(name(str));
      if(p != directory.end())
        cout << "Phone number: " <<  p->second.get();
      else
        cout << "Name not in directory.\n";

      return 0;
}
```

Here is a sample run.

```
Enter name: Rachel
Phone number: 555-0809
```

In the program, each entry in the map is a character array that holds a null-terminated string. Later in this chapter, you will see an easier way to write this program that uses the standard **string** type.

Algorithms

As explained, algorithms act on containers. Although each container provides support for its own basic operations, the standard algorithms provide more extended or complex actions. They also allow you to work with two different types of containers at the same time. To have access to the STL algorithms, you must include **<algorithm>** in your program.

Algorithm	Purpose
adjacent_find	Searches for adjacent matching elements within a sequence and returns an iterator to the first match.
binary_search	Performs a binary search on an ordered sequence
copy	Copies a sequence.
copy_backward	Same as **copy** except that it moves the elements from the end of the sequence first.
count	Returns the number of elements in the sequence.
count_if	Returns the number of elements in the sequence that satisfy some predicate.
equal	Determines if two ranges are the same.
equal_range	Returns a range in which an element can be inserted into a sequence without disrupting the ordering of the sequence.
fill and fill_n	Fills a range with the specified value.
find	Searches a range for a value and returns an iterator to the first occurrence of the element.
find_end	Searches a range for a subsequence. It returns an iterator to the end of the subsequence within the range.
find_first_of	Finds the first element within a sequence that matches an element within a range.
find_if	Searches a range for an element for which a user-defined unary predicate returns true.
for_each	Applies a function to a range of elements.
generate and generate_n	Assign elements in a range the values returned by a generator function.
includes	Determines if one sequence includes all of the elements in another sequence.
inplace_merge	Merges a range with another range. Both ranges must be sorted in increasing order. The resulting sequence is sorted.
iter_swap	Exchanges the values pointed to by its two iterator arguments.
lexicographical_compare	Alphabetically compares one sequence with another.
lower_bound	Finds the first point in the sequence that is not less than a specified value.
make_heap	Constructs a heap from a sequence.
max	Returns the maximum of two values.
max_element	Returns an iterator to the maximum element within a range.
merge	Merges two ordered sequences, placing the result into a third sequence.

Table 27-5. *The STL Algorithms*

Algorithm	Purpose
min	Returns the minimum of two values.
min_element	Returns an iterator to the minimum element within a range.
mismatch	Finds the first mismatch between the elements in two sequences. Iterators to the two elements are returned.
next_permutation	Constructs the next permutation of a sequence.
nth_element	Arranges a sequence such that all elements less than a specified element *E* come before that element and all elements greater than *E* come after it.
partial_sort	Sorts a range.
partial_sort_copy	Sorts a range and then copies as many elements as will fit into a resulting sequence.
partition	Arranges a sequence such that all elements for which a predicate returns true come before those for which the predicate returns false.
pop_heap	Exchanges the first and last–1 elements and then rebuilds the heap.
prev_permutation	Constructs the previous permutation of a sequence.
push_heap	Pushes an element onto the end of a heap.
random_shuffle	Randomizes a sequence
remove, remove_if, remove_copy, and remove_copy_if	Removes elements from a specified range.
replace, replace_copy, replace_if, and replace_copy_if	Replaces elements within a range.
reverse and reverse_copy	Reverses the order of a range.
rotate and rotate_copy	Left-rotates the elements in a range.
search	Searches for a subsequence within a sequence.
search_n	Searches for a sequence of a specified number of similar elements.
set_difference	Produces a sequence that contains the difference between two ordered sets.
set_intersection	Produces a sequence that contains the intersection of the two ordered sets.
set_symmetric_difference	Produces a sequence that contains the symmetric difference between the two ordered sets.
set_union	Produces a sequence that contains the union of the two ordered sets.
sort	Sorts a range.
sort_heap	Sorts a heap within a specified range.

Table 27-5.   *The STL Algorithms* (continued)

C++

Algorithm	Purpose
stable_partition	Arranges a sequence such that all elements for which a predicate returns true come before those for which the predicate returns false. The partitioning is stable. This means that the relative ordering of the sequence is preserved.
stable_sort	Sorts a range. The sort is stable. This means that equal elements are not rearranged.
swap	Exchanges two values.
swap_ranges	Exchanges elements in a range.
transform	Applies a function to a range of elements and stores the outcome in a new sequence.
unique and unique_copy	Eliminates duplicate elements from range.
upper_bound	Finds the last point in a sequence that is not greater than some value.

Table 27-5. *The STL Algorithms* (continued)

The STL defines a large number of algorithms, which are summarized in Table 27-5. All of the algorithms are template functions. This means that they can be applied to any type of container. The following sections demonstrate a representative sample.

Counting

One of the most basic operations that you can perform on a sequence is to count its contents. To do this, you can use either **count( )** or **count_if( )**. Their general forms are shown here.

```
template <class InIter, class T>
    size_t count(InIter start, InIter end, const T &val);
```

```
template <class InIter, class UnPred>
    size_t count_if(InIter start, InIter end, UnPred pfn);
```

The **count( )** algorithm returns the number of elements in the sequence beginning at *start* and ending at *end* that match *val*. The **count_if( )** algorithm returns the number of elements in the sequence beginning at *start* and ending at *end* for which the unary predicate *pfn* returns true.

The following program demonstrates **count( )**.

```
// Demonstrate count().
#include <iostream>
#include <vector>
#include <cstdlib>
#include <algorithm>
using namespace std;

int main()
{
  vector<bool> v;
  unsigned int i;

  for(i=0; i < 10; i++) {
   if(rand() % 2) v.push_back(true);
   else v.push_back(false);
  }

  cout << "Sequence:\n";
  for(i=0; i<v.size(); i++)
    cout << boolalpha << v[i] << " ";
  cout << endl;

  i = count(v.begin(), v.end(), true);
  cout << i << " elements are true.\n";

  return 0;
}
```

This program displays something similar to the following output.

```
Sequence:
true true false false true false false false false false
3 elements are true.
```

The program begins by creating a vector composed of randomly generated true and false values. Next, **count( )** is used to count the number of **true** values.

This next program demonstrates **count_if( )**. It creates a vector containing the numbers 1 through 19. It then counts those that are evenly divisible by 3. To do this, it creates a unary predicate called **dividesBy3( )**, which returns **true** if its argument is evenly divisible by 3.

```
// Demonstrate count_if().
#include <iostream>
#include <vector>
#include <algorithm>
using namespace std;

/* This is a unary predicate that determines
   if number is divisible by 3. */
bool dividesBy3(int i)
{
  if((i%3) == 0) return true;

  return false;
}

int main()
{
  vector<int> v;
  unsigned int i;

  for(i=1; i < 20; i++) v.push_back(i);

  cout << "Sequence:\n";
  for(i=0; i<v.size(); i++)
    cout << v[i] << " ";
  cout << endl;

  i = count_if(v.begin(), v.end(), dividesBy3);
  cout << i << " numbers are divisible by 3.\n";

  return 0;
}
```

This program produces the following output.

```
Sequence:
1 2 3 4 5 6 7 8 9 10 11 12 13 14 15 16 17 18 19
6 numbers are divisible by 3.
```

Notice how the unary predicate **dividesBy3( )** is coded. All unary predicates receive as a parameter an object that is of the same type as that stored in the container upon which the predicate is operating. The predicate must then return a **true** or **false** result based upon this object.

Removing and Replacing Elements

Sometimes it is useful to generate a new sequence that consists of only certain items from an original sequence. One algorithm that does this is **remove_copy( )**. Its general form is shown here.

> template <class InIter, class OutIter, class T>
>   OutIter remove_copy(InIter *start*, InIter *end*,
>   OutIter *result*, const T &*val*);

The **remove_copy( )** algorithm copies elements from the specified range, removing those that are equal to *val*. It puts the result into the sequence pointed to by *result* and returns an iterator to the end of the result. The output container must be large enough to hold the result.

To replace one element in a sequence with another when a copy is made, use **replace_copy( )**. Its general form is shown here.

> template <class InIter, class OutIter, class T>
>   OutIter replace_copy(InIter *start*, InIter *end*,
>   OutIter *result*, const T &*old*, const T &*new*);

The **replace_copy( )** algorithm copies elements from the specified range, replacing elements equal to *old* with *new*. It puts the result into the sequence pointed to by *result* and returns an iterator to the end of the result. The output container must be large enough to hold the result.

The following program demonstrates **remove_copy( )** and **replace_copy( )**. It creates a sequence of characters. It then removes all of the spaces from the sequence. Next, it replaces all spaces with colons.

```
// Demonstrate remove_copy and replace_copy.
#include <iostream>
#include <vector>
#include <algorithm>
using namespace std;

int main()
{
  char str[] = "The STL is power programming.";
  vector<char> v, v2(30);
  unsigned int i;

  for(i=0; str[i]; i++) v.push_back(str[i]);
```

```
// **** demonstrate remove_copy ****
cout << "Input sequence:\n";
for(i=0; i<v.size(); i++) cout << v[i];
cout << endl;

// remove all spaces
remove_copy(v.begin(), v.end(), v2.begin(), ' ');

cout << "Result after removing spaces:\n";
for(i=0; i<v2.size(); i++) cout << v2[i];
cout << endl << endl;

// **** now, demonstrate replace_copy ****
cout << "Input sequence:\n";
for(i=0; i<v.size(); i++) cout << v[i];
cout << endl;

// replace spaces with colons
replace_copy(v.begin(), v.end(), v2.begin(), ' ', ':');

cout << "Result after replacing spaces with colons:\n";
for(i=0; i<v2.size(); i++) cout << v2[i];
cout << endl << endl;

return 0;
}
```

The output produced by this program is shown here.

```
Input sequence:
The STL is power programming.
Result after removing spaces:
TheSTLispowerprogramming.

Input sequence:
The STL is power programming.
Result after replacing spaces with colons:
The:STL:is:power:programming.
```

Reversing a Sequence

An often useful algorithm is **reverse( )**, which reverses a sequence. Its general form is

template <class BiIter> void reverse(BiIter *start*, BiIter *end*);

The **reverse( )** algorithm reverses the order of the range specified by *start* and *end*.
The following program demonstrates **reverse( )**.

```
// Demonstrate reverse.
#include <iostream>
#include <vector>
#include <algorithm>
using namespace std;

int main()
{
  vector<int> v;
  unsigned int i;

  for(i=0; i<10; i++) v.push_back(i);

  cout << "Initial: ";
  for(i=0; i<v.size(); i++) cout << v[i] << " ";
  cout << endl;

  reverse(v.begin(), v.end());

  cout << "Reversed: ";
  for(i=0; i<v.size(); i++) cout << v[i] << " ";

  return 0;
}
```

The output from this program is shown here.

```
Initial: 0 1 2 3 4 5 6 7 8 9
Reversed: 9 8 7 6 5 4 3 2 1 0
```

Transforming a Sequence

One of the more interesting algorithms is **transform( )** because it modifies each element in a range according to a function that you provide. The **transform( )** algorithm has these two general forms.

template <class InIter, class OutIter, class Func)
    OutIter transform(InIter *start*, InIter *end*, OutIter *result*, Func *unaryfunc*);

template <class InItter1, class InIter2, class OutIter, class Func)
    OutIter transform(InIter1 *start1*, InIter1 *end1*, InIter2 *start2*,
                    OutIter *result*, Func *binaryfunc*);

The **transform( )** algorithm applies a function to a range of elements and stores the outcome in *result*. In the first form, the range is specified by *start* and *end*. The function to be applied is specified by *unaryfunc*. This function receives the value of an element in its parameter and must return its transformation. In the second form, the transformation is applied using a binary operator function that receives the value of an element from the sequence to be transformed in its first parameter and a element from the second sequence as its second parameter. Both versions return an iterator to the end of the resulting sequence.

The following program uses a simple transformation function called **reciprocal( )** to transform the contents of a list of numbers into their reciprocals. Notice that the resulting sequence is stored in the same list that provided the original sequence.

```
// An example of the transform algorithm.
#include <iostream>
#include <list>
#include <algorithm>
using namespace std;

// A simple transformation function.
double reciprocal(double i) {
  return 1.0/i; // return reciprocal
}

int main()
{
  list<double> vals;
  int i;

  // put values into list
  for(i=1; i<10; i++) vals.push_back((double)i);
```

```
cout << "Original contents of vals:\n";
list<double>::iterator p = vals.begin();
while(p != vals.end()) {
  cout << *p << " ";
  p++;
}

cout << endl;

// transform vals
p = transform(vals.begin(), vals.end(),
              vals.begin(), reciprocal);

cout << "Transformed contents of vals:\n";
p = vals.begin();
while(p != vals.end()) {
  cout << *p << " ";
  p++;
}

return 0;
}
```

The output produced by the program is shown here.

```
Original contents of vals:
1 2 3 4 5 6 7 8 9
Transformed contents of vals:
1 0.5 0.333333 0.25 0.2 0.166667 0.142857 0.125 0.111111
```

As you can see, each element in **vals** has been transformed into its reciprocal.

Using Function Objects

As explained at the start of this chapter, the STL supports (and extensively utilizes) function objects. Function objects are simply classes that define **operator( )**. The STL provides many built-in function objects, such as **less**, **minus**, etc. It also allows you to define your own function objects. Frankly, it is beyond the scope of this book to fully describe all of the issues surrounding the creation and use of function objects. Fortunately, as the preceding examples have shown, you can make significant use of the STL without ever creating a function object. However, since function objects are a main ingredient of the STL, it is important to have a general understanding.

Unary and Binary Function Objects

Just as there are unary and binary predicates, there are unary and binary function objects. A unary function object requires one argument; a binary function object requires two. You must use the type of object required. For example, if an algorithm is expecting a binary function object, you must pass it a binary function object.

Using the Built-in Function Objects

The STL provides a rich assortment of built-in function objects. The binary function objects are shown here.

plus	minus	multiplies	divides	modulus
equal_to	not_equal_to	greater	greater_equal	less
less_equal	logical_and	logical_or		

Here are the unary function objects.

logical_not	negate

The function objects perform the operations specified by their names. The only one that may not be self-evident is **negate( )**, which reverses the sign of its argument.

The built-in function objects are template classes that overload **operator( )**, which returns the result of the specified operation on whatever type of data you select. For example, to invoke the binary function object **plus()**, use this syntax.

```
plus<float>()
```

The built-in function objects use the header **<functional>**.

Let's begin with a simple example. The following program uses the **transform( )** algorithm (described in the preceding section) and the **negate()** function object to reverse the sign of a list of values.

```
// Use a unary function object.
#include <iostream>
#include <list>
#include <functional>
#include <algorithm>
using namespace std;
```

```
int main()
{
  list<double> vals;
  int i;

  // put values into list
  for(i=1; i<10; i++) vals.push_back((double)i);

  cout << "Original contents of vals:\n";
  list<double>::iterator p = vals.begin();
  while(p != vals.end()) {
    cout << *p << " ";
    p++;
  }
  cout << endl;

  // use the negate function object
  p = transform(vals.begin(), vals.end(),
                vals.begin(),
                negate<double>()); // call function object

  cout << "Negated contents of vals:\n";
  p = vals.begin();
  while(p != vals.end()) {
    cout << *p << " ";
    p++;
  }

  return 0;
}
```

This program produces the following output.

```
Original contents of vals:
1 2 3 4 5 6 7 8 9
Negated contents of vals:
-1 -2 -3 -4 -5 -6 -7 -8 -9
```

In the program, notice how **negate( )** is invoked. Since **vals** is a list of **double** values, **negate( )** is called using **negate<double>( )**. The **transform( )** algorithm automatically calls **negate( )** for each element in the sequence. Thus, the single parameter to **negate( )** receives, as its argument, an element from the sequence.

The next program demonstrates the use of the binary function object, **divides()**. It creates two lists of double values and has one divide the other. This program uses the binary form of the **transform( )** algorithm.

```cpp
// Use a binary function object.
#include <iostream>
#include <list>
#include <functional>
#include <algorithm>
using namespace std;

int main()
{
  list<double> vals;
  list<double> divisors;
  int i;

  // put values into list
  for(i=10; i<100; i+=10) vals.push_back((double)i);
  for(i=1; i<10; i++) divisors.push_back(3.0);

  cout << "Original contents of vals:\n";
  list<double>::iterator p = vals.begin();
  while(p != vals.end()) {
    cout << *p << " ";
    p++;
  }

  cout << endl;

  // transform vals
  p = transform(vals.begin(), vals.end(),
                divisors.begin(), vals.begin(),
                divides<double>()); // call function object

  cout << "Divided contents of vals:\n";
  p = vals.begin();
  while(p != vals.end()) {
```

```
    cout << *p << " ";
    p++;
  }

  return 0;
}
```

The output from this program is shown here.

```
Original contents of vals:
10 20 30 40 50 60 70 80 90
Divided contents of vals:
3.33333 6.66667 10 13.3333 16.6667 20 23.3333 26.6667 30
```

In this case, the binary function object **divides( )** divides the elements from the first sequence by their corresponding elements from the second sequence. Thus, **divides( )** receives arguments in this order:

divides(*first, second*)

This order can be generalized. Whenever a binary function object is used, its arguments are ordered *first, second*.

Creating a Function Object

In addition to using the built-in function objects, you can create your own. To do so, you will simply create a class that overloads the **operator( )** function. However, for the greatest flexibility, you will want to use one of the following classes defined by the STL as a base class for your function objects.

```
template <class Argument, class Result> struct unary_function {
  typedef Argument argument_type;
  typedef Result result_type;
};

template <class Argument1, class Argument2, class Result>
struct binary_function {
  typedef Argument1 first_argument_type;
  typedef Argument2 second_argument_type;
  typedef Result result_type;
};
```

These template classes provide concrete type names for the generic data types used by the function object. Although they are technically a convenience, they are almost always used when creating function objects.

The following program demonstrates a custom function object. It converts the **reciprocal( )** function (used to demonstrate the **transform( )** algorithm earlier) into a function object.

```
// Create a reciprocal function object.
#include <iostream>
#include <list>
#include <functional>
#include <algorithm>
using namespace std;

// A simple function object.
class reciprocal: unary_function<double, double> {
public:
  result_type operator()(argument_type i)
  {
    return (result_type) 1.0/i; // return reciprocal
  }
};

int main()
{
  list<double> vals;
  int i;

  // put values into list
  for(i=1; i<10; i++) vals.push_back((double)i);

  cout << "Original contents of vals:\n";
  list<double>::iterator p = vals.begin();
  while(p != vals.end()) {
    cout << *p << " ";
    p++;
  }
  cout << endl;
```

```
// use reciprocal function object
p = transform(vals.begin(), vals.end(),
              vals.begin(),
              reciprocal()); // call function object

cout << "Transformed contents of vals:\n";
p = vals.begin();
while(p != vals.end()) {
  cout << *p << " ";
  p++;
}

return 0;
}
```

Notice two important aspects of **reciprocal()**. First, it inherits the base class **unary_function**. This gives it access to the **argument_type** and **result_type** types. Second, it defines **operator( )** such that it returns the reciprocal of its argument. In general, to create a function object, simply inherit the proper base class and overload **operator( )** as required. It really is that easy.

Using Binders

When using a binary function object, it is possible to bind a value to one of the arguments. This can be useful in many situations. For example, you may wish to remove all elements from a sequence that are greater than some value, such as 8. To do this, you need some way to bind 8 to the right-hand operand of the function object **greater( )**. That is, you want **greater( )** to perform the following comparison

val > 8

for each element of the sequence. The STL provides a mechanism, called *binders*, that accomplishes this.

There are two binders: **bind1st( )** and **bind2nd( )**. They take these general forms.

bind1st(*binfunc_obj, value*)

bind2nd(*binfunc_obj, value*)

Here, *binfunc_obj* is a binary function object. **bind1st( )** returns a unary function object that has *binfunc_obj*'s left-hand operand bound to *value*. **bind2nd( )** returns a unary function object that has *binfunc_obj*'s right-hand operand bound to *value*. The **bind2nd( )** binder is by far the most commonly used. In either case, the outcome of a binder is a unary function object that is bound to the value specified.

To demonstrate the use of a binder, we will use the **remove_if( )** algorithm. It removes elements from a sequence according to the outcome of a predicate. It has this prototype.

template <class ForIter, class UnPred>
    ForIter remove_if(ForIter *start*, ForIter *end*, UnPred *func*);

The algorithm removes elements from the sequence defined by *start* and *end* if the unary predicate defined by *func* is true. The algorithm returns a pointer to the new end of the sequence, which reflects the deletion of the elements.

The following program removes all values from a sequence that are greater than the value 8. Since the predicate required by **remove_if** is unary, we cannot simply use the **greater( )** function object as-is, because **greater( )** is a binary object. Instead, we must bind the value 8 to the second argument of **greater( )** using the **bind2nd( )** binder, as shown in the program.

```cpp
// Demonstrate bind2nd().
#include <iostream>
#include <list>
#include <functional>
#include <algorithm>
using namespace std;

int main()
{
  list<int> lst;
  list<int>::iterator p, endp;

  int i;

  for(i=1; i < 20; i++) lst.push_back(i);

  cout << "Original sequence:\n";
  p = lst.begin();
  while(p != lst.end()) {
    cout << *p << " ";
    p++;
  }
  cout << endl;

  endp = remove_if(lst.begin(), lst.end(),
                   bind2nd(greater<int>(), 8));
```

```
   cout << "Resulting sequence:\n";
   p = lst.begin();
   while(p != endp) {
     cout << *p << " ";
     p++;
   }

   return 0;
}
```

The output produced by the program is shown here.

```
Original sequence:
1 2 3 4 5 6 7 8 9 10 11 12 13 14 15 16 17 18 19
Resulting sequence:
1 2 3 4 5 6 7 8
```

You might want to experiment with this program, trying different function objects and binding different values. As you will discover, binders expand the power of the STL in very significant ways.

One last point: there is an object related to a binder, called a *negator*. The negators are **not1( )** and **not2( )**. They return the negation (i.e., the complement of) whatever predicate they modify. They have these general forms.

not1(*unary_predicate*)

not2(*binary_predicate*)

For example, if you substitute the line

```
   endp = remove_if(lst.begin(), lst.end(),
                    not1(bind2nd(greater<int>(), 8)));
```

into the preceding program, then it will remove all elements from **lst** that are not greater than 8.

The string Class

As you know, C++ does not support a built-in string type, per se. It does, however, provide for two ways of handling strings. First, you may use the traditional, null-terminated character array with which you are already familiar. This is sometimes referred to as a C *string*. The second way is as a class object of type **string**, and this approach is examined here.

Actually, the **string** class is a specialization of a more general template class called **basic_string**. In fact, there are two specializations of **basic_string**: **string**, which supports 8-bit character strings, and **wstring**, which supports wide-character strings. Since 8-bit characters are by far the most commonly used in normal programming, **string** is the version of **basic_string** examined here.

Before looking at the **string** class, it is important to understand why it is part of the C++ library. Standard classes have not been casually added to C++. In fact, a significant amount of thought and debate has accompanied each new addition. Given that C++ already contains some support for strings as null-terminated character arrays, it may at first seem that the inclusion of the **string** class is an exception to this rule. However, this is actually far from the truth. Here is why: Null-terminated strings cannot be manipulated by any of the standard C++ operators. Nor can they take part in normal C++ expressions. For example, consider this fragment.

```
char s1[80], s2[80], s3[80];

s1 = "Alpha"; // can't do
s2 = "Beta"; // can't do
s3 = s1 + s2; // error, not allowed
```

As the comments show, in C++ it is not possible to use the assignment operator to give a character array a new value (except during initialization), nor is it possible to use the + operator to concatenate two strings. These operations must be written using library functions, as shown here.

```
strcpy(s1, "Alpha");
strcpy(s2, "Beta");
strcpy(s3, s1);
strcat(s3, s2);
```

Since null-terminated character arrays are not technically data types in their own right, the C++ operators cannot be applied to them. This makes even the most rudimentary string operations clumsy. More than anything else, it is the inability to operate on null-terminated strings using the standard C++ operators that has driven the development of a standard string class. Remember, when you define a class in C++, you are defining a new data type that can be fully integrated into the C++ environment. This, of course, means that the operators can be overloaded relative to the new class. Therefore, by adding a standard string class, it becomes possible to manage strings in the same way as any other type of data: through the use of operators.

There is, however, one other reason for the standard string class: safety. In the hands of an inexperienced or careless programmer, it is very easy to overrun the end of an array that holds a null-terminated string. For example, consider the standard string copy function **strcpy( )**. This function contains no provision for checking the boundary of the target array. If the source array contains more characters than the target array can hold, then a program error or system crash is possible (likely). As you will see, the standard **string** class prevents such errors.

In the final analysis, there are three reasons for the inclusion of the standard **string** class: consistency (a string now defines a data type), convenience (you can use the standard C++ operators), and safety (array boundaries will not be overrun). Keep in mind that there is no reason that you should abandon normal, null-terminated strings altogether. They are still the most efficient way in which to implement strings. However, when speed is not an overriding concern, using the new **string** class gives you access to a safe and fully integrated way to manage strings.

Although not traditionally thought of as part of the STL, **string** is another container class defined by C++. This means that it supports the algorithms described in the previous section. However, strings have additional capabilities. To have access to the **string** class, you must include **<string>** in your program.

The **string** class is very large, with many constructors and member functions. Also, many member functions have multiple overloaded forms. For this reason, it is not possible to look at the entire contents of **string** in this chapter. Instead, we will examine several of its most commonly used features. Once you have a general understanding of how **string** works, you will be able to easily explore the rest of it on your own.

The **string** class supports several constructors. The prototypes for three of its most commonly used constructors are shown here.

string( );

string(const char *str);

string(const string &str);

The first form creates an empty **string** object. The second creates a **string** object from the null-terminated string pointed to by *str*. This form provides a conversion from null-terminated strings to **string** objects. The third form creates a **string** from another **string**.

A number of operators that apply to strings are defined for **string** objects, including:

Operator	Meaning
=	Assignment
+	Concatenation
+=	Concatenation assignment
==	Equality
!=	Inequality
<	Less than

Operator	Meaning
<=	Less than or equal
>	Greater than
>=	Greater than or equal
[ ]	Subscripting
<<	Output
>>	Input

These operators allow the use of **string** objects in normal expressions and eliminate the need for calls to functions such as **strcpy( )** or **strcat( )**, for example. In general, you can mix **string** objects with normal, null-terminated strings in expressions. For example, a **string** object can be assigned a null-terminated string.

The + operator can be used to concatenate a string object with another string object or a string object with a C-style string. That is, the following variations are supported.

string + string

string + C-string

C-string + string

The + operator can also be used to concatenate a character onto the end of a string.

The **string** class defines the constant **npos**, which is –1. This constant represents the length of the longest possible string.

The C++ string classes make string handling extraordinarily easy. For example, using **string** objects you can use the assignment operator to assign a quoted string to a **string**, the + operator to concatenate strings, and the comparison operators to compare strings. The following program illustrates these operations.

```
// A short string demonstration.
#include <iostream>
#include <string>
using namespace std;

int main()
{
  string str1("Alpha");
  string str2("Beta");
  string str3("Omega");
  string str4;
```

```
  // assign a string
  str4 = str1;
  cout << str1 << "\n" << str3 << "\n";

  // concatenate two strings
  str4 = str1 + str2;
  cout << str4 << "\n";

  // concatenate a string with a C-string
  str4 = str1 + " to " + str3;
  cout << str4 << "\n";

  // compare strings
  if(str3 > str1) cout << "str3 > str1\n";
  if(str3 == str1+str2)
    cout << "str3 == str1+str2\n";

  /* A string object can also be
     assigned a normal string. */
  str1 = "This is a null-terminated string.\n";
  cout << str1;

  // create a string object using another string object
  string str5(str1);
  cout << str5;

  // input a string
  cout << "Enter a string: ";
  cin >> str5;
  cout << str5;

  return 0;
}
```

This program produces the following output.

```
Alpha
Omega
AlphaBeta
Alpha to Omega
str3 > str1
This is a null-terminated string.
This is a null-terminated string.
```

```
Enter a string: STL
STL
```

As you can see, objects of type **string** can be manipulated in ways similar to C++'s built-in data types.

Notice the ease with which the string handling is accomplished. For example, the + is used to concatenate strings and the > is use to compare two strings. To accomplish these operations using C-style, null-terminated strings, less convenient calls to the **strcat( )** and **strcmp( )** functions would be required. Because C++ **string** objects can be freely mixed with C-style null-terminated strings, there is no disadvantage to using them in your program—and there are considerable benefits to be gained.

There is one other thing to notice in the preceding program: the sizes of the strings are not specified. **string** objects are automatically sized to hold the string that they are given. Thus, when assigning or concatenating strings, the target string will grow as needed to accommodate the size of the new string. It is not possible to overrun the end of the string. This dynamic aspect of **string** objects is one of the ways that they are better than standard null-terminated strings (which *are* subject to boundary overruns).

Some string Member Functions

Although most simple string operations can be accomplished using the string operators, more complex or subtle ones are accomplished using **string** member functions. While **string** has far too many member functions to discuss them all, we will examine several of the most common.

String manipulations

To assign one string to another, use the **assign( )** function. Two of its forms are shown here.

string &assign(const string &*strob*, size_type *start*, size_type *num*);

string &assign(const char **str*, size_type *num*);

In the first form, *num* characters from *strob* beginning at the index specified by *start* will be assigned to the invoking object. In the second form, the first *num* characters of the null-terminated string *str* are assigned to the invoking object. In each case, a reference to the invoking object is returned. Of course, it is much easier to use the = to assign one entire string to another. You will need to use the **assign( )** function only when assigning a partial string.

You can append part of one string to another using the **append( )** member function. Two of its forms are shown here.

string &append(const string &*strob*, size_type *start*, size_type *num*);

string &append(const char **str*, size_type *num*);

Here, *num* characters from *strob* beginning at the index specified by *start* will be appended to the invoking object. In the second form, the first *num* characters of the null-terminated string *str* are appended to the invoking object. In each case, a reference to the invoking object is returned. Of course, it is much easier to use the **+** to append one entire string to another. You will need to use the **append( )** function only when appending a partial string.

You can insert or replace characters within a string using **insert( )** and **replace( )**. The prototypes for their most common forms are shown here.

string &insert(size_type *start*, const string &*strob*);

string &insert(size_type *start*, const string &*strob*,
                 size_type *insStart*, size_type *num*);

string &replace(size_type *start*, size_type *num*, const string &*strob*);

string &replace(size_type *start*, size_type *orgNum*, const string &*strob*,
                 size_type *replaceStart*, size_type *replaceNum*);

The first form of **insert( )** inserts *strob* into the invoking string at the index specified by *start*. The second form of **insert( )** inserts *num* characters from *strob* beginning at *insStart* into the invoking string at the index specified by *start*.

Beginning at *start*, the first form of **replace( )** replaces *num* characters from the invoking string, with *strob*. The second form replaces *orgNum* characters, beginning at *start*, in the invoking string with the *replaceNum* characters from the string specified by *strob* beginning at *replaceStart*. In both cases, a reference to the invoking object is returned.

You can remove characters from a string using **erase( )**. One of its forms is shown here.

string &erase(size_type *start* = 0, size_type *num* = npos);

It removes *num* characters from the invoking string beginning at *start*. A reference to the invoking string is returned.

The following program demonstrates the **insert( )**, **erase( )**, and **replace( )** functions.

```
// Demonstrate insert(), erase(), and replace().
#include <iostream>
#include <string>
using namespace std;

int main()
{
  string str1("String handling C++ style.");
  string str2("STL Power");
```

```
cout << "Initial strings:\n";
cout << "str1: " << str1 << endl;
cout << "str2: " << str2 << "\n\n";

// demonstrate insert()
cout << "Insert str2 into str1:\n";
str1.insert(6, str2);
cout << str1 << "\n\n";

// demonstrate erase()
cout << "Remove 9 characters from str1:\n";
str1.erase(6, 9);
cout << str1 <<"\n\n";

// demonstrate replace
cout << "Replace 8 characters in str1 with str2:\n";
str1.replace(7, 8, str2);
cout << str1 << endl;

return 0;
}
```

The output produced by this program is shown here.

```
Initial strings:
str1: String handling C++ style.
str2: STL Power

Insert str2 into str1:
StringSTL Power handling C++ style.

Remove 9 characters from str1:
String handling C++ style.

Replace 8 characters in str1 with str2:
String STL Power C++ style.
```

Searching a String

The **string** class provides several member functions that search a string, including **find( )** and **rfind( )**. Here are the prototypes for the most common versions of these functions.

size_type find(const string &*strob*, size_type *start*=0) const;

size_type rfind(const string &*strob*, size_type *start*=npos) const;

Beginning at *start*, **find( )** searches the invoking string for the first occurrence of the string contained in *strob*. If one is found, **find( )** returns the index at which the match occurs within the invoking string. If no match is found, then **npos** is returned. **rfind( )** is the opposite of **find( )**. Beginning at *start,* it searches the invoking string in the reverse direction for the first occurrence of the string contained in *strob* (i.e., it finds the last occurrence of *strob* within the invoking string). If one is found, **rfind( )** returns the index at which the match occurs within the invoking string. If no match is found, **npos** is returned.

Here is a short example that uses **find( )** and **rfind( )**.

```
#include <iostream>
#include <string>
using namespace std;

int main()
{
  unsigned int i;
  string s1 =
    "Quick of Mind, Strong of Body, Pure of Heart";
  string s2;

  i = s1.find("Quick");
  if(i!=string::npos) {
    cout << "Match found at " << i << endl;
    cout << "Remaining string is:\n";
    s2.assign(s1, i, s1.size());
    cout << s2;
  }
  cout << "\n\n";

  i = s1.find("Strong");
  if(i!=string::npos) {
    cout << "Match found at " << i << endl;
    cout << "Remaining string is:\n";
    s2.assign(s1, i, s1.size());
    cout << s2;
  }
  cout << "\n\n";
```

```
    i = s1.find("Pure");
    if(i!=string::npos) {
      cout << "Match found at " << i << endl;
      cout << "Remaining string is:\n";
      s2.assign(s1, i, s1.size());
      cout << s2;
    }
    cout << "\n\n";

    // find list "of"
    i = s1.rfind("of");
    if(i!=string::npos) {
      cout << "Match found at " << i << endl;
      cout << "Remaining string is:\n";
      s2.assign(s1, i, s1.size());
      cout << s2;
    }

    return 0;
}
```

The output produced by this program is shown here.

```
Match found at 0
Remaining string is:
Quick of Mind, Strong of Body, Pure of Heart

Match found at 15
Remaining string is:
Strong of Body, Pure of Heart

Match found at 31
Remaining string is:
Pure of Heart

Match found at 36
Remaining string is:
of Heart
```

Comparing Strings

To compare the entire contents of one string object to another, you will normally use the overloaded relational operators described earlier. However, if you want to compare a portion of one string to another, then you will need to use the **compare( )** member function, shown here.

int compare(size_type *start*, size_type *num*, const string &*strob*) const;

Here, *num* characters in *strob*, beginning at *start*, will be compared against the invoking string. If the invoking string is less than *strob*, **compare( )** will return less than zero. If the invoking string is greater than *strob*, it will return greater than zero. If *strob* is equal to the invoking string, **compare( )** will return zero.

Obtaining a Null-Terminated String

Although **string** objects are useful in their own right, there will be times when you will need to obtain a null-terminated character array version of the string. For example, you might use a **string** object to construct a filename. However, when opening a file, you will need to specify a pointer to a standard, null-terminated string. To solve this problem, the member function **c_str( )** is provided. Its prototype is shown here.

const char *c_str( ) const;

This function returns a pointer to a null-terminated version of the string contained in the invoking **string** object. The null-terminated string must not be altered. It is also not guaranteed to be valid after any other operations have taken place on the **string** object.

Strings Are Containers

The **string** class meets all of the basic requirements to be a container. Thus it supports the common container functions, such as **begin( )**, **end( )**, and **size( )**. It also supports iterators. Thus, a **string** object can also be manipulated by the STL algorithms. Here is a simple example.

```
// Strings as containers.
#include <iostream>
#include <string>
#include <algorithm>
using namespace std;

int main()
{
```

```
string str1("String handling is easy in C++");
string::iterator p;
unsigned int i;

// use size()
for(i=0; i<str1.size(); i++)
  cout << str1[i];
cout << endl;

// use iterator
p = str1.begin();
while(p != str1.end())
  cout << *p++;
cout << endl;

// use the count() algorithm
i = count(str1.begin(), str1.end(), 'i');
cout << "There are " << i << " i's in str1\n";

return 0;
}
```

Output from the program is shown here.

```
String handling is easy in C++
String handling is easy in C++
There are 4 i's in str1
```

Putting Strings into Other Containers

Even though **string** is a container, objects of type **string** are commonly held in other STL containers, such as maps or lists. For example, here is a better way to write the telephone directory program shown earlier. It uses a map of **string** objects, rather than null-terminated strings, to hold the names and telephone numbers.

```
// Use a map of strings to create a phone directory.
#include <iostream>
#include <map>
#include <string>
using namespace std;

int main()
{
  map<string, string> directory;

  directory.insert(pair<string, string>("Tom", "555-4533"));
  directory.insert(pair<string, string>("Chris", "555-9678"));
  directory.insert(pair<string, string>("John", "555-8195"));
  directory.insert(pair<string, string>("Rachel", "555-0809"));

  string s;
  cout << "Enter name: ";
  cin >> s;

  map<string, string>::iterator p;

  p = directory.find(s);
  if(p != directory.end())
    cout << "Phone number: " << p->second;
  else
    cout << "Name not in directory.\n";

  return 0;
}
```

Final Thoughts on the STL

The STL is now an important, integral part of the C++ language. Many programming tasks can (and will) be framed in terms of it. The STL combines power with flexibility, and while its syntax is a bit complex, its ease of use is remarkable. No C++ programmer can afford to neglect the STL, because it will play an important role in the way future programs are written.

The Complete Reference

Borland
C++
Builder

Part IV

The C++ Builder Integrated Development Environment

Part Four of this book covers the C++ Builder development environment. This includes using the integrated development environment (IDE), creating applications, and using the debugger.

The Complete
Reference

Borland
C++
Builder

Chapter 28

The Integrated
Development
Environment

C++ Builder has two separate modes of operation. The first is called its *integrated development environment*, or IDE. Using the IDE, editing, compilation, and execution are controlled by single keystrokes, mouse clicks, and easy-to-use menus. In fact, the IDE is so easy to use that its operation is almost intuitive. The other method of operation uses the traditional command-line approach. When using the command line, first you use an editor to create a program source file and then you compile it, link it, and run it. Many programmers still favor the command-line method of program development. However, most find that the conveniences offered by the IDE speed up and simplify development.

This chapter provides an overview of the C++ Builder's IDE. If you are new to C++ Builder and have never used an integrated development environment before, then you will find this tour helpful. For detailed information about using the IDE, consult C++ Builder's online help system.

The Four IDE Windows

When you first execute C++ Builder's IDE, four windows appear, as shown in Figure 28-1. (Most of the fourth window is actually hidden behind the Form1 window.) The IDE consists of four windows that float. They are

- The Menu window
- The Object Inspector window
- The Form window
- The Code window

If you have used earlier versions of Borland's C++ compiler, then it will be readily apparent that the IDE has changed quite a bit from its predecessor. It has more options and greater flexibility. The remainder of this chapter examines each of the windows that compose the IDE.

The Menu Window

The top window, or *menu window*, is the main controlling window in the IDE. It contains several menus that tell the IDE to do something, such as load a file, compile a program, or set an option. It also contains all the toolbars that provide fast and easy access to other key functions or shortcuts, such as saving the active window. Table 28-1 summarizes the purpose of each menu.

When you select a menu bar item, a pull-down menu is displayed that contains a list of choices. Some choices produce another pull-down menu that displays additional options relating to the first menu. Secondary pull-down menus operate just like primary pull-down menus. When one menu will generate another, it is shown with

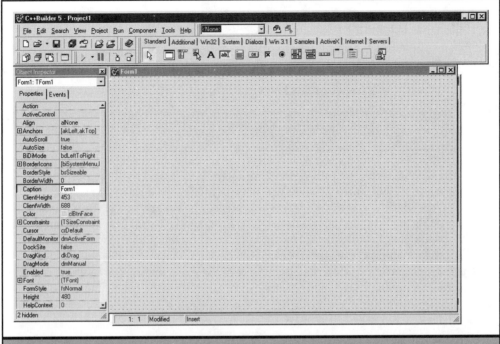

Figure 28-1.   *The C++ Builder IDE main windows*

Item	Purpose
File	Creates new applications; forms, frames, loads, and saves projects and files; handles printing; and exits the IDE.
Edit	Performs standard editing functions and sets object layout characteristics.
Search	Performs various text searches and replacements.
View	Accesses the Project Manager, object inspector, display units, forms, toolbar management and debugging information.
Project	Opens, closes, and builds projects.
Run	Accesses program control and additional debugging functions.
Component	Opens, closes, and inserts additional components, objects, and ActiveX controls.

Table 28-1.   *Summary of the Menu Window Items*

Item	Purpose
Tools	Manages configuration options for the environment, editor, debugger, and images.
Help	Accesses online help.

Table 28-1. *Summary of the Menu Window Items* (continued)

a dark arrow to its right. If a pull-down menu item is followed by three periods, selecting this item will cause a dialog box to be displayed that relates to the item.

The menu window actually contains two areas. The first is the very top menu row, which contains the standard menu items, File, Edit, and so forth. The second area holds the various toolbars that can be configured and used by the IDE. By default, the IDE shows all the toolbars on the menu window.

The following sections describe each entry in the main menu. The toolbars region is also briefly examined.

File

Highlighting the **File** option activates the **File** pull-down menu, as shown in Figure 28-2. Every menu item is organized into logical groupings. As you can see in the figure, the **File** menu is further divided into six groups dealing with these topics: new, open, saving and closing, including, printing, and exiting.

Selecting **New** opens the New Items dialog box, as shown in Figure 28-3. As you can see, there are numerous items that can be created. Even more items can be created by selecting one of the other four tabs, Project1, Forms, Dialogs, and Projects. Feel free to explore these other tabs to see the available items that the IDE can manage.

There are three other **New** menu items that can be selected from the **File** menu. These are the **New Application**, **New Form**, and **New Frame** items. These are shortcuts to the most commonly used items.

The next section of the **File** menu handles opening or reopening of files and projects. There are three items in this section, **Open**, **Open Project**, and **Reopen**. The **Open** or **Open Project** option prompts you for a filename and then loads that file or project into the IDE. If the file does not exist, you will be prompted to select the type of file to open (form, unit, textfile) and it will be created. The **Open** option also displays a list of files from which you can choose. Use the arrow keys to move the highlight until it is on the file you want to load and press ENTER to load the file, or double-click the desired filename. Note that the file type is not limited to a C or C++ source file. Make files, bitmap images, project files, and resource files are some of the possible file types. The **Reopen** option shows a list of previous items (history list) that have been worked on in the IDE.

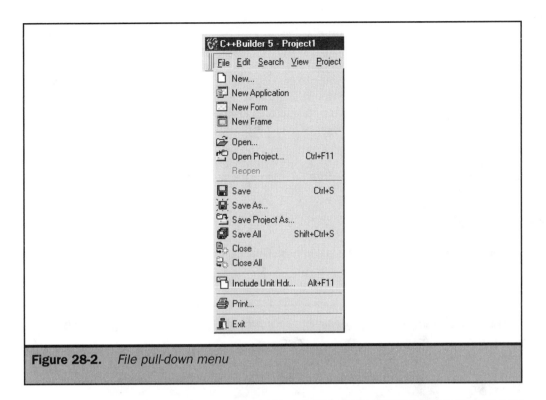

Figure 28-2.   *File pull-down menu*

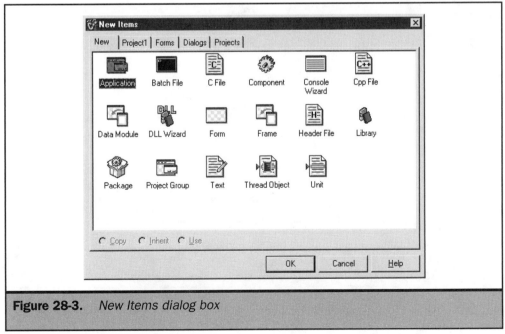

Figure 28-3.   *New Items dialog box*

The next part of the **File** menu handles save and close functions. This area enables you to save and close individual windows. The **Save** option saves the file in the active window. The **Save As** option lets you save a file using a different filename. The **Save Project As** option saves the current project using a different project name. The **Save All** option saves all the files that are open. The **Close** option closes and removes the current file and/or project. The **Close All** option closes all the windows.

The **Include** section enables you to insert **#include** statements into the current unit in the editor.

The **Print** option opens the Print Form dialog box. This is where the printer settings can be configured or modified before the file in the active window is printed.

Exit exits the IDE.

Edit

The **Edit** option performs several editor operations. Figure 28-4 shows the available options.

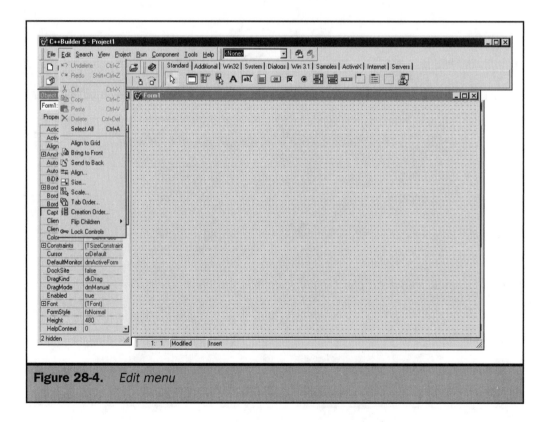

Figure 28-4. *Edit menu*

While only two options are shown in the first section, there are actually three available. The three options are **Undelete**, **Undo**, and **Redo**. If the active window is the code editor, then **Undo** and **Redo** appear. Select **Undo** to undo the most recent mouse or keystroke. Select **Redo** to redo the previous mouse or keystroke. If you are working on a form, then **Undelete** and **Redo** appear. Select **Undelete** to undelete an object that was just deleted. The **Redo** option works the same in the form window as it does on the code window. The number of undo steps can be set by adjusting the Undo Limit number in the **Tools** | **Editor Options** menu, under the General tab. This is where the Group Undo option for block undo operations can be set as well.

The next section contains the standard editing options: **Cut**, **Copy**, **Paste**, **Delete**, and **Select All**. These options function the same way in this IDE as in any Windows application.

The last section in the **Edit** menu is available only in the form window. If the code window is active, this section is grayed out or unavailable. **Align To Grid** aligns the selected objects to the nearest grid point. The **Bring To Front** option moves the selected object in front of all the other objects. **Send To Back** moves the selected object in back of all the objects on the form. **Align** opens a dialog box that can be used to align the selected objects in relation to each other. Alignment of the objects can be either horizontal or vertical. **Size** opens a dialog box and controls the width and height of an object on the form. The **Scale** option opens a dialog box where a percentage number can be entered for proportionally resizing the objects. **Tab Order** opens a dialog box where the controls on the form can be sequenced. The tab order is the order in which the cursor moves when the tab key is pressed. The **Creation Order** option opens a dialog box where you can specify the order in which nonvisual objects are created. These nonvisual objects are placeholders, including a database connection component and a system timer, to name two. **Flip Children** opens a submenu where either **All** or just the **Selected** objects are flipped. The controls can flip from a right-to-left image or vice versa. **Lock Controls** locks down all the objects in the current form. Once the objects are locked, they cannot be moved or resized.

Search

The **Search** menu option performs various types of searches and search-and-replace operations, as shown in Figure 28-5.

There are two sections in this menu. The top section deals with the searching or replacing of items. The **Find** option opens a Find Text dialog box, as shown in Figure 28-6, where the text to be searched can be entered. The dialog box allows searching for items within files by selecting the Find In Files tab. The **Find In Files** option opens the Find In Files tab, as shown in Figure 28-6, which allows you to search for text within files.

Replace opens a Replace Text dialog box. This dialog box looks very similar to the Find Text dialog box. However, **Replace** has a field where new text can be entered. **Search Again** repeats the preceding **Replace** or **Find** function. **Incremental Search** performs a dynamic search by moving to the next occurrence of the letter that was

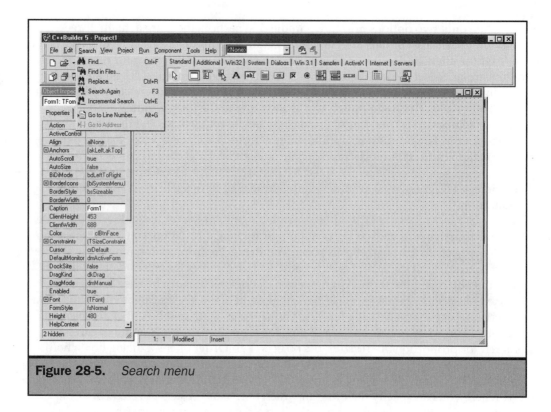

Figure 28-5. *Search menu*

pressed. When this option is selected, the code window becomes active and the status line changes to reflect Searching For. Every key that is pressed is searched for and the next occurrence of that letter is found. For example, as you type "tform1," the cursor

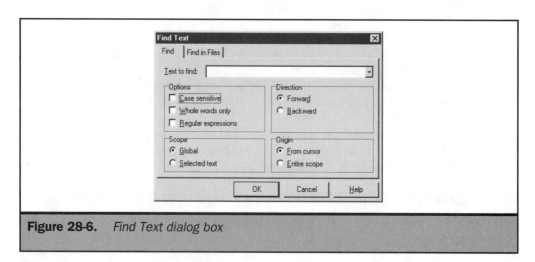

Figure 28-6. *Find Text dialog box*

moves to the first *t* found in the code window. When the *f* is pressed, the search engine locates the first instance of the combination *tf* and highlights that text. The **Incremental Search** continues this way until it no longer finds an occurrence of the specified string.

The last section allows for direct access to either a line number or an address. **Go To Line Number** allows a line number to be entered, and then the code on that line is shown. **Go To Address** shows a dialog box where an address in hexadecimal or decimal can be entered. You can also enter a function name directly. This option is available only in debug mode.

View

Highlighting the **View** option activates the **View** pull-down menu. As seen in Figure 28-7, this menu item allows you to display various windows. The first section deals with viewing other IDE components as described in the text that follows.

The **Project Manager** option displays all the files that make up the current project. This includes any forms and source code, as well as objects. It shows the name of the unit and the file location. The **Object Inspector** option will either reopen the Object Inspector window, if it was closed, or toggle between the Object Inspector window and the other opened windows. The **Alignment Palette**, as shown in Figure 28-8, shows the

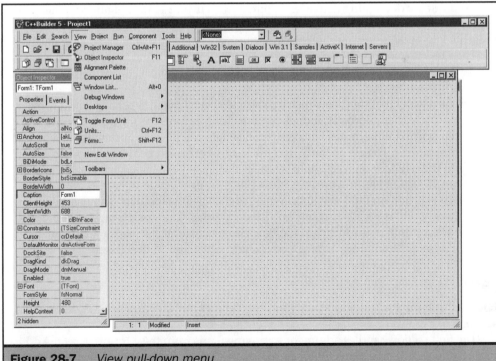

Figure 28-7.   *View pull-down menu*

Figure 28-8.   *Align window*

various ways that the objects on the form can be arranged or aligned. This menu item makes it very easy to organize and align all objects on a form.

The **Component List** option displays a scrollable list box where you can select a component or object to be added to a form. The **Window List** displays a list of all the opened windows.

The **Debug Windows** selection provides options for seeing all the various debug windows. These windows include: **Breakpoints**, **Call Stack**, **Watches**, **Threads**, and **CPU**. **Breakpoints** list all breakpoints. (Breakpoints are used when debugging.) The **Call Stack** displays the current call stack, which is useful when debugging. **Watches** are used during debugging activities to obtain the current values of any watched expressions. **Threads** lets you see the current thread, state, status, and location. **CPU** presents low-level debugging information.

The **Desktops** option lets you manage the IDE desktop windows and layouts. You can save layouts, delete layouts, and configure a specific layout, a feature that is used only during debugging.

The next section of the **View** menu allows access to the different unit and form windows. As with any project, it does not take long before a multitude of windows have been opened. It becomes very easy to lose windows behind other windows. The next three options, **Toggle Form/Unit**, **Units**, and **Forms**, all provide a method for getting to the window of your choice.

The next section lets you create a **New Edit Window** (code window).

The last section on the **View** menu toggles the various toolbars on (visible) or off. These other toolbars include: **Standard**, **View**, **Debug**, **Custom**, **Component Palette**, and the **Desktop**. These additional toolbars can be customized via the **Customize** option. These additional toolbars are covered briefly, later in this chapter.

Project

Highlighting the **Project** option activates the **Project** pull-down menu. There are five sections under this option, as shown in Figure 28-9.

The first section handles adding or removing items from the current project. **Add to Project** adds additional items into the existing project. **Remove from Project** removes items. The **Import Type Library** displays the registered type libraries on your computer

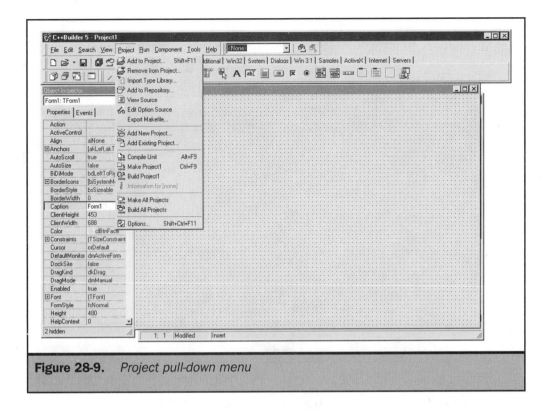

Figure 28-9.   *Project pull-down menu*

so that a registered type can be imported into a project. **Add to Repository** lets you create templates to add into the repository. **View Source** brings the source code window to the forefront. **Edit Option Source** lets you display/edit the project options file (**.bpr**) file for the current project. This file is shown in XML format. It is recommended that this file not be edited directly. The **Export Makefile** option creates a makefile for the current project. This makefile can then be used at the command line.

The next section of the **Project** menu deals with adding and modifying existing projects. There are two items here. **Add New Project** lets you create a new project of your choosing, and **Add Existing Project** loads an existing project.

The third section deals with compiling and building projects. **Compile Unit** compiles the code that is in the active window. **Make Project** compiles and links the current project, but only the items that have changed since the last build or make. **Build Project** rebuilds the entire project regardless of whether the files or forms have changed. The **Information for** option shows the program compilation and status of your project.

The next section is for making or building all the projects that are opened. There are two options here, **Make All Projects** and **Build All Projects**. The make all and build all options work the same as those for making and building the current project, except that these work on all the projects, not just the current one.

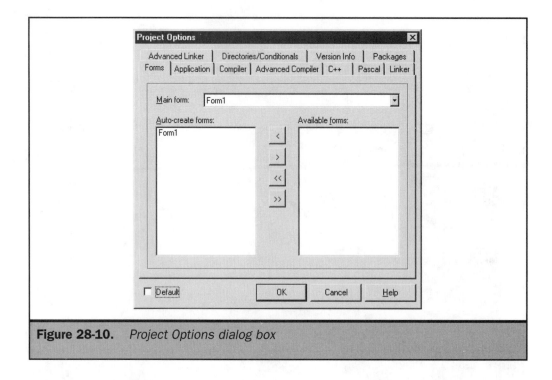

Figure 28-10.   *Project Options dialog box*

The last item is **Options**. When **Options** is selected, a dialog box opens. Figure 28-10 contains several tabs that enable you to fully configure the project.

Run

Highlighting the **Run** option activates the **Run** pull-down menu, as shown in Figure 28-11. The first section runs the current project and sets any command-line parameters. **Run** executes the current project. If there were any changes made to the source files, this option will first compile and link the project before executing. **Parameters** allow you to pass command-line parameters to the program when it executes.

The next section steps through the project in debug mode. **Step Over** starts the project in debug mode. Each time it is selected, it executes the next line in the code. If the next line calls a function, it executes the entire function as a single unit. **Trace Into** does the same as **Step Over**, except that it will follow the execution into functions one line at a time. **Trace To Next Source Line** stops the execution on the next source line of the application. **Run To Cursor** executes the application up to the point at which the cursor is located in the code window. **Run Until Return** executes the application until it returns from the current function. **Show Execution Point** places the cursor at the line in the code that is to be executed next. **Program Pause** pauses the execution of the application, and **Program Reset** stops the current application and frees up any memory.

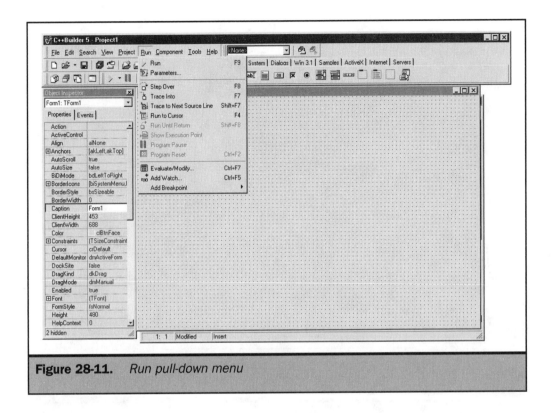

Figure 28-11. *Run pull-down menu*

The last section evaluates variables. **Evaluate/Modify** displays a dialog box where you can see or change a variable. **Add Watch** opens a dialog box where you can create an expression to watch or change an existing one. **Add Breakpoint** allows you to add a breakpoint into your code.

Component

The **Component** pull-down menu offers ways for managing components that are to be added to your project. Figure 28-12 shows the menu under the **Component** option.

The first section creates or manages components for your project. **New Component** opens a dialog box where you can create new components to be added into your project. **Install Component** lets you choose a predefined component to add into your project. **Import ActiveX Control** displays a dialog box, as shown in Figure 28-13, where you can select a registered control to be added to the active project.

The next item is **Create Component Template**. The **Create Component Template** item allows you to create template components that can be configured with specific values and added to your project.

The last section manages packages and configuration palettes. The **Install Packages** option allows a package or component to be selected. It displays a dialog box as shown in Figure 28-14.

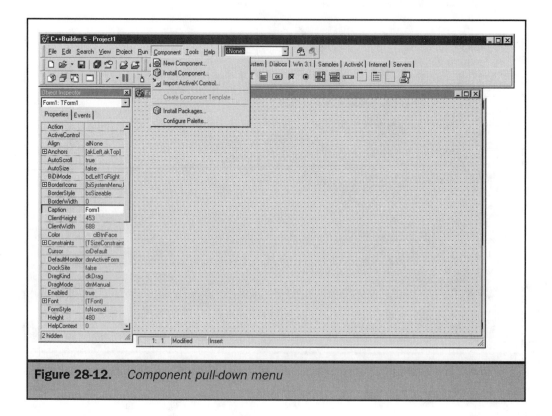

Figure 28-12.   *Component pull-down menu*

This dialog shows which packages have been installed and allows you to select other packages or remove an existing one. The **Configure Palette** option is a shortcut to the **Tools | Environment Options** item with the Palette tab opened. As shown in Figure 28-15, the **Configure Palette** option is for changing the way the component palette looks when it is opened. You can add, reorder, and remove pages and components from this option.

Tools

The **Tools** pull-down menu provides a convenient way to manage the IDE. The first section from the **Tools** menu edits the main components of the IDE. The Environment Options dialog box is shown in Figure 28-16. This dialog box configures the settings for the IDE. There are four tabs, Preferences, Library, Palette, and C++ Builder Direct, which can be configured and set for customizing the IDE. See the C++ Builder help files for more details on these tabs and their options.

The **Editor Options** menu item opens the Editor Properties dialog box. There are several tabs on this dialog box, as shown in Figure 28-17. These tabs provide a way to configure the IDE functions. Explore these options and the C++ Builder help files for more details.

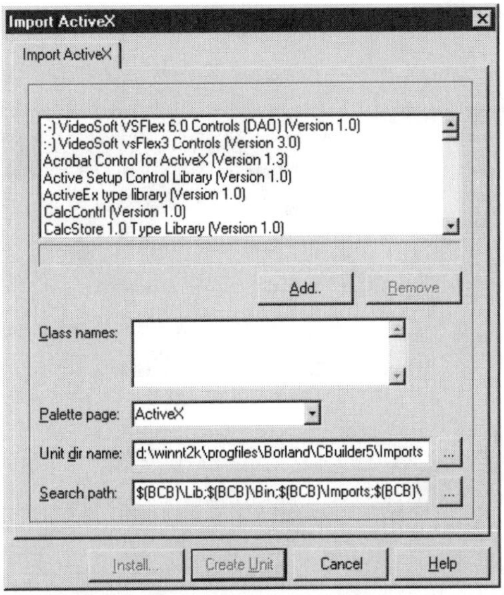

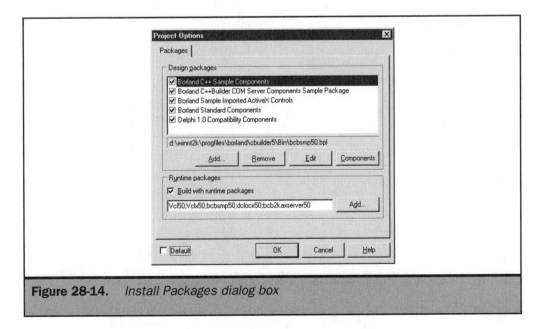

Figure 28-13.   *Import ActiveX dialog box*

The **Debugger Options** item opens the Debugger Options dialog box as shown in Figure 28-18. This menu item customizes the debugger options.

Figure 28-14.   *Install Packages dialog box*

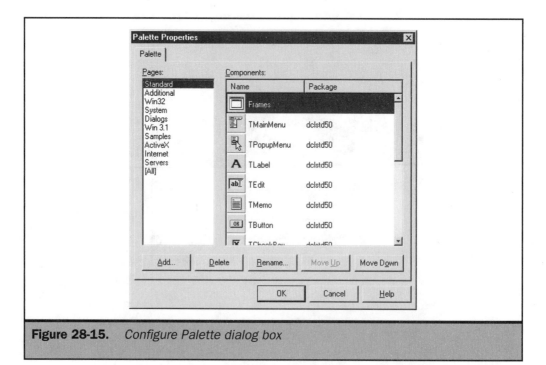

Figure 28-15. *Configure Palette dialog box*

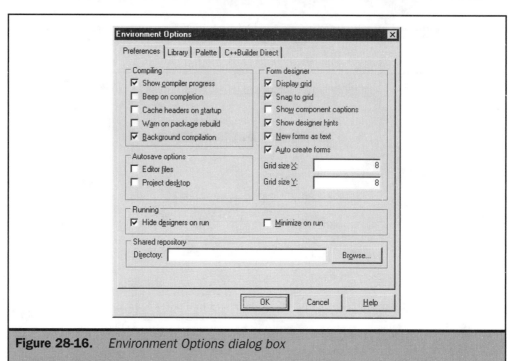

Figure 28-16. *Environment Options dialog box*

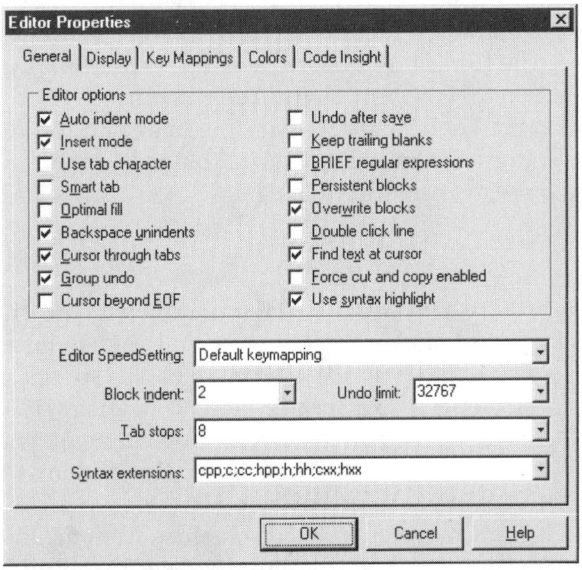

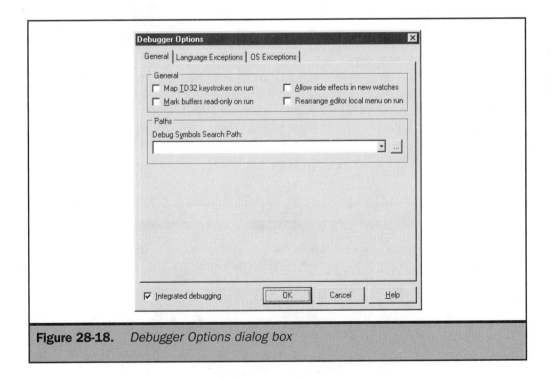

Figure 28-17. *Editor Options dialog box*

Figure 28-18. *Debugger Options dialog box*

The **Repository** adds, removes, and renames pages in the Object Repository. This setting affects how C++ Builder functions or behaves when starting a new project or creating a new form. The **Configure Tools** option opens the Tool Option dialog box. You can configure which tools appear on the **Tools** menu.

The last section on the **Tools** menu contains the **Image Editor**. C++ Builder comes with its own image editor for manipulating icons, bitmaps, resource files, and cursor files, as well as the component resource files.

Help

Highlighting the **Help** entry activates the **Help** pull-down menu. The top section of this menu accesses the built-in help files that come with C++ Builder. The **C++ Builder Help** option displays a standard help file with more details about C++ Builder. The **C++ Builder Tools** option opens up a specific help file dealing with tools that are built into the IDE. This file focuses on the Image Editor; depending on your version of C++ Builder, however, it may contain other items as well. The **Windows SDK** option opens the Windows Win32 Developer's Reference help file.

The next section has additional help that is obtained from the Internet. These are links to **Borland Home Page**, **Borland Community Page**, **C++ Builder Home Page**, **C++ Builder Developer Support**, and **C++ Builder Direct**. If you have an Internet connection, you can use these Internet links to obtain additional help.

The last item is the **About** option, which displays the version of C++ Builder.

Toolbars

The row of icons immediately below the menu bar is the toolbar. There are several toolbars, as shown in Figure 28-19.

If you look closely at the figure, you will notice that there are two vertical bars that are used for separating the various toolbars. If you right-click in the area of the toolbars, it displays a pop-up menu of the different toolbars that are available. As you can see in Figure 28-20, there are six available toolbars: **Standard**, **View**, **Debug**, **Custom**, **Component Palette**, and **Desktops**. You can customize the toolbars by selecting **Customize** from the pop-up menu.

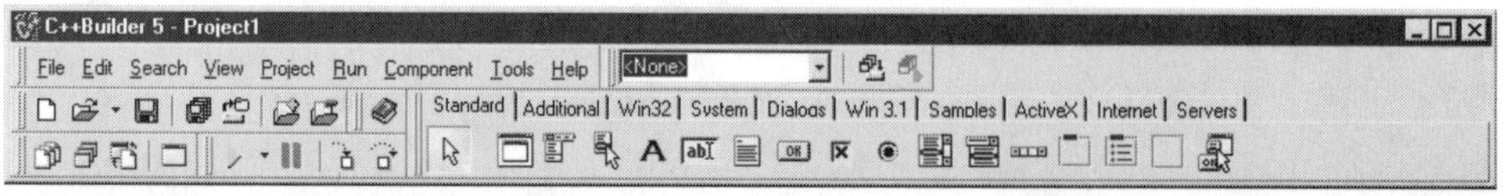

Figure 28-19.   *Toolbars*

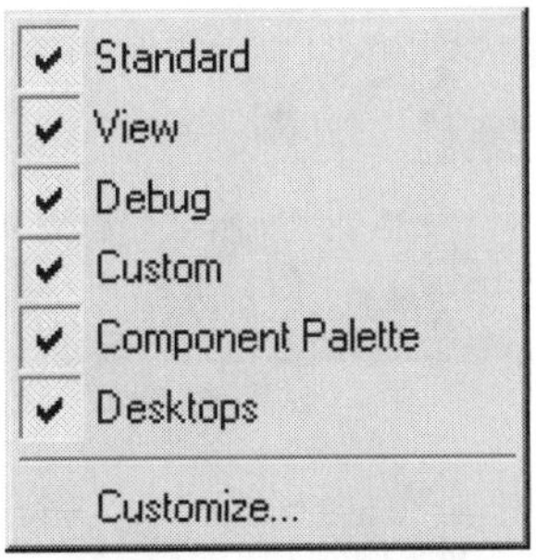

Figure 28-20. *Toolbars*

Object Inspector Window

The **Object Inspector** window is a detailed look at the properties associated with the active object. This window is the connection between the appearance of the application and the code that runs. This is where design-time properties for any object or component are set or modified. Events can also be added or modified. The drop-down selector at the top of this window contains a list of the individual components that are on the active form and shows the object type of the selected component.

The **Object Inspector** window contains two tabs: **Properties** and **Events**. The **Properties** tab displays a list of available properties and their associated values. This list will change dynamically for each object as the object is selected. For instance, a list box and a text box will have different properties. The **Events** tab, like the **Properties** tab, is tied directly to the selected object. This list contains the available events that the selected object can trigger. The list of events will change depending on the object chosen.

Form Window

This window is the artist's canvas. It starts when the IDE starts and presents a blank form. All objects are placed on a form. You can drag and drop objects on this form to build an application. Most of the components used for building an application exist on the **Component Palette** toolbar. As you can see in Figure 28-21, there are a lot of available components. Many are discussed in Chapter 29.

Code (Unit) Window

When the IDE first starts, this window is almost entirely hidden behind the form window. You can bring this window forward by either selecting the bottom portion

Figure 28-21.   *Component Palette*

of the window, which contains the status bar, or by **View | Window List** and select the unit window. This window is a text file window. All program coding is done in this window. Unit windows are also called *code windows*.

Using Speed Menus

C++ Builder includes special menus called *SpeedMenus* that are activated by pressing the right mouse button when it is over certain items. SpeedMenus are also called *context menus*. These menus can be activated when using any of the main windows defined by the IDE. For example, if you are in the Form window and you press the right mouse button, a SpeedMenu appears giving you more options for the form. SpeedMenus save several keystrokes and are generally quite useful.

Using Context-Sensitive Help

The IDE contains *context-sensitive* help that allows you to obtain information about any feature of C++ Builder by simply pressing the F1 key. This means it displays help information that relates to what you are doing at the time. More specifically, it displays information that relates to the current focus of activity. For example, if you highlight **Save** under the **File** option in the menu bar and then activate the help system by pressing F1, you will see information about the **Save** option. Also, if the cursor is positioned over the name of a library function, keyword, or preprocessor directive, pressing F1 gives you information about that item.

Before moving on, you might want to try the context-sensitive help feature on your own. As you will see, it is a powerful aid.

The
Complete
Reference

Borland
C++
Builder

Chapter 29

Developing Applications
Using the IDE

s explained in Chapter 28, C++ Builder's IDE (integrated development environment) is designed to streamline the development of applications. In this regard, it succeeds admirably. Using the IDE, you can design, construct, manage, and maintain all types of applications, be they large or small. Frankly, C++ Builder's IDE is one of the best there is.

Although logically organized, its power and sophistication can make the IDE seem quite intimidating to newcomers. If you have never used it before, it can be hard to know where to start or what to do next. To solve this problem, this chapter walks through the creation of two projects. The first is a console-based program, such as those shown throughout this book. The second is a Windows application. Of the two, the Windows application is the more challenging.

The IDE discussed here is the IDE that comes with the Standard Edition of C++ Builder. There is a Professional Edition available as well that offers the same functionality but a wider variety of components and objects for developing specialized applications. Most applications can be managed and created using the Standard Edition.

Before creating either application, we will begin by taking a close look at the types of projects that C++ Builder can support, and the various components that can be incorporated into a project. To follow along, start C++ Builder now.

Types of Applications

Several types of applications can be created with the IDE. To create an application, you will first select **File | New**. Doing so activates the New Items dialog box shown in Figure 29-1. There are five tabs that can be selected, and each tab offers different projects or other objects that you can create using the IDE. Let's examine the contents of each tab now.

New

The New tab is shown by default. Table 29-1 shows a list of the applications in this tab.

When you are creating or adding new files to an existing project, the IDE keeps all the code windows together within one main window. Tabs separate the individual code windows, as shown in Figure 29-2. The main window in this figure has four text files opened. Clicking a tab brings that code window forward. That the IDE keeps similar items together makes it easy to handle multiple code units.

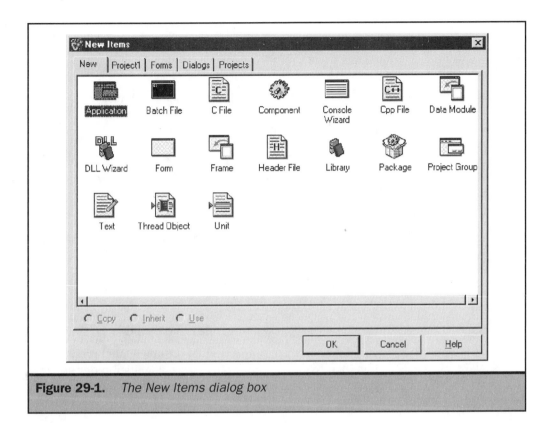

Figure 29-1.   *The New Items dialog box*

Application	Creates a new Windows application. An application consists of a form, code windows, and a project file. Any .c, .cpp, .h, or .hpp files are called *units*. The project file will have an extension of .bpr.
Batch File	Creates a batch file.

Table 29-1.   *Applications Created with the IDE*

.C File	Creates a new .c file.
Component	Creates a new component or object.
Console Wizard	Creates a new DOS-based console application. This wizard will be used later in this chapter to help develop a console application.
CPP File	Creates a new .cpp file.
Data Module	Creates a data module. This is a special form for organizing different data modules within one tool.
DLL Wizard	Creates a DLL file or application.
Form	Creates a blank form for the current project.
Frame	Creates a new frame for the current project.
Header File	Creates a new .h or .hpp file.
Library	Creates a library file or .lib file.
Package	Creates a new package and adds it to the project.
Project Group	Creates a *super* project group that groups related projects together. By having multiple projects together in one super group, you can create all the projects with one command.
Text	Creates a new text file.
Thread Object	Creates a new threaded object.
Unit	Creates and adds a new unit to the project. A unit is made up of both the .cpp file and its header file.

Table 29-1.   *Applications Created with the IDE* (continued)

Project1

The next tab in the New Items dialog box is the Project1 tab. This window shows the forms that are part of the current project.

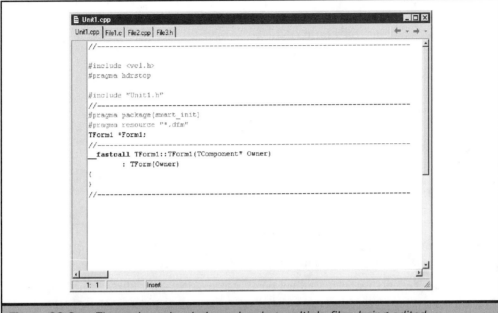

Figure 29-2. The main code window, showing multiple files being edited

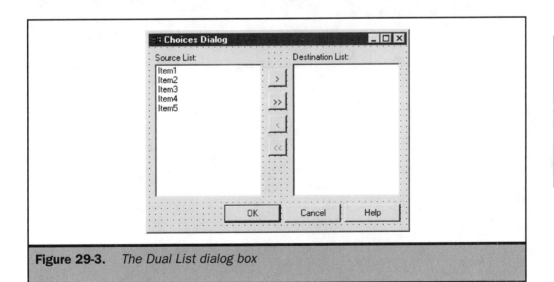

Figure 29-3. The Dual List dialog box

Forms

The Forms tab contains three forms that can be included in a project. Table 29-2 lists these available forms.

Dialogs

The Dialogs tab contains five items, which are summarized in Table 29-3.

Projects

The Projects tab contains four types of projects. These projects are summarized in Table 29-4.

About Box	Creates an About box for the project. This dialog box contains all the basic items that appear in a normal About box.
Dual List Box	Creates a dual list box, as shown in Figure 29-3. Again, all the basic information items or components are created for you; they just need to be configured.
Tabbed Pages	Creates a prebuilt dialog box for handling multiple tabs at the top.

Table 29-2. *Forms Tab New Items*

Dialog With Help (Horizontal)	A basic dialog box that contains the OK, Cancel, and Help buttons at the bottom of the dialog box.
Dialog With Help (Vertical)	A basic dialog box that contains the OK, Cancel, and Help buttons along the right side of the dialog box.
Password Dialog	A basic dialog box for handling passwords. Text typed in is shown as asterisks or hidden.
Standard Dialog (Horizontal)	A basic dialog box that contains the OK and Cancel buttons along the bottom of the dialog box.
Standard Dialog (Vertical)	A basic dialog box that contains the OK and Cancel buttons along the right side of the dialog box.

Table 29-3. *Available Dialog Boxes*

MDI Application	This is a standard multiple document interface (MDI) application. These applications are complex and require more designing or planning because they can spawn separate client windows within the main window of the application.
SDI Application	This is a single document interface or SDI application. This application shows only a single window.
Win2000 Client Application	Creates a client application for Windows 2000.
Win95/98 Logo Application	Creates an application that meets the minimum requirements for a computer running Windows 95 or 98.

Table 29-4. *Preconfigured Projects for the IDE*

The Component Palette

Once you have selected the type of application to develop, you will populate it with items selected from the Component Palette. These are the items that are available for building Windows applications. (You won't use the Component Palette for console applications.) The objects in the Component Palette support the Windows graphical user interface (GUI) portion of an application. As you will see, to use a component, you simply drag and drop it to the main form of your project. The Component Palette is shown in Figure 29-4.

To see the name of each component, move the mouse cursor over an icon and wait a few seconds. A tool tip appears showing the name of the component. The following sections present a brief overview of the components.

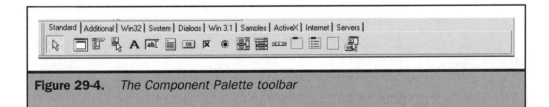

Figure 29-4. *The Component Palette toolbar*

Standard Components

The Standard Component tab is shown in Figure 29-4. It contains Windows control components (shown left to right in the order that they appear on the tab).

Pointer	This pointer is part of all the other tabs as well. You select this component when you want to select components on the form.
Frames	Displays a dialog box with a list of frames that are in the project.
MainMenu	This component creates a main menu bar. This item adds a main menu to your application.
PopupMenu	Similar to the MainMenu component, this creates a pop-up menu with a list of functions.
Label	Creates a label control.
Edit	Creates a text editing box.
Memo	Creates a larger editing area. Similar to the Edit component; however, this component allows for multiple lines.
Button	Creates a push button component, also known as a command button.
CheckBox	Creates a check box button.
RadioButton	Creates a radio button option.
ListBox	Creates a list box of choices
ComboBox	Creates a combo box, which is like a list box and an edit box. Data can be typed into this box, or a selection can be made from the drop-down list.
ScrollBar	Creates a scrollbar component for scrolling through a range of values.
GroupBox	Creates a container for grouping similar items on a form.
RadioGroup	Creates a container for grouping radio option boxes together.
Panel	Creates a panel for holding other objects, such as toolbars and a status bar.
ActionList	Creates a collection of actions that your program can use in responding to user events.

Additional Components

The Additional Component tab contains specialized windows controls, as shown in Figure 29-5.

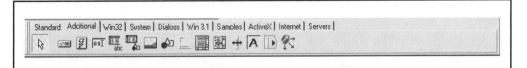

Figure 29-5.   *Additional components*

The components are explained here:

BitBtn   Creates a button with an icon as the face.

SpeedButton   Creates a button that graphically displays its state, such as selected, unselected, on, or off.

MaskEdit   Creates a maskable edit box. This type of edit box allows a mask to be set that enforces a special format, such as phone numbers or social security numbers.

StringGrid   Creates a grid that displays strings in a spreadsheet-like manner.

DrawGrid   Creates a grid that displays data in a spreadsheet-like manner.

Image   Creates a graphic component that holds a bitmap, icon, or metafile.

Shape   Creates a component that allows drawing of geometric shapes.

Bevel   A three-dimensional line or box.

ScrollBox   A container that displays resizable scrollbars.

CheckListBox   This is a list box that contains a check box next to each item.

Splitter   Creates a splitter, a line that allows you to resize controls at run time.

StaticText   A text box, like the Label component, that has its own handle.

ControlBar   Creates a layout tabbed area for docking toolbars.

ApplicationEvents   Creates an association between events and forms.

Win32 Components

The Win32 tab shows the user interface controls, as shown in Figure 29-6.

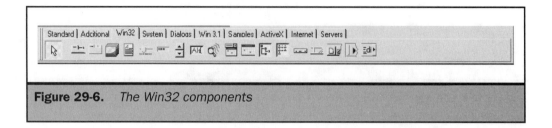

Figure 29-6. *The Win32 components*

These components are briefly explained here.

TabControl	Creates a tabbed page or notebook-like component.
PageControl	Creates multiple dialog box components.
ImageList	Creates an image collection list. Helps organize and manage all your images for your project in one location.
RichEdit	Creates a rich text memo component. This type of edit box supports more text properties, such as fonts, typeface, size, and colors.
TrackBar	Creates a vertical or horizontal track bar. A track bar is used as an adjuster-type control such as a zoom bar for zooming in and out of images and other items.
ProgressBar	Creates a progress bar. Most installation programs use this type of bar for showing progress of the installation activity.
UpDown	Creates an up and down button for incrementing and decrementing values.
HotKey	Creates a hotkey attachment to any component. Hotkeys are key combinations like CTRL-C, which is used for copying the selected item to the clipboard.
Animate	Displays an animation control window for managing and displaying AVI files.
DateTimePicker	Creates a list box for entering dates or times.
MonthCalendar	Creates a month calendar for showing and handling months.
TreeView	Creates a control that is indented and displayed in a tree fashion. Windows Explorer is an example of a tree view.
ListView	Creates a component that displays lists in a column.
HeaderControl	Creates a header above columns object.

StatusBar   Creates a status bar component that is usually displayed at the bottom of a window.

ToolBar   Creates a component that lets you manage buttons and other objects. This is usually placed right below the main menu bar.

CoolBar   Creates a bar that contains controls that can be moved and resized.

PageScroller   Creates a component that holds other components in a client area. These components can be scrolled either vertically or horizontally.

System Components

The System tab contains system control objects, as shown in Figure 29-7.
The components are briefly explained here:

Timer   Creates a nonvisual timer component. A nonvisual component is one that does not display anything when the application runs. This component can trigger events according to the system timer.

PaintBox   Creates a rectangle area with boundaries for painting.

MediaPlayer   Creates a VCR-style panel for handling multimedia files.

OleContainer   Creates an Object Linking and Embedding (OLE) area.

DdeClientConv   Creates an object where the application can connect to DDE servers.

DdeClientItem   Creates an object that contains the data for the DDE client to send to the server.

DdeServerConv   Creates a DDE server connection to a DDE client.

DdeServerItem   Creates the DDE server data to send during a DDE connection.

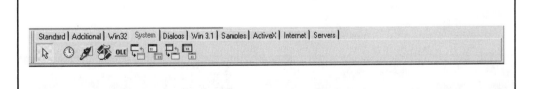

Figure 29-7.   *System components*

Dialogs Components

The Dialogs tab contains Windows' common dialog boxes, like Open and Save As, as shown in Figure 29-8.

The components are briefly explained here.

OpenDialog	Displays the Open dialog box.
SaveDialog	Displays the Save dialog box.
OpenPictureDialog	This component is identical to the OpenDialog component, except that it shows only graphic files in the open box and an area for previewing the image.
SavePictureDialog	This component is identical to the SaveDialog component, except that it saves graphic files. It also has an area for previewing the image.
FontDialog	Displays the font dialog box, where the font type, size, and style information are selected.
ColorDialog	Displays the color dialog box, where color information can be selected.
PrintDialog	Displays the print dialog box, where printing information is selected, such as a range of pages.
PrinterSetupDialog	Displays the printer setup dialog box for changing printer settings.
FindDialog	Displays the find dialog box for searching for a string.
ReplaceDialog	Displays the replace dialog box for finding and replacing strings.

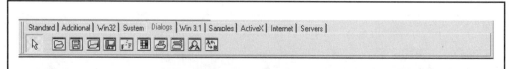

Figure 29-8. *The Dialogs components*

Win 3.1 Components

The Win 3.1 tab contains components that allow for backward compatibility with Windows 3.1 systems; they are shown in Figure 29-9.

The components are briefly explained here.

TabSet	Creates a component that contains tabs, like a notebook.
Outline	Creates a component that shows data in outline format.
TabbedNotebook	Creates a notebook-type tabbed page. The page contains multiple tabs, each with its own set of controls.
Notebook	Creates a multiple page notebook.
Header	Creates a multisection area for showing data. Each region or section can be resized.
FileListBox	Creates a scrolling list box of available files in the current directory.
DirectoryListBox	Creates a scrollable list of the available directories in a tree format for the current drive.
DriveComboBox	Creates a scrolling list box showing the available drives.
FilterComboBox	Creates a filter box where the file types can be specified, like the All Files (*.*) filter that is commonly seen.

Samples Components

The Samples tab contains customized, prebuilt components. These sample components can be added into the Component Palette as another tab. C++ Builder includes the source code for these samples on the C++ Builder CD. The sample control components are shown in Figure 29-10.

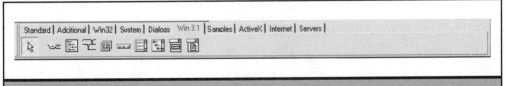

Figure 29-9. *The Win 3.1 components*

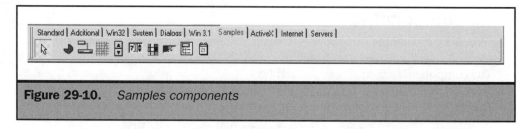

Figure 29-10.   *Samples components*

These components are, for the most part, self-explanatory. For more details on these sample components, see the source code under the **\CBuilder5\Examples\Controls\Source** directory.

Pie	Creates a pie chart.
TrayIcon	Creates a tray icon application.
Performance Graph	Creates a performance graph chart.
CSpinButton	CSpinButton component example.
CSpinEdit	CSpin edit control.
CColorGrid	Color Grid example.
CGauge	Gauge sample.
CDirectoryOutline	Directory outline example.
CCalendar	Calendar example.

ActiveX Components

The ActiveX tab contains ActiveX objects, as shown in Figure 29-11. The components are briefly explained here.

Chartfx	Helps create charts.
VSSpell	Helps create a spell checker program.
F1Book	Helps create a spreadsheet.
VtChart	Helps create 3D charts.

Standard | Additional | Win32 | System | Dialogs | Win 3.1 | Samples | ActiveX | Internet | Servers |

Figure 29-11.   *ActiveX Objects*

| Standard | Additional | Win32 | System | Dialogs | Win 3.1 | Samples | ActiveX | Internet | Servers |

Figure 29-12.   *The Internet components*

Internet Components

The Internet tab contains components that help create Web server applications; it is shown in Figure 29-12.

The components are briefly explained here.

ClientSocket   Creates a TCP/IP client. This component allows you to set the connection and manage it.

ServerSocket   Creates a TCP/IP server application. This application will listen for requests from other machines.

Servers Components

The Servers tab contains the Visual Component Library (VCL) wrappers for COM servers. These components are shown in Figure 29-13.

These components are self-explanatory based on their icons. As you can see, there are numerous wrappers available for various Microsoft Word objects, Microsoft Excel objects, and Microsoft Powerpoint objects, just to name a few. When a component is executed, the Microsoft application associated with it is executed.

Creating a Console Application

As explained, there are two general categories of programs that C++ Builder can create: console applications and Windows applications. Here you will learn to create, compile, and run console applications. (A Windows application is developed later in this chapter.)

Throughout this book, the code examples have been console applications. A console application does not use the Windows graphical user interface. Instead, a console application runs in a DOS session. Prior to the creation of Windows several years ago, all applications were console programs. Today, most commercial programs are Windows applications. However, console applications are still widely used for three main reasons. First, they make excellent teaching examples. As you may know, a Windows program contains a large amount of code that handles the interface to Windows. Such a program could not be used to demonstrate the essentials of a programming language. Second, many utility programs, such as file filters, are still coded as console applications because they do not benefit from a GUI environment. Finally, sometimes a console program is

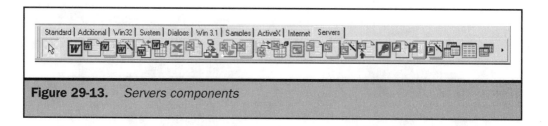

Figure 29-13.   *Servers components*

used to prototype the non-GUI portion of an application. Whatever the reason, nearly all programmers today still use and create console-based programs.

There are two ways of creating and building console applications: using the IDE or using the command line compiler. Even though this chapter is about the IDE, both methods are described because many (perhaps most) programmers use the command line compiler to compile console-based programs.

One last point: The instructions for compiling a console application given here can be used to compile any of the example programs shown earlier in this book. Just follow the instructions, substituting the program that you want to compile.

Using the IDE to Create a Console Application

When compiling console programs, such as those shown in Parts One, Two, and Three of this book, you will use the Console Wizard to set up C++ Builder to create console applications. This is necessary because by default, C++ Builder is set up to create Windows applications.

To start the Console Wizard, select **File** I **New** and then double-click the Console Wizard icon, as shown in Figure 29-14. This wizard helps configure the console application. The Console Wizard dialog box appears, as shown in Figure 29-15.

Let's take a look at the options. **Source Type** has two options, C or C++. The **Source Type** option sets the source code for the main module of the application. For this example, you will use C++. The other options available are **Use VCL**, **Multi Threaded**, and **Console Application**.

The **Use VCL** option enables the application to use objects from the Visual Component Library (VCL). This option can be used only in C++ applications. If chosen, it will include the **vcl.h** include file and will adjust the startup code and linker to use VCL objects.

The **Multi Threaded** option is for more than one thread of execution. This option must be specified if the **Use VCL** option is checked.

The **Console Application** option tells the IDE to create a console program.

The **Specify project source** option lets you select an existing source file, C or C++, to be used for the console application. As you will see, this option is useful for compiling the sample programs shown in this book.

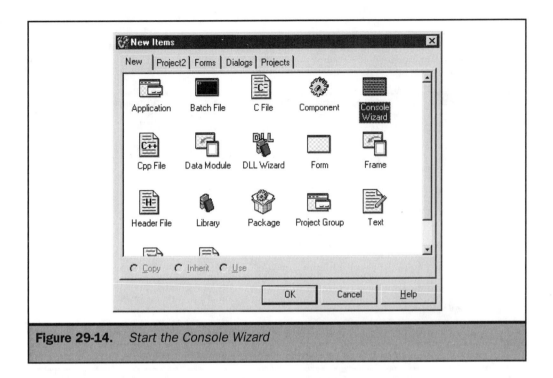

Figure 29-14. *Start the Console Wizard*

Select the **C++** option and the **Console Application** check box. Click **OK** to create a skeleton console application.

Figure 29-16 shows what the IDE looks like with the skeleton console application. As you can see, the Object Inspector window is blank and the only other window opened is the code window, labeled Unit1.cpp.

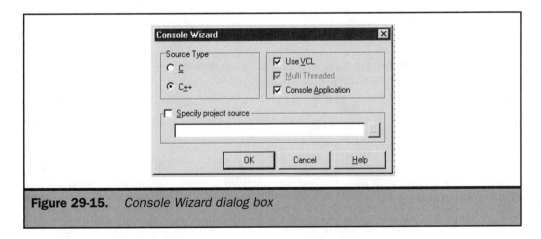

Figure 29-15. *Console Wizard dialog box*

THE C++ BUILDER INTEGRATED DEVELOPMENT ENVIRONMENT

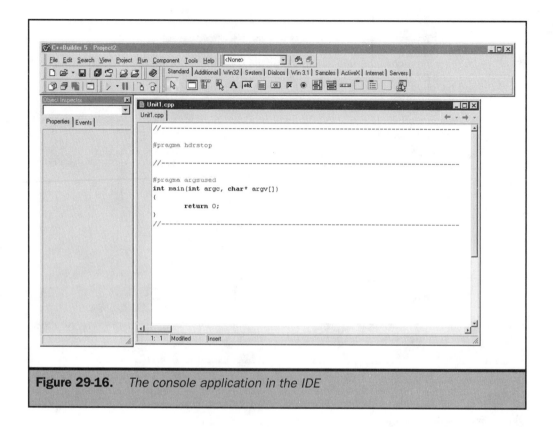

Figure 29-16. *The console application in the IDE*

The code window should look familiar to you. It is just a text editor with the basic C++ skeleton. Two lines of code have been added with which you are probably unfamiliar. The first is

```
#pragma hdrstop
```

which stops the list of header files available for precompiling. All include files listed above this line are eligible to be precompiled. (Precompiled headers save compilation time.) In the sample program, you will put other headers above this line. The line

```
#pragma argsused
```

disables a sometimes annoying compiler warning message. This message is generated when a variable is used in the code but not assigned any value. This **#pragma** disables this warning message:

Parameter *name* is never used in function *func-name*

It affects only the function that it precedes. It is included by C++ Builder to prevent a warning message if the parameters to **main( )** are not used.

At this point, the console application is ready for code. Like all first-time projects, it will just display a message. Since you are building a C++ program, you will use C++ coding syntax and language. Add the lines shown in bold into the code window.

```
//-----------------------------------------------

#include <iostream>
#pragma hdrstop
using namespace std;

//-----------------------------------------------

#pragma argsused
int main(int argc, char* argv[])
{
  cout << "My first console application!" << endl;
  return 0;
}
//-----------------------------------------------
```

Once those three lines have been added, save the program. Do this by selecting **File | Save All**. As with all projects, you should have a folder in which to store the project files. Browse to the location or folder where you want these files placed. If you need to create a new folder, right-click an empty spot inside the Save As dialog box and select **New | Folder** from the pop-up menu. Just remember where you put the project. You will need to locate the **.exe** file in order to execute the application. Name the source code **Firstcon.cpp** and the project **Firstcon.bpr**. These are the only two files saved. You are now ready to build this application.

You can run the program directly from the IDE by selecting **Run | Run**; since this application is small, however, the file will compile and execute too quickly to see the results. The best approach is to select **Project | Build**. The IDE compiles and links the code to create an executable.

To execute the console application, go to a command prompt and then to the folder where the project was saved. There you will find a **Firstcon.exe** file. Type **Firstcon** at the command line and you will see this result:

```
My first console application!
```

While this is a very simple example, the process of using the wizard and entering source code in the code window will be the same no matter how large the console application.

Compiling the Sample Programs in This Book

In the preceding example, you entered the program code by hand into a console-based skeleton provided by C++ Builder. However, often you will want to compile a file that is already existent, without having to type it in again. This is especially important if you are using the program files that accompany this book. These files can be downloaded from **www.osborne.com**.

To compile an already existent C++ file, simply create a console project as just shown. When the Console Wizard appears, select either C or C++ for the source type, depending upon the type of the program. Then, check **Specify project source** and then enter the name of the file in the edit box. This causes the file to loaded and made into the source file for the project. To try the program, compile and run it as described in the preceding section.

If you are working your way through the examples in this book, there is no reason to create a new console project for each one. Instead, when you are done with one example, just remove its source file from the project and then add the next program. To remove a source file, select the **Project** main menu entry and then select **Remove from Project**. You will see the Remove from Project dialog box. Simply highlight the file you want to remove and then click OK.

To add the new source file, select **Project | Add to Project**. This activates the Add to Project dialog box, which lets you select the file that you want to add. Once you have selected the desired file, you can compile and run the program. Thus, if you are working through the examples in a chapter, you can simply use the same project to run them by deleting the one you are through with and adding the next.

Using the Command Line Compiler

As mentioned, when working with console-based programs, it is often easier to use the command line compiler provided by C++ Builder. To execute the command line compiler, first open any DOS window and enter **bcc32** on the command line. The syntax for using the command line compiler is

bcc32 [*options*] *sourcefile* [*sourcefile2 ... sourcefileN*]

where *sourcefile* is the name of the file you are compiling and *options* are special options that affect how the compiler compiles your code. For instance, the **–c** option causes the compiler to just compile the source code. It will not link or create an executable. This option is useful if you want to check for syntax errors. To see a complete list of the available options, type **bcc32** at the command line. This lists all the options and provides a brief description of each.

The source file can be either a C or a C++ file. Thus, it can use either a **.c** extension or a **.cpp** extension. If no extension is given, the compiler first looks at the source file in the existing directory and if the file is found and the extension is **.cpp**, the compiler compiles it as a **.cpp** file. If the extension is anything other than **.cpp**, the compiler treats the file as if it had a **.c** extension. The *sourcefile2 ... sourcefileN* arguments are optional and are used when compiling multiple source files. In general, it is best to explicitly specify the extension to avoid confusion. Also, as explained in Part One, C programs must be compiled as C programs, so be sure to use the proper file extension.

Here is an example. To compile the file **Firtscon.cpp** created earlier, go to the directory in which the file is stored and enter in the following line:

```
bcc32 firstcon.cpp
```

The command line compiler displays the following information:

```
Borland C++ 5.5.1 for Win32 Copyright (c) 1993, 2000 Borland
Firstcon.cpp:
Turbo Incremental Link 5.00 Copyright (c) 1997, 2000 Borland
```

The compiler generates a **Firstcon.exe** file that can be executed by typing **Firstcon** on the command line.

The command line compiler can also compile multiple source files. For example, this line compiles and links the files **file1.cpp**, **file2.cpp**, and **file3.cpp**:

```
bcc32 file1.cpp file2.cpp file3.cpp
```

All the files on the preceding line are compiled first. If there are no errors, the compiler then links the object files together to create the executable. When multiple filenames are listed, the first filename in the list, **file1** in this example, is the name that is used for the executable. In this example, the executable is named **file1.exe**. If you want to change the executable name generated by the compiler, use the **–e** option. For instance, the preceding example would be rewritten like this:

```
bcc32 -enewname file1.cpp file2.cpp file3.cpp
```

When the compiler is done, the executable file will be named **newname.exe**.

Today, with the dominance of Microsoft Windows, most applications are written for a window environment and not for the command line. This brings us to the next sample application, a small address book Windows application.

Creating a Simple Windows Application

Although you can use the IDE to create console applications, as just described, its main use is to develop Windows applications. As you may know, Windows is a challenging programming environment. Windows programs tend to be large, contain many files, and use many resources. The main role of the IDE is to manage this complexity. As you will see, C++ Builder makes the sometimes difficult task of creating a Windows application as easy as possible.

Windows programming is a very large topic. A complete description of Windows would fill several books. Thus, it is not possible to teach Windows programming in this book. What we will do, though, is describe how to use the IDE to build a Windows application. Because the IDE provides a "point and click" interface to Windows programming, you can follow along even if you are a novice Windows programmer. Of course, to develop your own Windows applications, you will need a thorough understanding of Windows programming.

In this section, you will build a simple Windows application that allows you to enter in the name and address of a person. This is a simple Windows application that demonstrates these window elements:

Menus	Dialog Boxes	Toolbars
Images	Labels	Edit Boxes

These are the core elements that are part of nearly every Windows program.

The following sections work through the creation of the address book application, one step at a time. Because each step depends upon the preceding one, don't try to jump ahead. Just work through the example in the order presented.

Preliminary Steps

Before starting to work, it will be useful to see what the final goal looks like. This will help make sense of the various steps that you will be performing. Figure 29-17 shows the final outcome of the sample application. Although this application looks fairly sophisticated, the IDE does most of the work, and it is easier to create than you might at first suspect. You will use three easy-to-use tools to build the address book application: the **MainMenu**, **ActionList**, and **ImageList** components. These are the three critical pieces that streamline the design and development.

Whenever creating applications, it is a good idea to create a folder where you can save all your project files. So before beginning, use Windows Explorer to locate a place to store the project. Create a folder, and call it **AddressBook**.

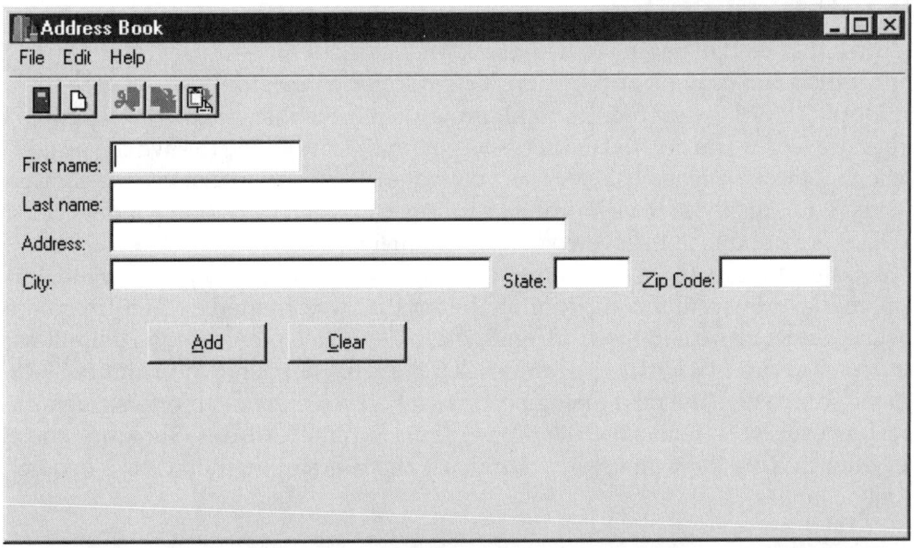

Figure 29-17. *Address book application*

Let's begin by defining the functionality incorporated into the address book. Its elements are shown here (not in any particular order).

Action	Description and Usage
Exit	Exits program.
New	Clears all fields and gets ready for a new data record.
Cut	Cuts text.
Copy	Copies text to the clipboard.
Paste	Pastes text from the clipboard into the fields.
Help | About	Every application should show its name and version.
Add	In a real application, this function should add the record into a database, but for this example, it will just display the information entered into a message box.
Clear	Empties the data fields.

Create the Application

Start the IDE. The IDE begins with a blank project that you will use as the starting point for the address book application. The first thing you should do is save the default project files. By saving the blank project, you establish the project's path to the appropriate folder you created earlier, and you make it possible to save the project by just clicking the Save icon. This way, as you make progress you can use the shortcut key, CTRL-S, to quickly save new changes. In general, when developing a project using the IDE, it is a good idea to save your work frequently.

Next, select **File | Save All**. Before clicking the default name given to the unit or source file, browse to the appropriate folder that was created earlier. If you are following along, browse to the **AddressBook** folder. Once there, use the default name shown for the **.cpp** file, **Unit1.cpp**, and click **Save**. This step, shown in Figure 29-18, saves the source file. The next dialog box asks for a project name. It offers a default name; however, you should use the project name, so enter **AddressBook.bpr** and click **Save**. After making these changes, you can use the shortcut method CTRL-S to quickly save any changes.

Building the GUI Form

Now that the foundation of the application is ready, you can begin to create the form. Resize the application to match Figure 29-17. The title of the form is **Form1** by default.

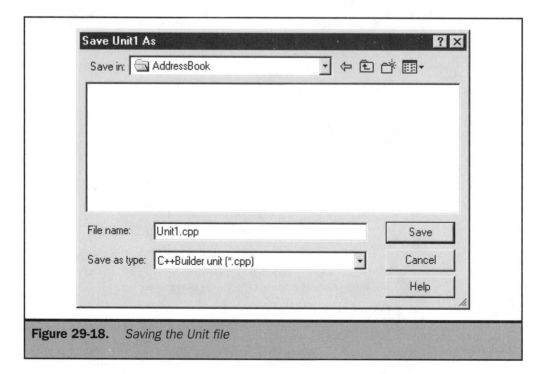

Figure 29-18.   *Saving the Unit file*

Let's change the title to **AddressBook**, which reflects the name of the application. You will use the Object Inspector, shown in Figure 29-19, to change properties of objects.

The Object Inspector contains the property settings for the selected object. In this case, the main form is the only selected item. The left column of the Object Inspector shows the property name, and the right column shows the values for each property. Change the Caption value from **Form1** to **Address Book**. To do so, select the value field to the right of the Caption. Enter the new form name and watch the form change the title to your new name.

Now let's add the fields to the form. Everything you need to build the basic form is located on the Standard tab on the toolbar. Locate the Label component. There are two ways of getting a component onto the form. One way is to double-click the component. When you do this, a default component is placed on the form. You can then drag this component anywhere you like and change its property with the Object Inspector. The other method for getting components onto the form is to select the component by single-clicking it. This activates the component. Now move the mouse to a location on the form. Click and hold down the left mouse button. While holding down the left mouse button, drag the mouse out; it creates an enlarged area that grows as the mouse moves. When you release the mouse button, a component is created. Use whatever method you feel comfortable using.

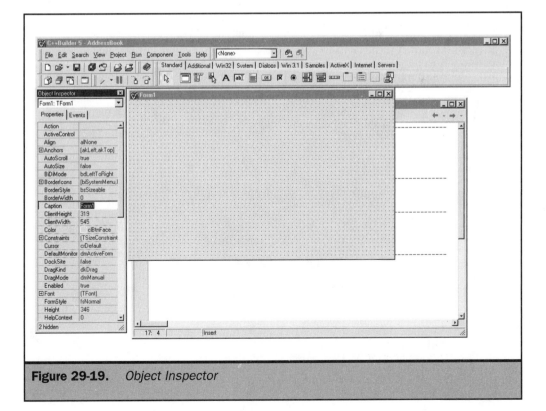

Figure 29-19.   *Object Inspector*

Adding Label and Edit Components

Now, add the labels and edit components required by the application. It does not really matter how these get entered, just as long as they match Figure 29-17. Here is a list of the items to add to the form along with their properties. When adding these items, you will need to change their properties to the values shown here. (The tab order will need to be set only if the labels and edit boxes are not laid out in the order shown.)

Component	Property	Value
Label	Caption	First name:
	Name	lblFirstName
Edit	Name	txtFirstName
	Text	(erase default value)
	TabOrder	0
Label	Caption	Last Name:
	Name	lblLastName
Edit	Name	txtLastName
	Text	(erase default value)
	TabOrder	1
Label	Caption	Address:
	Name	lblAddress
Edit	Name	txtAddress
	Text	(erase default value)
	TabOrder	2
Label	Caption	City:
	Name	lblCity

Component	Property	Value
Edit	Name	txtCity
	Text	(erase default value)
	TabOrder	3
Label	Caption	State:
	Name	lblState
Edit	Name	txtState
	Text	(erase default value)
	TabOrder	4
Label	Caption	Zip Code:
	Name	lblZipCode
Edit	Name	txtZipCode
	Text	(erase default value)
	TabOrder	5

Add all the preceding components to your form. The Edit component is the box that is white; it is where data will be entered. The Edit boxes should always go to the right of the Label. To arrange the components more easily, you can select multiple items by holding down the SHIFT key while you click the component. You can then use **Edit | Align** to help align the items.

Let's examine these properties before going forward.

Label Components

The Label component has many properties. However, in most cases, the only property of concern is the **Caption** property. The value of this property is shown when the application runs. When a Label component is added to a form, it has a default caption **Label1** or **Label***N*, where *N* is the next number in the labeling scheme. For example, the first label component added will be Label1, the next label component will be Label2, and so forth. So for each label component, the caption property will need to be changed to match the prompt string. Also, you will notice in the preceding list that the **Name** property is changed. The **Name** property is the internal variable name that the application uses to access this property and its value. While Label components do not generally change, giving them an internal name makes it easier to identify them later in the project. In the example, all Label component names begin with the prefix of **lbl** (short for label) followed by the name.

Edit Components

The Edit component handles user input. Like the Label component, this object also has many properties. Most of the default properties for an Edit component are okay to use. The three properties that will change for the program are the **Name**, **Text**, and **TabOrder** properties.

The **Name** property is the internal name of the item that the program will need to know in order to retrieve the information. In this example, Edit component names begins with **txt** (short for Text field). For example, the First name box will have an edit box that is named **txtFirstName**.

The **Text** property, by default, displays whatever is in the **Name** value. Since you want the box to be empty, you will need to remove these values. Just click the value box beside the **Text** property and delete the characters in the box.

TabOrder reflects the order in which the Edit components were added to the form. If the Edit components were added to the form in the order indicated previously, then the **TabOrder** property will be fine. Be sure to check this, though.

Once all the fields have been entered on the form and aligned the way you want them, save the project. Then, try the application by selecting **Run | Run**. After the project compiles, you should see a simple window displayed with your components on it. Try the TAB key to see how the cursor moves. This tests the **TabOrder** property to make sure the cursor will tab to the correct fields. Next, type information into the edit boxes. They should work too. Now, exit the application.

Using the ActionList and ImageList Components

Two of the most powerful components of the IDE are the **ActionList** and **ImageList** components. These two items add a great deal of flexibility to the application. They also contribute to the ability to create this application quickly.

ActionList Component

The **ActionList** component is on the Standard tab. It is the last item to the far right. If you are not sure which one it is, move the mouse cursor over the last icon and let it sit for a few seconds. A tool tip will appear to let you know the component's name. To add an **ActionList** component to the form, double-click it. It does not matter where this component is placed on the form. This is a *nonvisual* component, which means that when the application executes, this component does not display anything or is not visible.

> **Note**
>
> *The ActionList is a component that stores all the available actions that you want to use in the application. Once the actions are placed in this list, they can be selected easily and used in multiple events. The key is to place the actions you want in one location and then apply the action as needed to any object that accepts actions.*

To add actions into the **ActionList**, double-click the **ActionList** component. This action brings up the form and the action list window, as shown in Figure 29-20.

The **Editing Form1->ActionList1** window shows two columns. The left column shows the categories that you will create, and the right window shows the actions associated with each category.

There are two types of actions that can be added into this window, **New Action** and **New Standard Action**. The **New Action** creates your own action. The **New Standard Action** uses existing prebuilt actions, like **Cut**, **Copy**, and **Paste**, to name a few. These are standard window functions that everyone has come to expect in any Windows application.

The actions that you are going to add will be tied to an item on the menu bar and an icon on the toolbar. For this example, you will implement the actions as shown in the Table 29-5.

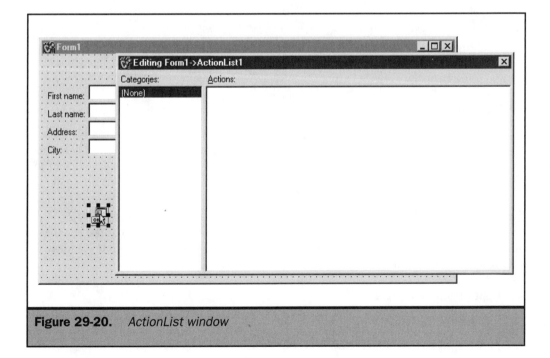

Figure 29-20. *ActionList window*

THE C++ BUILDER
INTEGRATED DEVELOPMENT
ENVIRONMENT

Action	Description
File | New	Presents a new or empty window.
File | Exit	Exits the application.
Edit | Cut	Standard Windows Cut function.
Edit | Copy	Standard Windows Copy function.
Edit | Paste	Standard Windows Paste function.
Help | About	Standard Windows About box.

Table 29-5.   *List of Actions*

To add the actions, right-click the ActionList window and select **New Action** from the pop-up menu. In the Object Inspector window, set these properties:

Caption	&New	This is what will be shown as the action name. The **&** character causes the next character to be underlined.
Category	File	Puts the New action under File.
Hint	Create new	Tip that will appear when mouse is over item.
ImageIndex	0	Ties Image # 0 to this action item.
Name	FileNew	This is the internal variable name. It is always best to combine the menu names so that you will know that this is New function from the File menu.

Once these properties have been set, your screen will look similar to Figure 29-21.

Next, add the rest of the items. The information you need is shown in the list that follows. To start the process, right-click in the **Editing Form1->ActionList1** window and select **New Action**. Add the following:

Caption	E&xit
Category	File
Hint	Exit program
ImageIndex	1
Name	FileExit

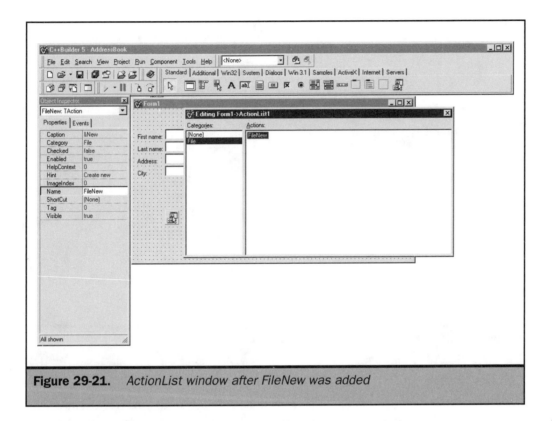

Figure 29-21.   *ActionList window after FileNew was added*

Now is a good time to save your application.

The next three items, **Edit | Cut**, **Edit | Copy**, and **Edit | Paste**, are standard Windows functions. These can be added easily to the **Editing Form1->ActionList1** window. Right-click in the **Editing Form1->ActionList1** window and select **New Standard Action** from the pop-up menu. The Standard Actions dialog box appears, as shown in Figure 29-22. There are quite a few standard actions that can be used. For this application, you will use the **TEditCut**, **TEditCopy**, and **TEditPaste** action items. To expedite the selection of all three items, simply hold down the CTRL key as you click each of the three edit controls. Then click **OK** to transfer all three into the **ActionList** window. By default, all the standard action items have their properties preconfigured. The only property you will need to change is the **ImageIndex** so that you can tie it to an icon. Select the **EditCut1** action and change its **ImageIndex** to 2, change the **EditCopy1 ImageIndex** to 3, and finally change the **EditPaste1 ImageIndex** to 4.

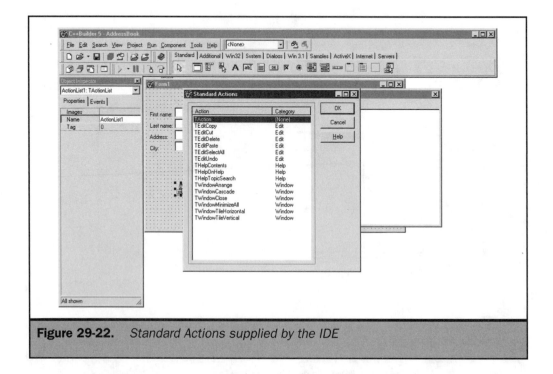

Figure 29-22. *Standard Actions supplied by the IDE*

There is one more action item that needs to be defined, **Help | About**. Right-click in the **Editing Form1->ActionList1** window and select **New Action** from the pop-up menu. Change the following properties:

Caption	&About
Category	Help
Name	HelpAbout

This completes the list of action items. You can leave the **ActionList** open for now, as you will use it again later.

ImageList Component

It's now time to add images for the application to use. To begin, add an **ImageList** object which is located on the Win32 tab. Double-click it to add it to the form. This component is a nonvisual component as well, so it doesn't matter where it is placed on the form. However, a good programming habit is to keep all the nonvisual components together, out of the way of other fields or visual components. It makes it easier to find them.

Double-click the **ImageList** component to open the **Form1->ImageList1 ImageList** window, as shown in Figure 29-23. This window helps manage icons that will be used on the toolbar. Now is the time to add the icons. C++ Builder supplies over 160 different images that you can use. For the application, you will need the following images:

Filename	Use or Description
Filenew.bmp	File I New function
Doorshut.bmp	File I Exit function
Cut.bmp	Edit I Cut function
Copy.bmp	Edit I Copy function
Paste.bmp	Edit I Paste function

These images are located in the directory

\Program Files\Common Files\Borland Shared\Images\Buttons

If you don't have these images, they may not have been installed on your computer. (Check the C++ Builder CD and install them if necessary.)

To add icons, click **Add** and browse to the preceding directory. Select the icons in the order that they are shown. Recall that the **File I New** property **ImageIndex** is assigned

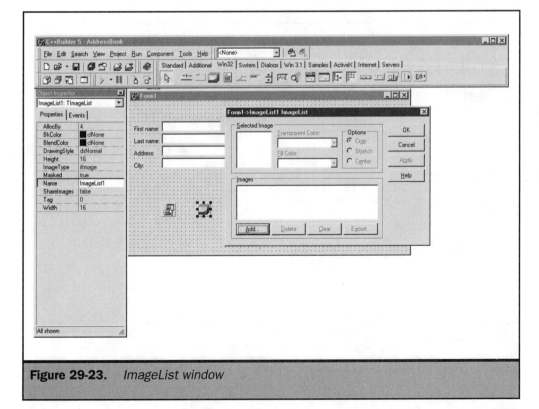

Figure 29-23.   *ImageList window*

the value 0. **File | Exit**'s property is assigned 1, **Edit | Cut** is assigned 2, **Edit | Copy** is assigned 3, and **Edit | Paste** is assigned 4. Find the file **Filenew.bmp** and click **Open**. A message appears asking if you want to split this image into two separate bitmaps. Answer **Yes** for each of the icons. Both the active and inactive icons appear in the image list editor as shown in Figure 29-24.

Each icon is maintained as a pair. The first part of the pair is the active icon, and the second part is the grayed-out icon. By splitting them into two separate bitmaps, you can choose which icon to use, the active icon or the grayed-out, inactive one.

Delete the inactive icon by selecting the grayed-out icon and clicking **Delete**. Now add these icons, in the order shown:

Doorshut.bmp
Cut.bmp
Copy.bmp
Paste.bmp

Each time, answer **Yes** to the two separate bitmap questions. Remember to delete the grayed-out icons as they are separated and added. As these icons are added, you

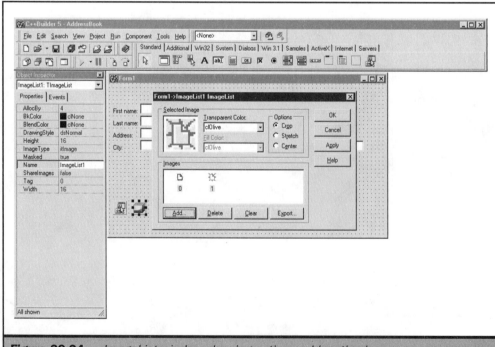

Figure 29-24. *ImageList window showing active and inactive icons*

should notice that they are given unique numbers. These numbers match the **ImageIndex** numbers that were given to the corresponding functions. For instance, the **File | New** function has an index of 0, which ties it to the icon of 0 or the **Filenew.bmp** file. If the icons are out of order, you can rearrange them by dragging them into the correct positions. Once all the icons have been added to the list, click **OK** to close the image list editor. Now you need to tie these images to the action list. To do this, single-click the **ActionList** component on the form and change the **Images** property value to **ImageList1**. Now would be another good time to save the changes that you have made. Once the changes have been saved, you can build the menu for the application.

Building a Basic Menu

The menu bar contains three top-level items, **File**, **Edit**, and **Help**. To build a menu, you first need to include the **MainMenu** component in the form. This component is located on the Standard tab. Double-click it to add it to the form. This component is also a nonvisual component and should be placed near the other nonvisual components.

The first thing is to tie the icons to the main menu component. To do this, select the **MainMenu** component on the form and change the **Images** property to **ImageList1**. Next, open the **Form1->MainMenu1** window (menu designer window) by double-clicking the **MainMenu** component. The menu designer window looks like Figure 29-25.

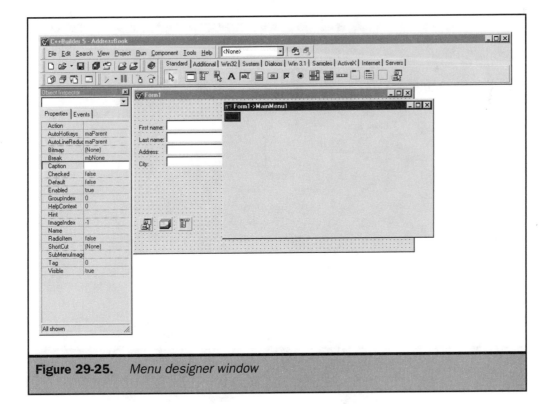

Figure 29-25. *Menu designer window*

Create the top-level items manually. You can pull the submenu items from the **ActionList** component. In the Object Inspector window, change the **Caption** property to **&File** and press ENTER. Now in the menu designer window, select the **File** item just added. You should see an empty item below it; select the empty menu item. In the Object Inspector window, select the **Action** property and click the down arrow. A drop-down list appears, as in Figure 29-26, which shows the available actions created earlier.

Select **FileNew** for this empty menu slot. Immediately, the menu item **New** appears in the menu designer window. You may have noticed that Windows applications usually have a separator line between the file submenu items and the exit program item. While the address book application really does not need one, it is easy to add a separator. Select the empty slot below the **New** item and in the **Caption** property type a hyphen and press ENTER. By doing this one little step, you have created a separator line on the menu. Now select the empty slot below the separator line and change its **Action** property to **FileExit**. This completes the File menu item and its submenu. Now let's add the **Edit** menu.

Select the empty slot right next to the **File** menu name and, in the **Caption** property value, type **&Edit**. Select the **Edit** item to open an empty slot below it and select the empty slot. In the **Action** property, select **EditCut1**. Notice that not only does it put the

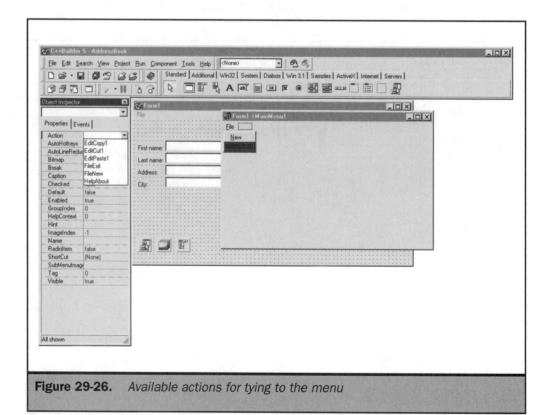

Figure 29-26. *Available actions for tying to the menu*

action item in the menu, it also adds the appropriate shortcut key. Now select the empty slot below the cut item and add the copy action item. Do the same thing for the paste function as well.

There is one more top-level menu item to add, **Help**. Select the empty slot just to the right of **Edit** menu item and type **&Help** for the **Caption** property value. Select the **Help** menu item, and select the empty slot below it. Now select the **HelpAbout** action item from the **Action** property. This now completes the menu. Close the menu designer window.

Now, save the project and execute the program. As you can see, even though you have added no code of your own, the application executes and displays the form and menu. If you look through the menu, you will see the icons and action items. Most of these items will be grayed out or inactive, but the standard window objects, like Cut, Copy, and Paste, are active.

Creating a Toolbar

The toolbar is the bar that appears right below the main menu and shows icons to represent functions, such as open a file, save a file, print, cut, copy, and paste, to name a few. You will need to include **FileExit**, **FileNew**, **EditCut1**, **EditCopy1**, and **EditPaste1** on the toolbar.

The toolbar component is located under the Win32 tab. It is the third item from the right. Double-click this component to add it to the form, right below the main menu, as shown in Figure 29-27.

You need to change the following properties:

Property	Value	Description
Images	ImageList1	Hooks the images into this toolbar.
Indent	10	Indents the toolbar 10 pixels. (This is a bit much, but it enables you to see how the indent works. Most of the time, a value between 3 and 5 works best.)
ShowHint	True	Shows tool tip hints—these are the hints that you created as part of the action list items.

Now add the icons to the toolbar. Right-click the toolbar and select **New Button** from the pop-up menu. The first icon to appear is the **FileNew** icon, which is maintained in the image list. Right-click and select **New Button** again and the **FileExit** icon appears. Next, add a separator to organize the icons by function. Right-click the toolbar and select **New Separator**. Now you are ready to add the Cut, Copy, and Paste icons. Right-click and choose **New Button**, three more times. The toolbar is almost complete. If you do not like how the icons are arranged, you can move the icons by using your mouse to drag and drop them where you want them. Move the exit icon (the closed door)

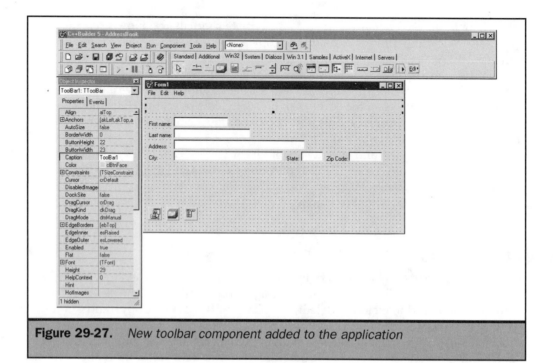

Figure 29-27. *New toolbar component added to the application*

to the far left, making it the first icon. Visually, the toolbar is complete. However, the icons don't do anything, yet. In order to make the icons functional, you need to tie each icon to an action from the **ActionList** component.

To set the following icon's **Action** property, first click the icon, and then set its action property as shown here:

Icon	Value
Door	**FileExit** (selected from drop-down action list)
New	**FileNew**
Cut	**EditCut1**
Copy	**EditCopy1**
Paste	**EditPaste1**

If the icons disappear or appear out of order, select an icon and change its **ImageIndex** to match the preceding list.

The toolbar is complete, and the standard Windows functions will now work when the application is executed. You can see how easy this can be once you have an **ImageList** component built. This is a good time to save the changes that you have made.

To see how the application is progressing, compile and run the application by selecting **Run | Run**. Try the toolbar, particularly the **Cut, Copy**, and **Paste** functions. All three work, and without you writing a single line of code. This shows the power of the IDE.

Building Command Buttons

Windows applications usually contain at least one push button or what is sometimes referred to as a *command button*. For the application you need two buttons: an **Add** and a **Clear**.

Add, in this application, will just pop up a message box showing the information entered into each field. (On your own, you might want to try tying this button to code that saves the information to a file, or a database product, like Microsoft SQL Server.) The **Clear** button will clear all the fields, just as the **FileNew** action item will do.

Begin by adding a **Button** component to the form. The **Button** component is located on the Standard tab; it is the one that looks like a button. Double-clicking the component will add it to the form. Drag the button to where you want it. Change these properties:

Property	Value
Caption	&Add
Name	cmdAdd

The **Name** property is the internal variable name that you will use when you add code to cause this button to function. Since buttons are sometimes known as command buttons, their names begin with the **cmd** prefix.

Now let's add the second button. Double-click the **Button** component. Again, drag this button over next to the **Add** button. Change these properties:

Property	Value
Caption	&Clear
Name	cmdClear

There is one more visual component that needs to be added to the project, and that is the **Help | About** dialog box. All Windows applications include an About box to show basic information about the program. You will include one in the application as well.

Adding a Help | About Dialog Box

The action list already has a **HelpAbout** item that you can use to activate an About box. To include an About box, you need to select **File | New**. Select the Forms tab and double-click the **About Box** form. The **About** window appears, as shown in Figure 29-28.

All the basic information is contained in this box. You just need to change or add information to complete the About box. Make the following changes:

Select item	Property	Value
Form	Caption	About Address Book (The easiest way to select the form is by clicking the grid.)
Product Name	Caption	Address Book
Version	Caption	Version 1.0
Copyright	Caption	Copyright 2001
Comments	Caption	Created by *place your name here*.

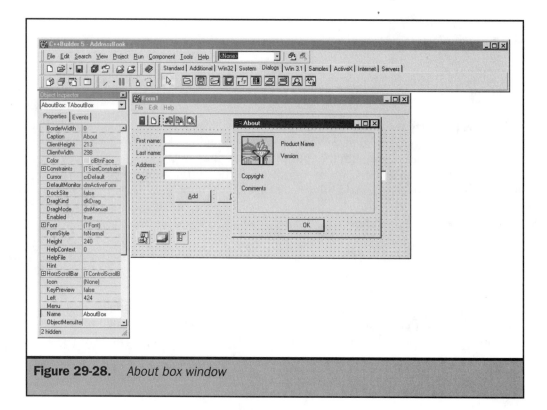

Figure 29-28.   *About box window*

You may have to stretch the Comments label component out in order to show the complete Caption. You are done visually altering the About box. Close the About box. When you do this, the **Save Unit2 As** dialog box appears. Save it as **About.cpp**. Now you need to tie it into the application. This is done by including the About unit into the source code file. To do this, select **View | Units**, from the View Unit dialog box select **Unit1**, and click **OK**. This brings the **Unit1.cpp** code window forward. You need to include the About box unit into the main form window. You do this by selecting **File | Include Unit Hdr**. The **Use Unit** dialog box opens. It only has the About item listed. Select the About item and click **OK**. You can now close the **About Address Book** window.

You now need to create an event that will activate this About box. To do this, go back to the form and double-click the **ActionList** component. The action list editor window appears. Select **Help** from the Categories column and then double-click the **HelpAbout** action item, in the right column. The code window appears and creates a skeleton function. Right where the cursor is located, enter this line of code:

```
AboutBox->ShowModal( );
```

This code will open the About box when the **Help | About** is selected from the application. The **ShowModal( )** function means that nothing else can be done until the **OK** button is selected on the About box. Your code window should like similar to Figure 29-29.

This completes the About box. Now, save the application and then compile and execute it. Try the **Help | About** menu item. You will see that it works and displays the **About Address Book** dialog window. Close the application.

Let's wrap up this project by adding the rest of the code. You will be pleasantly surprised to see that it does not take much code to make this a fully functional Windows application.

Adding Code and Finishing the Application

Now that the visual interface of the application is all done, you can concentrate on adding code to tie all the buttons and icons to events. Events represent actions, such as selecting a menu item or clicking a button. Open the **ActionList** component by double-clicking it. From the action list editor, select **File** from the Categories column and double-click the **FileNew** action. This opens the **Unit1.cpp** source file.

Now add the following lines of code into this function.

```
// Need to clear each edit boxes on the form.

txtFirstName->Text = "";
txtLastName->Text = "";
```

```
txtAddress->Text = "";
txtCity->Text = "";
txtState->Text = "";
txtZipCode->Text = "";
```

This takes care of the **File | New** selection. You still need to tie this code to the **Clear** button. To do this, double-click the **Clear** button on the form. This opens the code window and places the cursor inside the cmdClearClick event. Add the following:

```
FileNewExecute(Sender);
```

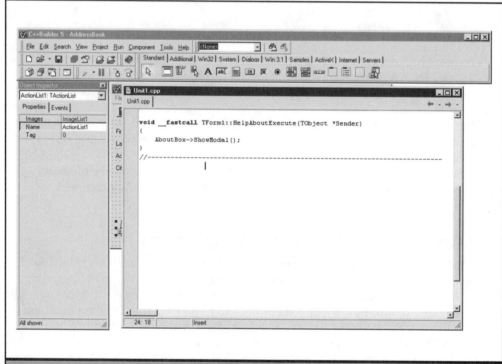

Figure 29-29.   *Unit1.cpp code window showing the About box code*

Since you have already taken the time to clear all the fields using the **File | New** function, you can call that function from here. This way you can reuse the code instead of duplicating it again in this function.

Next, save your application and execute it. Fill in the fields and then try the **File | New** menu item, the **New** icon on the toolbar, and the **Clear** button. They each perform the same function, which is to clear all the fields. Close the application so that you can continue building the application.

It's time to add code for the **Add** command button. In a real application, the **Add** command would do a lot more, like add the data into a database, but that is beyond the scope of this book. Double-click **Add** to place the cursor in the code window inside the add button event. Add the following lines of code.

```
ShowMessage("First name = " + txtFirstName->Text + "\n" +
            "Last name = " + txtLastName->Text + "\n" +
            "Address = " + txtAddress->Text + "\n" +
            "City = " + txtCity->Text + "\n" +
            "State = " + txtState->Text + "\n" +
            "Zip Code = " + txtZipCode->Text);
```

Now every button and event has been accommodated except for one of the most important: the one that exits the application. So you need to add the **File | Exit** event and tie it to the icon of the closed door on the toolbar, too.

To do this, double-click the ActionList on the form. Select **File** (categories) and then double-click the **FileExit** action. This brings the code window forward and places the cursor inside the function. Add this line of code:

```
Close( );
```

This completes the address book application. Save the changes and try it out by selecting **Run | Run**. Experiment with all the fields, icons, and buttons.

The very last step is to build or create the final executable. To do this, select **Project | Build AddressBook** to build the final code. That's it; the application is complete.

As you have seen, C++ Builder's IDE streamlines the creation of Windows applications. It does most of the work for you, allowing you to drag and drop objects onto a form. Before moving on, you might want to try adding additional functionality to the address book. For example, try adding a Sort button (which doesn't have to actually do anything). Also, try creating your own application from scratch. The best way to get adept at using the IDE is to create several small projects.

The Complete Reference

Borland
C++
Builder

Chapter 30

Using C++ Builder's Integrated Debugging Environment

C++ Builder includes a built-in source-level debugger in its integrated development environment. This chapter introduces the debugger and explores some of its most important features.

Preparing Your Programs for Debugging

Although C++ Builder's debugger is available for use at the press of a key, you must make sure that your programs are compiled for a debugging session. This means that you must compile and link your program with debugging information. By default, this is automatically the case. But if you need to turn on these options, here is how.

To add debugging information to your project, choose **Project**, then **Options**. Next, open the Linker page by selecting the Linker tab. In the Linking section, select the check box labeled **Create debug information**. Click **OK** to close the Project Options dialog box.

What Is a Source-Level Debugger?

To understand what a source-level debugger is and why it is so valuable, it is best to compare it to an old-style, traditional debugger. A traditional debugger is designed to provide object-code debugging, in which you monitor the contents of the CPU's registers or memory. To use a traditional debugger, the linker generates a symbol table that shows the memory address of each function and variable. To debug a program, you use this symbol table and begin executing your program, monitoring the contents of various registers and memory locations. Most debuggers allow you to step through your program one instruction at a time, and to set breakpoints in the object code. However, the biggest drawback to a traditional debugger is that the object code of your program bears little resemblance to the source code. This makes it difficult, even with the use of a symbol table, to know exactly what is happening.

A source-level debugger offers a vast improvement over the older approach in that it allows you to debug your program using the original source code. The debugger automatically links the compiled object code associated with each line in your program with its corresponding source code. You no longer need to use a symbol table. You can control the execution of your program by setting breakpoints in the source code. You can watch the values of various variables using the variables' names. You can step through your program one statement at a time and watch the contents of the program's call stack. Also, communication with C++ Builder's debugger is accomplished using C/C++-like expressions, so there is nothing new to learn.

Debugger Basics

This section introduces the most common debugging commands. To follow along, you need to create a new project. When the New Items dialog box is displayed, double-click **Console Wizard**. When the Console Wizard dialog box appears, set **Source Type** to

C++, and check the box next to the **Console Application**. Remove any other checks. Click **OK** to continue. The wizard generates a code window or editor window labeled Unit1.cpp. Save the project, **File | Save**, and call the project **test**. In the editor window, enter the boldfaced code that follows.

```
//-----------------------------------------------------------

#include <iostream>
#pragma hdrstop
using namespace std;

//-----------------------------------------------------------
void sqr_it(int n);

#pragma argsused
int main(int argc, char* argv[])
{
  int i;
  char ch[1];   //Use in cin to stop console app in window

  for(i=0; i<10; i++) {
    cout << i << " ";
    sqr_it(i);
  }
  cin.getline(ch,1);   //Pauses window until Enter is pressed
  return 0;
}

//-----------------------------------------------------------

  void sqr_it(int n)
  {
    cout << n*n << " ";
  }
```

After you have entered the program, compile and run it to make sure that you entered it correctly. It prints the values 0 through 9 along with their squares. Press the ENTER key to close the console window and return to the IDE.

Single-Stepping

Single-stepping is the process by which you execute your program one statement at a time. The two commands that accomplish this are **Step Over** and **Trace Into**, which are both found in the **Run** menu. To begin a debugging session, select **Step Over**. After starting the debugging session, you can also use **Trace Into** to single-step through your program. In addition to using the **Run** menu, the **Step Over** command can be activated by pressing F8 or by pressing **Step Over** on the toolbar, and the **Trace Into** command can be activated by pressing F7 or by pressing **Trace Into** on the toolbar.

You can also use **Trace Into** to begin the debugging session, but it creates a rather complicated window, containing a mix of assembly language and C++ code, as shown in Figure 30-1. To avoid this, start by using **Step Over**. Also, since this is a console application, a console window opens upon starting the program.

Notice that the line containing the **main( )** function declaration is highlighted. This is where your program begins execution. Note also that all the **#include** lines, the **#pragma** lines, and the **sqr_it( )**'s prototype are skipped over. Statements that do not generate code, such as the preprocessor directives, obviously cannot be executed, so the debugger automatically skips them. Variable declaration statements without initializers are also skipped when single-stepping, as they are not action statements that can be traced.

Press F7 several times. Notice how the highlight moves from line to line. Also notice that when the function **sqr_it( )** is called, the highlight moves into the function and then returns from it. The F7 key causes the execution of your program to be traced into function calls.

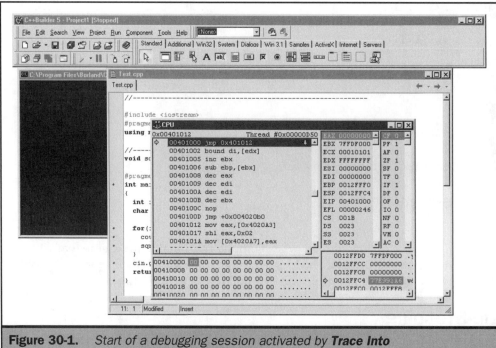

Figure 30-1. *Start of a debugging session activated by* ***Trace Into***

There can be times when you only want to watch the performance of the code within one function, and not follow execution into any other functions. To accomplish this, use the F8 (step over) key. Each time this key is pressed, another statement is executed, but calls to functions are not traced. Experiment with the F8 key at this time. Notice that the highlight never enters the **sqr_it( )** function.

Figure 30-2 shows the appearance of the edit window SpeedMenu. It provides numerous debugging functions, including the ability to run the program to where the cursor is as well as to toggle breakpoints.

Breakpoints

As useful as single-stepping is, it can be very tedious in a large program—especially if the piece of code that you want to debug is deep in the program. Instead of pressing F7 or F8 repeatedly to get to the section you want to debug, it is easier to set a breakpoint at the beginning of the critical section. A *breakpoint* is, as the name implies, a break in the execution of your program. When execution reaches the breakpoint, your program stops running before that line is executed. Control returns to the debugger, allowing you to check the value of certain variables or to begin single-stepping the routine.

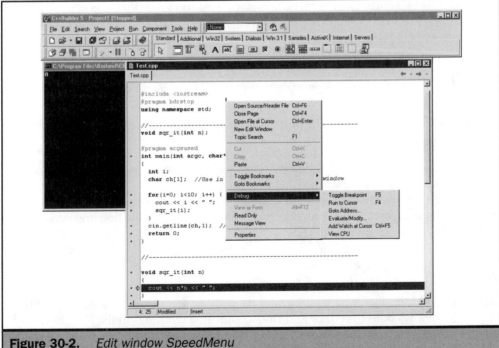

Figure 30-2. *Edit window SpeedMenu*

THE C++ BUILDER
INTEGRATED DEVELOPMENT
ENVIRONMENT

The C++ Builder debugger allows you to define the various different types of breakpoints shown here.

Type	Operation
Source	Stops execution when a line in your source code is executed.
Address	Stops execution when the machine instruction at a specified address is executed.
Data Breakpoint	Stops execution when the data at a specified location is changed.
Module Load	Stops execution when a specified dynamic link library (DLL) is loaded.

Here we will examine only the source breakpoint, because it is the most important and frequently used. (After understanding source breakpoints, you can easily explore the others on your own.)

There are two basic flavors of breakpoints: conditional and unconditional. Each is examined next.

Setting Unconditional Source Breakpoints

An unconditional source breakpoint always stops execution each time it is encountered. There are several ways to add this type of breakpoint. Position your cursor at the line where you want to place the breakpoint. Then, you may do any of the following:

- Press F5.
- Select the **Toggle breakpoint** option in the **Debug** menu of the edit window's SpeedMenu.
- Click the left margin of the edit window at the line where you want to add a breakpoint.

The line of code at which the breakpoint is set is highlighted. You can have several active breakpoints in a program.

Once you have defined one or more breakpoints, execute your program by choosing **Run** from the **Run** menu. Your program runs until it encounters the first breakpoint. As an example, set a breakpoint at the line

```
cout << n*n << " ";
```

inside **sqr_it( )**, and then run the program. As you can see, execution stops at that line. Figure 30-3 shows both the editor and **Breakpoint List** windows in the IDE. You may select **Breakpoints** from the **View | Debug Windows** menu to obtain this display. The

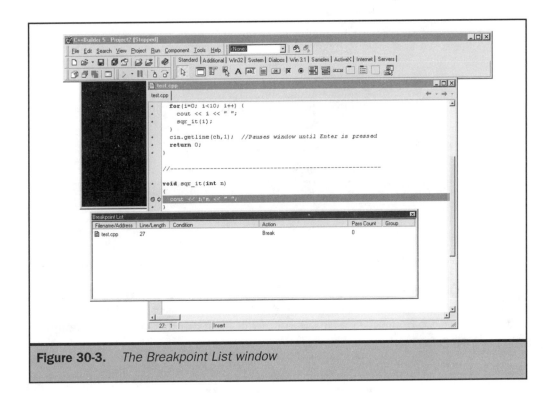

Figure 30-3.   *The Breakpoint List window*

Breakpoint List window lists all of the breakpoints and also indicates which of these was the last encountered.

There are several ways to remove a breakpoint. You may do any one of the following:

- Press F5.
- Select the **Toggle breakpoint** option in the **Debug** menu of the edit window's SpeedMenu.
- Highlight a breakpoint entry in the **Breakpoint List** window and then press the DEL key.

Setting Conditional Source Breakpoints

A conditional source breakpoint allows you to specify the conditions under which a breakpoint stops execution and the actions that occur when it does. Let's look at an example, using the program from the preceding section. To add a conditional source breakpoint, position your cursor in the editor window at the line where you want to establish the breakpoint. For example, position it in the **main( )** function at the line where the **sqr_it( )** function is called. Choose **Source Breakpoint** from the **Run | Add Breakpoint** menu. This action causes the dialog box shown in Figure 30-4 to appear.

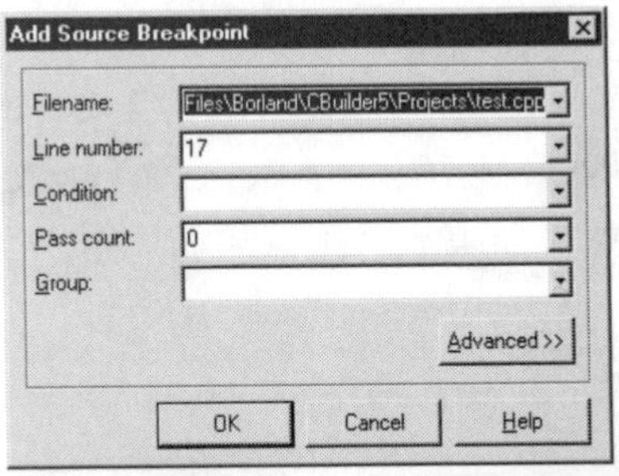

Figure 30-4.   *Add Source Breakpoint dialog box*

Now click Advanced in the lower-right corner of this dialog box. This activates the dialog box shown in Figure 30-5.

Sometimes you will want to establish a breakpoint so that it stops execution only after a specified number of iterations through a loop. This threshold is defined by setting the **Pass Count** field equal to the number of iterations that you wish to ignore. For this example, enter **4**.

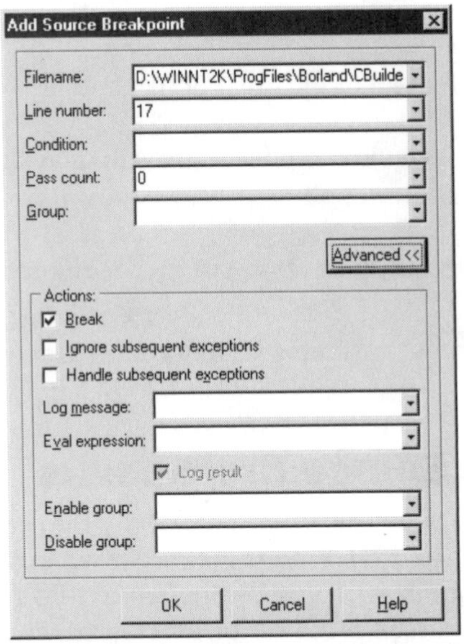

Figure 30-5.   *Advanced Add Source Breakpoint dialog box*

To see the conditional breakpoint in action, choose **Run** in the Run menu. The program begins execution and the breakpoint does not take effect until the **sqr_it( )** function has been executed three times and is ready to begin its fourth call, at which point it stops on the breakpoint.

Watching Variables

While debugging, you commonly need to see the value of one or more variables as your program executes. Using C++ Builder's debugger, this is easily accomplished. There are two methods for watching variables. The first is very quick and just shows the value of a variable; the second method involves using watches.

To quickly see the value of a variable, simply move the mouse cursor over the variable name in the edit window. Let the mouse cursor sit on the variable for just a few seconds and a little window will pop up showing the current value of the variable in question. The preferred method of watching variables is by using the **Watch List** Window.

First, activate the **Watch List** window by selecting **Watches** from the **View |
Debug Windows** menu. To add a watch, first activate the **Add Watch** dialog box. Here are two ways you may do this.

- Press CTRL-F5.
- Right-click in the **Watch List** window and select **Add Watch** from the SpeedMenu.

Once the **Watch Properties** dialog box is displayed, enter the name of the variable you want to watch. The debugger automatically displays the value of the variable in the **Watches** window as the program executes. If the variable is global, its value is always available. However, if the variable is local, its value is reported only when the function containing that variable is being executed. When execution moves to a different function, the variable's value is unknown. Keep in mind that if two functions both use the same name for a variable, the value displayed relates to the function currently executing.

As an example, activate the **Watch Properties** dialog box and enter **i**. If you are not currently running the program or if execution has been stopped inside the **sqr_it( )** function, you will first see the message

i: [process not accessible]'

However, when execution is inside the **main( )** function, the value of **i** is displayed.

Figure 30-6 shows the appearance of the editor, part of the console window, and the **Watch List** window when execution is suspended at a breakpoint. Notice that the editor window indicates the location of the breakpoints and the **Watch List** window indicates the value of any watched variables.

You are not limited to watching only the contents of variables. You can watch any valid C/C++ expression involving variables. However, the expression cannot use any **#define** values or variables that are not in the scope of the function that is being executed.

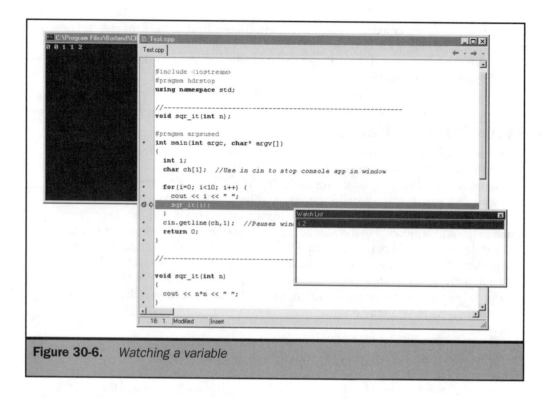

Figure 30-6.   *Watching a variable*

Watched-Expression Formats

C++ Builder's debugger allows you to format the output of a watched expression by selecting a format in the **Watch Properties** window. Table 30-1 gives a brief description of each format. If you don't specify a format, the debugger automatically provides a default format.

You can display integers in either decimal or hexadecimal. The debugger automatically knows the difference between **long** and **short** integers because it has access to the source code.

When specifying a floating-point format, you can tell the debugger to show a certain number of significant digits in the **Digits** field. By default the debugger will show up to 18 digits.

When a structure or a union is displayed, the values associated with each field are shown using an appropriate format. By selecting the **Record/Structure** format command, the name of each field is also shown. To see an example, close the existing **test** console program and create a new console application. Call the project **test2**. The complete listing follows. Try watching **sample**, using both the **Default** format and the **Record/Structure** format. You can include the variable, **sample**, as many times as you wish with each instance having its own format.

Format	Meaning
Character	Display as a character with no translation.
Decimal	Display in decimal.
Floating point	Display in floating point.
Hexadecimal	Display in hexadecimal.
Memory Dump	Show memory.
Pointer	Display as a pointer.
Record/Structure	Display class, structure, or union member names and values.
String	Display as a character with appropriate character translations.
Default	Display a format that matches the data type of the variable.

Table 30-1.   *Debugger Formats*

```
//------------------------------------------------------------

#include <cstring>
#pragma hdrstop
using namespace std;

//------------------------------------------------------------

struct inventory {
  char item[10];
  int  count;
  float cost;
} sample;

#pragma argsused
int main(int argc, char* argv[])
{
    strcpy(sample.item, "hammer");
    sample.count = 100;
    sample.cost = 3.95;

    return 0;
```

```
}

//-------------------------------------------------------------
```

After the three assignments have taken place, the output shown in the **Watch List** window looks like this:

```
sample: {"hammer\0\0\0\0", 100, 3.95}
sample: {item:"hammer\0\0\0\0", count:100, cost:3.95}
```

The first line uses the **Default** format, and the second line uses the **Record/Structure** format. As you might expect, you can also watch an object of a **class**. When you watch an object, you are shown the current value of any data that is contained within the object. As with structures and unions, if you use the **Record/Structure** format specifier, the names of each data item are also displayed. When you are watching an object of a class, all **private**, **protected**, and **public** data is displayed. For example, if the previous program is changed as shown here:

```
//-------------------------------------------------------------

#include <cstring>
#pragma hdrstop
using namespace std;

//-------------------------------------------------------------

class inventory {
   int i;  // private data
public:
   inventory() {i=100;}
   char item[10];
   int   count;
   float cost;
} sample;

#pragma argsused
int main(int argc, char* argv[])
{
     strcpy(sample.item, "hammer");
     sample.count = 100;
     sample.cost = 3.95;
```

```
return 0;
}
//----------------------------------------------------------
```

the following output is obtained when watching **sample** using **Record/Structure:**

```
sample: {i:100,item:"hammer\0\0\0\0",count:100,cost:3.95}
```

As you can see, even though **i** is **private** to **inventory**, for the purposes of debugging, it is accessible to the debugger.

Figure 30-7 shows the options that are available via the SpeedMenu of the **Watch List** window. As indicated, you may modify, add, remove, or disable watches.

Qualifying a Variable's Name

You can watch the value of a local variable no matter what function is currently executing by qualifying its name using this format:

filename.function-name.variable-name;

The *filename* is optional in single-file programs, and the *function-name* is optional when there is only one variable by the specified name.

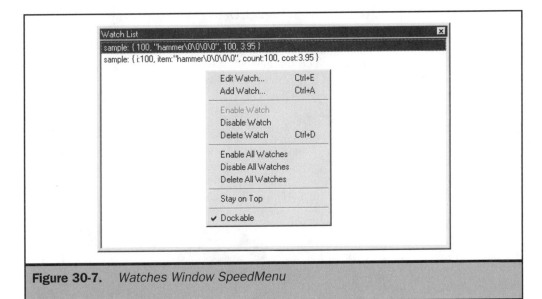

Figure 30-7. *Watches Window SpeedMenu*

THE C++ BUILDER INTEGRATED DEVELOPMENT ENVIRONMENT

As an example, assume that you want to watch both the **count** in **f1( )** and the **count** in **f2( )**, given this fragment:

```
void f1()
{
  int count;
  . . .
}

void f2()
{
  int count;
  . . .
}
```

To specify these variables, use

```
f1.count
f2.count
```

Watching the Stack

During the execution of your program, you can display the contents of the call stack by:

- Selecting the **Call Stack** option in **View | Debug Windows** menu.
- Pressing CTRL-F3.

This option displays the order in which the various functions in your program are called. It also displays the values of any function parameters at the time of the call.

To see how this feature works, create a new console application and enter this program:

```
//------------------------------------------------------------

#include <iostream>
#pragma hdrstop
using namespace std;

//------------------------------------------------------------

void f1(), f2(int i);

#pragma argsused
```

```
int main(int argc, char* argv[])
{
    f1();
    return 0;
}
//------------------------------------------------------------

void f1()
{
  int i;

  for(i=0; i<10; i++) f2(i);
}

void f2(int i)
{
  cout << "in f2, value is " << i << " ";
}
```

Set a breakpoint at the line containing the **cout** statement in **f2( )**, and then inspect the call stack. The first time the breakpoint is reached, the call stack looks like that shown in Figure 30-8.

Evaluating an Expression

You can evaluate any legal C/C++ expression by using the **Evaluate/Modify** window. This is shown in Figure 30-9. To obtain this window, you may do one of the following:

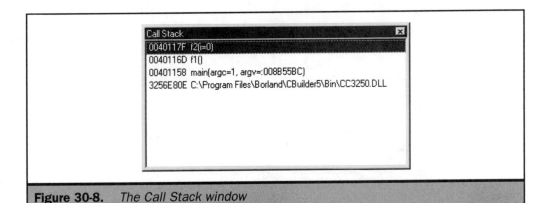

Figure 30-8.   *The Call Stack window*

- Press CTRL-F7.
- Select **Evaluate/Modify** under the **Debug** menu in the edit window's SpeedMenu.
- Select **Evaluate/Modify** from the **Run** menu.

To evaluate an expression, enter it in the **Expression** field. You will see its value in the **Result** field. Expressions can contain constants and variables defined in the program you are debugging. They may also call functions. However, you cannot use any **#define** value.

Pausing a Program

You may pause a program by choosing the **Program Pause** option in the **Run** menu. Execution of your program is suspended and you may then use any of the facilities that have already been discussed to troubleshoot a problem. To resume execution, select **Run** in the **Run** menu.

Using the CPU Window

One final debugging tool at your disposal is the CPU window. If you select **CPU** from the **View | Debug Windows** menu, the window shown in Figure 30-10 appears. This is divided into five separate panes:

- The disassembly pane shows how your source code maps to assembly code.
- The memory dump pane shows the contents of the memory available to your program.

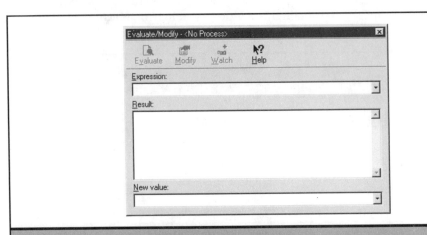

Figure 30-9. *The Evaluate/Modify window*

- The machine stack pane shows the contents of the program stack in hexadecimal.
- The registers pane shows the current values of the CPU registers.
- The flags pane shows the current values of the CPU flags.

To make good use of the **CPU** window requires an intimate knowledge of assembly language programming and the architecture of your machine. However, for those really difficult bugs, careful analysis of the **CPU** window may be your only resort.

A Debugging Tip

Before concluding this chapter, one piece of advice must be offered: Don't rely too heavily on the debugger. While great debuggers, such as that provided with C++ Builder, are an indispensable part of any programmer's arsenal, they should never be a substitute for good design and good coding practices. If you are using the debugger on a daily basis, then you are probably using it too much. Frankly, a poor implementation that is "fixed" through extensive debugging is almost always inferior.

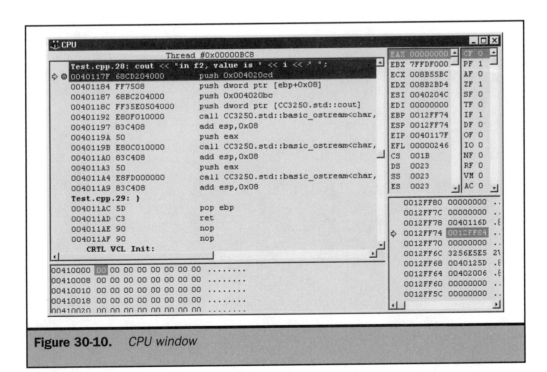

Figure 30-10. *CPU window*

Index

INTERNATIONAL CONTACT INFORMATION

AUSTRALIA
McGraw-Hill Book Company Australia Pty. Ltd.
TEL +61-2-9417-9899
FAX +61-2-9417-5687
http://www.mcgraw-hill.com.au
books-it_sydney@mcgraw-hill.com

CANADA
McGraw-Hill Ryerson Ltd.
TEL +905-430-5000
FAX +905-430-5020
http://www.mcgrawhill.ca

**GREECE, MIDDLE EAST,
NORTHERN AFRICA**
McGraw-Hill Hellas
TEL +30-1-656-0990-3-4
FAX +30-1-654-5525

MEXICO (Also serving Latin America)
McGraw-Hill Interamericana Editores S.A. de C.V.
TEL +525-117-1583
FAX +525-117-1589
http://www.mcgraw-hill.com.mx
fernando_castellanos@mcgraw-hill.com

SINGAPORE (Serving Asia)
McGraw-Hill Book Company
TEL +65-863-1580
FAX +65-862-3354
http://www.mcgraw-hill.com.sg
mghasia@mcgraw-hill.com

SOUTH AFRICA
McGraw-Hill South Africa
TEL +27-11-622-7512
FAX +27-11-622-9045
robyn_swanepoel@mcgraw-hill.com

**UNITED KINGDOM & EUROPE
(Excluding Southern Europe)**
McGraw-Hill Education Europe
TEL +44-1-628-502500
FAX +44-1-628-770224
http://www.mcgraw-hill.co.uk
computing_neurope@mcgraw-hill.com

ALL OTHER INQUIRIES Contact:
Osborne/McGraw-Hill
TEL +1-510-549-6600
FAX +1-510-883-7600
http://www.osborne.com
omg_international@mcgraw-hill.com